Malcolm Cowley

MALCOLM COWLEY

THE FORMATIVE YEARS

H A N S   B A K

THE UNIVERSITY OF GEORGIA PRESS   ATHENS & LONDON

© 1993 by the University of Georgia Press

Athens, Georgia 30602

All rights reserved

Designed by Richard Hendel

Set in Electra & Gill by Tseng Information Systems, Inc.

Printed & bound by Maple Vail Book Manufacturing Group

The paper in this book meets the guidelines for
permanence and durability of the Committee on
Production Guidelines for Book Longevity of the
Council on Library Resources.

Printed in the United States of America

97 96 95 94 93 C 5 4 3 2 1

Library of Congress Cataloging in Publication Data

Bak, Hans.

Malcolm Cowley : the formative years /
Hans Bak.

p. cm.

Includes bibliographical references and index.

ISBN 0-8203-1323-8 (alk. paper)

1. Cowley, Malcolm, 1898–
2. Authors, American—20th century—
Biography.   3. Critics—United States—
Biography.   I. Title.

PS3505.O956Z58   1993

811'.52—dc20

[B]   91-33786

                                             CIP

British Library Cataloging in Publication Data available

Photograph on title page is a detail of a photograph
taken by Jim Casey in 1929. Courtesy of Robert
Cowley and the Estate of Malcolm Cowley.

FOR ELLA AND SASKIA

Wanderers outside the gates, in hollow

landscapes without memory, we carry

each of us an urn of native soil . . .

Malcolm Cowley, "The Urn"

Contents

Preface

The reputation of Malcolm Cowley has long hung in the balance between the literary hagiographers and the political executioners. On the strength of *Exile's Return* (1934; revised and expanded edition, 1951) and his path-breaking efforts on behalf of Ernest Hemingway and William Faulkner, many have seen Cowley primarily as the chronicler and historian par excellence of a now legendary literary generation. Others, in particular the intellectual descendants of onetime anti-Stalinists, have recurrently reminded Cowley of his past political sins. Still others have accused him of writing politically motivated, ideologically predisposed, anti-American criticism or have exposed his supposedly pernicious influence on American literary history. Each critical approach, shaping Cowley according to its own intellectual needs, has found it difficult to see him whole and to do justice to the variety of his interests and the multiplicity of his achievement.

In recent years the nature of Cowley's achievement and the significance of his contribution to American literary history have begun to be more justly recognized. Lewis P. Simpson and George Core have written sensitive essays aimed at a comprehensive estimate of Cowley's influence as a man of letters. In a valuable but limited first study of Cowley's early career James M. Kempf has sought to redress misrepresentations of his influence and ideas. Henry Dan Piper and Donald W. Faulkner have provided perceptive introductions to compilations of Cowley's writings, while others have explored specific aspects of his variegated career as a poet, critic, editor, and historian of American literature.

The present study aims to give an impetus to an overall critical appraisal of Malcolm Cowley's influence as a man of letters. Based on a thorough examination of Cowley's published and unpublished writings, his private notebooks, and his voluminous correspondence with his literary contemporaries, it presents a detailed and comprehensive account of Cowley's early life and writings in order to come to a critical assessment of his total achievement. It presents and evaluates the documentary historical record against which the semi-autobiographical *Exile's Return* needs to be measured; but it aims to move beyond a critical biography of Cowley's early life. Between 1915 and 1930 Cowley first developed the set of literary values and assumptions that remained the cornerstone of his subsequent practice as a literary critic and historian. He also arrived at a broad conception of his role and function as a man of letters, to which he remained remarkably faithful throughout his long career. By considering his early life and writings in the light of his mature efforts on behalf of American writers and American writing, the present study hopes to show that the years before 1930 were truly the formative years of Malcolm Cowley.

Malcolm Cowley died at the age of ninety on March 28, 1989. In one of his last published essays, "Looking for the Essential Me" (1984; republished in *The Portable Malcolm Cowley* [1990]), Cowley, pondering the special handicaps and advantages of the aged memoirist, recalls one of the earliest "watershed moments" of his life. It occurred, he writes, when he was fourteen years old: "I stood alone on the east bank of the Mississippi at Quincy, Ill., where my grandmother lived. The river was a mile wide and from bank to bank its current moved past me solidly, relentlessly. A hundred yards from shore a water-soaked log bobbed up and down while being carried onward. The scene haunted me, I didn't know why, and later I dreamed about it. In the dream I had become that water-soaked log, but somehow the log had eyes to observe what happened on the bank as it was carried along. Still later, much later, I came to feel that I had found a guiding metaphor. The river was history and we were all involved in it as objects on its relentlessly moving surface. It would never turn back. Our only hope was to become more conscious of the spectacle as it unrolled." Later in the essay, telling of his ongoing search to discover "the shape of his life," Cowley contemplates himself at age thirty-two: "As late as 1930 I had regarded myself as one representative of a new generation in American letters, one person among many, and otherwise as a young man without special qualities. I was not a leader, not an exhorter, not an actor in the great events of our time, but chiefly an observer and recorder. I listened and remembered without trying to enforce my opinions on others. There is the possibility, however, that I was a more uncommon character than I suspected at the time." Without the pretense of a full-fledged biography, the present study pursues a parallel quest to that of the aged memoirist: to search for the "shape in time" of the life of this "uncommon character" as he moved from early youth to manhood and maturity, and to document his endeavor "to become more conscious of the spectacle" of history, specifically the history of American letters in his time, as he watched it unroll from his double perspective of immersion and detachment.

Acknowledgments

Many individuals and institutions have helped in many ways to bring this study to completion.

My greatest debt of gratitude is to the late Malcolm Cowley, without whose support and cooperation this study could not have been written. Mr. Cowley kindly granted me permission to examine and quote from his voluminous papers at the Newberry Library in Chicago, as well as Cowley material in numerous other libraries. Over the years he patiently and painstakingly answered my many pertinent and impertinent questions, both in writing and in conversation. In addition, he allowed me to study his notebooks at his home in Sherman, Connecticut, and made available original material from his personal files. His many valuable suggestions and his unflagging trust in my efforts have been the best possible encouragement. Lastly, I am grateful to both Malcolm and the late Muriel Cowley for welcoming me into their Sherman home and graciously sharing with me their luminous reminiscences about the literary past. It is a sad thought that, having witnessed the slow growth of this book with patience and generosity, neither of them lived to see it published.

The American Council of Learned Societies, the Fulbright-Hays Program, and the Newberry Library have provided grants and fellowships which enabled me to carry out a substantial part of my research in the United States during leaves of absence kindly granted by the Catholic University of Nijmegen, the Netherlands.

A special word of thanks is due to the staff of the Newberry Library, who have helped in more than material ways. My stays there have been an invaluable education; in more than one way this is a Newberry book. I am indebted to Diana Haskell, Lloyd Lewis Curator of Midwest Manuscripts, and, in particular, to Carolyn Sheehy, former Curator of Modern Manuscripts, who patiently helped me unearth the many treasures in the Cowley Papers and assisted me in countless, always efficient ways.

Next to the Newberry Library, I am grateful to the staffs of over fifty libraries and institutions, for permitting me to examine or quote from printed materials and unpublished letters and documents in their collections, for providing me with xerox copies or microfilms of material relating to Malcolm Cowley, and for promptly answering my many queries. Here I list only those that have provided me with material directly pertinent to this study, or that have kindly granted permission to quote from unpublished Cowley materials in their collections: American Academy and Institute of Arts and Letters, New York; Clifton Waller Barrett Library, University of Virginia; Beinecke Rare Book and Manuscript Library, Yale University; Rare Book and Manuscript Library, Columbia University; Charles Patterson Van Pelt Library, University of Pennsylvania; Fred Lewis Pattee Library, Pennsylvania State University; George Arents Research Library, Syracuse University; Golda Meir Library, University of Wisconsin-Milwaukee; Olin Library and Gordon Keith Chalmers Memorial Library, Kenyon College; Harry Ransom Humanities Research Center, University of Texas at Austin; Houghton Library, Harvard University; John Hay Library, Brown University; Joseph Regenstein Library, University of Chicago; Koninklijke Bibliotheek, The Hague; Library of Congress, Washington, D.C.; Lockwood Memorial Library, State University of New York; New York Public Library; Peabody High School, Pittsburgh; Princeton University Library; Library, University of Illinois at Urbana-Champaign.

I thank Daniel Aaron, Gay Wilson Allen, the late Marshall Best, Peter Blume, Eleanor Clarke, Felicia Geffen-Van Veen, R. W. B. Lewis, Henry Dan Piper, the late Robert Penn Warren, James M. Wells, and Alan D. Williams for graciously taking time out to talk to me, often at great length, about Malcolm Cowley; their views and reminiscences, even if not always directly reflected in this study, have greatly helped to sharpen my critical perspective on Cowley. In addition, I thank Robert Cowley, literary executor, for extending his father's permission to consult and quote from published and unpublished Cowley materials, and for his general support of my efforts. Unless otherwise credited, all photographs are reproduced by permission of Robert Cowley and the Estate of Malcolm Cowley. I am grateful to Gay Wilson Allen for making his personal correspondence with Cowley available to me, and I am indebted to Kenneth Burke for allowing me to have a microfilm made of his side of his correspondence with his oldest "sparring partner." I have also profited from discussion and correspondence with Donald Faulkner, Adam Gussow, and James Kempf, who freely shared thoughts with me about Malcolm Cowley. Ruth Nuzum kindly answered queries from her vast collection of Cowleyana.

Portions of this work were first published, in different form, as "Malcolm Cowley: The Critic and His Generation," *Dutch Quarterly Review of Anglo-American Letters* 9, 4 (1979), 261–83, © 1979 Rodopi, Amsterdam; "Malcolm Cowley and the Rehumanization of Art," *Georgia Review* 39, 3 (1985), 649–54; "The Fabulous Ostrich of Art: Malcolm Cowley's Notebooks of the Twenties," *The Visionary Company: A Magazine of the Twenties* 2, 2 & 3 (1987), 131–61; "Malcolm Cowley and Edgar Allan Poe: A Critical Controversy of the 1920s," *Horns of Plenty: Malcolm Cowley and His Generation* 2, 2 (1989), 18–26, 31–35; " 'Contest in Vilification': The Literary Friendship of Kenneth Burke and Malcolm Cowley," *Southern Review* 26, 1 (1990), 226–35; "Malcolm Cowley," *Dictionary of Literary Biography Yearbook: 1989* (Detroit, Mich.: Gale Research Inc., 1990), 179–94. I thank the editors and publishers of these periodicals for their support of this study.

Thanks are due to Tilly de Groot, Fleur van den Tweel, Diane Crook, Elly Kersjes, Nico de Milliano, Hélène Nieuwhof, Hans Beerens, Pamela Perkowski, and Manon Smits, who helped in the initial stages of research, typed substantial portions of the manuscript, or assisted in other practical ways. I am grateful to Els Bronzwaer-Schrover for bringing her expertise to bear on the sections dealing with French literature, and to Rosie Taggart for critically reviewing an early version of the manuscript. Jaap van der Bent kindly helped out proofreading. My friends René Dellemann and Jan Hertman offered practical support and spiritual comfort when it was most needed. Most of all I am indebted to Ger Janssens, teacher and colleague, for pointing me the path to Malcolm Cowley. His expert guidance and advice, and his unfailing belief in the value and outcome of this enterprise, have been indispensable; his good taste and high standards of literary scholarship I can only hope to emulate. Finally, I thank my parents and all those, near and far, who sustained me through the making of this study.

Malcolm Cowley

Prologue

An Urn of Native Soil

One of the compensating pleasures of old age, Malcolm Cowley wrote with a twinkle of self-irony at age eighty, is "simply sitting still, like a snake on a sun-warmed stone, with a delicious feeling of indolence. . . . A leaf flutters down; a cloud moves by inches across the horizon. At such moments the older person, completely relaxed, has become a part of nature—and a living part, with blood coursing through his veins. The future does not exist for him." The aged man for the moment finds himself in a state of passive receptivity, a "nirvana of dozing in the sun." This feeling of near-timelessness, of a deep sense of communion with nature, may seem rather incongruous in a writer whose works, like F. Scott Fitzgerald's, so strongly exemplify a "sense of living in history."[1] Considering that in his later years Cowley showed a renewed interest in the writings of Ralph Waldo Emerson and the perpetuation of the spirit of New England transcendentalism in modern American literature, one might be inclined to read in the experience evidence of a transcendent state in which, as Emerson wrote, the individual becomes "part and parcel of God."[2] To do so, however, would be to forego the fact that Cowley's sensibility was fundamentally pragmatic, historical and anti-mystical. At heart the experience here evoked is best understood as Cowley's enactment of one of the prerogatives of old age: a return in memory and spirit to the scenes of youth. In a memoir of his childhood written in 1982 Cowley recalls how, growing up in the hills and valleys of western Pennsylvania in the early 1900s, he often wandered alone in the woods, which "seemed to embrace me and say, 'You belong here, you are ours.'"[3]

In old age Cowley's return to the days of childhood took the form of, among other things, a large-scale revision and, in many cases, a thorough rewriting of his early poems, preparatory to the publication of his collected poems in 1968. "The spirit hasn't stirred in me . . . to write many new ones," he told Robert Penn Warren in the summer of 1967, "but I have a curious mania for revising old ones, as if I felt that each of the poems written long ago was begging me to chisel away at the rough stone and give it a final form. I'm senilizing my juvenilia." He did write several new poems, however, one of which he submitted to Henry Rago, then editor of *Poetry*, saying, it "will stand first in my collected book, to serve as an induction to the countryside."[4]

"Boy in Sunlight," the opening poem of *Blue Juniata: Collected Poems*, is an intensely personal evocation of the cherished landscape of childhood. It tells of a boy who, "having fished alone / down Empfield Run," finds himself at rest in a patch of sunlight, in a burned-over stretch of land that "used to be hemlock woods," where, having caught four trout, he

> now sprawls above the brook on a high stone,
> his bare scratched knees in the sun, his fishing pole beside him,
> not sleeping but dozing awake like a snake on the stone.[5]

The boy's position in nature unmistakably echoes the older man's "nirvana" of dozing "like a snake on a sun-warmed stone." For Cowley, the sense of being at home in nature was the most fundamental childhood experience, the antipode to the sense of exile and alienation at the heart of his adult experience. With advancing age, the future tended to recede, but the past became alive only more vividly. "Funny how my whole boyhood comes back now, stone by tree by running water," Cowley wrote to Conrad Aiken in 1961. In imaginative retrospection the older poet reached back to childhood for a sustaining sense of wholeness, lost in adult life but still cherished as his deepest and most precious memory, one carried throughout life as his "most essential baggage." It is "the secret voice of water trickling under stone" that the boy can hear; it is symbolically represented by the boy's instinctive oneness with the land:

> The land absorbs him into itself,
> as he absorbs the land, the ravaged woods, the pale sky,
> not to be seen, but as a way of seeing;
> not to be judged, but as a way of judgment;
> not even to remember, but stamped in the bone.
> "Mine," screams the hawk, "Mine," hums the dragonfly,
> and "Mine," the boy whispers to the empty land
> that folds him in, half-animal, half-grown,
> still as the sunlight, still as a hawk in the sky,
> still and relaxed and watchful as a trout under the stone.[6]

The attempt to approximate the "nirvana" of childhood, most nearly successful in advanced age, marked an arc-like movement toward completing the curve of Cowley's life. It is the closest the exile came to a complete return.

The importance of the landscape of childhood for a correct understanding of Cowley's development as a writer and of his unfolding interpretation of modern American literature is difficult to exaggerate. The "shapes of his childhood," to lift a Proustian thought from his poem "The Pyre," constitute the "patterns of his growth." Throughout Cowley's varied writings the country of childhood looms as an obsessive memory, a poetic landscape that forms a rich storehouse of values, myths, and symbols. It is "the landscape by which all others are measured and condemned." Many of Cowley's writings are infused with an undertone of wistful regret. "Nostalgia is one of the great motives of lyric poetry," Allen Tate once remarked to Cowley, who seldom used the phrase "my own country" without a haze of affection. The nostalgic note resounds eloquently in the last stanza of the title poem, "Blue Juniata":

> for sometimes a familiar music hammers
> like blood against the eardrums, paints a mist
> across the eyes, as if the smell of lilacs,
> moss roses, and the past became a music
> made visible, a monument of air.[7]

Although echoes of his childhood haunts reverberate throughout his works, Cowley never wrote a full-fledged autobiographical account of his younger years.[8] The richest account is in verse: the lyrical and elegiac first section, "Blue Juniata," of the collected poems. Together, these fourteen poems make up a personal mythology of childhood.

The poetic landscape of childhood at the heart of Cowley's writings can be located with geographical precision. Its emotive center is Belsano, a small village in Cambria County, Pennsylvania, on the western slope of the Alleghenies, seventy miles east of Pittsburgh. There, in the family's summer home, a big clapboard farmhouse called "Maple Home," one mile west of Belsano, David Malcolm Cowley was born on August 24, 1898, at four in the afternoon, during a thunderstorm.[9] In a "salute in prose" to Belsano, published in January 1929, Cowley described the exact geography of "my own country":

It is not an abstraction for politicians, a capitalized immensity like the Middle West, the South, New England, the Prairie States. My country is tangible, small, immediate: a Pennsylvania valley, or rather a high tableland cut by ravines, lying between Chestnut Ridge on the west and Laurel Hill on the east and south. By climbing to the highest branches of a pine tree on the knob behind our barn, one can survey the whole of my country, from the one steeple of Bethel to the stone house at Nolo, and from the high ground in the north, around Nicktown, to where, in the south, the coke-ovens of Vintondale cut the horizon with a wall of smoke.[10]

Cowley received most of his early education in city schools, but all of his summers were spent in the country, "fishing, shooting cottontails and pine squirrels, or simply wandering through the woods." Every May the family drove down from Pittsburgh in a buggy and, after spending two nights on the road, opened the farmhouse for the summer. While his father, a homeopathic physician, returned to grimy Pittsburgh to attend to his patients, mother and son remained on the farm, sometimes through October. The long rural summers gave Cowley a deep-seated attachment to country life; always he thought of the country around Belsano as his "real home" and of the time he spent there as his "real life."[11]

It was by all accounts a pastoral, idyllic childhood, if one marred periodically by loneliness and hunger. "I had the good fortune to be a neglected child, free as a weaned colt in an unfenced pasture," Cowley recalled. The boy's country duties were kept to a minimum; mainly, he was expected to take care of the family's two horses. For the rest, if he had not forgotten to keep the woodbox stored, he was allowed to roam the chestnut woods, usually barefoot, wearing "nothing but a blue-denim shirt and a pair of bib overalls" and carrying his fishing pole in search of trout under the stones in Empfield Run. Sometimes, wandering through the small village, he strolled back and forth between the church, the school, and the crossroad general store, where he listened to "tales of good crops and incredible fishing." It was the "absolute freedom" and "self-dependence" that made his boyhood special, Cowley recalled in 1983: "There was hardly a No Trespass sign in the whole of Cambria County. You could go anywhere your legs would carry you. . . . The only rule was you had to be home for supper."[12]

On hot summer days he often sought out the coolness of the swimming hole in Blacklick Creek, a hundred yards below the White Mill Dam. In 1929 Cowley described it as "a pool in the deep woods, black and still, with a school of minnows floating at the surface of the water, in the sunlight, and hummingbirds moving from flower to flower along the bank. Usually it was the haunt of silence." This pool of childhood figures in "The Living Water" as a symbol of the source of all vitality and life, the home to which the exiled wanderer seeks to return. There the poet hopes to find again "the arrowlike shadows of trout," "cool in their sunless kingdom":

> Climb,
> stumble and climb, for the source of it all is here—

> here the final and secret pool,
> with green scum at the edge of it,
> a cloud of midges over it,
> and bubbling from the depths of it,
> stirring the frogs' eggs and the fishes' eggs,
> here the source, the limpid and living water
> rising from white sand.[13]

The incantatory rhythm of the lines and the repetitive sentence structure give the poem the quality of a sorcerer's chant. As a poet Cowley liked to place himself in line with Edgar Allan Poe or Hart Crane. He pictured Poe as "a would-be sorcerer bent on making a charm or weaving a spell or composing a mantra." He spoke of Hart Crane as "the sorcerer of a primitive tribe" who aimed to produce "not poems only, but incantations or mantras that would have a magical power."[14] Cowley's poems about his Pennsylvania boyhood are infused with this very spirit. Aiming to recapture imaginatively the pristine, unadulterated landscape of childhood Cowley imbues these poems with a feeling of primitive magic. Later, as a critic, he singled out the same quality in William Faulkner's "The Bear" and Ernest Hemingway's "Big Two-Hearted River," feeling an instinctive kinship with writers whose values are similarly rooted in the land. For each of them the country of childhood was a magical kingdom with its own rituals and symbols, a country "stamped in the bone" as a way of judgment and perception. This affinity helps to explain the remarkable degree of empathy in Cowley's criticism of the literary achievements of his generation. As he observed in A Second Flowering, it enabled him to grasp intuitively certain values, images, and associations that might be misconstrued by critics of a different background. Reading Hemingway's Michigan stories Cowley recalled his favorite pastime of "walking through first-growth hemlock timber and feeling the short, warm, dry, a little prickly needles under bare feet." Reading Faulkner he was reminded of the first automobile chugging through Belsano in a whirl of dust, followed by "running boys, while men in overalls craned forward from the bench in front of the general store" where Cowley, like the young Faulkner, often listened to stories and legends of the past. Likewise, Cowley's attachment to the Pennsylvania landscape helps us understand the affinity he felt, in spite of political, regional or temperamental differences, with many southern writers, especially Faulkner, with his "brooding love for the land," but also with such onetime "Agrarians" as Allen Tate and Robert Penn Warren, as well as an independent southerner like Hamilton Basso. Conversely, it helps to explain why, in spite of literary kinship and admiration, Cowley never felt as close to such writers as Van Wyck Brooks or Edmund Wilson, whose personalities were molded by a background far less rural and more patrician. "We were most of us countrymen, in one sense or another," Cowley wrote later. "We were radicals in literature and sometimes in politics, but conservative in our other aspirations, looking back for ideals to the country we had known in childhood. I suspect that we were the last generation in which those country tastes could be taken for granted." [15]

The magic of Cowley's country speaks most clearly from its principal elements: trout, pine trees, and chestnut woods. These took on a value beyond their factual existence quite early and became "the totems of a tribe." "To catch a trout, to cut a virgin pine, or to shoot a twelve-tined buck was almost a ritual act: it was like sacrificing a white bull to the god Mithra," he wrote in 1929. Such a feeling for the ritualistic dimension of an active life close to the soil also sensitized Cowley to the overtones of ancient myth and "magic lore" in Ernest Hemingway; to read Nick Adams's fishing trip, in "Big Two-Hearted River," as "an incantation, a spell to banish evil spirits" was for Cowley an intuitive response as much as a reasoned criticism. Just as he credited Hemingway with "a sort of instinct for legendary situations," Cowley himself came to write a powerful contemporary fable of exile and return that carries the echoes of ancient myth and legend. [16]

Notwithstanding his essentially pragmatic sensibility, occasionally Cowley's feelings for the natural world of his boyhood carried an element of religious worship. Plagued by the summer heat of 1929, Cowley complained to his friend Kenneth Burke that he longed for Belsano, where "the house is cool and the hemlock woods are dark as a cathedral." Years later he recalled how, during a return visit in 1944, he had "worshipped among the last surviving first-growth pines." Once, in 1928, wishing to recapture the "tragic power" and "cold majesty" of his childhood country, Cowley climbed an old pine tree on a hilltop, from where, "perched on the highest branch," he could survey the surrounding countryside in silent contemplation, completely isolated and absorbed by nature: "[The old pine tree] stands some distance behind the farmhouse alone in a bare field, with its branches twisted northward in the direction of the prevailing winds. Branch after branch they spread like Egyptian fans of ostrich feathers or separate terraces of moss, hiding the ground from the watcher who has climbed to the top. There, a perpetual breeze creeps through the needles, exhaling the odor of dried herbs and a rustle of heavy silk." As his notebooks testify, the protective, moss-green bower high up in the old pine tree was one of Cowley's recurrent memories. It constitutes the "true moral norm" at the heart of his writings, much in the way the idyllic fishing expedition at Burguete is the moral core of Hemingway's *The Sun Also Rises*. He shared with Hemingway a feeling of nostalgia for the natural world of the past, unspoiled, orderly, secure. For Cowley, a lifelong aficionado of trout fishing, the activity always was, as he once remarked to Allen Tate, "a piety, an obeisance to lost youth." [17]

Already during Cowley's childhood, however, the magical landscape was rapidly becoming a vanishing pastoral dream. For youngsters growing up in the early years of the century, between the Victorian and the modern age, it was still possible to imagine America as a rural Jeffersonian paradise of self-sufficient, independent farmers who lived mostly by a system of barter and virtually without money. The farmers Cowley encountered as a youth "raised enough hay, buckwheat and rye to carry their cattle through the winter," he remembered in 1931. The wheat they grew, just enough for their year's supply of flour, was ground by waterpower at the White Mill, on the creek below the Cowley farmhouse. "They paid the miller in grain; and when they carried butter and eggs to the general store, they were given credit against their year's supply of calico, shoes, overalls and chewing tobacco." Such a primitive household economy did not make for prosperous living. There was, Cowley recalled in 1983, "real poverty" in Cambria County: "People ate what they could produce. Potatoes went into the root cellar. Apples were gathered, pressed into cider, and the cider boiled down into apple butter, which would stand on the shelves in the pantry. . . . They'd have a cow and a couple of pigs. In the fall you'd hear the pigs being killed by having their throats cut, their terrible wails going over the whole country. But by the end of the winter people actually didn't have enough to eat." [18]

The old spirit of pioneer individualism was still strong; with each man working for his own salvation, social feeling was at a low ebb. Bad roads, primitive schools, polluted trout streams, badly maintained churches, forest fires that went unfought—these were conspicuous symptoms of a lack of responsibility to the community. Yet, enough of the magic of a frontier existence remained for Cowley to think back on his country as a "mountain paradise," a fabulous land of deer hunters, lumberjacks and backwoods farmers, in which he situated "the myth of the pioneer." Old people in Cowley's youth still hummed the tune of half-forgotten sentimental frontier ballads: "Wild roved an Indian girl, Bright Alfarata, / Where sweep the waters of the blue Juniata." To the west of Belsano lay Duncan's Knob, which had been claimed and named by Cowley's great-great-uncle James Duncan, a deerslayer and "pine-butcher" who had hewn his cabin from the forest, log by log. His son Thomas had built the White Mill, first of the water gristmills in the region, and by marrying Cowley's paternal great-aunt Lizzie, had brought the Belsano farmhouse into the Cowley family. For an imaginative boy the farm must have formed a living link to the pioneer past. [19]

Most eloquently, the pastoral past and the pioneer spirit survived in the region's aging farmers, memorable old men who could vividly recall a time when "the hills were covered with first-growth pine, when water gristmills hummed in all the valleys, when panthers slunk after white-tailed deer, when every creek and run . . . was full of shadowy trout." Later, in poetic remembrance of things past, Cowley wrote two poems in tribute to these legendary pioneer-farmers who embodied the harsh practical spirit and sturdy individualism of an older time, who had attained a dignity of their own—like Dan George who, as a sergeant in the Army of the West during the Civil War, was wounded at Chickamauga and was a prisoner at Andersonville: "Dignity is an old man dribbling tobacco juice / on the yellow ends of his cavalry mustache." The ring of their voices, the slow-spoken "drawling singsong" of the Pennsylvania mountains, reverberated in Cowley's memory: "My country has no dialect of its own, but it has a verbal melody which is unmistakable, and the speech of these old men was a sort of chant that rose and fell like the slow Allegheny ridges." The magic of that chant is heard in the dramatic voices of Simon Overbeck and Dan George, carrying traces of the appeal of Edgar Lee Masters's *Spoon River Anthology* for the young poet:

> "Humpty Mert Miller,
> ran a water sawmill in Pine Flats,
> a hard man, a good hater, died fighting drunk.
> Bury me at his side—"
>   and three words more,
> remembered from a song—"where woodbine twineth" . . . [20]

"Overbeck's Barn" tells a representative and symbolic tale. Simon Overbeck had arrived fifty years before, with a brand-new wagon and a new wife, picked his "stumpy clearing" among the pine trees, and begun to strike down roots in the rich "black loam" of Pennsylvania. Hard on himself, ruthless in dealing with others, but respectful of the land, he managed to expand an empty and windowless cabin into a majestic farm. Now, on his deathbed, his life and identity having fused with his self-created empire, he is "seized / with sudden furious longing to destroy / present and past." Endeavoring to take the farm with him into death, he tries to set fire to the barn, but fails and dies in the attempt: "He clenched his chalky hands / as if they held the farm. His face went white." [21] With the death of the original homesteaders, the mountain paradise as a way of life died, too. But the ideal of a life in loving contact with the soil was stamped into the bones of the boy, on whom some of the stubborn independence and sturdy practicality of the Pennsylvania farmer rubbed off.

A more serious threat to the countryside was posed by the advance of industry and technology and the concomitant exploitation of natural resources. In 1907, when Cowley was nine years old, the Vinton Lumber Company began rapaciously cutting the second-growth pine, the first-growth hemlock, and the sugar maple trees covering Cambria County, leaving only birch and beech as worthless or unprofitable. Forest fires burning in the slashings turned thousands of acres into a veritable wasteland, "black meadows where ashes stirred in the breeze like the pollen of infernal flowers." Mine tipples and culm banks stood out like "toadstools on the bare hills"; creeks, poisoned with sulphur, ran an orange color. "It was as if my country had been occupied by an invading army which had wasted the resources of the hills, ravaged the forests with fire and steel, fouled the waters, and now was slowly retiring, without booty." This destruction profoundly stirred Cowley's imagination. In effect, it precluded a return to the world of childhood well before the adolescent began the long process of deracination that he later dated from the moment he entered the "international republic of learning," rootless and timeless, in high school and university.[22] Indeed, Cowley was an exile by historical necessity long before he became one by choice and interpretation.

Between 1907 and 1915, when Cowley departed for Harvard, the farming paradise of childhood was irretrievably lost. Paradoxically, but not surprisingly, the process of destruction yielded a rich poetic harvest. The center of despoilment was nearby Vintondale, seat of the coke ovens and of the Vinton Lumber Company with its big lumber mill beside the North Branch of Blacklick Creek. Vintondale, Cowley remembered, was "a hellhole." Owned by the coal company "lock, stock and constables," it was about "as ravaged and grimy as a town can be." On the South Branch of Blacklick Creek, about five miles from the Cowley farmhouse, lay a community made up of miners' cabins known as Mine No. 6. It had, Cowley wrote in answer to an inquiry from Robert W. Stallman, "no other name, no post office, no school at the time, no church, no place to buy anything except the mine commissary, no law except the mine superintendent, no fish in the poisoned stream, no tree within half a mile, and nobody except the superintendent who spoke English." A seemingly unpromising subject, it brought forth one of Cowley's finest poems. "Mine No. 6," first published in the *North American Review* of August 1922, was one of the "lucky" poems that found its proper and permanent form from the beginning. Straining a modern subject against a classical sonnet form, it underwent only minor revisions over the years. Published in the same year as T. S. Eliot's *The Waste Land*, the poem evokes Cowley's vision of the spiritual wasteland of modern life.

> They scoured the hill with steel and living brooms
> of fire, that none else living might persist;
> here crouch their cabins, here the tipple looms
> uncompromising, black against the mist.
>
> All day their wagons lumber past, the wide
> squat wheels hub deep, the horses strained and still;
> a headlong rain pours down all day to hide
> the blackened stumps, the ulcerated hill.

> Beauty, perfection, I have loved you fiercely
> —even in this windy slum, where fear
> drips from the eaves with April rain, and scarcely
> a leaf sprouts, and a wilderness in pain
> brings forth its monstrous children—even here
> . . . your long white cruel fingers at my brain.[23]

In "The Hill above the Mine" the dead are the only survivors in a barren landscape of destruction. Abandoned and forgotten in their graveyard on the hill—"sprawled on the ash-gray slope above the mine, / where coke-oven fumes drift heavily by day / and creeping fires at night"—they remain as silent witnesses of a despoiled paradise, awaiting the moment of apocalyptic resurrection, the only ambiguous consolation the poet can hold out to them.

> What have you seen, O dead?
>   "We saw our woods
> butchered, flames curling in the maple tops,
> white ashes drifting, a railroad in the valley
> bridging the creek, and mine shafts under the hill.
> We saw our farms lie fallow and houses grow
> all summer in the flowerless meadows. Rats
> all winter gnawed the last husks in the barn.
> In spring the waters rose, crept through the fields
> and stripped them bare of soil, while on the hill
> we waited and slept firm."
>
>   Wait on, O dead.
> The waters still shall rise, the hills fold in,
> the graves open to heaven, and you shall ride
> eastward on a rain wind, wrapped in thunder,
> your white bones drifting like herons across the moon.[24]

Mines, lumber companies, and forest fires put an end to the magical kingdom of marginal farmers and original settlers. Young men, instead of following in their fathers' footsteps, left the region to seek employment in the mills of Johnstown and Pittsburgh or followed the lumber companies into Kentucky or Virginia for new acts of despoliation. Others went farther west to find work in Michigan factories or Oregon sawmills. They became,

Cowley observed in 1929, "landless men, trees without roots—the homeless peasants of the machine."[25] What remained of the way of life of their fathers was a host of dying and abandoned farms, dotting the countryside as reminders of an irretrievable past.

> I watched for years a sidehill farm that died
>   a little, day by day.
> Branch after branch the dooryard maples died
> and a buckwheat field was gullied into clay,
>
> to the beat . . . beat of a loose board on the barn
>   that flapped in the wind all night;
> nobody came to drive a nail in it.
>
>   . . .
>
> The farm died when two boys went away,
>
> or lived until the lame old man was buried.
>   I came then, and once more
> to see how sumac overspread the pasture,
> to smell dead leaves and hear a gust of wind
> somewhere inside the house blow shut a door.[26]

A door on the past had blown shut, but the way had been opened for what Lewis P. Simpson has diagnosed as a "poetics of exile" at the heart of Cowley's writings.[27] It is in Cowley's poetry that the process of severance and alienation is depicted most lyrically and elegiacally. "Day Coach" opened the first issue of the avant-garde little magazine *Secession* in the Spring of 1922 and is one of Cowley's better-known experimentalist poems. Counterpointing stanzas of formal and metrical regularity with sections of free, poetic prose, the poem's seven parts chart a train journey from New York back into Cambria County, past all the "grimy remembered stations" whose very names resound with the magic of childhood (Luckett, Munster, Ebensburg, Beulah Road, Nant-y-glo), to Twin Rocks, then the railroad station for Belsano. As the poet-traveler settles back in his coach, "his mind in animal reverie, kept warm / by remembered things as by an overcoat," he feels unassailable in the assurance that "strangers" can touch "only the frayed coattails of his dream." Metaphorically, the journey is a quest for a lost childhood, as the train takes the poet back over the same water he had crossed before, into the prison of his exile:

> The lights of the train now move
> transversely across the water;
> across the water strides
> the shadow of the engineer;
> barred rows of window shine across the water
> as if they marked a prison that exists
> nowhere on solid earth, but always bears
> us the condemned across a world of water.

Arriving at the station of his hometown, the traveler finds that even in the country of his boyhood he is doomed to be a spiritual exile: wandering off by himself, "Feeling the weight of darkness on his shoulders, / he stumbled on with his burden of trees and hills."[28] Shouldering his burden of alienation, the poet comes to the realization, so central to his generation's experience, that you can't go home again.

The truth of this was brought home to Cowley with renewed force during several return trips he made over the years. Shortly after his mother's death in the autumn of 1937 the son came back to sell the family summer home and its belongings. Thirty years later he recalled the day of his definitive break with his Belsano boyhood in a poem, "The Pyre," which ends with a symbolic burning of the unsold furniture in the yard. In 1970, two years after he painstakingly revised many of the poems about his Pennsylvania past, a last return proved "a sad experience," as he told Kenneth Burke. His birthplace, once a big frame house sheltered from storms by two locust trees, had now been transformed into a roadhouse, "a piss-smelling ginmill," the old clapboards covered with "dirty vomit-colored asbestos shingles," the room where he was born converted into a barroom smelling of stale beer.[29]

Nostalgia for a lost landscape of childhood remained the strongest incentive for Cowley's pastoral lyrics, memory the supreme source of consolation. Poems infused with this elegiac spirit, notably "The Chestnut Woods" and "The Urn" (perhaps Cowley's best-known poem), are among his finest accomplishments in verse. "The Chestnut Woods," first published in the February 1923 issue of Harriet Monroe's *Poetry*, is a dramatic dialogue between two poetic voices, which, vaguely conceived as a man's and a woman's, speak for contradictory impulses within the poet. Here, as elsewhere, the chestnut trees are intended as "a symbol of the rich natural world" of childhood. The dialectic in the poem is between a longing to reach back to the "spring" of youth (as in "The Living Water") and a dawning awareness of its irremediable ruination under the onslaught of urbanization and industrialization. It appropriately concludes the series of Pennsylvania poems in the first edition of *Blue Juniata* (1929).

> While nobody's million eyes are blinking, come!
>
> > It is too late now.
>
> Come far, and find a place where orchard grass,
> blue grass and fescue, white and yellow clover
> tangle an orchard slope, and juneberries
> ripen and fall at the edge of the deep woods.
>
> > Highways and areaways,
> > eyes, numbers, unremembered days;
> > it is too late now.
>
> Since unremembered days the ferns have grown
> knee deep, and moss under the chestnut trees
> hiding the footprints of small deer. You ran
> and I ran after, till we reached the spring
> that flows from underneath the chestnut roots
> in a bright stream, we traced it through the laurel,
> crossing burned ground where briars clawed us back,
> then headlong crashing down a hill to find—
>
> > and lose again and now it is too late.
> > We have lived a long time under sheet-iron skies
> > in neon-haggard dreams where no moons rise;
> > the juneberries will be withered on the branches;
> > the chestnut woods are dead.[30]

"The Urn" most poignantly and beautifully evokes the poetics of exile at the core of Cowley's literary experience. For Allen Tate it was "one of the great 20th century lyrics." It is the concluding poem to a book of verse that was meant to be "the integrated record of a life."

> Wanderers outside the gates, in hollow
> landscapes without memory, we carry

each of us an urn of native soil,
of not impalpable dust a double handful,

why kept, how gathered?—was it garden mould
or wood soil fresh with hemlock needles, pine,
and princess pine, this little earth we bore
in secret, blindly over the frontier?

—a parcel of the soil not wide enough
or firm enough to build a dwelling on
or deep enough to dig a grave, but cool
and sweet enough to sink the nostrils in
and find the smell of home, or in the ears
rumors of home like oceans in a shell.[31]

To be a wanderer outside the gates, sustained by memories of home, was not only a leitmotif in Cowley's literary life, it also constitutes the cornerstone of his interpretation of the achievements and vicissitudes of the writers of his "lost" generation. Just as in his personal life Cowley put down new roots in the land—this time in the foothills of the Berkshires rather than in Pennsylvania—so his conception of culture as an organic outgrowth of the writer's environment and experience, his humanistic insistence on a meaningful correlation between art and life, and his perpetual effort to help establish a sustaining sense of literary community are all part of Cowley's ongoing attempt (in the words of Lewis P. Simpson) to "redeem the American writer from his condition of alienation." [32] Treading in the critical footsteps of the early Van Wyck Brooks, Cowley always conceived of culture as organically related to the soil from which it sprang. Consequently, as he later wrote in *Exile's Return*, "an artisan knowing his tools and having the feel of his materials might be a cultured man," and "a farmer among his animals and his fields, stopping his plow at the fence corner to meditate over death and life and next year's crop, might have culture without even reading a newspaper." [33]

Concomitantly, Cowley always conceived of writing, in practical and professional terms, as a craft with its own high standards of excellence and decorum, and of the literary artist as foremost an artisan with an expert knowledge of his tools. Typically, he liked to envision the writer as a manual craftsman, a worker at the writer's trade. As he wrote in 1979, he preferred to regard himself as "a wordsmith essentially, working at his forge and anvil, devoted to the craft of hammering his thoughts into what he hoped would be lasting shapes."[34] Because he early recognized the paradox inherent in each literary work—both of its time and place, and growing toward an autonomous existence apart from its creator and its context— Cowley would become an expert literary historian of his own time as well as an astute technical critic.

Cowley often associated the act of writing with the concrete world of nature. Much of *Exile's Return* was "tramped out . . . on walks in the woods or along farm lanes," its crystallizing thoughts first spoken aloud "to a respectful audience of trees."[35] The result is a style that remarkably resembles Hawthorne's, another writer deeply attached to the New England soil, who developed "a natural, a *walked* style, with a phrase for every step and a comma after every phrase like a footprint in the sand."[36] In Malcolm Cowley, the man, the style, the conception of culture, and the writer's life were one.

Sharing Faulkner's "admiring and possessive" love of the land, as well as his "compulsive fear lest what he loves should be destroyed," Cowley remained a country boy at heart. All his life he was a devoted gardener and conservationist. Though he spent a substantial part of his professional life in the cosmopolitan company of big-city writers and intellectuals, particularly in New York and Paris, such a milieu filled him with feelings of uneasiness and distrust. How deeply country tastes and habits remained an ingrained part of his character is difficult to fathom. Although he may have exhibited a degree of posturing in his way of confronting city intellectuals and academics, some literary acquaintances have perhaps concluded too easily that Cowley was playing a plebeian part, construing a facade of sophisticated provincialism to hide his weaknesses. Such a feeling may have informed John Peale Bishop's condescending epithet: "the plowboy of the Western world who has been to Paris." Alfred Kazin, too, recalling Cowley's manner of addressing young potential book reviewers from behind his editorial desk at the *New Republic*, underestimated the serious impact of a largely rural upbringing and read a trait of temperament as a consciously adopted pose: "Whenever you crossed Malcolm directly, he would sidle into his familiar role of the slow-moving and slow-talking country boy from western Pennsylvania, clear-minded and deliberate, definite as the gestures with which he tapped the last pinch of tobacco into his pipe and then looked out at you through the flame of the match as he slowly

and puffingly lighted up." Cowley, indeed, preserved the slow and deliberate habits of country speech, just as he retained "a farmer's blunt hands."
But his procrastinating manner was deceptive, as was the rocklike solidity
and lucid transparency of his prose. Behind the pipe-lighting posture were
twinkling, light-blue eyes shining with quick, good-natured intelligence. If
his conversation was punctuated with "a farmer's large silences" and lacked
the verbal fireworks and fast-paced witticisms of the citified intellectual,
his words when actually spoken usually displayed a careful consideration
and judiciousness.[37]

To be nourished on local values and traditions and to be simultaneously
uprooted was an important theme of Cowley's career, as well as an essential
ingredient of his vision of modern literature. It was Cowley's destiny, as it
was the destiny of many of his generation, to live as "an exile at home,"
to be an "alien tourist" in his own country. Like Faulkner, he was condemned to live as an "internal émigré." But more than Faulkner, Cowley
was conscious of sharing the tribulations of the writing profession with
his coevals: he was both a member of a specific generation and an autonomous individual committed to his own special talent and vision. This
tension between a writer's tribal inclination and his individualistic bent lies
at the heart of Cowley's career as well as of his interpretation of his literary
generation.[38]

Pittsburgh and Peabody High

1898–1915

In late August 1898 Dr. William Cowley was summoned to Norfolk, Virginia, to be at the sickbed of his younger brother David, who had served as a volunteer in Cuba during the Spanish-American War and had contracted camp fever. As a result, only his sister Margaret, Aunt "Tannie," slightly crippled and fated to be a spinster, was at hand in the Belsano farmhouse to help his wife Josephine give birth to their first child. "For nearly two days Mother moaned in labor," Malcolm Cowley wrote in 1982. "Aunt Margaret became terrified and locked herself in a closet. There was no telephone. Finally someone heard the moans, whipped up his horse, and summoned a company doctor from the nearest coal-mining camp. The doctor arrived during a thunderstorm, just soon enough to save two lives. But Mother vowed next morning that she would never bear another child." [1]

Josephine Hutmacher Cowley was born to a family of German immigrants on December 17, 1864, in Quincey, Illinois. Her father, Rudolph Hutmacher, had fled from Westphalia to America in 1850 to avoid conscription into the Prussian army. He set up as a wholesale ice merchant on Quincey Bay and prospered by shipping ice down the Mississippi, mostly to the Anheuser-Busch brewery in St. Louis. A successful trader, he built a pretentious brick mansion at the edge of Quincey, with a high cupola overlooking the cornfields, and married Rosa Josephina Stuckenberg, the daughter of German Catholic settlers in Louisville.

Their eldest daughter, Josephine spent an unhappy childhood as "household slavey" under her mother's strict regime. She suffered the drudgeries of keeping house for a family of five brothers and four sisters and received little formal education: she attended a parochial school for five or six years and for one year was instructed by the nuns of St. Mary's Academy. She grew to be a handsome woman, "with a high brown pompadour, Gibson Girl style, gray eyes set wide apart, and classical features except for a Hutmacher nose that flared at the tip," a physical trait that she passed on to her son. Partly due to her mother's severity and lack of affectionate attention Josephine always lacked social confidence and suffered from a "sense of unworthiness." Perhaps it was she who instilled in her son a habit of modesty and an aversion to haughtiness. When she finally mustered the courage to leave home, Josephine, thirty-three and desperate to be married, found work in Pittsburgh as a seamstress for "Young, Modíste," a relatively busy dressmaker. There, Josephine met her future husband (Miss Young was a patient of Dr. Cowley). Their backgrounds differed in all respects; even physically they were oddly matched. Four inches taller than her short, round husband, she always avoided being photographed beside him. Instead of publicly walking side by side, they went for buggy rides.[2]

On his paternal side Malcolm Cowley hailed from a family of Scotch-Irish Presbyterians, who around 1840 had emigrated from the North of Ireland and settled first in Allegheny County, and afterwards in Pittsburgh, "that world metropolis of the Scotch-Irish."[3] Great-grandfather Cowley had a truck garden on Troy Hill, raising vegetables for market, and lived next door to the legendary Carnegie family, then still very poor. Great-uncle William Cowley had been one of the original Carnegie partners. He had been the only member of the Cowley clan to fight in the Civil War, and had died of typhus, thereby "permanently removing the threat of wealth from the family."[4] William's fiancée, Margaret Mowry, subsequently married his brother David, Cowley's grandfather, who had broken with the family tradition of Presbyterianism and exchanged its aspiration to business success and military glory for the devout and mystical writings of Emanuel Swedenborg (1688–1772); David Cowley set up practice as a homeopathic physician in Pittsburgh.[5]

His son, William, was born on September 8, 1864, in Pittsburgh and, like his father before him, was a pious, devoted Swedenborgian and an honest but not very successful homeopathic physician. His father, Cowley recalled, was "an impractical, wholly lovable man," who into old age, though plagued with arthritis, retained the benevolent looks of "a little round Santa Claus." His office was located in the Wallace Building, a three-story apartment building of grimy yellow brick in the commercial center of East Liberty, Pittsburgh, on Center and South Highland avenues. With streetcars rumbling past until far into the night, with shops on the ground floor and a few cramped apartments occupied by music teachers and unprosperous physicians above, the building provided a rather inglorious, forbidding setting for a writer's boyhood.

After her marriage, Josephine Cowley surrendered her Catholicism and joined the Church of the New Jerusalem, though she never ventured far into Swedenborg's mystical writings or tried to understand his doctrines about the spiritual world. Forty years later, on her deathbed, she would ask to see a Catholic priest to receive absolution. "A restless, energetic woman, big-boned, full-bosomed, and proud of the strength in her arms," she never was fully accepted into the Cowley clan.[6] By temperament, social background, and education, she seemed a little out of place among the Cowleys, who still treasured memories of a more glorious past, when the family had the services of a coachman and two servants. Impoverished intellectuals of a sort—uncle Henry was a Swedenborgian minister and aunt Eliza had married an Englishman with ambitions for a similar vocation—the Cowleys cherished books and liked to discuss the mystical writings of the founder with others in the Swedenborgian community. Unused to manual labor and given to study and debate, the Cowleys of Malcolm's father's generation seem to have confirmed the popular view of Swedenborgians as "a dreamy and mystical people." Their impracticality was such that even their Swedenborgian friends spoke of them as "a little queer." The Cowley clan was privately condescending to Josephine, a simple and kindhearted woman who had no interest in books but was supremely skillful in practical matters.[7]

The impact of the family's Swedenborgianism on Malcolm Cowley's literary outlook and career is difficult to assess. Never formally instructed in its religious doctrines, Cowley was yet exposed to the philosopher's notions of divine providence, "conjugial" love, and the promise of spiritual reunion in a heavenly afterlife. "Graves played no part in our Swedenborgian family, / with my father's trust in celestial reunions," he recalled in a late poem.[8] Every day at noon, unless he was at school, his father read him a passage from Swedenborg's writings, to which he "scarcely listened"; and every night at bedtime, until he was twelve, Cowley was read a chapter from the Bible. Many of Swedenborg's writings were available only in Latin. The English translations used by Cowley's father could do little to fan the boy's interest; they were, Cowley recalled, "in leaden prose that put me to sleep."[9] But even if he could have understood the original, he might have sympathized with the verdict of an earlier admirer of the Swedish mystic, Henry James, Sr.: "Swedenborg's intellect was singularly deficient in *humor*. . . . Thus it is, that whether I read of heaven and its orderly peaceful vicissitudes, or of hell and its insane delights, and feel the while my moral sense amply satisfied, I must say that to my aesthetic sense . . . the result is very much the same in either case, being always very dull and prosaic, with the poetical element very nearly eliminated." [10]

It is not unlikely that the religious atmosphere of a Swedenborgian up-bringing worked its influence by indirection. From Swedenborg's theo-logical mysticism to theories of utopian socialism is not such a big step. In mid-nineteenth-century America Swedenborg's visionary predictions of the Church of the New Jerusalem as "a new social and spiritual order" found a sympathetic ear with many followers of Charles Fourier, for whom the social implications of Swedenborg's theology were easily apparent. [11] An early exposure to the Swedish mystic may well have prepared the way for Cowley's later dreams of a new social and economic order, built on justice and equality, which could satisfy man's spiritual as well as physical needs. Just as for the elder James the conjunction of Swedenborg and Fourier provided an opportunity for "a marriage of Society and God," so Cowley, basing his thoughts on the writings of Emile Durkheim and William Ernest Hocking, later inclined toward an explanation of religion in terms of soci-ety and, conversely, of communism in terms of religion. [12] Cowley wrote retrospectively that in the radical 1930s he had been "less Marxian than Emersonian." [13] Such insights, tied to the recurrent presence of Emerson in Cowley's later writings, tempt one to read his later interest in Emerson as a modified return to the Swedenborgian creed of his family.

Nonetheless, from early youth Cowley's temperament clashed with his father's predilection for the mystical and supernatural. If he inherited his father's love of reading, he took after his mother in his inclination toward the pragmatic. Though he "always respected" his father "for holding fast to his beliefs," Cowley had begun to reject his Swedenborgianism well be-fore he was fifteen. In 1943 he observed in a letter that he had "rejected all religious dogmas so long ago that the loss of faith seems to have been an experience of early childhood." And in a 1924 letter to Kenneth Burke he emphatically repudiated the notion of a personal immortality and a divine providence: "Such topics are sweet to meditate, in the country, in the dusk, when one is seventeen." [14] Much later he felt that, rather than a pervasive Swedenborgianism, it had been "the decay of the Protestant sects" that had largely determined his (and his coevals') religious back-ground: "pragmatism and instrumentalism was not for us a point of view to be adopted after struggles, but something taken for granted at first, and then questioned afterwards." Yet Cowley too, though not exactly raised in a Calvinist tradition, had "a Protestant ethic drilled into [him]." [15]

On the whole the effects of Swedenborgianism on his character were only indirectly religious. Having lost his belief in divine providence in early adolescence, his father's daily readings nevertheless impressed upon him a carefree confidence in life, "the habit of not worrying about tomorrow." Similarly, Cowley retained a strong belief in the sacredness of marital or, as Swedenborg called it, "conjugial" love; for twelve years it kept him from divorcing his first wife, in spite of mutual pain, even though he later felt he had had ample "cause for divorce and three times fell in love with other women." [16] In part his rejection of formalized religious doctrine may have come so soon and so easy, because Cowley, like Henry James, Jr., was (in the words of Leon Edel) exposed "much more to religious *feeling* than to religion itself." Still, Cowley never considered himself an atheist. "We all feel the need of some doctrine to color our live[s]. . . . All of us, even the confirmed William Jennings Bryans of science, feel the need of some religion," he observed in his notebook in the early 1920s. "I don't think there are any true atheists," he speculated almost sixty years later; "Everybody has some sort of God, if he is only an abstract principle." There came a time when Cowley believed, with Durkheim, that God is Society. But he continued to believe that there are "depths of the mind in which the Passion survives for most of us, religious or irreligious, as the archetypical story." [17] Religion, either in the sense of formalized doctrine or as intuitive faith, was not a guiding principle in Cowley's life. But it was not absent from it; rather, as it had been for Henry James, it was translated into a religious passion for art.

The seeds of Cowley's literary ambition lay in the experiences of early childhood. In his infant years Cowley enjoyed his mother's undivided attention. Josephine nursed her only child for sixteen months and, radiating maternal pride, used to parade him through East Liberty in snow-white dresses that she herself had embroidered. She instilled in her son an early feeling of difference, of being the "center" of the "mysterious world." Years later, aware of possible overtones of "the too-famous Oedipus complex," Cowley recalled the moments of strong affection when, having slept late, his mother let him climb into her warm bed. Even when they quarreled, he then reflected, they fought "as equals, almost as a married pair." If he "never quarreled" with his father, "never felt him to be a rival," the effects of his mother's unswerving devotion stayed with him all his life. In later years he recognized the pertinence of Sigmund Freud's observation in *The Interpretation of Dreams* that "a man who has been the indisputable favorite of his mother keeps for life the feeling of a conqueror, that confidence of success that often induces real success."[18] Before long, the boy's sense of specialness, of being fortune's favorite son, grew into a self-confident desire to be a famous and successful writer.

A shift in his relations with his mother occurred when Cowley reached the age of six. Spurred on by his father, an avid reader and admirer of Charles Dickens, he entered a new world closed to his mother. "You learned to read," she told him later, "and you weren't my boy any more." From here on she expended her nervous energies on countless practical projects, partly to make or save some money, partly to find an outlet for her thwarted affection. For three years, obsessed with poultry, she raised special breeds of chickens in Belsano, as well as guinea fowl, turkeys, pigeons, and geese. At other times she was seized with a passion for baking pies and loaves, sewing quilts, or collecting lamps and music boxes at country auctions. Once, on a visit to the farmhouse, Cowley found the parlor given over to a free-flying flock of canaries, which she hoped to sell at a profit.

Others now claimed their share of his mother's untapped affection. When Cowley was twelve she adopted the two-week-old illegitimate child of a distant relative. The little girl, Ruth, not only allowed Josephine to relive her early days of motherhood, but also was "affectionate, mostly obedient, always eager to help," where her son had at times been difficult, stubborn, and recalcitrant. In 1919 Ruth died of diphtheria at the age of nine, depriving Cowley of the nearest equivalent to a sister and leaving a searing emptiness in his mother's life. Later, she took into her home the little daughter of a miner whose wife had just died, and cherished her as her own child until the father could remarry. Once she gave shelter to a lively girl of fourteen who, Cowley recalled, "caused a scandal by leading boys behind the barn."[19] Her concern for the needy was reflected in her son's humanitarian sympathies during the depression years and in his willingness to help writers in need.

Cowley's parents were unpretentious and hardworking people, "not quite members of the respectable middle class." In their unassuming fashion, they strove to inculcate in their son the principles of conventional middle-class morality. Josephine, in particular, passed on some of her "unspoken standards" to her son, not alone "a practical sense of what things were worth," but the importance of "keeping one's word, paying one's debts, not being wasteful, and doing honest work even if it went unpaid." The one attempt she made to instill at least a modicum of culture into her son was her insistence that in spite of his short and stiff fingers he learn to play the piano. In his adult years Cowley still occasionally performed the Chopin waltzes and Beethoven sonatas he had played in early youth "with more brio than correctness." One of his earliest pieces of verse, "Chopin," published in his high-school literary magazine in March 1915, paid tribute to a favorite composer:

> Bearded professors in their musty schools
>> Have analyzed your every pulsing dance
>> Into its mingled chord and dissonance.
> I think those garbling pedants are but fools
>> And see a Polish warrior with a lance
> Stalk lord-like through each stately Polonaise,
> And after burning tones and chords that blaze,
>> Hear a still voice with half-abashed caress
>> Sing like a maiden in the wilderness. [20]

Cowley's musical training, such as it was, may well have helped to give him a feeling for the sound and rhythm of words.

Though the Cowleys lived in East Liberty, a generally prosperous area of Pittsburgh, and were able to afford an underpaid servant, their social status was insecure. Josephine felt somewhat abashed by the Pittsburgh ladies, and on the rare occasion when she invited them to afternoon tea spent "hours polishing the family silver and ironing the fine-linen tablecloths she had strained her eyes to embroider." The Cowleys, indeed, were regarded as "quite strange, if harmless, and too poor to clothe themselves properly." As a result, young Cowley felt a slight, if not a traumatic, sense of social maladjustment: "I didn't wear the right clothes or use the same words as my schoolmates."[21] Dr. Cowley was a good and generous man who allowed his medical services to go unremunerated too often. In the economic crisis of 1907 his income was cut in half, as steel mills closed down, patients stopped paying their bills, and banks refused to give out loans. For three winters Cowley walked the mile to school without an overcoat or a muffler. Eventually his mother bought him a raincoat at a bargain sale, but the memory of such early deprivations rankled.

Cowley grew up a rather lonely and neglected child. Once, in Belsano, his mother having been summoned to Pittsburgh by a family crisis, the eleven-year-old boy was left alone for an entire month and suffered serious malnutrition: the sores on his legs were later diagnosed as symptoms of scurvy. Even in the city he seldom saw his father except at bedtime for the daily ritual of Bible reading. His mother rarely bothered to inquire where or how he spent his time and often he was left to his own resources, free to indulge in reading or to explore vacant lots in the neighborhood. Since the Wallace Building was situated in a business area, there were no other boys on the same block, and thus Cowley was without playmates most of the time. As if in compensation, he chose to live in an "imaginary world peopled with Scottish clansmen and Robin Hood's band." The loss of his mother's attention at an early age, Cowley reflected as late as 1982, "made me a loner for many years that followed, down to this morning."[22]

The years of loneliness and poverty mark an important formative phase in Cowley's literary career. They triggered a desire to rise from such early humiliations "by force of ability," and help to explain his later "rage for putting justificatory words together." Such a period, Cowley wrote to Alfred Kazin in 1962, occurs in almost every literary life and is the writer's salvation as well as his sorrow; "the early humiliation is what winds him up and keeps him going." One should be grateful for it, Cowley felt, or at most, regret it was not worse.[23]

Loneliness helped to make Cowley a passionate reader. His early reading was voracious but indiscriminate. On cold winter mornings he raced through the twenty-five volumes of Scott's Waverley novels in his father's Pittsburgh waiting room; on rainy summer afternoons he climbed to the attic of the farmhouse in Belsano and devoured the bound volumes of ancient magazines full of stories of slavers, filibusters, and pirates, of African travels, the battle of Sedan, and of the Civil War.[24] From the circulating library in a local stationery store he borrowed trashy romances, which he consumed by the armload. From the East Liberty branch of Carnegie Library he borrowed books that made a more lasting impression, long historical novels filled with action and color, such as the Polish trilogy of the 1905 Nobel Prize-winner Henryk Sienkiewicz, whose *With Fire and Sword*, *The Deluge*, and *Pan Michael* he relished especially. Written in a vivid style of epic clarity and, despite their theatricality, possessed of real narrative power, such books helped give the young Cowley a "taste for history and geography" and catered to "his youthful romanticism."[25] Mostly, his early reading spurred his imagination and incited an early ambition to write books of his own. It provided him with subjects, scenes, characters, and an abundance of new words for what became an inveterate habit of his writing life: an "inner conversation" between the storyteller and the listener in himself. This lonely custom of conducting "imaginary conversations with imaginary playmates" heightened a sense of separateness from his co-evals and helped to give him, in his own words, "the sense of perspective that writers have to possess."[26]

‹ ‹ ‹   Malcolm Cowley attended elementary school in Pittsburgh from October 1904 through June 1911. He completed his first seven grades at Shakespeare School, where he was a good but not always diligent pupil. The principal, Miss Ella Hanlon, whom Cowley remembered with respect and affection, used to move him into a higher grade whenever he showed any disposition to study. For his eighth grade he went to Liberty School, attending a three-room "high-school class" headed by Miss Ruswinkle. There he wrote his first story, later published in the high-school literary paper, about Allison Crawford, then his best and almost only friend:

> He was two years older than I, a sandy-haired boy with a high, thin bridge to his nose, that gave him a look of quizzical contempt. I thought, and still think, that I had never met anyone so brilliant or so far beyond his years. At fifteen he wrote some stories that are still remembered by his high-school classmates. He also began to visit the red-light district that flourished on Second Avenue, chiefly because he thought it was the reckless thing to do. At sixteen he contracted gonorrhea, which was never cured. At seventeen he got into a street fight with an amateur boxing champion. He was kicked in the bladder, complications set in and he died a few months later. At twelve and thirteen, when I knew him best, he already seemed to carry with him an intimation, almost a halo, of early death.[27]

Allison Crawford was Cowley's first acquaintance with the picturesque and squalid heroism of the bohemian artist, the world-weary pose of the decadent aesthete, and the shocking indifference to prevailing moral standards of the dadaist. It was a type he would frequently encounter in the artistic milieu of Greenwich Village and the Quartier Latin, though by then his admiration was strongly qualified. In 1910, at age twelve or thirteen,

Crawford inspired Cowley with visions of reckless adventure and tragic, sordid love and embodied the glories of the literary life.

Apart from the four months in 1912 when he was enrolled in the Academy of the New Church in Bryn Athyn, a Swedenborgian school near Philadelphia, Cowley attended a public high school in Pittsburgh. From September 1911 through June 1915 he was at Peabody High School, then new, well-equipped, and numbering about a thousand pupils. Cowley was in the second class to graduate. Though the general atmosphere was "prosperous and middle-class," the attending pupils were socially and racially mixed and Cowley consorted with youngsters from various backgrounds. His later sensitivity to the formative influence of social class and background on a writer's character and career may well owe something to his early years at Peabody. In 1936 he looked back "with deep gratitude to the fact that I went to school with poor kids in the city and with farmers in the country." [28]

Cowley's literary ambitions materialized early. "I wanted to be a writer from the time I entered Peabody High School and began contributing to the school paper," he wrote to Stanley Young in 1944. Cowley was lucky in his choice of Peabody. Instruction, by all accounts, was excellent; it allowed him to be excused from taking English A when he later entered Harvard and enabled him to establish an excellent record during his freshman year. He hardly bothered to distinguish himself socially and athletically but soon managed to make himself conspicuous in Peabody's rather exceptional literary crowd. He began writing for the *Peabody*, the school's literary paper, in early 1913, was a member of Peabody's literary society, and became president of the debating club. In its January 1915 issue the *Peabody* reported "a clean-cut victory" for Peabody's visiting team in interscholastic debate with Central High School's home team: "Our speakers, Malcolm Cowley, Mollie Davidson, and Jacob Davis, seemed perfectly at home before the large audience, which applauded Central enthusiastically. Each one did well, and they won a unanimous decision by clear and logical argument. The debate was one of the best that have been held in the league." Cowley was also awarded a ten-karat gold medal for essay writing, and upon his graduation in 1915 ("with honors") was elected class poet.[29]

Between February 1913 and June 1915 Cowley contributed five short stories and seven poems to the *Peabody*. One of his earliest pieces of verse, "To Lotta on Her Double Chin," pictured the young ambitious poet-philosopher vainly and self-ironically yearning for an unattainable high-school love, but doing so in a mock-Romantic fashion that suggested an early talent for parodic wit:

> I cannot paint the smiling lines that creep
>> Through your pink nose; the blush that dyes your skin,
>> Nor tell the pert charm of your pointed chin.
> I know, but cannot tell just how you keep
> A crowd around you always. Words are cheap
>> And I am losing time, for as I sing
>> Of your two jewels made for languishing,
> Others are stealing favors I should reap.
> But my great day will come in twenty years
>> When those two dancing eyes of yours will blur,
>> At that far day when you will wear a rat
> And mourn your youthful grace with futile tears.
>> For then, my dear, I'll be Philosopher,
>> While you at forty, Lotta, will be fat.

Another poem, "True to Art," written in a similarly satiric vein, mocked the lack of realism in the romantic popular literature of the time, with typical cleverness and a touch of humor:

> The type of hero found in books
> Who wins his love by fighting crooks
> Beats out the rest of us for looks,
> Is captain of the Harvard crew
> And stands, when barefoot, six feet two,
> Some books tell how his life was passed
> And how he died, game to the last;
> But in most tales—I wonder why—
> He lives and lets the villain die.
> Still things are not quite what they seem
> In every matinee girl's dream
> And life, as usual, bursts the bubble:
> It's villains, who are quite the rage,
> Live long and die at last of age;
> It's heroes die of stomach trouble.

The short stories he wrote for the *Peabody*, if distinctly juvenile, also exhibit a precocious feeling for characterization and a remarkable narrative control. "The Best Story of the Year," published in June 1915, not only testified to the intensity of its author's adolescent ambitions but also showed that, from the first, Cowley was intrigued by the problems of art and craftsmanship besetting the writers of his age group. Inspired by his friendship with Allison Crawford, the story deals with the son of a poor music teacher who is pressured to realize vicariously the literary ambitions of the father. Finding himself without a subject and a style, the son secretly arranges with an older, more sophisticated, and already-published high-school writer to write a story for him, against payment. The ensuing literary fame places the son in a false position, as he is now expected to turn out a story every month. Crisis comes when his self-enamored ghostwriter makes stiffer financial demands than can be met. In despair, the son, who has meanwhile acquired a style of his own from copying and secretly revising his mentor's prose, dashes off a story about his recent humiliations that miraculously wins him greater popularity than before. In conclusion Cowley posited a typical literary moral: whereas the "intellectual" senior writer had "tried to write literature," the younger boy had "tried only to write a good story, and succeeded in writing a good story, a very good story, the best story of the year." [30]

Cowley's literary consorts at Peabody made up a motley but remarkable crew: Kenneth Burke, with whom he had also attended eighth grade, would go on to a distinguished career as a critic and philosopher of language; Jake Davis, vice president of the debating club, followed Cowley to Harvard and became head of a firm of diamond merchants in Pittsburgh; James Light would go on to Ohio State University, edit the collegiate magazine *Sansculotte*, and become theatrical director of the Provincetown Players in postwar Greenwich Village; Susan Jenkins, who became Light's wife and later married the novelist William Slater Brown, would write a book of memories of Hart Crane; Mary Blair would study at the Carnegie Tech School of the Theatre, become a leading actress with the Provincetown Players, and marry Edmund Wilson. Most of these classmates were editors of or contributors to Peabody's literary monthly, members of the literary society and debating club, and, as Susan Jenkins recalled, "loyal rooters" for the school's champion football team. It was an intellectually precocious and self-consciously brilliant group. A nonliterary classmate remembered how Cowley, Burke, and Davis used to terrorize the teachers "by being brilliant and knowing so much."[31]

At Peabody Cowley also had his initiation into literary politics. It occurred when he was seventeen, and it was, he later told Allen Tate, "an almost traumatic experience." On the brink of being named editor of the high-school paper, Cowley's appointment was overruled by the faculty adviser, who decreed that the editor was to be chosen by a vote of the class. Four candidates were named: Burke, Cowley, Davis—each excellently fitted for the job—and Russell Farrell, who had not even written for the paper. The outcome was predictable: Burke, Cowley, and Davis split the vote, and Farrell was elected.[32] In the long run, such experiences taught Cowley much about the folkways of the literary community and, as no college course could, convinced him of the necessity of tact and circumspection in his dealings with fellow writers. Though this knowledge eventually helped make him an eminently tactful literary politician, it was not enough to protect him against blundering at times into hot and hurtful situations.

Cowley's most intimate friend at Peabody was Kenneth Burke. They first met in 1901, when Dr. Cowley, the Burkes' family physician, had taken his wife and three-year-old son along for a visit. On their first day together, his mother later recalled, Cowley "went around the Burke parlor touching everything in reach while Kenneth followed repeating apprehensively, 'Don't touch, Musn't.'"[33] Though Burke was his senior by some sixteen months—he was born in Pittsburgh on May 5, 1897—in their early years Cowley appears to have been the more reckless and venturesome of the two, the natural one to lead and take initiatives. Round-faced, chubby-cheeked, blue-eyed, with a thick wave of hair and a solid, somewhat clumsy build, Cowley made a more daunting impression in adolescence than Burke, agile, of nimble mind, and of slighter build. Referring to a poem recited in high school, Cowley once spoke of them as "the mountain" and "the squirrel."[34] Pimpled, awkward, bashful, and self-questioning, yet given to boastful posturing as a shield against shyness, Cowley was inclined to adopt an attitude of protective and solicitous concern toward the sensitive, timid Burke. Burke remembered being admonished by Cowley in youthful arrogance: "You are at your best when you are like me."[35] Wholly engrossed in their own hesitantly developing personalities, yet persuaded of their secret distinction, the boys brooded on the mysteries of death and sex, and yearned for love. They naively assumed that the world-weary stance of the decadent aesthete would mysteriously endow them with artistic genius. Leagued in covert companionship against an insensitive adult society, they often met at night at the Carnegie Library in Schenley Park. Burke later recalled how he and Cowley read technical and theoretical "how-to" books on poetry, drama, and story writing, and took a particular fancy to authors on the librarian's list of "restricted" modern literature: Ibsen, Shaw, Wilde, Dostoyevski. When the library closed at ten o'clock, the two walked home together, a stretch of some three miles, along Ellsworth Avenue, conducting heavy-handed philosophical discussions, punctured by shouts and fierce gesticulations, on the literary and amorous topics closest to their hearts.[36]

They were entirely different in character and intellectual disposition. Bristling with ideas, Burke's ceaselessly fermenting and punning mind was already marked by what Stanley Edgar Hyman has called an "endless fertility, suggestiveness, an inexhaustible throwing off of sparks." Whereas Burke's mind tended to move from concrete instances and specific works to general concepts and hidden principles, thus making him one of the boldest synthetic and "truly speculative" thinkers of his era, Cowley had primarily a poet's and historian's sensibility. His mind, as Allen Tate noted in an early review, was "basically concrete and unspeculative."[37] Unlike Burke's intellectual fireworks, Cowley's writing habits were careful and laborious and involved slow and painstaking revision. Their handwriting reflected their different personalities. Where Burke wrote a cryptically illegible hand, resembling secret hieroglyphics and having the look, as Cowley once remarked, of minuscule mouse droppings or sparrows' footprints in the sand, Cowley's handwriting was classically round, bold, and lucid. Already as youngsters their temperaments were so unmistakably their own that there was little danger of one succumbing to the other's influence. Though their early views on art and life were developed in close communion and correspondence, each remained his own man and followed the direction of his intellectual and emotional disposition. Whereas in their early years Cowley appeared the bolder leader, even if he was occasionally daunted by Burke's complexity and soon had intimations of inferiority, in the end Burke proved the more persistent quester and innovative explorer. Without a doubt they aided each other in their intellectual development and reinforced each other's inclination toward the literary life. Convinced that true friendship demanded radical frankness, they felt that tact and consideration would reduce them to mere acquaintances. Accordingly, they tended to be unsparing in analyzing each other's characters and criticizing each other's literary efforts; in the ring of letters they were each other's principal sparring partners. Though their friendship would suffer injuries along the way, it continued, intact and unabated, until Cowley's death. Their literary correspondence extends over seven decades and constitutes a unique chapter in American literary history.[38]

‹ ‹ ‹   Cowley grew up during the period Van Wyck Brooks has famously labeled "The Confident Years." It was a time when the majority of Americans lived in a moral atmosphere of belated Victorianism "even stiffer and stuffier than Victoria's English reign" and still retained an unshakable faith in the reality and certainty of universal and eternal moral values. The period basked in a spirit of rational, scientific optimism and was marked by faith in automatic social evolution. Technology produced miracles like the first automobiles and movie houses. Cities grew rapidly and agricultural-industrial production soared, holding a promise that, in Cowley's words, the world would grow "in wealth and wisdom toward the goal of universal peace." The moral protestations and pleas for reform of the muckrakers barely affected the social and religious foundations of the system: people retained their confidence in "the basic rightness of things as they were." There was no reason to doubt that social ills could be adjusted, as long as young boys grew up to become honest and hardworking men who strove for success by a diligent pursuit of their personal interests and thereby ensured the progress of society.[39]

To Cowley, in the throes of adolescence, such a moral atmosphere seemed oppressive and debilitating rather than reassuring. By the time of his graduation from Peabody in the summer of 1915 he had come to question most of the values and traditions of his upbringing. Countless arguments about God and religion had led him to reject his parents' Swedenborgianism; at seventeen he was "converted to indifferentism." He repudiated prevailing morality as the cloak of a prudish puritanism. To want to be a poet was in itself an act of filial disloyalty and rebellion; he was, he later wrote in a long, confessional poem, "a bad son, but a poet"— " 'My world has deeper colors than yours,' / I boasted, 'and the words will come / to match the colors.' "[40] In a society ruled by scientific, impersonal laws, Cowley felt geared toward a future that seemed the epitome of boredom and security. Nor did Belsano promise a more inspiring future. Young men of Cowley's age either could move away and become landless, homeless servants of technology or could stay behind and succumb to "the yoke of women and the past." For a youngster with artistic aspirations the country offered only the options of exile or imprisonment. In 1915, with other incipient artists of his age, Cowley felt as if he were on a train smoothly gliding toward a destination he would never have chosen for himself.[41]

There were signs, however, that the complacent surface of Victorianism was cracking. For all its apparent moral certainty the Progressive period was, in the words of Alfred Kazin, "an upheaval, a sudden stirring, a breaking of the bonds between the old order and the new." The years of Cowley's adolescence witnessed the gradual disintegration of moral and religious confidence. As Henry F. May has shown, this disintegrative process, most commonly associated with the revolution in morals and manners of the postwar years, was already well under way before, and then sharply accelerated by, World War I. If, in art and literature, this breaking up of traditional standards led Ezra Pound to proclaim, in 1913, the imminence of an "American Risorgimento" and Van Wyck Brooks to announce America's cultural "Coming-of-Age," for a younger generation the joyful expectation of an artistic renaissance was often dimmed by a mood of puzzled search and self-questioning.[42]

In a time when literary standards were predominantly British and literature was regarded as "an effeminate upper-class affair open chiefly to men with a Harvard education," it was Cowley's reading of the *Smart Set* that opened up new literary vistas. The *Smart Set*, originally an upper-class magazine of cosmopolitan sophistication, allowed young writers of Cowley's midwestern middle-class background to breathe vicariously an artistic atmosphere of subtle, aristocratic affectation. In 1913, in particular, the magazine, then under the editorship of Willard Huntington Wright (H. L. Mencken became co-editor, with George Jean Nathan, in 1914), had a "tremendous" impact on young Cowley. It exposed him to an impressive array of modern European writers, none of whom he had before encountered in an American magazine: Arthur Schnitzler, James Joyce, D. H. Lawrence, Max Beerbohm, Frank Wedekind, Mikhail Artzibashev, Gabriel d'Annunzio. "It seemed," Cowley recalled, "that a new world was being revealed to us, that it was time to smash the Victorian gods, open all the windows, go floating off on a cloud of dream toward golden Vienna and Paris the City of Light."[43]

In early adolescence Cowley thought the *Smart Set* "the wittiest, the most deliciously wicked of American magazines." No doubt this was partly due to the presence of H. L. Mencken, whose irony and idol-smashing were perfectly attuned to Cowley's dissatisfied adolescent sensibility. At fourteen, he "worshiped" Mencken, read every author he recommended, and "took his word for gospel." It was Mencken who set him dreaming of becoming a critic: "I would praise good books, tell the bitter truth about the others, recite little German lyrics, and drink tremendous seidels of Löwenbrau." By the end of his high-school years, however, Cowley had begun to turn against the Sage of Baltimore and come to find "his perpetual mockery a rather slender diet." By 1919 he regarded him as his "bitterest enemy," spoke of him as "the greatest existing menace to American letters," and would "cheerfully have hanged him to the nearest lamp-post." By 1927 he felt that, as a critic, Mencken was puerile and immature, and showed "the keen literary judgment of a peewit."[44]

At seventeen, the intensity of Cowley's literary ambition was unmistakable; indefinite were the form and direction it was to take. "We were launching or drifting into the sea of letters with no fixed destination and without a pilot," Cowley observed in *Exile's Return*. Eager to establish a mode of writing that could give artistic expression to his own youthful sense of life, he lacked experience and suitable models to emulate. The effect of his high-school instruction in literature, Cowley later felt, was little short of disastrous. It implied that America was "beneath the level of great fiction," that only foreign authors were worthy of admiration, that wisdom and beauty were the exclusive property of Europe and the past. If he wanted to write about his own contemporary reality, he was made to adopt "a standardized Amerenglish as colorless as Esperanto," instead of a language properly rooted in his own time and place. In high school, Cowley wrote in a famous passage, he and his coevals were subjected to a "process of deracination," which ended by making them "homeless citizens of the world." Only the examples of Edgar Lee Masters and Carl Sandburg proved that in America art could be made out of a narrow midwestern provincialism. It was they who incited Cowley to write verse.[45]

Seeking guidance, Cowley plunged into an extensive course of reading that continued through his college years. From Dickens, Scott, and Sienkiewicz he went on to Keats, Swinburne, Kipling, Stevenson, Meredith, Hardy, and Gissing, then to Maugham, Conrad, and the writers first sampled in the *Smart Set*. James Light introduced him to modern dramatists like Ibsen, Shaw, Strindberg, Wilde, Hauptmann.[46] From there he passed on to Chekhov, Dostoyevski, and the Elizabethan dramatists and, later, steeped himself in the writings of the French symbolists, in particular Baudelaire and Laforgue. At Harvard he was exposed to the influence of such American moderns as Amy Lowell, Conrad Aiken, and T. S. Eliot. Such explorations were neither original nor idiosyncratic. Most important, they exposed Cowley to the sensibility of modernism, "ironical, intro-spective and self-questioning." Though he barely understood the aesthetic assumptions and intellectual premises underlying the modern spirit, his reading dramatically changed his literary taste in that it led him to discover "subtler methods and more difficult standards in literature than those of the *Saturday Evening Post*."[47] The process of discovery of and adjustment to the modern spirit was by no means easy or untroubled; Cowley's search for aesthetic guidance was marked by an uncertainty and ambivalence that continued through the 1920s.

Toward the end of his high-school years Cowley had evolved his own peculiar notion of the "modern": its crux lay in the "sense of paradox." Whereas a classical writer's reactions were emotionally logical and thus predictable, the modern writer, Cowley observed in a later notebook entry, was embarked on a "constant round of convolutions": he subverted his readers' expectations by inverting logic. Cowley and Burke had first de-veloped this "theory of convolutions" at Peabody. Motivated by a desire to be different and advanced at all costs, they adopted a chain of literary enthusiasms, then quickly discarded or inverted them as soon as less mod-ern followers had caught up. They praised Oscar Wilde when others were still mired in Victorian or Edwardian dullness; as soon as others had ad-vanced to Wilde, they denounced him in favor of Strindberg, Schnitzler, or Flaubert. In the end they lost track of whom to praise or to condemn and were caught in a vicious circle: the ultimate "convolution" was to be like everybody else, while cherishing a sense of secret distinction as apprentice writers who could appreciate the "modern" and understand the "sense of paradox."[48]

Such theories helped prepare Cowley to understand a mode of the artis-tic life he later subsumed into his interpretation of the "religion of art." It was the perfect theory for young writers with grand ambitions but without as yet much to say: "We wanted merely to live in ourselves and be writers." By 1915 Cowley had come to feel that "artists" were different from ordi-nary "lifelings"; they constituted a special, secret order, a freemasonry of initiates who lived in a world of their own and maintained only the most tenuous of connections with the "real world."[49] From here it was but a step to embracing the aesthetics of symbolism and the belief of salvation by art alone. Upon his graduation from Peabody High in June 1915 he found the door to a life devoted to the possibility of modern art in America wide open; beyond it loomed a long process of uneasy and ambiguous accommodation.

‹ ‹ ‹   Cowley spent his first weeks after commencement in wistful idleness, cherishing the memory of a "jubilant" class night, attending graduation parties and consorting with other "outs" in Pittsburgh. Acting against his parents' wishes, he had applied for a scholarship from the Harvard Club of Western Pennsylvania and was anxiously awaiting news from the committee. He had scored excellent marks for English and Latin in his entrance examinations and his hopes were high. Meanwhile, he took classmates Susan Jenkins and James Light on outings on the Allegheny River, haunted the moving-picture palaces, and wrote plaintive letters to Kenneth Burke, berating him for not writing old classmates and criticizing his poems for retaining too much *Smart Set* artiness. With Burke gone—he had moved with his parents to Weehawken, New Jersey—Cowley felt lonesome. His letters were filled with ironic self-lamentations. On June 24, 1915, he complained: "I often have that empty feeling at the pit of my stomach, which takes the bassoon part in the series of unconnected dissonances with no discoverable tonic or dominant which seems to make up life." At school they were on terms of such exclusive intimacy with each other that they kept themselves from broad acquaintanceships with other schoolmates. He now advised Burke to meet many strangers and resolved to devote himself to friendships during his freshman year at Harvard.

By the end of July he was back in Belsano. The country gave Cowley a curious shift in perspective. From Belsano, Pittsburgh and Cambridge seemed "far off towns," and he feared that ultimately the attractions of country living would prove the deathblow to his literary ambitions: "I would be quite content to stay here, managing my own farm and bossing a hired man, until literary ambitions seemed as far off as New York city," he wrote on July 20. Thoroughly absorbed in summer activities on the farm, he seemed to lose his sustained capacity for writing and thinking: "the pen is becoming a strange weapon to me." Art flourished best in an atmosphere of languishing decadence; rural Belsano seemed fatally uncongenial to literary creation: "I have no moods. I write no poetry. The country is decidedly healthy, and health produces no modern literature." [50]

As his letters testify, many of the conflicting impulses that governed Cowley's career were germinally present at this stage. City and country exerted contradictory pulls, and the attractions of rural living seemed to cancel the realization of his literary dreams. The demands of the writing life collided with his social instinct for companionship and the impulse to immerse himself in the active, practical reality of life. Indeed, the seeds of his later ambivalence about a life exclusively devoted to art had been sown even before he entered Harvard: "after all," he reflected, "the passion to write novels cannot fill a whole life. There must be something else, or one cannot even write novels."[51]

In mid-August, upon learning that his application for a scholarship had miscarried, he returned for a short visit to Pittsburgh. If Harvard fell through, he decided, he would follow James Light and Susan Jenkins to Ohio State. Some days later, back in Belsano digging ditches, he learned he had been awarded a $150 scholarship after all: "It seems to me that Harvard is my fate," he wrote to Burke.[52]

As long as he remained engrossed in country life—early September was threshing time and Cowley was busy helping the neighboring farmers harvest grain—his interest in writing waned. He was fully confident, however, that his stay in Cambridge would bring it back. "Wait a month till the metropolis has fascinated me," he wrote Burke on September 3, "till I begin whirling in the squirrel cage of success." He was expected to arrive at Harvard on the twenty-sixth and planned to stop off in New York to visit Burke and "resume my position as foil to your wit." It had been a long summer of separation and Cowley was anxiously anticipating a reunion. When Burke reacted with less than unqualified enthusiasm, Cowley's response was typical of the tone of their early friendship:

Kenny, you are much too complex. First you try to frighten me away with your cordiality, and then to keep me off with your distrust. I shall pay neither of them the compliment of my regard and will come anyway—if I can. I ought to enjoy the visit very much. It won't be a matter of unalloyed enjoyment. It won't be a matter of ecstacies. A person who would ecstacize over me has to be either very discerning of character or a little off in the head. You—who are gifted and cursed with the intensity of an Irish nature, will have either a pleasing surprise or a bitter disappointment, depending on which convolution you are in at the time. And I, the German-English-Irish-Scotch moderate, will find the visit about as I expected. But don't take such a humble opinion of your own attractions, or you will have, instead of friends, people who merely pity you.[53]

Cowley's departure for Harvard signaled a decisive step in his formative years as a writer. Though his rebellion against his parents had never been fierce or violent—a matter of silently disregarding their advice rather than one of open hostility—his choice of Harvard meant a definitive break with the Swedenborgian world of his parents and the cultural standards of his past. Much too humble and sweet-tempered a man to stand in the way of his son's desire, his father, who had been deeply disappointed when Cowley refused to stay at the Swedenborgian school in Bryn Athyn, now could not help regretting his choice of a college "dominated . . . by godless Unitarians." As for the son, his motives for choosing Harvard were clear: "I earned myself a scholarship to Harvard, because I had heard that other writers went there."[54]

2

The Emergence of a Harvard Poet

1915-1917

In 1915 Harvard University basked in the glow of a "golden age." Under the liberal presidency of Charles W. Eliot, a zealous educational reformer and expansionist, Harvard had experienced years of unprecedented growth and intellectual prestige. Eliot had introduced the "elective system," which allowed undergraduates complete freedom of choice in the matter of courses.[1] By the time Cowley entered Harvard the elective system had been abandoned by Eliot's successor, Abbott Lawrence Lowell, then in his sixth year as president, in favor of a policy of "concentration and distribution," the familiar system of majors and minors prevailing at most American universities today. Though Lowell initiated even more new construction than Eliot, his greatest achievement was to establish higher standards of education at Harvard. The university, he had pleaded in his inaugural address, ought to produce "not defective specialists, but men intellectually well rounded, of wide sympathies and unfettered thought." Lowell's attempts to improve instruction and the emphasis he placed on the value of strenuous intellectual effort attracted, so Samuel Eliot Morison believed, the devotion of the younger generation and made Harvard under his presidency "an exciting place" for students and teachers alike.[2] Cowley's later distrust of any narrowly specialized methodology, whether in science, philosophy, or criticism, and his concomitant ideal of the intellectual as "a universal man," may well owe something to his experience at Harvard under Lowell.[3]

By 1915 such Harvard teachers of Olympian stature as William James, Josiah Royce, and George Santayana were no longer part of the intellectual scene, but they had engendered an intellectual atmosphere of skeptical humanism, experimental pragmatism, and aesthetic pluralism that remained palpable in Cowley's Harvard days.[4] Barrett Wendell and Irving Babbitt were still around as reminders of a vanishing era; though Cowley did not study under them, their conservative opinions were part of the

intellectual currency of any undergraduate seriously interested in literature. Babbitt's denunciations of the romanticist tendencies of modern culture, in particular as exemplified by the French symbolists Baudelaire,
Rimbaud, and Verlaine, paradoxically helped to introduce these poets to
many students who otherwise might not have heard of them until much
later but who now gladly turned to them in their revolt against traditional
culture.[5] Wendell, an Anglophile defender of New England gentility and
a symbol of puritanism and patrician snobbery to the young, had written
A *Literary History of America* (1900), which breathed such a patronizing
air of New England superiority that it was often derided as "A Literary
History of Harvard College." Wendell's book, T. S. Eliot felt in 1920, virtually amounted to "an admission, in a great many words, that there is no
American literature."[6] Wendell's condescending attitude toward American
writing in effect still prevailed during Cowley's stay at Harvard. "When
I was in college," Cowley recalled in 1984, "American literature was at
one of its low points in critical and scholarly estimation. . . . In academic
circles here and abroad it was still a question whether the body of prose
and verse produced by Americans truly constituted a national literature
or whether it was no more than a provincial branch of English writing. I
can't remember that so much as a single course in American literature was
offered to Harvard undergraduates. The authors to be emulated by young
Americans were Shaw, Wells, and perhaps Compton Mackenzie."[7] It was
not the least important part of Cowley's achievement that, as critic and
chronicler of his generation, he helped raise America's understanding of
the nature and the merit of its own literature.

Among American universities Harvard was no doubt the best training
ground for writers; any other university was, in Cowley's words, "a second
choice." Among the many illustrious literary predecessors at Harvard were
Van Wyck Brooks, Edward Sheldon, John Hall Wheelock, and Maxwell
Perkins, all members of the class of 1907; T. S. Eliot, John Reed, Walter Lippmann, Heywood Broun, Alan Seeger, and Robert Edmond Jones
all belonged to the famous class of 1910. Other literary alumni included
Conrad Aiken, Robert Benchley, S. N. Behrman, Witter Bynner, Stuart
Chase, Bernard DeVoto, Arthur Davison Ficke, John Gould Fletcher,
Hermann Hagedorn, John P. Marquand, Samuel Eliot Morison, Stuart
Sherman, Harold Stearns, and Wallace Stevens. Among those of Cowley's
own age group were E. E. Cummings, who had graduated magna cum
laude in 1915 and was still around during Cowley's freshman year for a year

of postgraduate work, and John Dos Passos, then in his senior year. Edward Weeks, who later became editor of the *Atlantic Monthly*, recalled meeting Cowley at Harvard in 1919.[8] Cowley's closest literary friends at college were S. Foster Damon (class of 1914), Robert Hillyer (class of 1917), and John Brooks Wheelwright (class of 1920).

At the time Harvard had an excellent reputation in the field of "composition." George Pierce Baker taught play writing to a carefully selected group of students in his English 47 workshop, and sympathetic mentors of undergraduate students like Charles Townsend Copeland and Dean Russell Briggs were famous and inspiring teachers of composition whose classes Cowley attended. Besides reading Elizabethan drama under Baker, Cowley studied literature under John Livingston Lowes and philosophy under William Ernest Hocking, Lucien Lévy-Bruhl, and Raphael Demos.[9] In literary criticism, however, the program at Harvard was painfully deficient. A student of Cowley's generation could receive excellent training in the principles of historical scholarship and criticism under such renowned professors as George Lyman Kittredge, a Shakespeare scholar who had done pioneering research in Anglo-Saxon literature and the history of the English language, or William A. Neilson, a specialist in medieval literature and Elizabethan drama. He might learn the principles of prosody in Bliss Perry's course in lyric poetry, but there was hardly any way to obtain training in aesthetic or formalist criticism. At Harvard, as at most other universities, there was no serious critical method of aesthetic analysis and judgment before I. A. Richards developed his *Principles of Literary Criticism* (1925) and initiated the teaching of "practical criticism."[10] Training in a formalist, aesthetic appreciation of art could be obtained outside academe, by following one's own critical bent or the example of poet-critics like Eliot and Pound; or it could be obtained in an altogether different cultural milieu like that in France, where in the early 1920s Cowley was exposed to a method of critical analysis (*explication de texte*) that, largely through the endeavors of the "new" critics, became the dominant mode of literary teaching in American universities in the decades after World War II. But a young writer at Harvard in the late 1910s, struggling for criteria to make literary judgments of the modern writers, could only resort to his own literary sensibility, to personal impressions and intuitions. In the absence of a critical vocabulary and approach to deal seriously with the formal properties and the technique of modern writing, it was part of Cowley's achievement to help create the language and standards of criticism by which such qualities were to be judged. But Cowley's criticism always held a strong historical dimension and retained the marks of impressionism; his personal literary sensibility remained its cornerstone.

‹ ‹ ‹   Arriving in Cambridge in late September 1915, an innocent, smiling boy from a Pittsburgh public high school with a scholarship and a face full of pimples, Cowley needed the bulk of his freshman year to get his social and intellectual bearings in the complex new order of things at Harvard. During his freshman year he roomed with two Jewish students, John Rothschild and Jake Davis, his friend from Peabody. With them he occupied a suite in Gore Hall, one of the new freshman halls initiated as part of President Lowell's social program for the college, which was to bridge the gap between rich and poor students. On an open quadrangle facing the Charles River, Gore Hall contained a dining hall, a common room, and suites for from one to five persons, holding modern comforts and conveniences. In the freshman dormitories one could find accommodation for as little as $35 a year. Tuition was $150; it was raised to $200 in 1918. Board at Memorial Hall, the big common dining hall, was $5.50 a week. Prospective students were advised that they needed a minimum of $500 to get through the academic year. "Harvard, though it sailed under false colors as a gentleman's finishing school, was really a poor boys' college," Cowley observed in 1967.[11]

During his first semester Cowley took on a load of six courses: a survey course in English literature, a "rather advanced" composition course (English 22), and courses in French, historical German, European history, and the history of philosophy. The new experience of attending college lectures roused his intellectual enthusiasm, but after a month his initial ardor had cooled and he had begun to doubt the relevance of much that he was being taught. "When I graduate from Harvard I mightn't know anything worthwhile, but I'll at least be educated," he cynically reflected.[12] Soon enough, his attitude toward lectures and exams became more pragmatic. Knowing he would have to carry himself through college on scholarships, Cowley developed a knack for getting good marks and established an excellent record in his freshman year, standing second in a class of 685. "I had a gift for remembering almost anything for 24 hours, displaying my knowledge in a blue book, then wiping it as from a blackboard," he mused almost sixty years later. Unwilling to be known as a grind—"I wanted to be distinguished by careless brilliance and for getting drunk in Boston"—

he did most of his studying "in secret" and often worked in the library at the Harvard Union, hardly used by other students.[13]

After a month Cowley had sampled enough of Harvard's social and literary life to report on his impressions to Burke. His initiation into the pleasures and pains of student life had taken place, he wrote, during the festive exuberance attending Harvard's smashing victory over Yale in the annual football derby, 41–0. Thoughts of the drinking spree that followed still filled him with disgust: drunk to the point of sickness, he ended up in the Stillman Infirmary. More important, he had begun to discover that Harvard had an exciting literary life and to take pride in its intellectual preeminence. There were, he claimed, only three universities in America, two of which, Yale and Princeton, were not "awfully good." Harvard men might find "an infinite number of faults" with their university, but this did not shake their conviction of "the one shining fact that Harvard is America's greatest university." He had found that there was "a remarkable lot of good verse" being written at Harvard, mostly in the form of free verse and sonnets; there was even "a Poet's Club." He also had begun to discover the complex college club system and was actually competing in the dramatic club's publicity competition. Requirements for belonging, however, were stiff. To be eligible for membership in the *Deutscher Verein* one had to write a comic poem in German "on special invitation" and the *Cercle Français* demanded that one act in a French play. Both organizations, Cowley had learned, were "infamous for booze and smutty stories. I must belong." But his principal interest was in the six undergraduate magazines and the opportunities they offered for realizing his ambitions. A few days after his arrival he had attended a smoker for candidates held by the *Harvard Illustrated,* but had found the requirements for making the staff of the paper "tremendous and impossible"; he had "more hopes" for the *Harvard Advocate.* A few weeks later he summed up his impressions of Harvard journals. The *Advocate* was "a remarkably poor magazine," he judged, even if it published some good poetry. The *Monthly* had "a lot of good stuff in it." The atmosphere at the office of the *Crimson* he found "invigorating." "I would like to get on the staff of all these three papers," he announced ambitiously. He admired the *Lampoon* for being "independent in what it says," and considered it "really one of America's best humorous publications, in or out of college." The *Illustrated* was "not of much account," but in the *Music Review* he had relished the "original compositions and articles on Scriabin and on Mussorgsky's songs."[14]

Staggering under a load of six courses, however, Cowley had little time or energy left for outside activities. His literary endeavors were limited to commenting on the poems sent to him by Burke or shown to him by his roommates. Though he was often afraid to speak his mind, he was tentatively discovering a penchant for criticism. He had been advertising Burke's poems to his fellow students and was convinced that, given time, he would be able to found "a culte de Burke" at Harvard with himself as "stage manager."[15]

Meanwhile Burke had been promoting Cowley's verse at what had been his exciting literary debut: an evening with Theodore Dreiser. The evening had been "an epoch," Burke reported; he had had "the fullest hours of [his] life." Dreiser had been cold and perfunctory, but Burke had managed to worm himself into conversation with the older writer, only to make the "very gratifying discovery" that "you and I could give him kindergarten-lessons in convolutions." Cowley's poem, an early piece of imitative verse written under the spell of Edgar Lee Masters, had been read to the guests but had met with a lukewarm reception: "It was neither enthused over, nor was it condemned. Dreiser, who is a great admirer of Masters, said it was the usual waves that one could expect to follow in his wake. But please don't think I am exulting over you. I was very pleased to find myself up in arms to defend you. I am honestly sorry the poem did not make a stronger impression."[16] Feigning indifference, Cowley dismissed the niggardly verdict of "that American behemoth of letters," and instead heartily recommended three plays by Arthur Schnitzler, *Intermezzo*, *The Lonely Way*, and *Countess Mizzi*, all "extremely psychological," he argued, in addition to being "sexual." Thirteen years later, when Schnitzler had become "a romantic memory" associated with his "first eager foray" into modern literature, Cowley analyzed the appeal of his plays to the younger generation:

We read them in our college days, at a time when the modern drama was a prevailing fashion, when German seemed a language of the sophisticated, and when Vienna was the city of ultimate enchantment. Schnitzler to us was the modern drama, and he symbolized Vienna. Being very young, we failed to understand the half meanings in his plays; we disregarded most of their realistic elements; we prized them only for their glamour, for a sort of thick persistent charm, for their portrayal of a civilization that was tolerant, sentimental, rather witty and delightfully corrupt. We planned a visit to Vienna; we dreamt of young women—*süsse Mädl*—with yellow hair, brown eyes and a tolerant smile.[17]

Cowley's own poetic productivity, meanwhile, was at a low ebb. He was writing only sporadically and had taken to polishing up old poetry. On November 14 he sent a sample of his revisions to Burke. The poem, a "Rossettiesque sonnet," with its struggle to master a perfect regularity of meter and rhyme, its pose of weary decadence, and its daring sexual suggestiveness, showed that the "modern" note in Cowley's verse was still strongly colored by a spirit of decadent aestheticism. Its conventional diction marked the immaturity of the juvenile poet:

> Let the great master's crashing harmonies
> > Rouse the brave soul within the concert hall,
> > Let Margaret sing to stately Parsifal,
> And Chopin whisper in his minor keys—
> There is a time and place for such as these.
> > Bach and Debussy, Haydn, Mozart, all
> > Are masters, yet there is a time they pall
> And the tired soul seeks simpler melodies.
>
> And when the warm spring night rests on the land
> > When blood is young and youth is in the raw
> > There is one music we can understand—
> So whisper softly in some woman's ear
> > Go with her to the cabaret, and hear
> The frantic rhythms of the orchestra.

For the time being, neither Cowley's poetic nor intellectual efforts met with much encouragement. His verse was not appreciated in his composition class, and though he had made excellent marks in English literature, he scored only B-plus on a philosophy test: "I confess myself mediocre." The net result of his studies so far, he skeptically reflected, was only a pedantic ability to use "moderately strange words" like ontology, subinfeudation, hylozoism, empiricism, dialectics, and eclecticism. For the time being, his only real success was in debating. With Jake Davis he made the debating team, which he rated "somewhat of an accomplishment," since only three freshmen were elected. Before long, the freshmen beat the seniors in what the chairman judged to have been "the best interclass debate he ever heard."[18]

In spite of his own scholastic troubles Cowley took it upon himself to advise Burke. After Peabody High School, Burke stayed out of college for a year to work in a bank, his father hoping his son would opt for a career in business. Knowing, however, that Burke was wavering between enrolling at Columbia University or Ohio State, Cowley intimated that he would be "damned glad" to have his friend by his side in Cambridge: "Harvard won't be exactly suited to you. You will find many defects—all Harvard men spend their spare hours picking the University to pieces in the *New Republic*. But the faults of Harvard are the faults of the American university. And many of its virtues are its own."[19]

Cowley planned to spend Christmas with relatives in Washington, D.C., but it did not take much pressure from Burke to persuade him to accept an invitation to spend some time in Weehawken, where Burke's parents lived in an apartment on the Palisades overlooking the Hudson River and Manhattan. Burke was eager to show Cowley "a very assertive Bohemian restaurant" he had discovered; it was done "in the futuristic way—its yellow, for instance, is as shameless as that on the seat of the El cars." Rapturous over the aesthetic splendors of New York, Burke managed to make his invitation irresistible: "I am dying to show you the city just as a work of art. I cannot express it—it is too sweeping—and thus I want to purchase the consolation which comes of merely showing it to someone who can rhapsodize with me. To be out on the river by the Cortlandt Street Dock about a quarter to six is simply agonizing. . . . And the skies—I often wonder if the skies are especially gorgeous here, or if I had not awakened to them in Pittsburgh."[20] Burke's letter doubled Cowley's desire to see his friend in New York while en route to Washington. He was "dying" for a good philosophical discussion, especially since he felt college life was turning him into "a brute": "All I do is study, eat, sleep, take a shower, go to classes, eat, and study. I know more about Friedrich Hohenstaufen and Hildebrand and the Cluny movement than I do about such interesting matters as imagist poets or Bohemia."[21]

To effect an early release from college Cowley proposed a clever scheme. Burke had been reading Louis Wilkinson, a British novelist who had come to New York after the outbreak of the war in Europe and who had published some stories in the *Smart Set*. Burke had written the novelist a beginner's letter, which had led to a first meeting. Cowley's plan was founded on this literary acquaintanceship. Burke, he proposed, was to write a letter inform- ing Cowley of a "splendid opportunity" to meet Wilkinson, who, in turn, could arrange for an interview with Theodore Dreiser, ostensibly Cowley's "favorite novelist." He would take the letter to the dean and try to get off on the twentieth. Burke's letter "worked like a charm." The dean allowed Cowley to leave three days early, making an exception on account of his "remarkable record." Once in New York Cowley planned to rest, walk, and talk. Dreiser he did not want to meet, even if he could: "Such a colossus could have no interest in a Harvard freshman." Wilkinson, however, he would like to meet, if only "out of a desire to hear a great man talk." [22]

Cowley spent Christmas at the home of his great-uncle Alexander McKenna, trying to make himself agreeable to his second cousins in Wash- ington. McKenna was not only "transcendentally good"; he also proved a very generous man, presenting his nephew with a gift of a hundred dollars. The McKennas did much to help Cowley get through Harvard. Great-aunt Lydie complemented his scholarships by sending him a check for three hundred dollars on three successive Christmases. [23]

‹ ‹ ‹   Back in Cambridge for his second semester Cowley decided to drop a course at midyear and to devote more time to literature. As always, rivalry with Burke helped to goad his ambition. Notwithstanding Cowley's expectation that some of his friend's poems would be "too advanced" for the *Little Review*, Burke had managed to get some poems published in an obscure little magazine. When, furthermore, Cowley discovered that a fellow freshman regularly submitted work to the *Smart Set*, he was driven to "a literary renaissance": he wrote three poems. He submitted a satire to the *Smart Set* and a poem to the *Harvard Monthly*, expecting both to be rejected; they were. Eight days later he quoted to Burke, as proof of his poetic renaissance, part of a reworked version of an early "awfully sensu- ous" pastoral lyric, "In the Garden," a poem that Burke had rightly judged was "distinguished . . . for immaturity":

> Ah wonderful starless, moonless night,
> Ah night of the blossoming South,
> You hide the flower of my delight—
> The heavy eyes that my eyes seek,
> And the flush that comes and goes on her cheek,

> And the warmth of her flowerlike mouth—
> Ah the whispering silence of the night,
> The starless night of the South.[24]

Cowley had now become enough of a Harvard man to boggle at Burke's plans to attend even a single semester at a "provincial university" like Ohio State; it had, he objected, "no past at all." He himself had come to appreciate Harvard's august traditions and ancient history, and to savor its flavor of late nineteenth-century English decadence. "I am coming to love the past—to love Oxford and Cambridge. Some of their lustre is reflected to Harvard." As symptomatic evidence he adduced "the masterful conceit" of Harvard men. Moreover, Boston was near and held out the promise of cultural and social attractions; the city, Cowley noted, had "a disgustingly sensual night-life which would inspire any decadent poet." The very nature and reputation of Harvard was inspiring and lent its students an aura of prestige: "Even street whores are highly respectful to Harvard men." He clinched his argument by evoking the university as the quintessence of modernity: "The whole idea of going to Harvard is a paradox. Normal Americans go to Yale."[25]

Cowley could never assent to Burke's decision to enroll at Ohio State (Burke eventually spent the fall 1916 semester there, together with James Light and Susan Jenkins, then transferred to Columbia), but their friendship was too precious to be so easily disrupted. Despite reciprocal vilifications and insults, whether in jest or in earnest, it remained his strongest antidote to loneliness—there were times, he lamented, when he felt "as desperate as some Latin Quarter Impressionist." But Burke was far away and in order to combat "that damnable loneliness which is the greatest danger here," Cowley sought out a group of fellow students with whom he could socialize and conduct intellectual discussions. He liked to play first fiddle: "as long as I can talk—and I am naturally the best talker in the crowd—I am happy." The group must have comprised an odd assortment of intellectual poseurs: one was "an idealistic humanist," Cowley reported, another defended the double standard, a third wavered between Orthodox Christianity, Unitarianism, deism, agnosticism, and indifferentism, and, as capstone to the company, there was Cowley himself, "a skeptical Hedonist with a philosophy of negation."[26]

Studies and exams continued to interfere with literature and formed a perpetual occasion for complaint. Though he expected to be eligible for a substantial scholarship at the end of the year, Cowley recurrently lamented that exams were "not aesthetic" and were too time-consuming. He still entertained hopes of sometime rooming with Burke but also longed to leave the conformist atmosphere of the freshman dormitories and, for the following academic year, had snobbishly decided to exchange his Jewish roommates for a "clever, charming, selfish, young, average Yankee." Eager to improve his living conditions and to move upward in Harvard's social hierarchy, he had selected a room in Russell Hall, on Mount Auburn Street, on the Gold Coast—"oh magic name." There the new private dormitories were more spacious, comfortable, and expensive (some had swimming pools and squash courts), and drew the richer undergraduates, who tended to shun the college dormitories in the Yard. "I am developing into a disagreeable prig and a good deal of a snob," Cowley admitted to Burke.[27]

For all the burden of his studies Cowley's heart remained with literature. In February he made the "important" discovery of a book by George Moore about his early life in Paris, *Memoirs of My Dead Life* (1906), which fanned Cowley's ambition for a certain mode of the literary life: "No one can lay claim to being an artist who has not read the *Memoirs* or at least lived them." Halfway through his second semester he began to plan decisive moves for making his way into Harvard's literary scene. In early March he announced to Burke that he was "out for the *Advocate.*" He also regularly attended meetings of the Harvard Poetry Society, which had been organized in 1915 by S. Foster Damon, shortly before Cowley's arrival in Cambridge. The Poetry Society, Cowley reported to Burke, numbered some thirty members, "most of them skilled sonneteers" and "connoisseurs of verse."[28]

During his first two years at Harvard Cowley was able to observe the college literary ferment in one of its more picturesque manifestations. A group of poets, or would-be poets, who subsequently became known as the Harvard Aesthetes, languished in the pallid atmosphere of a type of decadent aestheticism and were trying, in Cowley's words, "to create in Cambridge, Massachusetts, an after-image of Oxford in the 1890s." Cowley's composite and ironic portrait has often been cited:

> They read the *Yellow Book*, they read Casanova's memoirs and *Les Liaisons Dangereuses*, both in French, and Petronius in Latin; they

gathered at teatime in one another's rooms, or at punches in the office of the *Harvard Monthly*; they drank, instead of weak punch, seidels of straight gin topped with a maraschino cherry; they discussed the harmonies of Pater, the rhythms of Aubrey Beardsley and, growing louder, the voluptuousness of the Church, the essential virtue of prostitution. They had crucifixes in their bedrooms, and ticket stubs from last Saturday's burlesque show at the Old Howard. They wrote, too; dozens of them were prematurely decayed poets, each with his invocation to Antinoüs, his mournful descriptions of Venetian lagoons, his sonnets to a chorus girl in which he addressed her as "little painted poem of God." In spite of these beginnings, a few of them became good writers.[29]

The Harvard Aesthetes experienced their halcyon days during the undergraduate years of E. E. Cummings, whose early verse was tinged with their spirit, and John Dos Passos, who for a time adopted a touch of the Aesthetes' pose and moved on the fringes of the group, which consisted largely of contributors to the *Harvard Monthly*. Cowley did not directly befriend Cummings or Dos Passos at Harvard—as graduate students they were "outside the horizon of a freshman"—but he saw both of them, along with most of the Harvard Aesthetes, at meetings of the Poetry Society.[30]

Despite the blustering tone of his letters to Burke, Cowley was somewhat daunted by his senior colleagues-in-verse at the Poetry Society and, feeling it would be "a presumptuous act" for a freshman to freely address them, he tended for the time being to move on the periphery. He listened to Robert Hillyer—already an established Harvard poet (he was the only undergraduate to have a book of verse published by Harvard University Press)—declaim his poems; he heard Dos Passos shyly read his verse; and he witnessed S. Foster Damon recite his unorthodox poetry in the dimly lit room of the *Harvard Monthly*. Cowley was never formally a part of the Aesthetes, though he, too, could not prevent his early verse from being tainted by their influence. Wary of belonging to a group, he tended to observe, witness, and record their literary vicissitudes from a critical and ironic distance, rather than participate and follow suit. Unlike Cummings and Dos Passos, who were regular contributors to the *Monthly*, most of Cowley's publications were for its rival, the *Advocate*, for which he wrote over thirty pieces of verse and prose. There is little in his early letters that points to an awareness on Cowley's part of the Harvard Aesthetes as a special literary phenomenon; such an awareness grew by hindsight, once he was able to adopt "the long view" in the early 1930s. Only then did he recognize their type of aestheticism as an extreme manifestation of romanticism and a precursor of the "religion of art" he lashed out against in the fervor of his radicalism.[31]

In the early months of 1916, however, Cowley was not entirely unaffected by the atmosphere of decadent aestheticism he encountered at Harvard. In late March he recommended to Burke the stories of Lilith Benda in the *Smart Set*, which he relished for being clever exploitations of vulgarity and horribly "fin de siècle." In the same letter he exulted over a "blessed vulgarian" he had met at the *Advocate* who shared his interest in Ernest Dowson and who "swears beautifully, is a scoffer, a nigger-hater, everything that is cheap and much that is able." At times Cowley liked to adopt an aesthete's pose of decadent vulgarity; more commonly he felt that the conservative literary climate at Harvard stood badly in need of modernization: "You and I, Kenny, could in time overturn literary standards here . . . and we could make the *Advocate* a radically poetic magazine."[32]

Ambition, however, could not stifle the self-doubts that besieged the young poet at regular intervals. Whatever his hopes for publication in the *Advocate* he more than once despaired of the quality of his writings and lamented that all he had been inspired to do was rehash and revise earlier work. He came to gloomy but ironically prescient conclusions: "No, Burke, I won't be the great one of the crowd. I repeat it, the burden rests on you. I am too willing to become a hack." If original work were not forthcoming—his latest poem, "a trifle in the 'Smart Set' style," proved that he was "less a poet than ever"—he decided he would try to earn a name for himself by translating German free verse for the *Advocate*. If he ever was to amount to anything as a poet, he told himself, he must forswear reading the *Smart Set*.[33]

The poetry Cowley wrote at this time reveals that, like many apprentice poets, he possessed a talent for absorbing and reflecting literary influences without giving them too much conscious thought; his understanding of them was intuitive rather than theoretical. The same letter that expressed his doubts about himself announced his first publication in the *Harvard Advocate* of March 31, 1916. The poem, "To Certain Imagist Poets," demonstrates his uneasiness with the languishing decadence of the Harvard

Aesthetes and demands of modern poetry a more vigorous realism and a subject matter that spoke of the world he knew:

> Why do you write of your delicate lusts
> And your ephemeral sensations?
> Why don't you write of a village street
> With scampering dogs, and scampering boys, and houses sleeping
>   in the light,
> With tired horses standing before the blacksmith shop—
> They prick up their ears when Bob Marks rattles past in his
>   buckboard,
> Dust rises in banks and settles on the drooping maple leaves—
> Why don't you write of a village street in August?
> I am tired of delicate sensations.

In his own unsophisticated fashion Cowley was already pleading the need to express—as Hemingway was to write—"what you really felt, rather than what you were supposed to feel, and had been taught to feel." [34]

The fortnightly *Advocate* was Harvard's oldest publication; it was founded in 1866 as a college newspaper and "advocate" of students' interests, but in the 1890s had shifted to primarily literary concerns. Its rival, the *Harvard Monthly*, was founded in 1885 by George Santayana and others, boasted a distinguished roll call of editors and contributors, and enjoyed a superior reputation in the field of poetry. But the *Advocate*, perhaps as much as its rival, was a "nursemaid of genius." Besides William Vaughn Moody, Edwin Arlington Robinson, and John Hall Wheelock, it published undergraduate writings of Theodore and Franklin Delano Roosevelt, George Lyman Kittredge, Charles Townsend Copeland, Van Wyck Brooks, Maxwell Perkins, Hermann Hagedorn, Conrad Aiken, E. E. Cummings, T. S. Eliot, and Wallace Stevens. A healthy rivalry marked the relationship between both magazines: "The Monthlies," Cowley recalled, "thought that the board of *The Advocate* . . . was composed of journalists, clubmen, athletes, and disciples of Teddy Roosevelt, a former editor, with not a man of letters among them. The Advocates suspected that the Monthlies were aesthetes . . . scruffy poets, socialists, pacifists, or worse." [35]

Once his first poem had been accepted Cowley soon became a regular contributor to the *Advocate*, publishing free-verse poems side by side with regular, polished sonnets. In the pages of the conservatively inclined

Advocate such poets as Cummings and Cowley showed an awareness of the possibilities of modern verse. Whereas Cowley, in spite of early misgivings about the form, at least tried seriously to explore free verse, to the majority of *Advocate* critics vers libre meant little more than "whimsical formlessness" and "sordid realism": in 1916 an editorial rejected the "undisguised unwholesomeness of the *new manner in poetry*" as "unfit for human consumption."[36]

Cowley's attitude toward free verse was as yet ambiguous and inconsistent. In January he observed to Burke that he was rapidly tiring of conventional verse: "After writing free verse, there seems to be something gaudy and cheap about [the] recurrent rhyme of the old lyrics." Several months later he confessed that, as a rule, he did not like free verse, since it bred a disturbing amount of bad poetry. Having read "ream after ream of broken prose," he mockingly proposed that a "law" be passed prohibiting poets other than Walter Arensberg, John Gould Fletcher, Amy Lowell, Burke, and himself from forsaking meter. "Do you really wonder that I have come to despise free verse and despise myself for writing nothing else?" He soon realized that, if he wanted to stand a chance of publication and election to the Poetry Society, he would have to continue writing regular verse more in accord with the accepted mode. His next two poems to appear in the *Advocate* were written in metrical regularity and conventional rhyme schemes. "Execution" deals with a timeless subject against a vaguely Spanish-Catholic backdrop; "On Rereading Wordsworth" betrays the influence of the English Romantic poets whom Cowley had been reading under John Livingston Lowes. The latter evokes a contrast between the harsh reality of the bustling city life outside the poet's window and the barren landscape of solitude in Wordsworth's nature poetry. This tension between the demands of life and the attractions of literature forms a recurrent motif in Cowley's early writings.

> I turned the pages. From below arose
> > The multitudinous noises of the street,
> > The shouts of boys, the constant tramp of feet,
> The echoes of the trade that ebbs and flows.
> The town stretched out beneath me with its woes,
> > Plying its business in the summer heat.
> > I saw the fool, the drudge, the drab, the cheat,
> In all the bustle that the city knows.

> But as I read, I felt the clear, cold breeze
>   From the bare northern hillsides, and I saw
> The driving storm clouds, and the bending trees,
>   And the dead leaves that drifted without law;
> And heard the whistling gull's monotony,
> And roaring under jagged cliffs, the sea.[37]

Taking stock at the end of his freshman year Cowley felt that Harvard had effected many changes in his personality, outlook, and habits. Whereas in Pittsburgh he had recurrently indulged in late-night poker games and "nocturnal, almost matutinal conferences" with Burke, at Harvard he had developed a passion for health and physical exercise: he now went to bed at ten, rose at seven, ate regularly, took an hour of "strenuous exercise" each day and despised physical flabbiness. He was also rapidly becoming a real "university man," a development he viewed as both "dangerous" and "pleasing." In early May he summed up in a letter to Burke the changes Harvard had brought: "Harvard has made me healthy. It has made me respect myself, and yet at the same time made me snobbish. It has ruined me as an author, and made me a much better citizen. It has taught me to kiss girls without blushing. The old views I had are dropping off one by one. Perversity I now adopt only as a pose to amuse people, and even then I soon drop it. I have come to believe that the Allies are right. If all goes well, I shall join the Harvard Regiment and later go to Plattsburgh. I even entertain ideas of becoming a professor. You see I have changed."[38]

‹ ‹ ‹ Coming to Harvard when the college was in an "ineffably snobbish" period Cowley could not avoid becoming tainted by a prevailing spirit of anti-Semitic feeling.[39] Besides its social and intellectual snobberies, Cowley later recalled, Harvard had its "ethnic snobberies, with a deep social prejudice against Jews, Boston Irish, and Radcliffe students." His own class of 1919, he reflected upon another occasion, "must have reached nearly the acme and zenith of Harvard snobbery."[40]

Cowley had begun to absorb the current strain of anti-Semitic sentiment shortly after his arrival at Harvard. His very first letter to Burke reported that he was becoming "a Jew hater"; he had talked to a student from Andover and had come away with the conviction that Harvard would "some day be ruined by the damn Jews." A naive freshman from a public high school, Cowley was intimidated by the boys from rich, exclusive prep schools like

Andover, Exeter, and Groton: "I lick their boots," he wrote to Burke on November 9. Partly from a sense of personal insecurity and social inferiority, partly from an instinctive longing to relieve his loneliness and belong to the crowd, Cowley adopted some of their racial and social prejudices. Thus he considered his roommate Jake Davis a "besotted fool" for joining the Menorah Society and "advertising his Judaeism." Seven months later he observed in a similar vein that he was "always willing to be interested in a Jew who is afraid to acknowledge his race. I know I should be if I were a Jew."[41]

It is not unlikely that Cowley's ethnic prejudice was caused partly by literary and intellectual envy. He found himself in scholarly competition with "a bunch of bright Jews" and was irked by their outstanding academic performance. On April 5, 1916, he expressed himself more elaborately than before on the "pertinent subject" of Jews. At Harvard there were few Jewish intellectuals, he maintained, and there were none on the staff of the *Advocate* or the *Monthly*. They were "mostly a race of ill-bred grinds," who imitated "the jolly good fellows of Harvard in a tawdry way," ran after chorus girls, played poker, and boasted of their wickedness. There *were*, however, "intelligent Gentiles, some of them very intelligent."[42]

For all the force of its rhetoric, Cowley's ethnic prejudice did not run very deep. Partly a bid for social acceptance, partly a defiant pose adopted to irritate the more sensitive Burke, it was essentially restricted to his early years at Harvard. Once its usefulness as a veneer of social distinction had passed, it wore itself out soon enough. With the exception of an isolated, unexpected flare-up on the eve of his return to Harvard from France in 1917, Cowley's subsequent correspondence does not show any continued anti-Semitic sentiment. Its emergence during his Harvard years, short-lived as it was, indicates that Cowley was as yet insufficiently aware of a potentially dangerous side to his nature: a chameleonic inclination to adopt the sheltering colors of his environment. As his future career would show, unrestrained by moral sensitivity or the upbraidings of friends, that inclination might lead Cowley, often against his better judgment and notwithstanding private misgivings, into indefensible positions.

By the end of his freshman year Cowley was thoroughly steeped in the Harvard atmosphere and had adopted many of the stereotypical traits of the Harvard student, both good and bad. Indeed, he was assimilated so rapidly that at times he feared a loss of individuality and, as a consequence, despaired of his ability to write. Typically, he analyzed himself by speculating on the effects Harvard would have on Burke. Whereas he himself was "never very much of a literary man" and "always nourished conservatism in [his] heart," Burke was "an original from the core" who stood in no danger of losing his individuality but needed the social pressures and herdlike atmosphere of a year at Harvard for balance. Burke would not run the risk of becoming a university man, Cowley felt, but Harvard might draw him out of his isolation by forcing him to socialize and involve himself in the larger life about him. Such a life, Cowley was convinced, would make Burke a better writer by carrying him outside of himself and providing him with new subject matter: "As it is, all you know, all you can express yourself about, is Self, sex, and the business of writing."[43]

Cowley's analysis of Burke tells us as much about himself as about his friend. Intuitively, he sensed the nefarious effect on a writer of limited experience, and he felt the tension between the pressures for social conformity and the demands of the individual, between human desire for interdependence and artistic necessity of isolation. Already, he seemed distrustful of a self-contained subjectivism in art and a mode of writing dissociated from life.

‹ ‹ ‹   Cowley spent the summer of 1916 in Belsano. Even before his last examinations in June anticipatory thoughts of the "old town" filled him with "near-sentimentality." Overcome with an "infinitely sweet longing" for Belsano, he hoped to see Burke there and with him to "travel the dusty road and swim in the little creeks and crawl down Chestnut Ridge just as the sun is setting."[44] Back in Belsano, Cowley became thoroughly absorbed in the rural scenes of his boyhood. From Cambria County, even Bohemian living in Greenwich Village lost its aura of enticement. As yet, he felt, he was "not ready for the Square," nor was he willing to relinquish his boyhood too soon. Typically, Cowley was inclined to be nostalgic even before he had been properly severed from his youth. "I am still a boy, and you know it," he explained to Burke; "I still like to swim, and canoe, and flirt in a cheap way, and roughhouse. I want to live a healthy life until I am strong enough to stand the late hours of Bohemia, which I cannot stand now. And when I remember that I can be a boy only once, and that once I have deserted the old life, I can never go back to it, I am quite content to stay here and enjoy myself. I am content to let the dear old *Advocate* publish my corsetted verse (they do it regularly now), to study a little, and to bide my time."[45]

Cowley's mood of nostalgia soon spent itself. He was quick to recognize the childishness of his own thought, even if he felt that he had "learned to mask its inanity" rather well. On the Fourth of July he complained that he was "bored to death" and lonely. Over the summer he kept in touch with old friends and classmates, corresponded with Susan Jenkins and James Light, and tried unsuccessfully to impress female acquaintances with his poetry and "prose libre." For two full weeks he chased around the country with one of the local characters who intrigued him deeply, Leaird ("Doc") Altemus. Altemus was a widow's son who lived on a farm four miles from Cowley's home and who had run the farm since he was fifteen; eventually he managed to become a doctor. Altemus, Cowley had written Burke in an early letter, provided one with "an agreeable insight into the life of a dashing young buck. He drinks, fucks, swears, works like hell, is popular with girls, makes a good fraternity at Bucknell, and is sure of an average of 92 in his studies. His philosophy is the unconscious acme of the double standard, and he always plays a fellow square, and is honorable to a decent girl." Now, for a fortnight, gossiping, drinking, and keeping late hours, the two consorted on intimate terms. "Intellectual conversation none. Simply smut and profanity and reminiscence and personalities—and action."[46]

The one book he read during the summer that filled him with enthusiasm was Thomas Mann's *Buddenbrooks*, which he struggled through in German. He was, rather naively, impressed by Mann's ability to create characters that were "as interesting as the people I meet, and much easier to understand." But he found that Mann was especially good on "the art-degeneracy theory." In the story of the sensitive Hanno—the last offshoot of a prominent bourgeois family whose artistic streak undermines his vitality and erodes his will to live—Cowley, the decadent aesthete, was tempted to read a portent of his own career: "I think I am even a whole generation beyond little Hanno. For generations and generations our family has nourished artists, musicians, drunks, degenerates, insanity, and worst of all, the religious spirit. I ought to be a regular genius."[47] Mann's pessimism was infectious and inculcated a mood of languishing despondency. As the summer advanced, a plaintive note crept into Cowley's letters. "A hell of a lot I care about my poetry after the sixth beer or the first kiss," he mocked himself on August 12. "God, Burke, am I a pessimist? Independently I am going Schopenhauer one better. Nietzsche's conclusions do not interest me much, for I am too confirmed an individualist to worry about the future of the race. And my own future—if immortality were offered me,

I would not accept it, yet I do dread dissolution. Life is too short . . . we never get a chance to get tired of living."[48]

In early September, preparing to return to Harvard, he realized he had "really absolutely wasted" his summer. The one piece of writing he had undertaken was a fictive autobiographical sketch of Malcolm Cowley "as he might have been if born in 1860." The story would have included several concerns "very near" to him: "Omar Khayyamism, drunkenness, futility, love of our section of the country, London literary life, farming and various other things." Luckily, perhaps, the sketch does not survive. In all, he had done little reading over the summer, written nothing worthwhile; even his letters to Burke had been but "purely extempore affairs." He had not even had an affair to boast of. He was relying on a meeting with Burke en route to Cambridge for some badly needed "medicine" for his moods of pessimism and despondency.[49]

But rather than Burke it was the literary recognition he gained during his sophomore year that proved the more effective cure. Back in Cambridge in early October, Cowley faced the luxurious problem of having to decline one of two scholarships of two hundred dollars each. He decided to retain the Harvard University scholarship and hoped to find a means of transferring his other grant, from the Harvard Club of Western Pennsylvania, to Burke. He moved into a new room at 19 Russell Hall on Mount Auburn Street and struck up a new friendship with Robert A. Cunningham, a boy from Newton, Massachusetts, who was handicapped by a slight limp. Cunningham became Cowley's regular social companion in his sophomore year. Though he eventually made it to the staff of the *Crimson*, Cunningham had little or no ambition to write. Cowley thought him "an estimable fellow" who had "a wonderful smile" and was "the soul of decency." Both of them, he told Burke on November 28, were "united in a common admiration for our college, and a common interest in feminine psychology."[50]

Dwelling in close proximity to the social elite on the Gold Coast, Cowley's conceit soared to new heights and he was inclined to adopt a pose of haughtiness and condescension. On November 1 he proclaimed: "I am a snob—hurrah, a true snob. What pleasure it gives me to think I can cut absolutely anybody I want to. What a feeling of superiority it gives me to have my boots blacked by the janitor of my Gold Coast dormitory instead of by an ordinary Dago. And just think—I hope to be invited to join a fraternity, and I am going to refuse—not because I don't want to join a fraternity, but because this one isn't good enough for me. Could anything be farther from the boy who used to associate with the social outcasts of a socially outcast high school[?] I bought a fancy vest yesterday."[51] Burke recoiled in disgust. He railed against his friend's "colossal cheapness"— "As a masterful man you are nothing but a little snotty-nosed smarty. You disclose common ambitions, common standards, and common vices"— and virulently denounced Cowley's "ridiculous hatred of Jews" and his "parvenu" snobbishness as the manifestations of "a typical subordinate."[52]

Indeed, in the rigid social hierarchy of Harvard, more was needed than a room on the Gold Coast and a pose of social and racial snobbery to be accepted as an insider by those at the pinnacle of the social pyramid. Cowley realized as much. Burke had given him "an undeserved bawling-out," he protested. He had by no means been proclaiming himself one of the "ins." On the contrary, he knew how thoroughly his friend disliked his "show of snobbishness," but loved to irritate him with it. To be an "in" was a matter of birth, clothes, speech, training, and money, Cowley instructed Burke. Money alone was no guarantee of admittance; he could point to millionaires' sons who were "decidedly not in the running." To be an "in" at Harvard was an "awesome thing beyond [his] ambition."[53]

Cowley was well aware that the crucial division in the student body was between those from privileged social milieus who had attended private preparatory schools and boys from middle-class or poor families who had attended public high schools. The former immediately enjoyed privileged social standing in their freshman years. A boy from a public high school would continue to be treated with social condescension, notwithstanding a respectful academic record or success in literature or athletics. In 1974 Cowley recalled how George Brownell, one of the "big" men in his class, had one day instructed him to "bathe every day and always wear a clean shirt. . . . The fact was that I did bathe every day, usually twice, and I did wear clean shirts, but other people don't see us as we are . . . I was a high-school boy from Pittsburgh and hence unclean."[54] Nonetheless, it was not until his senior year that Cowley came closest to being ostracized. He came through his first two years relatively unscathed, if coated with a thick veneer of gentlemanly snobbishness.

Prerequisites for success in the Harvard club system were rigid and complicated.[55] Cowley, doubtless aware of the hopelessness of his case, might claim that the club system was beyond his ambition, yet he could not refrain from toying with the possibility, and had secret hopes of making at least the Dickey.[56] Rubbing elbows with the social elite on the Gold Coast, Cowley could not help feeling uneasy about his own social status. Knowing himself barred from eligibility to any of the Harvard clubs—he made neither the Institute nor the Dickey—Cowley, as if in compensation, was tempted to adopt the manners and modes of those inside the club system. Since he was neither an "in" nor a complete outsider, his social position at Harvard remained uncertain and amphibious.

Loneliness was less a problem than before. He had Cunningham for companionship, and he moved within the circle of the Harvard Poetry Society, which served him much in lieu of a club. As a sophomore he was a full-fledged member of the group of poets gathering under the eaves of the Harvard Union; his contributions in prose and verse were now appearing regularly in the *Advocate*. Meeting many of the Harvard Aesthetes in their own den, however, hardly filled Cowley with unqualified enthusiasm. The *Advocate* and the *Monthly* he found but "cowardly, castrated sheets," and he was only moderately impressed by the poets he met at the Poetry Society. His only real "find" was Royall H. Snow, a freshman from Chicago who had been published in *Scribner's Magazine* and possessed a "wonderful collection of rejection slips" from the *Smart Set*. Though Snow had not read what he should, Cowley judged him "a sound critic" and thought he would "pass every test for membership in our coterie." On October 24, after attending a meeting of the Poetry Society, Cowley arrived at a higher estimate of the Harvard poets: "There has been poetry at Harvard in the past, and there is poetry there now. Norris, Paulding, Snow, Raisbean, Cutler—lord, you'll hear of them all some day." Their tastes, however, collided with his own. He had read aloud some of Burke's poems, but had been forced into explanations and apologies that had left his audience with the fatal impression that Burke was "a most interesting fellow who wrote most interesting, amusing poetry."[57]

At this time Harvard poets were divided into two factions. On one side were the "Ancients," represented most eloquently by Robert Hillyer, later a staunch literary conservative; on the other were the "Moderns," represented by such poets as Cummings, Damon, Dos Passos, and Wheelwright. Though the aesthetic direction of his own poetry was still far from certain, Cowley was critically and temperamentally already entrenched on the side of the Moderns. The Moderns, he observed in retrospect, believed that poets ought to write in their own language about things they had seen or felt, whereas the Ancients were content to write about what

they had read, "in the language of Lord Alfred Keats-Rossetti." [58] Many of
the Harvard poets of Cowley's day, in particular descendants of old Boston families like Cummings and Wheelwright, were sensitive to (and often
satirical about) the cultural heritage of a university that had its roots in
seventeenth-century New England. But they were also attracted to the rebellious bohemianism of Greenwich Village and late nineteenth-century
European decadence. Typically, as Alan Wald has noted, their poetry
combined an awareness of tradition with a penchant for rebellion. In 1917
Stewart Mitchell, a poet-editor of the *Monthly*, brought together some of
the best Harvard verse, Modern and Ancient alike. *Eight Harvard Poets*,
published with the financial help of Dos Passos's father, featured the work
of Cummings, Damon, Dos Passos, Hillyer, Mitchell, William A. Norris,
Dudley Poore, and Cuthbert Wright. Norris, one of the Ancients brought
in at the request of his friend Hillyer, reputedly was so horrified by his
appearance in such "modern" company that he bought up and destroyed
every copy of the book he could find. [59]

Cowley's own work was now beginning to draw attention. On October 10, 1916, the *Advocate* published the first of three fictional sketches to
appear during his sophomore year. Slight in itself, "Then Fear Crept in at
the Window," the story of a newlywed farm wife who finds herself besieged
by imaginary terrors in an isolated mountain shack on the first night of her
husband's absence, showed a budding talent for suspenseful narrative. [60] In
early November a Harvard reviewer, writing in the *Crimson*, singled out
one of Cowley's poems in free verse, "To a Girl I Dislike," as "the best in
the issue." It satirized the conventional sweetness of adolescent love lyrics
by subverting its self-created expectation of romantic pastoral love:

> Ever since I was a very little boy,
> I have known a path that wound away through the birches
>   and hemlocks;
> And I remember
> How I always feared to follow it,
> And liked to dream instead what lay at its end—
> An Indian burying-ground, perhaps;
> Or a cave of robbers, stored with fabulous riches;
> Or a rotting cabin that had nursed some great hero.
> And one day I followed the path,
> Walking slowly out of fearfulness;

Starting back when I roused a covey of quail
From the maple scrub around the spring;
Only to find at the end of it,
Among the hemlocks and mossed birches,
A pigsty—
Like a piece of yellow glass set in filigreed platinum,
Or like your heart
Beneath the mysterious immobility of your beauty.[61]

At the end of the month Hermann Hagedorn—"I hope you know that most distinguished poet and dramatist"—wrote an unsolicited letter to the *Advocate* praising the "freshness" of its poetry and singling out Cowley, along with two others, for special mention. In December the *Advocate* published two of Cowley's poems, both again set in a rural Western Pennsylvania landscape. "To a Chance Acquaintance," in free verse, recalled an amorous tryst between a dreamy lover of wide horizons and a provincial girl whose words hold out the promise of a stunting life. "A Letter to Jim" struck a conversational tone and, freely rhyming, evoked the nostalgic delights of long hikes on Chestnut Ridge and the pleasures of physical labor in the woods.[62]

In mid-December Cowley attended a joint meeting of the New England Poetry Society and the Harvard Poetry Society. The event, which featured Amy Lowell, the legendary advocate of the New Poetry, was a modest occasion and Cowley came away with a cluster of satirical impressions and a glowing compliment. The New England Poetry Society, he reported to Burke, consisted primarily of "Amy Lowell and her enemies." But listening to "the mountain queen . . . haranguing a half-dozen subjects and enemies," Cowley could not help being impressed by Lowell's poetry as much as by her personality: "Last night the poetry of the Harvard Poetry Club hopelessly outclassed that of the semi-professionals, except, I must admit, Amy. . . . And My Lord, those women were ugly. Amy stood with her back to the fire, puffing away at a Fatima, and looking very much like a volcanic mountain in eruption. Accent on mountain. . . . I like Amy, and because I like her, I am beginning to like her poetry." Some of his admiration may have been roused by Lowell's complimentary observation that Royall Snow and Cowley seemed to be "the only two poets who wrote modern verse among the members of the Harvard Poetry Society." Before long Cowley became one of several young poets who received Lowell's criticism and encouragement. Her *Six French Poets* (1915) helped to introduce him to French poetry, while later, acting as a literary agent of sorts, she sold some of Cowley's verse to *Poetry* and the *Dial*. In a 1936 review of S. Foster Damon's biography of Lowell for the *New Republic*, Cowley praised her as "the commanding general of the new poets." Though he had grown skeptical of the merit of her poetry he continued to admire her strength of personality and her "genius for organizing, genius for human relations, genius for command."[63]

Cowley's first book reviews appeared in the November 22 *Advocate*. These are hardly substantial essays, though it is remarkable that in his first piece, a review of a translation of Chekhov's *The Darling*, he found a basic approach for the hundreds of reviews to follow. After giving factual information about the book Cowley discussed Chekhov's subject matter and his characters, then branched out into a consideration of the writer's outlook on life as exemplified by his fiction, analyzed its appeal to an American audience, and concluded with a discussion of the contemporary literary scene in America in the light of the writer's example.

Cowley's earliest reviews displayed the conventional belief that art should first and foremost be judged as a representation of life. Thus he praised Chekhov's characters for their "surprising reality" but objected that Chekhov seemed incapable of portraying "a woman we can admire." This inability he related to Chekhov's pessimistic outlook. It was an attitude, Cowley implied, that could easily lead to unhappy literary results: "A writer of tales can believe that life is useless if he will; he can believe that tedium and disappointment is the common lot, yet he cannot lose interest in life, or else he will lose his ability to depict it." Such an insistence proved axiomatic. Chekhov's view of life was peculiarly Russian, Cowley observed, but many Americans shared a similar attitude toward existence. Why, then, was there no American Chekhov? The answer, Cowley thought, lay in the nefarious effects of American journalism, which demanded that the writer "view everything in the light of the story it will make. No American writer," he declared, "can take life as it is and tell about it. Every one of them, even the tedious Mr. Dreiser, insists on twisting life in the attempt to form an organized plot." In an accompanying review of W. Somerset Maugham's *Of Human Bondage* Cowley praised the novel for possessing "an unmistakable air of reality," but here defined his criterion of realism

more precisely. What he admired was not the minute external verisimilitude of the naturalists—Maugham had "avoided Theodore Dreiser's great
mistake"—but a degree of behavioristic or psychological realism: the air of
reality in Maugham sprang from "the author's careful observations of the
actions that characterize a person," the details of behavior that laid bare
a character's "soul."[64] Earlier, he had preferred Schnitzler to Dreiser for
similar reasons.

These early reviews, full of impressionistic vagueness, pointed the direction in which Cowley's talents would develop. They displayed his capacity
for singling out a writer's strengths and weaknesses in a few sharp phrases,
showed an emerging interest in a writer's outlook on human existence,
suggested a rudimentary humanism in his demand of a correlation between art and life, and revealed a gift for lending a book dramatic relevance
by placing it in the context of the present. The reviews also showed that
his talent for conceptual thinking and exact theoretical definition was not
strong.

To Burke, Cowley acknowledged the slender theoretical basis on which
he had approached the novels and granted that "the theory of the novel"
was "of infinitely greater importance" than the criticism of specific works of
art. Typically, his early speculations were predicated on assumptions about
art and the literary life that were instinctive rather than theoretical. He
agreed with Burke that "the novelist's art [was] the highest," but demanded
of the writer a broad experience and a wide acquaintanceship with people
and was inclined to see his own gregariousness as better equipment for
the writing life than Burke's comparative isolation: "a novelist has to know
people. And to know them, he has to meet people. I think at present I have
a better knowledge of many kinds of people than you have, although your
mind is more naturally bent to character analysis." He believed he owed his
advantage to Harvard, since Harvard was the only university with "a really
distinctive attitude." "You can always tell a Harvard man," he reminded
Burke, "but you can't tell him much." Knowing Burke was planning to
leave Ohio State, Cowley proposed his ideal of Burke and himself together
at Harvard with renewed fervor. He promised to "boom" Burke, introduce
him to all the "literary lights" and help him around the *Advocate* office.
The year after, Cowley would then be willing to swap universities and bury
himself with Burke in the "wilds" of Ohio State: "You and I together and a
library close at hand—what does it matter whether we are in Paris, Petro-
grad, Columbus or New York?" Meanwhile, he triumphantly announced,

his literary sterility had disappeared, since he had discovered "a subject of infinite interest. I am writing my own history."[65]

‹ ‹ ‹   Over the Christmas break Cowley voyaged to New York, accompanied by Royall Snow, whom he introduced to Burke. He spent a day with Burke in New York, then journeyed on to Pittsburgh, where he saw old friends from high-school days, and to Belsano, where he consorted with James Light and Susan Jenkins, who had spent the fall semester at Ohio State with Burke. He also met some of their fellow students and seized the opportunity to boast about the *Advocate* and flaunt his Harvard sense of superiority by proclaiming "a lot of childish socialism."[66]

Back in Cambridge, Cowley made every effort to help smooth Burke's path to Harvard. Pulling as many strings as he could, he consulted with the dean, discussing Burke's chances of obtaining a scholarship and of entering Harvard without taking entrance examinations. He advised Burke to apply for a scholarship from one of the regional Harvard clubs, wrote a glowing letter of recommendation to a potential sponsor in one of the Pittsburgh banks, and even tried to find a suitable roommate for Burke. Sensing the latter's hesitation he stressed the importance of an orientation visit to the college. Burke visited Cowley in Cambridge in late January. Cowley did his utmost to present the university in the best possible light. In one of his invitational letters, he proposed to arrange a meeting with the dean and suggested they attend a Monday night lecture by Charles Townsend Copeland, "the English professor of great ego," and get a taste of Boston's cultural offerings by taking in a theatrical performance—he mentioned Oscar Wilde's *The Importance of Being Earnest* as one possibility. But Cowley's efforts did not pay off. Much to his regret Burke let deadlines for applications pass and, starting with the spring semester, transferred from Ohio State to Columbia. The following year, in January 1918, he left a promising scholastic career—he had hopes of being appointed to the Columbia faculty—and went to room with James Light and Susan Jenkins in Greenwich Village.[67]

Cowley's writings were now beginning to appear in little magazines published beyond the boundaries of Harvard. Though he could boast rejection slips from five magazines, "ranging from the *Seven Arts* to *Saucy Stories*," two poems he had written the previous fall—"Wistfulness" and "The Harbor at Night"—were published in *Slate* early in 1917. *Slate*, an advocate of educational reform, was edited from New York by Jess Perlman, who managed to keep the magazine afloat for the first five months of 1917. Besides Cowley and Burke it featured early writings by Floyd Dell, Scott Nearing, Louis Untermeyer, Haniel Long, Witter Bynner, and Royall Snow. About this time, too, Max Lincoln Schuster published some of Cowley's earliest verse in an intercollegiate little magazine called *Challenge*.[68]

Cowley himself showed more enthusiasm for an avant-garde venture by some of the undergraduate students from Ohio State whom he had met over Christmas. In the fall of 1916 they had laid plans for the foundation of a collegiate magazine called the *Sansculotte*. Its moving spirit and editor in chief was James Light; among the associate editors was Louis Lozowick, who, after World War I, became a leader of the Russian Constructivists and disappeared in the Great Purge of the 1930s. *Sansculotte*, derisively called "No Breeches" after the most radical supporters of the French Revolution, represented the orthodox avant-garde opinions of the time; it stood, Cowley recalled, for "pacifism in politics, bold realism in fiction, and hurrah for free verse."[69] The first issue, dated January 1917, contained an editorial proclamation of the magazine's commitment to a radically aesthetic position; its language was enthusiastic but shrouded in vague and inconsistent generalities:

> Our faith is in the essential goodness of man's powers, in the worth of his purposes, in the value of art for full and satisfying life. We attempt to envisage ourselves in respect of the living controls of the past, and to appreciate our position in our time. We are individuals speaking each for himself, but speaking each with a definite relation to the others. We believe that the underlying reality in life is given meaning and force by art, that art and literature are the interpreters, the coordinators of what meaning there is in men and their surroundings, that they absorb, assimilate and nourish the foundational sense and purpose of human existence. . . . Our care is for literature for its own sake, as far as possible. Our aim is an artistic one purely.[70]

Sansculotte ran for three issues only, in January, February, and April 1917, and, following the fate of numerous little magazines during the war, folded for lack of money. The second issue carried some poems by Ludwig Lewisohn, then on the faculty of Ohio State and a sympathetic mentor of the venture. Another amused but somewhat bewildered observer of the magazine, though he did not contribute, was James Thurber, then a student at Ohio State. George Bellows and John Sloan saw enough in the venture to contribute a free cover drawing each. But mostly James Light called on his friends to fill the magazine's pages. Apart from contributions by the editorial board, the bulk of its contents were made up of the writings of Burke, Cowley, Snow, and Susan Jenkins.[71]

Cowley followed the magazine's fate with a good deal of skeptical interest. He subscribed to most of its editorial philosophies, especially its general emphasis on the value of art for life, its commitment to life "in our time," and its stress on the independence of its individual contributors within the context of a group; however, he was critical of the language in which the statement had been couched. Cowley was represented in all three issues of *Sansculotte*, contributing a total of five poems and a prose sketch. One poem was rejected by Light because it "sounded like a sophomore Villon"; since Cowley had written the poem at Peabody, he took the criticism as a compliment. The prose sketch, "The Author of His Being," is set in Cambria County. Grotesque in mood, it explores the brutal underside of life in the Midwest and relates how the illegitimate son of a shiftless drunkard, out of fear and resentment, refrains from saving his father from death by freezing.[72] Among the poems was "Kisses," which had moved Amy Lowell to praise the modernity of Cowley's verse; it reveals a penchant for precise, imagistic notation:

> Like fox-grapes after the first frost,
> Lucy's kisses are wholesome, and fragrant and a little tart.
> Clara's sweetest kisses are sticky and ostentatious—
> Like shoeblacking.[73]

To Cowley's delight Light also published one of his earliest poems, "The Oldest Inhabitant," a tribute to his pioneer ancestor Thomas Duncan written at Peabody. The poem, in free verse, laments the despoliation of the Cambria County countryside by mines and forest fires, and lovingly evokes the vanished woodlands of Chestnut Ridge; it shows a tendency toward proselike diffuseness that marks even some of Cowley's more successful poems. The last lines of the poem read:

> You were my own kin, Thomas Duncan,
> And I sometimes wish that instead of bending over my desk,
>   hour by hour,

> I could trudge like you beside my wagon over the timbered
>   Alleghenies,
> To carve new empires out of the eternal hills.[74]

Cowley's poems in *Sansculotte* display an early adeptness at mastering different verse forms, but are hardly distinguished; though written with care and possessed of incidentally felicitous phrases or images, their final impression is one of distinct juvenility.

Several poems appearing in the *Harvard Advocate* of February 1917 show greater sophistication. Cowley continued to toy with free verse, but his predilection was for strict, regular forms, like the sonnet, the ballad, or other stanzaic narrative verse. "Ragtime," published side by side with "Ante Mortem," an experiment in vers libre, was a characteristic effort to counterpoint a conventional form with the wild and primitive rhythms of contemporary music:

> These tunes they hum today are ages old.
>   Shushan and Babylon were in their might
>   When once they played them in the fire-light
> That reddened lost glades of the Congo wold.
> They made the seething jungle blood run cold,
>   Until the warriors stole into the night,
>   Lusting for blood, to slay in secret fight,
> While tom-toms pulsed in rhythms manifold.
>
> The battle dance around the fire is gone;
>   The warriors' very bones have bleached away.
> But though their open savagery is done,
> The savage rhythm of their chants lives on;
>   Lives in the frantic tunes the fiddlers play
>   To drunken mummers in the cabaret.[75]

Another poem, "An Old Fellow to his Friends," strikes a typical pose of world-weariness as it speculates upon the possible effect of the poet's death on his friends. A "philosophical discussion" in verse, it was inspired by a talk Cowley had had with Burke over Christmas and had subsequently turned into blank verse; in it Cowley tried to integrate a tone of conversational ease with the formal restraint of iambic pentameters. The second stanza will suffice as an illustration:

> Forget the silence and the darkened room,
> Old friends, when I am dead. Perhaps instead
> You all might meet as we all used to meet;
> With cards and glasses and a haze of smoke—
> And then the time to jest and jibe at me.
> Then tear apart my poems as of old,
> Show their essential weakness; take my prose,
> That never could grow up, and jeer at it.
> And when all that is criticized enough,
> Turn to my person, laughing louder still;
> Bring forth my foibles and my prejudices. . . . [76]

In March, Cowley's hopes for literary success were fulfilled. His contributions to the *Harvard Advocate* were sufficiently numerous and impressive for its author to be elected to the magazine's editorial board. He was admitted at a ceremonial banquet on March 20. At the occasion the Harvard litterateurs were particularly impressed by the reading of one of Cowley's sonnets. "From the Diary of a Restoration Gentleman" was "a grand success"; it was traditional enough to elicit Barrett Wendell's comment that it was "literature" and to earn the glowing (if drunken) praise in French of Robert Hillyer—as well as the sober applause of many others.

> We passed a stupid night at Lanterloo,
>   and afterwards, when day did first approach,
>   Sir Reginald advised a hackney coach.
> Then home to sleep, and glad the night was through.
> At twelve, I to the Mall, where there were few
>   Wenches who did not flee at my approach,
>   Or who shewed pleasure if I cared to broach
> A quiet supper at the Rose for two.
>
> Then to the play. The boxes were all full,
>   The pit was jammed, but I could not forgive
> A clumsy cast, and Lord! the lines were dull.
>   Then wine and cards and home I know not how . . .
> I wonder if such fops as I will live
>   Such stupid lives two centuries from now? [77]

Reflecting Cowley's reading in Restoration and Augustan literature, the poem displays a penchant for satire that marks several of his early writings, including one of two short stories published in the *Advocate* early in 1917. In "The Wages of Death" the satire was aimed at Cowley's own ambitions as well as at the standards of the magazine and book-publishing world. The story explores the conflict between public success and artistic integrity, a theme that soon enough surfaced in Cowley's own career. Rejected twice by his beloved Doria, Harold, the young protagonist, turns to fiction with redoubled efforts. He dreams of writing best-sellers, but one after the other his stories are rejected: the editor of *The Romantic* finds them too classical and pompous, the conservative editor of *The Arctic Monthly* too frivolous and colloquial. Then Harold learns that Doria has been foully murdered by an unknown killer. In a flash of inspiration he gives himself up for the murder of his beloved. Immediately publicity surrounds him and he is offered "gratifying royalties" by three publishers: "Any volume of tales written by such a notorious criminal was bound to be successful. Respectable matrons read it instead of divorce proceedings. Flappers thought him more wicked than Verlaine. Old maids gave up their favorite Oscar Wilde. When an officious librarian barred the book from the Boston Public Library, its sales redoubled." Basking in literary glory, Harold sits through the courtroom proceedings, speculating on the artistic uses to which the scene of his trial can be put. On the day before his execution, he receives a check for fifty thousand dollars from his publisher.[78]

Cowley remembered several of his Harvard teachers, especially Dean Briggs and John Livingston Lowes, with great fondness. But the teacher who made the most lasting impression was Charles Townsend Copeland. "Copey" was a legendary Harvard character whose advanced composition course, English 12, attracted scores of young talented writers, many of whom would go on to distinguished careers in letters. Known as a sympathetic mentor and friend to undergraduates, Copey was less the scholarly intellectual than an excellent lecturer and teacher. Failure to publish and lack of appreciation from his colleagues kept him in the rank of instructor for years, yet few teachers gathered such a dedicated following among students. Many of them, including Cowley, remembered him as their "favorite English instructor." Before joining the Harvard English department Copey had been an actor, had written a biography of Edwin Booth, dropped out of Harvard Law School, and worked for seven years on the staff of the *Boston Post*. Giving free rein to his histrionic talents, Copey loved to perform while teaching. His public readings of Poe, Twain, Kipling, and Dickens were famous; in the opinion of one historian they managed to give even "the most illiterate a taste for the English classics."[79]

Cowley took English 12 in his sophomore year; as he reported to Burke, he found it "remarkably interesting." Copey purposely kept his composition course limited to about thirty students, whom he met in his own rooms in Hollis Hall. He was known as a devastating critic of students' work, one who had a keen eye for detail and could infallibly distinguish good from awkward prose. Years later Cowley remembered "those awful moments in the afternoon when one went to Copey's room by appointment to read aloud one's latest theme, while Copey dozed in his chair, perhaps with the dying sunlight reflected from the south window on the polished membrane that covered his enormous skull. At the end of the reading he would dictate his comments for the student to copy on the folded back of the theme. Once when I had described the swirling dust in a downtown Pittsburgh street, he dictated slowly, without unfolding his hands, 'Don't you remember the smell of dried horse dung? Why didn't you put that in?' And once when I read him a sententious article written for the *Advocate*, in which one wondered how the country knew who . . . he shook his head and groaned, 'Malcolm, when are you going to stop using those knew-whoings and one-wonder-ings?' I stopped that afternoon."[80]

When Copey gave him his first two A's at the end of March, Cowley was exultant, exclaiming in a letter to Burke: "I began to feel so much like a successful poet that I was going to write immediately and tell you that you weren't more a genius than I after all." When his friend seemed skeptical about the value of Copey's praise Cowley explained its importance: "Copey is almost a parent of present-day American literature. Our writing today is done by Harvard men, and Harvard men of prominence in literature always take Copey's course."[81]

Copey's instruction was not restricted to his classes. For almost forty years he kept "open house" one night a week after ten. To be admitted to Copey's inner circle was a much-coveted privilege and it was with appropriate pride that Cowley announced to Burke in March 1917: "Copey has finally opened his gates to receive me." One of Cowley's early unpublished pieces of verse, "Copey's Room," evoked the atmosphere of these evenings.

> A low-beamed ceiling, and a glowing fire;
> Old photographs that peer out of the gloom;

Pamphlets and books invading everything;
Chairs deep as death; the calm that calm minds bring:
Call it a vision of the student realized
If you like words—or call it just a room.

The current of life has passed it by—it seems
Two doors shut out the world and what it says;
A murmuring fire makes reminiscences
Of waves along the beach—wind in the trees;
And now the gloom is live with memories:
An old man's memories—and a young man's dreams.

The minutes pass in clockticks—I forget
That through these double doors young men have come
As old as life—bowed down by fear of living;
That they have talked as I talk—and then some,
Having felt unknown worlds in your advice,
More than you meant to say—Truth, Sacrifice—
Have stridden through the doors some minutes later,
With a set smile, and saying banal things,
To die for God and kin—and dreams much greater.[82]

Besides their essays, students were required to submit five hundred words of translation from any language every week. Rumor had it that Copey never read them. Cowley once submitted five hundred words of sheer "gibberish"; they elicited no comment. In the 1920s, having gained a reputation as an expert translator of French literature, Cowley was persuaded of the value of translating for the beginning writer. In 1958, outlining his own proposal for an advanced writing course in the Hopwood Lecture at the University of Michigan, he recommended a course in translation as an ideal preparation: "translation is a most effective means of learning the spirit and resources of one's own language. There is no better way of acquiring a prose style, except possibly the writing of verse." Copeland did not exert any demonstrable influence on Cowley's literary thought, but his flair for showmanship and his capacity for playing on an audience helped Cowley understand that a communicable art must depend to a large extent on the spoken voice. The leading principle that Copey inculcated in his pupil was that "good prose should be speakable prose," a goal Cowley pursued through his long career.[83]

‹ ‹ ‹   Though there is little in Cowley's college writings or his early correspondence that explicitly prepares us for his interpretation of his Harvard experience in *Exile's Return* (1934), the evidence available suggests that, divested of its political coloration, Cowley's retrospective account is historically accurate. In college, Cowley argued in *Exile's Return*, the process of deracination that had started in high school continued relentlessly. Little or nothing of what he was taught in the classroom had any connection with the rapidly changing urban-technological society outside the university walls or with the intellectual upheavals of the years between 1912 and 1917. To an impressionable student the university appeared a "high disembodied realm" of books and ideas, in which raw human experience was refined into "the dead material of culture." In such a milieu regional and ethnic differences blurred into a cultural and intellectual universalism with a distinctly elitist flavor, which induced young writers like Cowley to disregard the literary potential of their personal backgrounds and experiences. The values instilled in Harvard men, Cowley later felt, were essentially "leisure-class" ideals; a student of his own educational and social background ran "the risk of losing [his] own culture . . . and of receiving nothing real in exchange." As the record indicates, to resolve the discrepancy between both worlds and to counteract a feeling of social unease, Cowley was inclined to accept the "unspoken doctrines" of his socially privileged fellow students, and allowed some of their prejudices to color his own attitudes. Cultivating a pose of snobbery, he tended to wear his culture, not as something natural, but as "a veneer, a badge of class distinction." As he later wrote, in college Cowley "never grasped the idea that culture was the outgrowth of a situation."[84]

Most of his early poems implicitly support Cowley's thesis in *Exile's Return*. Typically, they exploit the "dead material of culture," as in "Execution" or "From the Diary of a Restoration Gentleman." At most, in "To a Chance Aquaintance" and "A Letter to Jim," they use a native Pennsylvania landscape for backdrop. Only "The Oldest Inhabitant," written in high school, and the unpublished "Copey's Room" anticipate the argument in *Exile's Return* with any degree of explicitness, the first by seriously exploring the poet's roots in the pioneer history of Pennsylvania, the second by picturing the university (metonymically represented by the professor's study) as a stagnant, lifeless world of art and learning in opposition to the "current of life" outside its protective walls.

Cowley's overriding concern at Harvard was with literature. If, as a student, he had "every chance to combine four years of sound classical discipline with a personal observation of city morals and sociology and politics in action,"[85] he was indifferent to such an opportunity, preferring to spend his time with literary friends at the Poetry Society or in the editorial offices of the *Advocate*. If with Burke he exulted over the city as a "work of art" and evoked its "multitudinous noises" and "woes" in an occasional poem, he failed to grasp the social and economic underpinnings of its picturesque surface.[86] His letters display little or no interest in the social and political problems that preoccupied Harvard students like John Reed or John Dos Passos, nor did the full significance of Harvard's New England legacy dawn upon him as it did upon Cummings and Wheelwright. During his student days Cowley's understanding of the historical roots of the university and the socio-economic forces shaping his Harvard experience were but hazy at best. It was not until his awareness of them had deepened and accelerated under the impact of the Great Depression that he developed a coherent vision of his cultural and social position at Harvard. Partly because that vision was predicated on a newly raised social consciousness and inspired by a personal need to fit the disparate parts of his past into a meaningful framework, in *Exile's Return* Cowley was tempted to overplay the importance of social and economic factors and to underplay the intensity of his ambition to make an impact on Harvard's literary scene.

In the spring of 1917 history did not permit Cowley to pursue his literary interests unperturbedly and finish his college education in the regular fashion. As World War I dragged on in Europe and American participation became increasingly imminent, Cowley was moved to act and, in the process, physically severed from his native culture.

3

The Spectacle of War

France, 1917

In the spring of 1917, even before the United States declared war, a majority of the Harvard population openly and strongly supported the Allied cause. As Harvard's share in the national "preparedness" program President Lowell had from the first urged students to enroll in the special training camps set up in Plattsburgh, N.Y., and in April and May 1917 special finals were held, allowing students to leave for active service or to join the Harvard R.O.T.C. Most undergraduates participated in some form of wartime service; by May 1918 enrollment had dropped to one-fifth of the normal.[1] At Harvard, as at other universities, the attitudes of the student body toward the war were by no means uniform or unambiguous; in effect, they ran "the full gamut from pacifism to jingoism." The editorial staff of the *Harvard Monthly* was split about evenly into opposing camps of pacifists and patriots. Unable to find a compromise the editors were forced to suspend publication in April 1917. The *Harvard Advocate*, less riveted with dissension, continued publication, in spite of wartime shortages and the pressures of conscription. As the oldest Harvard publication, it felt it had a special wartime duty to maintain "a sane continuity in the artistic life of the college."[2]

Whatever their attitudes, in the spring of 1917 virtually all young Harvard writers were eager to get to Europe and personally witness the war. Many volunteered for ambulance or military transport service in a foreign army. Even if they rebelled against the war in principle, they were still conscious of emotions pulling them toward participation in a great experience. E. E. Cummings's sympathy with the peace movement and his scorn for the mounting war hysteria did not prevent him from volunteering for the Norton-Harjes Ambulance Service on the day after the U.S. Congress declared war; typically, his decision was inspired by a desire to direct his own fate and a fascination with the new experience in store. S. Foster Damon shared Cummings's pacifist ambivalence about the war but promptly exchanged his role as captain of the Harvard fencing team for that of bayonet instructor at the Plattsburgh training camp. Neither

John Dos Passos's pacifism nor his radical sympathies could prevent him from attempting to enlist in the army, and when he was disqualified on the grounds of defective eyesight he volunteered for ambulance service with Norton-Harjes and later with the Italian Red Cross. Indeed, by the end of the spring most of Cowley's literary colleagues at the Harvard Poetry Society were involved in the war effort.[3]

The prospect of American intervention had also set off a fierce debate between militarists and pacifists at Columbia University. Kenneth Burke, already an avid reader of philosophy and ambitious to write a novel, was half-heartedly drawn into the debate. A "half-socialist," Burke was inclined to view the war as "silly" and irrational. His skepticism about the war, however, seemed fed as much by the jingoistic excesses of the press as by actual pacifist opposition; the war hardly diminished his literary ambitions. Cowley, like Burke, was appalled at the contradiction between the high German culture of the past and the nation's current militarism; but unlike Burke, his horror at the desecration of European culture did not foster much apparent skepticism about the war. In his last review for the *Advocate* before his departure he wrote: "That Germany, often called in the past the most civilized of all nations, has murdered, plundered, turned pirate, and broken all human obligations, is apparent to all observers. But how her actions harmonize with her peculiar culture has up to now remained a puzzle." In his correspondence with Burke, too, Cowley gave few indications that he shared his friend's ambivalence. In early May 1916 he was already convinced of the rightness of the Allied cause and pronounced his intention of joining the Harvard Regiment and entering the Plattsburgh training camp. A year later, on March 31, 1917, he announced that he was "definitely signed up with the regiment."[4]

Caught up in the prevailing contagious mood of patriotism, Cowley was prepared to don a uniform, evidently without giving much thought to the larger purposes of the war. For him, as for many, the war was a call to excitement and adventure sanctioned by the rhetoric of heroism and idealism.[5] In "Ballade of French Service," a poem written in anticipation of his French venture, Cowley expressed his relief at being able to exchange the boredom of his Cambridge life for the color and excitement of wartime France. Even his friends' pacifism, the poem implied, could not shake his conviction that his move was right. With Burke, Damon, Light, and Wheelwright staying behind, Cowley must have felt he was taking a historical lead. The poem, however, despite its half-ironic tone, hardly moves beyond conventional romanticism. A representative stanza reads:

No more to stroll for half the day
Along the careless Avenue;
No more to doze the night away
Reading of deeds that others do.
Cards, wine, avaunt! Get out! I'm through.
I'm going to drive an ambulance—
A Ford, mind—for a year or two
Along some shell-swept road in France.[6]

During his first two years at Harvard, Cowley had repeatedly run up against the limitations of his experience and had despaired of becoming a writer on such a slender diet. Now the war held out the promise of firsthand observation of the reality of danger, injury, and death, a rich store of experience to be mined in future writing.[7]

‹ ‹ ‹   Shortly after Congress declared war upon Germany, Cowley enlisted as a volunteer in the American Ambulance Field Service. His gesture of commitment received cordial endorsement from his senior mentors. Charles Townsend Copeland presented him with a book inscribed with a Latin motto—*solvitur ambulando*—that perfectly fitted his student's pragmatic bent, while G. B. Kirk, the "tyrant" of Peabody High, wrote him a letter of recommendation and a note of self-pitying regret at being unable to go over and fight the Germans in person. Cowley was particularly pleased with a "most flattering commission" he received from one of his Harvard instructors, Frederic Schenck, who was impressed enough by Cowley's writing skills to give him a "soft-soaping" to the head of the ambulance service. Cowley was commissioned to write letters about his war experiences with the understanding that, if they were good enough, Schenck would publish them.[8]

Pending his departure Cowley spent a few days in New York, where he was introduced to a new comrade of Burke, Matthew Josephson. In his memoirs Josephson has recalled how, upon their first meeting, Cowley was "not much more than eighteen, ruddy and chubby-faced, and looked like a big overgrown country boy. . . . But within this awkward rustic-looking youth with the broad smile, there was a keen student of poetry who wrote with grace and clarity when he put pen to paper." Josephson, two years younger than Burke, was the son of Eastern European Jewish immigrants who had settled in the 1890s in Brownsville, the Jewish section of Brooklyn. By dint of hard work his ambitious father had worked his way up from a successful career as a printer to the ownership of a bank and a position of civic leadership in Brownsville. Josephson scorned the banking career that his parents expected him to pursue and, like Burke, disregarded his elders' expectations by becoming a defiant poet-rebel. Callow and precocious, the young Josephson went on to a distinguished career in journalism and biography. He became one of Cowley's lifelong friends.[9]

Burke and Josephson, who first met at a meeting of Columbia's literary society, were regular companions at the university: "We were quite vigorously involved in a constant muddle of intimacy and scrappiness," Burke recalled. Burke's sharp and complex mind challenged Josephson's adolescent literary opinions and helped to expand his intellectual horizons. Like Cowley, they were given to posing as world-weary decadents or vulgar cynics but were also filled with literary idealism and motivated by the determination to be good writers: before long, the three considered themselves the hard-core triumvirate of the younger literary generation in America. But while Cowley was preparing to face the battlefields of northern France, Burke and Josephson decided to try to impede the American war effort, and in the summer they joined the Guillotine Club, a Greenwich Village group of pacifists and socialists opposed to the war. Soon, however, they turned away in disgust over the organization's autocratic procedures.[10]

Cowley sailed from New York on Saturday, April 28, 1917, on the *Touraine*, a French passenger liner. Also on board were E. E. Cummings and William Slater Brown, who struck up a close friendship during the voyage. Cowley saw much of them during the 1920s but did not meet them during the crossing. After an "unexciting" ten-day passage the *Touraine* steered safely through the submarine zone. The atmosphere on board was one of "assumed carelessness." After disembarking at Bordeaux, the volunteers went by train to Paris, and on May 11, Cowley was writing to Burke from the American Field Service Headquarters at 21 Rue Raynouard, a château set in a five-acre park at the top of a hill at Passy, looking down past terraces and formal gardens, through old chestnut trees, to the Seine. The château, loaned to the service by a French countess, served as a social center and mail office for volunteers on leave from the front.[11]

From its inception the American Field Service was, as many besides

Cowley have observed, "an enterprise of a strongly literary, or academic, nature." Among college students, in particular, the Field Service rapidly rose in prestige. Harvard men were most numerous, followed by students from Yale, Princeton, and Dartmouth. Among private preparatory schools Andover contributed the largest delegation. Many who enlisted in the volunteer service expected to meet there with their former cronies. As Charles Fenton has observed, "membership in the Field Service was on the whole an extension and a renewal of the acquaintanceship one had made at prep school and college, with a fraternity aspect that included hazing of new men and the celebration at the front of Yale's upset victory over Harvard in 1916." Thus Cowley's interpretation, in *Exile's Return*, that the ambulance and transport units served as "college-extension courses for a generation of writers" must be seen in a social as well as a literary light. If he had suffered a sense of social uneasiness at Harvard, he might predictably encounter much the same experience in the Field Service.[12]

Upon Cowley's arrival in Paris a reorganization of the Field Service caused a delay in the assignment of volunteers to specific camps and units. Cowley was thrilled at being able to spend some time in Paris. With Bob Cunningham, who had enlisted in the service with him, he wandered amid the jostling crowds down the boulevards, relished the girls at the Folies Bergères and the Olympian Music Hall, and attended a French cabaret. The show, he reported to Burke, like a genuine American innocent abroad, was only "a little above the level of one of your Weehawken vaudeville shows." To his surprise, nothing in the program was indecent even by Pittsburgh standards. Instead, a great deal of nationalist poetry had been recited in glorification of *La France*.[13]

Cowley had come over with the romantic expectation of driving an ambulance, but fate decided otherwise. Soon after the United States entered the war, Commandant Doumenc, the head of the Automobile Service of the French Army, put in an emergency request to the American Field Service, hoping to secure the assistance of American volunteers in the transport of munitions and matériel for the French troops. He was in need of seven thousand camion drivers. Helped by the fact that in the early months of 1917 the ambulance service was so popular that it stood in danger of becoming overrecruited, the inspector general of the Field Service, A. Piatt Andrew, responded affirmatively to the request. Thus the Franco-American Military Transport Service, known as the Réserve Mallet, was launched. The need for camion drivers was explained to the volunteers who arrived in Paris in early May. Cowley and Cunningham agreed to join the newly formed transport units because they were persuaded they "could be of more use there." In two months the Mallet reserve grew to eight hundred volunteers. In the period of Cowley's service, between July and October 1917, the reserve, carrying ammunition, engineering supplies, and shells on a twenty-four-hour basis, played an important role in the Allied victory of the Chemins des Dames attack. In later battles, too, the transport units rendered essential help.[14]

Cowley and Cunningham were assigned to T.M.U. 526 (a somewhat peculiar abbreviation of Transport de Matériel Etats-Unis) and were placed at first in a transport section of forty volunteers, eighteen of whom, Cowley wrote to his parents, were "young buds of Yale's chief preparatory school— Andover." By the third week of May, Cowley was in training camp at Dommiers, a village eight miles southwest of Soissons and fifteen miles behind the front lines. Here, volunteers were given military schooling, including setting-up exercises, elementary infantry drill, lectures about the organization of the French army, and practical training in the handling and repairing of cars.[15]

On May 18 Cowley started to jot down his observations in a war diary, expecting to rework his notes into publishable reports.[16] "Well, we're out of it and into it," he mused, surveying his trip from Cambridge, which he had left in a springtime drizzle, to New York, where flags were waving along Wall Street, through the submarine zone and the busy traffic of Bordeaux and Paris, to his camp behind the lines. For the moment, surrounded by contradictory information, no one in camp seemed sure of their immediate destiny: "From a milieu of rumors and uncertainties I have come into a milieu of other rumors and uncertainties." The volunteers were entitled to seven days' leave every three months, were issued a ration of pipe tobacco every ten days, and received a daily allowance of a quart of sour *pinard* and two francs from the French government. "I suppose we are real soldiers now," Cowley observed.[17]

Cowley's sense of war was naive. Born in 1898, he had been raised on stories about the Spanish-American War and of how his mother had held him, a little baby, against the window to watch the files of soldiers march through the avenues of Pittsburgh, as they returned from "That Splendid Little War" that had sent Frank Norris and Richard Harding Davis scampering off to Cuba in search of titanic adventure and romantic glory. Cowley's innocence about wartime military life soon received its first blow.

On his second day in camp his lieutenant halted midway through a lecture on the construction of the motor truck and marched the volunteers over to the road to watch a contingent of ragged soldiers in blue returning from the front. The fresh recruits saw a cavalry unit of dirty, unshaven men who sat lolling on their horses, a poignant contrast with the "prime dragoons" they had seen marching through the streets of Paris—"we wondered a little about the empty saddles," Cowley remarked. The infantry troops followed: "Route step, no order, little gaiety. Just dirt and the indifference bred of three years in the face of the enemy." These, reputedly, were some of the finest soldiers of France, but Cowley could not help wondering: "Would we be anything like them in a year?" In the rear the troops were still marching in rank. As the flag came by, the lieutenant-instructor saluted and a military band struck up the "Marseillaise." "We were evidently important enough to deserve attention," Cowley noted in his diary, with as yet only the faintest inkling of the political and psychological impact the mere presence of American volunteers was having on a dispirited French army.[18]

Cowley's individualistic bent collided with military discipline. Once, he received a stinging reprimand from his *chef* for wearing a shabby old coat to morning drill. Feeling humiliated by the complacent air of military authority with which his *chef* had addressed him, Cowley made a gesture of rebellious defiance, and in his diary indulged in fantastic dreams of future vengeance.[19] His response on this occasion was informed by a puerile pugnacity and a streak of Pennsylvania stubbornness. Cowley was often quick to resent encroachments upon his personal liberty and temperamentally resisted attempts to subject a precious individualism to the straightjacket of discipline and authority, be it of a military unit, a literary faction, or a political party.

Cowley was hardly "a blooming success" at driving an unwieldy five-ton Pierce-Arrow truck; for a while he had to be satisfied with being only a second driver. His awkwardness as a motorist exposed him to much ridicule and pestering from fellow drivers. For two weeks, until he was transferred with Cunningham to another section, he was made to feel uncomfortable and "unhappy." "Man, I was in for it at first," Cowley later confessed to Burke. "I was perhaps the poorest driver in camp, and everybody came to regard me as a general nincompoop. But a little judicious profanity and a great deal of silence, and above all our old friend Time have worked very well together." Indeed, except for his ineptness Cowley was "quite satisfied" with life in his particular section. He had run into Robert Hillyer and

Elisha Whittlesey of the *Advocate* and the *Monthly* and rejoiced in having, for the time being, "some literary company." He also enjoyed talking with the poilus, from whom he received "sidelights about French life that I think the average tourist misses." [20]

One of the noteworthy events of Cowley's period in training camp, which was located near territory evacuated by General Paul von Hindenburg in the spring retreat, was a visit to the abandoned German trenches and dugouts. Cowley described the visit in a report for the *American Field Service Bulletin* that upon his return to the United States he rewrote and expanded for newspaper publication.[21] The visit left a deep impact on the young soldier's impressionable mind.

During his visit Cowley had occasion to note how on the side of a narrow ravine the Germans had built an entire "dugout city." Compared to the makeshift *abris* of the French, the German dugouts were veritable "palaces," which seemed "constructed to last a hundred years." As a first step in the methodical process of Prussianizing the French country, the German invaders had attempted to annihilate everything indigenously French. Everywhere Cowley was struck by the sights of "total destruction": graveyards despoiled, houses dynamited or razed by shells, orchards chopped down, wells poisoned. In a nearby village only the outlines of walls still stood erect and "heaps of crumbling stones, all dazzlingly white, lay in the May sunshine," making the ruins resemble "the picked skeleton of some great beast on a tropical beach." Everywhere he noticed "the same attempt to rear a civilization exclusively Germanic" on the ruins of France. This "Kultur" seemed "childishly anxious to justify itself" with copious inscriptions glorifying the German God, King, and Nation, and blaming Great Britain for the present destruction. As the convoy returned to camp through the Aisne valley, a splendid sunset drowned the West— "The reed-bordered river curved majestically among the meadows. Here and there was a clump of poplars such as Corot loved to paint"—and, with a surge of affection for the French landscape and the art it had engendered, an epiphany came to Cowley as to the futility of the German attempt: "And it seemed to me suddenly that even if the invader did succeed in destroying every vestige of past civilization in the country and killed every human being, they would hardly succeed in their work of Germanization. In the end the land itself would conquer them, just as it had conquered Celts and Romans, Franks and Northmen in past centuries, making them over into its own spirit." Independently, if as yet tentatively, Cowley had begun to feel his way toward a conception of culture as the organic "outgrowth of a situation" that was to be a keystone to his literary thinking.

Many of Cowley's diary entries hold the germs of the interpretation he retrospectively put on his wartime service in *Exile's Return*. Often they imply the "spectatorial attitude" Cowley later posited as the quintessence of his war experience; they are written from the perspective of an observer witnessing an impressive spectacle without fully comprehending its scope or nature. Such verbs as "watch," "see," and "observe" proliferate, as Cowley, mindful of his commission to report on his experiences to the home front, is inclined to view his personal impressions as representative of his coevals and unconsciously slips into the habit of adopting a plural "we" for his narrative point of view. The use of a diary phrase like "we of the Camion Service" anticipates Cowley's use of the generational "we" in *Exile's Return*. In his diary entries and his pieces of wartime reportage Cowley first developed a sense of himself as the recording instrument of a communal experience; it grew into his characteristic narrative voice—that of the spokesman, chronicler, and interpreter of a generation of American writers. The poem "Poilus," which registers Cowley's impressions of the hardships and endurance of the French soldiers, evinces the spectatorial, communal perspective explicit in a representative passage from *Exile's Return*:

> Regiments at times pass through our village
> And, filthy with the caked mud of the front,
> They lie along the roadside, or else hunt
> Their billets in damp cellars, or in stables;
> And there, forgetting their abandoned tillage,
> Their mining, or their clerking, or their law,
> They sleep like beasts together in the straw . . . [22]

. . . Sometimes for three days at a time, a column of men and guns wound through the village where we were quartered. Chasseurs slouching along in their dark-blue uniforms, canteens and helmets banging against their hips; a regiment of Senegalese, huge men with blue-black faces, pink eyeballs and white teeth; then a convoy of camions in first and second gear, keeping pace with the moving files. Behind them, dust rose from an interminable line of seventy-fives drawn by great bay horses, with very blond Flemish artillerymen riding the caissons; then came a supply train; then, in horizon blue, an infantry regiment from Provence, three thousand men with sullen features; then rolling kitchens and wagons heaped with bread the color of faded straw. The Annamites, little mud-colored men with the faces of perverted babies, watched from the ditches where they were breaking stone; the airplanes of three nations kept watch overhead, and we ourselves were watchers. It did not seem that we could ever be part of all this. The long parade of races was a spectacle which it was our privilege to survey, a special circus . . . given for our benefit.[23]

Before leaving training camp Cowley paid a visit to the aviators of the famous Lafayette Escadrille, which had its hangars within two miles of his camp. The spirit of reckless, heroic adventure he encountered there stood in poignant contrast to the mood of fatigue and exhaustion that prevailed in the French army. The French, Cowley wrote home, were "quite tired" of the fighting. "No militarists over here," he observed to Burke early in June. After three years most soldiers had lost whatever idealism or exhilaration they had felt at the outset of the war; what had remained was a sense of numbness and waste, a "dead nausea." There had been several mutinies, Cowley reported to his parents, such as that of the 168th and 169th regiments, which had refused to go into the trenches.[24] In an atmosphere of widespread discontent the appearance of fresh American troops gave a tremendous boost to Allied morale. "The United States army was certainly received here enthusiastically," Cowley wrote to his father on July 9. "And you may believe me, it is needed." He was sure that the young American conscripts would see "a deal of bloody fighting." It was not until he came to write *Exile's Return* that Cowley realized that American volunteers were also serving a political purpose: they were used to mitigate the mutinous mood and were "displayed as first-tokens of victory." "We were treated well, that was all we knew. We were seeing a great show."[25]

Cowley left training camp at Dommiers on June 12. From Dommiers he was transferred to Jouaignes, a little town almost due east of Soissons, where camp was "within range of the German shells." Yet for the first few weeks life in camp was slow and relaxed, the work not overly arduous or dangerous, and soldiers had a relatively easy time of it. Around three each afternoon the section proceeded to the shell depot to load the camions. "We carry seventy-fives—the shells, not the guns; occasionally asphyxiating shells, some fuses, and for the most part barb wire and trench flooring," Cowley wrote to his father. The real work did not start until after ten o'clock, when night had fallen and the convoy wound itself, in pitch dark without lights, along muddy or dusty roads to the front. At a place from one to three kilometers behind the frontline trenches they rested, while their camions were being unloaded by French territorials; then they returned to camp and to sleep.[26]

Cowley's report on his first camion trip for the *American Field Service Bulletin* is saturated with the spectatorial attitude.[27] On this particular trip, it was past midnight before the camions were unloaded and they could return by an unknown road in the chaotic dark. As Cowley and Cunningham, his relief chauffeur, slowly made their way back under the constant noise of explosions, a heavy *marmite* exploded just ahead of their car. "Some of the red hot pieces fell very near and lay smoking in the road. Immediately the American craze for souvenirs came to the fore; and a half-dozen of the boys were racing for the fragments, and picking them up gingerly in their helmets." Some miles ahead Cowley was poignantly confronted with the harsh human reality beneath the touristy spectacle of the war:

> Right by the bridge I saw something lying across the road. Bob, who was driving, swung out. As we passed, I turned a flashlight toward the obstruction. A middle-aged Territorial . . . was lying there in a little spot of bloody mud. A fragment of shell had torn a great hole in his side. I turned the light away, and we went on in silence. . . . Then other ruined villages we passed, and other marching troops; all the time, star-shells rose and flamed over the lines. I was not watching them much, however. I was remembering the man at the bridge-head. For, after all, the dust and the galloping batteries . . . marching troops, and star-shells formed only the panoply of war; that middle-aged Territorial lying in his own blood was its immediate reality.

Such moments left their impact. Gradually a more realistic estimate of the nature of the war began to supplant Cowley's naive enthusiasm: "in America we don't realize exactly what it means to be at war for three years," he wrote to Burke in early June. "These wars of today are no longer the toy wars of the Middle Ages."[28] On the contrary, the war, he now saw, was senselessly destroying what had for centuries been defended as the good and noble and permanent in Western culture. On one of his expeditions Cowley passed the walls surrounding the immense park of the Château de Soupir; they were broken by shell holes and bordered by abandoned dugouts. Within he witnessed an emblem of the cataclysm that was sweeping the monuments of an entire cultural heritage toward destruction, in particular the neoclassical splendors of eighteenth-century France:

> We caught a glimpse within the walls of a landscape once as well ordered as a New England parlor. Fauns and nymphs, gods, kings, and philosophers were grouped at appropriate intervals; an artificial lake had been fixed just where it was needed to break the monotony. The château itself, in harmony with its park, had been of that ornateness which is somewhere between mere ostentation and real splendor.
>
> At present, it was only a gutted shell. Half the ornamental poplars and yews were shot down; the busts had gone, many of them, to form parts of *abris*, while those that remained were peppered with shrapnel. Quite unfeelingly, the German artillery had scattered about shellholes without any regard for decorative effects. Yet in all its ruin, the park was unconquerably polite and rococo. It reminded one strongly of the powdered *marquises* who preserved on the scaffold the manners of the drawing-room.[29]

The memory of the formal gardens of Soupir, destroyed by trenches, shellfire, and machine guns, stuck in Cowley's mind. It surfaces in *Exile's Return* and, some years after the war, inspired one of his finest poems. "Château de Soupir: 1917" appeared in the January 1922 issue of *Broom*; a comparison of the poem with the 1917 prose passage is illustrative of the changes in the postwar temper:

> Jean tells me that the Senator
> came here to see his mistresses,
> and having passed the gilded door,
> was ushered regally—Jean says—
> past genuine Flemish tapestries,
> velvets and mahoganies,
> to where the odalisque was set,
> the temporary queen, Odette.
>
> . . . An eighteenth-century château
> rebuilt to meet his lavish taste,
> painted and gilt fortissimo;
> the Germans, grown satirical,

had hidden a machine-gun nest
underneath the banquet hall.

The trenches run diagonally
across the alleys and the lawns,
and jagged wire from tree to tree;
the lake is desolate of swans;
in tortured immobility,
the deities of stone or bronze
await a new catastrophe.

Phantasmagorical at night,
yellow and white and amethyst,
the star-shells burn, and Verey lights,
and silent waters of the mist
submerge the landscape, till we feel
like drowned men, tragical, unreal.

And recent ghosts appear: Odette,
in skirt ballooning at the hips,
tosses a hasty kiss and slips
away to taunt the Senator
who, strong with marc and anisette,
his red beard waggling in the wind,
pursues her like a matador.

The mist creeps riverward. A fox
barks underneath a blasted tree.
An enemy machine-gun mocks
this ante-bellum comedy
and then falls silent, while a bronze
Silenus, patron of these lawns,
stands riddled like a pepper-box.[30]

In the prose passage the tone is objectively descriptive, the perspective spectatorial, and what little irony that exists is directed first of all at the senseless indifference of German destructiveness, and only secondarily at the overly refined exquisiteness of the "powdered *marquises*"; the over-all effect is one of regret at the tragedy of destruction. In the poem the stanzas describing the château are embedded in a context satirizing the decadence and tasteless pomposity of eighteenth-century French aristoc-racy. The war is still seen as a colorful, "phantasmagorical" spectacle, affecting the men with its tragic unreality. This time, however, the whole poem is not only heavily ironic, but also its target has shifted: the German enemy now have "grown satirical," like the poet, and the principal thrust of the poem is against the civilization being destroyed by the war, the "ante-bellum comedy" whose patron stands "riddled like a pepper-box." After the war Cowley, with many others of his generation, adopted a sardonic and ironic point of view toward the old order of things, for the preservation of which the war was supposedly fought but which had become effectively discredited in the eyes of a younger generation.

In 1917 Cowley's letters from France were as yet mostly devoid of any such skepticism. Instead, he sometimes struck a note of ironic flippancy that made his war experiences seem curiously trivial. At times he com-plained of the absence of any real peril in his war work—there was "not enough danger to frighten a cotton tail," he observed to his father—or joked that he hoped to get wounded just badly enough to receive the *croix de guerre* and avoid the *croix de bois*. At other times he prided him-self on his fluency in French and his command of obscene words—"we have a wonderful opportunity to learn the language"—or boastfully gave Burke the "dope" on Paris: he sketched the bookstalls along the Seine, snorted that the river was hardly bigger than the American Youghiogheny, described the elegant women of Paris, and in adolescent pride outlined precisely on what streets the concentration of prostitutes was thickest.[31]

Not surprisingly, Cowley's letters and reports exposed him to the ridi-cule of his friends back home, who received the impression that his French venture was but a holiday trip. Irritated by such responses, Cowley was prompted to justify himself. He had at first been "in the midst of a little throe of militarism," he confessed; but actual service had turned him into "as much of a slacker" as James Light. But, he reasoned, whereas Light was trapped in a dull routine of working in a munitions factory, and para-doxically advancing the very militarism he claimed to hate, Cowley at least was in a new country, doing work he found congenial ("I always did like big lumbering things like camions"), and having his daily routine "very faintly spiced with adventure." The war, he felt, was having a liberating effect on him. "I thank God constantly that I have crossed the water," he wrote Burke on July 31. "Not that my soul has been transfused with wonder, but just that I have been drawn out of my fixed orbit." Most importantly, he was aware that he was an eyewitness to events that were "going to dominate the history of the world for the next century." Cowley's analysis of the war was neither profound nor sophisticated, yet he realized that it was illusory to hold that a postwar society could actually resume life on its prewar foundations or be built on the social and political ideals for which the war was nominally fought: "For all we Americans realize too little that at the end of the war every nation—yes, even the United States—will be too exhausted in men and money, too much in need of quick recuperation, to go on with the old happy-go-lucky state of affairs. We Americans are fighting for personal liberty, and yet after the fighting is over, out of sheer need of efficiency, we shall have to forego it." The very thought of the brutal regime that would follow a German victory sickened him: "In the captured portions of France they are making even the little children work in the fields from five in the morning until seven at night." Though French morale was low, Cowley continued to hold that the conflict was "about as clearcut between right and wrong as any war ever is." But over and above all loomed his awareness that participation in the war was the crucial formative event of his generation, a watershed moment in history that a young ambitious writer could afford to miss only at the risk of finding himself an alien in the postwar world. "At present . . . everyone should serve his time on the Western Front. That is the great common experience of the young manhood of today, an experience that will mould the thought of the next generation, and without which one will be somewhat of a stranger to the world of the present and the future." [32]

At other times his tone was pert and defiant. "Why not become a blooming slacker yourself and join our nobly lazy service," he challenged Burke on July 12. Camp, indeed, gave him plenty of opportunity for loafing and literature. Besides *The Red Badge of Courage*, he read Dostoyevski's *The Idiot*, W. L. George's *The Stranger's Wedding*, and two novels by Arnold Bennett. He began to make serious explorations of French literature and was anxious to remain informed about the literary situation at home. In early June he asked Burke to send him current issues of *Poetry*, the *Little Review*, and the *Seven Arts* and, if extant, the last issue of "Sans Breeches." A few weeks later he announced his discovery of a "splendid" anthology of French verse from 1866 to 1888, in which he found much to relish: Rimbaud, Verlaine, and "bawdy" Baudelaire, as well as lesser-known French symbolists like Léon Valode and Catulle Mendès. In early July he read a three-volume anthology of contemporary French verse in the *Librairie*

Delagrave, which altered his appreciation of French culture. Though he was still persuaded that France was "no more intellectual" a nation than America—"The chief thing I can see is that America is the best country in the world. . . . The fabled universal education and culture of France is fabled," he had observed on June 20—Cowley was now deeply impressed by the sheer quantity of good verse written in France between 1866 and 1914, much of it "unsurpassed in English." His discovery was the more significant in that, for the first time, it made him realize that many of the avant-garde tendencies in modern Anglo-American poetry had their aesthetic roots in nineteenth-century French symbolism—a commonplace of literary history today, but a startling discovery to an American apprentice poet on the Western Front in 1917: "As one reads from Baudelaire to Mallarmé," he told Burke, "one gets the origin of all English verse movements, averaging ten to twenty years later. A lecture of Amy Lowell's on Vers Libre and the strophe—I saw where she stole it; from an excuse for his own methods written by Gustave Kahn in 1897." Art movements, he thought, would show "an even more startling sameness in their origins," but he lacked the knowledge to substantiate what was as yet a mere hunch.[33]

Though Cowley remained vaguely ambitious to write a novel, already he envisioned the ideal literary life to be that of a gentleman farmer-poet who would own his hundred acres, write "reams of verse," get drunk on his own hard cider, and live with a congenial woman. Though conceived in irony, the ideal would stick.[34] Meanwhile, he vainly tried to peddle French war stories from *Le Journal* for translation in American magazines and continued to write up the more colorful incidents of his experience. At the end of July he finished an article on the celebration of Independence Day in camp, which he intended for publication in *Outlook.* Piatt Andrew liked it well enough to have it published in the *American Field Service Bulletin.* The article reads almost like propaganda for the Field Service. Though it makes occasional references to the grim reality of the war, it is filled with the proper sentiments of patriotic pride and evokes an atmosphere of jovial solidarity and international camaraderie that made the Field Service seem jolly and ideal. In Cowley's romanticizing imagination the Fourth of July celebration, which included games and sports like fencing, baseball, tilting at a water bucket, egg and spoon races, and Arab music and dancing by Tunisians stationed nearby, took on "a truly medieval tone." Both participant and observer, he was overwhelmed by a double sense of the war as both horrendously real and curiously unreal: "One rather missed the torchlights and smoky rafters. Except for these, it was easy to imagine, looking down the long, littered tables, that one was at a banquet in some Norman castle when Edward III was king. Always, however, when the laughter died down for a moment, the guns that were defending Craonne or Moulin de Laffaux would drown the lesser clatter of the tinware." There were moments when the war seemed exactly such a theatrical "spectacle" as the exotic revelries on Independence Day.[35]

Cowley described another such moment in "The Luck of Green Americans." Toward the end of July the Germans launched a series of attacks aimed at recovering from the French a recently conquered vantage point near Craonne. This action put an end to the volunteers' "unhappy loafing" of the last few weeks. The American camions were summoned to supply a thirty-five-mile stretch of front and the volunteers were kept "on the march" virtually without interruption. On July 28 Cowley's convoy found itself at a munition *parc*, waiting to be unloaded of its cargo of shells by "seedy" territorials wearing gunnysacks over their heads. To relieve the weariness from driving since four in the morning, Cowley and five of his companions—without permission—decided to watch a nearby German bombardment at close range. For a while he relished the picturesque effects of shells bursting six thousand feet in the air, "leaving white puffs of smoke like giant chrysanthemums." As the explosions drew nearer, Cowley and his companions calmly watched, affecting "a boredom they did not feel." Not until the shells began whistling past their ears did they seek refuge in an abandoned trench. After a short silence a new bombardment burst forth close by. Cowley reported on the scene in a passage he later revised for *Exile's Return*:

> Everybody crowded back into the shelter of an overhanging bank on one side of the road. Now shells were falling at regular intervals of time, approximately every two minutes. Each time one exploded, a few red-hot fragments would fall into the road in front of us. Then would ensue a wild scramble after them as souvenirs, and many burnt fingers were the result. A minute later everybody would rush back under the bank to wait for the next shell. The territorials, who had seen too much war to risk their lives for thrills or souvenirs, had, in the meanwhile, disappeared into dugouts.

Later the platoon received official felicitations "for the coolness and courage they displayed during the night of July 28, 1917, while unloading trucks in a *dépôt* subjected to heavy bombardment." When he came to rewrite the passage for *Exile's Return*, Cowley, much in the spirit of Alan Seeger's "Rendezvous with Death," pointed up the spectatorial aspect: "our lives were charmed. Spectators, we were collecting souvenirs of death, like guests bringing back a piece of wedding cake or a crushed flower from the bride's bouquet." [36]

At the time Cowley realized that his reaction to the war might seem disappointing, even callous and insensitive, to his friends back home. In a nearly apologetic tone he wrote to Burke that he had "not yet seen piled corpses. Here behind the lines one gets more the pictorial effects of the war." At the end of July he reported that a nearby hospital seemed to receive "especially favorable notice from our German friends. Three nights ago one of its barracks was reduced to kindling wood and sausage meat— I mean the patients." If such horrifying scenes stirred Cowley's pity and humanitarian concern, he mostly kept such sentiments to himself and refrained from expressing them in his letters. His indignation focused more readily on the stupidity of fellow volunteers from rival colleges, some of whose "innocent pranks" had resulted in the gratuitous deaths of scores of French poilus. [37]

In the first week of August, Cowley went on leave in the expectation that the war would "doubtless last a year or more." This he had deduced from newspaper reports on the situation in Russia, where the revolutionary embers that would flare up in the November uprising were already smoldering. Cowley spent most of his leave enjoying the luxuries absent at the front: food, beer, and featherbeds. With Cunningham he traveled to the coast at Trouville, where the British army was stationed in force, visited Le Havre, and relished Paris. By his own admission Cowley spent "some of the best days of [his] life" in Paris, but he failed to realize his dream of renting a room in Montmartre where he could, uninterrupted by Americans, read French poetry for a week. He did, however, speak French to his heart's content and, much to his delight, could now conduct a conversation with more ease than Burke, who had already devoured French novels when Cowley's command of the language was as yet "non-existent." [38]

Cowley's wartime service in France intensified his awareness of the uniqueness of his literary friendship with Burke. "Our differences, great as they are, are really insignificant compared with our similarities," he reminded Burke in late June. "I think . . . we sometimes came as near to perfect frankness as one can get." But Burke, he now felt, had also "rather spoiled" him for new friendships. Since leaving Peabody and his Pittsburgh comrades, Cunningham was "the nearest to a real friend" he had encountered and Cunningham, he was beginning to realize, was "holding him [back] intellectually." Indeed, despite many shared enjoyments, Cowley continued to feel "intellectually imprisoned" with Cunningham. As a young poet he felt different from the herdlike mass of his military companions yet was uncomfortable with the concomitant feeling of separateness and loneliness. A desire to belong often prevailed over an urge to assert his individuality and independence. Set apart yet drawn toward companionship, he felt uncomfortably pulled between the need for artistic isolation and the desire for social integration. At the end of August, after nearly four months' absence from home, he came to "the sudden acute realization" that he did not have a single friend among the two hundred men in camp. He confessed his ambivalent feelings about himself to Burke in an incisive piece of self-analysis:

I have really decided that I am an out—I mean an intellectual—by nature. All of which makes the last two years a blank in my life. But not an utter blank, for I certainly had need of finding out just what the companionship of his fellows—social, not intellectual—means to the artist. It means a constant struggle with his own nature; a constant repression of his impulses; and an acceptance of standards, which, while true to others, are false to him. The mere discovery of this fact cannot annihilate instantly the desire to stand well with my fellows. It can annihilate, however, the possibility of standing well with my fellows, since it further complicates my actions and makes inconsistency the rule rather than the exception. All this has a retroactive effect on the social desires. . . . Behold in me in a few [years] a hermit like yourself.[39]

His discomfort was aggravated rather than relieved over the next few weeks, as boredom and demoralization took their toll. Throughout September, Cowley was caught up in a dull routine of sleeping, eating, driving, cleaning, and repairing camions. On September 18 he observed: "The wastage of lives in war seems infinitely less important just now than the wastage of time." For weeks on end his letters to Burke were merely perfunctory and were filled with complaints of spending profitless hours lying around the barracks or shooting craps. Camp, he reported, had turned into a "gambling hell." Soon he had run out of money and had to refuse invitations to play. "Christ, I'm demoralized . . . I can't help it—give me time and I always prove myself one of the crowd: average."[40]

To put an end to boredom and "the half-assed discipline," Cowley contemplated several alternatives promising greater danger. One moment he was tempted to enlist in the U.S. Army, the next he inclined toward an adventuresome career in aviation as a "machine-gunner" or "bomb dropper"—"I envy those young devils who are scampering off to this highest of high adventures."[41] When, toward the end of September, the Field Service was about to be taken over by the U.S. Army, Cowley decided not to enlist but to spend some time in Paris after his release at the end of October. Afterward he would try to get into aviation. Five days later his plans changed again. Rumor had it that a new ambulance section was recruiting volunteers for service in Italy, Switzerland, and possibly Russia. The vision of a trip to Russia excited him—"Travel and adventure, but not an adventure in which the chances of death would be above sixty percent, as in aviation." Should the new ambulance service materialize, Cowley would enter it; otherwise, he would in all likelihood come home to be secretary of the *Advocate*, he wrote to Burke on September 23. His morale was at rock bottom. Burke, who besides conducting fierce discussions on the subject with Josephson, had apparently been reading Randolph Bourne's diatribes against the war in the *Seven Arts*, sent him a letter disparaging "the poor war." Cowley was somewhat dismayed—"If even the intellectuals turn against it, and the third convolution men, what friends will it have left?"—but was too "lazy and dispirited" to effectively retaliate.[42]

Despite his inertia Cowley managed to write. Though his experience presumably lacked the color and heroic glamor he craved, his prose sketches and poems for the *American Field Service Bulletin* reveal him as "the most prolific and polished of the truck-driver writers." In September, Cowley reported to Burke that Piatt Andrew had printed some of his "bad poems" in the bulletin; he had also contributed to an American page in *Le Poilu*, a French army publication.[43] One ballade, "We Had Great Argument," was typical in its attempt to romanticize his war experiences; by casting them into the form of a conventional ballad, Cowley managed to surround them with an aura of timeless heroism.

> After a tardy sun had set
> We four untried lieutenants chose
> The back room of the town *buvette*;

And there, until the next sun rose,
We each discussed, in meaty prose
The meaning of the firmament
And all such things that no one knows.
That night we had great argument.

It was no trouble to forget
Dress and society and pose;
The girls we knew; Marthe and Odette;
Marie and Madelon and Rose;
We did not give a thought to those;
Or other things; War, or the Rent;
Our lives; the price of furbelows.
That night we had great argument.

A crimson sun came like a threat;
We drained our glasses and arose;
Roused the good old folk and paid our debt;
And rode off northward toward our foes.
Our feckless youth was at a close
And hell grew nearer as we went;
Yet life seemed good to us—because
That night we had great argument.

A German trench on the Ailette
Next day cost half our regiment,
And all my jolly friends—and yet
That night we had great argument.[44]

Cowley's weeks of "absolute boredom" in camp during September yielded at least one rather successful poem, "To a Dilettante Killed at Vimy." Besides expressing Cowley's self-ironic awareness of the immature idealism with which he had gone off to war, it evinces an incipient sensitivity to what Paul Fussell has called the "potential of ironic meaning" inherent in the war itself.

Years of small sorrows and of small endeavor;
Years of great plans, and mental cowardice;
And we that hoped they would not last forever:—
That's all. To cut the whole thing short, came this.

> And yet the petty muddle you made of it;
> The pose; the brave dreams foundered in a sea
> Of idle talk, now seem to us resolved
> Into clean metal by catastrophe.[45]

As his French venture drew to a close Cowley continued his explorations of French writing. Perhaps under the impact of his weariness with the war he now viewed the "decadent" writers of the 1890s with much more ambivalence than he had shown at Harvard. Joris-Karl Huysmans's A *Rebours* (1884) in particular fostered his skepticism about the whole movement of decadence. Cowley's ambivalence mostly concerned Huysmans's esoteric affectation and, by implication, the trivial escapism at the basis of his art. Typically, his objections were moral as much as aesthetic:

> A Rebours is Wilde exposed. Huysmans is terrible in his hates and his disgusts. Authors he doesn't like, he gives to his servants for toilet paper. He likes childish things, however, the pictures of Gustave Moreau, Poe, Baudelaire, trite English expressions because they are English. He demonstrates the banality of the whole decadent movement. There is some difference between him and the youth who smokes Fatimas instead of Camels because they are 'distinctively individual,' but not much. He is the sort of person who would have one wife in Turkey and eight in Massachusetts; who would read Arsène Lupin in the original French, if he is English, and Victor Hugo, and Dumas; he is, in other words, an ass.[46]

Cowley's objections reflected his own uneasy struggles to dissociate himself from the ideals of the literary life implied in Huysmans's book. Despite such skepticism, however, he continued to cherish many of the symbolists and early moderns. His likes and dislikes laid bare the inconsistent and contradictory premises of his literary taste. In September he sampled several of the writings of Henri de Régnier (1864–1936) and found them models of stylistic elegance, "polished like a gem; as brilliant and as limited." In October he read *Education de Prince* by the French playwright Maurice Donnay (1859–1945), which he thought "excellent" and relished for being "perfect Schnitzler." In early November he discovered Romain Rolland (1866–1944). The recipient of the 1915 Nobel Prize for Literature, Rolland had taken a controversial stand in opposition to the war and in the 1930s became a leading spirit on the international radical scene. In

1917 Cowley considered Rolland's epic cycle of novels, *Jean-Christophe* (1904–1912), "the one book to which I am giving my approbation today."[47]

By early October demoralization among the volunteers was such that recruiting officers of the U.S. Army were not very successful: most men in Cowley's section refused to enlist. "You can't imagine with what a feeling of absolute negation I play cards," Cowley wrote Burke in the depths of his indifference. Earlier, Cowley's nocturnal expeditions had inspired "a great poetic emotion" and evoked associations with the romantic adventure stories about trappers and Indians by the English author G. A. Henty, a boyhood favorite. Now, even the nighttime maneuvers with faulty camions in cold, wind-driven rain seemed "conventional" when set against the "thousands of war diaries" he had read. Once the Field Service had been incorporated into the American army and American authorities were in charge, Cowley expected "real strictness" in the matter of censorship and the maintenance of military discipline. He resented the American "business-like" attitude toward soldiering and denounced the strict enforcement of military rules as "a form of Prussianism." It made enlistment in the American forces seem repulsive.[48]

By the middle of October, Cowley was slowly climbing out of the depths. He expected to be released from service on the twenty-eighth and was already dreaming of an armchair in Cambridge. Anticipating his return Cowley expected to burst in upon his friends "fresh and bustling as a wind from an abattoir." He felt skeptical about how much he had profited from his French trip and thought he had "more of a past than of a future." He expected to resume the old life and talks with Burke and to meet Josephson again. To his discredit the mere thought of returning to Cambridge was sufficient to resuscitate, gratuitously and indefensibly, a dormant anti-Semitism: "I often wonder if a complete elimination of the Hebrew race would not be the best solution of the problem."[49]

Before his release from actual service the Field Service volunteers were engaged in full force to support the big Aisne offensive along the Chemins des Dames. For months Cowley had complained of having so little to report that all his letters had been but "masterpieces of futility"; now there was news to tell. Ever since the German offensive in July, preparations for a French counteroffensive had been in progress. During August and September new gun bases, roads, bridges, and munition depots had been constructed and the camions had transported huge quantities of ammunition to the new depots, leaving the Aisne front "clogged with batteries—all sizes." In early October, Cowley wrote to his mother that work had been "difficult lately, even exciting." Every thought of boredom vanished in the face of strenuous, dangerous work. In addition to the threat of German shelling, ongoing rain and fog made for hazardous driving along slippery, muddy roads in the pitch black of the night. As preparations continued, tension rose and rumors multiplied about the date and aim of the actual attack. The artillery preparations, it turned out, had been "the greatest on record." When the attack—on Malmaison—finally broke, it lasted for more than a fortnight. "Sixteen days and nights we had our ears battered and our sleep disturbed," Cowley reported to Burke. Later, he wrote an account of the "push" in his "Camion Service Notes," parts of which were subsequently published in the *Harvard Advocate*.[50]

By October 29 Cowley had been released and was writing from the University Union in Paris, basking in idleness and luxury. He was aware that now he could no longer procrastinate and must decide whether to return to the United States for good or only for a few weeks' leave. But before going home, Cowley was determined to enjoy Paris while his money lasted. For a start he bought a preventive against venereal disease and took a room at the Royal Palace Hotel, a pension near the Luxembourg Gardens, at a ten-minute walk from the crooked streets and cheap restaurants of the Latin Quarter. In early November, lapsing into his pose of decadent vulgarity, he boasted to Burke of his adventures among the French cocottes at the Café du Dôme and La Rotonde, famous rendezvous for artists and *bohémiens*. Compared to American street women the French cocottes struck Cowley as "a superior type"—one of them had shown an interest in books, recommended a performance of *The Merchant of Venice*, and relished *Jean-Christophe*. Cowley was so impressed by the prostitutes he met that he felt like making "all my correspondence about them." At La Rotonde, where "harlots and greasy Serbian artists passed me laughing," he talked to Russian poet-painters and learned about the prewar fame of the place, when Serbians, Russians, Japanese, and Americans made it a redoubtable meeting place for the international avant-garde; compared with the lively café of earlier days, however, the Rotonde in 1917 seemed relatively "sad." Cowley's first taste of international bohemianism did not immediately fill him with delight. Instead he felt somewhat intimidated and out of place, "awkward and aimless," among the older and experienced inhabitants of bohemia.[51] Despite his ambivalence, Cowley had briefly acted as a true vanguard scout for the hordes of expatriates who were to follow to Paris in the 1920s.

‹ ‹ ‹   In the early 1930s, when he came to write *Exile's Return*, Cowley had reason enough to think back upon his six months of French service as "almost ideal." As a volunteer he had enjoyed privileges and a degree of freedom and prestige unattainable to regular soldiers. Under the relaxed conditions in the French army he had been spared "the severe and stupid forms of discipline" imposed on American soldiers. On noncombatant duty, he had been relatively safe from the dangers of war, yet close enough to be thrilled by them vicariously. Having no real personal stake in the cause of the war, he had yet learned "the virtues of men at war"—courage, extravagance, fatalism. What physical hardships he had suffered had been compensated for by reasonable food, "congenial" work, and furloughs to Paris. He had had his first taste of bohemia at "the capital of world culture," and been introduced to a foreign language and culture that would leave an indelible mark on his literary and cultural thought.[52]

The historical record suggests that in France Cowley was mostly a detached observer, whose understanding of the war was naive and rather superficial, and whose occasional twinges of conscience could not stifle his "monumental indifference" to the cause for which Americans were dying. Even at the time he was aware that he was witness to "mostly the pictorial effects of the war." It was only by hindsight that Cowley could see his French venture as the next step in the process of deracination that had started in high school and continued through college. The war, he then advanced, had "physically uprooted" his age-group, "plucked" it from its native soil, and "scattered [it] among strange people." Behind its "curious attitude of non-participation" in the war had lain its continuous awareness of "another country, . . . the country of their childhood, where they had once been part of the landscape and the life, part of a spectacle at which nobody looked on." Service behind the lines had instilled a fear of boredom and a taste for excitement that would persist into postwar civilian life. The war had acted like a potent drug sharpening the senses: "Danger was a relief from boredom, a stimulus to the emotions, a color mixed with all others to make them brighter." The proximity of death had given "a keen, precarious delight" to their perception of reality. In *Exile's Return* Cowley posited this new sense as one of the important literary consequences of the war: "It revivified the subjects that had seemed forbidden because they were soiled by many hands and robbed of meaning: danger made it possible to write once more about life, adventure, death." [53]

Limited as his own experience of the war had been, it yet enabled Cowley to intuit with remarkable precision what many—volunteers and conscripts, spectators and participants—acknowledged as the essence of their war experience. There is, indeed, ample evidence that Cowley was justified in presenting his personal, "spectatorial" sense of the war as exemplary for the writers of his generation. As Cowley was among the first to note, the writings of Hemingway and Dos Passos, as well as those of Cummings, Faulkner, Fitzgerald, and MacLeish, could be used effectively to support the thesis of *Exile's Return*.[54]

Still, Cowley's account of the war in *Exile's Return* must be seen in the light of his radical sympathies of the early 1930s. His emphasis on the volunteer service as a frivolous and irresponsible flight of adventure, "a goddam crazy Cook's tour of Western Europe," fitted in with the self-critical mood of the times.[55] In September and October 1933, as he was writing the book, Cowley had publicly conducted an acrimonious debate on the war with Archibald MacLeish, in which he had discredited the war in unmistakable terms, and concluded: "It is time for us to admit that you, MacLeish, and I, Cowley, and Hemingway, Wilson, Dos Passos, Ramon Guthrie, our relatives who crashed in airplanes or died by machine-gun fire, our friends who were crippled—that all of us fought in vain." [56] As Charles Fenton has suggested, in such a mood it was not uncommon to mock what seriousness of commitment American volunteers may have felt and to sneer at their service as "a comfortable, rather ridiculous sinecure." On the whole, work in the Field Service was perhaps more arduous and dangerous, commitment stronger, and morale higher, than Cowley's slightly deprecatory account suggests.[57] Such flaws of emphasis, however, cannot impair its general accuracy. Half a century after the American entrance into the war Cowley's interpretation of his and his generation's sense of the war had proved its validity and could be maintained without substantial modification.[58]

By choice of narrative form, tone, and critical intention, however, Cowley's account in *Exile's Return* underplays elements that are crucial for our understanding of his development as a writer. In France he had had his first intimations of the aesthetic origins of modernism in late-nineteenth-century French symbolism. But if he had sampled Baudelaire and Rimbaud, he had also relished a writer of social vision like Romain Rolland. He had made the first tentative steps toward formulating a conception of culture as a living human, social, and historical organism, which became a fundamental assumption of his literary practice. In his awareness of the war as "the great common experience" of his generation, Cowley had evinced a dawning capacity for intuiting the historical importance of the present, which would serve him well as literary chronicler of his times. He had been made aware of the ineluctable alienation inherent in the artistic and intellectual life, as his literary sensibility and individualistic temperament had clashed with the uniforming social pressures of the group. In his war-time writings he had, for the first time, begun to adopt the perspective of spokesman for a generational experience and begun to write on the tangent plane of the idiosyncratic and the representative, of the personal and the communal.

When he returned to America in November 1917, Cowley underestimated the impact the war was to have on his subsequent life and career. Though he vaguely felt he might be "out of place" in a postwar world, he did not consider himself profoundly altered or affected. Yet six months of "organized Byronism" behind the French lines had infected him with the "poison" of irresponsibility, travel, and excitement that would predictably disqualify him from resuming life on its old terms. A spectatorial attitude was carried over into civilian life as Cowley, like many of his coevals, assumed a cynical and disillusioned stance of social disengagement and political noncommitment, a stance for which the absurd spectacle of the peace treaty provided ampler justification.[59] Cowley's commitment would be mostly to the realization of his literary aspirations, his determination to be a practising professional writer in America. Coming home, he launched upon a difficult period of readjustment that ended only temporarily with a renewed acquaintance with his "second country" in the early 1920s.

4

Harvard and New York

1918

In November 1917 Cowley disembarked in New York. He was wearing his "gorgeous" Field Service uniform, carrying a collection of souvenirs from the front, and had fully sixty-five cents in cash. Burke and Josephson met him at the dock and immediately took him to their favorite hangouts in Greenwich Village: the experimental little theater of the Province-town Players and the back room of the Hell Hole, "the grubbiest drinking parlor west of the Bowery." Here Cowley launched into stories of his adventures behind the lines and among the *poules* in Paris. The friends were duly impressed. "Hearing him," Josephson re-called, "we were all the more highly resolved to get to France, war or peace." [1]

Cowley's war stories, however, failed to di-minish Burke's and Josephson's skepticism about the war. Neither did his friends per-suade Cowley to change *his* attitude; in early December, back in Pitts-burgh, he grumbled that the "pages of pacifist literature" they had advised him to read struck him as so many "tergiversations and peripaties." "Again I am one of the lick-the-Germans-first crowd," he told Burke. Nonethe-less, Cowley felt uncomfortable with the atmosphere of patriotic heroism in which he had been welcomed back in Pittsburgh and soon grew dis-gusted with playing the role of "bunk hero." He remained disturbed by the thought of a possible German victory but boggled at enlistment. In-stead, he applied for balloon service with the aviation corps, which would spare him the "enforced companionship of barrack life" and give him the status of an officer, yet relieve him of the necessity of command-ing others. Moreover, the balloon service was "dangerous enough to be honorable, yet hardly suicidal." When he failed his physical examination (because of a weak muscle in his right eye), he felt "much irritated and dispirited." [2]

The war provided Cowley with both a new stimulus for writing and a handy subject. Shortly after his return from France he started a small leather-bound pocket diary in which he recorded memorable "words, phrases" to be used in future poems, army impressions in vers libre, and even the skeletal outline for a semi-autobiographical novel, "A Son at Harvard." The book was to hold the story of Robert Grossman, of Johnstown, Pennsylvania, a self-contented and snobbish Harvard aesthete who, out of dissatisfaction with his life, "goes off with the Ambulance" to France. There he experiences a "sort of religious impulse" which draws him out of his self-disgust and egotism and makes him decide to "get killed and be mingled with the soil of France." Signed up with the Foreign Legion, he suddenly finds himself possessed of the urge to write: "Literature has become the most important thing in the world for him, and he stands ready to sacrifice everything including his dream of French burial." He decides to transfer to artillery school, but is killed just after his application has been accepted. "Whereupon," Cowley concluded his draft, "I have great fun with the way the news of his death is accepted at home."[3] The novel was never written, but the impulse to digest personal experience through semi-autobiographical recreation was typical, while the ironic twists in the projected plot bespoke Cowley's nascent postwar cynicism.

In Pittsburgh, in December, Cowley spent several afternoons in the reference room of the Carnegie Library writing up his war experiences. In January he tried to peddle several of his war stories and managed to place the account of his visit to the abandoned German trenches with a Pittsburgh newspaper. Decked out in his "handsome" camion driver's uniform he carried his manuscript, together with a collection of photographs from the front, to the offices of the Democratic *Post* and the Republican *Gazette Times*. Impressed by the photographs as much as by his writing, the editor of the *Gazette Times* accepted the story. It ran on January 6, 1918, as a full page in the Sunday paper, under the caption: "U. S. Volunteer Tells of French Battle Front Visit—No Union Hours." The article was lavishly illustrated with five pictures, the centerpiece displaying Cowley in his military uniform, a trench coat draped casually over his arm. A patriotic editorial honored him as a Pittsburgh hero. Cowley expected to receive ten dollars for the article; he was paid five, the first money he earned by writing. That same month the *Advocate* printed his report on the October Aisne offensive, "The History of a Push."[4]

The war also inspired new poems. In mid-December Cowley sent Burke "Ostel 1917," a poem subsequently published in the *American Field Service Bulletin* and later republished in *Youth: Poetry of Today*. He had again "turned vers librist just to show that I can write the nasty stuff." An early entry in his pocket diary displayed his eagerness to *épater les bourgeois* in the Midwest: "To shock Chicago let us write a scornful poem on the cornfed Indiana towns, claiming as their only virtue the fact that a good cyclone would obliterate them and leave nothing but the prairie." When he surveyed his total production in verse, however, Cowley was disappointed at the scant number of poems worth keeping. He now saw that even his most individual poems, like "The Oldest Inhabitant," still owed too much to his "various preceptors," in particular, Edgar Lee Masters. A month later, making a critical estimate of his work, he realized that his penchant for the innovative and unorthodox was kept in check by his predilection for formal control: "The whole series [of poems] shows a procession formatically towards and away from the sonnet. I am always form-conscious. Even the last two or three things I have done in vers libre are as organic as a sestina. Yet always I am striving to be unorthodox. I think however that my tendency towards organization and regularity is more fundamental than my heterodoxy. And even this latter is only formatic, and hardly ever extends to the substance of what I write."[5] Typically, Cowley oscillated between experiment and convention, being both attracted to and repelled by the more extreme experiments of modernism.

By the end of December, Cowley had grown "desperately bored" in Pittsburgh and was eager to "escape" to Washington Square before returning to Harvard. In Pittsburgh he had felt "a bit drab and discouraged," and he hoped the Village would prove the tonic he needed, even if money or a job were not forthcoming. One of his "chief ambitions," he ironically observed, had always been "to starve in a garret for my Art." Notwithstanding such bohemian aspirations, Cowley was not prepared to make Burke's radical sacrifices for the life of art: Burke had failed his midyear examinations at Columbia because he had been engrossed in the letters of Gustave Flaubert. Cowley, who thought Burke "quite an ass" for throwing away "the tangible proofs of a semester's hard work," insisted that his friend's propensity was for scholarship as much as artistic creation. Only a doctoral degree, he advanced pragmatically, would yield Burke a guaranteed income. Cowley's objections could not keep Burke from dropping out of college and independently pursuing a career in literature and criticism. He was determined to "work like a sisyphus" in order to be "a genius"—"This is my final showdown," he told Cowley. "I am in it for life and death this time." Borrowing money from his father, he rented a small room in the Village, where, living sparsely on rations of oatmeal and milk, he hoped to begin his "existence as a Flaubert." Burke's drastic steps, Cowley granted, succeeded in "touching the imagination."[6]

Before returning to Harvard, Cowley spent several weeks in New York. Over the next three and a half years he regularly resorted to the Village, alternating his last two semesters at Harvard with forays into New York bohemia. Thus, while he was still a Harvard undergraduate, his literary horizons were already expanding beyond the confines of the *Advocate* and the Poetry Society. In New York he moved in the circle of writers, artists, and actors gathered about the Provincetown Players—George Cram Cook, Susan Glaspell, Eugene O'Neill, Hutchins Hapgood, Edna St. Vincent Millay, and her sisters, Norma and Kathleen. He had been introduced to them by his old Pittsburgh friends James and Susan Jenkins Light, who, after marrying, had moved to New York from Ohio in October and attached themselves to the experimental theater group. James Light, a versatile youth of handsome, intellectual appearance (he was once described as a "sad-eyed, dreamy young man with a faint mustache, heavy eyebrows and a futuristic expression") stayed on with the Provincetown Players, as both actor and director, until the group's dissolution in 1921. Susan Jenkins Light, a "vivacious and comely" woman with bobbed hair, helped out by reading unsolicited plays and assisting at the box office. In New York the Lights lived in a seven-room apartment at 86 Greenwich Avenue. It was nicknamed "Maison Clemenceau" (or "Clemenceau Cottage"), after the French premier who had lived there in exile before the revolution of 1871. Burke had a little cubicle there, which later became Josephson's. Other roomers included the painter Charles Ellis, the writer Djuna Barnes, and the photographer Berenice Abbott. Jim Butler, stepgrandson of the painter Claude Monet, was a regular visitor, as were Eugene O'Neill, Floyd Dell, Dorothy Day, a newspaper reporter and militant suffragist, and her friend Peggy Baird, recently divorced from the poet Orrick Johns. The place, Josephson recalled, was a veritable "Village gristmill."[7] It was to Clemenceau Cottage that Cowley naturally gravitated whenever he came to New York. It was his stepping-stone to bohemia, the place where he could consort with old Pittsburgh friends as well as make new Village acquaintances; it was there also that he met his first wife.

In mid-February Cowley was established in his new Cambridge quarters at 20 Randolph Hall, one of the better private dormitories on the Gold Coast. Afraid of sinking back into a stunting routine of studying much and writing little, he decided to direct his Harvard existence as much as possible toward literature. Though he still toyed with the idea of going to Italy as a volunteer in the Red Cross Ambulance Service, he was more than ever committed to the writing life. As he scrutinized his old Boston environment with a fresh eye for its artistic possibilities, Cowley was less disappointed than he had feared. He discovered a good French bookstore, but the Boston Public Library and Harvard's own Widener he found "criminally" deficient in modern novels. To quench his thirst for bohemia, however, there was the city's Italian quarter, boasting several Village-style restaurants, saloons that served stout on draught for a nickel a glass, and even one "Bolsheviki joint."[8]

To meet his college requirements Cowley took on a load of five courses: a course in Elizabethan drama with George Pierce Baker, a history course on the age of the Tudors and Stuarts with Roger B. Merriman, a course in French with Louis Allard, in ethics with William Ernest Hocking, and Dean Briggs's famous course in poetry. He made A's in all five. A sixth course in German he soon dropped; after the "beautiful clarity" of French, he found it hard to appreciate the "inversions and perversions" of German. Authors like Mann and Schnitzler, whom he admired, existed for him "in spite of the language they write in"; German was "a tongue fit only for Kant and for lyric poetry." Cowley's comments, though emotional and not very sophisticated, nevertheless showed that his aesthetic tastes were developing in the direction of clarity, discipline, and precision. Studying French literature, he told Burke, he had begun to see "what a consciously developed medium is the French language. Germany never had a Rabelais in the XVIe century to introduce all sorts of Latin words, Greek words, technical words, manufactured words; or a preciose school in the XVIIe century to purify it; or an eighteenth-century Voltaire to make clarity a deity. . . . Grillparzer has been compared to Racine. My God, to read the two at once! G[rillparzer] is wildly beautiful at times, it is true, but his diction sprawls all over itself like an adolescent elephant."[9]

As a first step toward the literary life, Cowley set out to meet the poet Conrad Aiken. He had just read *The Jig of Forslin* (1916) and was deeply impressed. He recommended the volume to Burke as "a study in form" and praised Aiken's ability to "infinitely" modify his polyphonic verse with the demands of each new mood. Aiken's poems, he observed in an unpublished review a year later, were "symphonies, divided into movements, connected by recurring themes, diversified by a complicated counterpoint." Cowley saw this search for a poetical analogy to musical form as "one of the great modern tendencies in the arts. Form has been recognized as the common language of the artistic world; music comes nearest to being pure form."[10] There were other than formalist reasons for Cowley's enthusiasm for *The Jig of Forslin*. He was aware that Aiken was one of the first to use Freudian psychology as a poetic framework and was thus able to deal with subjects not commonly considered suitable for poetic treatment: hence, Cowley noted with ironic approval, the profusion of rapes, suicides, vampires, and prostitutes in Aiken's verse. Nine years later he understood that such elements were part of Aiken's exploration of the subconscious, his "search for the dark countries that lie inside of Man." Here lay a source of distrust, however, for despite his admiration, Cowley disliked what in 1927 he called the "hot-house atmosphere" of Aiken's verse: only by viewing "any one man as representative of his race" and "our smallest acts under the species of eternity" had the poet been able to avoid a hermetic egocentrism. Cowley's appreciation of Aiken's verse is important as one of his earliest explorations of the aesthetics of modernist poetry. Predictably, his attitude was ambiguous: he admired its formal innovations and technical accomplishment, but distrusted its self-enclosed subjectivism. The latter was a basic element of the modernist creed, with which he never was entirely comfortable. Cowley did not fully grasp the theoretical implications of Aiken's poetics until much later, but his early understanding carries the seeds of what, from a perspective of sixty years, he termed Aiken's "religion of consciousness." [11]

In 1918 Cowley's enthusiasm for *The Jig of Forslin* sent him to Aiken's Boston publisher, Edmund Brown, to request the poet's address. In response to a letter from Cowley, Aiken proposed they meet for dinner in the lobby of the Hotel Touraine; the young apprentice was to look for "a man in an orange necktie who wasn't a fairy." Years later, Cowley recalled their first meeting: "On that unseasonably warm evening in February 1918 I saw the necktie as he came in the door; it was brighter than his Valencia-orange hair. For the rest he wore the Harvard uniform of the period: white button-down oxford shirt and brown suit. His forehead was high . . . his jaws square and his eyes were set wide apart. The impression he gave me was a mixture of shyness and pugnacity." Cowley was fascinated. Aiken was nine years older, he had resigned from Harvard in 1911, shunning a public performance as class poet, and fled to Europe. He was a good friend and admirer of T. S. Eliot and a poetic rival as well as champion of his verse; in 1914 he had carried a typescript of "The Love Song of J. Alfred Prufrock" to London and had been instrumental in launching Eliot by introducing him to Pound. In 1918 Aiken was married, had two children, and had already published four volumes of verse. He was then living on "the unfashionable side of Beacon Hill," but moved to South Yarmouth on Cape Cod the year after, choosing to put a "skeptical distance" between himself and the literary coteries of imagists and vorticists he had found in Boston and London.[12]

At their first meeting Aiken struck Cowley as "a development, a successful development, of most of my present tendencies." He was the author of "remarkable poetry that doesn't sell," and like himself, an "enthusiastic admirer" of Louis Wilkinson's novels. Years later Cowley recalled that Aiken and he "both liked Boston in decay, we admired the French symbolist poets, we wanted to achieve architectural and musical effects in our poems (I in theory, Conrad in practice), and we were fascinated by the political maneuvers of the poetry world without wishing to take part in them." A second meeting was "all about How to Sell Poetry." Aiken provided Cowley with inside information on a number of Boston publishers, but it was reading Aiken's poetry criticism for the fortnightly *Dial* that made Cowley truly exultant: "He rips everybody to pieces; you must read him. He is getting so unpopular that he can't get anything published in a magazine."[13]

In Conrad Aiken, Cowley found his first ideal of the literary vocation. He admired the older poet's independence of mind, his disdain for literary commerce, and his refusal to compromise his standards. Above all he admired Aiken's wholehearted dedication to the life of letters. In retrospect Cowley realized how lucky he had been to have gained admittance to a poet who "seldom opened himself to literary strangers," shunned writers and editors on principle, refused to partake in literary politics, and lived his artistic life, as he said in *Ushant*, his autobiography, "*off-stage*, behind the scenes, out of view."[14] Cowley's 1918 meetings with Aiken were the beginning of a lifelong literary friendship. Over the years Cowley was a consistent champion of Aiken's verse and regularly engaged in efforts to remedy the neglect of his work by the larger public.

After Conrad Aiken, perhaps the most influential literary mentor of Cowley's early years was S. Foster Damon, a regular literary companion at Harvard. Damon was Cowley's senior by five years; he had graduated in 1914 and was still in Cambridge doing graduate work. Damon served as an important catalyst in awakening the relatively staid literary milieu of Harvard to modern art and letters. A poet and musician, he was an editor of the *Harvard Monthly* and the *Music Review*, and a founding father of the Harvard Music Society. He had helped organize the Harvard Poetry Society, and in 1917 had appeared in *Eight Harvard Poets*. Cowley had seen and met Damon at meetings of the Poetry Society in his sophomore year and had joined him on excursions to Boston for sessions at Jake Wirth's German saloon on Stuart Street. In the late 1960s Cowley recalled Damon at Harvard as a most "adventurous reader" who, like a knight errant of modernism, liked to guide his coevals to new discoveries. It was through Damon that Cowley first came to read Ezra Pound's *Ripostes*, the poetry of Stephen Crane, Melville's *Moby-Dick*, the less familiar poems of William Blake, the poems of the obscure Thomas Holley Chivers, the work of Gertrude Stein, and, perhaps Damon's outstanding gift, the poems of Jules Laforgue. Though Cowley could not share Damon's enthusiasm for either Stein, Blake, or Chivers, like many others he was indebted to Damon for exposing him to numerous modern authors still outside his youthful ken.[15]

In 1918 Cowley associated with Damon most frequently. More than once he visited Damon's room above the Western Club, where he lived with Philip Hillyer Smith, later Cowley's neighbor in Sherman. In early March he attended a session of the New England Poetry Society with Damon and Royall Snow. With Amy Lowell's departure, however, the society could no longer muster Cowley's enthusiasm; its new president, Josephine Preston Peabody, was hostile to the New Poetry and represented everything he opposed: "her pet aversion is Aiken; my pet aversion is her." Instead, he personally paid his respects to Lowell, to whose house he gained admittance through Damon, who in turn had been introduced to Lowell by John Brooks Wheelwright. Regularly, Amy Lowell invited Damon, Cowley, and sometimes Royall Snow to Sevenels, her big house in Brookline, for dinner. There the youthful poets read aloud their manuscripts and were "praised and scolded" by their patroness or, puffing away at her Manilla cigars, sat listening to Lowell demolish her literary enemies. Damon also led Cowley into Boston society circles and gave him glimpses of the fashionable and dilettantish world of the Cambridge debutantes. Cowley's feelings for Damon approached adulation. Though upon occasion he found him "irritatingly aesthetic and disgustingly supercilious," he was impressed by Damon's esoteric knowledge and thought him "a very sound poetic workman."[16]

After Foster Damon, Cowley's closest friend at Harvard was John Brooks Wheelwright. Wheelwright was a highly unconventional Boston Brahmin, an Anglican High Churchman who became a modernist poet, an architectural historian and, during the last years of his life, a fierce devotee of revolutionary socialism. An eccentric dandy and a convivial bachelor, Wheelwright was an obstreperous nonconformist with a quirky sense of humor, and the composer of "elliptical and often wilfully unmelodic verse." Wheelwright's contentiousness led to his expulsion from Harvard in his senior year, reputedly for misspelling a word. His poetry was long unappreciated. Upon his premature death—in 1940 he was run down by a drunken driver on Massachusetts Avenue in Boston—he was commemorated in one of the media as "the most famous unheard-of poet of his time."[17]

For Cowley, it was the exhilarating company of "moderns" like Aiken, Lowell, Damon, and Wheelwright that made life in Boston intellectually exciting. For the rest, he was appalled by its literary and political conservatism. The city was a "hotbed of Toryism," he told Burke. "Can you imagine a place where people wax violent still over vers libre? Or a place where the mere mention of the words Socialist or Bolsheviki or Radical must be in a whisper?" But if he was skeptical of Boston's tories, Cowley also looked down upon the high esteem accorded Village bohemianism: he was irked to find that in certain circles "anyone who has lived in Greenwich Village . . . is a little of the hero." Already, he took but a dim view of the countless "miniature Greenwich Villages" that were mushrooming all over the nation and drawing into their orbit countless artists, socialists, anarchists and syndicalists, besides "students from the nearest university come to see Life."[18]

Between tory conservatism and the various manifestations of would-be bohemianism, Cowley sensed, truly "modern" writing was left in a vacuum. He now regretted the demise of James Light's venturesome if immature *Sansculotte*. "There is a tremendous need for a magazine, not merely wild and Hebraic like the *Pagan*; not run by a temperamental woman, like the *Little Review*, and not inspired with nothing but love of the masses and other dirt, like the *Liberator*, but which would print decent stuff by (us) new men." Aiken had persuaded him that Harriet Monroe, editor of *Poetry*, and William Stanley Braithwaite, the popular anthologist of contemporary poetry, were quietly conspiring "to stifle the new poetry at birth" by silently passing over poets like Aiken, John Gould Fletcher, and William Carlos Williams. The latter's *Al Que Quiere!* (1917) Cowley had found promising as "the framework and the suggestion of much good poetry, much excellent, superexcellent poetry." Ultimately, he was persuaded, only a magazine that published new creative work yielded "the best sort of critical encouragement."[19]

Dovetailing with his critique, Cowley sent Burke a blueprint of a new literary magazine, "a post-bellum Sansculotte." The new periodical was to serve as a forum for "our circle," and thus advance the general cause of avant-garde writing; but Cowley was also personally ambitious to get published. The magazine was to be run by some ten editors, each of them a shareholder. In return for their financial support they could use the paper as an outlet for their personal work. As potential editors Cowley suggested acquaintances whose taste and judgment he respected or whom he expected to be sympathetic to the project: Damon, Aiken, Snow, Wilkinson, Lowell, Edna Millay, Floyd Dell, Charles Ellis, Jim Butler, the artist Stuart Davis, Burke, Light, and himself. In matters of editorial policy, the magazine was to have "no political creeds, and damned few artistic." Cowley expected to find a willing publisher in Edmund Brown of the Four Seas Company, who had already demonstrated his sympathy for modern writing by bringing out books by Aiken and Williams. A low subscription price was to guarantee a large circulation. Publishers' advertisements, to be encouraged by "a corking good set of book reviews," were to keep the magazine afloat financially. Even numbers could be made up of "the best contributions we can find"; the odd numbers could serve to introduce a new young writer (like Damon, Cowley, or Burke). Such an issue, Cowley dreamed, was "practically equivalent to publishing a book." He had already solicited the support of several people in Boston (including Aiken and Snow) and was convinced the venture was "both serious and feasible."[20] In the end, however, as Cowley's energies were channeled into more profitable directions, his interest in the project waned and nothing came of it.

In line with his earlier observations on the French language, Cowley was now discovering a congenial aesthetics in the verse of Alexander Pope, with whose satirical wit and strict yet elegant diction he felt affinity. On March 25 he announced that he was "meditating the establishment of a new classicism" consisting of a set of maxims inversely related to Pope's. As yet Cowley's conception of a new classicism remained imprecisely defined: it chiefly involved "a certain attendance to form," in particular a "perfect abandonment" of conventional poetic diction and rhetorical devices. For the moment classicism to Cowley was not "a matter of any particular rules, but just of Rules": "No more wild flights of fancy, no more exaggerated ego."[21]

To exemplify his "theories" Cowley set to work on a unified sequence of poems that, in ironic tribute to Edgar Lee Masters, he conceived of as "a Cambridge Spoon River." The series was to be opened by a sonnet winking at Dryden and Pope, "From the Diary of a Restoration Gentle-man," and to include a poem on the Common Cupboard, a restaurant Cowley frequented, one on student life in Randolph Hall, and another en-titled "C_2H_5OH," the chemical formula for ethyl alcohol. In March 1918 the *Advocate* published two poems from Cowley's "Boston Anthology," the first an ironic dramatic monologue on Louisburg Square, the second nostalgically contrasting the carefree irresponsibility of Cambridge student life with the reality of the war in France. The latter, "Sentimental," was planned as the concluding poem in the series: "Outside my dugout, star-shells flame and sizzle, / And near the lines a few stray shells are falling; / I try to sleep, and slumber off recalling / The elms of Cambridge in a summer drizzle." [22]

While Cowley was struggling to rekindle a new classicism, his en-thusiasm for French poetry was fanned by Ezra Pound, who, in the *Little Review* of February 1918, introduced fourteen French poets to an American public, mostly by copious presentations of their work—Jules Laforgue, Tristan Corbière, Arthur Rimbaud, Remy de Gourmont, Henri de Régnier, Emile Verhaeren, Francis Vielé-Griffin, Stuart Merrill, Lau-rent Tailhade, Francis Jammes, Jean Moréas, André Spiré, Charles Vil-drac, and Jules Romains. Cowley had already made the acquaintance of most of these poets in France or through Damon and owned *Poètes d'Aujourd'hui*, a two-volume collection of contemporary French verse compiled by Adolphe Van Bever and Paul Léautaud. But Pound, Cowley recalled, was "a marvelous impressario" with "an assured manner that overwhelmed his readers," and his 1918 article for the *Little Review* had "a lasting influence on younger American poets." Spurred on by Pound, Cowley vainly tried to obtain the works of several of these French poets in Boston. He next appealed to Burke to make a "pilgrimage of New York" for him and, "at any price," buy copies of Tailhade's *Poèmes Aristophaniques*, Jammes's *Le Triomphe de la Vie*, and the complete works of Rimbaud. Rimbaud and Tailhade, he eulogized, had "a tremendously dirty view of life" and delighted in the sacrilegious, the perverse, and the obscene. He described Tailhade as "a poet of barrooms, old women with ulcers on their anuses . . . old men whom the exhilaration of a shower bath sets running after little girls, the third sex, and other matters of the sort." Such, Cowley felt, were "quite legitimate poetic subjects," not at all irreconcilable with his demand for a classical control of form. [23]

In April 1918 the *Harvard Advocate* published a long poem by Cowley that suggests that his criticism of modernity in American writing easily took the form of parody. In "A Theme with Variations"—its very title implied an Aiken-like effort at musical analogy—Cowley treated the same poetic theme in four different ways, each of them parodying a specific "modern" mode. One section ridiculed the rank and luxuriant Oriental mysticism of "the Spectric School," another recast the poem in a mode of free verse favored by Joseph Kling's Greenwich Village magazine the *Pagan*. A third section parodied the treatment the theme would have received at the hands of William Carlos Williams, though it did so "with apologies":

> I wish I could pass out
> lie with my toes towards the daisies
> it must be cool even now
> down there.
>   Next autumn
> there'll be wind, frost,
> biting rain.
>   I'll be peppy.
> August is like last night's
> Stale Pilsener.

The parodic sting of the opening section ("As Written by Miss Edna St. Vincent Millay on Her Typewriter") was not assuaged by any such apology:

> My thoughts had festered in the heat
> Three months; I could not do a thing.
> The pavement boiled beneath my feet
> Three months; I could not even sing
> And wondered what the fall would bring.
>
> But yesterday at dusk, the lost
> North wind sprang up after a rain,
> And when I woke, I saw the frost
> Had patterned lacework on the pane,
> And on my lips were songs again.[24]

Millay's poetry, Cowley wrote to Burke at the end of April, was "tremendously overrated, . . . she borrows her freshness from the modern Celts and her charm from Sara Teasdale." Lacking intellectual substance, her verse seemed an effusion of "baby talk." Millay's "Renascence," which in 1912 had just missed winning the five-hundred-dollar *Lyric Year* poetry prize, he sneered at as "pantheism grown senile." Cowley saw a good deal of Millay and her younger sisters, Kathleen and Norma, when he moved in the circles of the Provincetown Players, but he had little or no "intellectual contact" with her. "Her great admirers were somewhat older or younger," he recalled. " 'We' regarded her as a conservative in poetry, and ourselves as radicals." For all his intellectual and poetic strictures, Cowley was no more able than many in the Village to resist the sexual charms of the Millay sisters and, for a while, was half in love with Norma Millay, a serious actress who played major parts for the Provincetown Players.[25]

In the end Cowley's junior year at Harvard boiled down to "a very happy semester." In Randolph Hall he lived *"en gentilhomme"* and among the Harvard litterateurs he was attaining a position of near-prominence. One of his professors, Roger B. Merriman, was impressed by Cowley's gift of gab displayed during an evening of discussion at his home, while Merriman's assistant, Frederic Schenck, who had earlier been instrumental in arranging Cowley's commission to write war reportages, continued to feel "a great enthusiasm" for his work. An advisor to the Signet Society, a prestigious literary club, Schenck now passed down word that Cowley was to be cultivated. In late February, Cowley was taken to lunch at the Signet by Tim Whittlesey, a young Harvard poet who had been with him at Jouaignes, and introduced to "the sons of various millionaires, who talked of going horseback riding just before tea." Though he did not expect to be nominated for membership, the event brought home to him that the snobbery he hoped to have "conquered" was still "powerful." During the semester he attended various social affairs, including two punches given by the *Lampoon* and the *Crimson*. The private plays performed by the new candidates for membership catered to Cowley's taste for vulgarity; they contained "some of the wittiest smut."[26]

Moving in Harvard's social and literary limelight, Cowley eventually "passed muster": in April he was elected president of the *Harvard Advocate*. During his absence in France the *Advocate* had suffered a crisis that led to the resignation of four of the editors: upon his return to Harvard, Cowley found the magazine "in a bad way" and hardly up to the level of the *Peabody*. With most of his former editorial colleagues serving in the army Cowley was one of the few writers left who possessed "somewhat of an established reputation," and the remainder of the *Advocate* board, in-cluding its secretary, Jake Davis, now looked to him as its potential savior. At a meeting of the *Advocate* board on April 26 Cowley was deputized to run the paper and offered the presidency. "I always wanted to run a paper," he cheerfully reported to Burke. "No doubt it will be just as rotten as ever, but inevitably my opinion of it will go up." [27]

By early May he was firmly in the presidential seat. To breathe new life into the magazine Cowley enlisted the help of Foster Damon and John Brooks Wheelwright. With their assistance he "struck a blow for the Mod-erns" by inviting Amy Lowell to read her latest poems at a smoker given by the *Advocate* on May 2, 1918. Some weeks later Lowell recalled the meet-ing in a letter to a friend: "I was, as usual, smuggled into an upper chamber, and kept quiet with cigars while they heckled me in true undergraduate fashion. I think I held my own; I tried to." Lowell, Cowley recalled, was undaunted by any of the attacks: "wreathed in smoke, [she] crushed the hecklers as if with bolts from a fat thundercloud." [28]

Editing the *Harvard Advocate* suited Cowley perfectly. It fitted his prag-matic bent and gave him an opportunity to develop his talents for organiza-tion and critical selectiveness. Moreover, it early taught him to watch out for new poetic talent. In 1957 he recalled how, as editor of the *Advocate*, he kept "one eye cocked" for Stephen Vincent Benét, then "the bright star not only of Yale but of all the Eastern colleges." Though he continued to correspond about a postwar *Sansculotte* with James Light and Royall Snow, his enthusiasm for the venture was mostly transferred to the concrete prob-lems of running a Harvard paper. By May 25 the earlier project seemed to have lost his interest: "I think the Advocate promises more fun, even if it is a priori condemned to be no Seven Arts." Still, he was determined to make the *Advocate* into "a whooping good paper." [29]

‹ ‹ ‹   Cowley's plans for the summer included a rural walking trip and a few weeks of fishing and canoeing in June with Kenneth Burke before going off to six weeks of military camp on July 1. In the early half of June Cowley hiked with Foster Damon to a small hilltop cabin near Can-dor, New York, where Burke was to join them later. There, ostensibly because he found himself "ennuied to distraction," Cowley composed a half-satirical poem for Norma Millay, on whom he had had a secret crush since he had met her in the Village during the winter: "One complains /

About the middle of vacation / Because one misses osculation." Cast in the form of a letter, the poem was never sent, one suspects for artistic as much as amatory reasons. Unexpectedly, the cabin at Candor, owned by Jim Butler, became the location of an amusing literary hoax. It originated as a countermove to the Spectra hoax, a literary sensation of 1916 that had reached the front page of several newspapers. A book called *Spectra* had purported to present the work of a new literary school founded by two Pittsburgh poets, Emanuel Morgan and Anne Knish. The book was solemnly reviewed in the *New Republic* by Witter Bynner and some of Morgan's and Knish's verse appeared in *Others* and the *Little Review*. The secret was let out by Martyn Johnson in the *Dial* for April 25, 1918, and the names of the poets were disclosed as the pseudonyms of Witter Bynner and Arthur Davison Ficke; their objections against modernism (in particular the Imagism of Amy Lowell) had taken the form of parody. An interview with Bynner in the *New York Sunday Times* for June 2 had proclaimed the complete success of the hoax. Judging the joke to be "a victory for the Ancients," Cowley and Damon plotted a Modern counterattack, "to see if the hoaxer couldn't be hoaxed." [30]

In a single day, June 15, 1918, they ground out the complete works of an imaginary poet, variously dubbed "the plowboy poet of Tioga County" and "the bard of the rushing Catatonk." Cowley invented an appropriate name, Earl Roppel, and provided the country background of what approximated a poetic alter ego. Adopting colloquial rhythms and clumsy syntax for Roppel's country speech, they composed a letter to Witter Bynner, then a member of the English department at the University of California at Berkeley:

> My dear Mr. Bynner: I venture to write you to express my profound admiration of your book *Grenstone Poems* [1917]. . . . I got your book out of the free library at Owego and read it all through that night and I like it very much though I do not understand it all. It gives you such a picture of life. Now, Mr. Bynner, what I want to say is this: I write some and I feel I write different from most. . . . There is no one here who I can show my poems to. All my friends would laugh and their not the kind of poems to show the preacher because sometimes I fear I am not as strong in my faith as I should. . . . And now I am drafted and have to leave next week. This seems to cut off all that my life has

been. Before I go I would like to have the opinion of someone I feel knows what poetry is on my poems. . . . Please say what you think because I know they are not as elegant as they would be if I put more time on them but I feel I should write about what I know.

With the letter came a sheaf of Roppel's poems. His ghostwriters, Cowley later recalled, had tried to "adumbrate the utterly inane" and to burlesque the "false innocence" of Bynner's lyric poetry. Each wrote about half of the poems, Damon's "gift for mischievous parody" appearing to advantage in "Moonlight," a poem supposedly much indebted to Bynner:

> Last night when I was in our surrey,
>   Driving home with my best girl,
> I saw the moon run down the fence-row,
>   Like a fat squirrel.
>
> The horse stopped at the darkest turning
>   When no one that passed by could see
> Although the moon hung like a lantern
>   From a long branch in the tree.
>
> And when the cold snowflakes are falling
>   I'll think of that fair eve in June,
> When we three were alone together,
>   I and Lucy and the moon.

Another poem, "Memories," comprised a quasi-imagistic vignette of the rural poet's mother: "I think of my mother / As moving toward the kitchen door, / The dirty water circling in her dishpan / Yet I find she possessed / A book with flower-stained leaves." Still another poem showed the poet philosophically musing after a long, toilsome day on the farm:

> At night I sit beside the stove,
>   So tired I cannot see.
> But at my plowing all the day
>   The great thoughts come to me.
>
> They say that men have dreampt strange dreams
>   In mansions in the city,

And I am not as rich as they,
    Nor am I half as witty.

Yet all the day in the hot sun
    Visions come crowding strong as death,
As sweet as those that Jezus had
    When he was young at Nazareth.

Shortly after the rural bard had been conceived, his begetters were joined by Burke and Berenice Abbott. The latter was promptly enlisted in the poetic plot and persuaded to copy out the plowboy poet's verse and letter in appropriately "unformed, ingenuous" handwriting. On June 28 a slightly revised letter was sent to Amy Lowell, including "Venice," written by Damon as a pastiche of her free verse poem "The City of Falling Leaves."

O Venice!
Venice of the seventeen hundreds!
Cocked hats and carnivals and sonnets in strange pattern.

.   .   .   .

I wish for the city of waters
All day at work in the
    parched cornfield
And for the freedom of the carnival,
At night in the shifty kitchen
Venice! Masks! Stilettoes!

A similar letter was sent to Conrad Aiken. There the jokers left off. Soon after the company scattered, Cowley to enter military camp, Damon to carry out an assignment with the Red Cross, Burke to work in a shipyard. Any letters for Earl Roppel, they instructed the postmaster at Candor, were to be forwarded to 86 Greenwich Avenue in New York, Burke's address in the Village.[31]

All three recipients of Earl Roppel's verse were wholly taken in. Aiken expressed "a measured critical appreciation" of Roppel's talents, recommended Keats and Tennyson, and presented him with an inscribed copy of Palgrave's *Golden Treasury*. Amy Lowell offered detailed criticism of the poems, which she found "distinctly of the modern type." She seriously separated out the original from the weak and commonplace elements and urged Roppel to study the principles of versification and "modern" poetry criticism in her own *Six French Poets* and *Tendencies in Modern American Poetry*. She asked Roppel's permission to submit the poems to *Poetry* and felt confident that Harriet Monroe would accept them.[32]

Witter Bynner's response exceeded all expectations, though at first, with no letter forthcoming, the hoax seemed to have miscarried. Finally, in July 1920, Cowley explained the joke in an article for the *Literary Review of the New York Evening Post*, entitled "The Real Earl Roppel—The Brief and Meteoric Career of the Genius of the Catatonk." The hoax, he wrote, had been born of the "happy boredom" of a rural summer, its parents two young poets wishing to "bamboozle" the authors of the Spectrist school.[33] Upon reading Cowley's revelation Bynner wrote him a letter, returning Roppel's poems and disclosing the full extent of his efforts to locate Earl Roppel.

Upon receiving the poet's oeuvre, Bynner had written several letters of criticism and advice to Roppel in Candor, New York, but his letters were returned from the Greenwich Village address to which they had been forwarded, marked "No such person." Bynner persevered and wrote for information about the poet to the postmaster at Candor, the Authors' League of America, and the librarian of the Free Library at Owego, ten miles from Candor. At the end of November the librarian informed Bynner that no Earl Roppel had ever borrowed books from her library and that her enquiries with the superintendent of schools at Candor and several local residents had yielded no result.[34] Bynner proceeded undaunted and advertised Roppel's poems among his colleagues at Berkeley. Arthur Farwell of the music department was so charmed by one of them, "Sunset," that he was eager to secure Roppel's permission to set it to music. Bynner again wrote to Roppel, asking permission on Farwell's behalf and suggesting that the poet stipulate his share of the monetary returns. In April 1919, with as yet no sign of Roppel's existence, Bynner solicited the help of Louis J. Stellman of the *San Francisco Bulletin*, which soon featured a story about the case: "Bynner Seeks Lost Mystery Poet in N.Y." Farwell was quoted characterizing "Sunset" as "the best patriotic song-poem in America" and Bynner came out with the verdict that "Earl Roppel's letter and verses have a freshness and sincerity which make it impossible for me to believe someone is trying to play a joke on me." The writer of the article agreed that "a marvelously clever man alone could counterfeit them." Though a closer look at the New York address led Bynner to suspect that one of the Washington Square bohemians was trying to get even with the originator of the

"Spectrist" school—for a while he suspected Edna St. Vincent Millay—
he continued to believe that the poems were "the genuine products of unspoiled bucolic genius." The poem (retitled "The Flag") was finally set to
music and sung by a chorus of three thousand trained voices to a huge
San Francisco audience: "Flag of our country, strong and true, / The sky
is rosy with your bars; / But as they fade it turns to blue / and radiant with
your stars."[35]

Through 1920 Bynner pursued the plowboy poet. In January he wrote
to the War Department in Washington, D.C., explaining that Roppel's
verse was "of such remarkable beauty that I could not believe it the work
of the country boy he purported to be"; however, no record of Roppel's enlistment in the army within the last six years could be found. Undaunted,
Bynner wrote further letters of inquiry to the commanding general of the
U.S. Marine Corps, the chief of the Bureau of Navigation at the Navy
Department, and finally to the landlord of 186 Greenwich Avenue—all
to no avail.[36] When, soon after, Bynner read Cowley's disclosure in the
New York Evening Post, he communicated with Cowley in a spirit of good
sportsmanship and confessed to having found the entire affair "extraordinarily amusing." Bynner expressed his appreciation of Cowley's own verse
and formally invited him to join the Poetry Society in New York, which,
as its president, he was trying to revitalize. Cowley was tickled with the
belated success of his hoax. Bynner, he told Amy Lowell, had "fallen" for
Roppel's verse "like ten tons of lead off the top of the Woolworth Building."
Some years later Bynner confessed that he had "never ceased regretting"
the plowboy poet's death; he felt that Cowley, in spite of his satirical intentions, had produced "some damn fine poetry." Roppel, Cowley agreed in
1923, was "a nice experiment and he deserves to be resurrected."[37]

‹ ‹ ‹   In July and August 1918[38] Cowley spent six weeks in the barracks
of the Harvard R.O.T.C., taking a summer course in military science that
consisted of "mostly sham battles and bayonet drill." In the fall he returned
to Cambridge, but was prevented from taking up his regular studies when
the increasing demands of the war persuaded the U.S. government to put
all college students in uniform. As a result Harvard opened in the fall
with "everyone but the near-sighted, the flat-footed and the very young"
in the Students' Army Training Corps (S.A.T.C.).[39] Released from serious
study Cowley spent the last two months of the war in a frolicsome mood
of carousal with Damon and Wheelwright. One evening in September,

Wheelwright was arrested for driving his Model-T Ford in the streetcar reservation on Commonwealth Avenue and Cowley spent a night with him in Brighton Jail. For a week he stayed with Damon and laid plans for the *Advocate*. On September 23 the S.A.T.C. demanded his presence, "shutting off all joy and leaving lamentation in its stead." Two days later Cowley was a corporal and shortly after handed in his application for the Field Artillery Officers' Training School at Camp Taylor, near Louisville, Kentucky. On October 19 he learned he had been accepted. That afternoon he wandered about Boston with Wheelwright and Damon, drunk. They fell asleep in the upstairs lounge of the Harvard Club and, the next morning, had breakfast at the Copley. In late October, before entering military camp, Cowley spent an "ecstatic" week with Damon, Wheelwright, and Susan Jenkins Light in New York, sleeping little, dancing, and drinking so much that his nerves were "positively susceptible to the slightest sensation." He courted Norma Millay, attended a performance of Tolstoy's *Redemption*, frequented Luke O'Connor's saloon in the Village, and for most of the week felt "very much the genius and the mystic." On October 31 Cowley was back in Pittsburgh, which he found "very dull and cheerless." Revved up by his New York visit, he was eager to shock and during dinner with his parents "explained the newest poetry and the inevitable revolution." Shortly thereafter he left for Camp Taylor where, between exercises, he worked on drafts of "Château de Soupir," "O'Connor's at One O'Clock," and a never finished "Song for the Birthday of a Revolutionist."[40]

The elation Cowley had felt in New York was intensified by news from Amy Lowell. Since the summer she had endeavored to place some of Cowley's poems with literary magazines, a service she performed for several of her youthful satellites. At the end of July she reported her failure to sell Cowley's poems to the *North American Review* and announced she would try to place them with *Poetry* or the *New Republic*. Should she fail, she promised to go to New York in person and read Cowley's verse aloud to the editors, a practice she had found "an efficacious way of placing things" ("Amy could read pretty good poems as if they were masterworks," Cowley observed in 1936). On October 24 she informed Cowley that Harriet Monroe had accepted three of his poems and advised him to accept Monroe's suggestions for changes as the most expedient way of getting into *Poetry*. Cowley promptly wrote to Monroe, expressing his pleasure at her acceptance of his poems and giving her "carte blanche" for any changes. That same day, on November 1, he dashed off a note to

Lowell from the Wallace Building in Pittsburgh, congratulating her on her "ability as a salesman. You have sold the impossible—namely three of my poems to Harriet Monroe. She offered only twenty dollars, which seems niggardly, but no poet seems able to make his own terms—with one conspicuous exception."[41] On his own strength Cowley managed to get two of his war poems published in *Youth: Poetry of Today*, a magazine started in October 1918 by Royall Snow, Jack Merten, and Donald B. Clarke. All three were Harvard undergraduates, but *Youth* was not otherwise associated with the university. Besides Cowley's verse it published contributions by Aiken, Fletcher, Lowell, and E. A. Robinson. In November the *Harvard Advocate* published "Bayonet Drill," a page of verse consisting of a sonnet each by Cowley and Damon, a former bayonet instructor. Cowley's sonnet, marked by occasional crudities of form and a supercilious touch of anti-Semitic sentiment, satirized the fake battles fought in the S.A.T.C.[42]

Armistice Day, November 11, 1918, found Cowley at Camp Taylor. At first he was caught up in the exhilarating sense of relief that came with the end of the war. For a while it actually seemed possible that democracy had really triumphed and Wilsonian ideals realized. Soon, however, as the mood of joyful intoxication passed, the debacle of Versailles and Wilson's Fourteen Points would bring home to Cowley and his literary friends that the "composite fatherland" of international democracy was rapidly "dissolving into quarreling statesmen and oil and steel magnates." Awaiting formal demobilization, Cowley was prevented from resuming his Harvard studies. Instead he drifted to New York, "the homeland of the uprooted."[43] For the next ten months he resided in Greenwich Village; then he returned to Cambridge to complete his university education in the fall of 1919. The time he spent in the Village—"The Long Furlough" as he dubbed it in *Exile's Return*—was anything but an academic vacation or a professional sinecure. The period marked his first confrontation with the practical and social circumstances attending the artistic life, with problems that, in the sheltered milieu of Harvard, had barely existed. College had habituated him to the decorum of the literary life by fanning and focusing his ambitions, providing easy outlets for publication, allowing him to test his poetic and editorial talents and permitting him to relish, within the limitations of its literary ambience, the joys of a certain prominence as a writer. Now he had to face the problem of finding a congenial social position as a writer in postwar America, of striking a balance between the distractions of bohemian living and the professional practice of the writer's trade.

5

A Humble
Citizen of
Grub Street

Greenwich Village

1919

Freshly demobilized, Malcolm Cowley joined the bands of young aspirants in the arts who came flocking to Greenwich Village in the immediate aftermath of the war. In 1919 the maze of crooked streets and alleyways to the south of West Fourteenth Street still retained much of its prewar reputation as a laboratory for new values and free life-styles. Since the war, however, the place had undergone a change of character that made it less of an ideal refuge for writers and artists. Not only had wartime inflation forced up the cost of living, but greater accessibility had increased the Village's commercial potential and driven up the rents and value of real estate. With the Village rapidly becoming a hangout for fakers, eccentrics, and exhibitionists ("a sideshow for tourists," Floyd Dell called it), and Prohibition turning it into a place of continuous revelry, the serious artist and old-style bohemian felt increasingly ill at home there.[1]

Before the war Village life was marked by a contagious spirit of challenge and change. Political radicalism and artistic experimentation went hand in hand with an ease and flexibility that would be the envy of radicals in the 1930s. Many saw no conflict in championing the causes of socialism, anarchism, free love, imagism, birth control, syndicalism, futurism, feminism, and free verse alike. The war, however, drove a wedge between the political and aesthetic currents of rebellion. By 1919 old-style bohemians were speaking nostalgically of "the good old days"; radicals were either defeated by the reactionary backlash of the war or forced to go underground to reemerge at the end of the 1920s. "The Village," Cowley observed in his pocket diary shortly after his arrival there, "is becoming an institution." Political radicals, he noted, were driven out by "their enemies to whom free love is a luxury instead of a convenience and to whom radicalism is an affectation."[2]

In 1919 Cowley found the Village full of what he called "former people," those who once fought with fervor and idealism for social, political, and sexual causes but who now seemed spent and weary. The older Villagers, in turn, took a dim and ironic view of the young arrivals, whom, in contemptuous mockery, they dubbed "the Half-Villagers." When Cowley went to live in the Village, however, he did so without any intention of becoming a bohemian. He went there because the Village seemed to offer a most congenial ambience for the life of literature. Living was cheap and rents still were relatively low; the top floor of a tenement house could be rented for thirty dollars a month. The Village also promised the companionship of literary friends committed to modern writing and persuaded of the need to consort together in the face of hampering social and moral conditions. New York, moreover, seemed "the only city where a young writer could be published."[3] Countless little magazines mushroomed in and around the Village, while such new publishers as B. W. Huebsch, Mitchell Kennerley, Alfred A. Knopf, Albert and Charles Boni, and Horace Liveright showed an increasing hospitality to modern writing. Later, when he wrote about his time in the Village in *Exile's Return*, Cowley was careful to distinguish the inhabitants of "bohemia" from the dwellers on Grub Street, the territory of those struggling to eke out a living by writing. Grub Street, he then observed, was "a way of life unwillingly followed by the intellectual proletariat." Bohemia constituted "a revolt against certain features of industrial capitalism"; it was "Grub Street romanticized, doctrinalized and rendered self-conscious; it is Grub Street on parade." Having come to the Village not to be a rebel but to pursue his writing career, Cowley was one of the "young men on the make, the humble citizens not of bohemia but of Grub Street."[4]

Cowley had come to pursue his literary apprenticeship, but it took some months for him to adjust to the practical realities of postwar life. The war, he later wrote, had left him with "a vast unconcern for the future and an enormous appetite for pleasure." Released from active service, he lingered for several months in the intoxicating mood of an extended soldier's leave and plunged headlong into the distractions of Village life. He became, in his own words, a member of "the proletariat of the arts," subsisting on scanty meals and borrowed money, meanwhile feverishly enjoying himself and jeopardizing his health.

You woke at ten o'clock between soiled sheets in a borrowed apartment; the sun dripped over the edges of the green windowshade. On the dresser was a half-dollar borrowed the night before from the last guest to go downstairs singing: even at wartime prices it was enough to buy breakfast for two—eggs, butter, a loaf of bread, a grapefruit. When the second pot of coffee was emptied a visitor would come, then another; you would borrow fifty-five cents for the cheapest bottle of sherry. . . . Dinner provided itself, and there was always a program for the evening. On Fridays there were dances in Webster Hall attended by terrible uptown people who came to watch the Villagers at their revels and buy them drinks in return for being insulted; on Saturdays everybody gathered at Luke O'Connor's saloon, the Working Girls' Home; on Sunday nights there were poker games played for imaginary stakes and interrupted from moment to moment by gossip, jokes, plans; everything in those days was an excuse for talking. There were always parties. . . . Eight hours' foresight was sufficient.[5]

In the spring of 1919 Cowley suffered badly in the notorious epidemic of Spanish influenza. His physical resistance was weakened by poverty and hunger, and for a while his health was in a critical state. Lionel Moise, a reporter on the *New York American*, virtually saved his life when Cowley was "delirious" with influenza: "he cradled me in his arms as if I were a rag doll and carried me into the hospital." The flu, Cowley later wrote, left him "weak in body, clear in mind, revolted by humanity" and by the life he was leading. Out of the hospital, he realized he could not go on living "on borrowed money, on borrowed time, in a borrowed apartment." There was no longer an army or university to shelter him; a young writer possessed of literary dreams but without money, Cowley was out on his own and would have to pay for his next meal himself.[6]

Such considerations became more pressing when in the early months of 1919 Cowley fell in love with a Greenwich Village artist, Peggy Baird. He first met Baird around Christmas 1918 at a party at Clemenceau Cottage, the home of James and Susan Light; soon after he moved into her Village apartment, where the two began "living in sin without paying the rent for our room." Marguerite Frances Baird was born in 1890, the daughter of an impecunious jeweler in Babylon, Long Island. After attending the Art Students League, she married Orrick Johns, a one-legged poet from St. Louis who in 1912 caused commotion when *The Lyric Year*, an annual anthology of verse, awarded its $500 first prize to his poem "Second Avenue," bypassing Edna St. Vincent Millay's superior "Renascence." For a while Johns shared a room on the south side of Washington Square with Floyd Dell. Later he fell in with the circle of poets gathered about Alfred Kreymborg's *Others*.[7]

Peggy Johns, as she was familiarly known among the artists of the Village, had been much at home in the flexible and open climate of the prewar Village. By nature a free and independent spirit, she sided with many of the causes championed by the New Women. In the autumn of 1917 she and Dorothy Day, her closest friend, went to Washington, D.C., with a band of representatives of the National Women's Party to picket the White House. They were arrested and imprisoned in a Federal jail for several weeks, during which they went on a hunger strike and were treated brutally. Emancipation seemed to come naturally to the opinionated, easygoing Peggy. Reputedly one of the first Village women to bob her hair, she mocked conventional notions of femininity and, without being a radical feminist, insisted on a woman's right to economic independence. "A woman in these days can't afford to be feminine unless some nice kind of man has an income of ten thousand to spend on her," she wrote to John Brooks Wheelwright in 1921. "A good majority of the present day women have got to be ready to face any emergency and to stand on their own feet at any moment."[8]

Though Baird had shown some talent as a student under Robert Henri at the Art Students League, she appears to have been more at ease with the disorderly freedom of bohemian living than with the discipline of art. She had a wide acquaintanceship among the writers, editors, and artists of the Village and was a popular drinking companion to many of them, including the reticent Eugene O'Neill. "She never really learned to draw," Cowley recalled, "but she met everybody in the Village, all the best artists." A cartoon by Herb Roth, picturing a session of the Liberal Club in 1914, shows Peggy Baird in the company of Floyd Dell, Alfred Kreymborg, Orrick Johns, Becky Edelsohn, Bernard Gallant, Grace Potter, and Paula Holladay.[9]

The woman Cowley started courting in the winter months of 1918–1919 was a dyed-in-the-wool *bohémienne*, "tiny and curved with a tilted chin," eight years his senior, whose marriage had just drifted to a close and who seemed perfectly at ease in the ambience of Village freedom. To a pink-cheeked fledgling writer recently released from college and the army, an experienced woman with the charms and vitality of Peggy Baird must have appeared simultaneously daunting and appealing. To Baird, a

recent divorcée struggling to make an independent living as a watercolorist
in the Village, Cowley must have seemed an ambitious young writer on
the make, whose fresh charm and bumptious naivety could not conceal a
stubborn determination of purpose and an attractive solidity of character.
Possessed of a thick mane of dark hair, a small moustache and shiny, intelligent blue eyes, Cowley made a handsome appearance in the Village—
he struck Josephson, for one, as a "burly farm boy who wrote with a very
light touch and a pleasant turn of wit." [10]

It was Peggy who helped Cowley gain a wide literary acquaintanceship
in the various circles and coteries in and around the Village. Late in the
spring of 1919 she took him to Grantwood, New Jersey, where a new locale
for the New York avant-garde had begun to spring up around the magazine
Others. Since the foundation of their magazine in 1915, Alfred Kreymborg
and William Carlos Williams had habitually consorted there with such
poets, painters, and critics as Man Ray, Orrick Johns, Walter Arensberg,
Marcel Duchamp, Mina Loy, Robert Sanborn, and Maxwell Bodenheim.
Though Cowley was never formally a member of the *Others* group—none
of his poems appeared in the magazine—through Peggy he came to know
most of them. [11]

It was again Peggy who helped launch Cowley on his reviewer's career
by introducing him to persons holding strategic positions in the magazine
world of New York. One of the literary editors on Martyn Johnson's fortnightly *Dial*—a magazine devoted to politics and economics rather than
literature and the arts—was Clarence Britten, a Village friend of Peggy's
who agreed to let Cowley try his hand at reviewing half a dozen novels in
fifty to a hundred words a piece. Upon publication the reviews would yield
one dollar each. In *Exile's Return* Cowley related how he carried the books
to a bench in Union Square, hastily leafed through them, made his notes,
and sold the novels to a secondhand bookseller for thirty-five cents each.
Next morning he wrote the reviews, then started out "on the search for a
few dollars more." [12]

For the *Dial* Cowley was allowed to write a substantial number of what
he later regarded as "deservedly anonymous" brief criticisms. During the
year he also wrote several longer but still unsigned reviews, as well as
surveys or omnibus discussions that appeared as "Notes on New Books,"
"Books of the Fortnight," or "Casual Comment." Robert Morss Lovett,
who had started his term as editor of the *Dial* in 1918, remembered Cowley
as "one of the most engaging" young writers to come to the *Dial* offices

in 1919. Lovett's memory suggests that Cowley may well have been the fastest reviewer on record: he "sometimes appeared early in the day to collect no fewer than three volumes for review. At noon the reviews were on hand, the pay check issued, the volumes exposed for sale at Frank Shay's bookshop—and Malcolm was lunching."[13]

Cowley's earliest review for the *Dial* was a merciless consideration of an anthology of American student verse that forms a virtual compendium of Cowley's critical touchstones at the age of twenty. Except for the verse of Stephen Vincent Benét and "a good piece of Imagism" by Royall Snow, Cowley looked in vain for "the lyrical realism" of Aiken, the "whimsical realism" of Eliot, and the "starker realism" of Masters. He complained of the poets' "almost universal conservatism" and their unpardonable "technical carelessness." They were victims, Cowley held, of a mistaken and juvenile conception of poetry, "the theory so assiduously spread abroad by Sara Teasdale and H. L. Mencken—that poets are best when young, and require almost no training."[14]

Chance occasionally brought him a book or topic that truly commanded his interest, but more commonly Cowley was forced to write on subjects not of his own choosing. He always approached even his slightest reviews in a spirit of honest workmanship, but his interest in them was necessarily limited. Once in a while an evaluative phrase, an introductory paragraph, or a concluding statement lifts the review above the merely perfunctory and provides a glimpse of the young critic's maturing insights and opinions. An omnibus review of war novels reveals Cowley's impatience with an exclusive treatment of the "pleasant," "heroic" side of the war; by 1919 he had come to share his generation's bitterness about the war and unequivocally demanded an unromantic account of events. He spoke admiringly of Siegfried Sassoon's indignation at "the system that lets war come to pass," but apparently cherished no hopes for a revival of the reformist zeal of the Progressive era. In a review of a novel by Ida M. Tarbell he dismisses the muckrakers of those days as a "courageous but rather priggish set," a "gallant lot of crusaders who acted on the assumption that America was Holy Land and Big Business the infidel in possession thereof, but who today seemed as far off and abortive as the Jacquerie."[15]

Just as in fiction Cowley demanded an "uncompromising truthfulness," honesty of workmanship, and "the power to visualize" characters and "make them live," so in poetry he made demands of craftsmanship and precision. What was needed, Cowley argued, was a professional and scientific study of the principles of poetry and poetic criticism. He observed that "a course in writing poetry . . . still remains to be given" and hoped that a serious study of "poetic exactitudes" would help to furnish "that much-needed article, a new saddle for Pegasus." In January 1921, reviewing a book of verse by Robert Hillyer, Cowley reiterated his plea for a course in what he termed "practical poetics" as indispensable for a mature conception of the art of poetry.[16] By repeatedly expressing such sentiments, Cowley helped to swell the chorus of critical voices that ultimately led to the publication of I. A. Richards's *Principles of Literary Criticism* (1925) and, a decade after Cowley's first plea for such a book, Richards's influential *Practical Criticism* (1929), which revolutionized the teaching and understanding of literature and laid the groundwork for the emergence of the New Criticism.

An occasional unsigned review, even if remunerated, was hardly sufficient for two young people to subsist on. On May 14, having gone three weeks without income from work, Cowley noted in his pocket diary: "No money, little food. . . . Some damned pride keeps me from asking everyone for help." Then one morning, while crossing Sheridan Square on an empty stomach, Cowley fainted on the sidewalk. He scrambled to his feet, spent his last money on a roll and a cup of coffee, and took the incident as a warning. Years later, he recalled that his collapse made him surrender his "pride in living on the underside of society and [his] dream of being a free artisan working at his typewriter as if it were a cottage loom." Inclined to romanticize his beginnings as a writer, Cowley visualized himself as a worker at the writer's trade, analogous to the words of an old ballad: "When I was a bachelor I lived by myself, / And I worked at the weaver's trade, / And the only, only thing I did that was wrong / Was to woo a fair young maid." Even though he had done his best to shield his Peggy from "the foggy, foggy dew," as the ballad says, Cowley felt he had been "remiss" as a provider. In the spring of 1919, when Peggy's friends no longer seemed willing to lend her money, Cowley saw himself forced to compromise and find a job.[17]

Answering want ads, he found various hack-writing assignments. He wrote an occasional article for the *New York Central Magazine*, a house organ of the New York Central Railroad. For a time he worked as theater editor for the *Official Metropolitan Guide*, a giveaway weekly, for $12.50 a week; as its drama critic he wrote a regular column, "The Week in the Theatre," a job that strained his talents for improvisation, since he wrote the reviews "without ever seeing a play, for my boss kept all the tickets." In June he found himself working as a proof and copy reader for *Iron Age*, a New York industrial catalogue, at $42.50 a week, "a mere bagatelle." Peggy was adding to their income by acting as agent to Clara Tise, an illustrator boarding with the Cowleys, and collecting a royalty of twenty percent on the proceeds. "We are both of us on the make," Cowley reported to Burke, who had fled the city and gone to spend the summer in Jim Butler's rural cottage in Candor, four hundred miles upstate; "[we] rush about all day, write an hour or so at night, and spend the remaining two hours before bedtime in floundering deeper into debt." [18]

While Burke was struggling to be "an American Flaubert" in the country, Cowley tried hard to reconcile himself to life in his cold-water apartment in an old brick tenement house at 107 Bedford Street, which was "rat-infested" and stalked by three cats. The boarders there were but a "queer assortment" of Village radicals and artists, Cowley noted in his diary, but, he added, "in a way we are all comrades in misfortune." Peggy was regularly sought out by friends in distress for advice in matters of divorce or unwanted pregnancy. Their landlady was once arrested for passing bad checks, and Peggy rushed about to collect money and obtain a lawyer. Part of the "queer and jolly household" at Bedford Street was Clara Tise— "a curious and charming little person," Cowley observed in his diary. "Her body is exquisite and her pride is naive. Nothing of the New Woman here. She draws charming little nudes of no permanent value; looks up to Peggy as a miracle of efficiency; in general just accepts people, including men." To his relief, there were bourgeois restrictions to the bohemian freedom: "The crowd lives together, eats together, but fortunately has the grace to retire to individual bedrooms." [19]

Lionel Moise and Dorothy Day were regular visitors and companions in revelry. Moise, "big, curly-haired, broken-nosed," had worked for the *Kansas City Star* in 1917 when Hemingway was a cub reporter there. Cowley recalled him as a talented reporter who was also "a poet, a cop-slugger, a heartbreaker, a singer of barroom ballads, and a great teller of barroom stories"; in addition, "he liked to stand with his foot on a brass rail and discuss the art of writing fiction." Much as Cowley liked him, he thought him "one of the many brilliant reporters of the time who had half-baked themselves by reading Nietzsche." Day, suffragist friend of Peggy Baird's, was also a reporter and an aspiring novelist. When she received a hundred dollar advance on an unfinished novel about Greenwich Village, the occasion was celebrated riotously (*The Eleventh Virgin* was published, and reviewed by Cowley, in 1924). One night a street murder took place in front of the Cowleys' place. Another evening he attended a dancing wake to mourn the approach of Prohibition; among the mourners were Harold Loeb, Alfred Kreymborg, Harold Stearns, Norma Millay, Ivan Opffer, and Laurence and Clotilde Vail. On "Prohibition night" he broke the glass door at Luke O'Connor's saloon.[20] But between domestic disorders, a hectic social life—Peggy's friends, some of them artists, others hangers-on, continuously drifted in and out of the apartment—the drudgery of work at *Iron Age,* and the distractions of the city on the eve of Prohibition, it was hard to find time and energy for serious writing.

Between November 1918 and November 1919 only two of Cowley's poems reached print,[21] and he grew discouraged with the intellectually stunting life he was forced to lead. "Above the eyes, I am a dead man. A little drink, a little sex; kaffeeklatsch and nine hours a day for $42.50 a week; all that is the round of my existence." As a positive side effect of work at *Iron Age* he was beginning to take an interest in the mechanism of printing and could converse with ease on linos, monos, widows, shys, pied pages, and pica ems. Indeed, when he reviewed his last six months in the Village, not all was lamentation and regret: he missed much about Harvard, but he realized that he had "gained the ability to see Harvard in perspective"; more importantly, he noted in his diary, he had "gained also some knowledge of writing as it is practised; I have a trade."[22] Cowley's interest in the processes of printing over the years grew into a firm belief that the mechanics and economics of bookmaking were a legitimate area of concern for the man of letters. In his long career he regularly wrote on the "business" of literature, reviewed conditions in the publishing world, and reported on new developments affecting what he early learned to think of as "the writing trade."

In the early summer of 1919 Cowley sought out the downtown offices of the *New Republic,* where Francis Hackett was editing a strong and lively book section. For some years Cowley had been an avid reader of the magazine and if he seems to have been mildly indifferent to its political concerns, he was fully conscious of its intellectual prestige.[23] Unaware of the crucial role the *New Republic* was to play in his future career, Cowley carried his notebook with clippings of his writings to Hackett, "a big, red-faced Irishman looking like Jupiter in pince-nez glasses," who summarily turned him over to Mary Updike, his assistant. Glancing at Cowley "as if she were pouring a saucer of milk for a starved kitten," she assigned him a book to be reviewed in five hundred words. The *New Republic* paid two cents a word.[24]

Cowley's first signed review for the *New Republic* was a critique of Reginald Wright Kaufman's *Victorious*, a novel about World War I. Faced with a subject that he could speak on with authority, the young reviewer adopted a tone of grandiloquent condescension not wholly warranted by the relative lack of sophistication displayed in the review. He boldly accused American writers of timidity in their treatment of the war and urged them "to venture into the deep waters of the epic." Measuring the accuracy of Kaufman's picture of the war against his own firsthand observations, Cowley found the novel "a signal and magnificent failure." He criticized it as a rhetorical falsification of reality, condemned its shoddy workmanship, and felt Kaufman's work betrayed the sensational muckraking journalist rather than the artist: "He sees the world through yellow glasses."[25]

When needed, Cowley could find literary encouragement in discussions and communications with his friends. Cowley, Burke, and Josephson drew sustenance from common miseries and shared ideals. Together, Josephson recalled, they formed an "Anti-Logrolling Society" as a challenge to "the vices of puffing and mutual admiration" rampant in the literary world. The three would compete with each other in writing a sonnet upon a common theme within a fixed time limit and make it "as banal or mock-sentimental as possible." Then they would read aloud and mercilessly criticize each other's efforts. Burke, Josephson remembered, was "a master of this vinegarish sort of criticism," while Cowley, a notorious composer of dirty limericks, was "the most resourceful in writing occasional or light verses on a selected subject." Such meetings, jocular and frivolous as they were, helped to crystallize the direction of their aesthetic ideals and served to cement their literary friendship: despite occasional fallings-out, they remained "a trio of loving little friends, who never failed to say their worst for one another."[26]

Over the spring and summer what had started out as a casual affair in the feverish excitement of demobilized existence grew into a serious commitment: on August 12, 1919, Malcolm and Peggy were married. Early marriages were not uncommon among Cowley's literary friends. That same year Burke married Lillian Mary Batterham, a girl who had come to Greenwich Village from North Carolina. The year after, Josephson met and soon married Hannah Geffen, a young reporter on the *New York*

American. For a younger generation never really steeped in the rebellious mood of the prewar Villagers, Josephson believed, early marriage was in part "a concerted movement of reaction against *la vie de bohème*." [27]

From the start, living with Peggy demanded adjustments that threatened to interfere with Cowley's commitment to writing. Josephson's reminiscences suggest Cowley's early difficulties in finding a workable balance between Peggy's bohemian habits and the discipline required by the literary life:

> In her younger days the amusing Peggy was very pretty. Malcolm, as it happened, had very tidy personal habits bred in him by his (partly) Pennsylvania-Dutch forebears. Peggy, however, liked to live in charming disorder. If they were forced to borrow ten dollars in order to eat, she might spend most of it on flowers. She also loved to keep all-night poker games going on in the kitchen of their cold-water flat, which was also its living room. On occasion, I would come in to see Malcolm in the evening and find his home in complete disarray, a noisy game of cards in progress, and soiled dishes, empty wine bottles, and also flowers everywhere about. But in a corner of the kitchen, Malcolm had set up a small table with a portable typewriter and his papers and books. Here everything was beautifully neat and clean, so that his little writing corner was in marked contrast with the rest of the place. At times, he would go to his corner and set to work doggedly—for he had great resolution—while the poker game raged around him all night. [28]

Moreover, Peggy's flexible notions of marital fidelity easily collided with the more conservative ideas about marriage Cowley derived from his middle-class upbringing. Though he had long since taken his distance from his father's Swedenborgianism, Cowley entered upon marriage with a strong sense of responsibility and a deeply ingrained belief in "conjugial love." Never entirely at ease with the sexual experimentalism rampant in the Village, he felt he was taking upon himself the traditional role of the provider, the responsibility for keeping two persons alive. Despite Peggy's drinking, her irregular personal habits, and her "notoriously unfaithful" behavior over the years, it was only after twelve years that Cowley could bring himself to divorce her. However harassing their domestic and marital situation may have been, Peggy Baird was not, Cowley loyally recalled, "a bad wife for a young writer." Inclined to accept people and things as they came, she did not lay any exorbitant claims on her husband, but allowed him to pursue his ambitions and inclinations in the way he thought best. Moreover, she was content to share the financial insecurities attending Cowley's struggles to live by his pen and for years got along on slender means.[29]

‹ ‹ ‹   The year 1919 was, in the words of Robert Morss Lovett, a time of "yeastlike fermentation": a general strike in Seattle had failed, but strikes among the Boston Police, the steel workers, and the coal miners came in its wake, soon leading to the eruption of the Red Scare, the Palmer Raids, and the deportation of radicals. The year 1919, Cowley observed in 1927, signified nothing less than a "crisis" in the history of American civilization. "It was the time when our national credulity was finally exhausted. We were asked to believe that each of us had individually won the war, and thereby made the whole world safe for democracy. We were asked to believe that the country would suddenly become sober and infinitely richer by act of Congress. That bearded communists were the root of all economic evil. That we should pay ten dollars for a hooded nightshirt, and thereby save America for the white Protestant blondes. That great corporations existed only for Service. All this, and a great deal more, we managed to accept. But somehow in the process our whole capacity for belief was damaged beyond repair. An age of disillusionment began, and shows no signs of drawing to a close." Still later Cowley noted that, taken together, the events of that year constituted a cultural "counterrevolution, one that affirmed the moral dictatorship of congressmen from rural districts and left political power in the hands of businessmen with narrow aims." Reactionary politics, failed moral leadership, and general conservatism, he claimed in A Second Flowering, made young writers feel like "an oppressed minority, orphans and strangers in their own country."[30]

In 1919, however, Cowley appears to have been largely unaffected by the nation's political turbulence and its unsettling social atmosphere. If, during the time he lived in the Village, he felt alienated from a prevailing cultural and social reality, he gave only vague and inarticulate expression to such feeling in his correspondence. Like others of his age group, he was mostly indifferent to politics. The Treaty of Versailles, he recalled, was "so monstrous that it was hard to decide—it scarcely seemed worth the labor of deciding—whether or not the treaty should be signed." Rather, he aimed to preserve a personal integrity through the "privilege" of art—

"to write a poem in which all was but order and beauty, a poem rising like a clean tower above the tin cans and broken dishes of [his] days." Vaguely dissatisfied with cultural and societal conditions, Cowley could thus hope to attain a vicarious sense of mastery and control in the creation of a perfect poem, in the realization of significant form.[31]

In the summer of 1919 Cowley fell under the spell of Jules Laforgue (1860–1887), an early symbolist poet whose works he had been shown in early 1918 by Foster Damon.[32] In a retrospective essay from 1963 Cowley recalled how his enthusiasm for Laforgue was shared by many of his fellow poets at the time. Burke for years had been exploring modern French poetry and, after leaving Columbia, had been sending Cowley "Laforguean complaints and moonstruck rhapsodies in free verse." Later Cowley learned that Allen Tate, Hart Crane, Louise Bogan, Rolfe Humphries, and Yvor Winters had independently discovered Laforgue at approximately the same time. Laforgue's influence on Cowley, however, was markedly strong. As with Eliot, the French poet came to him as a "liberating force," a style and a voice to be absorbed, imitated, and transformed into a voice of his own.[33]

In part Cowley was indebted to Laforgue for a new sense of language: an unorthodox amalgam of Latinate erudition and casual colloquialisms, a combination of "learned words from philosophy, medicine and the natural sciences with familiar expressions, street slang, and newspaper phrases beautifully misapplied." In 1919 Laforgue's language seemed refreshingly innovative and modern; in his diary he spoke of his discovery of "a new apostrophic prose." Cowley admired the poet's ingenious verbal playfulness, his surprising neologisms (like *violuptés*), his "free but singing rhythm," and his experiments with stanzaic and metrical structure, including the use of snatches from popular songs.[34]

But Cowley found more in Laforgue than a new style and technique. His fascination came largely from his discovery of a congenial sense of life, an affinity of poetic sensibility. Laforgue's influence, Cowley later wrote, was based on "an instinctive sympathy amounting almost, at the time, to an identity of spirit." Struggling to leave his own adolescence behind, Cowley found in Laforgue a poet who dealt with adolescent emotions "ironically, but, *au fond*, with as much respect as if they were mature emotions." Laforgue actually raised the ambivalent yearnings and ironic insecurities of a bookish adolescent to the level of high art. His poems thus suggested "a style, a literary attitude to life" exemplified in "irony, paradox and a parade of learning." His coldly aloof yet yearning adolescents, his ironic disdain for the very world that fascinated him, his mixture of levity and seriousness, gave Cowley a tone, a pose, a strategy, in life as in art.[35]

A number of poems he wrote at this time strongly reflect the influence of Laforgue.[36] "Sunday Afternoon (After Jules Laforgue)" was the first of Cowley's poems to be accepted and published by the *Little Review*. The magazine had status and prestige among the young avant-garde writers—it had published Sherwood Anderson, Pound, and Joyce—and Cowley, eager to make his appearance in such company, carried his poem to its office on West Sixteenth Street. Editors Margaret Anderson, "beautiful, the woman of the couple," and Jane Heap, wearing tailored clothes and "savagely bobbed hair," together read his poem and "accepted it on the spot." It was published in the summer of 1919. A deft adaptation of Laforgue's "Dimanche," the poem assimilates Laforguean elements of technique and sensibility in its evocation of the bored and weary state of mind of a languishing bohemian artist. The first of its seven stanzas reads:

> Sunday in my bedroom staring
> Through the broken window pane,
> I watch the slanting lines of rain,
> And since I have an empty purse
> Turn to philosophy again:—
> The world is a potato paring
> The refuse of the universe
> And man excrescent,
> Adolescent.[37]

"Nocturne" likewise accommodates much of the form and spirit of Laforgue. Besides striking the adolescent note, the poem, in true Laforguean fashion, alternates two voices in dramatic counterpoint—that of a young woman longing to be released from a dreary and confined life by a princelike, gallant lover, and that of a young man, meditative and aloof, resisting her advances. As a key Cowley later inserted an epigraph from Laforgue: "Ces enfants, à quoi rêvent-elles, / Dans les ennuis des ritournelles?"[38] In "Time," published in 1920 in the *Little Review* as one of "Four Horological Poems," Cowley followed Laforgue's practice of experimenting with a Latinate vocabulary. It was in such poems, he later felt, that he was "breaking through into modernism." The middle section of the poem reads:

Twilight. And still the clock
ticks viciously at every second;
the minutes walk
slowly across the field of consciousness;
an hour is a time unreckoned;
precise and categorical,
the seconds hammer on the wall.

At their touch, the flesh disintegrates:
the mind is a cerebrum, a cerebellum,
in tangles like a ball of cotton waste,
like bundles of dirty linen or bales of shoddy.
The seconds drip from a great height,
exploding one by one against my nerves,
against the broken armor of my body;
each second is eroding like the rain
its bit of flesh or deliquescent brain.[39]

Not until 1963 did Cowley, with some embarrassment, publish another juvenile poem as historical evidence of Laforgue's influence on young American poets of the time. Laforguean in its very title, "Variations on a Cosmical Air" was written in 1919. It uses, among others, Laforgue's device of incorporating snatches from popular songs in ironic counterpoint with the preceding stanza; it also features the self-indulgent adolescent philosopher-poet, wearily masking his yearning for love in a pose of mock aloofness and a show of erudition. Two stanzas read:

Love is the flower of a day,
love is a rosebud—anyway,
when we propound its every feature,
we make it sound like horticulture,
and even in our puberty
we drown love in philosophy.

But I'm coming around in a taxi, honey,
tomorrow night with a roll of money.
You wanna be ready 'bout ha-past eight.

As celibates we cerebrate
tonight, we stutter and perplex

our minds with Death and Time and Sex;
we dream of star-sent, heaven-bent
plans for perpetual betterment;
tomorrow morning we shall curse
to find the self-same universe.

> *Frankie and Johnny were lovers—*
> *Lordy, how those two could love!*
> *They swore to be true to each other,*
> *just as true as the stars above.* [40]

Laforgue suggested to Cowley new ways of dealing poetically with a mood of disenchantment and a squalid urban setting; he hinted that one way of coming to grips with unhappiness and disgust for one's environment was to cloak one's feelings in irony, "a sort of crooked sentiment, a self-protective smirk." If, to an older Cowley, such sentiments seemed "questionable," they yet formed an authentic ingredient of the young poet's voice. Under the influence of poets like Laforgue Cowley and his fellow poets were inclined to "erect the sordid into a kind of religion. We worshipped the cluttered streets, the overflowing ash-cans, the houses full of people and rats; we felt something like veneration for the barrooms then in the last months of their legal existence; and our writings, too, had the smell of sawdust, youth, squalor and Luke O'Connor's beer-and-stout." [41] A poem he wrote on Luke O'Connor's saloon illustrates the degree to which Laforgue's spirit and technique were attuned to life in Greenwich Village. It also suggests that Cowley's unhappiness easily turned into nostalgia for the country of childhood from which he now seemed irrevocably severed.

Always I felt a love for sordid things,
alleys and courtyards, airless tragedies,
whispers in closets, poverty, amours
in the live darkness, swift and sinister.

These gangs parading, drunken, pale, these girls
who meet their kind like cats in areaways,
these cluttered streets of theirs, and filthy rooms,
and death around the corner I have found
voluptuous.

> The crowd is here tonight;
> the nickel-in-the-slot piano plays
> *Oh, take me back, please take me back to*—where
> do broken-voiced pianos hope to go?
> A floozie sobs tonight, "I'm lonely, please, I'm awful lonely,"
> Arthur, give me a drink,
> and Arthur humming as he mops the bar.
>
> Tonight I too am lonely for the soil:
> *Oh, take me back, please take me back*—to home,
> innocence, the family, marriage, these
> ancestral dreams, these melodies of the race.[42]

In 1919–1920 Cowley's enthusiasm for Laforgue was at its height. Though Laforguean echoes were audible in several poems written later in the decade—as in "Translucent Fingers"—by 1923 Cowley's fervor for his French master had waned. By then Laforgue had ceased to be a liberating force on Cowley's style and sensibility and a provider of a congenial strategy in life.[43]

‹ ‹ ‹ When in *Exile's Return* Cowley came to write his semi-autobiographical account of his time in Greenwich Village, he did so in terms that have helped to foster the myth of Greenwich Village as a place of frivolous, irresponsible living, a seat of social and artistic revolt, and a storehouse of avant-garde values and fashions that were later adopted by large segments of the American middle class. But as one who had lived among the rebels and artists of the Village, written a widely accepted account of the history of bohemia, and analyzed the unwritten code of life and culture in the Village, Cowley has perhaps too easily been identified as a full-fledged member of bohemia, one in accord with the Village ethic of rebellion against middle-class provincialism.[44] Though Cowley's account in *Exile's Return* may have helped to popularize a glamorous and romantic conception of bohemia, its tone was actually more complex and ambivalent, as he managed to clothe his retrospective analysis in both nostalgia and irony, infusing it with an undertone of emotional endorsement while taking his critical distance. In effect, his correspondence of those years reveals his time in the Village as one of uneasy accommodation to

frustrating conditions of life and work, a period when the possibility of
failure loomed large.

In 1919–1920, Cowley later wrote in *Exile's Return*, Greenwich Village
was already hardening into a bohemian cult which, if it did not actually
create the revolution of morals and manners of the postwar years, provided
the forms and standards of conduct that, cleverly exploited by commerce
and industry, set the tone for the reckless and gay 1920s. Greenwich Village
was fast on its way to becoming a caricature of its former self, a "doctrine"
or "system of ideas"—with a history that could be traced to the nineteenth-
century France of Théophile Gautier and Henry Murger's glamorizing
Scènes de la Vie de Bohème, and with underlying assumptions that could be
analyzed and summarized, in ironic oversimplification, as an itemized list
of ideas. The "Greenwich Village Idea," in Cowley's retrospective analysis, encompassed such notions as salvation by the child, self-expression,
paganism, living for the moment, liberty, female equality, psychological
adjustment, and salvation by exile.[45]

In 1919 Cowley was acutely aware of the difference in mood and outlook
between the artists, radicals, and bohemians who had lived in the Village
before 1917 and those of his own age group. His awareness of a generational difference—he thought consciously of the two age groups as "they"
and "we"—may well have been sharpened by his marriage to Peggy Baird,
friend and companion to many of the older Villagers. A New Villager
married to an Old Villager, his perspective was bound to be amphibian,
helping him to gain an inside knowledge while enabling him to retain an
outsider's critical distance—a doubleness of perspective that helps to explain the tone of ambivalence in his treatment of the generations in *Exile's
Return.*[46]

From a perspective of the early 1930s, Cowley could not help casting an
aura of admiration over the older Villagers. They, in effect, were the men
and women of true revolt, who attempted, at the cost of personal suffering
and defeat, to blaze new trails in politics, art, morality, and religion. From
a radical perspective their moral courage and their conjunction of social
and artistic ideals came to seem rather attractive, and Cowley found it difficult then to credit his own age group with similar virtues; by comparison,
they seemed conventional, unadventurous, and undefiant. Their "belief
in political action" destroyed by the war, they held that "society could
never be changed by an effort of the will." Even so, their mood of postwar
disillusionment seemed to Cowley different from the earlier rebels' joyless

cynicism in that it was admixed with a sense of release and reckless confidence. "We had lost our ideals at a very early age, and painlessly," he wrote in *Exile's Return*. "If any of them survived the war, they had disappeared in the midst of the bickerings at Versailles, or later with the steel strike, the Palmer raids, the Centralia massacre. But they did not leave us bitter . . . it was fun all the same. We were content to build our modest happiness in the wreck of 'their' lost illusions, a cottage in the ruins of a palace."[47]

As early as 1927 Cowley was convinced that the postwar disenchantment of his coevals was less the result of the war than of the moral and political debacles of its aftermath. From a later perspective than the 1920s and early 1930s, he evinced increasing skepticism about the widely current image of his generation as "lost" and "disillusioned," an image he himself had helped establish. In *A Second Flowering* he suggested that the postwar disillusionment of his generation was, in effect, a badge of dubious distinction more justifiably bestowed on its English and European contemporaries; it was they who, after years of trench warfare, were truly entitled to tragic desperation, who "had a right to be tired and cynical." The sense of loss or dislocation felt by his American coevals was "chiefly an attitude to be proclaimed in a style full of bounce." Cowley later saw them not as disillusioned but as "disaffiliated" writers whose "capacity for illusion had not been destroyed, but merely displaced." With the political and moral beliefs of an older generation effectively discredited, they turned from social and public ideals to personal and artistic aims. A whole generation, Cowley felt, retreated into a "new illusion": that success could be achieved in individual life "without any thought of society," by making money, attaining to fame or creating enduring works of art.[48]

In 1919 such impulses drew Cowley more deeply into the orbit of the French symbolists. What attracted him to French symbolism was its high ideal of conscious craftsmanship, and its anti-social, aristocratic aloofness from the world. Gustave Flaubert was easily appropriated as a literary hero; in July 1919 Cowley read *Madame Bovary*. He was impressed with Flaubert's "mania for style, architectural form, *le mot juste* . . . and aesthetic perfection." Flaubert respected his art so highly that he made it into "a sacred calling, a priesthood devoted to the religion of art."[49] The all-absorbing devotion of such artists as Flaubert—"Art is vast enough to take complete possession of a man"—inspired young Cowley with a high-minded sense of literary vocation. If he felt at odds with his native culture, he sought in art the emotional and psychological sustenance which others found in tradition, faith, or church. The creed of symbolism thus provided him with more than an aesthetic ideal; it represented a literary ethics and an implicit guide to conduct. With Josephson and Burke, Cowley, for the time being, was content to model his ideals of the life of art on those of Flaubert, Baudelaire, Rimbaud, and Laforgue.[50]

6

Harvard Revisited

1919–1920

On August 20, 1919, Cowley traveled to Belsano to spend several weeks on the family homestead before returning to Harvard for a last semester. He went by himself, leaving Peggy behind in the noise and squalor of New York, to break the news of his marriage to his parents. His first extended stay in the Village had made him anxious to reestablish contact with the country. Sitting in the sordid, shoddy ambience of Luke O'Connor's saloon, he had been "lonely for the soil" and had felt "mastered by a love of clean youth and chimeric innocence."[1] Back in Belsano, he rested and relaxed, caught up with his correspondence, fished for trout, helped out on the farm, and pruned young pine trees. Unfailingly, at first, the country proved refreshing and invigorating.

But trouble was brewing. Aware that his parents were bound to disapprove of his unexpected early marriage to a Village *bohémienne*, Cowley had chosen not to inform them until after he reached his majority (he had married twelve days before his twenty-first birthday on August 24). In Belsano, he unwisely procrastinated broaching the subject. Crisis came on September 2, when his mother, having grown suspicious from the correspondence her son kept receiving from the Village ("Peggy writes me once a day, as regular [as] sex," Cowley wrote to Burke from the family farm), forced him to disclose the ill-kept secret. On receiving the news, Cowley noted in his diary, his mother "burst into sudden hysteria, collapsed on the floor, tore at her breasts." Though his father's disapproval was expressed in calmer ways, the remainder of Cowley's visit was strained and filled with reproachful silences. As evidence of their displeasure, for the time being his parents stopped sending checks.[2]

If, later, they faithfully resumed fulfilling their parental obligations, Cowley's parents never were entirely comfortable with Peggy. Mrs. Cowley in particular could not help but feel that her only son and "hope for the future" was betraying her and her husband's ideals by allowing himself to live "in obstinate poverty" with a divorced and disreputable woman. She "detested" Peggy as a Greenwich Village type, one who not only was "irreligious," but a bad and slovenly housekeeper to boot. Though she re- 143 mained polite whenever she met Peggy, Cowley did not return home to Belsano as often as he may have wanted to, and for the duration of his first marriage saw his parents only during short summer trips to the farm.[3]

For all the tension, Cowley's weeks in Belsano served him much like a retreat; away from New York, alone in the country, he was able to arrive at a clearer perspective on himself, his marriage, his hopes for a literary career, his friendship with Burke. What he found was not wholly encouraging. His twenty-first birthday was an extra inducement for stocktaking. But the immediate occasion was a disappointing week he had spent with Burke before setting off for Pennsylvania. The meeting forced him to conclude that their present responsibilities as married men struggling to make a living interfered with their writing ambitions and prevented them from continuing their friendship on its old level of frankness and intimacy. Their talks had centered on "wives and sustenance" and their "intellectual engines" had seemed, for the time being, to be "running on different tracks." Family life, Cowley wrote to Burke on his birthday, "has a tendency to make a man much more self-sufficient. Public opinion affects him less; he has always the probable approval of his wife to fall back on, and so he craves less the approbation of his friends. I talk like Guffey's Fifth Reader."[4]

In response to Cowley's comment Burke, in mock-Romantic fashion, sent him a poetic lament for a lost friendship, "Lines Written in Dejection near Weehawken on the Occasion of Receiving a Letter from a Friend." The poem triggered a five-page letter from Cowley, analyzing what he felt to be a painful crisis in their friendship. It was a lengthy document of despondency. Needing Burke's friendship for emotional and psychological sustenance as much as for literary self-confidence, Cowley urged that their friendship be given a chance to survive its present crisis.

> We have not lost the faculty of talking to each other. If we had anything to say, we could still say it—anything such as we once mumbled for hours. We haven't got it; measured by our ideals of adolescence, we are failures. . . . Not on the basis of the work we have done, which is Promising, as anyone would tell us; rather because we have been caught up in the machinery of life. . . . In the same mail that brought your letter, I had an almost parallel communication from Peggy. She is having her troubles and discouragements and depends on me to carry her through. Little Does She Know that she is leaning on a Hollow Reed. . . .

We are failures in each other's eyes, and that makes us uncomfortable. However we can still seek out some Sub-Matty, who won't see through us and who will admire us as accomplished litterateurs. And I believe that the literary companionship of our respective wives is just about on that order, which is a cruel thing to say and for God's sake don't repeat it. But such companionship—as far as writing and discussing the universe goes—won't satisfy us forever. Some day we are going to be able to talk again, and I think that the thing which now makes us uncomfortable is the high standards of past discussions. We haven't those things to say today; the platitudes stick in our throats.

. . . I don't know how much faith you have left in me, but I still believe that you are going to pull through. And if either of us becomes a success—even in his own eyes—our relationship can get back on a more comfortable basis. Meanwhile beer and poker and kaffeeklatsch; smuttitudes on married life, and discussion of salaries. I have a great feeling for institutions which you lack; our relationship had become institutional in my eyes, and even if I knew quite well it was hollow, I refused to speak. Now I suggest that we leave it on an institutional basis for a little while, counting on the chance—which is a good one—that it will swing around. Personally I don't feel capable of cutting apart from you. It would be too much of a blow at my self-respect. However if that is what you want, don't answer this, and we'll meet in a year with a little fresher outlook.[5]

It soon appeared that their literary friendship was less in danger of dissolution than in need of reestablishment on a different, more mature basis. From a literary and intellectual perspective Cowley put a high premium on his friendship with Burke, higher perhaps even than on his relationship with Peggy. Cowley was deeply, fraternally attached to Burke. Since childhood he had learned to think of their destinies, in life as in art, as inseparably intertwined. Seeing them almost as mental and emotional twins, he had repeatedly insisted on the virtual interchangeability of the different stages of their intellectual development. Though Cowley continued to see the future course of his literary career as closely interlaced with Burke's, a greater degree of distance seemed a necessary step toward a healthy independent perspective.

In October 1919 Cowley returned to Harvard, while Peggy stayed in New York. He was determined to round off his studies in a single semester, even if it meant taking on a load of six courses, including biology, philosophy (Lucien Lévy-Bruhl and Raphael Demos) and literature (John Livingston Lowes and Dean Briggs). With checks from home no longer forthcoming, Cowley managed to find sufficient funds with the help of an insignificant scholarship, but depended for most of his expenses on small loans from Harvard College.[6]

At first Cambridge brought relief. The frustrating conditions of life in the Village seemed far away, now that he was once more established in relatively luxurious living quarters on the Gold Coast, at 24 Mount Auburn Street. He had found "a charming little room with green painted walls and a student lamp," furnished and including maid service, for $7.00 a month. By alternately taking his meals at the Signet Club, the Harvard Union, and Memorial Hall, at an average of $1.25 a day, he could hope to get by on a modest income. "No leisure, but at least comfort, and assurance that my next meal will be waiting for me at six o'clock with a napkin ring beside my plate, a waiter at my elbow, and a flood of dull conversation sweeping over me, soothing as a bath in Lethe." The resumption of his Harvard life made Cowley realize that neither he nor Peggy were "made for unhappiness." The allurements of a quiet life away from New York even made him consider settling down in or around Boston: "Existence is cheaper here; the air is purer, and there are trees." For the moment his longing for domestic and marital stability seemed stronger than his literary ambitions: "A few tugs from Pegasus, tethered in the closet with a pile of dusty books, but the household cat will purr him to calmness."[7]

Cowley was less divorced from the values of his middle-class background than he may have thought. True, he had chosen to pursue a career as a poet, in itself an act of filial defiance: even in high school his mother had reproached him for wasting his time on poetry and held up to him the example of a cousin who had managed to become a prosperous jewelry salesman. His marriage to Peggy had further severed him from his parents, though there was never a radical break. But what persisted were deep-seated cravings for a rural life of middle-class comfort, economic security, marital happiness, and professional recognition. Like others of his literary generation, Cowley was at heart as much "bourgeois" as "bohemian."[8] The effort to reconcile divided loyalties and longings was an important impetus behind his early career; it drew him both toward and away from New York. Through the 1920s and 1930s he tried to strike a workable balance by maintaining an apartment in the city, the seat of his operations as a professional writer, editor, poet, and translator, while settling down to a quiet, domestic life in rural surroundings.

Upon returning to college Cowley was not permitted to resume his Harvard life on its old terms. Whereas he had been cultivated in the spring of 1918, his months in Greenwich Village now seriously reflected on his social and literary standing at Harvard. At first his cordial good spirits seemed to win the day, and Cowley felt more or less reestablished among the social elite: "College has incidentally been a study in *snobisme*, with myself as one of the principal actors," he reported to Burke. "When I returned everyone seemed to hesitate a little before speaking to me. After all, you must know, I had been entangled in shady dealings . . . there were whispers of a woman. But my greetings were so artless and frank, my heartiness so aggressive, that really . . . and I am once more a member, even though humble, of the Ruling Class."[9] Cowley, however, was not as fully accepted back into social life as he was tempted to believe. In retrospect he recalled his last semester at Harvard as a time of bruised feelings and social humiliations, a painful confrontation with Harvard's conservatism and snobbish exclusiveness. In addition, some of his cherished friendships suffered. Foster Damon was one who disapproved of Cowley's marriage; though they remained on speaking terms, their friendship cooled and they saw less of each other after 1919.[10]

It was in the Signet Society that Cowley experienced the full rigidity of Harvard's social stratification.[11] During his months in Greenwich Village the secretary of the society had informed him of his election as an honorary member. Cowley was glad of the opportunity to eat at Signet, but coming from the Village he was barely tolerated in Signet's reactionary circles. "I was treated as if I had smallpox," he wrote years later to his old friend and Harvard roommate Jake Davis. Two of Signet's members had come to see Cowley in the Village and had brought back reports of a disreputable life and a disreputable wife. An editorial he had written for the *Advocate* in 1918, in which he had "made the mistake of praising wartime socialism," now opened him up to suspicions of cherishing Bolshevik sympathies. Merely to have lived in Village bohemia was enough to brand him a revolutionary among Signet's "doughty warriors for capitalism." His Village friends, struck by his "usually beaming face," had named him "the Beamish Boy"; his table companions at the Signet now dubbed him, less mercifully, "the decayed cherub." Cowley's "royal freeze-out" at the hands of Signet members left bitter memories. Yet, humiliating as the experience had been to one with a deep need for social acceptance and a strong impulse toward companionship, it had also been instructive: as he acknowledged to Jake Davis, it helped Cowley shed some of his social innocence and gain a subtler understanding of the politics of human relationships. But the experience also made him look back with renewed warmth and nostalgia to his happier years at Peabody.[12]

If Cowley's last semester left him with ambivalent feelings about his alma mater, throughout his life he stayed a critical but loyal son of Harvard. He remained faithful to the many literary friendships he first formed there, to his cherished teachers (Copeland, Lowes, Briggs) and to the intellectual traditions of the college. But he was distrustful of its social elitism and was not left with any strong affection for his class of 1919. Among his later friends and acquaintances in the literary world were countless Harvard men, but few from his class: its members distinguished themselves in finance, business, law, or engineering rather than in literature.[13] For most of his life Cowley refrained from attending class reunions. When, in 1944, he made an exception to attend its twenty-fifth, he suffered the same social exclusion as before. The event brought home to him once more that his class had "never jelled"; all the "pectin" had dissolved when the class was dispersed by the war. Illustrative of this lack of cohesiveness, Cowley felt, was that two of his friends, Jake Davis and Bob Cunningham, barely knew each other. It was not until the fiftieth class reunion in 1969 that he became a regular attendant, "partly from morbid curiosity." In 1974 the Signet Society honored Malcolm Cowley with a testimonial dinner.[14]

In November 1919 Cowley made it into the pages of *Poetry* when Harriet Monroe published the three poems Amy Lowell had sold to her thirteen months before. In August he had tactfully inquired of Monroe about the fate of his poems, confessing that he was "very hard up" and was anxiously awaiting "the grand-'n-glorious day" when the check for twenty dollars should arrive—"it will be the first money my poetry has ever brought me." At the end of September he learned that his poems at last were "nearing the light." In mid-October he received the proofs; they looked, he thought, "inexpressibly beautiful." In November the poems appeared in *Poetry* as "Three Portraits."[15] The series marked a belated tribute as well as a symbolic gesture of farewell to an earlier model, Edgar Lee Masters. Two of the poems have a midwestern pastoral setting of country dances and bucolic carousal; both deal with amorous trysts presented in ironic counterpoint. "Danny," the third poem, deals with the frustrated ideal-

ism and the sense of displacement of a naive soldier returning home from
the war. Besides eliciting praise from Conrad Aiken and Haniel Long, a
poet he had recently met, two of the poems, "Barn Dance" and "Danny,"
were republished by the *New York Sunday Tribune*. Encouraged by this
"very flattering" reception of his verse, Cowley submitted another batch
of poems to Monroe, including "About Seven O'Clock" and "Château
de Soupir: 1917," which he had earlier described to her as a "war fantasy, which, though a trifle surannée, is probably the best thing I have ever
done." He reported on work in progress, hoping to muster the editor's enthusiasm for "a Fantastic Etude, a long, sinister poem that interests me
more than anything I have done for ages." [16]

The private pleasures of poetic creation, however, were matched by a
desire for involvement in the world about him. Cowley had early distrusted
the hermetic isolationism of the modern artist and felt that engagement
with a wide range of experience was prerequisite for the creation of a living
and human art. The tension between withdrawal and involvement also
surfaced as a theme in two poems he wrote during his last Harvard term.
"Nantasket" suggests that Cowley was struggling to incorporate the larger
social world into his verse; it shows that since the writing of "Three Portraits" a year before, Cowley's diction, control of tone, and sense of form
had grown more complex and sophisticated. The poem mocks the fashions
and pretensions of postwar youth flaunting their new manners and sexual
mores under the not too compassionate auspices of a sardonic Nature, on
Nantasket beach near Boston:

> And now Society comes marching by,
> Young Kuppenheimer gods in bathing suits
> And flappers with their bonnets stuck awry:—
> Sand filters into patent leather boots;
>
> The sun is scorching painted cheeks; the sea
> Growls at the littered beach complainingly. [17]

"Colloquy with Himself," an inferior poem, expresses Cowley's ambivalence more directly. The impulse of the modern artist to renounce social
and public life in favor of the privacy and freedom of a spiritual existence, the poem seemed to imply, might well demand too high a price of
unreality, lifelessness, and loneliness. [18]

A young writer in financial straits, Cowley found a welcome if modest complementary source of income by writing occasional brief reviews for the *New Republic.* Written during the fall in Cambridge, they were published in the winter and early spring of 1920: "I must have been the only undergraduate who was a fairly regular contributor to *The New Republic,*" Cowley mused in the 1970s.[19] The short reviews, impressionistic and subjective pieces of criticism at best, are marked by a worldly wise presumptuousness paraded in a tone of unearned maturity. Yet they carry the germs of the writer's maturer sensibility. The apprentice reviewer clearly endeavored to engage the reader's attention, if by somewhat flippant means; he also evinced a characteristic inclination to criticize in images and metaphors as much as by sustained intellectual analysis. A concern with "truthfulness" and "honest workmanship" ranked with a demand for insight into human nature as touchstones of his critical judgment.[20]

Predictably, none of Cowley's earliest writings strive to develop a poetic or aesthetic theory. Yet it is possible to find in them the germs of ideas and critical tenets that evolved into basic assumptions. Among his papers is an undergraduate essay, written for English 72 and dated December 19, 1919, in which he analyzed the poetics of romanticism and imagism by contrasting Wordsworth's preface to the second edition of *Lyrical Ballads* with Richard Aldington's introduction to Amy Lowell's *Some Imagist Poets.* These two documents, Cowley argued, were "the most important pronunciamentos of a century and a half of English poetry." He insisted that they could not be seen as "independent phenomena," dissociated from their historical, cultural, and social context. The one generality to be concluded from them, he felt, was that "poetry is valueless detached from reality." Both Wordsworth and Aldington, he noted with approval, had wanted to "rescue" poetry "from the grip of the salons or the Browning Clubs, and bring it back not so much to The People in the abstract as just to people." Besides a distrust of abstractions and a demand that poetry deal with a living human reality, the paper expressed Cowley's wariness of doctrinal dogmatism and its fatal interference with poetic practice: "These [theories] are pet hobbies; the poets who hold them sin by attachment to them, ride them to death."[21]

Cowley's last reviews for the *Advocate* included a discussion of J. C. Squire's *Poems, First Series* and a cocky report on a number of theatrical productions presented by the English 47 workshop at Agassiz House on February 6, 1920. The latter review is one of Cowley's rare performances as a drama critic. Though he composed a number of one-act plays and gained a profound admiration for seventeenth-century French drama, in his long career Cowley never ventured deeply into drama criticism, nor was he ever an inveterate theatergoer. From the first it was poetry, fiction, and criticism that held his primary interest. Cowley's last poem to appear in the *Advocate*, "Eighteenth-Century Sonnet," pursued the conventional mode of satirical verse that had earlier made him popular at the Harvard Poetry Society. Written along the lines of "Diary of a Restoration Gentleman," the poem marks a fitting moment of farewell to the kind of verse Cowley was leaving behind in order to deal with the contemporary reality of urban life in a more modern mode: "Mine is a city muse; I tune my lyre / To sing no triumphs of a fox-mad squire." [22]

Through Cowley's last term at Harvard his friendship with Burke continued in a somewhat precarious state. For Cowley, paradoxically, the value of their friendship increased as they were further apart. Meeting Burke in the flesh he tended to become "inarticulate," but away from Burke he found himself conducting "many imaginary conversations." Through the fall and winter his discussions with Burke and their evaluations of the shifting terms of their friendship continued. They resumed their old habit from Pittsburgh days of swapping grand philosophies of life, god, and the universe, Cowley responding to Burke's erudite and witty speculations with a mixture of smutty banter and ironic seriousness. There were moments of painful discovery—"Kenneth, I fear my affection for you is alas! greater than yours for me. . . . Perhaps I need a friend more than you"—as well as comical misunderstandings. [23] In February, realizing that their misunderstandings resulted less from an incompatibility of ideas than from a fundamental difference in personality, Cowley reached out to Burke with a gesture of reconciliation, evoking the memory of their common Pittsburgh adolescence.

Remember Pittsburgh and the walks up Ellsworth Avenue? One scene comes to my mind especially clearly; it was on a long driveway in Highland Park; you had just developed another new Weltanschauung as all-embracive as Kant's and founded, I believe, on a sentence in *Diana of the Crossways*. We fell from world generalizations to theories about us twain and decided that you progressed by revolutions, I by sane, steady development. And now by sane steady development you have reached the logical resolution of your attitudes; I have lost most of my pimples, grown a moustache, and had a revolution. I feel offended because you don't understand me but I don't know why. For both you and I realize that your discernment has always been brilliant and microscopic. You would sympathize with the biologist who builds a theory of the descent of man on the number of chromosomes in the male reproductive cell; everything depends on whether there are 23 or 24. Or to put it another way, you see one facet of every personality, and build a theory of every personality on that facet; your universe reminds me of a Jonsonian comedy of humours. But now I am building a theory of you on one facet of a very complex personality. . . . Every once in a while you shock me. I shall never for a moment forget the time I sent you some platitudes of Herbert Kaufman's for a joke, and you took them seriously and questioned my mentality. . . . Yet I continue to write you because for all our disagreements I never learned how to talk to anybody else, and I don't know why you continue to write me.[24]

The bond cemented in childhood had weathered a first—minor—crisis. Despite Cowley's repeated, at times sentimental insistence on their affinities and common interests, their friendship flourished by the grace of their substantial differences as much as by their similarities.

Cowley's last weeks at Harvard were rushed and far from pleasant. After Christmas, Peggy joined him from New York. Together again after more than two months, they took up living quarters in a shabby old house near Central Square. It was hardly an idyllic reunion with his final six examinations coming Cowley was swamped with work. To make matters worse Peggy had fallen seriously ill in New York and continued in frail health for the rest of their stay in Cambridge. For several weeks, Cowley remembered, "I led a rather desperate life, shopping for dinner, cooking it, serving her in bed, then going back to my books." During January he immersed himself in the Elizabethan dramatists—Marlowe, Webster, Tourneur, Ford, Middleton—and, for pleasure, reread Shakespeare; he was "agreeably surprised" to discover the germ of Laforgue in *Hamlet*. At the end of the month he was steeped in the literature of Romanticism, reading Goethe, Coleridge, and Wordsworth. Between struggling to write, nursing a sick wife, running the household, and studying, Cowley had dif-

ficulty readjusting to married life. At one point in his studies he plunged
into biographies of Goethe and Shakespeare to learn about their "marital
difficulties." But he failed to find there the clue to a workable balance between being a devoted writer and a dedicated husband: "What's the moral:
I'm not Goethe or Shakespeare either."[25]

When his six examinations came Cowley went "breezing through them."
He had reason to be proud of his record: he made four As and two Bs—
enough to earn his Phi Beta Kappa Key, which was mailed to him after he
had left Cambridge.[26] In February 1920 Cowley was graduated from Harvard "as of 1919." He earned a regular bachelor of arts degree but could be
satisfied with his academic performance: despite several long-term interruptions, he had finished his college education in a little less than six
full semesters (his sophomore year having been ended prematurely by his
departure for France), scattered over five calendar years.

‹ ‹ ‹   Cowley's departure from Harvard in early 1920 coincided with the
beginning of an important literary connection. In November 1919 the fortnightly *Dial* was put under new editorial direction. Some months before,
Clarence Britten, an associate editor, had gained enough confidence in
Cowley to ask him to undertake a substantial signed critical review. Cowley
wrote the review, submitted it shortly after his return to Cambridge and
heard no more. In the late autumn the old *Dial* was permitted to die but
was immediately resuscitated as a new monthly magazine by two Harvard
graduates dispassionately devoted to art and literature and in possession of
considerable wealth, Scofield Thayer and James Sibley Watson. The refurbished *Dial* grew into the leading, most prestigious literary journal of
the decade; it was, Cowley felt in retrospect, "the best magazine of the arts
that we have had in this country."[27]

From the moment of its transformation Cowley and Burke were present
in the pages of the "new" *Dial* as representatives of a young generation
with an outspoken interest in modern, avant-garde writing. The *Dial* was
a crucial factor in the formative phase of the two writers' careers. From
the start both were ambitious (and competitive) to be associated with the
magazine. In January 1920, when the *Dial*'s first issue appeared, Burke
claimed priority: one of his stories was accepted, at the fabulous sum of one
hundred dollars. In ironic celebration of his friend's attainment Cowley
composed a "magnificent" satirical ode—"On the Occasion of My Being

Printed in the Dial, by K*nn*th B*rk*." The fourth stanza illustrates the spirit in which Cowley received Burke's success:

> Some day he too may leave the bench of scholars
> > And live with men
> Some day he too may earn a hundred dollars
> And I shall treat him with a father's kindness, when
> He comes at last through the supremest trial
> And sees his poems printed in THE DIAL.[28]

Cowley's association with the *Dial* was in the nature of "a long and close collaboration." Though, unlike Burke, he never served in any editorial capacity and though his opinion of the literary taste and merit of the magazine fluctuated with changes in the literary atmosphere, Cowley remained eager to write for the *Dial* for most of its life span. Indeed, it was largely (but not exclusively) through his contributions to the *Dial* that he was able to establish his position as a serious critic and poet in the 1920s. He respected the magazine's "standards of serious work and decorum" and struggled hard to meet them. The level of reviewing in the publication, he told Burke in 1922, was "encouragingly high"—"I am not the only one to believe that the book reviews are the liveliest part of the Dial."[29] Writing for the *Dial*, Cowley consciously tried to write better, to go beyond the ephemerality of a mere review and to reach a seriousness of consideration, a catholicity of taste, and a sophisticated cosmopolitanism worthy of the magazine. Not counting the numerous "briefers" that Cowley continued to write for the new magazine, his best and most substantial pieces of criticism in the 1920s were written for the *Dial*, as were some of his better poems.

In general Scofield Thayer could muster more enthusiasm for Cowley's critical writing than for his poetry; this may explain why considerably less of Cowley's verse appeared in the *Dial* than in other (mostly "little") magazines, such as *Poetry*, the *Little Review*, *Broom*, *Secession*, or *transition*. If Thayer could be "highstrung and moody," James Sibley Watson had a more endearing character marked by modesty and tolerance; for the Cowleys he came close to being a personal friend. "If you meet Watson of the Dial, you will like him immensely," Peggy wrote to John Brooks Wheelwright in 1921. "We both grew very fond of him in the short time we knew him, but he is horribly shy—without affectations." On the whole, Cowley's relationship with the editors of the *Dial*—Thayer and Watson, but also Gilbert Seldes, Stewart Mitchell, Alyse Gregory and, of course, Burke—was a good one. Only Marianne Moore, who assumed editorial responsibility in 1925, irritated his professional pride with her recurrent demands for alterations in his manuscripts. In late 1928, a year before the magazine's demise, Cowley became so irked by her editorial habits that he decided to stop writing for it.[30]

For Cowley the literary tone and ambience of the *Dial* seemed not so far removed from the spirit of his Harvard days. Over the years he continued to think of the *Dial* as a latter-day reincarnation of the aesthetic *Harvard Monthly*. Cowley's association of the *Dial* with the aestheticism of the *Monthly* may in part have been inspired by Thayer, who not only had been active on the *Monthly* but also looked the Harvard Aesthete incarnate—in the words of Alyse Gregory, he was "slender of build, swift of movement, always strikingly pale, with coal-black hair, black eyes veiled and flashing, and lips that curved like those of Lord Byron." Though at times Cowley felt as ambivalent about the *Dial* as he did about the Harvard Aesthetes, to write for the *Dial* may well have seemed an indirect mode of allegiance to the literary traditions of his alma mater.[31]

Cowley's first piece of criticism to be published in the *Dial* was the last one he had done for Clarence Britten, a review of two novels by Sheila Kaye-Smith—and proved to be the only item from the old *Dial*'s "barrel" (the stock of accepted but as yet unpublished manuscripts) to be retained by the new editors. Thus his article served as "the only link between the old and the new" *Dial*.[32] But if, as Cowley seemed to hold, the *Dial* represented a contemporary cosmopolitan variant of Harvard aestheticism, his very first contribution expressed his impatience with the introverted aestheticism of modern art: "Modern art subsists to a remarkable extent by taking in its own washing. Novelists adopt poets for heroes, who write sonnets on pictures, for which musicians compose orchestral settings. Painters contribute fantastic portraits of all these folks and become in turn the heroes of new novels; the circle is complete." Cowley was relieved to find, in Sheila Kaye-Smith, an author who dealt with the reality of "life" and who explored "authentic, unliterary experience." If he was modern in his concern with formal and stylistic perfection (Kaye-Smith's sentences were "hammered in bronze; each one perfect, each sufficient to itself"), he was conservative in his demand that art be humanistic, realistic, mimetic.[33]

In his next review for the *Dial* Cowley expressed a similar wariness of the exclusive aestheticism and narrowed range of experience of the modern

artist. He praised Romain Rolland's mastery of large-scale forms and struc-
tures—"Rolland is a monumental architect, . . . not an intaglio worker or
even a sculptor"—but was disappointed at Rolland's choice of a sculptor-
artist for his protagonist: "you had hoped for one hero at least not sicklied
over with the pale cast of art." Cowley's early impatience with the subjectivist, self-enclosed aestheticism of modern art foreshadowed his ambivalence about the merit of what, in the 1930s, he called the "Art Novel." [34]
His early reviews for the *Dial* suggest that this ambivalence (though politically colored in the 1930s) was less the result of a conversion to radical
politics than a natural outgrowth of a persistent literary attitude.

By the middle of February, Cowley was ready to leave Cambridge. "The
exams are finished," he announced on the ninth; "One short thesis and my
connection with college will be severed definitely." But between an empty
purse, an ailing wife and "no destination except, vaguely, New York,"
Cowley's prospects were dim. An unexpected act of generosity brought
relief: two days before the Cowleys planned to leave, a sealed envelope containing ten dollars and a message from Charles Townsend Copeland was
delivered to their attic room. Copey's ten dollars helped to pay the Cowleys' way to Grand Central Station, where they arrived with just enough left
to pay the taxi fare to Greenwich Village. Their former landlady, Katherine
Tyng, had offered to put them up for two or three nights in her basement
room. [35] On the threshold of the 1920s the Cowleys had no choice but to
resume a precarious existence as struggling artists and dwellers on Grub
Street.

7

Greenwich Village

1920–1921

Shortly after their return to New York, the Cowleys, with the help of one of Peggy's friends, Bessie Breuer, found a small three-room apartment on the top floor of a tenement at Eighty-eight West Third Street; it was situated over the elevated and rented for sixteen dollars a month. A bed was borrowed, chairs were begged, a writing desk was purchased at a Salvation Army store, and the Cowleys were established once again in Greenwich Village. The first half of "Winter Tenement" recreates Cowley's life with Peggy at Eighty-eight West Third Street, in the early months of 1920:

> When everything but love was spent
> we climbed five flights above the street
> and wintered in a tenement.
> It had no bathroom and no heat
> except a coal fire in the grate
> that we kept burning night and day
> until the fire went out in May.
>
> There in a morning ritual,
> clasping our chilblained hands, we joked
> about the cobwebs on the wall,
> the toilet in the public hall,
>   the fire that always smoked.
> We shivered as we breakfasted,
> then to get warm went back to bed. . . . [1]

For all the moments of fun and exhilaration, Cowley's seventeen months in Greenwich Village were marked by a recurrent feeling of frustration and unhappiness; the prevailing tone in his correspondence of those months is one of lamentation and discouragement. Though as a poet and reviewer he was productive enough to be assured of a modest income, he grew progressively ambivalent about success. Dismayed by the gap between his literary aspirations and the conditions of his life, he felt increasingly skeptical about the role of the artist in America.

Always an inveterate complainer and self-deprecator in his letters and notebooks, Cowley had reason to feel despondent. He had suffered badly in the notorious flu epidemic of 1918 and had lived through an ensuing period of poverty. He had married a disreputable *bohémienne*, a cause of estrangement from his parents and an occasion for ostracism by his prosperous Cambridge friends. During his last semester at Harvard he had lost the nearest equivalent to a sister, when Ruth, the girl taken in by his mother when Cowley was twelve, died of diphtheria at the age of nine. In "The Pyre," a late poem commemorating the selling of his ancestral Belsano home upon his parents' deaths, Cowley acknowledged his attachment to "his little sister" and transformed her death into an emblem of the demise of his own boyhood.[2]

Most of all Peggy's infidelities and her recent illness had seriously strained his marriage, an unstable union from the start. While Cowley had been struggling to bear up under social and academic pressure in Cambridge, Peggy, in New York, had been unfaithful, presumably with Orrick Johns, her first husband. She had contracted syphilis and passed it on to Cowley. At a time when antibiotics were not available for the treatment of venereal disease—penicillin was not discovered until 1928—syphilis was considered lethal and certainly (in Cowley's words) "the most sinister of diseases." A source of shame and humiliation, it was associated with images of leprosy and mutilation, of madness, the possibility of a slow, disgraceful death. For half a year Cowley and Peggy subjected themselves to courses of medical treatment at free clinics in Manhattan and became intimately familiar with conventional remedies of the time—mercury and Salvarsan. For the duration of the treatment they were locked to each other, much like "prisoners in the same cell." After six months they were pronounced cured and discharged, but the emotional and psychological wounds were slow to heal. More than fifty years later Cowley still recalled the intense feelings of estrangement brought on by the disease, as if through the experience he had been given a "passport into the underworld." In the free medical clinics of Manhattan he had witnessed a realm of suffering and pain that made him feel as if he had become "the comrade in spirit of all the horribly diseased people I saw."[3]

"Free Clinic," a poem first published in the *Little Review* of April 1920, was based on this experience and, in a detached yet immediate fashion, registers Cowley's mood. The poem opens with a coldly precise image of the clinic's waiting room; it pictures a dehumanized world of straight lines and right angles, from which all playful variety of form has been excluded.

From among the "rows of soiled faces" on the benches in the waiting room the poet, like a Whitmanesque observer, selects a few for sardonic presentation. Between the image of Mrs. Magrady, suffering from cancer and "dumped on the seat / like a barrel of ashes," and that of two perfumed shopgirls, "one with a rose / stuck in a ragged buttonhole, and one with a petaled sore," the poet finds it hard to preserve a sense of human dignity and cynically mocks the notion of a benign providence—"God is an old woman / with dropsy— / or perhaps / you were not created / in His image?" The poem ends with an evocation of the cruel paradox in the poet's suffering:

> Against a colorless skin the brazen
>   loveliness of a tumor,
> fistula, chancre, chancroid—
>   it is not
> because I admired their beauty,
>   no, tormented
> by the search for the white absolute,
> by the nostalgia of the immaculate
> conception . . . I therefore[4]

Though one must be careful not to read poems too directly as chapters in a spiritual autobiography, several of Cowley's poems help to illuminate aspects of his inner life during his Village days in 1920. Apparently his self-insight deepened considerably, and his belief in the sanctity of "conjugial love" was profoundly shaken. "William Wilson," its title derived from Poe's short story about a young man's struggle with his doppelgänger, envisions the poet embattled with his newly encountered shadow self, a "man of straw and many fires, / Iago doubled with Othello"; it ends with an image of the crumpled pillow on the poet's bed, "where once, immortal as a stone, / true love lay strangled by Othello." Two other poems recreating Cowley's life with Peggy in the Village deal with the demise of marital love and describe the deflation of an illusion—"our love that we had thought so holy." Both "Interment" and "Winter Tenement" envision the death of love as an act of strangulation by a vengeful angel and end with an image of disillusioned loneliness and separation.[5] Other poems recapture moments when Cowley, walking the streets of Greenwich Village, was beset with visions of death and felt trapped in the relentless advance of a cancer-like disease. Such moments made him want to lash out against the "tyranny" of Time—"Each second is eroding like the rain / its bit of flesh or deliquescent brain." "So Perish Time," one of "Four Horological Poems" published in the *Little Review* in the summer of 1920, is a plaintive, quasi-philosophical meditation on Time and Death written in the mode of Jules Laforgue.[6] Other poems, such as "Deathbed" or "Mortality," picture life as a protracted and potentially disgraceful process of dying.[7] At times, even the pursuit of poetic beauty lost its urgency, its significance dissolving in the face of death and decay.

> Beauty too white,
> too perfect for this mind infected with
> all the venerealities of sense!
> O all-sufficient loveliness:
>
> I cling
> vainly to the marble of your flanks,
> vainly to the knees of beauty, knowing
> before the ecstasy that my clenched fingers
> will loose their perilous grip, that I shall fall
> awkwardly to adjust myself about
> my skeleton.[8]

The majority of Cowley's poems from this period breathe bleak despair and radiate emptiness, sterility, and imprisonment. They were written out of loneliness and pain, from a new awareness of the reality of death, by a poet who not only had lost many of his illusions about Love and Beauty, but who had surrendered the vestiges of his childhood faith in a Divine Providence and who was no longer sure of the possibility of salvation.[9]

‹ ‹ ‹ Notwithstanding his personal and marital malaise, Cowley was soon writing again. Reserving his more respectable work for the *New Republic* and the *Dial*, he was occasionally prepared to engage in hackwork. Thus, in the spring of 1920 he turned his recent experiences as a house hunter in the Lower West Side to advantage in an article for the *New York Evening Post*. It describes how Manhattan house hunters, discouraged by the increasing commercialism and the high rents in the region around Washington Square, had begun to invade the Lower West Side, reducing a former artists' paradise to just another section of the "exclusive suburb" of Manhattan. Cowley did little to discourage or correct the current image of the Village as a place of bohemian revelry and affectation. Perhaps it was a sense of barely having risen beyond a form of middlebrow bourgeois journalism that prompted him to adopt for once a pseudonym: David Malcolm.[10]

Another assignment for the *Post*, an article on dramatist Laurence Housman, younger brother of the famous poet A. E. Housman, was cast in the hybrid form of the portrait-interview, and combined conversational informality with the detachment of serious criticism. Cowley presented Housman's confident prediction that American poetry would "progress along national lines" but that it had "not yet risen out of self-consciousness." He sympathized with Housman's critique of Imagism as lacking distinction of style and agreed that there was "something sacramental about the process of getting hold of the absolutely right word." When he considered Housman's career in the light of his own struggles as a beginning writer, Cowley was struck by the former's success in fashioning a unified whole out of the discordant elements of his life. Such a unity, he thought, was "perhaps the only mark of a successful life"; it was a feature conspicuously absent in his own.[11]

The few letters that passed between Cowley and Burke during the summer of 1920 confirm that Cowley was plagued by a lack of focus and direction in his life. A letter he wrote to Burke in early June, representing "the history of an evening," was fragmentary and haphazard in the way it drifted from subject to subject and oscillated between conventional spelling and "fonetty Kinglish" in the experimental mode of E. E. Cummings's poetry. Style and form were an appropriate reflection of his life at the time—meandering, confused, filled with trivial details, plagued by frequent interruptions, submerged in the rush and routine of a hectic Manhattan existence. He regularly complained of feeling intellectually numb—"My mind moves torpidly like a lizard in a stagnant pool"—and occasionally engaged in the experiment of automatic writing, hoping to trick a recalcitrant subconscious into producing "pearls" of poetry.[12]

Any effort at serious writing seemed fated to be thwarted by Peggy's Village friends, who assiduously drifted in and out of the apartment, holding out a perpetual invitation for carousal and distraction. Temptation could not always be resisted and often Cowley participated in the Village revelries of playing cards, drinking, gossiping. At other times distaste outweighed exhilaration. In several letters written in June he poured out his disgust at the crowd of assorted Village artists, sculptors, poets, and abstract painters with whom he found himself consorting. He seemed repelled as much by their indiscriminate sexual behavior and the ruthless ease with which they disrupted each other's marital and familial lives as by their fake and fraudulent pretensions in the field of art. He was disturbed to find that the new Village mores of freedom and independence were too often attained at the cost of human decency and consideration, and he despised those of Peggy's friends who derived their tentative Village "group identity" from the cheap and artificial bonds of alcohol and gossip.[13]

Two older Harvard writers, Joe Gould and E. E. Cummings, at about this time represented for Cowley the worst and the best possibilities of the artistic life in Greenwich Village. Gould was supposedly engaged in composing a gigantic "Oral History of Our Time," which purported to be a truthful record of the conversations overheard on his peregrinations through New York. Though his quasi-historical endeavors remained unpublished, he managed to become a legendary part of Village lore. A redoubtable vagrant and notoriously sloppy eater and drinker, Gould, a regular visitor at Eighty-eight West Third Street, embodied exactly the kind of eccentric pseudoartistry Cowley had come to detest. By contrast, Cummings stood aloof from the many Village writers only too eager to enjoy the privileges of the artistic life without possessing talent, endurance, and commitment. Cowley, sufficiently impressed with Cummings's serious dedication to his art, wanted to become "more than an acquaintance" of the poet: "people who are producing anything are so rare in this town."[14]

In the early summer of 1920 Cowley made a twofold proposition to Burke, clarifying his ambitions in "Art" as well as "Life." In the realm of art he agreed to join in the foundation of a "school," provisionally called *The Courve*, a neologism supplied by Burke. It was to be dedicated to the expression of various modes of spatial and temporal motion and aimed to integrate experiments in seemingly disparate branches of art—poetry, painting, sculpture—in an attempt to incorporate the new contemporary realities of city life, technology, and the machine into a radically modern art. Conceived in a spirit of freakish sport, the school seemed to embrace the whole range of experimental modes from that of Marcel Duchamp, Man Ray, and E. E. Cummings to Jules Romains's unanimism and F. T. Marinetti's futurism. Several months later Cowley proposed to preempt an issue of the *Little Review* for "our cute little movement." It was to be filled with poems and a satirical play by Cowley and Burke, drawings by the painter Charles Ellis, and a "Manifesto against Manifestoes." Though the "school" never materialized, the notion of a group manifesto soon surfaced in more effective form. For the moment the idea itself was most important as belying Cowley's earlier skepticism and bespeaking rather an unambiguous allegiance to modernist experimentation.[15]

Together with his plans for *The Courve*, Cowley launched a proposal for "Life" that resuscitated his old dream of living as a writer in the country, where he would be surrounded by kindred spirits yet able to maintain his professional contacts with the city. He had spent several bucolic weekends with Peggy in and around Haverstraw, just north of New York City, fishing for "legendary trout." The farming country there was within thirty-five miles of Forty-second Street, and Cowley toyed with the idea of renting a house there: he to raise a vegetable garden, Peggy to sell flowers. "The little money necessary for existence can be raised through a carefully cultivated typewriter and one or two trips a week to the city." This "vita nuova" combined "all the best features . . . mountains, woods, groundhogs, trout, literature." Cowley hoped that Burke would want to share in the venture with him: "We might run a community garden but the houses should be separate."[16]

Dreaming of Haverstraw, he found himself still mired in New York, writing reviews for the *New York Evening Post* on an odd assortment of topics: miscellaneous British poets, Theodore Dreiser, the French poet Paul Claudel, the Yiddish dramatist David Pinski. The free-lance market might yield a modest income, but it was uncertain work at best and hardly remunerative enough to permit full-time residence in the country. For a while Cowley complemented his earnings through a variety of odd jobs. On a fairly regular basis he wrote for *Export Trade*, a commercial-industrial New York magazine. For two weeks he worked as a stagehand at the Provincetown Playhouse at twenty dollars a week. During several performances he made an appearance on stage, playing a black ghost in Eugene O'Neill's *The Emperor Jones* and a white ghost in *Where the Cross Is Made*. For this he received ten dollars a week. The performances marked the beginning and end of his acting career, but the experience may have stimulated him to write several one-act plays. One of them, "Barn Dance," was seriously considered for production by the Provincetown Players. Written early in 1920, the play was intended as a "throwback to 1915" and owed much in spirit to Sherwood Anderson and Edgar Lee Masters.[17]

In June 1920 Cowley was offered a salaried position, at forty dollars a week, as copywriter at Sweet's Catalogue Service. Unwilling to surrender his independence, yet equally reluctant to stand in another person's debt, he accepted the job, expecting to resume full-time free-lancing in the fall. However, he stuck it out for a full year, working for seven hours daily at the office, writing poems and reviews at night and on the weekends. Copywriting for Sweet's was neither enervating nor inspiring. Over the summer business was slow, and while reading the *American Machinist* and contemplating the "artistic use of turret laths and slotters," Cowley occasionally found time to write poems during office hours. But soon enough he felt trapped in a dull routine and complained of leading "a spiritually uneventful existence." A month after accepting the job, he gave in to temptation and rented a ten-dollar-a-month, five-room house at Haverstraw until November. Though it left him "quite penniless," he could at least take comfort in the bucolic splendor of the chestnut blossoms ("like long drooping fingers") and the plentiful meadow flowers, while Peggy exploited their commercial value by selling them to a Greenwich Village flowershop at a profit of half the proceeds.[18]

If Cowley's spirits invariably revived in the country, they sank whenever he was in New York. He missed the company of Burke, who was spending the summer in Maine, and was occasionally peeved by the presumptuous behavior of Matthew Josephson, who seemed to delight in speaking of Burke in a proprietary manner, thereby feeding Cowley's fears that a cherished friend was slipping away from him. On July 20 he found it necessary to remind Burke once again of their shared Pittsburgh past and evoked the nostalgic memory of the "bucolic billboards" along Ellsworth Avenue. "I tell you there was something fine in the spectacle of two adolescent egos rubbing each other's fur and reciting philosophies like alternate phonographs." Cowley looked back sentimentally upon a time when they had been "like young priests confessing one another"; now, he could already taste "the proud isolation of the coffin."[19]

His despondent mood persisted over the summer. Several of his poems recapture the feeling of having lived "too long in windless exile from the meadows." In late August he admitted to Burke that his "fit of Viennese melancholy, this lavender-and-old-rose regret for other days" was largely the result of his inability to adjust to his precarious financial condition. "This week Peggy lost seven dollars, and as a result I had to hock four cameos and wrap the pawn ticket carefully around the fountain pen ticket and the ticket for my Phi Beta Kappa key." Forced to keep working for Sweet's, he was discouraged by the scant amount of writing he got done and regretted having surrendered his free-lance independence. The market, he now saw, had been "excellent," and would have enabled him to make as much as forty to fifty dollars a week; "it was only my inability to stick it out that dished me."[20]

That summer Cowley accepted an offer from Henry Seidel Canby to review on a regular basis for the *Literary Review of the New York Evening Post*, a weekly literary supplement that Canby had started early in 1920 with the assistance of William Rose Benét, Christopher Morley, and Amy Loveman. For ten dollars a week Cowley was to consider the weekly supply of leftover books and decide if any were deserving of a brief review. The arrangement, Cowley believed, for a while made him "the only salaried book reviewer in New York." Though over the next few decades Cowley and Canby would often find themselves on opposite sides of literary disputes—Canby speaking up for the prewar generation of Frost, Lewis, O'Neill, and Cather; Cowley taking "slingshot in hand" for the postwar writers of his own age group—he owed the older editor and critic a lasting debt for personal tolerance and generosity.[21]

From July through December 1920 the majority of Cowley's reviews appeared in Canby's *Literary Review*. They considered a wide array of topics, ranging from books of poetry by John Gould Fletcher, Robert Hillyer, D. H. Lawrence, Haniel Long, and Francis Brett Young, to a book of plays by Alfred Kreymborg ("the Dickens of the New art"), a volume of Argentinian plays edited by Edward Bierstadt, the diaries of court ladies in eleventh-century Japan introduced by Amy Lowell, and a book on "the world's timber" (an early indication of Cowley's interest in arboriculture and the conservation of natural resources). Two reviews—one of *Youth and Egolatry* by Pio Baroja, a member of the prewar European "generation of the disillusioned," the other of a contemporary history of modern French writing—were informed with Cowley's nascent awareness of the concept of literary generations and the social, historical, and literary forces responsible for their emergence. A later review (of Roland Dorgelès's war novel *Wooden Crosses*) displayed an early distrust of propaganda in fiction, praised the writer for realistically setting down military cowardice and heroism side by side, and observed that after four years the war already seemed "haloed with antiquity."[22]

Recalling his combined life as a salaried copywriter and hand-to-mouth literary journalist and poet, Cowley felt that in those days he exhibited a "somewhat special cast of mind." He was ambitious enough yet wary of success and fearful of becoming "a celebrated writer appearing in glossy magazines." Rather, he was content to "live obscurely, limit [his] needs, and preserve [his] freedom to write something new and perfect at some moment in the future." In the light of that expectation he deemed hackwork permissible, provided it was "honestly performed" and did not necessitate a compromise of integrity. Setting higher standards for himself than his wages warranted, he could hope to realize in his writing those qualities conspicuously absent in his personal life—"punctuality," "neatness," "logic," and progression.[23] If the chances of realizing his ideal of the literary life seemed increasingly slender, he could at least feel a redemptive pride in work well done and poems published.

‹ ‹ ‹   Cowley's aesthetic development during this period was reflected mostly in his review-essays for the *Dial*. On the threshold of the 1920s his sharpest and most buoyant criticism was reserved for the English Georgian poets. In several reviews he lashed out at their poetic abuses or used them as occasions to present his own ideals in poetry. Between 1912 and 1915 the Georgians had helped to liberate English poetry from the excesses of decorative Victorian verse, archaic diction, rhetorical flourish, and fin de siècle weariness. In the postwar years, however, with their poetry deteriorating into glibly competent verse lacking emotional intensity and imaginative force, the rustic simplicity of the Georgians came to seem increasingly irrelevant to an ironic younger generation.[24] In the *Dial* of May 1920 Cowley spoke out against the Georgians in unmistakable terms: "Eight years ago when the Georgians first appeared as a group, it seemed that they were discovering more strident harmonies, subtler dissonances. But with the publication of each new anthology, the disappointment is cumulative. Every two years a volume bound in fresh brown boards, printed on fresh paper, but with the contents so familiar, so delicately trite, reaching with such skill to new heights of inanity." Cowley mocked the Georgians as the last in a worn-out tradition of pastoral lyricism: "O nightingale! . . . O feathered pedant! O banal rhapsodist confused by the tic-tac of iambics! You leave me, O ecstatic bore, homesick for the hoot-owls and whippoorwills of an Ohio dusk." If Cowley was guilty of caricaturing the Georgians as lark lovers exclusively concerned with misty moonlight and the trilling notes of nightingales, he did so in order to advance a well-considered plea for poetry as a "mature art"—"Too much of contemporary verse expresses the emotions of a girl of twelve in words of one syllable. . . . when the Georgians erected this throbbing naiveté into a sacrosanct school, they were striking at the fundamentals of their art. Accept their premise, and poetry takes rank as a medium of expression somewhere between the movies and fancy needlework."[25]

Cowley's attacks on Georgian poetry were hardly prescient or radical; they were rather representative of the impatience of a younger generation with the literary products of its elders.[26] The burden of his complaint against the Georgians was that they had left the poetic premises from which they had started: precise craftsmanship, lucid and concrete expression, vigorous realism, and freedom from what Pound had denounced as "emotional slither."[27] Cowley's critique, however, did not imply wholehearted approval of more modern modes. If he objected to the facile charm of Georgian pastoral verse, he was equally uncomfortable with the tendency of modern literature toward wilful obscurity, the excessive search for originality, and the concomitant tendency to overcultivate the subtleties of private consciousness at the expense of bolder, universal themes.[28] Thus he did not unambiguously prefer D. H. Lawrence's more experimental poetry to that of a recent Georgian arrival like Francis Brett Young, in whose smooth verses he heard "nightingales melodize insinuatingly." Neither did he wholly approve of *Wheels*, an annual poetry anthology edited by Edith Sitwell that purported to be an early harbinger of the "modern" postwar spirit. Its "diapered sophistication" was hardly preferable to the "senile innocence" of the Georgians. Technically up-to-date and more refined than its *Yellow Book* predecessors, *Wheels* yet signified to Cowley only a "less malignant form" of the "malady" of the 1890s, a return to "the harlequinades and harlotry" of decadence.[29] Illustrative of Cowley's response to Georgianism was his exhortation to the English war poets, led by Siegfried Sassoon, to "demobilize" their intellects and utilize their knowledge of modern techniques to write civilian verse that dealt honestly with social reality in peacetime: "Even in a world at peace there are common thoughts waiting for some one bold enough to express them and there are abuses that stink to heaven as much as the corpses along Bapaume Road."[30] Moreover, Cowley observed that the Georgian novelists (Bennett, Mackenzie, Wells), like the poets, had failed to negotiate contemporary reality with "honesty" or depth. They belonged to "a generation notoriously incapable of solving problems," and were not artists so much as "determined pamphleteers on Sex or Peace or Education or Feminism."[31]

In his early reviews Cowley displayed a special adeptness as a critic of poetry; not infrequently, his criticism reflected problems encountered in the writing of his own verse. In the winter of 1921 Cowley continued his examination of the tendencies of modern poetry in a review of Aldous Huxley's *Leda*. It also marked a personal investigation of the validity of the ironic adolescent stance in poetry that he had first encountered in Jules Laforgue. Adolescence, in Huxley's words, was "a chinless age . . . an age feebly skeptical, profoundly unhappy." In Cowley's definition—one given urgency by his recent personal experiences—it encompassed "the stage at which one measures the traditional precepts into which one has been educated against the immoral realities of experience; depending on which force proves the stronger, one becomes idealist or realist." A third path open to the artist was the one of Laforgue: the refinement and prolongation of the stance of adolescence. In *Leda* Huxley had successfully followed Laforgue's path, but Huxley's future achievement, Cowley thought, was staked on his ability to forsake Laforgue and to "strike out in a totally new direction." Cowley's critique reflects his own uneasy efforts to proceed beyond the ironic sensibility of Laforgue to a more serious, critical, and emotionally mature art.[32]

In January 1921 Cowley reviewed *Alchemy*, a third book of poems by his Harvard acquaintance Robert Hillyer. He was impressed enough by the book to make a special visit to John Dos Passos, urging him to review the volume for the *Freeman*.[33] Cowley's review constitutes his most elaborate early statement on modern poetry; it advanced assumptions that remained basic with him and shows that Cowley, like others of his generation, was moving independently along aesthetic paths first marked out by Eliot and Pound. Where before he had lashed out at the Georgians, he now turned against H. L. Mencken for advancing a fatally influential conception of the "ideal poet" as one who was "adolescent, instinctive and untaught." By contrast Cowley envisioned the poet as a supreme and conscious craftsman, whose "tools"—an expert knowledge of techniques and forms, of metres, rhymes, assonance, alliteration—were as essential to the poet's craft as files and wrenches to the plumber. Cowley advanced Hillyer as the example of a mature, professional artist, whose verse was guided by "skill" and critical self-awareness as much as by the mysterious workings of "inspiration." His book, Cowley thought, could be used as "a textbook in some course in practical poetics that still remains to be given." If Cowley's language often remained that of impressionistic criticism, his primary focus was on poetic technique. A formalist emphasis on technique over content, he claimed, was a badly needed corrective: "In this day we have had almost too much of writers with Messages; we are in need rather of poets whose knowledge and whose training are thorough enough so that they can set down simply and melodiously what they think and feel and what their eyes see."[34]

Though Cowley's aesthetic notions were essentially homegrown, emerging from his practice as a poet and his discussions with such literary friends as Burke and Josephson, they ran roughly parallel to the poetic principles that Pound and Eliot had been advancing for some years.[35] Cowley's affinity with the aesthetics of Pound and Eliot is apparent in a combined review of books of poetry by John Gould Fletcher and Conrad Aiken for the *Dial* of June 1921, which was in effect a brief treatise on the question of poetic influence, the importance of tradition, and the futility of striving for artistic originality. Though inferior in depth and complexity, it is Cowley's nearest equivalent to Eliot's "Tradition and the Individual Talent."[36] In part the essay is a rebuttal to Babette Deutsch's review of Aiken's *House of Dust* in the March 1921 *Dial*, in which she had disclosed disturbing echoes of T. S. Eliot in Aiken's verse. Taking Fletcher and Aiken as a case in point, Cowley argues the admittedly "banal" truth that "poets learn from their contemporaries as well as from their predecessors." He mocks Deutsch's assumption that poems might "spring, fully adorned, from the forehead of any casual Jove" or that the poet was "a modern St. Simeon Stylites, who, standing aloof on a pillar, draws masterpieces from the wells of Inner Consciousness." Instead, he pleads for a recognition of the validity of conscious imitation and the overriding value of tradition: 'The poet is . . . a builder at work on the unfinished edifice of literature. He contributes an arch or a nave or the portion of a wall, and passes on; the important question is not his identity but whether he has done his work well. The workman who succeeds him builds further upon what has already been constructed, as Laforgue built on Baudelaire and as T. S. Eliot has built on Laforgue. There are periods of general demolition—and they are very necessary—in which the false work of several generations is torn down, but never is one forced to begin again on new foundations. For to be completely original, one would have to invent a language of one's own; even the idiom in which we work is a sort of crystallized poetry. . . . These things are banal, but they are irritatingly true." Typically, Cowley saw the advancement of literature as a collaborative venture. Aiken and Fletcher, he thought, recognized this axiomatic truth: "In a generation so proud of its independence that it gets nowhere, they have been content, for a little while, to work together towards a common aim." Early, Cowley looked upon writers and poets as a community of individual craftsmen, each devoted to his or her own special talent and vision, yet all engaged in a common literary endeavor and each building on, and in turn transforming, the cultural accretions of the past.[37]

Cowley's early attempts to define his critical position on modern writing were rounded out by three reviews published during the summer of 1921 in the *Dial*. In two of them he attacked the influence of Freudianism and related theories of psychoanalysis on contemporary fiction (and, by extension, on poetry and criticism). His skepticism dovetailed with his wariness about the overcultivation of subjective consciousness and private sensation. In July he praised A. E. Coppard for a careful workmanship that was "not subconscious" but based on "aesthetic judgements." Coppard had happily avoided "the *Bovarisme* of the present generation," a modern sensibility based on "neurosis rather than on false romance," which Cowley held responsible for "the novel of nerves" and "the cult of the disagreeable" rampant in contemporary fiction.[38] *Bliss*, a volume of short stories by Katherine Mansfield, came close to being dismissed on similar grounds as "a book of neurotics; a literary corridor of the psychopathic ward." What saved Mansfield from becoming "a literary specialist in nervous disorders" was her ability to combine an openness to modern experiment with an appreciation of traditional craftsmanship, apparent in the vividness of her characterization and her discovery of a "new and necessary form."

Cowley's review of Mansfield, typical in its ambivalent approval, displays a characteristic early tendency to borrow musical terms and analogies for technical analysis—he recurrently spoke of "movements," "themes," "counterpoint," "harmony," "variations," and a "coda." His adoption of such terms derived in part from discussions with Burke, whose experiments with short stories based on theories of musical and geometrical form already anticipated his later method of "perspective by incongruity"; partly it derived from Cowley's appreciation of the musical effects in Conrad Aiken's verse. More important, his use of such terms signified an attempt to find a new critical vocabulary that was precise and lucid, yet could accommodate the more radical experiments in structure and form he found in much of modern writing. Employing such terms for critical analysis Cowley responded intuitively to a quality in modern writing that Edmund Wilson, following Poe and Valéry, singled out as one of the principal aims of a modernist, symbolist aesthetics: the attempt to approach in language the indefinite and suggestive quality of music.[39]

A similar use of musical analogy is evident in a review of Amy Lowell's *Legends*. In retelling and re-creating ancient legends, Cowley noted, Lowell had perfectly assimilated them to her own contemporary vision by writing "programme music" around the legends, by using them as "themes," and by adding "harmony and counterpoint and variations." In the process she bestowed upon them "all the prodigality of orchestral detail." Cowley, speaking of "lyrical interludes" and of "narrative interspersed with choruses," admitted that his search for such analogies was prompted by a troubling "deficiency in critical vocabulary." In the end, his reluctance to pass judgment on Lowell's verse bespoke a certain ambivalence about the possibility of literary art in America: "In a city of literary failures one mistrusts established reputations. I have come to believe that one's estimate of Miss Lowell is bound up with one's estimate of American poetry in general. The new and excellent qualities of our literature are abundantly represented in her work, as is also our national tendency to be ragged. We must wait till the indefinite time when American literature has been judged before judging her. She is, at any rate, one of the three graces or nine muses upon which our poetry stands or falls."[40]

Cowley's approach to modern literature in 1920 and 1921 was clearly far from systematic. Rather, he faced each new book as a new problem in practical criticism and in each instance groped to define his often impressionistic response to a new literary tendency. For the time being his attitude remained confused and ambivalent. The full confrontation with modernity was yet to come. Over the next few years Cowley's isolated and intuitive responses slowly crystallized into an attitude that, if it never reached the scope or profundity of a critical theory, yet held the germs of his future assumptions as a literary critic and historian.

‹ ‹ ‹   Between the daily drudgeries at Sweet's, the distractions of Village life, and the pressure of grinding out reviews, Cowley found little time to compose the poetry on which he put so high a premium. Only two of his poems reached print between August 1920 and December 1921, both in Canby's *Literary Review*. As time passed and Cowley found himself still struggling to preserve "the integrity of an undisturbed life," the dream of producing lasting work was counterbalanced by the nightmare of a wasted life. Several unpublished prose sketches reflecting his mood suggest that more than once he was afraid of frittering away what talents he possessed and of hardening into the mold of a middle-class existence. Other sketches radiate disgust with the atmosphere of drunken dissipation and sexual profligacy at Village parties, poker games and dances, or they envision the wastage of genuine artistic talent and moral character in the reactionary social and political climate of the Harding years.[41] Two poems Cowley was working on in May 1921—"For a Methodist Hymnal" and "Poem for Two Voices"—suggest that he dreaded a deadening of intellectual and emotional resources as long as he continued living in the margin of an uncongenial society, imprisoned in stunting routines, and cut off from the countryside. The latter poem, a musical counterpointing of two contradictory impulses in the poet, suggests that it was "too late now" to rediscover "the spring / that issues miraculously from the chestnut roots," since the poet was already so immersed in the alienating realities of urban-technological life that "the city turns / like awkward vast machinery in my head / like vast wheels turning in a void."[42]

Soon it became apparent that only a change in the conditions of his life could bring Cowley closer to the realization of his literary ideals—and France beckoned. In March 1921, helped by recommendations from his Harvard mentor John Livingston Lowes and former *Dial* editor Clarence Britten, Cowley was awarded an American Field Service Fellowship for a year of graduate study at the University of Montpellier in southern France. The fellowship consisted of twelve thousand francs (about one thousand dollars), including a fifty-percent reduction in cabin-class steamboat fares, and held the possibility of a one-year extension. On April 30, 1921, as an act of courtesy, he attended the Field Service's second annual reunion at the Hotel Pennsylvania in New York.[43]

Newly invigorated by the prospect of a year abroad, the Cowleys plunged into a frenzy of preparatory activity. On March 17, 1921, Peggy reported the good news to Foster Damon: "It will be wonderful for both of us. Malcolm hasn't had any time to write since we have been married, which has worried me considerably. Now he will have two whole years." Peggy on her part planned to resume painting and had hopes of an exhibition at a New York gallery.[44] In late April, in search of extra money to finance the venture, Cowley traveled to Cambridge to sell his piano and triumphantly deposited $250 in a Boston bank. He visited John Brooks Wheelwright, who promised to lend money, and he paid his respects to Amy Lowell. In early May she wrote to tell him she had much enjoyed his visit and had found her faith in his promise as a writer undiminished: "It seemed like old times. I feared that New York had changed you, but I found it had not, unless, perhaps, for the better. You are one of the people I count on for the future. See that you do not disappoint me." She expected him to meet her literary rival, Ezra Pound, and promised to announce his arrival in France to Jean Catel, professor at the University of Montpellier and American literature critic for the *Mercure de France*. Six weeks later she wrote again, agreeing to act as Cowley's literary agent for the duration of his stay in France. She reported that Scofield Thayer had expressed his enthusiasm about Cowley's criticism for the *Dial* and she urged him to continue his *Dial* reviews from France.[45]

Before his departure Cowley was prompted to put his friendships in order. In late May he wrote to Foster Damon, apologizing for allowing their friendship to lapse into silence, promising to make up for lost time and announcing his provisional date of departure: July 12. "The booze gets worse. People quarrel constantly. Gene O'Neill was in town and left. Dos Passos is en route for Constantinople. Scofield Thayer goes to Southern France. There will be a general European exodus in July." It was hard not to read such departures as confirmations of the rightness of his own plans. A month later he wrote again, hoping to see Damon before sailing and promising to set him up as a free-lance writer by introducing him to New York editors and advertising agencies—"I will give you $25 for one advertising poem—and make a profit of it."[46]

The prospect of a European adventure also appears to have had a stabilizing effect on the Cowleys' marriage. In late March, Peggy spoke of their domestic situation as "our quiet family life"; news of the recent separation of James and Susan Light elicited Cowley's comment that soon he and Peggy would "gain a reputation of being the only happily married couple in the universe." In early May he traveled to Pittsburgh to attend at the sickbed of his father, who was seriously ill—"death prognosticated"—and stayed on until his condition improved. It was Cowley's last visit home before sailing.[47]

Such compliments as Cowley had received from Amy Lowell and Scofield Thayer, while enhancing his confidence in his literary promise, did little to dispel a persistent mood of despondency. In one of his last communications with Burke before departing he confessed to being "unhappy." "I don't know what it is; it resembles more than anything else the *mal du siècle* of the Romantics. One gets up, putters around the house, putters around the office, putters around the house, goes to bed. . . . One tells a client professionally about a boom in building that one doesn't believe in—and while waiting for his reply wonders when the devil it is going to end. . . . I feel as if I were . . . dying at the top; nothing can save me now short of a new life."[48]

Caught up in a trivializing routine, Cowley felt increasingly low-spirited. In a culture devoted to consumerism and materialism his poetic gifts might easily be turned to a profit—the advertising manager of Moon-Glo Silk had solicited a poet's services and Cowley, recommended by the editors of the *Dial*, had bargained a thirty-five-dollar submission price and a hundred-dollar acceptance price for a brief poem—but the very ease of such cheapening of his talents only intensified his disgust. Finding little or no opportunity to seriously pursue his intellectual and artistic interests, Cowley could see no way out but to join the exodus of American writers and artists to Europe. In June he listed the names of Village friends and acquaintances who were either actual or prospective expatriates in a letter to Burke—Cummings, Dos Passos, Dorothy Day, Mary Reynolds had already left, soon to be followed by Djuna Barnes, William Slater Brown, Alfred Kreymborg, Scofield Thayer, Ivan Opffer, Harold Stearns, and countless others; even Joe Gould, he reflected, seemed likely to stop by in France to borrow money.[49]

Expatriation was in the air that spring and summer. The self-constituted leader of those seeking salvation abroad was Harold Stearns, a thirty-year-old journalist and a Village acquaintance of the Cowleys. Stearns had probed into the causes for the prevailing mood of cultural disaffection and had publicized his pessimistic findings in a flamboyant book, *America and the Young Intellectual* (1921). Faced with the repression and hypocrisy of a culture dominated by Prohibition, puritanism, and the machine, so Stearns argued in his title essay, the young intellectual could find no outlet in the national life for the "moral idealism" he possessed in such large measure. Asking himself "What *Can* a Young Man Do?," Stearns concluded that in the pursuit of literature and the arts the field was virtually "closed." There was but one solution for a young writer not content to resign to philistinism and provincialism: "Get Out!" and take ship to Europe, where "life can still be lived."[50]

On July 4, 1921, Stearns suited the act to the word and theatrically embarked for France, there to pursue the vigorous intellectual life he found lacking in his homeland. Shortly before his well-publicized departure he finished editing *Civilization in the United States*, a symposium by thirty prominent American intellectuals—including Lewis Mumford, H. L. Mencken, Robert Morss Lovett, J. E. Spingarn, Van Wyck Brooks, Conrad Aiken, Walter Pach, George Jean Nathan, George Soule, and Ernest Boyd—that was published in 1922. A sweeping and near-unanimous indictment of the whole of American culture, it aimed at a critical examination ("without sentimentality and without fear") of American civilization. Stearns's contributions set the tone. America, he maintained, suffered from "emotional and aesthetic starvation"; it was plagued by "intellectual anaemia or torpor." Art had either lost out to the pursuit of materialism, or it had become "an instrument of moral reform" in the custody of "women." There was no opportunity for a *"disinterested"* intellectual life, nor were American intellectuals sustained by an institutional structure. As a result, intellectuals were forced into "individualistic isolation" and eccentricity, divorced from the national life and left *"déraciné."* [51]

Van Wyck Brooks's contribution, "The Literary Life," was a continuation and partial restatement of the critique of American culture he had expounded in *America's Coming-of-Age* (1915) and in subsequent essays for the *Seven Arts*, where he had criticized the thwarting effects of an exploitative and acquisitive materialism on the spiritual life, lamented the withering of artistic talent in infertile soil, and pleaded for a new leadership in letters. Surveying the last fifty years of American literary history, Brooks was disturbed by "the singular impotence of its creative spirit" and drew a bleak conclusion: "The blighted career, the arrested career, the diverted career are, with us, the rule. The chronic state of our literature is that of a youthful promise which is never redeemed." [52]

Cowley had had firsthand experience of what Brooks had denounced as the "failure" of American culture to offer to the artist a sustaining milieu, but he did not share the mood of pessimism and skepticism that radiated from this collective indictment by his intellectual elders. Their disillusionment with America, after all, largely emerged from a prewar cultural idealism—the hope of a "new republic" and the fulfillment of "the promise of American life"—that was never properly entertained by Cowley and his coevals. In *Exile's Return*, Cowley treated their symposium with ironic condescension; from his 1934 perspective he was impressed by the "limited vision" of the participants, found them "ridiculously ignorant" of the interests of his own age group, and "weak and discordant" in what remedies and solutions they proposed. Stearns was presented rather ironically as a reincarnation of "Alexander marching into Persia and Byron shaking the dust of England from his feet." [53]

In 1921 Cowley was not ready to make Stearns's kind of sweeping indictment of American life. If he went abroad in part out of impatience with the reactionary moral, social, and political climate of the Harding years, he did so less as an act of cultural repudiation than as a rebellious search for positives. As he later was to write, he left America less out of a feeling of being "driven into exile" than as a seeker for a more congenial "spiritual home." He engaged in his European venture less in a mood of disillusionment than in a spirit of youthful energy and gusto. [54]

Like Matthew Josephson, who embarked in September, Cowley went to Europe first of all to expand his personal and literary horizons and to extend his apprenticeship as a writer. His last year in Greenwich Village had convinced him that life in New York offered inadequate opportunities to do serious work and to develop his talents and abilities. France held out the promise of a greater hospitality to the arts, congenial working conditions, and freedom to pursue his literary education. The French, it seemed, had always treated writers and artists deferentially, no matter how eccentric or unorthodox, and regarded them as "useful members of the commonwealth." France, moreover, beckoned as an international center of culture where one could profit from the stimulus of interaction and communication with fellow artists. Paris, in the words of Ezra Pound, was the "intellectual and artistic vortex" that was such a lamentable deficiency in American culture. [55]

From New York, Cowley had been able to keep up with literary developments in France through such reports as Pound's "Paris Letter" for the *Dial*.[56] Moreover, Cowley and his literary friends were faithful readers of current French literary periodicals like the *Mercure de France* and the *Nouvelle Revue Française*, in which they had followed the quarrels between diverse schools and coteries in literary France and received the impression of "a great intellectual ferment in Paris." [57] More important, in France the spirit of Gustave Flaubert and Remy de Gourmont seemed still alive, promising a life of artistic integrity and an uncompromising search for perfection. As Cowley observed in *Exile's Return*, "France was the birthplace of our creed. It was in France that poets had labored for days over a single stanza, while bailiffs hammered at the door; in France that novelists like Gourmont had lived as anchorites, while imagining seduction more

golden and mistresses more harmoniously yielding than life could ever re-
produce; in France that Flaubert had described the quaint mania of passing
one's life wearing oneself out over words, and had transformed the mania
into a religion." [58]

Indifferent, for the time being, to social and political purposes, Cowley
sought in France both an artistic method and a way of life, hoping through
art to find an ethics of the literary life. For Cowley, as for Josephson, the
application of formalist, aesthetic standards to art was to be carried over
into life; both sought fulfillment through cultivating an aesthetic ideal. [59]
Since such an attitude carried all the moral, social, and spiritual implications of a "religion," moving from personal and aesthetic issues to larger
cultural and societal concerns was ultimately only a logical continuation of
such a search. Embarking for France in search of personal values, Cowley
might hope to return with a set of ideals that had applicability beyond the
personal. He might hope to carry home an understanding of new ways to
integrate the American writer into the very social and cultural ambience
he was now so anxious to leave. On July 8, 1921, a few days after the
spectacular departure of Harold Stearns, with most of his friends either
abroad or about to follow, Cowley and his wife unobtrusively joined the
artists, intellectuals, and writers who went "streaming up the longest gang-
plank in the world," part of "a great migration eastward into new prairies
of the mind," embarked on what he later felt was "almost a pilgrimage to
Holy Land." [60]

8

Pilgrimage to Holy Land

France, 1921–1922

The two years Malcolm Cowley spent in France, from the summer of 1921 to the summer of 1923, were years of literary fermentation and intellectual ripening that helped to clarify his attitudes and crystallize his ideas. In part, France was to Cowley what it was to Ezra Pound: a "laboratory of ideas," a place where "poisons can be tested, new modes of sanity discovered." Not only did it seem, as Gertrude Stein was to say, that "Paris was where the twentieth century was"; also, in the early 1920s, it was possible to believe that Paris stood fair to become "the intellectual capital of the United States." For Cowley as for Gertrude Stein, France functioned as a necessary "second" country, one that helped him to understand the nature and extent of his allegiance to American culture. Unlike Stein's, Cowley's expatriation was never meant to be permanent; strictly speaking he never was an "exile." Financially, culturally, and intellectually, he remained dependent upon American sources. Paradoxically, but not uncommonly, his foreign venture enhanced his perspective on America, led to a revaluation of the aesthetic potential inherent in his native culture, and prompted him to redefine his role as an American writer.[1]

Cowley's French venture proved an "ambiguous encounter." Innocently expecting to find the France of Gustave Flaubert and Remy de Gourmont, Cowley was confronted with a "mad steeple-chase" of quarreling factions and exposed to "the feverish intellectual development of half a century" in a fraction of that time.[2] It was in France that Cowley encountered the modern spirit in all its various and contradictory manifestations. His response to the complex literary situation in contemporary France revealed the paradoxes in his literary thinking, sharpened the ambiguity of his reaction to modernism, and brought out the contradictory elements in his personality.

Cowley felt relieved to have escaped New York. He knew that his disenchanting experiences in Greenwich Village had taken their toll and demanded to be digested if he ever was to do serious writing again. To Burke he wrote: "I really should sum up New York for myself if I want to kill it in my mind, otherwise it will live on like Harvard. And it was a much more unpleasant experience than Harvard College and needs more definite punctuation." Resolved to put the recent past behind him, he planned to "embalm" his New York impressions in a story and projected a poem as a "summing up of my adolescence." After New York he needed an intermezzo of "absolute idleness" to restore his emotional equilibrium and revive his intellectual resiliency. In effect his first five months in France were a time of adjustment and recuperation, in which his productivity was at a fairly low ebb. Three months after leaving America he confessed to John Brooks Wheelwright that "after another year of New York I should have been ready to saw off the part of me above the bridge of the nose and bury it." At the end of November he was still plagued by painful memories of New York and admitted to Burke the period had left him emotionally and intellectually drained: "I see very clearly that my eighteen months in New York were as effective as eighteen enemas. They cleaned me out." As late as September 1922 he complained that his time in the Village "played hell with me. I still haven't digested it." [3] Eventually Cowley's time in France proved most fertile; under its impact he published over thirty poems and developed along lines that left permanent traces on his literary and intellectual outlook.

On board the *Niagara*, a second-class steamer of the French Line, the economic advantages of a temporary removal to a France in the grip of postwar inflation were already apparent. For as little as $125, Cowley wrote from the ship, one enjoyed the privilege of becoming "one of the 86 aristocrats of the vessel," a privilege that included five-course luncheons and six-course dinners, with wine, cigars, and cognac, at prices unheard of in New York. Even during the crossing Cowley could feel Paris beckoning with the promise of opportunity in art and life. To express his exhilaration he vaguely planned a story on the course of a ship that never touched land but always pushed its bow into "new seas." [4] In retrospect Cowley described the mythical lure of Paris as that of a contemporary Olympus, the place where one could meet the entire "pantheon" of modern artists worshiped by the younger generation—James Joyce, Gertrude Stein, Picasso, Brancusi, Matisse, Pound, Valéry, Gide, and Stravinsky. [5] The immediate reality of Paris, however, proved different. For the moment it seemed as if Cowley had been transported back to rather than away from Greenwich Village. Arriving from Le Havre in a hot Paris on July 19 he made his way to La Rotonde, right in "the heart and nervous system" of American expatriate activity. There he found the painter Marsden Hartley; Djuna Barnes, future author of *Nightwood*; Arthur B. Moss, onetime editor of the Greenwich Village *Quill*; Percy Winner, a Village friend of Matthew Josephson's; Edna St. Vincent Millay; and, he told Foster Damon, "seemingly, everyone else who had ever got drunk at the Provincetown Players. We fled." Paris, indeed, seemed to harbor the same atmosphere of artistic pretense, moral abandon, and sexual profligacy he had reacted against in New York, and Cowley was dismayed to find the city a mere extension of Village bohemia. "It is hard to describe to you the Brevoortness, the O'Connorness of the Dome and the Rotonde," he wrote to Burke; only the names of the bartenders seemed changed. At a recent soirée he had met Sinclair Lewis and Robert McAlmon, later an influential publisher of American expatriate writers, and had reestablished contact with Mina Loy, a poet friend of Djuna Barnes and a former Village cohort of the Cowleys, Royall Snow, Lorimer Hammond, a colleague from Sweet's, and Harold Stearns. Lewis, Cowley told Burke, talked just like the characters in his novels, "only it is better in conversation. It is Middle West, with a twist. Sometimes he forgets the twist." Stearns, who "kept calling for a whore, kept protesting that he was too bashful to speak to one," already seemed bent upon the self-defeating life of dissipation, café sitting, and selling tips on racehorses to American tourists that made him the pantaloon among more serious American expatriates.[6]

If there were times when Cowley plunged headlong into the Montparnassian café life (one party, he told Burke, had ended at five o'clock with onion soup at Les Halles), his initial response to Left Bank expatriate activity was to take refuge from the "artiness" he found there and to seek an opportunity to lead the serious life of a self-respecting professional writer. His reaction showed that he approached the writer's vocation with the strenuous work ethic, the moral discipline, and the intense ambitiousness that marked the careers of the great writers of his generation.[7]

Apart from the American colony at Montparnasse the Cowleys found Paris "quite as charming as the guidebooks." They visited museums, paid their respects to Ezra Pound, were impressed by the vital spirit of French history in contemporary Paris, and made a trip into the French countryside to visit their Village friend Jim Butler in Giverny, an artists' village on the Norman border some fifty miles west of Paris.[8]

Stimulated by a new environment, Cowley was eager to get to work. "Let us begin the Renaissance," he exhorted himself one afternoon in Paris. Searching for "a new path" to follow in fiction, he drew up a prospectus for a story based on the long journey from New York to Paris. It was to embalm Cowley's impressions of the "noise, bustle, hysteria" of Manhattan, the city of the "living dead," and, surrendering realism to phantasmagoria, would encompass the account of a fabulous trip "in search of other stars." Cowley expanded its last part into a full-length story and submitted it to Art Moss for publication in *Gargoyle*, the "improved Paris edition" of the Village *Quill*. "The Journey to Paris" was partly intended as "an amusing satirical voyage, on the order of Dean Swift." It aimed to parody Burke's Freudian fictional experiments as well as John Brooks Wheelwright's "passion for arbitrary and non-sensical events." Foremost, however, "The Journey to Paris" was an imaginative enactment of Cowley's personal hopes for a magnificent French venture. It described a Gulliver-like voyage through a surreal seascape, past islands harboring exotic cultures, all the way to Paris, the ultimate city of magic.[9]

In mid-August, after a month in Paris, the Cowleys traveled south to Dijon and stayed six weeks before passing on to Montpellier. Sauntering over the city's medieval cobblestones, they relished the historical splendor of Dijon, the old capital of the dukedom of Burgundy; its ancient glory was still palpable among the royal palaces and costly churches. Boarding with a French family, M. and Mme. Lachat, Cowley hoped to settle down to serious work and to make good the promise of an oncoming "renaissance." For the time being, however, he found that his "muse" was "tethered." Historically interesting, Dijon yet was dull after the social gaiety of Paris. In Dijon, Cowley told Wheelwright, "our family Wrote and Painted. . . . There's a lot of Architecture, but one can't drink Architecture. There are a lot of excellent drinks, but no company in which to consume them."[10] Accordingly, he corrected and revised old poems, finished his story for Art Moss, and wrote a potboiling article on American trade in Dijon, which he asked Burke to sell for him to *Export Trade*. He also composed three satirical odes—on Harold Stearns, Ezra Pound, and Sinclair Lewis— reflecting the ironic bemusement with which he had recently observed American expatriates in Paris. He sent the poems to Henry Seidel Canby, who published them in the *Literary Review of the New York Evening Post* in January 1922.[11]

The most important offshoot of Cowley's six weeks in Dijon was an article printed on the front page of Canby's *Literary Review* on October 15, 1921. "This Youngest Generation," Cowley's first full-fledged literary essay on a self-chosen subject, marked his first formal performance as the champion and chronicler of his literary age-group. For the first time, a critic was making a concerted effort to define the nebulous ideas and aesthetic assumptions of the generation that had come to maturity in the wake of World War I. Part of the article's boldness, indeed, apart from its contention that such a generation existed, lay in its claim to future stature for a group of writers who were as yet largely unrecognized and who were yet to publish their most substantial work. But the article also signified an act of personal stocktaking, undertaken at a moment of transition, when the impact of the new cultural climate was yet unfelt but when New York already seemed "centuries away." [12] The article brought to a focus the disparate elements in Cowley's development to date. He used them synecdochically in a manner anticipating *Exile's Return* and combined them into a composite picture of the ideas of his coevals.

Cowley's understanding of what he had passed through and rejected was more precise than his awareness of where he wanted to go. Looking for the distinctive traits of generational cohesion, he pointed out that the younger writers did not share the social concern and reformist idealism of their "elder cousins." They were out of sympathy with "the belated revolt of the Georgians," and they spurned causes like feminism, Freudianism, and communism. In an ironic resumé of his own apprentice years Cowley drew up a "fever chart" of the literary childhood diseases of a representative member of his generation:

At sixteen he contracts his first bad case of Chesterton, complicated within three months by Oscar Wilde. Temperature, 105; pulse, very rapid. Before he recovers he is overwhelmed, first by Shaw, then by Schnitzler, and, finally, by the dramatic criticism of George Jean Nathan. Seventeen is the age of sophistication; he is older at seventeen than at any other time before fifty. He reads the *Smart Set*. He is trapped by H. L. Mencken into reading Hugh Walpole, and so is conducted into the whole world of Georgian novelists. The period that follows is one of subnormal temperatures; it is ended disastrously by a new fever of ecstaticism under the influence of Arthur Machen. Shortly afterwards he learns to read French and a new world opens before him. His temperature does not return to normal . . . till he has dipped into Freud and Marx. . . .

On the positive side Cowley credited his generation with "more respect, if not reverence, for the work of the past," in particular the "modern" past of the Elizabethan dramatists, French classical drama, and the satirical humanism of Swift and Defoe. It exemplified a clear "progression away from London" and a pronounced interest in avant-garde French writing. In the latter, Cowley acknowledged, his generation was less in revolt against, than carrying forward, a tendency initiated by its immediate elders: Lowell, Pound, and Eliot. "Pupils" of Flaubert and de Gourmont, the younger writers rejected an "inchoate" Dreiserian naturalism, displaying instead "a new interest in form" and a high respect for literary craftsmanship. Their aesthetic "catchwords" were "form, simplification, strangeness, respect for literature as an art with traditions, abstractness": ideals rooted in a French rather than an English tradition. His generation was lucky in being spared the fatal misfortune of American writers in the past: the lack of "a definite and receptive public." For creating such an audience it owed much to the very writers—Mencken, Dreiser—against whom it was revolting. In an effort to name the individuals composing "this youngest generation," Cowley trod carefully, singling out those among his literary friends who showed the most promise and had achieved publication, however modest: John Dos Passos, E. E. Cummings, William Slater Brown, S. Foster Damon, and Kenneth Burke.[13]

"This Youngest Generation" was an astute, if in places flippant and naive, inventory of the aesthetic assumptions of Cowley's literary consorts. Conspicuously, Cowley refrained from discussing his personal aesthetics and underplayed the nascent misgivings about the modernist creed he had exemplified in his reviews for the *Dial*. As such, the essay pointed up the uncertainty of Cowley's own aesthetic direction. With implicit self-reference, he acknowledged that "the coquetting of a young writer with various literary movements is of little value unless they cancel each other off, thus leaving room for the development of his individual talents." Defining the aesthetic contours of an age group, Cowley yet strongly stressed the individualism of each member, emphasizing idiosyncracy and diversity within a loosely generational framework. If there were "common habits of thought," there was "no solidarity" among its individual components, nor was there an intellectual or social focal point in the form of an "official magazine" or a "semi-official café or tearoom"; his was "a generation without a school and without a manifesto." Though such remarks might easily be (and would soon be) construed as pleas for the very creation of such a school, magazine, or manifesto, Cowley was in effect resisting the evolvement of any coterie or group spirit. His essay exemplified an early wariness of being pressed into an intellectual or literary framework. In part because he knew how easily he was inclined "to take color from [his] surroundings," Cowley was cautious to safeguard a free and independent development of his talents.[14]

It was not until he came to write *Exile's Return* that Cowley more precisely grasped the social and political implications of the aesthetic preferences of his age group. Also, in 1921 Cowley did not seem to realize that his coevals' new respect for literature as "an art with traditions" did not yet extend to their own native culture. In this respect he unknowingly revealed how thoroughly he shared, at least for the time being, what Alfred Kazin has described as his generation's "detachment from the native traditions." It was, indeed, not long after finishing his essay that Cowley complained to Burke of feeling "out of contact with my own traditions." His sense of cultural alienation, however, was never particularly traumatic; in effect, soon after departing from America he became conscious of the "urn of native soil" in his cultural baggage.[15]

By early October the Cowleys were established in Montpellier, where for 120 francs a month they rented a three-room apartment at the Villa Marcel, with cooking facilities, a tiled floor, and buff wallpaper. Situated at a twenty-minute distance from the Mediterranean, Montpellier was a quiet, provincial university town, surrounded by the timeless classical beauty of a stark subtropical landscape. "All the forms of the landscape are different from those of the North," Cowley observed to Damon; "there are rocks everywhere, grey in the sun. The trees are twisted: stone pines, cedars of Lebanon, olives, ilexes—or else they are neatly tailored cypresses. The villas have sloping roofs of red tile. . . . Blue sky, blue sea—as advertised. Grey olive trees, grey rocks, feathery grey pines. Everything very hard and unreal in the sunlight." The town itself seemed to breathe the classical spirit of the landscape. It was composed of "a mass of little streets, the width of one's outstretched arms, that climb tortuously up a hill. Occasionally they open out into a formal square, with palm trees and sycamores and a fountain, always with two swans. Or there will be an equestrian statue of Louis XIV, dressed as a Noble Roman." [16]

In Montpellier the Cowleys settled down to a calm, domestic life of regular work, study, and unpretentious diversion. "Since one can't run up to Paris for the week-end, one takes one's enjoyment at home," Cowley wrote somewhat wistfully to Wheelwright in October. "We have been going to the movies once a week," Peggy added in a letter of her own; "I spend the majority of my time doing housework, tending my flowers and painting. . . . My French is abominable. . . . Malcolm is writing little or nothing. . . . I get sore once in a while about it, but actually don't think it is anything but a long relaxation after New York." At times, indeed, Montpellier was too quiet for Cowley's convivial tastes and he found himself thinking with "faint regrets" about New York. He missed his friends and urged Wheelwright to look up Burke, whom he thought would be lonely "with nothing to occupy him but his feuds." At other times the university ambience triggered nostalgic memories of Harvard. For the moment, indeed, Cowley found himself transported back to the uncluttered freedom he had known in high school and at college. Undecided about what courses to take, he found the curriculum open to foreigners "a mixture of erudition and puerility." For ten days he was wrapped up in the Tenth Congress of the National Union of the Associations of French Students, to which he acted as an American delegate. Carrying a big American flag, he seemed back in more frivolous student days; if his snobbishness had worn thin, he still liked to pose and playact. "I sympathize with the French in their dislike for Britishers and swear the eternal amity of America. They know enough not to take things too seriously, whereby the game becomes amusing." [17]

Cowley remained eager to establish his name as a critic and poet. In September he urged Burke to keep him informed of the latest changes in the literary markets in New York. From Dijon he sent a "consignment of merchandise," a batch of twenty-four corrected poems, to Amy Lowell and anxiously requested her criticism: "Some of [the poems] have passed through a metamorphosis that would strain even Ovid's imagination. About the result I am very much in doubt. I, who have criticized so much, am myself much in need of a critic." The first results of Lowell's efforts at salesmanship were discouraging. On October 14 James Sibley Watson of the *Dial* told Cowley that he had returned his poem "Day

Coach" to Lowell, but had asked her to send in another selection of Cowley's verse. Two weeks later Lowell reported that she had mailed nine of Cowley's poems to the *Dial*, adding that she did not have much hope of placing many of them—most magazines, she thought, would consider them too free or unorthodox. Lowell perceptively diagnosed a characteristic weakness of Cowley's verse. Too many of his poems, she said, were "dangerously like prose" and "not quite rhythmical enough." She offered practical criticism and concluded that what Cowley most needed to learn was the skill of "teasing a poem up, and then teasing it up some more, until [he had] wrung the final essence out of it, all the subject will bear and all its implications." [18]

Cowley was disturbed by Lowell's well-considered critique. As he confessed to Foster Damon, he found it difficult to defend himself against the charge of carelessness, since he was consciously writing "on the border of free forms." In early December he defended his poetic practice to Lowell, explaining that his loose and irregular rhythms were due to an affinity with French rather than English prosody: "To tell the truth, the meters that sing themselves in my head are rather against the traditions of English poetry. Since Coleridge, trimeter and tetrameter have been extremely free measures, but in pentameter there has always been a tendency to count the syllables. . . . the only other modern poet I can point to who uses the crowded and irregular pentameter is D. H. Lawrence. Perhaps that is why his verse has always fascinated me." [19]

At the end of November, Lowell informed Cowley that she had sold "Mountain Valley" to the *Dial* for ten dollars. It was his first poem to be accepted by Thayer and Watson, and one of several poems marketed from France in which Cowley returned to the Pennsylvania farming country of his childhood. The poem illuminated Lowell's criticism as well as Cowley's apologia:

> Lost in this mountain valley, we have struggled
> Too long for bread. Here corn grows sparse and yellow.
> The valley is too narrow, and we have driven
> Our ploughs vainly against the flanks of the hill.
>
> There is no more use in struggling, O my brothers;
> Let us lie down together here and rest.

Some day when the crust of the earth has grown as cold
As the dead craters of the moon, these hills will wrinkle
Like the wrinkles on a forehead; they will draw
Together like a finger and a wrinkled thumb,
Squeezing the valley between them, and there will be
For us magnificent sepulture, O my kin.

Already the hills lie
Staring down at our cornfields covetously.

The sale of a poem about which Cowley had private reservations provoked cynical reflections about the relationship between literary merit and the principles governing the literary marketplace. To Burke he remarked that an ironic side effect of expatriation to the French provinces was that it gave one enhanced literary standing in New York. "It is the duty of any writer who wishes to sell himself to this age to travel three thousand miles away from it," he pontificated in a spirit of mockery.[20]

Cowley's speculations were fed in part by his recent experiences with *Broom*, a new international magazine of avant-garde art, which had been launched, shortly before, in New York by Harold Loeb and Alfred Kreymborg, the poet who had edited *Glebe* and *Others*. The editors soon decided to publish the magazine from Rome, where printing costs were lowest, while maintaining a New York office presided over by Nathaniel Shaw and later by Lola Ridge and Edward Storer.[21] Cowley had been aware of the new venture before his departure for France. He had urged Burke to contribute to the magazine and had offered to submit several of his manuscripts to Kreymborg, whose departure for Europe roughly coincided with his own. In late September Kreymborg informed Cowley from Rome that *Broom* had accepted "Château de Soupir: 1917" and was eager for more. Cowley promptly sent in a "modern, complete, and up-to-date version" of the poem, which appeared in *Broom*'s third issue. Kreymborg rejected three of Burke's stories, however, thereby confirming Cowley's impression that removal to foreign parts improved a writer's market value. Acting as Burke's European agent, Cowley negotiated with Kreymborg about his friend's contributions and sent Burke a letter of encouragement, in which he speculated on the mechanics of engineering a reputation for the "youngest generation": "Unrecognized genius is a commodity which does not exist in America. Our great problem is rather to be geniuses and to continue to be geniuses after forty. . . . The critics have proclaimed—until they now believe it themselves—that we are in the midst of a renaissance. And having proclaimed the renaissance they look busily around—like you and me—for the other half of this youngest generation. You are one of the few young American writers who writes. You cannot long be overlooked."[22]

In late September, Kreymborg sent Cowley the first issue of *Broom*, dated November 1921, for comment. Despite its homely title, the new magazine was lavish in appearance and extravagant in size. Its exterior, indeed, was "the best yet," Cowley observed to Foster Damon. The contents, however, were disappointing. In a "manifesto" written by Kreymborg, the editors promised to publish the best of contemporary writing, painting and sculpture—from Continental Europe as well as England and America— and to give "the unknown, pathbreaking artist . . . at least an equal chance with the artist of acknowledged reputation."[23] Kreymborg and Loeb, however, appeared to have fallen for those among a slightly older generation who had attained some national or international reputation. Moreover, there was little sign of an editorial policy that could distinguish *Broom* from other magazines devoted to the American and European avant-garde, notably the *Dial*. Cowley's response was tepid at best. The prose in *Broom*'s debut, he reported to Foster Damon, seemed "a weak edition of the Dial," the art was "very modern" and the poetry "not bad." But the issue as a whole lacked potency: "there was no wad shot." To a young writer in search of personal values, *Broom*'s undistinguished eclecticism failed to make good the promise of a radical clean sweep implied in its title.[24]

For the time being, Cowley remained nebulous in his literary thinking. In a letter to Burke he admitted he felt "vague about the aims of literature and the worth of modern literature. Vague about politics. Vague, more especially, about my own intentions in art and life." At the end of October he complained that he had been "alarmingly empty-headed" since his arrival in the Midi. In his mood of discouragement and self-deprecation he was inclined, as often, to seek refuge in nostalgia and to dream of pastoral trout-fishing moments in Cambria County, much in the way Hemingway dreamed of the piney woods of Northern Michigan from a table at the Closerie des Lilas. On October 27 Cowley sent Burke a first draft of "The Willow Branch."

> From the bulk of it,
> From the green fields stretching against the sky, from the

immense white sunlight beating down on them,
I have hidden myself away, under the green water
Where silver fishes nibbled at my thighs:
I can imagine them saying:
We have swum upstream for three days and three nights,
We have proceeded downstream for three days with the current,
Never could we find an end to the world;
It is shaped like a willow branch, but no one can swim to
    the tip of it.

The fishes hid away beneath a stone.

For the rest, however, the rumors of an oncoming poetic renaissance he had detected at Dijon proved "false." Once in Montpellier, he "reached down into the void and found it was infinite." He had no intellectual concepts to measure against Burke's and could do nothing but surrender to a mental state of "undelicious idleness and chaos." His only piece of writing was "a very mediocre article" on the Rabelais fêtes held in Montpellier on November 6, 1921, at which a monument to the great satirical humanist of the French Renaissance, a sculpture by Jacques Villeneuve, was unveiled by the French president; Cowley duly reported on the event and the concomitant festivities for the *New York Tribune.* By the end of November his despondency seemed to have touched bottom. Eager to break out of a self-imposed insulation, he sought out Jean Catel, of the *Mercure de France,* and began making the acquaintance of the local poets, artists, journalists, and intellectuals. He followed French politics from a distance and every morning read of the legislative debates in the French Parliament. In a letter to Burke he gave his spectatorial impressions of cultural and intellectual life in the Midi provinces: "Provincial towns are the same everywhere. The Midi hates Paris and is determined to prove that the intellectual center of France is south of the Loire. For which reason people here are aggressively intellectual. . . . They write for a literary paper published in Montpellier, which tries to patronize Picabia and Tristan Tzara equally. It is sanely progressive—you know, like Harriet Monroe. People do little sketches in Provençal or Languedoc or Catalan, and innumerable woodcuts. 'Go to Paris and you gain wit in losing your own.' But if they were a little richer, they would go to Paris."[25]

An unexpected companion in Montpellier was Stewart Mitchell, who had been editor in chief of the *Harvard Monthly,* had contributed to *Eight*

Harvard Poets in 1917, and three years later had become managing editor of the *Dial*. Like Cowley he was at Montpellier for a year of study but came "chaperoned" by his aunt, with whom he resided in the best local hotel. In Montpellier, Mitchell, a homosexual, lived a disciplined, rather ascetic life, which earned him Cowley's mild derision. Mitchell's poetry was too "austere" for Cowley's taste; it lacked visual concreteness and had "nothing to do with people." He liked Mitchell's personality better than his verse, even though he found him "weak and luxurious" and already sensed in him a tremendous strain: "American. Nice boy. Suicide."[26]

Much of Cowley's time in Montpellier was taken up by "the mysteries of French pedagogy": he attended sixteen to eighteen classes a week, wrote numerous French themes, studied French grammar and pronunciation and read such French classical authors as Corneille, Molière, Racine, and Boileau. His academic schedule was aimed at an early March examination, after which he planned to complete a *thèse de doctorat*, a project he hoped to turn to personal literary advantage. Already he was thinking of remaining in France for a second year, finances permitting. For the moment, his hopes were justifiably high: chances seemed bright of having his Field Service fellowship renewed and everything he had written in France since the summer had sold well. With poems and articles in *Broom*, the *Dial*, the *Literary Review*, and the *New York Tribune*, with occasional articles and interviews for *Export Trade*, and with the writing of advertising poems, Cowley's works during his first half year in France earned him all of $227.50. "My problem seems rather to write the stuff than to sell it," he told Burke. Finances remained precarious, however, and the Cowleys had to live cautiously and sparsely throughout their stay in France.[27]

After half a year in France Cowley finally felt he had shed New York; the city had now "sunk so far below the horizon that, if I wished to write a story about it, I should have to begin by documenting myself." The calm provinciality of Montpellier, unlike the snobbish milieu of Harvard, relieved Cowley of social insecurity and allowed him to feel his natural self. He no longer sported a cane, he repudiated exotic liqueurs, and he dressed simply and soberly: "very few affectations. . . . I think I am very near to my natural." Ten days later he added: "Six months more of New York and I should have been fifty, but in this calm Protestant town I begin to drop my factitious years."[28]

Entrenched in the provincial quietude of Montpellier, Cowley seemed worlds removed from the literary ferment of cosmopolitan Paris. Geographical distance, however, allowed him to maintain a skeptical distance from the vicissitudes of the American expatriate colony and the internecine warfare of French literary coteries and gave him an opportunity for independent thought and study. The beneficial effect of a relative detachment from Paris's tempestuous literary life was confirmed by a letter Cowley received from Matthew Josephson in early December. Josephson had arrived in Paris in late October and immersed himself headlong in the literary excitements of the city. He consorted with the crowds of expatriates gathered about the Montparnasse cafés and made concerted efforts to meet the young French writers: Tristan Tzara, André Breton, Philippe Soupault, and Louis Aragon. In early December, Josephson ecstatically described his newfound literary consorts to Cowley: "we have decided to attach ourselves to the Dadaists, of whom thrills may be wrested at the lowest cost. . . . My claim is that these young men, when they break away from the rubbish of Dada will be the big writers of the next decade. They are working at more or less the same problems that we are, although they abjure technique, and accuse each other in turn of toadying to the Academy. . . . I find it all very stimulating." [29]

But while Josephson was falling under the spell of dadaism, Cowley's literary thought went in an opposite direction. From late October 1921 Cowley's studies in French literature and history began to have a noticeable effect on his intellectual outlook and his attitude toward modern art. Under the impact of his readings of seventeenth-century French dramatists, Cowley was increasingly drawn into the orbit of French classicism. Realizing that he was "one of those people who need a tradition to work in, who need (a) a form and (b) an audience before they can write," he found a critical foothold in the aesthetics of French classicism and the practical conventions of its theater. The appeal of classicism was particularly strong in the winter and spring of 1922. Its attraction was neither surprising nor unprecedented. In the early months of 1918 Cowley had already meditated the establishment of a "new classicism" based on his readings of Pope. Over the years his aesthetic preferences had further evolved in the direction of the classical virtues of clarity, elegance, and precision. His discovery of French classicism was, in effect, less the adoption of a new aesthetics than a logical outgrowth of literary preferences and intuitions deeply ingrained in his sensibility. As late as 1967 Cowley still spoke of himself, in a letter to Robert Penn Warren, as "a bloody old classicist." [30]

In the winter of 1922 Cowley began to draw up aesthetic maxims of his own, but he had trouble defining his subject clearly: the "laws" of his aesthetics still remained "in the air." He knew, however, that he was growing wary of theories of disinterested aestheticism and denounced as "dangerous" Arthur Machen's "theory of ecstasy." Instead, he had recently attended a performance of Molière's *Tartuffe* by the Comédie Française and had found the play "an utter delight." A month later he observed in a similar spirit: "I think nothing so beautiful at present as a play by Racine."[31]

Cowley's attempts to formulate a personal philosophy of art were unpretentious and hardly methodical, less the building of a theory than the articulation of an attitude. "Without the ambition of Aristotle, I try to arrive at a formula which will at least satisfy me," he had written to Burke in the fall of 1921. "A focus is what I want," he observed in January 1922. "I want standards, common principles, a certain amount of common knowledge without which a classical literature cannot exist." Rather than toward Pope, he was now drawn toward the aesthetic maxims of Nicolas Boileau-Despréaux (1636–1711).[32] Boileau's *Art Poétique (The Art of Poetry)* admirably filled Cowley's earlier demand for a textbook of "practical poetics"; its pragmatic and rational humanism was surprisingly congenial. In early December, Cowley had snapped up a secondhand edition of Boileau and in a letter copied out those aesthetic maxims that he felt still had contemporary relevance. Rather than adopting Boileau's aesthetics for his own, Cowley empathized with many of his attitudes. In canto 1 of *L'Art Poétique*, Boileau emphasized "the light of reason," precision of style, and control of diction; he spoke of clarity of thought as a preliminary for clarity of expression and voiced his distrust of excessive originality. He expounded his belief in "the power of a word set in the right place," exemplified an overriding "reverence for language," admired "elegant playfulness" and "fine cadence" in verse, and admonished writers to revise and polish ceaselessly, to be open to criticism, and to "be simple but with artistry; be great without pride, agreeable without artificiality."[33]

Cowley found much in Boileau that suited his purposes and that also might serve the larger cause of contemporary letters. To Burke he defended Boileau as the eminent theoretician of the circle of Molière, Racine, and LaFontaine, and argued that "the first two pages of the Art Poétique would make a telling criticism of—let us say—D. H. Lawrence. His watchwords were Truth, Nature, Good Sense. We are changing all those watchwords, but we have to think carefully before denying them, and Boileau makes one think." Cowley, indeed, felt a remarkable affinity, temperamental as much as aesthetic, with the writers of Boileau's time, with their high-minded seriousness and their liking for satire, invective, and vulgarity: "I feel at home in the seventeenth century, as if I had just been introduced to a very pleasant company of very kindred minds. The two sides of it: the grand tragedies in which one could use only noble words, and the low comedies in which one could say anything; there are two waterproof compartments in my mind like that, and I have always felt ashamed of their existence. How regally I should have licked King Louis' ass, meanwhile composing the satire for publication after his death."[34]

In early January 1922, stimulated by his readings of Boileau, Cowley began a series of notebook investigations of contemporary aesthetics. His observations reflect the uncertainty of a young critical mind in search of a literary focus. Faced with an overwhelming array of modern styles, a kaleidoscopic variety of aesthetic theories and a highly fragmented literary landscape, Cowley struggled to find his own path in the labyrinth of modernism. As much as a systematic investigation of his own mind, his efforts, from the first, typically took the form of an attempt to chronicle and define the literary ideas of his age group, much as he had begun to do in "This Youngest Generation." The opening entry of his earliest notebook reads:

> The Current of Ideas.
> 1. No critical undertaking is more difficult than to define the literary ideas of my own contemporaries. They are young and they have published little. Their texts are scattered through the files of unperiodical reviews in four languages and a dialect. Few of these texts are critical, for my generation has difficulty in defining its ideas; sometimes I think it is afraid to define them. Nevertheless these ideas exist, and I have been able to observe their effect on my own mind if nowhere else.[35]

Cowley's observations on contemporary aesthetics were partly inspired by a satirical desire "to hold the ideas of others and ourselves up to a mild ridicule." He himself, however, was too deeply implicated in the very ideas he wished to satirize. Before long he acknowledged as much to Burke, granting that in his notebook he was ridiculing both what he approved and what he disapproved of. As much as an attack on ideas held by Burke, Josephson, and others, his notebook considerations were "an examination of my own mind and a denigration of my own ideas, inasmuch as I had accepted them from other people."[36] As he had admitted earlier, Cowley was perhaps dangerously inclined to adopt the protective coloring of his intellectual surroundings. His ambivalence about modernism was at least in part an attempt to safeguard his intellectual and literary independence.

In the aesthetic assumptions of French classicism, Cowley now discovered a congenial critical perspective from which to judge modernity; conversely, what he cherished in modernism pointed up the deficiencies of the classical ideal. Measuring by the standards of Boileau, Racine, and Molière, Cowley found many tendencies in modern art touched with "ridicule." Art did not merely originate in religion, he observed; more pertinently, contemporary art was "tending to replace religion," and the modern artist was "redeemed by Faith," in himself and in his art. A corollary of this tendency was apparent in the artist's way of life: "The Artist of the Younger Generation is an Ascetic," he observed. "He is poor by preference; when he descends to making money his omnipresent conscience chastens him. To the rule of poverty he adds that of chastity, for he believes firmly that the energy he denies to sex can be devoted to his work. If he marries it is with the injunction of St. Paul in mind."[37] However ironic, such notebook entries confirm that Cowley's search for a literary ethics and aesthetics partook of the religious. His conception of the modern artist as a religious novitiate suggests that his later analysis and qualified repudiation of the "religion of art" in *Exile's Return* owed less to his radical politics in the 1930s than to an early ambivalence about modernism.

A corollary of this religiosity of modern art was what Cowley called the "New Rosicrucianism," a cult of incomprehensibility and obscurity: "Do you know," he told Burke, "I was always rather ashamed of myself because I wasn't sufficiently unintelligible. Now I see that the most ridiculous feature of modern writing is the fear of being understood. We wish to be the priests each of our own little sect, and each sect has its Rosicrucian secrets, only to be revealed to the proselyte who has passed through the seven stages of the novitiate." Too often, Cowley believed, obscurity was merely a cloak for slipshod thinking: instead, complexity should lie in "the difficulty of the thought and not in the novelty of the word, in the general design of the piece and not in an individual sentence." Against obscurantism and self-contained aestheticism Cowley posited clarity and communicability: "literature remains the art of conveying ideas and shows no disposition to adopt either Dada or Rosicrucianism." Thus at an early stage Cowley was predisposed to reject part of the tenets of Dada. In the same spirit, he criticized Eliot for writing, in "Gerontion," poetry that was too esoteric and obscure: "If Mr. Eliot had named his poem 'Pantaloon' he should have carried the same meaning to several times as many people; he preferred to be rosicrucian, and I have no wish to be. I want an audience." [38]

Likewise, Cowley responded with growing uneasiness to the symbolist aesthetics he had embraced earlier. Where the symbolist endeavor to approach in language the "purity" of music led to extremes of individualism and inaccessibility, it could now count on his disapprobation. [39] In line with Boileau, Cowley stressed the communicative function of art and rejected the dissociation of the artist from his public. "I feel more than ever the need of intelligent society. Not being a romantic I have no wish for magnificent solitude. I want to write comedies and satires, and comedies and satires require an audience," he observed to Burke. The creation of such an audience was to Cowley the sine qua non of a living modern literature. The purpose of magazines, lectures, polemics, and poetry societies, he wrote in his notebook, was precisely the formation of "an intelligent public." Believing that art existed in a context of history, society, and tradition, Cowley envisioned a primary task of criticism as one of mediation between artist and audience, between contemporary art and its historical tradition. A notebook entry entitled "Credo" reads: "A critic believes that public and artist are interdependent. A critic believes that art has a history and can progress. Otherwise why be a critic?" [40] Such beliefs proved axiomatic.

Cowley's understanding of classicism was as yet rather naive and unsophisticated. Most typically he was inclined to define his classical ideal in opposition to romanticism: classicism, he wrote to Burke, was "the product, or at least . . . the modern expression, of thickly-settled countries where man has influenced the landscape to such an extent that it is an expression of man's emotion. Classicism is an expression of man as a social animal. Romanticism is the expression of man as a solitary animal, and of landscape as independent of man. It is the natural expression of the more unkempt countries; Russia, Scandinavia, the United States." In his notebooks he observed: "Classicism can exist alone; it is total; on the contrary romanticism is a corrective doctrine since it demands a classicism against which to revolt." [41] In opposition to romanticism Cowley evolved a set of classical "axioms": "Art is a function not of the individual but of a civilization. Art is a civilization defining itself. If art is a definition of a civilization, criticism is a definition of art." Apart from the intrinsic organicism of the classical ideal, Cowley appears to have understood it as largely the attainment of formal properties: "If anyone asked me what I desired, I should say that it was, in two words, a concrete classicism. Concrete by its dependence on simple and familiar objects, and on emotions decomposed to their elements. Classical by discipline, by clarity, by a dependence on the intelligence." Later, he defined "the highest quality of literature" as "elegance," a standard of intrinsic excellence and formal perfection: "The quality of a work of art which is absolutely right judged by the standards inherent in it." T. S. Eliot, despite his Rosicrucianism, possessed it to a high degree; Carl Sandburg was virtually devoid of it. The prototype of elegance was Jean Racine.[42]

Cowley conceived of "elegance" as both an artistic and an ethical ideal. His enthusiasm for a "concrete classicism" was an integral part of his search for the ideal literary life. By now his vision of "the Perfect Life" encompassed a farm, a literary magazine, a theater, a Maecenas (to finance the theater and the magazine), and "about a dozen companions." Cowley was convinced of the feasibility of his ideal: "Merely to state the idea is to go a long way towards its realization."[43]

Much of February 1922 was consumed by preparations for university examinations. For two weeks Cowley doused his mind with names and dates from French literature and history; his efforts were rewarded with a diploma of French studies, for which he received a *Mention très honorable*. In its wake he set to work on a number of articles for the *Dial*, hoping thereby "to keep the wolf from my open French windows." In between he enjoyed the "physical delights" of French food, while his countryman's eye reveled in the early arrival of the Midi spring. In early March, Cowley made a short trip into the Pyrenees with Stewart Mitchell, Peggy, and a young English woman. Crossing the border into Spain, they were thrilled by the barren beauty of the Pyrenean landscape, had a jolly snow fight at an altitude of five thousand feet, and sampled native oranges in the valleys. The Cowleys continued southward along the Spanish seacoast, enjoyed the "magnificent" cuisine of Catalonia and, after a "glorious" trip, returned to Montpellier in an anticlimactic drizzle. Money was going so fast they were "spending it like water"; the first of June still loomed as "judgment day."[44]

Before setting out for the Pyrenees, Cowley completed a review of *Fir-Flower Tablets*, a book of translations from classical Chinese poetry by Amy Lowell in collaboration with Florence Ayscough, a distinguished sinologist. No other volume of poetry affected him so deeply at the time or came so close to incorporating his ideal of classicism. "Unfortunately for my reputation as a judicious critic, my emotions were quite unmixed," he wrote to Lowell. "Perhaps [the Chinese poems] affected me so much because I was just in the state of mind to receive them." To Burke he observed in a similar vein: "Really that book of Chinese poems produced a tremendous effect on me. Obviously classicism means clarity, honesty and (as Ezra Pound added so sagely) freshness." He was so enthusiastic about the book that he reviewed it twice, for Art Moss's *Gargoyle* and for the *Dial*. Peggy shared Cowley's ardor: "For days we chanted over bits which especially pleased us, as if there were some strongly perfumed flower in the room which had to be noticed and admired constantly," she wrote to Foster Damon.[45]

Cowley's eulogistic consideration of *Fir-Flower Tablets* in *Gargoyle* was infused with moral fervor for the new literary paths it seemed to open. Taking the Chinese poems as "the expression of a civilization" rather than as the product of individual genius, he sharpened his conception of a classical, organic culture but also pointed up Boileau's deficiencies as a literary godfather: "These poems are clear, balanced, simple, restrained. . . . They are the expression of a culture which extends to the smallest acts of daily life, and as a result of which even these smallest acts become poetry. Boileau himself would have admired them, for they are . . . classical in the truest sense. They are classical without ceasing to be lyric, an achievement to which Boileau never attained." The book, so Cowley believed, appeared at a propitious moment when it could exert a beneficial effect upon contemporary literature. It proved that it was possible to be "classical without being dusty" and "without pouring beauty into a rigid mould." In the *Dial*, Cowley upheld the classical ideal against "the doctrine of our romantic Freudians" and concluded that the poetry in *Fir-Flower Tablets* offered "a resolution of our too-favourable antinome between romanticism and classicism, for it is a literature both universal and concrete, both human and humanistic; a literature that is classical without being mummified."[46]

Cowley's conclusion implied a recognition of his own need to move beyond a facile mode of dualistic thinking. In his notebook and correspondence with Burke he now pursued with particular doggedness the question of the relative importance of form and matter. Rejecting both a monistic formalism and a monistic materialism, he demanded instead a "perfect marriage" of form and matter. Such a "dualist" position, however, remained "vague," he reflected, since it failed to recognize that "form is not one but many, and that the *matter* of a work of art may often itself be a form." The one way to circumvent the dilemma, he told Burke, was to decompose both terms of the antinomy into several elements and to erect a "pluralistic" aesthetic.[47] If his own definition of form did perhaps less to dispel vagueness than he hoped, his "pluralistic" approach at least allowed him to remain sensitive to the formalist and aesthetic properties of modern art while continuing to develop his interest in literary subject matter. It opened the way to an eclectic study of literature, one encompassing the values, ideas, and sensations of the artist, as well as the social and historical context of art.[48]

Cowley's thoughts on the subject remained rather muddled. His youthful observations on aesthetics lacked the complexity, depth, and consistency to push them beyond the formulation of a personal attitude into the groundwork for a viable literary theory. Realizing that his propensity was not for theoretical exposition, he saw his natural affinity with classicism as the manifestation of an essentially pragmatic sensibility: "My brain is a practical brain, a brain that likes to work on definite lines, a brain that thinks about means rather than ends. . . . It is the classical brain which builds a perfectly proportioned edifice, which writes prose that is simple and clear, and poetry studiously incorrect. It does not question enough; it respects ability and authority. It is the brain of Boileau and Pope and Congreve."[49]

In early April, Cowley summed up his position in a long letter to John Brooks Wheelwright. In art as in morals, he observed, the present was "an age of reaction." Not only were happy marriages becoming "fashionable" again, modern painters like Picasso were reverting to the classical art of Ingres, writers were resuscitating the classicism of France and England, composers were rediscovering seventeenth-century Italian music, and sculptors were instigating a new primitivism. Temperamentally geared to classicism ("My mind is ordered, exact, and limited. It would have been more appreciated in the age of Congreve"), Cowley felt that he was going against the romanticist grain of his day and age: "I said once that our age was feeding from the putrescent corpse of romanticism," he had written in his notebook; "I was wrong; romanticism is as much alive today as is the romantic nationalism which it engendered." If his attempts at theory were confused, his analysis of contemporary culture was shrewd, containing as it did the germs of *Exile's Return* and anticipating the thesis developed by Edmund Wilson in *Axel's Castle*. Future critics, he now observed in his letter to Wheelwright, would speak of the modern age as "the logical unfolding of the romantic movement." He pointed to the work of William Carlos Williams, the dadaists or the Baroness Elsa von Freytag-Loringhoven as contemporary proof of a "romanticism carried to the limit of formlessness, immediacy, and unintelligibility." Defining romanticism as "the idea that matter is more important than form, the emotions than the intellect, and complex and inexpressible concepts more than clear concepts," he rejected the "mystical nationalism" of works like Waldo Frank's *Our America* and repudiated such writers as Floyd Dell and Sherwood Anderson for greeting Freudianism as "a final victory over conscious thought." As an antidote he exhorted Wheelwright to help instigate a new classical literature: "Let us demand a literature which preserves the virtues of classicism without its vices. A literature, in other words, which still possesses the sentiment of nature, which remains emotional and imaginative, but in which the emotions and the imagination are not given free license. A literature which may strive for complex effects, but which gains them with sentences and paragraphs which are absolutely lucid. An architectural literature, from which is disengaged an impression of proportion (or studied disproportion) as from a fine building. A literature, finally, which is a literature and not a theft from life."

In France, Cowley was increasingly preoccupied with the possibility of a national American culture. In his notebook and his correspondence with Wheelwright he lamented the absence of "clear ideas" in American letters and brashly condemned the pessimistic cultural analyses of *Civilization in the United States*, many of which, he felt, could easily be reduced to a single syllogism: "Puritanism is bad: America is puritan = America is bad." Against the "haziness of our unintelligentsia," which he blamed on subserviency to English culture, he maintained that "America is not, unlike England, incongenial to ideas. It is a land of sunlight and clear forms—no fogs—and it welcomes clear ideas when it finds them." In his notebook he wrote: "The forms of its buildings are distinct and logical, and if American thought followed its natural lines, it too would be distinct." [50]

The justification for Cowley's expatriation was more and more to be found in the creation of a viable cultural climate in the United States. "One should aim," he told Wheelwright, "at creating an atmosphere in which many ideas can be born and be polished by rubbing against each other." Cowley's ideals soon began to be reflected in his writings. An essay on "The French and Our New Poetry," commissioned by Canby, displayed his nascent literary nationalism. Studying French literature with an eye to its possibilities for American writing, Cowley found that, conversely, French critics were intensely interested in modern American poetry and that a lively debate on its merit was being conducted in French literary magazines. His essay discussed the critical reception in France of the "New Poetry" of Lowell, Frost, Sandburg, and Masters, poets in whom the French discovered "preeminently national" qualities. Cowley chose to read the French response as a significant indication, not merely of the "intrinsic progress" of American verse, but of the growing international prestige of American literary culture since the war. Whereas in 1914 a comparison between American and English poetry had been "all to our discredit," a recent article by Jean Catel had greeted "without reserves this splendid adventure which the poets of the New World are furnishing under our eyes." It was high time, Cowley implied, for Americans to reclaim these modern poets from the French and to recognize their achievement: "our poets reclaimed Poe and Whitman from the French only a dozen years ago; this reclamation is the basis of our contemporary poetry."[51] It was one of the typical ironies of Cowley's expatriation that his enthusiasm for his native culture was enhanced by the appreciative observations of a French critic.

Two articles Cowley wrote in the early weeks of April displayed his antipathy to current romanticism and his continued allegiance to the ideals of classicism. The first, "A Brief History of Bohemia," was occasioned by the centenary of Henry Murger, the author of Scènes de la Vie de Bohème ("Scenes of Bohemian Life"). Intended as a "plea for classical life as a basis for classical art," it took the form of a blistering, satirical attack on contemporary bohemianism, the origins of which Cowley traced to mid-nineteenth-century French romanticism. Much of its emotional impetus derived from his personal observations of bohemian life in Paris and in New York. In Cowley's verdict, Murger was "responsible for an ideal of artistic life which has wasted several generations of talent; an ideal which has peopled more sanitariums, jails, and venereal wards than it has ever filled museums." Nothing was further removed from a life of classical elegance than Murger's vulgarized and romantic falsification of a life of misery, debauchery, and starvation. At the present, Cowley observed, "romantic" bohemia had become not merely "an esoteric cult, like Theosophy or New Thought," but an international capitalist enterprise that had become "as much the property of the bourgeoisie as any other business-venture."[52] Cowley's essay formed the germ of his analysis of contemporary bohemianism in Exile's Return. One of his earliest well-researched attempts to locate the origins of a contemporary cultural phenomenon, it indicated that his social and historical consciousness antedated his conversion to radical politics in the 1930s. His second article favorably reviewed a French study by Charles Perromat of the life and works of the Restoration playwright William Wycherley. Even more than his critique of romantic bohemianism it testified to Cowley's classical aesthetics and illustrated the historical bent of his criticism. It reflected his predilection for representationalism in art and upheld his by now axiomatic belief in culture as the outgrowth of a social and historical situation. Cowley praised Perromat for recognizing the organic relation between art and milieu and for viewing Restoration drama as an expression of the age that produced it.[53]

Through Burke, Cowley submitted both essays to Van Wyck Brooks for publication in the *Freeman*. His choice of the *Freeman* was revealing, but not surprising. As early as November 1920 he had written to Brooks, brashly offering his services to the newly launched magazine as "the whole of the youngest generation of critics." He had advertised himself as a reviewer who "specialized chiefly in modern literature"—he named Joyce, Eliot, and Jules Romains—and who delighted in "a swashbuckling attack" on the Georgians. He was eager to write for the *Freeman*, he said, because its reviews had an "agreeably acrid taste" and managed to avoid "too much formality." Where the *Nation* was "pompous," the *Dial* "arty," and the *New Republic* "economic," the *Freeman* allowed one "to express one's own mind rather than the personality of the editor."[54]

Cowley's essays on Murger and Wycherley met with a receptive editorial response. By 1922 Brooks was moving rapidly toward a position of outspoken hostility to what he saw as the sterile aestheticism and obscurantism of the contemporary avant-garde, and the terms in which he would soon condemn its experimental formalism in the *Freeman* sounded remarkably like Cowley's earlier rejection of the "Rosicrucianism" of modern art. Cowley's articles appeared in the *Freeman* in June and July 1922. John Brooks Wheelwright, who shortly before had met Brooks in New York, reported that Brooks had spoken enthusiastically of Cowley's essays and had praised the "Gallic clarity" of his style. Brooks had initially mistaken Wheelwright's mentioning of "Burke and Cowley" for a reference to Edmund Burke and Abraham Cowley. But once he understood that Wheelwright was speaking of "the two white hopes of his own generation," he immediately set out to enlist Cowley in his campaign against the current wave of pure aestheticism.[55]

Cowley's attitude to Brooks, however, was ambivalent from the first.

If he shared Brooks's misgivings about modernism—its pure formalism, its esoteric obscurity, its divorce of art from society—and if he was tentatively moving toward a Brooksian ideal of an organic national American culture, there was still more to differentiate than to unite the two. It was one of the ironies of Brooks's career that, having expended the best of his critical energies analyzing the causes of cultural failure and calling for a new national literature, he should turn away from contemporary writing at the very moment when a vital new generation of American writers was appearing on the scene. By 1924 Paul Rosenfeld could justifiably lament Brooks's "perpetual absenteeship" from contemporary letters. Ten years later Cowley compared Brooks's generation of critics to literary obstetricians: "They gathered about the great unhappy body of the nation, they laid their spells upon it and adjured it to labor intellectually and bring forth a native American literature. When the baby was born many of the doctors were looking the other way." Brooks's absenteeism created a critical vacuum that was filled by a rising young generation of critics, among them Edmund Wilson, Allen Tate, Kenneth Burke, and Malcolm Cowley, who resented Brooks's indifference to modern literature and were wholeheartedly committed to contemporary American writing.[56]

Cowley's early strictures against Brooks mellowed over the years, as he became one of Brooks's most loyal, if not uncritical, apologists.[57] Indeed, Cowley's critical practice ultimately owed as much to the example of early Van Wyck Brooks as to Eliot and Pound. He came to share not only Brooks's conception of an organic culture but also his concern with the creation of a vital sense of community among American writers. Both men were concerned with the status of the writer in America and his relationship to the culture at large. Common purposes brought them together in the 1930s, but where Brooks's attempts were largely directed at the recovery of a "usable past," Cowley's were primarily aimed at chronicling and interpreting the present. Where Brooks celebrated and exhorted, Cowley more soberly criticized and analyzed. Though both gravitated toward a study of literary culture in terms of the lives and careers of leading individuals, their use of historical and biographical materials was radically different: Brooks often used the work of art to illuminate the artist's personality or the larger cultural situation,[58] while Cowley used biographical material essentially to illuminate the writer's artistic achievement. Brooks's critical imagination, it has often been said, was social and ethical rather than aesthetic; his strength was not in technical criticism and his critical sensibility, unlike Cowley's, was never attuned to poetry.[59] Cowley's sensibility from the first combined a sensitivity to the social and historical context of art with the technical and formalist ideals of craftsmanship formulated by Eliot and Pound. Throughout the 1920s, the years of his apprenticeship, he uneasily wavered between Pound's aesthetic formalism and Brooks's cultural criticism. Ultimately, in a typically eclectic and pluralistic approach to contemporary writing, he aimed to synthesize both and, with other writers of his generation, attempted to engraft a technical concern with the form and texture of modern literature onto the ideal of an organic native American culture.

In 1922 Cowley's concern with a hard-edged and rigorous "new classicism" and his concomitant anti-romanticism placed him in line with Eliot as much as Van Wyck Brooks. His understanding of the classical ideal, however, was always more secular and less metaphysical than Eliot's; for him it did not imply, as it did for Eliot, "a belief in Original Sin—the necessity for austere discipline" in a moral and religious sphere.[60] Still, Cowley's search for "standards" and "common principles" in criticism, together with his need to work in a tradition, his self-acknowledged respect for "authority," and his explorations of the issues of classicism and romanticism, for the time being allied his efforts with those of Eliot; as he observed to Burke, his own ideals were "really reactionary."[61]

Cowley's mounting ambitions in criticism led him to explore its nature and function more precisely. In letters and notebooks he lashed out against the fallacy that the theoretical development of an aesthetics might interfere with artistic creation. Aesthetics was "an art, a science, a metaphysic," he believed, and formed a "crown" to all the other arts. "Criticism is one of the fine arts insomuch as it is the creation of an ideal," he observed in his notebook. "Criticism which consists only in applying a preconceived ideal is certainly not an art. Criticism is an art, inasmuch as it is a philosophy; otherwise it is only a more or less skilled profession." Cowley's high-minded observations were not always matched by his practical achievements, but they were marked by an open-minded eclecticism and a wariness of doctrinalism that became seminal features of his work. In the last analysis, he felt, there was "no perfect criticism. Each book requires individual treatment."[62]

Cowley's practice was not wholly consistent with his theoretical observations. While in his notebook he acknowledged the restricted validity of an excursion into "psychological," "moral," or cultural criticism,[63] his actual consideration of modern poetry foreswore any such nonaesthetic divagations. In a review of two books of poetry for the *Dial*, he ridiculed the practice of critics of the "school" of Sainte-Beuve to deviate into extraneous matters—an author's pedigree, his thumbprints, or his income-tax forms—and voiced his determination to approach works of art "as if we knew nothing of the authors." What he looked for was a quality of "inevitable rightness"—what he described to Burke as "perfection of the work of art as judged by the standards it sets itself." Thus, Cowley was early aware of what seemed an inescapable paradox: whereas he defined art as not merely the expression of a personal sensibility but of a whole civilization, a definition that opened the way to a consideration of extraliterary elements in criticism, he continued to judge specific works of art by a standard of intrinsic elegance and to regard them as autonomous entities. In a letter dated June 2, 1922, he confessed to Burke that his formulation of a personal aesthetics had been stalled before an irresolvable difficulty: "despite the statement that art is creation and not representation, I still find that I judge works of art by their truth-to-life. . . . And I don't know whether to change my theory or my practice." [64]

‹ ‹ ‹   While Cowley was struggling to resolve the inconsistencies of a personal aesthetics, one of his essays unexpectedly provided the intellectual inspiration for the founding of a new literary magazine. In early December 1921 Gorham B. Munson informed Cowley that his article on "This Youngest Generation" had impressed him with "the feasibility of operating a review which will provide a forum for just those writers and their kin." He solicited Cowley's ideas and advice on a magazine "devoted solely to literary expression. . . . Its spirit can be indicated by saying that your essay might well be a prospectus for the aims of the venture." [65] Munson had come to Paris in the summer of 1921, after having spent several "years of muddle" in Greenwich Village, where he had struck up a literary friendship with Hart Crane, been published in Joseph Kling's *Pagan*, and developed an ardent enthusiasm for the work of Waldo Frank. He had come to Europe to extend his self-education but, as so many others, had much "ambition without a clear goal." Cowley's essay apparently gave Munson the intellectual focus he needed and provided the initiating ideas for what he conceived of as a *"tendenz* review." [66]

Though in his essay Cowley had stressed the individualistic bent and the lack of esprit de corps among the members of his age group, Munson appears to have mistaken the essay for a fervent plea for the creation of a group organ. In Paris, Munson had enlisted the cooperation of Matthew Josephson, whom he had met through Hart Crane, a mutual friend. Through Munson, Josephson in turn met Man Ray and Tristan Tzara, the reputed founder of Dada, who rapidly fired Josephson's enthusiasm for the French dadaists. Though Josephson told Cowley in early December that Munson and he were "fairly good friends," their relations actually were strained from the start. Distrustful of Munson's literary taste, an opinionated and overly ambitious Josephson seems to have wanted to appropriate editorial control and, availing himself of Munson's "diplomatic bent," to direct the magazine toward a militant modernism.[67] Still, with Josephson providing the necessary literary connections—unlike Munson he was personally acquainted with most of the writers mentioned in Cowley's essay— and Cowley supplying the nearest equivalent to an aesthetic platform, the new magazine seemed off on a propitious start.[68]

Cowley responded cautiously to Munson's plan for the new magazine. Though Munson had plainly stated his intention to use Cowley's formulation of the aesthetic ideals of his coevals as the official program for his magazine, Cowley's private endorsement of those ideals had been less than complete even at the time of writing. Under the influence of French classicism his skepticism about modernism had only grown. At this point, also, Cowley seemed unaware of Josephson's intentions to appropriate the magazine for dadaist agitation and the propagation of an aggressively modernist art. Instead, he saw the new venture as feasible insofar as it helped to advance his ideal of a "classical literature"—by providing a market for his and his allies' writings, by creating a receptive audience, and by focusing the activity of its contributors without pressing them into a group or school.[69]

During the early months of 1922 preparations for the inaugural issue moved ahead. Hoping to avail himself of low printing costs in Austria, Munson traveled to Vienna before returning to New York, from where he planned to edit future issues, though the magazine was to be printed and distributed from Europe. In February, Munson told Cowley that Burke was "very sympathetic" to the venture, in particular to its "massacring aspects." In early March he sent Cowley a circular announcement of the new magazine, which after a visit to the "Sezession" Art Gallery in Vienna he had named *Secession*. *Secession*—"I don't like the name," Cowley told Burke—was to be "the first gun for this youngest generation," the writers who were "moving away from the main body of intelligent writing in the United States since 1910" and who were "defending a new position from which to assault the last decade and launch the next." The circular quoted Cowley's formulation of the aesthetic catchwords of his generation, and announced *Secession*'s polemical intentions. Besides poems, stories, and criticism, it would publish "insults and vituperations" and "expose the private correspondence, hidden sins and secret history" of more solemn and eclectic rivals like the *Dial*, *Poetry*, *Broom*, and the *Little Review*. Munson wanted his review to be "intransigent, aggressive, unmuzzled" and to make "a little history."[70] He would not be disappointed.

After such a martial sounding of trumpets, the first issue of *Secession*, which appeared in April 1922, was mild, if lively. Largely it seemed an act of obeisance to the French dadaists, showing Josephson's early editorial dominance. In a critical essay written under a nom de guerre—Will Bray—Josephson, with infectious exhilaration, explored the provocative implications of dadaism for American writing. He minimized the nihilistic despair of the young French writers, and found them rather a "talented, extravagant, intolerant, fun-loving" counterpart to his own generation of secessionists. Like the French avant-garde writers, Josephson urged, American writers should frankly experiment with modern phenomena and "be at least as daring as the mechanical wizards who exploited the airplane, wireless, telegraphy, chemistry, the submarine, the cinema, the phonograph, what-not." He offered sensitive appreciations of Aragon, Breton, Eluard, Soupault, and Tzara—Tzara's poems, he claimed, were "as naturally expressive of the beauty of this age as Herrick's are of the 17th Century"—and praised them for employing the aesthetic uses of "all the instruments of the time, the streetcar, the billposter, the automobile, the incandescent light." In conclusion he expressed an Emersonian confidence in the possibility of a vital and independent contemporary American culture: "The complexion of the life of the United States has been transformed so rapidly and so daringly that its writers and artists are rendered a strategic advantage over their European contemporaries. They need only react faithfully and imaginatively to the brilliant minutiae of her daily existence in the big cities, in the great industrial regions, athwart her marvelous and young mechanical forces."[71]

Munson's contributions were rather more solemn. The promised unmasking of rival magazines was limited to a scathing attack on the *Dial* (ominously entitled "Exposé No. 1"), which centered on its diffuse eclecticism, its hospitality to Paul Rosenfeld's "acres of vague impressionistic excrement," and its championing of "an established writer" like Sherwood Anderson. In a rather heavy-handed editorial Munson advanced a primarily aesthetic position on modern literature but felt ambiguous about such "pure" and "abstract" writing as that of Tristan Tzara. *Secession*, he announced in conclusion, existed for writers "preoccupied with researches for new forms" and aimed at an American audience that had outgrown the social and psychological realism of Sinclair Lewis and Sherwood Anderson, as well as the genteel impressionism of Paul Rosenfeld and Louis Untermeyer. To cinch his editorial policy he referred readers to Cowley's essay in the *Literary Review* for "an important origin and a general program for *Secession*." As if to corroborate Cowley's authoritative position in the venture, the issue opened with "Day Coach," a poem Munson retrospectively rated as "the best thing in the issue, and one of Cowley's finest efforts." [72]

Cowley was less than happy with such an honor. "Day Coach" was admittedly one of his more radical modernist experiments; the poem was conceived along the lines of Burke's structural experiments with geometrical form, and Cowley had struggled hard to make its form "more satisfying logically, more integralistic." [73] But for all its formal experimentalism the poem as a whole is lucid and intelligible and deals with a recognizably human experience. It presents the rapid succession of impressions of a man traveling by train from New York to Cambria County, Pennsylvania, and develops one of Cowley's persistent themes: the impossibility of a return to the lost haunts of childhood. As such, the poem was rather out of key with the predominantly dadaist contents of the issue.

Naturally, Cowley was "disappointed" in the first issue. By April 1922 he had moved toward an aesthetic position diametrically opposed to Dada and related manifestations of contemporary "romanticism." Munson had invested Cowley with responsibility for the editorial policy of a magazine exemplifying much of what he strongly reacted against. Josephson, in particular, seemed to be moving in opposite directions from Cowley, Burke, and even Munson. In a letter to Burke, Cowley observed that *Secession* 1 displayed a disturbing "logical breakdown" in what literary consensus existed among its contributors. Munson's use of his name and article, Cowley wrote to Wheelwright, were but "a doubtful compliment." [74]

Predictably, Cowley's position brought him in conflict with Matthew Josephson. Unaware of Will Bray's identity, Cowley virulently denounced

Bray's apology for the dadaists in a letter to Josephson, pointing out its linear opposition to his and Burke's approach; a magazine that published both without batting an eye, Cowley fulminated, laid itself open to the very charges of eclecticism Munson had made against the *Dial*. Cowley's plea for a cerebral classicism, for a literature of "ideas" rather than "sensations," and for the attainment of clear, logical form elicited a violent response from Josephson. In a series of effervescent and outspoken letters he rejected Cowley's distinction between romanticism and classicism as an essentially meaningless form of academic "hockey-playing"—one could speak with equal right of "the romanticism of Molière and Congreve, and the classicism of Dada"—and he denounced contemporary aesthetics as but "a futile business." He advocated "the destruction of informative-aesthetic criticism" and proposed instead to "convince people by hypnosis, by a quivering finger, by advertising methods!!" Josephson's vociferous and exuberant posturing, so different from Cowley's balanced efforts to attain an intelligent and concrete criticism, climaxed in true dadaist fashion with a letter typed on Italian toilet paper.

In Josephson's verdict, Cowley's poetry was decidedly antimodern. "Mountain Farm," a poem published in the May 1922 *Broom* that laments the decay of the irrecapturable rural past of Cowley's childhood, he deemed but an old-fashioned piece of Frostian pastoralism, while poems like "Day Coach" or "Two Swans," which Munson had accepted for *Secession* 2, demonstrated that Cowley, like Proust, was still "slave to a procession of experiences" and lacked a "central directing brain." In a time when artists were forsaking verisimilitude and representationalism for a "purely formal" art, Josephson argued, Cowley's mode of poetry remained conservatively "descriptive," "impressionistic," "sentimental," and "representative." On June 18 Josephson, charged with editing *Secession* 3, put an end to the epistolary feud by opening its pages to Cowley for a frank exposition of his views on modern poetry. Cowley preferred to retaliate with a blatantly nonsensical poem (entitled "Poem") burlesquing Josephson's aggressively sponsored anti-art. Failing to see the joke, Josephson accepted it for publication. As for his critique of Cowley's verse, the bulk of Josephson's statements struck Cowley as imitative and empty, eminently usable for his projected "Ridicule of Contemporary Aesthetics."[75]

One manifestation of the modern spirit that persistently aroused the satirical wrath of Cowley and his friends was the overwhelming popularity of Freudian theories of sex and psychoanalysis and their repercussions for literature and morality. Distrustful of a literature excessively concerned with man's subjective nature and his subconscious drives, at times Cowley seemed equally uncomfortable with the new sexual mores of the times. All recent wives, he observed mockingly to Wheelwright, seemed determined "to be the perfect friend, the companion, the playfellow, and to share equally the erudition and the vices of the husband."[76] From the fall of 1921 through the spring and summer of 1922 Cowley collaborated with Burke on a poetic drama ridiculing the literary and moral excesses of "Ultra-Modern Love." Their principal targets were such Freudian popularizers as Havelock Ellis, James Oppenheim and, in particular, Floyd Dell, one-time editor of the *Masses* and soon-to-be author of *Love in Greenwich Village* (1924). Dell had explored the new sexual mores in several novels, among them *Moon-Calf* (1920), and had become a self-constituted prophet of free love and a crusader against sexual repression. He was jocularly dubbed "Freud" Dell by Cowley and Burke. Their joint play was intended to "thoroughly puncture Dell's innards," as Burke put it. Provisionally entitled "Hamlet: For an Operetta," the play was a satirical composite of various elements. Besides Dell's preachings on free love, it ridiculed falsely romantic notions of poetic inspiration. Hamlet, the play's protagonist, was conceived as a prototype of the sensitive young poet, the eternal Laforguean adolescent, who finds himself trapped between Ophelia (seen as the exemplar of traditional virginity, desirous of yet shrinking from "Life, Experience, Reality") and Berenice (the "villain," Lesbian, mannish, fearless, and aggressive, with short-cut hair, gloves, and cigarettes, a prototype of the New Woman modeled after Berenice Abbott, Norma Millay, and Ida Rauh, whose antimale preachings and female seductiveness toward Ophelia inspire Hamlet to acts of murder).[77]

The play remained unfinished, despite the time and energy spent on it. Though long-distance collaboration may simply have been an insurmountable obstacle to success, the play also suffered from a lack of clarity in conception. It was conceived "with all the artificiality of an opera," including duets, recitatives, solos, and arias, but also as a spoof of the traditions of Elizabethan drama—it was to end, Cowley wrote, in "a grand orgy of murder and bombasticism." Because the play was only worked at fragmentarily and intermittently, its satirical targets kept shifting with the current concerns of its creators. In May 1922 Cowley complained that the play had become surrounded with "a fatras of discordant ideas." By this time he had come to think of it more seriously, as "an excellent step toward

the foundation of a classical theater: it was free from geography, not especially dependent on time; simple in emotion and somewhat complex in
thought, and depended entirely on certain self-established conventions."
He surrendered the manuscript to Burke for revision and completion, urging him to attempt publication in *Broom* or the *Little Review*, or else to
appropriate an issue of *Secession*, so as to make "a jolly stink."[78] Though
Cowley recurrently suggested taking up the play once more, to all intents
and purposes there the matter rested.

But Cowley's satirical indignation continued unabatedly. In his notebook he lambasted the antirationalistic worship of "Surrender" among
contemporary writers and denounced the members of "the psycho-analytic
school" (in particular Waldo Frank and Sherwood Anderson) as producers
of "yoni-literature." Their books, he wrote, were reminiscent of "the sensations of a woman who lies on her back and surrenders her body to the
unnamed Lover, so that she may attain to the Clean, the Naked, the Real.
She expresses herself in the terms of a mysticism in words of one syllable.
She digs in the mine of her subconscious and finds that grey impalpable
mineral from which dreams are made. She calls them Art." Against an out-
pouring of intuitional impulses or subconscious drives Cowley posited a
definition of art that, however facetious and even dadaistic in its language,
was serious in its demand of a literature feeding less on the subjective self
than on social and human reality, "the vastly more interesting structure of
the actual world." Cowley's formulation became a favorite axiom: "Art is
a beast which pastures not on dreams or the Libido but on the violently-
coloured prairies of a world which exists, surprisingly enough, in time and
space. Art is the fabulous ostrich which eats sand and shits bricks: hence,
the Pyramids."[79]

The first public offshoot of Cowley's projected "Ridicule of Contemporary Aesthetics" was a satirical portrait of an imaginary young artist
bedazzled by aesthetic questions. Harold Loeb, after suggesting revisions
to point up the caricature, accepted it for *Broom*, where it appeared in
October 1922. "Young Man with Spectacles" is a humorous composite
sketch containing recognizable touches of Cowley, Burke, and Josephson.
Cowley's bespectacled young man is buffeted by contradictory modernist creeds and theories until he is left speechless with befuddlement. The
ideas he advances and abandons with startling rapidity are a clever and
colorful collage of passages from Cowley's personal notebooks and extracts
from his recent correspondence with Burke and Josephson. Indeed, as a

caricature of Cowley's own confused efforts of recent months to draw up a personal aesthetics the article is a little jewel of self-irony. But its ridicule is also aimed at those who were similarly struggling to find a foothold in the quicksands of modernity. For the time being, Cowley had found such a footing in the values and ideals of classicism; it was, significantly, the one feature that was exempted from his satire.[80]

By May 1922 Cowley's opinion of *Broom* had risen considerably. After Alfred Kreymborg's resignation Loeb had tentatively begun to shift the magazine's direction from a catholic eclecticism to a more outspoken commitment to the younger American writers. Among the slightly older American generation, he valued the cerebral poetry of Wallace Stevens and Marianne Moore, while he denounced the writings of Frank and Rosenfeld for containing "passages of purple prose and self-indulgent sentiment until the reader felt that he was sinking in a sea of hot tar." But he was particularly eager to secure contributions from the members of a younger age group—Cowley, Josephson, Burke, Cummings, Crane, and Brown. In European literature, too, Loeb decided to opt for the work of the younger French, Italian, German, Russian, and Central European writers.[81] With such an editorial policy Loeb could be assured of Cowley's approbation.

Loeb tentatively formulated his new editorial line in *Broom*'s May 1922 issue. In "Foreign Exchange" he explained the motivations behind the current exodus of artists from America and discussed the effect that foreign culture was having on American writers in France. Following Flaubert and de Gourmont, Loeb wrote, the expatriates displayed "a meticulous attention to form." More important, the European perspective led to "a revaluation of America," which was accelerated by French admiration for the more spectacular manifestations of American culture: advertising, motion pictures, skyscrapers. From such artists as Jean Cocteau, André Salmon, and Blaise Cendrars, American writers could learn "how to apply the lesson of the new American civilization to literature." He urged them to remain American, yet to "acquire French clarity, ease, and style"; by creating a vital literature out of the manifestations of contemporary culture the expatriates could perform "an invaluable service" to American letters and put an end to the isolation of American artists from the community.[82]

Loeb's hopes for a synthesis between a French ideal of formal elegance and a Brooksian cultural nationalism seemed profoundly congenial to Cowley. In early May he wrote to Loeb to express his critical appreciation of the latest *Broom* and pointed out the affinity between Loeb's article and the ideas advanced in "This Youngest Generation." Loeb replied that he was unaware of Cowley's essay, but expected "great things" of his co-evals, "above all a positive note to contrast with the persistent weeping over the fact that America is not Europe, or rather is not an imagined Europe which surely does not exist now if it ever did." He was particularly pleased by Cowley's praise since it pertained to the very issue that he felt had "approximated the ideal picture" toward which he hoped to steer the magazine. *Broom*, he observed to Cowley several weeks later, was slowly attaining "an underlying unity or personality."[83]

Broom's new editorial direction was consolidated in its next number by Matthew Josephson, whose "Made in America" pugnaciously buttressed Loeb's position. It was only necessary to respond freely and flexibly to a "bewildering and astounding American panorama," Josephson argued, for the artist to create "a new folk-lore out of the domesticated miracles of our time."[84] Josephson's exuberantly affirmative viewpoint convinced Loeb that the two might "advantageously cooperate." During the summer the alliance between Josephson and Loeb was clinched: in August 1922 Josephson became associate editor and *Broom* was transformed into "a 'fighting organ,' sponsoring the avant-garde of postwar Europe, the German as well as the French experimenters, and the youth of America."[85] Whatever his sympathies with Loeb, Cowley was as yet far from an unqualified endorsement of the avant-garde. Over the next few months he was drawn deeper into its orbit and came to share partial responsibility for the direction of both *Broom* and *Secession*; his skepticism about modernism, however, never vanished and his commitment to the avant-garde was never as unequivocal and vociferous as Josephson's. It was a measure of his literary pragmatism as well as of his ambivalent allegiance to avant-garde aesthetics that, while involved with *Broom* and *Secession*, he continued to write for the *Dial* and the *Freeman*.

‹ ‹ ‹   For much of May 1922 Cowley waited anxiously for news about the renewal of his fellowship. His financial situation remained precarious, necessitating a perpetual search for complements to his income. Skeptical of attaining early success, Cowley was yet pragmatic and ambitious enough to want to maintain a hundred-percent sales record—he prided himself on having marketed all of the articles he had written in March and April. Still, he continued to need the support of wealthier friends such as John Brooks Wheelwright and Stewart Mitchell, both of whom extended intermittent loans. Mitchell, in addition, commissioned Peggy to paint his portrait in watercolors for as much as sixty dollars. In May he reported that the portrait was exhibited at the Independents' Gallery in New York. He also solicited some of her watercolors for the *Dial*.[86]

At the end of May, Cowley learned that his American Field Service fellowship had been extended for a year. Though the renewal relieved him of immediate financial worries, he greeted the announcement with mixed feelings. Lately he had been "frightfully homesick" for the rural America of his youth—"a country where No Trespass signs can be disregarded, and where there are troutstreams"—and had realized with renewed poignancy the nature of his cultural allegiance: "My talent is not cosmopolitan, and I have no desire to spend my life in France." Cowley still cherished his dream of a rural literary life and agreed with Burke that "the ideal life for an American writer is somewhere within two hours of New York." Burke, who had recently fathered his second child, had purchased a farm near Andover, New Jersey, which would remain his permanent home; he had proposed that Cowley settle on a neighboring farm. Though Cowley had earlier protested that Burke's life was becoming "too much of a piece" and had urged him to transport himself to Europe, he was sorely tempted by his friend's rural ideal of literary community.[87]

By the end of his sojourn in Montpellier, Cowley was growing tired of the sober solemnity of classicism; he had begun to feel that he had exhausted the intellectual and social possibilities of provincial life in southern France and seemed ready for a transfusion of new literary and intellectual energy. Though he complained in early June that he had done "no thinking on aesthetics" of late, still he felt that intellectually Europe was "tremendously stimulating," that under its influence his ideas were "clarifying slowly," and that even life in the French provinces was giving him "an excellent perspective on America."[88] Such intellectual benefits were considerably enhanced during his second year in France, once Cowley had left the classicist backwaters of Montpellier to confront the flood tides of the European avant-garde in full force.

9

A Summer of European Travel

1922

Early in June 1922 Malcolm and Peggy Cowley returned to Paris. They stayed for nearly two months, before embarking on a summer of travel that would take them to Brussels, Munich, Vienna, Berlin. After a year in Montpellier, Paris was immensely stimulating. "I feel continually as if I were drunk, although I drink nothing at all," Cowley told Wheelwright. Gossiping, drinking, or playing bridge with the American colony at Montparnasse, Cowley was once again struck by its eccentric similarity to Greenwich Village. Though he found the Parisian variety more palatable, his attitude remained ambivalent. Like cocaine, he told Burke, the city left one either "tremendously elated or sunk in a brown fit of depression." Under its influence, he told Loeb, serious work was "just as impossible as with any other drug habit." Despite his misgivings Cowley was aware of the special fascination of the city: "Paris has rarely or never produced great literature. There are exceptions: Baudelaire, Verlaine, but the rule is pretty safe. However, Paris has been the condition of great literature." For Cowley, one came to Paris to be stimulated, but one's serious writing had to be done elsewhere. Remaining in Paris, one seemed fated to stoop to the mediocrity of *genre boulevardier* or the antibourgeois caperings of the dadaists.[1]

In Paris, Cowley was given an unexpected opportunity to meet a number of established French writers. Ivan Opffer, an artist from Denmark whom Cowley knew from the Village as an acquaintance of James and Susan Light, had been commissioned by John Farrar of the *Bookman* to draw "from Life" a series of lithograph portraits of great European men of letters; he now proposed that Cowley do the accompanying interviews in French, a language in which he was not proficient. Cowley, whose funds were running low, accompanied Opffer on his first assignment, a portrait of Henri Barbusse, whose antiwar novel *Le Feu* (*Under Fire*, 1916) had raised a good deal of political dust. Not all of it had settled down in

1922, for upon approaching Barbusse's country house, Cowley and Opffer were promptly detained as a pair of bomb-throwing suspects before being allowed to meet the writer. While Cowley asked questions and took copious bilingual notes, Opffer tried to catch Barbusse's facial expression. The interview was dispatched to the *Bookman* and resulted in an assignment to do six other profiles.[2]

Under cover of his now formal commission, Cowley met, besides Barbusse, André Salmon, Georges Duhamel, Charles Vildrac, Paul Fort, Pierre MacOrlan (pseudonym of Pierre Dumarchey), and, at his own proposal, James Joyce. A projected visit to Anatole France miscarried because the author refused to receive visitors. Most of the interviews were conducted during June and July, but Cowley took the summer and fall to give his articles a definitive form; they appeared in the *Bookman* at irregular intervals between October 1922 and January 1925. In the articles, Cowley told John Farrar, he aimed "to *define* each man" by giving "a personal impression" buttressed by exclusive information gained from firsthand sources.[3] Cowley's pen-portraits were but lightweight specimens of literary journalism, limited in depth and slight in critical substance. Yet they illuminate Cowley's early belief in literature as preeminently the expression of a personal sensibility, and show that from the first he thought of writing as an integral activity in which character and imagination, integrity and vision, were inseparably bound up together. In a modest fashion, also, the articles give evidence of Cowley's growing tendency to view a writer's oeuvre and career as one and to relate the work of art to the larger social and cultural milieu. His meetings proved an invaluable education; they initiated him into the complex network of French literary life and politics, and those with Barbusse, Salmon, and Joyce, in particular, sharpened Cowley's own evolving attitudes.

In Barbusse Cowley confronted, perhaps for the first time, a sensitive social visionary and left-wing political activist whose work and personality bespoke a profoundly radicalized human engagement. Cowley's essay radiated admiration, as he sketched Barbusse's rise from relative obscurity to overnight celebrity with the controversial *Under Fire*. Barbusse had plunged into political activism, Cowley implied, without surrendering literature to propaganda. He applauded Barbusse's determination to write literature bearing on "contemporary ideas," endorsed his repudiation of "pure literature" and praised him for combining a politically advanced mode of writing with an open and bold interest in formal experimentation.[4] Such an appreciation adumbrated the stand on literature and politics Cowley would take in the 1930s but in 1922 its radical implications remained unexplored. Nonetheless, Barbusse appears to have seen in Cowley a fraternal artistic and political spirit. In a letter he told Cowley that he looked upon the Americans as "the arbiters of the historical situation of Old Europe," but had found them "badly informed" about the "profoundly rational and equitable ideas" of the French avant-garde. Cowley, in turn, entertained hopes of translating Barbusse's forthcoming novel and helped to straighten out communications between the French writer and his American publishers through Max Eastman, then in Paris as a representative of Hearst International.[5]

Radically different from Barbusse, André Salmon—paradoxically but not surprisingly—seemed even more congenial to Cowley. Salmon was a close associate of a group of writers and artists—André Derain, Picasso, Apollinaire, Max Jacob, Pierre MacOrlan—who in the years before 1914 had virtually initiated the new modern art movement in France. In 1922 he was relatively unknown in America, though the *Dial* had recently published a eulogistic consideration of his latest novel, *La Négresse du Sacré-Coeur*, by Cuthbert Wright. Cowley was enthusiastic about Salmon's novels—"To me personally they opened new worlds of literature"—and proposed to translate parts of *La Négresse* for *Broom*. (In 1929 Salmon's novel was published in an English-language translation by William Slater Brown as *The Black Venus*.) Salmon, in turn, gave Cowley a lively personal account of the efforts of Apollinaire and Picasso to originate a radical modernism: he was, Cowley told Burke, "just what I was looking for"—a writer with an almost "superstitious reverence" for Apollinaire, who gave him "wonderful dope" on current French letters that could be exploited in future articles.[6]

Salmon's informal lectures enhanced Cowley's sense of the importance of specific age groups in literary history and deepened his understanding of a literary generation: it was, he observed, "not a coterie or a society for mutual admiration" but "a group of men whose common age has given them a common point of view, and a common aim which is not necessarily the destruction of every other generation." In America, he thought, one could distinguish "the generation of hopeful intellectuals" of the *New Republic*, the "discouraged intellectuals" of the *Freeman*, "the generation of psychoanalysts" of the *Seven Arts*, and, most recently, "the critical generation" of *Secession*. Despite the doubtful perspicacity of his analysis, under the influence of his Paris meetings Cowley was already feeling his way toward a history of contemporary letters in terms of its constituent age groups.

Undoubtedly Cowley projected many of his own preoccupations onto Salmon. Thus he credited Salmon's generation with having created "a new ideal of the artistic life." It had repudiated the symbolists' aristocratic and disdainful aloofness from common life in favor of a new critical formula: "Art must be given back to life." Impressed by the range of human experience Salmon took for his subject matter and by the variety of literary genres he commanded—Salmon wrote with the same integrity for a mass audience on Parisian murder trials as for a specialized public on modern art—Cowley upheld Salmon as "a type unfortunately rare in modern times: a man of letters who has taken all literature for his province."[7]

Georges Duhamel corroborated Cowley's preference for a literature concerned with human and social reality. Duhamel's wartime experiences as an army surgeon, he believed, had deepened his human sympathies and given him a "delicate compassion" for the suffering he had witnessed. Duhamel wrote "as if with a scalpel," Cowley said, and applied his sharp analytical gifts to individual life as well as to "the diseased organism of society." Still other of Cowley's personal convictions were reflected in the poet Charles Vildrac. He depicted Vildrac as an artist who managed to rise above the factional quarrels of literary Paris and sympathized with Vildrac's denunciation of the modern "affectation of intellectualism" as a "cult of the pure and heartless intelligence" (a verdict anticipating Cowley's later response to the anti-human cerebralism of Paul Valéry). Vildrac also sharpened Cowley's ideal of a new classical literature. In a letter to Amy Lowell, Cowley had observed that his efforts on behalf of a "new" classicism were not to be confused with "Neo-Classicism as now rampant in France." In the *Bookman* he endorsed Vildrac's condemnation of French academic neoclassicism as "a purely bookish attitude" that produced theories of art but was unable to function as the foundation of a vital modern literature—an attitude that adumbrated Cowley's later response to the sterile academicism of the New Humanists. He concluded by positing Vildrac as a contemporary poet who was "classical" in the proper sense: "Writing about the most daily of incidents in the language of the street, he has the ability to raise them to the level of high tragedy. His poems and his plays are simple, graceful, severe . . . he writes what he has to write, without theories or affectations. He is emotional but not emotionalist and simple without being simplist."[8]

Cowley's impressions of James Joyce were less than undividedly positive. In 1922 the cafés of Paris were buzzing with gossipy discussions of the recently published *Ulysses*, and Cowley decided to devote his *Bookman* portrait not so much to a "conventional" analysis of the book as to a discussion of its critical reception. He informed John Farrar that he intended to "write up Joyce from the standpoint of his audience" and to provide American readers with "a collection of the bromides that one hears in a Parisian conversation on *Ulysses*." Cowley's approach, facile as it sounded, seemed partly inspired by a recent altercation with Foster Damon. On July 15, 1922, Damon wrote Cowley that even a hasty reading of the book's last chapter had persuaded him that it was nothing if not "disgusting." Cowley responded that he had not given *Ulysses* the careful reading it deserved, but he objected "on principle" to Damon's repudiation of the book on the grounds of moral or sexual obscenity: " 'Disgusting' is an adjective that reveals less about the book than about the critic." He challenged Damon's right to attack "the authors of immoral literature" and urged him not to develop into "a Boston spinster. Take off them skirts." On September 21 Damon granted that *Ulysses* was "saved by its technique" but persisted in his general hostility: "There seems to be neither humor, nor pathos, nor phantasy. It is Realism at its most painstaking worst." For a truly modern masterpiece Damon referred Cowley to *Moby-Dick*.[9]

Cowley's article for the *Bookman*, based on several meetings with Joyce during the summer, was written in November 1922. Though Farrar judged the portrait "excellent," he did not publish it until July 1924. Opening the article with a satirical sketch of the contradictory and inane reactions to *Ulysses* by expatriate café-sitters, Cowley himself viewed Joyce with considerable, if ill-defined, ambivalence. Mindful of the pains, the sacrifices, and the setbacks marking Joyce's struggles to get his early books published, he admired Joyce's uncompromising dedication to his art, his readiness to fly in the face of "all the forces of custom and decorum and propriety," and his unceasing efforts "to make every word perfect." He presented Joyce as a ceaseless explorer of new paths, who in *Ulysses* had pushed fiction to "the limit not alone of the epic novel but of naturalism and frankness; even, in the true sense, of romanticism." Joyce's ambitious achievement demanded to be measured against Homer's, Cowley felt, but such a comparison was not unambiguously to Joyce's advantage: "either his work is the Odyssey of modern times or it is presumption."[10]

All in all, Cowley's impressionistic portrait was a rather slender and niggardly tribute. The sketch was sprinkled with unexplained touches of condescension, which latently anticipated Cowley's later severer strictures against Joyce. It was not until he rewrote and expanded his portrait to make it an integral part of *Exile's Return* that he understood more precisely what he had found so "intolerable" about Joyce's genius in 1922: his original objections had been less against the technical attainments of Joyce's work than to the moral and human implications of a Joycean aesthetics, which, in *Exile's Return*, he chose to see as a belated manifestation of the symbolist religion of art.[11]

Cowley's weeks in Paris served to clarify and confirm evolving tendencies in his literary thought to date. His meetings with a wide variety of European writers pointed up his humanist and classicist predilections, in art as in life, and reinforced his skepticism about the implications of the symbolist aesthetics at the root of modernity. By exposing him to a broad range of artistic modes and possibilities, they enhanced his sensitivity to the plurality of literary life and creation and supported his propensity for an open-minded approach to the varieties of literary experience. When, shortly after his Paris interviews, he met the more radical avant-garde, he was able to confront it with a sharpened critical perspective.

During July the French capital seemed given over to Americans. "In Paris American was the official language," Cowley told Damon; "nobody spoke French in Montparnasse but the waiters." Cowley appears to have found the American colony in Paris a self-contained community of eccentric individuals, most of whom remained rather isolated from the main cultural movements in France. Many of them did not avail themselves of the chance to establish contacts with French writers—when William Carlos Williams, arriving in France in 1924, asked Robert McAlmon to introduce him to the avant-garde French poets, he was puzzled to learn that McAlmon presumably did not know any of them well enough to function as an intermediary.[12] It was a seminal feature of Cowley's European years that he purposely shunned entrapment in a ghetto-like community of American expatriates but actively sought to associate with major French writers both inside and outside the avant-garde. Like Josephson and Burke, he was a serious student of French literature, of the past as of the present, and through criticism and translation would do much to introduce contemporary French writers to an American audience. In addition, he used his European sojourn to study and talk with the major modern artists of the time—among the "saints" of modernism whom Cowley discussed in *Exile's Return*, he had met Pound, Joyce, and Valéry in Paris—and was perpetually concerned with exploring the impact of European modernist aesthetics and ideas on the young American writers of his generation.

‹ ‹ ‹   By the end of July, Cowley had grown tired of Paris and its American colony. Apart from his *Bookman* interviews he had done no serious work, his funds had once again hit rock bottom, and the city left him intellectually exhausted. The low cost of living and the promise of settling down to work made him decide to spend the rest of the summer in the Austrian Tyrol. On July 24 the Cowleys were in Brussels, where they lingered to await remuneration for several reviews and brief mentions Cowley had written for the *Dial*. By way of Cologne, Munich, and Innsbruck they arrived in Imst, Austria, on August 13, where they put up at the Gasthof Post, an eighteenth-century château converted into a hotel. Shortly before their arrival, William Slater Brown had left the Gasthof Post for Germany, and Josephson had moved on to Reutte to spend time with a clan of French and German dadaists. In the summer of 1922, Cowley remembered, "young American writers were drifting everywhere in West Europe and Middle Europe; they waved to each other from the windows of passing trains." [13]

Having come to Austria to work, Cowley found a nation in the grip of a wildly fluctuating inflationary economy and a political turmoil that carried the seeds of a future world war. With the krone selling seventy-four thousand to the dollar and taking staggering daily plunges, the Cowleys for once could live in princely leisure, relieved from economic pressure. The shadow side of inflation, however, was less bracing. Not only were speculators and exploiters garnering immense profits, but a new breed of tourists was busily doing its part to aggravate the human misery. "Tyrol is overrun with foreigners, all seeking the same economies, and they are taking the food from the mouths of the inhabitants," Cowley wrote to Foster Damon. These profiteers of the exchange—*Valutaschweine* he later dubbed them— were wandering parasitically from country to country in search of "the lowest prices and the most picturesque upheavals of society." The spectacle of poverty and despair to which inflation was reducing the average Austrian family stirred Cowley's social conscience by its contrast with his personal well-being. Though his modest expenditures hardly ranked him with the ruthless profiteers, still Cowley felt implicated in what he later described as "the army of exploitation." To Burke he voiced his humanitarian concern with the sufferings of the people: "The Austrians . . . haven't enough to buy food. Here in Imst even . . . I see them dining on a slice of rye bread washed down with water. . . . They confide to you how dear things are, and you have to agree with them, although personally and familially you are spending less than a dollar a day at the best hotel."

Political tension was acute. Riots were "in the air," Cowley told Damon; tourists were growing unpopular, foreigners threatened with violence. In an atmosphere of human misery and social unrest, writing became next to impossible. "All I can think about is poverty, political economics, and the exchange," he confessed to Burke a few days after his arrival in Imst. Instead of writing, Cowley told Damon, "one broods over politics and consigns Wilson, Clemenceau, Lloyd George, and especially Poincaré to hell. A pretty world they've left us." Three days later he admitted to Burke that his impressions of the Austrian situation had enhanced his skepticism about a formalist aestheticism and strengthened his belief in the need for a literature concerned with the social and political realities of the present: "I don't see how such a thing as pure literature can come out of Austria for the next ten years." [14]

The Austrian situation, however, can hardly be said to have channeled Cowley's thought toward political radicalism. The sharp edge of his guilt and compassion wore off fast enough. "It took me just ten days (10) to harden my heart," he observed to Burke on August 27. "I suppose we'll stay now till the revolution, governmental decrees, rising exchange, or cold weather force us out." His political impressions were too shallow, the twinges of his social conscience too faint, to have more than a fleeting impact. As during the war, his attitude toward the unsettling human and political atmosphere in postwar Europe remained essentially "spectatorial." Cowley saw "the picturesque rather than the enduring." After ten days he had digested enough of the Austrian situation to resume writing in the face of it. [15]

A degree of social guilt also informed Cowley's poem "Valuta," which he mailed to Harold Loeb from Imst in early September:

> Following the dollar, ah, following the dollar, I learned
>   three fashions of eating with the knife, and ordered
>   beer in four languages from a Hungarian waiter

> while following the dollar eastward along the 48th
> degree of north latitude—where it buys most,
> there is the Fatherland—
>
> following the dollar by gray Channel seas, by blue seas
> in Italy, by Alpine lakes as blue as aniline blue, by
> lakes as green as a bottle of green ink, with ink-
> stained monumental mountains rising on either hand;
>
> I dipped my finger in the lake and wrote, *I shall never*
> *return, never, to my strange land*

Often cited and anthologized to illustrate the typical expatriate attitude, "Valuta" has perhaps been read too easily as a serious reflection of Cowley's expatriate experiences. In effect, Cowley aimed to satirize those parasitical tourists swarming over Europe, to whom America, seen through a screen of admiration, had come to seem a mythical country of fantastic skyscrapers and ingenious mechanical appliances, of majestic farmlands and astounding riches, of subways, folksongs, and popular movies. If Cowley was occasionally guilty of such nostalgic falsification, not for a moment did he intend his European stay to be permanent, as his poem claimed. In late October he clarified his position in a letter to John Farrar: "I have joined no band of expatriates and show every intention of returning to New York. . . . The chief advantage of two years in France is to give you a taste for America. . . . The only expatriates in Paris are the people who arrived on the last boat and Harold Stearns. As for the rest . . . say, if you want to hear good, nasal, limey-hating Amurricns, if you want to hear Amurricn spoken in all its ungrammatical purity, come to Paris."[16]

Cowley was in Austria on an ironic mission for *Secession*. While the Austrian situation had convinced him of the undesirability of a pure aestheticism, he was carrying manuscript material for the third issue of a magazine aggressively sponsoring a radical avant-garde aesthetics. His disappointment over its first issue notwithstanding, Cowley had retained a lively, if skeptical, interest in its possibilities. In April 1922 Gorham Munson had written to Cowley that the response to the first issue had given him "visible evidence that Secession was not locating above a vacuum." He had promised an "immensely stronger" second issue and by May had enlisted Burke's active cooperation on the magazine.[17]

Secession 2, published in July 1922, included four poems by E. E. Cummings, Burke's "The Book of Yul" (a story that Cowley had privately praised as the one complete vindication of Burke's experimental theories of form), and two poems by Cowley—"A Solemn Music" and "Two Swans" — the latter of which Josephson had criticized as old-fashioned representationalism. Munson deemed them "astonishingly perfected," and Wheelwright thought they were "complete and inevitable."[18] There was also a prose translation of Tristan Tzara, a short story by Josephson, and a piece of nonsensical humor by William Slater Brown. Munson concluded the issue with another blast at rival magazines; against the idiosyncratic *Little Review* and the "anthological" *Broom*, he presented *Secession* as a coherent "group organ," revealing once again how immediately, if mistakenly, his magazine was a response to Cowley's "This Youngest Generation." In a broadside he reaffirmed *Secession*'s militant avant-gardism: "*Secession* has swerved aside and shot ahead of its American contemporaries—straight into the dangerous rapids of modern letters. It disdains life-belts."[19]

Cowley remained uneasy about being publicly identified with the ideas behind *Secession*. To John Brooks Wheelwright, who had naturally assumed Cowley to bear editorial responsibility, he protested that he had "no formal connection with [*Secession*], none whatsoever." The admittedly "excellent" second issue, however, mitigated his earlier skepticism. To Wheelwright he wrote: "[*Secession*] aroused a great deal of discussion, more than any other magazine of its type. It stands for something definite, is not a collection of the second-rate work of great men. . . . It is an organ for poetry and polemic, an undignified organ, much more mobile than *Broom* or the *Dial*. I want to talk it over with you—badly." To Burke, freshly appointed associate editor, he expressed himself in similar terms: "I do *not* agree with you that Secession should be solid—entirely. I think it should change its character from issue to issue as much as it can while still remaining our own organ. It should always contain serious work, but should do stunts and polemify and all that."[20]

Secession 3, however, again reversed Cowley's appreciation. In September he traveled to Vienna, having agreed to proofread the issue and supervise the printing and distribution of five hundred copies, at a total cost of twenty-five dollars. It was not until he saw the contents of the issue that the irony and inconsistency of his mission stood revealed. Josephson had used his editorial *carte blanche* to advance a pugnacious radical experimentalism and give free scope to his Dada friends. There was a poem by Philippe Soupault and nonsensical, associational prose sketches by Hans Arp and "Will Bray," as well as Josephson's experimental story about a Manhattan sexual voyeur, "Mr. Peep-Peep-Parrish," printed over Munson's objections. In a haphazard series of editorial comments Josephson lambasted *Vanity Fair* for allowing Paul Rosenfeld's "rosy, disheveled, sentimental" and "rapturous" prose to pass for serious criticism, for transforming Apollinaire into a "chic" and "dashing" literary fashion and for butchering Tristan Tzara's "Some Memoirs of Dadaism."[21] Besides a fragment from Waldo Frank's forthcoming *City Block* and Burke's "First Pastoral," the issue included a poem by William Carlos Williams and Cowley's nonsense poem in burlesque of Josephson. The satirical intent of Cowley's poem, however, went virtually unobserved amid the predominantly dadaist contents, which made the issue into a polemical tract for a literature based on mysticism, subconscious drives, and associational processes of thought.[22]

At the end of September, Cowley returned from his proofreading mission to Vienna and in an angry letter to Burke fulminated against the contents of *Secession* 3. The issue, he said, "stinks of bad writing, Dada, and the ghetto." Cowley's disaffiliation from the avant-garde radicalism of *Secession*, his uneasiness about being publicly identified with the *Secession* collective, and his ongoing preference for a classical aesthetics were revealed nowhere more strongly than in his comments to Burke: "The whole weakness of Secession is the fact that it is supposed to be a group organ and that the group falls apart in the middle. I often contradict myself, but if there's one thing I believe in, it is good writing. With you I have been trying to work towards solidity and elegance, towards a to-some-extent classical reaction against the muds and fogs of contemporary literature. . . . I repeat that the third number of Secession has got to be suppressed and that Matty alone cannot edit another number. Otherwise to save our self-respect we have got to secede from Secession." The fervor of his disapproval, however, was but a measure of the seriousness of his commitment to the magazine. Whatever his objections, he still saw *Secession* as a feasible instrument for the creation of a receptive audience and a congenial literary milieu for the members of his age group: "The purpose of Secession is not really to be the organ of a group but to form a group which as yet does not exist. The purpose of a group is to be an audience for poetic drama and to make intelligent literature possible."[23]

While Cowley's endorsement of *Secession* was temporarily suspended, his relations with Loeb and *Broom* were rapidly improving. In late August, Cowley traveled north to Reutte to visit Josephson. Memories of their epistolary quarrel of several months past made him approach the meeting with apprehension, but what resentments still lingered were quickly obviated by Josephson's charm and conviviality. Though Cowley still resented Joseph-son's airs of superiority, his brash posturing was contagious and helped persuade Cowley of the need to "do stunts and polemify" in *Secession* while reserving *Broom* for more serious work. As they discussed the future of both magazines, Josephson was impressed by Cowley's editorial com-petence and recommended to Loeb that he be made a contributing editor on *Broom*. Cowley later recalled Josephson as "a very good editor [with] a gift for making discoveries, for taking risks and for getting himself into hot water, as if he carried a steaming kettle with him through Europe." [24]

In early September, Cowley traveled east to Innsbruck to meet Harold Loeb, who was transferring *Broom* from Rome to a cheaper printing estab-lishment in Berlin. Loeb was accompanied by Kathleen Cannell, a habitué of modern art circles in Paris, and Loeb's informal assistant and advisor on matters of art. Cowley took an immediate liking to Kitty Cannell, an at-tractive woman of sound and independent taste; it turned out they shared a host of New York acquaintances. His impressions of Loeb, however, were reserved. To Burke he described him as the scion of a wealthy Jewish family with international contacts in finance, philanthropy, and art, a type he had first encountered in his first year's roommate at Harvard, John Roth-schild. Adopting a tone of ironic bemusement, he sketched how Loeb had attained to the captainship of the Princeton wrestling team before joining a "pre-Rape-and-Raphael sort of circle" of art lovers near Haverstraw, where Loeb had occasionally seen Cowley stroll past his cabin in search of trout. After running the Sunwise Turn bookshop in New York, Cowley wrote, Loeb had launched *Broom* with Kreymborg's help, confident that the latter "would edit a vastly superior Others" but soon finding that Kreymborg had turned "scared and conservative." He sketched some of the conflicts that had led to Kreymborg's resignation (about which he had earlier expressed regret) and noted that Loeb seemed eager to "add us to his staff." Cowley depicted Loeb as an editor of uncertain taste and judgment, a man under the successive artistic and sexual influences of his friends. As an essayist, however, he felt Loeb was "infinitely more logical" than Josephson. [25]

Loeb's memory of his meeting with Cowley in Innsbruck mixed irony with admiration: "My opinion of Cowley . . . had risen during the years. No one wrote better letters or contributed such consistently good material to *Broom*. And I was not disappointed when he finally arrived, looking like a cross between Foxy Grandpa and the darker Katzenjammer Kid.

Malcolm refused to be hurried. When a question was put to him, the lines between the eyes deepened and the quizzical expression froze. Nothing else happened. Often the silence seemed interminable. But when he finally spoke, his words meant something." Loeb offered Cowley a modest position on *Broom* as a wandering scout and contributing editor. With Josephson established in Berlin, Cowley was to avail himself of his French contacts, round up new material, and translate it; in return he would find *Broom* a hospitable outlet for his own writings. After some hesitation—he grumbled about the magazine's low rates of payment—Cowley accepted. On September 9 he wrote Loeb that he was "very enthusiastic" about his new connection with *Broom* and saw the magazine as "the perfect medium for what I have to say." His enthusiasm was understandable enough. Not only did Loeb seem willing to publish whatever Cowley submitted, his new arrangement with *Broom* was also "a comfortable lever for meeting anyone I want to know in Paris." He could now exult, indeed, in a profusion of "markets" for his writings: he had the *Dial* for "literary ideas," the *Freeman* for "political ideas," *Broom* for "cultural ideas," and *Secession* for "poetry and polemic."[26]

Cowley's commitment to *Broom* was buttressed by his growing approval of its artistic course. As Loeb had written to Lola Ridge in early May, *Broom* had become "an organ with a *strongly held* point of view." During the summer Loeb had allowed Josephson to strengthen his editorial hold over *Broom*'s direction. In a series of articles Josephson had propagated the "pure" and non-referential poetry of Paul Eluard, the use of American popular culture by Philippe Soupault, and the experimental *roman poétique* of Louis Aragon. He had praised Isidore Ducasse, author of the blasphemous *Les Chants de Maldoror* (*The Lay of Maldoror*), then being serialized in *Broom*, as the precursor of "a literature of great fertility, freedom, invention, aggressiveness" and the explorer of "the cavernous recesses of the mind and the momentous display of the unconscious." Though there was much in Josephson's aesthetics (and *Broom*'s contents) about which Cowley continued to feel ambivalent, his skepticism was diminishing and by late September, only two days after he had reaffirmed his classical ideals to Burke, he observed that he agreed with Josephson that Louis Aragon was "doing vastly interesting work."[27] More importantly, he was increasingly sympathetic to *Broom*'s cultural nationalism and its support of an avant-garde machine aesthetics, an editorial line that had grown markedly stronger since Loeb's "Foreign Exchange" and Josephson's "Made in America" in the May and June issues.

Broom's September 1922 issue contained a lengthy article by Loeb, in which he expounded his optimism for the emergence of a vital and indigenous American culture. The essay had a profound effect on Cowley. The recent indictment by American intellectuals of America's cultural inferiority to Europe, Loeb argued, did more to inhibit than to foster the rise of an autochthonous culture in the United States. He forswore all imitation of European art and searched for the signs of a native culture unadulterated by European ideals or traditions. Genuine artistic expression in America, Loeb held, was rooted in "the mysticism of money," an American religion of business and moneymaking. The indigenous manifestations of technology and business—whether in architecture, advertising, engineering or the popular arts—had "an aesthetic value of no mean order." Loeb spoke of "aesthetic pleasure in the balanced masses and curved belt lines of machinery" and praised Marinetti, Wyndham Lewis, and the French dadaists for recognizing the aesthetic potential of a machine age. He spoke of jazz as a universal art form and of Negro spirituals as America's "real folk music." The "mysticism of money" engendered a vital new language ("vigorous, crude, expressive, alive with metaphors, Rabelaisian, resembling Elizabethan rather than Victorian English"), a new narrative technique founded on speed and dispensing with "logical continuity" (a mode best exemplified by the popular Nick Carter stories) and a new stock of "conventionalized characters," including the "greatest living dramatic artist," Charlie Chaplin. Such, Loeb felt, were the hopeful signs that American culture was entering "a classical period."[28]

Loeb's essay elicited an enthusiastic response from Cowley. The "new" *Broom* obviated all his objections against its aimless eclecticism and its new editorial line held his full approval. To Burke he had already indicated that "as expatriates expatiating on America as a literary subject" Loeb and he were fully in agreement. Writing to Loeb himself he grew positively ecstatic: "*Broom* is an international magazine of the arts," he wrote. "But *Broom* is also, by reasons stronger than any of us, an American magazine of the arts. As such it has to represent a definite attitude and a set of definite ideas. It needs a sort of manifesto, which I always thought was lacking. But by God it isn't any longer, not since your article on the Mysticism of Money. There was a set of clear ideas, ideas which are fresh to American literature and which ought to revitalize it. . . . Here is *Broom's* declaration of principles; all that remains is to apply them. . . . The article on the whole was bully. I make a more personal comment on it when I say that it affected my own thinking." [29]

As a direct offshoot of Loeb's essay, Cowley composed a satirical portrait of an imaginary young American intellectual, "written specially for *Broom.*" He advertised his sketch as "venom and bile against the generation of Harold Stearns. Twelve hundred words of fine hate." "Young Mr. Elkins" was partly directed against the rhapsodic impressionism and mystical nationalism of Paul Rosenfeld. More directly, it aimed to ridicule the anti-American indictments of the thirty intellectuals of *Civilization in the United States.* Stearns was Cowley's principal target. A young man mystically spawned and culturally conditioned by American civilization— "It suckled him with Shredded Wheat. It draped Kuppenheimer Klothes about his shoulders. It gave him an Underwood typewriter"—Mr. Elkins spurns the culture that produced him; he thunders against "billboards, Billy Sunday and Methodism, proportional representation, Comstock, elevated railroads. . . . the commercial ugliness of cities." At thirty-four he is "a single tired wrestler at grips with American civilization and determined to talk it to death." In his portrait Cowley criticized those who refused to take seriously America's indigenous cultural expressions, however crude or popular, but who strove instead to transform American culture into a replica of Europe: Elkins "dreams of an America which has imitated the best of Paris and Berlin and London, an Anglo-Franco-German America ruled by philosophers and economists and rising clean from the sackcloth-and-ashes of puritanism into the leisured humanism of European culture, into a naked dawn. And what he dreams he writes, in his deeper room, sulkily, on a typewriter which is the most finished product of a mechanical civilization." The paradox inherent in Stearns's cultural renunciation was underlined by the irony of Cowley's concluding image: annoyed by the cacophonous chaos of an urban-technological America, Mr. Elkins rises "nervously" and closes his window upon the very culture that has shaped him. [30]

In early October 1922 Malcolm and Peggy Cowley traveled north to spend three weeks in Berlin, where Josephson was opening up the new offices of *Broom.* Germany, like Austria, was in the grip of inflationary madness. The mark was taking daily downward plunges, and Cowley remembered how, at a monthly stipend of a hundred dollars, Josephson in Berlin could dwell in luxury and leisure. Josephson, in turn, recalled how with limited means the Cowleys "played at being Monte Cristo" for the duration of their stay in Berlin. Through Josephson, who in turn had received the tip from one of his Dada friends, the Cowleys had been recommended a cheap hotel near the Berlin Tiergarten, the "Hotel am Zoo." The Josephsons, much dismayed but appreciative of the Dada joke, had discovered that the hotel was patronized by a host of Berlin streetwalkers, but they decided not to enlighten the Cowleys and spoil their surprise. Upon arrival, however, the Cowleys outjoked the jokers by setting up permanent quarters in the "mournful bagnio," much to the amusement and consternation of visiting friends like Harold Loeb, Kathleen Cannell, and Mina Loy, who came accompanied by her fourteen-year-old daughter Joella.[31]

Cowley was depressed by the spectacle of moral degradation and human exploitation he witnessed in postwar Berlin. With its economic system in ruins, Weimar Germany seemed to have abandoned all human and social values. This, indeed, was the bleak and "godless" Germany of George Grosz's *Ecce Homo*, drawings from which were reprinted in a special German issue of *Broom* (February 1923). Grosz depicted, in Cowley's words, "a society without redeeming features. Glory had been lost in the War, honor in the betrayal of the revolution and sanity in the crazy years when ten million marks would not buy a package of cigarettes. There was no standard left except pure effrontery." Fourteen years later Cowley recalled Berlin in the autumn of 1922 as a city "peopled with cripples and fairies, with bacon-fatty Polish profiteers, with hungry street girls (half of them Lesbians), with demobilized and demoralized German officers who looked as if they belonged in a hospital rather than a night club. The general atmosphere was that of a frenzied carnival in an asylum for incurables."[32]

It was in Berlin that Cowley first met Louis Aragon, who had come north from Austria to seek out Matthew Josephson. Cowley had already begun to admire Aragon's writings, but he was bowled over by the Frenchman's vitality and charm, an unusual combination of "cruel wit and literary erudition." Aragon, Cowley recalled, was "more brilliant than anyone else I had known." Striding into a restaurant on the Kurfürstendamm, in the midst of a corrupt and dehumanized city, he seemed "like a first intruder from the world of living men, like Orpheus in hell." Aragon belonged to a generation of French writers whose war-induced disillusionment, far from leaving them morally broken, had given them a perversely jovial ability to feel at home in a disorderly postwar Europe: in 1922 Aragon relished Berlin as "the most modern city of Europe. . . . Advertising is everything here. The electric signs are luminous over the Potsdamer Platz; the radio blares everywhere in this town. . . . The bars and music halls . . . are decorated with an applied form of Cubist or Expressionist art, while the subway stations must have been designed by Arnold Böcklin." For all his admiration, Cowley was not prepared to share Aragon's appreciation of Berlin as a manifestation of "the most admired disorder"—rather, his three weeks persuaded him that "it was an insane life for foreigners in Berlin." At the end of October he and Peggy took an express train back to France.[33]

10

Life Among the Dadaists

France, 1922–1923

After a short stopover in Paris, where he gathered material for *Broom* from André Salmon and Pierre Reverdy, Cowley spent two weeks in Montpellier to wind up his scholastic affairs. Once again he found the Midi ambience intellectually immobilizing. "I cannot understand how I stayed a year in this town or how I ever had the strength to leave it," he told Loeb. "The air is poison. It is like living in molasses; it is sweet and an enemy of motion." After a summer of travel the enforced stability of Montpellier engendered a bleak self-assessment. Cowley was disturbed by his failure to make a responsible use of his "absolute liberty" and to work out a "scheme of life" by which he could think and write to his contentment. His ambitions, he feared, might well outrun his talents—"this is the period of my life when I realize poignantly that I am not Shakespeare; the beginnings of middle age." In early November he sent Loeb his latest poem, "Mortuary," which recalls his earlier despondency in Greenwich Village but also reflects the anxiety he was then feeling about finding a viable mode of life that could procure a mainstay against artistic dryness—"death is rigid being the achievement of a pattern; death is a finished pattern of / wrinkles round the eye." He also translated material by Pierre Reverdy for *Broom*. Finding Loeb personally "sweet and generous and very pleasant to work for," Cowley remained strongly committed to *Broom* and fearfully followed its fortunes in the dizzying tumbles of the German mark.[1]

In mid-November 1922 the Cowleys settled down in Giverny, a small Norman village on the river Epte, some fifty miles west of Paris, where they planned to spend the winter and spring. Jim Butler, a painter friend from the Village and the stepgrandson of Claude Monet, helped them find a studio and two rooms over a blacksmith shop. Giverny was an artists' colony that had known its prime before the war; it still harbored an assortment of artists and craftsmen and occasionally was startled by boisterous invasions of young artists from Paris. Once in a while, the eighty-two-year-old Monet could still be observed working at his easel near the water-lily pond that inspired his "Nymphéas" paintings. After months of European rovings the Impressionist charm and serene tranquility of the Norman landscape worked like a balm: "A long hill running east and west, with little copses and wheatfields. A huddle of stone cottages. A little river bordered with poplars, damp green fields, then finally the Seine. Giverny should be familiar to everybody; it has been painted for the Luxembourg, the Metropolitan, the Autumn Salon, and the Independents; by Cezanne, Monet, T. E. and J. Butler and Robert W. Chambers." Cowley was soon perfectly acclimatized to the countryside; predictably, he found his northern environs "much more sympathetic than the Midi." Jim Butler, a natural outdoorsman, often joined Cowley on trout-fishing expeditions in the Epte or went canoeing with him past the local water mill, Giverny's architectural pride. After writing or studying in the mornings, Cowley would bicycle into the softly rolling countryside, where he was struck by the way in which the landscape reflected the difference in character between the Normans and the French: "On the west bank were straggling towns, the homes of farmer-freebooters who feared nobody, not God or the French; on the east bank the villages were close-huddled each about its church, for spiritual warmth and self-protection." Here, it seemed, was another confirmation of Cowley's belief in cultural organicism.[2]

From Giverny, Cowley laid ambitious plans: fortnightly trips to Paris, a thesis on Racine, a book of poems, a series of portraits for *Broom*, criticism for the *Dial*. Typically, he was inclined to put more irons in the fire than he could effectively handle. For the moment, he seemed to realize as much: "I want to do too much. If I had come here to write a novel or a thesis, I should write it. Under the circumstances, with divided aims, I shall probably accomplish little."[3] In a long career Cowley was to spend a large part of his energy on a host of minor literary projects. Only rarely did he manage to take time out for a consecutive and undisrupted effort at a larger enterprise; the majority of his books would be remoldings of earlier fragmented writings, with the finished product showing little trace of patching.

Cowley's association with *Broom* and *Secession* did not preclude a continued allegiance to the *Dial*. At the end of May 1922 Gilbert Seldes had pronounced his trust in Cowley's "infallible taste and editorial judgment" and shown his willingness to let Cowley "continue the establishing of [his] critical position" in the pages of the *Dial*.[4] Over the summer he wrote two reviews, which appeared in the *Dial* in October and November 1922. Considerations of recent books of poetry by Maxwell Bodenheim, Conrad

Aiken, and Carl Sandburg, they amounted to an analysis of what Cowley saw as three major tendencies in American poetry, a personal modification of Amy Lowell's tripartite division. In a witty and caricaturistic review of Bodenheim, Cowley put him down as the "American prophet of the new preciosity." Aiken and Sandburg he saw as representatives of, respectively, a genteel, polished, Anglo-Saxon tradition and a rough-hewn "ril Amurricn" strain in verse. The second review ("Two American Poets") probed into the meaning of the term "American" in poetry. "It is a temporal rather than a spatial adjective," Cowley wrote to Scofield Thayer; "it belongs definitely to the generation of 1914; an earlier writer like Poe, or a later like Cummings is just a poet; Amy Sandburg Frost is an American poet." In Cowley's eyes "American" did not so much designate an authentic national quality as mark a historical period. Moreover, as he advanced in "Two American Poets," since the term could encompass the poetic extremes of Aiken and Sandburg as well as a host of widely divergent writers, each of whom defended a different conception of "Americanism," one could only conclude that "except as a party label" there was no American poetry. There was, he explained, "no poetry so deeply rooted in our soil and tradition that a foreigner can never fully understand it. . . . America remains a thing seen and not a manner of seeing. America is not a point of view, a style, or a mode of thought, but a subject merely. . . . American poets do not exist, but (to witness Sandburg and Aiken) there are capable poets in America."[5]

By the time of the publication of "Two American Poets" in November 1922, however, Cowley's attitude toward nationality in art was altering drastically. In early January 1923 he observed to Burke that since the writing of the piece in August he had "evidently right about faced on the question of the importance of American material." The change, he felt, was mostly "psychological." "America in the distance begins to loom up as a land of promise, something barbaric and decorative and rich. The form-matter pendulum has taken another stroke, and I begin to believe strongly in the importance of using contemporary material." Several weeks later he returned to the subject in a letter to John Brooks Wheelwright, which shows how, under the influence of his European experience, his sense of a specifically American tradition in literature was deepening:

"Two American Poets" was written in August. Since then I have greatly changed my attitude towards American traditions. I should no longer say that there is no American poetry in the sense that there is French or Chinese poetry. I even disagree with you when you state that America begins with the Civil War, and I think if you reread Huckleberry Finn or the beginning of Moby Dick you would revise your statement. From certain documents it would even seem that American characteristics were already pretty well defined in Revolutionary days. I begin to admire Sinclair Lewis, having recently read Main Street and Babbitt, and I do not think that critics are at all discerning when they say that he writes from hate only. He has done more than Whitman to create a national consciousness. Nationalism is not a spook. Spooks don't hit you on the head with a brick or prevent you from eating in restaurants. Nationalism does just that to the French in Munich. Nationalism is just as real as bricks or restaurants. A few of its manifestations are desirable.[6]

Cowleys' nationalist orientation was confirmed by his *Bookman* interview with Pierre MacOrlan, who convinced Cowley that in a wavering Europe badly in need of moral and economic regeneration America was in effect "the bulwark of the present order." America's new importance on the international scene, MacOrlan asserted, had enhanced the status of its literature in Europe.[7]

Cowley's increasing Americanism was strongly apparent in his contribution to the January 1923 issue of *Broom*. During the fall of 1922 the contents of *Broom* had emphatically come to support the aesthetic program for an indigenous American art advanced in Loeb's "The Mysticism of Money."[8] Its November issue had contained an exuberant attack by Josephson on the failure of Stearns's thirty symposiasts to appreciate "the unaffected beauty and wisdom of the American *milieu*." It was high time for American artists, Josephson had pleaded, to recognize the aesthetic potential of "that effervescent revolving cacophonous milieu . . . where the Billposters enunciate their wisdom, the Cinema transports us, the newspapers intone their gaudy jargon; where athletes play upon the frenetic passions of baseball crowds, and skyscrapers rise lyrically to the exotic rhythms of jazzbands which upon waking we find to be nothing but the drilling of pneumatic hammers on steel girders." Josephson had advanced American advertising slogans as "the most daring and ingenuous literature of the age."[9] *Broom*'s December issue had featured Cowley's satirical attack on "the generation of Harold Stearns," but the magazine's national focus reached a pinnacle in its all-American January number, with contributions by Kenneth Burke, Jean Toomer, Robert Sanborn, William Carlos Williams, Kay Boyle, Elsa von Freytag-Loringhoven, Gertrude Stein, Hart Crane, Marianne Moore, Matthew Josephson, and several lesser-known American writers.

Cowley was represented by an article in celebration of the American watercolors of Jules Pascin (1885–1930).[10] Cowley's enthusiasm for Pascin had been roused during his summer stay in Paris. At the end of July he had written to Loeb, proposing to do an article on Pascin for *Broom*: "It is caricature of the highest sort, savantly distorted; civilization revealed by the line of a uniform and race by the color of the eyeball. Sure choice of the picturesque: Mexicans in Texas, niggers in Florida, Jews in New York, Irish in Boston. . . . After Waldo Frank and Mr. Stearns, here at last is a worthy commentary on American civilization." Loeb had agreed that, "treated as plastic comment rather than pure art," Pascin might make the subject of a "very acceptable" article.[11]

"Pascin's America" was written in the late summer, before Cowley's skepticism about the avant-garde had begun to subside; amid the predominantly experimental contents of *Broom*'s American issue, it was conspicuous for its moderately conservative defense of Pascin's social and human realism and for its resistance to a modernist machine aesthetics. Pascin, Cowley wrote, "was neither futurist nor unanimist but human." He praised Pascin for recognizing the infeasibility of a pure aestheticism as well as the dependency of art upon human experience—the implications of his art were "social, economic, personal," Cowley noted, for into his work Pascin put "all his experience . . . and not a circumscribed portion labeled Aesthetics." He commended Pascin for rejecting tarnished legends about America and, rising to a tone of Emersonian affirmation, ranked Pascin with those mythmaking artists who, each in his personal fashion, had helped to shape America's conception of itself: "Before Walt Whitman America hardly existed; to him we owe the pioneers, the open spaces, in general the poetry of square miles. Bret Harte created California and Twain the Mississippi. Woodrow Wilson, Chaplin, the James brothers; each created a separate America, an America which frightened pleasantly or amused us, a Godrighteous America for which we fortunately did not die. America is a conception which must be renewed each morning with the papers. It is not one conception but a million which change daily, which melt daily into one another."[12] Cowley was evoking an openness to the multiformity of American culture and cultural expression that became a hallmark of his criticism. His treatment of Pascin carried the seeds of his later insistence on the social and humanizing function of art and anticipated his conception of the artist as a creator of myths and values that serve to make man's natural and social environment humanly habitable.[13]

‹ ‹ ‹ From Giverny, Cowley made weekly or fortnightly train trips to Paris to immerse himself in the fast-paced cosmopolitanism of the city. "Paris was a great machine for stimulating the nerves and sharpening the senses," he recalled in *Exile's Return*; "everything seemed to lead toward a half-sensual, half-intellectual swoon." Still, Cowley approached Paris with a divided mind, as his rural predilections were brought into conflict with his appreciation of the cultural excitements of the modern city. "Paris is a town I enter with joy and leave without regret," he observed to Burke in early February; "it is a town where one spends weekends which occasionally last a lifetime." Finding the city both "fantastic and unlivable," Cowley preferred to approach its urbane cosmopolitanism from the serene pastoralism of rustic Giverny. The tension between city and country, so central a theme in his verse, was an important leitmotif in his entire career.[14] Its dominant geographical pattern—a pendulum movement between Belsano and Pittsburgh, Giverny and Paris, Sherman and New York—reflected a deep-seated ambiguity about urban living and a nostalgic longing to remain in touch with the rural landscape of his childhood.

On one of his excursions to Paris in mid-December, Cowley was introduced by Matthew Josephson to his French dadaist friends, the group surrounding the magazine *Littérature*—Louis Aragon, André Breton, Philippe Soupault, Tristan Tzara. Whatever his reservations about their aesthetic theories, Cowley found it hard to resist their infectious vitality, their youthful defiance, and their exhilarating taste for novelty and scandal. Aragon and Tzara, in particular, he found personally likable; both became his good friends and were regular visitors in Giverny. Where six months before he had virulently denounced Dada as a violation of his classical ideal, he now concurred with Josephson that the dadaists were "the most amusing people in Paris." Aragon initiated Cowley into the Dada art of staging disruptive pranks and manifestations when he took him to a performance of *Locus Solus* (1914), a play by Raymond Roussel that aroused the "unbounded enthusiasm" of the Dada group. Cowley reviewed the performance (and the dadaist response) for *Broom* and at length described the spectacle to Burke. He took the play as an experimental piece of sur-realist and absurdist theater that violated all the standards of clarity and logic governing traditional French culture. The play roused the fury of the Parisian literary establishment but was promptly appropriated by André Breton and his consorts as a masterpiece of pointlessness. On several con-secutive nights Breton brought along the staff, collaborators, wives, and mistresses of *Littérature* to conduct a volley of tumultuous applause when-ever the audience showed signs of disapproval or the actors made a trivial remark that could be blown up into comic universality. In the end the police tried to put a stop to their riotous behavior only to be held at bay by Breton's delivery of a "magnificently hostile oration" in defense of the liberty of the spectator. Cowley, who had observed the fracas in sympa-thetic but ironic bemusement, granted there was "something magnificent" in the very pointlessness of the play and confessed he had found the whole manifestation "utterly mad" but also "huge fun." [15]

What partly attracted Cowley to Dada was its exuberant, if ironic, affir-mation of the ultramodernity of American civilization, its celebration of American technology and popular culture as the genuine expressions of a dynamic urban-industrial society. At the end of January 1923, exactly a year after the peak of his classicist infatuation, he revealed how thoroughly he had absorbed the provocative excitement of Dada. His nationalist wrath was roused by Kenneth Burke, who in a letter had observed that America, lacking cultural richness and dignity, had become "the wonder of the world simply because America is the purest concentration point for the vices and vulgarities of the world." From among the skyscrapers of Manhattan, Burke's perspective on America had remained critical, but essentially un-changed. From his friend's European perspective, however, "the dragon of American industry" had come to seem "a picturesque and even noble monster." Accordingly, an indignant Cowley fulminated rather incoher-ently against what he, somewhat wrongheadedly, saw as Burke's defection to the anti-Americanism of Harold Stearns:

America is just as Goddamned good as Europe—worse in some ways, better in others . . . Wave old Glory! Peace! Normalcy! . . . America shares an inferiority complex with Germany. Not about machinery or living standards, but about Art. *Secession* is less important than *Littérature* because it is published in New York . . . the only excuse for living two years in France is to remove this complex, and to discover, for example, that Tzara, who resembles you like two drops of water, talks a shade less intelligently than you. To discover that the Dada crowd has more fun than the *Secession* crowd because the former, strangely, has more American pep. . . . THE ONLY SALVA-TION FOR AMERICAN LITERATURE IS TO BORROW A LITTLE PUNCH AND CONFIDENCE FROM AMERICAN BUSINESS. American literature—I mean Frank, Anderson, Oppenheim, et al.—is morally weak, and before it learns the niceties of form its morale has to be doctored, or all the niceties in the world will do it no good at all. . . . New York is refine-ment itself beside Berlin. French taste in most details is unbearable. London is a huge Gopher Prairie. You give me a pain in the ass. Mr. Burke, meet Mr. Stearns. You'll be crazy about each other. You have *so* much in common.[16]

If on occasion Cowley's attitude rose to jingoist extremes, more com-monly his literary nationalism was tempered with criticism. Though as he told John Wheelwright he had begun to "potter with Amurricn material," his exploration of native themes was often satirical and rarely devoid of irony. Essentially his attitude was that of "a critical patriot," whose loyalty to American culture was laced with skepticism. His position was clearly exemplified in "Portrait by Leyendecker," written for *Broom* during January 1923; it was conceived as a fantastic variation upon *Babbitt* and was, appro-priately, dedicated to Sinclair Lewis. Cowley's Leyendecker man—named after the artist Joseph Leyendecker, best known for his *Saturday Evening Post* covers and as the creator of the "Arrow Collar Man"—satirically ex-emplifies the consumerist ideal of life (standardized, uniform, smiling) conjointly propagated by American advertisements. He is the inventor of Duplicator, Inc., a patented method of duplicating his magic smile upon millions of lips, and the composer of a poem made up entirely of advertis-ing slogans. Cowley had methodically extracted the slogans from an issue of the *Saturday Evening Post* and rearranged them in dadaistic fashion to create an ironic impression of "inexplicable sadness." Forty-five years later he included Leyendecker's poem in *Blue Juniata: Collected Poems* as "Voices from Home: 1923."[17]

In that same January of 1923 Cowley sent Burke a poem for *Secession* that played on American popular culture in a similarly ironic fashion. Adapting the rhythm of a popular jazz lyric to the subject of a burial ceremony, Cowley created "an impressive funeral jig." Its effect was utterly dadaistic—"WORMS crawl out and the WORMS crawl in / to BUILD them a dwelling beNEATH the skin." But as if to underline that such radical experimentalism did not preclude a classical allegiance to formal elegance and control, he sent in a companion poem on love that was beautifully finished and proportioned:

> There is a moment after the embrace
> when happily fatigued we do not speak
> when still my cheek is resting on your cheek
> when hearts throb still and limbs still interlace
>
> . . . .
>
> There is a moment logical and white
> behind the wall of flesh. It is as if
> falling agreeably from some high cliff
> I floated in a limitless sea of light
>
> among impersonal forms and came to rest
> within the personal limits of a night
> where chair and bed loom comfortably trite
> where still my heart is beating on your chest.[18]

Over the winter Cowley was drawn more deeply into the orbit of the dadaists. He discovered that whatever cohesion the Dada movement had possessed in its heyday was rapidly disintegrating; the group was already plagued by internal dissensions that would cause its ultimate dissolution. In early February, Cowley attended a Dada manifestation at which Aragon, Breton, Francis Picabia, Georges Ribemont-Dessaignes, Jacques Rigaut, and Tzara banded together for the first time since their falling out eighteen months before. At the occasion Cowley was formally taken up into their ranks; he contributed a signature and a poem to their manifestation and Tzara translated "Valuta" for one of the Dada sheets. "I suppose I am now officially a Dada," Cowley announced to Burke on February 8, 1923. The uncertainty of his proclamation pointed up his ambivalence. From the first he tried to maintain a critical distance. His commitment was never as vociferous or wholehearted as Josephson's. Rather, he displayed an eclectic openness to the diverse and complex literary life of Paris, regarded Dada as merely one of its manifestations (if a most contagious one), and made a point of meeting many writers of various persuasions. Thus, while he consorted with the dadaists, he continued to befriend such "hated enemies" of

Dada as Salmon and MacOrlan, and "in the most fraternal manner" conversed with Vildrac and Duhamel, writers less than sympathetic to Salmon and MacOrlan.[19]

Yet it was impossible not to find the dadaists stimulating, refreshing, even liberating. Underneath their nihilistic posturing and theatrical activism Cowley discovered a "surprisingly disinterested" devotion to art and literature. Their loud proclamations of disdain for all morality, Cowley saw, could not conceal that they were "animated by fierce moral convictions." The dadaists, he observed in his notebook, "seek to regenerate literature by absurdity, for theirs is a moral generation." In particular he admired their high sense of principle, their personal integrity, and their refusal to compromise with a commercial literary culture. Fierce individualists, they yet displayed an attractive sense of literary community: "They are a form of cocaine and personally take no stimulants except their own company." In Cowley's eyes the dadaists evinced a natural capacity to work (and fight) together, which seemed alien to an American tradition of artistic and spiritual isolation but appealed to his feeling for literary and social companionship. Yet he also recognized that for all their brilliance (Aragon, in particular, he judged "immensely talented") they would never accomplish greatness unless they broke away from the group.[20]

From the first, however, there were limits to Cowley's admiration. He could not share the dadaists' predilection for the city and distrusted their free sexual mores and bohemian life-style. More importantly, if from the dadaists he acquired "a pretty rigorous conception of literary ethics," he felt uneasy about its artistic implications. "*Dada c'est le jemenfoutisme absolu*," he wrote to Burke. "It is the negation of all motives for writing, such as the Desire for Expression, the Will to Create, the Wish to Aid." Through its whimsical individualism Dada seemed doomed to ultimate futility— the pursuit of one's individual caprices, the staging of practical jokes. Even at the time, Cowley recognized the internal contradictions of Dada: "A writer who was truly dada would disdain collective action as he would disdain any other attempt to influence the mind of the public." Regarding the world, in Cowley's later words, as "a hostile force to be fought, insulted or mystified," the dadaists were yet morally bound to the very public they pretended to disclaim.[21]

Though Cowley's early response carried all the germs of his repudiating analysis of Dada in *Exile's Return*, his understanding in the winter and spring of 1923 remained shallow and impressionistic. At the time, he responded intuitively to its mood of carefree excitement and youthful rebellion but did not explore its intellectual assumptions or historical roots very deeply. He did not actually read most of the Dada manifestoes until, a decade later, he was in the midst of writing *Exile's Return*.[22]

Contrary to his intentions, Cowley did not always manage to keep his distance from this infectious movement. As he granted in retrospect, he "could not help absorbing [dadaist] notions of literary conduct, as if from the atmosphere." Through Dada, he told Burke in late January, he was "infected with the desire to write excitingly." The dadaists, he thought, had "affected not [his] thinking but [his] writing profoundly"; he assured Burke that he had "not substantially revised" his ideas on art and criticism. When Burke expressed his "purest disgust" with his friend's apparent infatuation with "the arrant and sterile modernity" of Dada, Cowley became more emphatic: "I haven't swallowed Dada hook and sinker; my instincts are classical and intellectual. I'll save my soul if it can be saved."[23]

In the early months of 1923, then, Cowley was at best a reluctant espouser of dadaism. Though some of his dadaist caperings became part of literary lore, to cut a dashing figure as a dadaist did not come naturally or spontaneously to him. Cowley was temperamentally unsuited for the slapstick iconoclasm of Dada; his dadaist posturings always seemed slightly strained. Ultimately, Dada's impact went less deep than his enthusiasm for a classical humanism. Cowley's profound respect for form, intelligence, and clarity made him skeptical of Dada's extreme romanticism, its wilful obscurity, its abolition of logic, and its veneration of the subconscious— he never followed Dada into surrealism. Conversely, Dada's affirmative vitality, its moral fervor, and its effervescent involvement with the present pointed up the tepid anemia and tiresome dignity of Cowley's classical ideals.

Despite (or perhaps because of) Dada, Cowley's ambivalence about the modern continued unabatedly. On January 6, 1923, he voiced his exasperation to Burke: "What is the 'modern' note that distinguishes authors of the present 'advance guard'? Those terms are so distasteful to me that I can't repeat them without quotes, and yet I possess the current weakness for modernity. And the modern note at present is the substitution of associational for logical thought. Carried to its extremity among the Dadas, the modern note is the substitution of absurdity for logic." In his notebook,

too, Cowley expressed his ongoing uneasiness about the seemingly contradictory manifestations of the modern spirit. At moments he seemed ready
to renounce all of them in equal measure:

> Of all periods Modern is the most irritating. It is full of stage prop-
> erties, cranes, locomotives, subways, billboards. Evidently to write a
> poem about the stockyards is to write a modern poem. Or to write a
> poem whose grammar is arbitrarily bad. Or to make drawings without
> perspective. To distort is modern. To be obscure is modern. To omit
> punctuation and connectives is the white shirtfront of modernism.
> The inevitable reaction follows. It becomes modern to be reaction-
> ary, and Mr. Kreymborg is praised for writing sonnets. Somebody
> discovers that Racine is a great author, from which principle some-
> body else draws the conclusion that Estlin [E. E.] Cummings, or
> even T. S. Eliot, is not a poet. It becomes strictly modern to praise
> the seventeenth century, and the word Modern is used as a cloak to
> hide timidity.

At other times he seemed to realize the futility of rowing against the current of his times: "We are modern because we can be nothing else . . .
When we write our contemporary civilization is the subject imposed."[24]

For all his misgivings, the Dadaists at least helped Cowley gain a better
appreciation of Matthew Josephson. Josephson's capricious personality
notwithstanding, Cowley liked him for his charm and vitality and was willing to make allowances for his conceit and indiscretion. Josephson's "grand
manner," his fighting with waiters, his methods of quarreling, his habit
of insulting people—all these, Cowley believed, were but mannerisms
aped from the French dadaists. On the positive side he credited Josephson
with a "lively interest in literature," an uncompromising independence,
and a refreshing capacity for indignation. Josephson, Cowley told Burke,
"treads where angels fear to"; he seemed ready to "compromise even the
Holy Ghost or Charles Evans Hughes." He also realized, however, that
Josephson was unpredictable.[25] Recent developments had put Cowley on
his guard.

In the early months of 1923 the tensions that had long simmered between Munson and Josephson came to a boil. A notorious literary and
personal feud ensued, causing a rift between *Broom* and *Secession* and dis-
rupting what little cohesion and solidarity existed among the contributors.

The controversy centered about Munson's and Josephson's diverging attitudes to Waldo Frank. In the fall of 1922 Josephson, acting on behalf of
Broom, had supported an earlier rejection by Loeb of a long critical mono-
graph on Frank by Munson. Josephson had next written a scathing "note"
for *Broom* on two of Frank's books, an article Cowley deemed "really the
best he ever wrote." Munson's bitterness about *Broom's* "unprofessional"
treatment of his work intensified when he was tentatively approached by
Josephson to become *Broom's* American agent, only to learn through the
grapevine that Cowley was to be *Broom's* new editorial assistant. Munson
had never ceased to resent Josephson's appropriation of the contents of
Secession 3, his inclusion of a story vetoed by Munson and Burke, and his
failure to insert a note stating his exclusive editorial responsibility. Moreover, he had begun to grow less than satisfied with Josephson's panegyrics
to American machinery and advertising.[26]

The fracas was brought to a head in late 1922, during an informal editorial gathering at Cowley's home in Giverny, where Josephson was spending
the Christmas week. He was carrying new manuscript material for *Secession* 4, sent to the Berlin office by Munson and Burke from New York. By
this time Josephson had grown "lukewarm" at best toward *Secession* and,
as Munson suspected, may well have been deliberately procrastinating
on the issue. Among the manuscripts accepted by the New York editors,
he took violent exception to a group of six poems by "Richard Ashton,"
pseudonym of Donald B. Clarke, a poet Cowley had known at Harvard
(Clarke, with Royall Snow, had edited *Youth: Poetry of Today*). Josephson's
indignation was roused particularly by one "very long and bad romantic"
poem called "The Jilted Moon" and, with Cowley's blessing, he decided
to delete everything but its title and the last two of its twenty lines: "To me
you are no more than Chinese, o moon, / Are no more than Chinese."
The mutilation of Clarke's poem was a violation of editorial decorum:
Cowley held no editorial power whatsoever and Josephson was formally
and morally bound to print material accepted by the New York editors.
To Cowley and Josephson, however, the slaughtering of the poem was an
amusing practical joke, utterly Dada, and as such permissible. But Munson could muster little sympathy for the sportive polemics they felt should
mark *Secession*. Increasingly out of touch with the very spirit that had given
birth to his magazine, Munson solemnly blacked out the truncated poem
from all issues of *Secession* that reached him in New York. From then

on, Josephson considered his relations with *Secession* effectually broken, though he did not bother to inform Munson of his abdication until after his return to America in the spring.[27]

Though from the first Cowley was determined to stay on the sidelines of the Munson-Josephson feud, temperamental and literary predilections did not allow him to remain *au dessus de la mêlée* as much as he may have wanted to. In early January he wrote an exasperated letter to Burke, complaining that the one-sided information he received from Josephson in Berlin made it impossible for him to judge the situation fairly and objectively. Like Josephson, however, Cowley had never had a high opinion of Munson's literary and critical taste and resented his veneration of Waldo Frank. He confessed to Burke that he was beginning to be "prejudiced" against Munson, whom he feared was "climbing into Olympus over our several backs." Munson's "bandwagon stunts" were beginning to do "more harm than good." In a fight, Cowley thought, he would "instinctively support" Josephson against Munson.[28]

In the winter of 1923 Cowley's exasperation was roused in particular by Munson's propagandistic sponsoring of *Secession* in a recent issue of Norman Fitts's *S4N*. In "The Mechanics for a Literary 'Secession' " Munson called for "a prompt deviation into purely aesthetic concerns." There were "bitter necessities" calling for *Secession*, Munson believed, among them the "aesthetic sterility" of the generation of Dreiser, Anderson, and Dell, and the timid anemia and "general flabbiness" of American criticism. More emphatically and programmatically than before, Munson presented Cowley as the spokesman for a nucleus of writers ready to "strike out freely into immediately aesthetic concerns," and he used Cowley's description of the aesthetic "catchwords" of his generation as the foundation for his "secessionist" platform.[29]

Secession had caused quite a stir in the literary world upon its inception, but Munson's article put the cat among the pigeons. In the *New Republic* Louis Untermeyer, like Paul Rosenfeld one of *Secession*'s favorite punchbags, looked with "surprise and outrage" at "a younger generation that not only knocks at our doors but threatens to batter down the very structure in which we are just beginning to feel comfortable." He described the adherents of *Secession* as a band of "New Patricians," whose reaction against the "undisciplined emotionalism" and "inchoate naturalism" of an earlier generation had led them to a new intellectual formalism, a preoccupation with technique and "a rigorous and crystallized aestheticism." Their principal interest in criticism, he warned, might well lead to "imaginative sterility." [30] Untermeyer's critique was buttressed by Van Wyck Brooks in the *Freeman*, who argued that "formal qualities alone, and especially the 'abstract form' of our contemporary cerebralists, will never constitute a literature." Form was dictated by subject matter, Brooks pontificated, agreeing with Untermeyer that "without guiding ideas a literature is doomed to sterility." In order to create significant literature, a writer needed what the Secessionists lacked, "some faith, some cause, some idea outside of himself." Without it, Brooks feared, the Secessionists were "simply leaving one wilderness for another." [31]

Though the publicity roused by *Secession* helped to bring Cowley's name before a larger audience, his position was still too ambivalent for him to feel at ease being publicly identified with a radically aesthetic platform. Indeed, Brooks's plea for a literature marked by both intellectual substance and significant form could not but hold Cowley's sympathy. After all, Cowley had privately criticized Burke's experiments with "abstract form" in terms that closely echoed Brooks's critique and had warned his friend against "working in too narrow a formula." Mostly, however, Cowley resented Munson's soapbox oratory. He privately denounced Munson's propagandizings of *Secession* as "a Cause, a movement" for being "pink tea stuff," and fulminated against his presentation of *Secession* as a coherent group. "Secession was never a Movement or a School," Cowley observed to Norman Fitts. Its contributors were much too disparate to be treated as a coterie or "composite personality"; instead, each of them should be judged "on his own merits." [32]

By mid-January Cowley was growing increasingly wary of the literary feuding among his friends and detested the way in which their literary relations were being poisoned by trivial conflicts of personalities. He revealed his personal discomfort in a letter to Wheelwright, warned him against playing "too many literary politics," and stressed the need for a clarification of positions and ideas:

> There is a fundamental weakness in Secession: namely, that it doesn't agree with itself. Munson believes in the sanctity of criticism. Josephson believes in criticism as a burlesque. Brown seems to work on a basis of Joyce, and everyone else to believe that Joyce is an ex-

pression of the last generation. Munson, Our Founder, reveres Waldo
Frank, a sentiment which I should hardly share. I like Sinclair Lewis,
have begun to potter with Amurricn material, think that among the
Dadas Louis Aragon has really accomplished something, have been
changing my ideas rapidly, don't know just where I stand. However
I believe in good writing and believe equally that neither Munson
nor Josephson writes good prose. The title of this chapter is A House
Divided.[33]

Cowley's naively idealistic desire to clarify the conflicting ideological assumptions behind *Secession* drew him deeper into the Munson-Josephson
vendetta than he had bargained for. Hoping to clear the air, he sent Munson a frank letter stating his position on *Secession*. His good intentions were
thwarted by Burke, who showed Munson Cowley's earlier epistolary confession of bias in favor of Josephson. Munson's reply, however, was less ran-
corous than Cowley had reason to expect. It calmly explained the factual
inducements to his quarrel with Josephson, but also included a devastating
critique of Josephson's ideas on advertising and on Waldo Frank, subjects on which Cowley's attitude was roughly consonant with Josephson's.
To Munson, Josephson was "simply another pest cluttering up the field,"
one who made a "fetish of originality," displayed "the fallacious mental
mechanisms of Rosenfeld, Upton Sinclair, and F[ranklin] P. A[dams],"
and who had a fundamental "disrespect for criticism." Josephson's propagation of machine-age America, Munson felt, went "no deeper than the
romantic's thrill upon finding strange materials to exploit." Munson expressed his high opinion of Cowley's poetry, reaffirmed his belief in the
validity of polemics in *Secession*, and supported a proposal of Cowley's for
a dadaist "stunt afternoon" at the Greenwich Village Theater. In conclusion he cited Waldo Frank's verdict that *Secession* was "the most significant
group-manifestation since the *Seven Arts*."[34]

Munson's letter contained enough truth and good sense to remove the
sting from Cowley's prejudice but also pointed up the gulf between both
men's literary loyalties. What little goodwill Munson's letter created, however, was soon destroyed by news from Harold Loeb, who disclosed that
malicious gossip, aggravated by Munson's habit of passing around confidential letters, had implicated Loeb, Cowley, and Burke in the feud against
their will. Munson, Loeb concluded, was "just a dirty politician" whose
conduct possessed "an odor decidedly putrescent." By mid-March the tone

of the quarrel had sunk so low that Cowley was ready to throw in the towel: "I'm so discouraged about this feud between Munson and Matty, with wrongs on both sides, . . . that I feel very much like dropping both Secession and Broom . . . and this in spite of the fact that they are the only two American magazines which interest me in the least."[35]

Cowley's discouragement was complete when he was informed by Loeb that *Broom* would suspend publication with its March 1923 issue. For several months the fate of *Broom* had hung in the balance—there had been editorial tensions between Loeb and Lola Ridge (culminating in her threat to resign if a poem by Gertrude Stein were to be included in *Broom's* American number) as well as financial problems resulting from the fluctuations of the German mark, a rise in printing costs, and frictions with Loeb's sponsoring rich uncles. In January, Loeb had personally voyaged to New York in a desperate attempt to straighten matters out but had met with no success.[36] In a letter to Loeb, Cowley poured out his disappointment at *Broom's* premature demise: "Write *finito* on Broom, probably the most interesting magazine which Americans ever published. Its poetry from the first outranked every other American magazine—or English—; its reproductions were vastly superior; it translated what nobody else dared to translate. Its native fiction was weak, but that could hardly be called your fault. See how many complete files of Broom you can collect; they will be valuable." To Burke, too, he affirmed his belief in *Broom's* avant-garde importance: "If Broom had no rudder, or too many of them, its course was always interesting. It was the appearance of Broom which made the Viennese letters of Hugo von Hofmannsthal appear so hopelessly stodgy. It was less dignified than the Dial and wrong more often, but more interesting (I repeat the word)."[37]

‹ ‹ ‹   By early 1923 Cowley could boast a reputation as a leading contributor to the avant-garde little magazines. In the retrospective appreciation of Gorham Munson, he was "one of the literary fledglings most likely to mature into a true man of letters."[38] Munson's appraisal was corroborated by the publication of *Eight More Harvard Poets* (1923), an anthology of Harvard verse that marked the first appearance of Cowley's poetry in book form. The volume was formally edited by Foster Damon and Robert Hillyer, both of whom served as English instructors at Harvard and whose verse had appeared in the earlier *Eight Harvard Poets* (1917). Most of the work behind the scenes, however, was done by John Brooks Wheelwright in collaboration with Damon. Moral and practical support was given by Amy Lowell; financial backing was guaranteed by Wheelwright's aunt, Louise Brooks. When arrangements with Harcourt, Brace and with Houghton Mifflin fell through, the book was published in January 1923 by Brentano's.

Since October 1921 Cowley, one of the first to be invited to contribute, had conducted a busy correspondence about the book with Damon and Wheelwright. Throughout its preparations he enthusiastically advised on the practical and financial organization, the selection of contributors, the solicitation of materials, the arrangement of publication, and publicity. Damon and Wheelwright proved generous editors; they were convinced of the superiority of Cowley's verse and allowed his eleven poems to out-number the other selections. Cowley, in turn, offered mild objections to their choice of poems that merely served to "express Harvard," and insisted upon the inclusion of "Day Coach" and "Fifteen Minutes" as a "mod-ernist" counterweight to the "moderately conservative" remainder of the volume. Besides Cowley's and Wheelwright's, the book featured poems by Norman Cabot, Grant Code, Jack Merten, Joel T. Rogers, R. Cameron Rogers, and Royall Snow.[39]

Critical reaction to the book was bracing and gave proof of Cowley's rising reputation as a poet. James Light, Stewart Mitchell, and John Dos Passos wrote in to praise Cowley's and Wheelwright's contributions. From England, Conrad Aiken wrote to Wheelwright that the book had "historic interest" but lacked "intrinsic value," with the exception of Cowley, who seemed to him "most like a professional" and "pretty compactly and ma-turely himself." He repeated his verdict in a personal letter to Cowley: "I liked immensely your things in 8 Mere Harvard Poets. Far and away the best in it: too good for it." Wheelwright, too, considered Cowley's selections the best in the book and, countering Cowley's misgivings about the lack of authenticity and underlying unity in his poems, insisted they were "most consistent and coherent" and expressive of "a perfectly distinct personality."[40]

Among the grumbling voices were Milton Raison's and Mark Van Doren's. Raison, writing for the New York Herald Tribune, was alone in his preference of Wheelwright; Cowley's verse he deemed "too pretentious" and lacking in intellectual substance. Mark Van Doren, writing in the Nation, felt uncomfortable with Cowley's experimentalism and objected that he attacked "sensational" themes with "all the ruthlessness of a knight who has given an oath to Lady Psychology." Most reviewers, however, concurred with the critic of the *Times Literary Supplement* that Cowley stood out "the subtlest and withal the strongest," followed at some distance by John Wheelwright. William Rose Benét picked out both for managing to "convey the special color and oddity of their own personalities," but concluded: "The man I most bank on is Cowley." Kenneth Burke agreed and in the *Dial* pointed up Cowley's overriding interest in form: "It is Malcolm Cowley who will run ahead of his ticket. His poems are the work of a man keen on the formal elements of writing . . . in addition to their cautious line-for-line texture, they manifest a functional relationship between the parts, a sense of the beauty in balancing movement with countermovement." In the appreciation of the young Newton Arvin, writing in the *Freeman*, Cowley was by far superior in "the individuality of his idiom" and "the depth and richness of his human implications." In a rancorless review for the *New Republic*, Gorham Munson felt that only Cowley attained to "a well-proportioned height of maturity." His verse, Munson noted, had "an underlying rigidity like fresh clean marble." Cowley, he concluded, seemed "already a very considerable poet."[41]

Eight More Harvard Poets received its most perceptive criticism from Hart Crane, who over the years had appreciatively followed Cowley's poetry in the little magazines. In *S4N* Crane singled out the "convincing manners" and "fresher reactions" of Cowley and Wheelwright from the "familiar nostalgias and worn allusions" of the other poets. Crane's verdict was witty and astute. Cowley's "genial pedestrianism" opened the way for a modern " 'pastoral' form," Crane felt. He praised Cowley for displaying a gift for "ironic nuance" and "a faculty for fresh record, city and road panorama," but felt he had occasionally carried his classicist predilections too far: "For one who can so well afford to stick closer to home, he deliberately allows French and 18th century influences to intrude too notably . . . yet practically all of his poems achieve consistent form. . . . Cowley seems to be civilized in the same sense as the older Chinamen."[42]

Cowley was pleased enough by Crane's comments to thank him in a letter for "the most intelligent criticism" the book received. Cowley, in turn, had begun to detect in Crane the makings of an innovative and important contemporary poet. For several months he had spoken favorably of Crane's poetry to friends and now he expressed his admiration to Crane: "You write with a bombast which is not Elizabethan but contemporary, and you are one of two or three people who can write a 20th Century blank verse, about other subjects than love, death and nightingales in other patterns than ti tum ti tum ti tum ti tums. Salutations." He praised Crane's "Poster" ("Voyages I") in *Secession* 4, as superior to the poems by Williams and Stevens in the issue and singled out "O brilliant kids" as "the most simple, the most brilliant combination of noun and epithet that I have seen these many years."[43] Cowley's letter was the beginning of a difficult but cherished friendship.

Cowley was now drawing attention as a poet of skill and promise in wider quarters. In February 1923 *Poetry* magazine published a group of six of his poems that Amy Lowell had sold to Harriet Monroe the previous summer. Monroe's preference for Cowley's "country poems" corroborated Hart Crane's impression that Cowley's poetic forte lay in the achievement of a modern pastoralism.[44] Together, the six poems gave evidence that Cowley's deepest and most authentic emotions, as well as his most individual nuances of tone and diction, were rooted in a nostalgic attachment to the land. The leitmotif in the poems is that of separation from the rural landscape of his childhood—as always the sustaining source of vitality and identity—conjointly with the wastage of human life and love in an infertile urban ambience. In "Prophetic" the process of severance from the country culminates in an apocalyptic vision of urban destruction:

> With blocks of broken asphalt where the streets ran once,
> And granite and brick spilling in heaps across them,
> With girders bridging the rain-washed ravines, it would be
> More pains than the worth of it to make ten level farms
> > out of Manhattan Island.
> But in the old graveyards,
> And under the site of stables and slaughter-houses,
> What excellent gardens![45]

Other editors, too, now showed themselves eager to print Cowley's verse. John Farrar of the *Bookman* accepted "The Strange Companion" (an early version of "William Wilson") for future publication and John McClure published "History" in the *Double Dealer*. It was the only one of Cowley's poems to appear in its pages. Norman Fitts had earlier expressed a desire to infuse the "left wing" of S4N with "fresh new good blood" by publishing Cowley's work, and for its summer 1923 issue accepted "Carnaval in Provence" (later retitled "Carnaval in the Midi"). In April, Cowley received an invitation to contribute to Harold Monro's London magazine *Chapbook* and sent in "Processional of the Third Season."[46]

Now that *Broom* had folded and *Secession* seemed seized with convulsions, Cowley became more ambitious to strengthen his position on the American literary market. His hopes were set in particular on *Vanity Fair*, which he considered "the only 4-cent a word magazine which is open to the vague possibility of publishing good critical work." In March he talked to John Peale Bishop, a good friend of Edmund Wilson (then managing editor of *Vanity Fair*), in Paris. At the end of the month he received a letter from Wilson, soliciting such of Cowley's "unmistakably effective" poems as "our readers would be capable of understanding." Wilson's appraisal betrayed a suspicion of Cowley's dadaist propensities: "You are not sufficiently bizarre to warrant our exhibiting you on that ground alone and I should hesitate to publish in *Vanity Fair* some of the best of your poems which I have seen because they would be likely to puzzle people without amusing them as freaks."[47] Wilson soon resigned as an editor and Cowley never made it into *Vanity Fair*, except as a translator.

Cowley also wrote to Burton Rascoe at the *New York Herald Tribune*, hoping to find an opening as a reviewer or translator in its book section. He proposed to do a series of articles, analogous to his *Bookman* portraits, in which he aimed to convey "the feeling of exhilaration that one gets in the Parisian literary world of today." In May he sent Rascoe his translation of an article by Louis Aragon, explaining that most of the young French writers shared Aragon's belief that "nothing of importance is coming out of England, that America is infinitely more alive, but that official American literature is if possible more stupid than official French literature." He had translated the article, Cowley told Burke, "to give foreign weight to the good propaganda." From France, however, Cowley was overestimating the interest of American editors in French appreciations of American culture: both Rascoe and Canby turned down his Aragon translation.[48]

Luckily, Cowley's association with the *Dial* seemed assured enough. In March 1923 he learned from Gilbert Seldes in Paris that Kenneth Burke, who was substituting as managing editor in New York, would be asked to remain on the editorial board after Seldes's return from Europe. Seldes was willing to have Cowley write one long review for the *Dial* a month. Cowley's opinion of the magazine remained high. "After three years of the new Dial it seems hard to imagine a world in which the Dial did not exist," he told Scofield Thayer. "It is the rock of American literature, on which schools, movements and other magazines are founded. It has been called conservative, and that is perhaps its greatest triumph. . . . The public who would call the Dial conservative was formed by reading the Dial." Wary as ever of premature success—"Recognition by the general public is our national form of artistic euthanasia"—Cowley felt the *Dial* had made the prospects for American literature brighter by assisting in the rise of "a number of special publics," each serviced by different avant-garde magazines. In reply Thayer praised Cowley's reviews in the *Dial*, admitting to a preference for his criticism over his poetry, and invited him to become his private editorial secretary, a position previously held by William Slater Brown but politely declined by Cowley on the pretext of not knowing shorthand.[49]

With Burke an editor and Cowley a regular contributor, their correspondence pertained more often to *Dial* affairs. Cowley explained that he preferred to review modern poetry and poetry criticism, gave advice on how to improve the *Dial*'s book-review section, and carried on an epistolary debate with Burke on the nature of criticism and reviewing. From the first, Cowley's conception of criticism was less pretentious and less theory-oriented than Burke's: "You believe that a critic should judge a book according to aesthetic laws which he formulates. In effect, you believe in using the book as a text for an essay on Form. More modestly, I believe in defining a book. . . . your essays in aesthetics parade under a false name. They are good essays but bad reviews." He observed that book reviewing remained "a distinctly minor medium" even if it was attracting "a number of the best intelligences in America. . . . Our critics are almost invariably more intelligent, more creative, than our artists." Despite their disagreements Burke remained eager to have Cowley's longer criticism for the *Dial* and regularly sent him books for brief review in the magazine's back pages (over the years Cowley wrote at least eighty "Brief Mentions"). In March, Burke accepted two of Cowley's poems for the May 1923 issue. Both "The Fishes" (a reworked version of "The Willow Branch") and "Starlings" explore a conventional subject of lyric nature poetry, but are freely experimental in form. "Starlings," for example, is Cowley's attempt to apply "dada technique" to a "Georgian subject":

> Starlings wheel and descend at nightfall, choosing maybe
>   a bamboo copse or a cedar of Lebanon. They cross the
>   face of the winter sun like a smoke.

A cloud of descending starlings: it takes the successive
    postures of a ball, a cane, a mandolin (or rather a
    guitar), a string of frankfurters, a candy-poke, finally
    a balloon which collapses with a rush of escaping gases.

Out of the centre of a cloud is heard the twittering of birds.[50]

The last three essays Cowley wrote for the *Dial* during his French
sojourn confirm his ongoing uneasiness with various tendencies of literary
modernism—its symbolist aesthetics, its intellectualism, its expressionism. In March 1923 the *Dial* belatedly published a long essay by Cowley
on Marcel Proust, one of two essays by which the magazine commemorated the death of Proust in November 1922.[51] Cowley's shifting appreciation of Proust illustrates the difficulty that a young critical intelligence
experienced in coming to grips with a major exemplar of "modern" literature. Cowley had been reading Proust off and on since the spring of
1922. Though he had found Proust's labyrinthine sentences and complex
syntactical convolutions hard to digest, he commended *A la Recherche du
Temps Perdu* (*Remembrance of Things Past*) to Foster Damon and observed
to Burke that Proust "somewhat reconciles me with the novel as a form."[52]
By late November, Cowley's appreciation of Proust had grown more critical. He now believed that Proust's poetic effects derived from an antisocial
cultivation of his private sensibility and, granting the magnificence of the
separate parts of *A la Recherche du Temps Perdu*, found fault with its lack of
temporal sequence and linear structure. To Burke he wrote: "Proust bathes
everything in some luminous mental fluid which does not alter the facts
but makes them stand out in unfamiliar relief, as if seen by moonlight. . . .
The brain of Proust is a tool which he has fashioned to serve his egoism."
Proust, he felt, was the "foremost specimen" of "an inferior category of artists."[53] Cowley's appreciation of Proust was circumscribed by his inability
to shed a predilection for narrative sequence and artistic representationalism. In his *Dial* essay he described *Remembrance of Things Past* as, in
essence, a "historical novel," which, though ostensibly concerned with the
history of one man's personal consciousness, yet provided a faithful record
of late nineteenth-century France. He acknowledged, however, that the
book was so complex as to defy any single fictional category. Though he
toned down his earlier verdict, he still found the book "episodic, fragmentary." Proust's modern associational devices of form and structure were

"masterly," he granted, but defeated by the very length of the book, which he judged "its greatest imperfection."

If Cowley was divided in his judgment of Proust's style and technique,[54] he was adamant in his repudiation of symbolism as a way of life. Cowley saw Proust as an artist who had carried the aesthetic and ethical implications of the symbolist creed to the limit. Proust's ideals of the artistic life, he observed, had become anachronistic: "if any age can claim him it is certainly not ours." He ended his *Dial* essay with a damning picture of the artist completely withdrawn into the privacy of his hermitage, wholly engrossed in the manic process of translating his "uncontemporary and unique sensibility" into an autonomous monument of art. A decade later he incorporated the passage into *Exile's Return* to point up the "anti-social" and "anti-human" implications of symbolism: "Observe the life of Proust, so different from the ideal of contemporary writers. He spent most of it in bed, in an interior room hermetically sealed to prevent drafts. . . . He rarely saw the daylight. His work-room was lined with cork to deaden every noise. . . . His own death was only a process of externalization; he had turned himself inside out like an orange and sucked it dry, or inscribed himself on a monument; his observation, his sensibility, his affectations, everything about him that was weak or strong had passed into the created characters of his novel."[55]

At Cowley's insistence Burke persuaded Seldes to publish his article on Proust as an essay rather than a book review. Cowley, who self-righteously believed that he was "one of the ten Americans, or perhaps five, who [had] read the collected works" of Proust in the original, obviously considered his essay an important statement on modern literature. But when in March 1923 he saw a copy of the *Dial* at Sylvia Beach's bookstore, Shakespeare and Company, he thought the piece "insufferably pompous" and "full of fine writing."[56]

Cowley was not alone in disliking the pomposity of his "Monument to Proust." Ernest Hemingway used its title in a rather obscene poem published in *Der Querschnitt*, a German magazine edited by Hans von Wedderkop. In the poem Hemingway attacked the *Dial* for paying pompous homage to Proust and built an alternative excremental "monument" to Pound: "The Dial does a monument to Proust. / We have done a monument to Ezra." The poem may well have been intended as an oblique attack on Cowley as much as on Proust or the *Dial*. Cowley first met Hemingway on one of his visits to Ezra Pound in Paris, where Hemingway had come to seek out Pound's tutelage. Some time after, Hemingway took Cowley to the International News office, for which he then worked as a news reporter. Cowley's success as a poet of some reputation and a regular contributor to the *Dial* and the avant-garde little magazines may well have roused the spite of Hemingway, several of whose manuscripts had been declined by the *Dial*. (His first book, *Three Stories & Ten Poems*, was to appear later that year.)[57] Cowley had published a half-satirical poem on Pound in the *New York Evening Post* and his admiration for Pound was strongly qualified. Hemingway later incorporated a scathing reference to Cowley in a draft of "The Snows of Kilimanjaro." Having seen Cowley on the terrace of the Dôme in the company of Tristan Tzara and having learned that Cowley was a regular associate of the dadaists, Hemingway put him down as a typical expatriate wastrel.[58] Still later, he placed Cowley in an unfavorable light with Marianne Moore, who as editor of the *Dial* had rejected several of his stories, by repeating confidential editorial information Cowley had received from Burke.[59] Though there were frictions between both writers through the 1930s, Hemingway revised his opinion of Cowley in later years and considered him one of the few literary critics worthy of his respect.

Cowley's second *Dial* essay showed that by 1923 his appreciation of Eliot, like that of Proust, had grown more critical. Even more so than Proust, Eliot was a touchstone of Cowley's shifting appreciation of modernism. Searching in the network of modernism for a common denominator, Cowley readily acknowledged Eliot as its undisputed American leader. A notebook appraisal, antedating the publication of *The Waste Land*, seemed prescient enough: "Ibsen was never more dead; the definition of modernism is undergoing another change. . . . Its different aspects have been referred to as cubist, neo-classical, abstract, fantastic; but the one term which includes all its tendencies is Intellectualism. . . . He never meant to, perhaps, but Eliot has become the leader." Eliot's influence, Cowley maintained, could be traced in dozens of contemporary poets, most of whom were "too independent to be called his followers." Conspicuously omitting himself, he named Aiken, Bishop, Crane, Cummings, and Elinor Wylie.[60]

For the young Cowley, Eliot came closer than any other poet to realizing his ideal conception of the modern poet as a ceaseless explorer of ever-new poetic theories and forms, who regarded his poems as "intellectual problems" and who, having explored the possibilities of a new principle, "moved on" to "new frontiers," leaving its application to his disciples.

Eliot's formalism was clearly congenial to younger poet-critics of Cowley's persuasion, as was his defense of "the conscious mind" against "the dark Freudian wish." The publication of *The Waste Land* in late 1922, however, caused an important modification in Cowley's appreciation of Eliot. The change seemed Cowley's as much as Eliot's. Formally and technically, *The Waste Land* might fulfill all the requirements of "a great modern poem"; its intellectual substance, however, elicited "private reservations." In the winter and spring of 1923 *The Waste Land* in fact ran counter to Cowley's whole emotional and intellectual predisposition. The dadaists, committed to the present, had fanned Cowley's conviction that "values are created by living men"; now Eliot's poem seemed to imply that the present was "prematurely senile," incapable of expressing its "impotence" in language of its own, and thus "forever condemned to borrow and patch together the songs of dead poets." A youthful Cowley was not prepared to follow Eliot on his "desert pilgrimage toward the shrines of tradition and authority." Cowley's inclination to let the exuberant exigencies of the present prevail over the solemn legacies of the past was to be rectified in the future. For the moment, however, he demanded that writers deal with contemporary reality, and "instinctively" rejected Eliot as his guide.[61]

An impatience with amorphous and undisciplined emotionalism informed Cowley's third *Dial* essay, a consideration of an anthology of contemporary German poetry. Principally, his review, written in early May but not published until August, entailed a condemnation of German expressionism, which he described as "no more than a violent restatement of romanticism." Most fatally, it conflicted with his demand for an art meaningfully concerned with the contemporary social and human world. Expressionism, he wrote, was "an attempt to express the pure Self, independently of every element imposed on the poet from without; in other words it is a revolt against every form of society." Cowley's analysis of expressionist verse carried the nonpolitical germs of his repudiation of the symbolist or "Art Novel" at the height of his political radicalism: "Instead of describing the infinite diversity of the exterior world it confines itself to the soul, and souls are uniform and simple. To express the inmost Self is the narrowest of all formulas."[62]

During his last months in France, Cowley's search for a personal aesthetics remained marked by intellectual indeterminacy and a lack of theoretical foundation. In March 1923 he received a letter from Burke challenging his conception of criticism as a form of "definition" that might involve formal as well as moral, psychological, or historical elements. Burke protested that Cowley's critical practice was doomed to remain on a level of newspaper journalism as long as it was marked by his disinclination to judge a book by previously formulated aesthetic laws. He recommended the writings of Benedetto Croce, whose *Aesthetic* (1902) had appeared in English translation the year before, but Croce's doctrine of art as the subjective and nonconceptual expression of intuition predictably conflicted with Cowley's classicist predilections and his defense of "the conscious mind." "My disagreement with every point of [Croce's] Breviary of Aesthetics is so profound," he wrote to Burke, "that I thought of writing an Aesthetic Breviary of my own by the simple process of turning each of Croce's statements backwards."[63]

Burke's preoccupation with the formal properties of writing made him look "with alarm" upon Cowley's Dada-inspired infatuation with American subject matter. When Burke argued that subject matter was bound by "a priori definitions and limitations" that should "originate in formal considerations," Cowley responded with critical hesitation, confessing his uncertainty about "form and matter." Several weeks later he returned to the subject, admitting that between a conception of art as autonomous creation to be judged by its intrinsic excellence and a conception of art as representation to be judged against its cultural, social, and historical background, he found it hard to strike a balance: "A work of literature . . . should be judged for its excellence, not for its representative value. . . . [Yet] a house is not independent of its environment; neither is a book. As soon as one allows a book to be judged against its special background instead of as a phenomenon existing in an imagined vacuum:—at that moment one allows the whole mechanics of representationalism to creep in, which is the logical defect of my position."[64] Cowley had once again run up against an endemic paradox of art: the seeming incompatibility between art as expression and art as creation.

‹ ‹ ‹   Meanwhile there was always Paris and *la vie littéraire*. In the spring of 1923 Cowley was a regular client at the terraces of Montparnasse. Occasionally he dropped in at Sylvia Beach's bookshop—he had become a member of her library on January 15, 1923—and once sat for his photograph at the Paris studio of Man Ray, together with Matthew Josephson. Ray remembered them as young littérateurs "eager to absorb the Paris atmosphere but prudently keeping a foot on American shores." Among the many Americans in Paris, Cowley saw Gilbert Seldes, who was working on *The Seven Lively Arts*, and talked with John Peale Bishop. He met John Dos Passos, who "spoke well" of Burke, and had lunch with E. E. Cummings, whom he found in full sympathy with *Secession* and *Broom*. While seeing these and others—Royall Snow, Robert and Elsa Coates, Matthew and Hannah Josephson, Harold Loeb and Kitty Cannell, John and Elinor Nef, Lewis Galantière, Wheelwright, Hemingway, Pound—he continued to seek out the dadaists, especially Tzara and Aragon, as well as French writers and artists outside the Dada group: Pascin, Salmon, and Valéry. Valéry, who was to exert a deeper influence on Cowley than he could have realized upon their first meeting in 1923, already impressed him by writing poetry as if it were "a laboratory experiment in thought."[65]

In mid-April Tzara arranged for Peggy to hold an exhibit of her paintings and drawings at Galérie Six, a Paris art gallery run by Madame Soupault. Peggy had drawn portraits of nearly all their artist friends, and her newest watercolors, Cowley thought, were "extremely interesting." The exposition, he reported to Burke, was exhausting ("our house was full of people for two weeks before the event") but "came off nicely." In early June, on the terrace of the Dôme, Tzara introduced Cowley to Theo van Doesburg, a Dutch artist who later achieved renown as the founder of the avant-garde movement De Stijl. At the time of his meeting with Cowley he was editing, under the pseudonym of I. K. Bonset, a Dutch dadaist magazine, *Mécano*, which was distributed from Leiden and Paris. Van Doesburg impressed Cowley as "a pleasant, enthusiastic, rather simple fellow, less ironic in his temper than the French Dadaists." Asked to contribute to van Doesburg's little magazine, Cowley submitted, in true Dada spirit, three rather scabrous "madrigals"—featuring Masochistic Mazie, Sadic Sam from Alabam, and Fetishistic Fanny—written for his own and his friends' entertainment. The poems were published in a two-page issue of *Mécano*, where they appeared together with a story by Kurt Schwitters, translated by van Doesburg. Cowley's reputation as an adept impromptu composer of dirty epigrams and limericks was spreading into unexpected corners of the international avant-garde.[66]

In early April, John Brooks Wheelwright, the recently appointed overseas agent of *Secession*, arrived in Giverny. He brought editorial suggestions from Munson and Burke in New York and carried manuscript material for the next two issues of the magazine, numbers 5 and 6, which Wheelwright had offered to have printed at his own expense in Florence, Italy. Having spent a "wildish winter" in New York with the American contingent of *Secession* (Munson, Burke, Slater Brown, Edward Nagle, Gaston Lachaise), Wheelwright had conquered much of his earlier skepticism and grown more sympathetic to the magazine. He had defended *Secession* against Brooks and Untermeyer in the *Freeman*, and had been sent overseas by Munson to prevent further tampering with *Secession* by Josephson. Munson had virtually given Wheelwright editorial carte blanche, a move he soon had cause to regret.[67]

Falling in with Cowley and Josephson in Giverny, Wheelwright was rapidly infected by the dadaist atmosphere. In early April he went over the material for *Secession* 5 and 6 with Cowley and Josephson. They agreed it was "pretty poor. No life to it." From New York, Wheelwright had brought over a public apology to Richard Ashton for the mutilation of his poems, which Munson wanted published in *Secession* 5. At Cowley's insistence the note was not accepted; he maintained that the injury was "intentional" and not, as Munson's statement implied, accidental. Wheelwright was easily persuaded and, on his own authority, published a long editorial comment in *Secession* 5 wickedly maintaining that "the bosses in New York apologise to Ashton but the Satanists can not, their injury was intentional"; in addition, he embedded the entire text of "The Jilted Moon" in a scathing satirical analysis of Ashton's verse.[68]

Cowley objected to the bulk of the material accepted by Munson and Burke for the fifth issue. "Most of the number is dead," he reported dutifully to Burke. He declined to bear editorial responsibility for the issue and emphasized as much to Wheelwright: "I shouldn't like my name to appear as sponsoring this number, considering that the larger part of it was chosen definitely in New York, and much of it against my own strong prejudices." Cowley's request was partly inspired by his strong misgivings about Wheelwright's ability to handle the mechanical and editorial ends of magazine publishing, but for reasons of his own he refrained from interfering. "I wondered what the issue would look like after being set in type by Italian printers who couldn't speak English and then proofread by the worst speller who ever failed to graduate from Harvard," he recalled in *Exile's Return*. The result, he reflected, "would at least be arbitrary, surprising and utterly *dada*."[69]

From Italy, Wheelwright flouted Cowley's disclaimer of responsibility and inserted a note to the contrary in *Secession*: most of the material

for issues five and six, he pontificated, was "accepted and rejected with
the advice of Malcolm Cowley." On his own authority he set out to revise a lengthy, technical essay by Munson on E. E. Cummings and had
the issue printed in Florence. When Munson saw *Secession* 5 in New
York, he flew into a rage: his apology to Ashton had been suppressed, his
opinions on Cummings had been corrected, and the entire issue (mistakenly numbered 6) teemed with typographical errors and misspellings.
Cowley, too, had reasons to be unhappy. Not only had Wheelwright discarded his refusal of responsibility, but, in the confusion of bringing out
two issues simultaneously, Wheelwright had unintentionally maltreated
Cowley's own poems. In May, Cowley had asked Wheelwright to withdraw
two poems—"Old Melodies: Love and Death"—he had earlier submitted
for *Secession,* since one of them was shortly to appear in the relaunched
Broom. He had sent "Into That Rarer Ether" as a substitute contribution. But Cowley's request reached Wheelwright too late, thereby feeding
Munson's suspicion that by publishing the same poem in both *Broom*
and *Secession* Cowley was deliberately "playing unfairly" toward his magazine. Wheelwright was sincerely annoyed by the accidental mistreatment
of Cowley's contributions, and by this time began to suspect that he might
not be the ideal man to edit a little "art paper." [70]

Though his voice weighed heavily with Wheelwright, Cowley could
never be sure in how far his friend would actually follow his advice. Thus,
Secession 6 contained a long poem by Wheelwright that Cowley had advised him not to include in number 5. The only item endorsed by Cowley
was a burlesque detective story by Robert Coates, "The Crimson Emer-
ald." Cowley's own "Into That Rarer Ether" duly appeared, preceded by
an apologetic note from Wheelwright.

Wheelwright's incompetent handling of Hart Crane's tripartite "For the
Marriage of Faustus and Helen" has become legendary. In retrospect Munson presented Crane as a "victim of the Josephson-Cowley-Wheelwright
imbroglio," but Cowley could plead innocence. He had strongly urged
Wheelwright to publish Crane's poem, adding as his personal judgment:
"The best of the three movements is unfortunately the second, which
appeared in Broom." [71] Wheelwright appears to have mistaken Cowley's
verdict for a suggestion to exclude the middle section in *Secession* and print
only parts 1 and 3. When Crane, who set great store by the symphonic
unity of his poem, saw that *Broom* had printed only the second part, he
demanded Munson withdraw his poem from *Secession* unless assurance

could be given that it would not be subject to gratuitous editing. Wheel-wright, however, printed a dismembered two-part version of the poem, complete with typographical mistakes, thus butchering its unity a second time and violently outraging Crane. When the issue reached New York a shamefaced Munson could only excise, with a razor blade, the entire poem from its pages. He made amends to Crane by publishing an integral version in *Secession* 7.[72] After his involvement with *Secession* 6, Cowley's relations with Munson and his magazine were effectively severed, though resentments would blaze up again in the near future.

Meanwhile, through the spring of 1923, Loeb conducted busy epistolary negotiations with Cowley and Josephson to check out the practical feasi-bility of a revival of *Broom*. Cowley was enthusiastic, but cautious, having no wish to see the new magazine perpetuate old quarrels and proposed that *Broom* become a quarterly. Loeb, on his side, promised Cowley that the new *Broom* would "more or less represent your group," but he wanted to be assured of Cowley's "wholehearted cooperation." At the end of March he wrote to Cowley: "With you helping I shall be happy to delegate the American editorial responsibility to a group and to collaborate thoroughly on policy." In early April, Josephson left Europe to take over the American end of *Broom* and try to find a new angel, printer, and distributor. Before sailing, Josephson had talked over practical arrangements with Cowley, who now envisioned for himself a position on the magazine with stronger editorial responsibility. To Loeb he agreed to act on an American board of associate editors consisting of himself, Josephson, and, as a most likely third candidate, Slater Brown. In April Cowley and Loeb spent a week together making a walking trip through southern Burgundy, and Loeb visited Cowley in Giverny to go over manuscripts left over from the "old" *Broom*; he was impressed by Cowley's "editorial ability" and feeling for style: "Often he cleaned up a smudgy sentence by the transposition of a word." By the end of May, Josephson had found a new financial supporter and printer of *Broom* in his brother-in-law Maxwell Geffen, and prepara-tions were progressing for the first number of the revived magazine. On May 20 Cowley reported to Burke that the refurbished *Broom* meant "a direct bid for our own crowd with its far dependencies"—Burke, Cowley, Josephson, Coates, Crane, Jean Toomer, Glenway Wescott, Yvor Win-ters, and Wheelwright. He still believed that *Broom* could fill a separate function side by side with *Secession*, but he also realized that such was hardly feasible unless Munson and Loeb could be convinced that "both magazines are necessary."[73] He was now fully prepared to stand by *Broom* and Loeb and pledged his active support upon his return to America.

‹ ‹ ‹   During Cowley's last months in France the influence of Dada culminated in his friendship with Louis Aragon. In April 1923 Aragon had resigned from his job with the *Paris-Journal* and come to spend two months in Giverny to work on a new book. In May and June, Cowley saw Aragon almost daily. Together they tramped up and down the country roads, while Aragon, an indefatigable talker, recited poem upon poem, recommended books, and proclaimed his literary ideas. Cowley was no better able to resist the influence of Aragon than had Josephson, on whom, Cowley believed, Aragon had "imposed all his ideas." Cowley's relationship with Aragon approximated that of disciple and master. In early June he admitted to Burke that he had fallen under the dadaist spell of Aragon, but maintained that his influence was "less literary than moral." In a tone of near-adulation he praised Aragon's precocious literary genius, his "splendid disdain" for the social and moral conventions of his background, his capacity for zestful indiscretion, his contempt for literary commerce. Most of all, Cowley was impressed with the intensity of Aragon's commitment to art: "He lives literature. If I told him that a certain poem of Baudelaire's was badly written, he would be capable of slapping my face. He judges a writer largely by his moral qualities, such as courage, vigor, the refusal to compromise. He proclaims himself a romantic." Of all the writers he had met in Europe, Cowley observed, Aragon was "the only one to impose himself by force of character."[74]

Aragon's influence brought out the contradictory elements in Cowley's attitude. Against his classicist predilections he was now drawn toward the very romanticism he had sharply discredited a year before. Under Aragon's tutelage, he read such English and French romantics as Monk Lewis, Lord Byron, Gérard de Nerval, and Pétrus Borel, seeking ways to apply their literary methods to contemporary subject matter, and demanded of writers that they display, in their attitude to art, "high courage, absolute integrity and a sort of intelligence which was in itself a moral quality."[75] As his notebook testifies, he also recognized, however tentatively, that such a moral stance had its social and political repercussions: "The moral judgment has been reinstated. . . . Once you have admitted that literature has a moral value, you must admit the right of the state, or of society, to have some control over literature. But one differs with society. One desires a new society. The next step is to take an interest in social laws, to become anarchist, royalist, communist. It will not be long before this step is taken."[76] He also showed himself ready to accept the personal consequences of his "highly moral" attitude:

> To deny that literature has any moral value is of no danger to morality, but it is a fashion of denigrating literature. Art for art's sake . . . a cowardly attitude in which one takes refuge, as if to say, "My opinions really don't matter to you, they are only artistic questions." My opinions matter, and I claim the right to be jailed for them if necessary. Art has a moral function. To say: he lived, he died, he loved has no meaning except the meaning that artists give it. They make life interesting, give it dignity and history. Their conception is not always the same as that of the society to which they belong, and in these cases society has a right to impose its own point of view. Artists are dangerous. I hope to be dangerous; otherwise why bother to be an artist?[77]

Cowley's newly adopted moral stance fortified his belief that art had the power to affect society and bestow meaning and dignity upon human life. Extending artistic judgments to life itself, Cowley now seemed prepared to transpose his moral idealism from the literary into the social and political world: "We must proclaim our political opinions," he wrote in his notebook, "beg for a censorship, write an Open Letter to President Harding, attack the liberal magazines, beg people to abstain from voting, or otherwise we must resign ourselves to conducting petty literary quarrels with Ezra Pound and Robert McAlmon and Floyd Dell." At the end of June he sent a flamboyant letter to Burke, reiterating his notebook fulminations, announcing his belief that "the time has come for us to write some political manifestoes," and proclaiming his wariness of being "ticketed" in a narrowly literary fashion: "We are not critics or short-story writers; we are poets; in other words we are interested in every form of human activity." Glowing with revolutionary fervor, Cowley confessed he was "eaten with the desire to do something significant and indiscreet. . . . In a country as hypocritical as the United States, merely to enumerate the number of laws one has broken would be a significant gesture."[78]

Filled with a drive for defiant public action, Cowley now seemed eager to prove that even an American writer could out-Dada the dadaists if he chose to do so. Two of his "significant gestures" have become part of literary lore and have done much to fix a public and historical image of Cowley as an American dadaist *extraordinaire*. The first took place in Giverny in the company of Aragon, Loeb, Cummings, and Dos Passos. After a bibulous dinner the company resorted to Cowley's studio above the blacksmith shop to resume drink and argument. Once there Cowley, commonly slow-spoken and chary of words but now inflamed with dadaist ardor, delivered an exuberant oration on book fetishism and the illogical accumulation of bad review books on his shelves. Whipping himself up to a climax of mock-indignation, he pulled an assortment of books from his shelves—volumes of "irritating modern poetry and prose" by Elinor Wylie and Jean Cocteau, and dispensable French university texts—and, to shouts of encouragement by Aragon, Cummings, and Dos Passos, tore them apart and heaped them in a pile on the asbestos apron before the stove. Denouncing the books as only good for a bonfire, Cowley set fire to the pile; it smoldered and filled the room with smoke until Cummings, undaunted by his recent arrest in Paris as a "*pisseur Americain*," walked over and urinated on the flames. Later that night, Loeb challenged Cowley to a wrestling match but, his Princeton championship notwithstanding, found his opponent "unmovable." In the end Cowley and Aragon marched Cummings and Dos Passos to the Vernon railway station. They missed the last train to Paris and had to put up at a local hotel. Cowley walked back to Giverny in the early dawn, accompanied by Aragon vociferously reciting poetry.[79]

Cowley's dadaist ardor peaked during the public fervor of Bastille Day, July 14, 1923. Driven to a pitch of high excitement by his imminent departure and the general madness of a Paris swirling in the ecstasy of "a vast plebeian carnival," Cowley with Peggy joined a group of revelers at the Dôme: Laurence and Clotilde Vail, Peggy Guggenheim, Harold Loeb, Kitty Cannell, Jim Butler, and Louis Aragon. With Cowley they formed the nucleus of a party that was joined intermittently by Robert and Elsa Coates, Ivan Opffer, Harold Stearns, Robert McAlmon, and Tristan Tzara. Before long the conversation turned to the Rotonde, a café patronized by anarchists and revolutionists; its proprietor was rumored to be a police informer who had behaved insultingly toward American women. When Laurence Vail proposed that the entire company move over to the Rotonde and "assault" its *patron*, Cowley was seized with a passionate desire for significant action. After the provocateurs had regrouped at the Rotonde, Aragon began a speech denouncing stool pigeons in general and the proprietor in particular. As the waiters, anticipating trouble, gathered about their boss, Laurence Vail spit forth a stream of insults and Harold Loeb, pipe in mouth, looked on in embarrassment. All of a sudden, Cowley, presumably revolted by the proprietor's "look of a dog caught stealing chickens and trying to sneak off," shot forward and landed "a glancing blow" on the man's jaw. In the ensuing chaos he was hustled out of the café. For the moment nothing happened. Cowley seemed ready to forget the entire affair and persuaded several of his companions to shift their activities to other quarters. Long past midnight, Cowley returned to the scene of the crime, shouted a new volley of insults at the proprietor, and was promptly arrested and escorted to the police station.

At the *gendarmerie* Cowley faced a double charge: not only had he unprovokedly assaulted a *patron*, but—a more serious, if incorrect, charge— he had also forcibly resisted a police officer. Soon friends (Laurence Vail, Louis Aragon, Jacques Rigaut) came to the rescue, bringing Cowley's identification papers and, twice over, bribing the police officer to drop the second of the charges. Cowley spent an anxious night in jail awaiting a preliminary hearing the next day. Upon that occasion a group of his friends, sobered up and escorted by nine elegantly dressed and highly respectable-looking women (among them Clotilde Vail, Kitty Cannell, and Peggy Guggenheim), testified that Cowley had acted under provocation by the *patron* and solemnly swore he was a gentleman writer of irreproachable character. The presiding police magistrate was duly impressed. The *patron* had only his own personnel to back him up, whereas Cowley had at least ten presumably disinterested witnesses. In the end it was André Salmon, who as reporter of Parisian murder trials for *Le Matin* was on good terms with the police, who did the most to get Cowley off the hook in time for his departure to America. Robert McAlmon, who had scurrilously testified against the *patron* at the police station, believed that Cowley had been saved a six-month term in jail.[80]

Overnight, Cowley was a dadaist celebrity—though one somewhat baffled by the sudden admiration bestowed upon him by his French acquaintances. Upon reflection he could only conclude that, unknowingly, his act had sublimely exemplified all the Dada precepts: "I had acted for reasons of public morality . . . I had been *disinterested*. I had committed an *indiscretion*, acted with *violence* and *disdain* for the law, performed an *arbitrary* and *significant gesture*, uttered a *manifesto* . . . I had shown *courage*." For the first time in his life Cowley became "a public character." Between dinners, cocktail parties, interviews for the newspapers, and invitations to contribute to dadaist magazines in Holland, Belgium, Germany, Hungary, and Russia, Cowley's last weeks in France were busier and more exciting days than he had ever known.[81]

Beyond the circle of his European admirers, however, Cowley's act was less cordially seen as a display of irresponsible tomfoolery. The *New York Tribune* featured an editorial with a headline—"Prize American Literary 'Eggs' Boil Over in Paris Latin Quarter"—that captured the spirit of gusto behind Cowley's gesture, but pointed up its facetious futility. Gorham Munson, who had reasons for malice, remembered that in New York, Burke was made visibly uncomfortable by Cowley's pugnacious antics and felt "as if he were watching a literary suicide." Munson rightly believed that Cowley was temperamentally unsuited "to act dada" and found his capering "painfully stupid" and "pediculous"; for him Cowley's act exhibited an "elaborate straining for spontaneous foolery."[82] Harold Stearns, the frequent butt of satire by Cowley and Josephson, retrospectively belittled their dadaist shenanigans as merely "untempered emotionalism overcoming weak judgement." In a vengeful reminiscence he decried their Dada-inspired Americanism as "a strange form of New Nationalism," one quickly surrendered upon their return: "Impolite and aggressive Americans abroad, they became European and Russian yearners when they got back home."[83] Robert McAlmon gave a similarly spiteful account of *l'affaire Cowley* in his 1934 memoir, *Being Geniuses Together*. There had never been any love lost between McAlmon and the members of Cowley's group. Ever since his Village days McAlmon had regarded Burke, Cowley, and Josephson as affected cerebralists in possession of a forbidding erudition and had preferred the poetic company of William Carlos Williams, with whom he edited the little magazine *Contact*. Burke, Cowley, and Josephson, on their side, continued to feel cool and hostile toward McAlmon through the 1920s and beyond. With William Slater Brown—who in 1928 summed up his opinion of McAlmon's writing ability in a famous couplet: "I would rather live in Oregon and pack salmon / Than live in Nice and write like Robert McAlmon"—Cowley was persuaded of McAlmon's literary insensitivity and later wrote that "he never in his life wrote as much as a memorable sentence."[84]

As a result of the well-publicized fisticuffs, Cowley was either acclaimed or reviled as an American dadaist, his personal objection to the aesthetic assumptions of Dada notwithstanding. Because the incident belatedly gained anecdotal notoriety—not in the last place because Cowley himself blew up its symbolic value in *Exile's Return* while underplaying his continued allegiance to a classicist aesthetics—the glaring incongruity between his privately held classical opinions and his public posturing as a Dada activist has not been properly recognized.[85]

Nothing so points up that incongruity as the fact that during his last six weeks in France—while he was seized with fervor to perpetrate significant public action—Cowley was privately composing a lengthy essay on the classical theater of Jean Racine. It formed an act of intellectual justification to himself and the American Field Service for having spent two years abroad: it was to hold, he observed half-ironically to Burke, "the rubies of my wisdom." A separate notebook devoted largely to his studies in French classicism gives evidence of the subject's continuous attraction and of the elaborate research he had done at Montpellier and, more irregularly, at Giverny. Besides notes for a comparative thesis on the seventeenth-century French and English theater (Wycherley, Congreve, Molière, and Racine), it contains extensive bibliographical annotations, a chronology of the career of Racine, an analysis of the conventions of Racinian theater, a listing of Boileau's "Laws of Tragedy," and elaborate quotations from Racine's critical prefaces to *Andromaque* (1667), *Bajazet* (1672), and *Phèdre* (1677). Two longer notations—"About a Performance of Racine" and "The Morality of Racinian Tragedy"—were later expanded and revised for the essay on Racine. Returning to Racine in the midst of his flirtations with Dada, Cowley's former enthusiasm rose to new heights. "Racine can be tremendous," he wrote to Burke; his poetry was "something to tear the guts out of you."[86] With mounting admiration he worked on his "monumental" essay from late May until the first week in July, pouring into it many of the insights into art and aesthetics he had accumulated over the past two years. Thus the essay stood as a summing up of the literary values and beliefs he had developed in the course of his French sojourn.

Cowley opened his essay with a classical epigraph from André Gide— *L'art est toujours le résultat d'une contrainte* ("Art is always the result of constraint")—and argued that Racine's disciplined art was inseparable from the social and cultural conditions that produced it. More strongly than before, Cowley emphasized the interdependence of art, artist, audience, and milieu: "only an existing tradition and an audience educated in this tradition can make the classical theatre possible." Racine, in this respect more fortunate than contemporary artists, approximated an ideal— the writer fully integrated into and sustained by his social and literary milieu—that Cowley subsequently strove to realize in an American ambi-ence.

Positing the classical ideal as one of "absolute perfection," Cowley noted that a tragedy by Racine was produced by a definite age and milieu, yet constituted an autonomous entity transcending its historical moment. Racinian tragedy, he observed, was "stylized" to the point of becoming an "abstract painting of an emotion," yet it remained a unified and living organism. Racine's abstractness, moreover, was different from the non-representational obscurantism Cowley resented in the modernism of a contemporary like Gertrude Stein: "To be abstract a literature need not be unintelligible. . . . An abstract literature is one in which ideas or emotions, expressed with the greatest possible exactness, are combined into a unity which possesses a formal value and which is something more than a copy of experience." Running counter to the pure aestheticism in vogue among his contemporaries, Cowley admired Racine for recognizing the inextricability of aesthetics and morality as well as for his fundamental and affirmative humanism. For Racine, as for Cowley, art created value and lent meaning and dignity to human life: "The Racinian tragedy, for all its plastic value, is moral to a supreme degree. It is moral . . . because it reasserts, in the face of doubts which assail us continually, the importance of man's destiny, the reality of his passions, the dignity of the human ani-mal. . . . Our actions have no more meaning than is conferred on them by art or religion. . . . After Racine the mass of contemporary literature seems tangential and petty; he takes our attention violently, and it is precisely the violence of his tragedies that makes them a moral spectacle."

In conclusion Cowley presented Racine as preeminently "the classi-cal type" and ventured a personal definition: classicism "is an approach, through the discipline of arbitrary conventions, to a form which is perfect and abstract. At the same time classicism remains intelligibly human. It is concerned with people instead of nature or the supernatural; it considers the moral rather than the picturesque value of their actions; it does not avoid their most rigorous ideas or their most violent emotions. It is an ideal that is tenable in any age, today more than ever, for by following its prin-ciples one can create a literature which is fresh and unimitative, which is contemporary and which avoids the excesses of contemporary sentiment." For all the desirability of a "classical" contemporary literature, Cowley also acknowledged, as he wrote Burke, that "the whole classical movement is only a part of literature and not the ideal for everybody." Accordingly, he ended his essay on a tangent, making a bow to contemporary romanticism: "Dignity grows tiresome. In spite of its claim of being total, the classical ideal is no more complete than the romantic; the very nature of it is to exclude and eliminate. A world grows up outside its barriers. Its conventions become laws; a generation is born which wears them as chains; either they strangle the theatre or else are broken away. As long as a nation retains its vitality classical and romantic periods succeed each other. The desire for change is the most durable convention. Unquestionably the last age was romantic." [87]

If Cowley remained "a classicist *au fond*," a part of him also remained disposed to the rebellious romanticism he encountered among the dadaists. Thus as an antidote to the tiresome dignity of classicism, he might amuse himself by composing obscene songs and limericks or drafting, in his notebook, a dadaistic "Open Letter to Gertrude Stein," in which he denounced her "doctrinary modernism," fulminated against her obscurantist "*snobisme*," and dubbed her "the bulkiest bore of our century." [88] Yet he always retained an eclectic openness to modern experimentation. In the end, he was less opposed to the avant-garde than skeptical of certain of its manifestations: he still wanted to be part of modern literature but hoped to shift its course into more desirable directions.

Cowley thought highly enough of his essay on Racine to have it privately printed in pamphlet form. Shortly before embarking for the States, he signed a contract for two hundred blue-covered copies at an estimated cost of thirty-five dollars. After his departure, the printing and proofreading of the pamphlets were supervised by Harold Loeb. The French printer, however, failed to make good speed—partly because Cowley could not pay the printing bill—and the business dragged on through the summer and fall. In mid-September, Cowley submitted a slightly amended version of the essay to Van Wyck Brooks, commenting, "By the definition which I made myself, I cannot be a classicist, but I admire Racine immensely." The essay appeared in two consecutive issues of the *Freeman* in October. By late November the French bills were paid and the pamphlets sent off to Cowley in New York. [89]

Friends who received the pamphlet were almost unanimously enthusiastic. Charles Townsend Copeland gratefully accepted Cowley's dedication—"To Copey in default of a better gift." Glenway Wescott wrote to say that "your Racine study seems to me very important and finely done." Scofield Thayer enjoyed the essay and said as much in a letter. Foster

Damon thought the piece "very stimulating" and found it strengthened his conviction that "Stravinsky and his circle were classicists." He proposed Cowley "set up as a founder of the New Criticism," provided such would not interfere with his poetry. William Slater Brown shared Damon's enthusiasm, and believed Cowley showed the makings of an excellent critic precisely because he was a creative artist first. Only Gorham Munson, who not long before had eulogized Cowley's poetry in the *New Republic*, was severely critical. He was unconvinced that Cowley had "seen through to the end the passional and moral significance of Racine" and criticized his approach to classicism for being "too structural or formal." Feeling that in places Cowley tended to "waver and glide too rapidly," Munson pointedly charged that Cowley had failed to consider the inroads made by science into poetry, morality, and religion: "The issue between classicist and romantic is out of the hands of the artist. . . . The battle is being fought out in the at present immensely more intelligent world of scientists. They are giving us a new universe: the stabilities which propped up classicism are gone." [90]

Whatever the limitations of his essay, Racinian tragedy remained an important critical and literary touchstone in Cowley's writings. At the height of his "red romance" he recurrently reverted to Racine as the prototype of elegance and good writing. And in the late 1950s, in a long essay on Hawthorne, he argued that *The Scarlet Letter* gained "a new dimension" from being read as "a Racinian drama of dark necessity." [91] Throughout Cowley's career his explorations of French classical drama in the early 1920s remained part of his intellectual baggage, exemplifying an impressive literary erudition that radiated from his work in a quiet and unobtrusive fashion.

‹ ‹ ‹   During his last six months in France the prospect of returning to America filled Cowley with relief and apprehension. Prior to his departure he aimed to collect translation rights, make himself the "agent for half a dozen French authors," and carry home "a batch of suggestions" to American publishers. Upon his return he planned to spend "a hectic fortnight in New York" to dispose of translations and get commissions for articles, then to retire to his parental farm in Belsano for the summer, to write and to fish. Afterward—reviving a persisting dream—he hoped to purchase a cheap farmhouse near New York. "The program solaces me with leaving Europe," he told Loeb in early February. [92]

But hopes exceeded possibilities. Translation rights were easy enough

to come by: in late February Pierre MacOrlan granted him, on generous terms, the rights for the English translation of his works. Cowley had
already translated four episodes from *On Board the 'Morning Star'* for
Harold Loeb; they were published in the August 1923 *Broom*. For later
issues he translated work by Aragon, Vitrac, and Soupault. From France he
asked Burke to look into the New York market for translations and, in early
March, earnestly requested particulars about a farming property Burke had
recently located near Andover, New Jersey. After years of wandering from
one habitation to the next, he was eager to "return to something settled."[93]

More immediately, his problem was how to finance the voyage home.
Over the spring he wrote, at two dollars a piece, a series of brief reviews for
the *Dial*, in addition to a number of longer critiques. In early May he tried
without success to peddle a translation of Aragon to American magazines
and was upset by his failure to gauge its sales potential on his native market.
At the end of May, seeing no immediate prospect of future betterment,
he appealed to James Sibley Watson of the *Dial* for a $200 advance. He
was depressed at his inability to make more money by writing than he had,
and could only conclude: "As a money-maker I'm a mediocre poet, and
as a poet I'm a mediocre money-maker." Though, by his own calculation,
he had earned as much as $654 during the preceding year, he anticipated
with anxiety the day of return to a hackwriting existence in Manhattan.
"I get stagefright every time I think of New York," he confessed to Burke.
"How in hell's name are we going to live?" The situation was not quite as
desperate as he imagined—though he did not particularly relish the idea
of resuming office work, there was the assuaging prospect of a part-time job
on *Broom*—but the practical incommodities of the moment were depressing enough. To pay off his small remaining debts in France he was forced
once more to appeal for a loan to John Brooks Wheelwright. In early July
he received the $200 he had requested from "Doc" Watson. Shortly after,
he arranged for passage on July 28.[94]

The efforts to scrape together funds for his return voyage brought home
to him how bracing, comfortable, and, above all, unencumbered had been
his life in France. "Liberty—nearly at an end," he noted in a letter in
early June. He received high-spirited letters from Burke and Josephson describing the bibulous delights to be enjoyed in Prohibition America, but
even the promise of "a good bat" upon his return ("I suppose I'll need it. I
haven't been drunk since October 1922") could not make New York seem
anything but "a distant and difficult mirage." Cowley's misgivings were of

a complex kind. His two-year exposure to a wide array of varying and often conflicting aesthetic theories and manifestoes had brought a clarification of ideas without giving him the fully defined philosophy of life and art he had sought. The acceleration of his intellectual and literary development had exposed his dangerous inclination—proof of underlying insecurity and confusion—to adopt the protective coloring of his intellectual and literary surroundings. "We are both showing ourselves the rebellious slaves of environment, even our rebellion being determined by our slavery," he had observed to Burke in late January, adding a few days later: "It frightens me to see how dependent on environment I am."[95] Inclined to absorb and reflect rather than dominate and direct his literary ambience, Cowley struggled to control the pressures of environment throughout the decade, as lengthy entries in his notebooks testify. If, in moments of despondency, he felt much like a literary chameleon, his ideas actually showed greater consistency than he thought; he never lost his belief in the primacy of human intelligence and its ability to control human experience. "Man progresses by rationalizing his world," he wrote in his notebook around 1924. "Wild forces are directed to man's uses, brought under the light of logic . . . good actions are deliberate actions, while bad actions are those forced on us by circumstances. The good man is he who controls the greatest number of factors in his own life." Such a principle of individual morality likewise infused Cowley's literary preferences and helps to explain his dislike of "authors like Sherwood Anderson and D. H. Lawrence whose doctrine is one of surrender to our instincts. Surrender, drift, passivity, a feeling which is generally compensated by mysticism."[96]

On the threshold of his return to America, Cowley feared that a resumption of his former life as a "humble citizen of Grub Street" might undo the moral and literary gleanings of his last two years. The disorderly excitement of his European years made him long for "some stable environment in which one's ideas could develop in more orderly progression." Yet he also remained wary of a narrowing of intellectual interests and a contraction of the circle of experience: "To take no interest in politics or economics, but to speak solely of literary things. But the literary things, losing their roots in general life, wither." Where writers chose to follow "the fallacy of contraction," Cowley observed in his notebook in a passage later incorporated into *Exile's Return*, they violated what he defined as "the aim of literature": "the work of expanding the human mind to its extremest limits of thought and feeling."[97] In line with such a broad conception, he defined "the man of letters" in his notebook as "a man whose province is all of literature, a man who devotes himself to letters as one might devote a life to God or the Poor; a man for whom literature is an end in itself. Examine the career of such a man—Dryden, Boileau, Poe, Baudelaire, Duhamel, and you will find that he is primarily a poet." His definition shows that Cowley's thought remained marked by contradictions. If, in accordance with his earlier symbolist ideals, he demanded of the writer an almost religious devotion to literature as "an end in itself," he also believed, as he had observed to Burke and later wrote in *Exile's Return*, that the man of letters "should concern himself with every department of human activity, including science, sociology and revolution." By 1923 Cowley had become convinced that literature desiccated when it lost its "roots in general life."[98] The political pertinence of such a belief did not become clear until after the crash of 1929; divested of political coloration, however, it remained an axiom of his literary creed.

Whatever his apprehensions, Cowley benefited enormously from his French venture. He had considerably broadened the scope of his experience, gained in knowledge about life and art, and grown in critical and literary self-assurance. His personal acquaintanceship with a broad range of artistic modes and possibilities had corroborated his propensity for an eclectic and pluralist approach in criticism; literature, he already saw, was "a house with many windows." His experiences with *Broom* and *Secession* had publicly placed him in the vanguard of modernity, exposed to him the pitfalls of literary politics, and pointed up the difficulty of preserving a sense of literary solidarity even among the members of his own generation. Having come in search of the artistic life, Cowley saw his ancient dream of a professional writing life in a rural retreat with urban proximity reinforced by his European sojourn. From his early acquaintance with the French he always retained a feeling for the unity of culture and the interrelatedness of all aspects of the literary trade. His studies in French classicism fostered his understanding of culture as the organic outgrowth of a social, historical, and personal situation and gave him a literary ideal—a writer fully integrated into and sustained by his milieu—an ideal he hoped to realize in his native ambience. For the time being his understanding of the relationship between art and society remained superficial and incomplete; its social and political repercussions were hazily intuited at best. But the groundwork had been laid for the "little bundle of beliefs" that he carried with him through life—a fundamental humanism, a belief in the social and communicative function of art and in the "reciprocal connection" between artist and audience, and a conviction of the need for a meaningful correlation between literature and contemporary life.[99]

Cowley returned home hoping to recreate in New York the "atmosphere of intellectual excitement and moral indignation" to which he had responded with fervor in the Paris of the dadaists. His hopes for such a cultural transference were fanned by the reports he received from Josephson, who since his return in the spring had been making concerted efforts to launch Dada in the United States and to act out his celebration of an American machine-age aesthetics on native soil. "America is getting nuttier and nuttier," he wrote to Cowley in July. "The country is falling our way . . . the most colorful and preposterous life in the world is being lived in America." Sympathetic to Josephson's aims, Cowley was a willing ally. What he did not perceive at the time was that his hopes for such a cultural transference were built in part on a delusion: after all, to believe that a vital culture could be transplanted from one country to another as if it were a marketable commodity was in itself a blatant violation of his classical belief in cultural organicism. In France, Cowley had rediscovered the aesthetic potential of America and attained a new conception of his role and position as an American writer. But in the process he had come to see America through a screen of nostalgia and idealism, in "a vision half-remembered, half-falsified and romanced." He had embarked on a search for a new literature celebrating the picturesque qualities of contemporary American life in an age of business, industry and technology—the towering skyscrapers, the roaring machines, the glamorous movies, the nervous rhythms of jazz, the banal advertising slogans—but his understanding of the human and social realities behind the glittering façade was superficial and deficient. It was one thing to lyrically invest the products of a commercial and technological society with artistic vitality and potential; it was another to have to eke out a daily living as a writer in the anonymity of Manhattan. Predictably, also, Cowley's rural tastes were bound to clash with his extravagant if ironic "bravos for the spectacle of American business." In "The Peppermint Gardens," a poem capturing Cowley's mood on the brink of his return, he voices his tiredness of the classical, "ordered beauty" of a cultivated European landscape—a landscape cultural as much as rural—and expresses a nostalgic preference for the wild disorder of "a country where briars sprout / under the crazily twisted gum trees, / an imprecise, untutored country / where all the gardens are inside out."[100]

Cowley had sought "salvation" in cultural exile, only to discover the inutility of expatriation. As he would find soon enough, the cultural dilemmas he had dramatized by his departure from America survived his coming home. He had yet to discover that expatriation was less geographical or external than psychological or internal. It was painfully possible to be a spiritual exile at home.[101]

II

Dada in
New York

1923-1924

Cowley left Paris on August 2, 1923, the day of President Harding's death, to confront an American literary and cultural climate equally dispiriting as the one he had left two years before. Ten days after leaving Paris, he landed at the French Line Pier of New York, hardly realizing the incompatibility of the mental picture of America he carried home from France and the reality of living and writing in the shadows of Manhattan's downtown skyscrapers. Eight years later, in the early stages of *Exile's Return*, he wrote, "everything I learned in France, the whole course of my thinking, had prepared me for an uncomfortable season of readjustment." The ethical and aesthetic beliefs with which he returned proved but a "dubious" foundation for such high-minded purposes as he envisioned for himself: "I was returning to New York with a set of values that bore no relation to American life, with convictions that could not fail to be misunderstood in a country where Dada was hardly a name, and moral judgments on literary matters were thought to be in questionable taste." In retrospect Cowley was forced to acknowledge that the attempt to act out Dada in New York was fated to miscarry: "Looking back at the early autumn of my return, I cannot help feeling that most of my decisions, though made for the highest moral reasons, were ill-suited to the circumstances and costly in their results."[1]

Cowley arrived in New York in the highest of spirits but with empty pockets. Before long, however, the Cowleys were established on the top floor of an old house owned by Frances Gifford, a friend of Peggy, downtown at 16 Dominick Street, close to the Woolworth Building; it must have been, Cowley recalled, "the most battered and primitive lodging in New York."[2] In the first flush upon his return Cowley relished the cultural offerings of the city and let himself be enchanted by the spectacle of New York in the age of business and the machine: "Allagazam, allagazam, the great show is about to begin. The fire-trucks dizzily skidding, the journey through mammoth caves, the song of riveting hammers, the death-defying leaps from beam to beam on the fortieth storey. Allagazam, step up. See the genuine gangsters, the old pretzel women, the ghetto, the

African village, the business men dictating to three stenographers and a dictaphone. Come out with the crowd, tonight, aw, be a sport. Buy the elixir of happiness, only fifty cents at my bar. Step up, allagazam."[3] Laced with irony, Cowley's celebration of the city shows that his enthrallment was mostly with the colorful surface of modern urban life. As in the war, he was still inclined to adopt a spectatorial attitude toward contemporary reality; he viewed the city as a "great show," enacted for his benefit, with a superficial understanding of the reality behind the glittering, kaleidoscopic panorama. In accordance with the aesthetic beliefs he had evolved in France, if Cowley was to succeed in artistically negotiating this urban scene, he still had to find a way of integrating his rhapsodic savorings of the aesthetic splendor of the city with an appreciation of the deleterious social effects and the human expenditure of an urban-technological reality. A writer who insisted on the inseparability of literature from contemporary life must find a way of overcoming the alienation implicit in his spectator's role in order to attain an organic integration of artist and milieu.

Cowley's most pressing need, however, was to find a source of income. Not only did the debts he had incurred in France "weigh heavily" on his conscience, but above all he needed to find a job that would provide for his and Peggy's elementary needs without depriving him of the time or energy to write. Faced with the choice between free-lance authorship and a regular office job, Cowley's fear of surrendering to commercial compromise proved stronger than the deterrence of a daily nine-to-five routine. Knowing that as a free-lance writer his work might be affected by the need to sell, he chose to make his money in a different sphere—the world of advertising copywriters—saving his remaining hours for what he hoped could be "the disinterested practice of the art of letters." Cowley's justification for adopting a split mode of existence—by day a copywriter in the service of a business civilization, by night a free and independent writer with an aversion to corrupting his talents—seemed a violation of his aesthetic creed. Not until some two years later did he realize that he had opted for a self-defeating life-style: "when one's writing ceases to have a functional relationship to one's life, when it becomes a way of spending otherwise idle evenings, it loses part of its substance." Only then did he dare to face the occupational and commercial hazards of a free-lance existence.[4]

At the end of August, Cowley resumed work with Sweet's Catalogue Service, serving as proofreader, copywriter, and "general utility man" at a modest salary. On the whole, the office was friendly and the job "a pleasant sort of refuge"; it did not involve much arduous work except during the two months before publication of the catalogue. Cowley was reemployed in the midst of the annual prepublication rush; for his first six weeks he was kept working from nine to ten hours a day. "The prospect is disheartening," he complained to Wheelwright; "I cannot write." To Loeb he wrote: "From August 29 till October 5, I was working so hard that my sole recreation was to play a rubber of bridge and drop off to sleep."[5]

Cowley's reminiscences do not contain much evidence that he experienced any sense of incongruity in being employed at Sweet's—"Copywriting for Sweet's Catalogue was merely stating the facts about honest products"—but an entry in his notebook of the time expressed more ambivalent feelings. Exploring the artistic possibilities of American advertising, Cowley sounded much like a man trying to convince himself of an ironic truth he only half believes in: "Advertising is a group art, an anonymous art, and it is the cathedral of 1923, erected to the deity whom all of us worship: bow down, brethren, before the possession of a butler, a chauffeur, four motorcars, Success! . . . Advertising is the literature of a religion with a creed: buy more. Increase your wants: that way lies happiness. It is exactly as true as the opposite doctrine of Epicurus."[6]

Contemplating the literary situation of America under Calvin Coolidge, Cowley found that, on the surface, literary conditions seemed encouraging enough. On the wave of a booming national economy, American literature, too, seemed on the threshold of "a period of excitement and inflation." There was a profusion of writing jobs, of publishers, and of literary markets. But Cowley, infused with a spirit of defiant activism retained from the dadaists, was dissatisfied with a lack of moral fervor in the literary climate and with the apparent failure of American artists to seriously negotiate the urban-technological scene before them. Too many, he felt, chose to withdraw into a riskless mode of life, to escape into expatriation or the past. In his notebook Cowley whipped himself up to moral indignation as he demanded an infusion of new literary oxygen:

> Poets should be suppressed . . .
>
> Poets, if one defines the term in accordance with its application, are people with a certain weak attitude toward the world they live in. They cannot digest it. They cannot make it poetry. Poetry is an acid which eats away values and deposits new values, like salts, on the open plumbing of new civilizations. A civilization without poetry is un-

bearable. Poets find that American civilization is unbearable because they lack the force to transmute it into poetry. . . .

The game is so easy, so tame; there are no risks; we have allowed them to take a title which belonged to more adventuresome spirits; now let us make the title worthless. To cast ridicule on poets by every means at our command, to attack them, physically if necessary, to clear the air so that breathing is possible![7]

"People need to be shocked, have pins stuck in their buttocks, be made to think," Cowley had fulminated to Witter Bynner on the eve of his departure from Giverny. His dadaist desire to provoke and activate was only fanned when, back in America, he felt himself surrounded by a literary atmosphere of aimless apathy. In his notebook he returned to what he now had come to think of as "an inevitable project"—"the analysis of this literary age"—and diagnosed a present "crisis in literature." He was persuaded that "all the machinery for a literary renaissance" was at hand, yet he looked about in vain for the writers of the new *risorgimento*. Fashionable authors like Anderson and Dreiser he decried as "muggy and ill-defined Rousseauists" who lacked discipline and uncritically worshiped freedom and the libido. But even the writers with whose aims he felt in sympathy— he named Edmund Wilson as "an excellent example"—seemed "overcome by inertia, without direction," and tended to be "reactionary in the sense of being antagonistic to their age." By contrast, Cowley envisioned the forthcoming "genius" of the times as one fully alive to the multifarious possibilities of the contemporary scene, at home in many different fields of human endeavor but enslaved by none, and marked by a sparkling enthusiasm for life: "Now the genius of this age, if he appears, will work with the instruments provided by this age: he will know science, and business, and applied psychology; he will even make use of publicity, as a tool. His mind will be keen, but he will forge ahead by virtue of a certain zest in living, which we seem to have lost. I ought to make the portrait of this shining, mechanical, electric creature."[8]

Cowley's Emersonian hopes for reanimating a sluggish cultural milieu centered on *Broom*. On October 5 the nineteenth edition of *Sweet's Architectural Catalogue* appeared, after which Cowley assumed a more active role in *Broom's* precarious adventures, both as editor and writer. Since Josephson's return to America in the spring he had reestablished *Broom* in New York with the aid of Maxwell Geffen, who was willing to extend a line of printing credit despite the fact that in America publication costs were twice as high as in Europe (to improve the chances for survival, *Broom*'s size was reduced and the number of pages decreased from ninety-six to sixty-four). Josephson had strongly steered *Broom* toward a celebration of the contemporary scene, making it into an effective instrument of what Burke ironically called "our Great Young New American Movement," and, in addition to Burke and Slater Brown (formally *Broom*'s third associate editor), he had managed to persuade a considerable number of writers and artists to stand by *Broom* and offer material for the first few American numbers.[9]

By early October, Cowley's more active help was sorely needed. A month earlier Josephson had written to Loeb: "Cowley is in the mess of returning to America and reestablishing, otherwise he would be a bulwark. . . . I must say that he has been very helpful and concerned; that France in the last while changed him much for the better." With Cowley's assistance Josephson had drawn up an editorial program for *Broom* involving the presentation of more American writers and artists and fewer translations from Europe. In the first American *Broom*, published in July 1923, Loeb surveyed the "internal evolution" of the magazine's editorial policy over the past two years and described the "nucleus of American writers of the youngest generation" to which the new *Broom* was now openly committed. Loeb emphasized their "whole-hearted disapproval" of the preceding generation of Anderson, Dreiser, and Lewis and pointed up their affirmative Americanism: "They keep an open mind toward the phenomenon of contemporary industrialism, and devote themselves to the more immediate task of men of letters: writing well." They were distrustful, Loeb said, of "current panaceas" for social and political ills and abjured "the doctrines of poets on economics and of novelists on psychoanalysis." Instead, they displayed an "unusual concentration on problems of form and style." Singling out Burke, Josephson, and Cowley as the core of *Broom*, Loeb analyzed the distinctive features of each:

> Kenneth Burke, perhaps stimulated by research in plastic mediums for what Clive Bell calls "significant form," has been studying its elusive equivalent in writing. His stories, which discard the old binding of plot or narrative, obtain unity by what he calls a super-plot. . . .
> The experiments of Malcolm Cowley are even more diversified. He believes that every literary conception has an ideal form. In the search

for it he has evolved nearly as many forms as he has written poems. He is not afraid to write about contemporary phenomena, and does not share the fashionable gesture of horror toward them. Matthew Josephson is another who is able to discover food for poetry in the "crackle of typewriters, comptographs, dictaphones and phonographs" or "dropping dishes in the effervescent crater" of that part of the restaurant one does not think about. His talent is not quite so intellectualized as Burke's or Cowley's, not so dependent on theories based on reason, but more instinctive, drawing directly on the subconscious. . . . All of these have a love of rhetoric, of mouth-filling explosive phrases, unlike the emotional breast-juggling of recent years and more akin to the eloquence of the Elizabethans.

At last, Loeb concluded, *Broom* was giving up its "vagabond career" and settling down "in the country to which it belongs." Ironically, if unintentionally, Loeb's survey of the first two years of *Broom* marked his final contribution to the magazine.[10]

Cowley was represented in the first American issue of *Broom* by his translations of four episodes from Pierre MacOrlan's *On Board the 'Morning Star'*, as well as by the last in his series of imaginary portraits, "Snapshot of a Young Lady," which he had worked on between March and June in Giverny. Louis Aragon liked it well enough to undertake a French translation. The story is a fantasy burlesque of a detective story; it surrenders realistic conventions of verisimilitude as well as traditional devices of plot, chronology, and linear narrative structure, and parodies the improbable mixture of astounding riches, horrendous crime, and sentimental love that marked the plots of countless popular tales and movies of the time.[11]

Broom's September issue even more strongly reflected the editors' flamboyant appreciation of contemporary American culture. It featured essays on the American motion picture by Philippe Soupault, Robert Alden Sanborn, and William Slater Brown, sections from Jean Toomer's *Cane* and from William Carlos Williams's *In the American Grain*, as well as poems by Glenway Wescott and Isidor Schneider. Cowley appeared with his dadaist improvisation (first published in *Secession*) of a funeral jig set to the rhythm of a popular ragtime tune, "Memphis Johnny," and Josephson with "Brain at the Wheel," an ironic poetic tribute to the genius of automobile tycoon Henry Ford. Cowley was enthusiastic about the September *Broom* and said as much to Loeb: "The second American issue of *Broom* impresses me very favorably. It has a great deal of unity, and ought to make a very definite, if hostile, impression."¹²

The emphasis on autochthonous forms of American cultural expression continued in *Broom*'s third American issue. It featured American art by Edward Nagle and Joseph Stella, as well as a series of photographs and paintings by Charles Sheeler, ranging from his "Still Life" of a black telephone to his pictures of Bucks County barns. There was a group of sonnets on American prostitutes by E. E. Cummings, "Five Americans," a second section from Williams's *In the American Grain*, and a portrait by Brown and Nagle of the idiosyncratic Joe Gould, followed by what purported to be "Chapter CCCLXVIII of Joseph Gould's History of the Contemporary World, to be published posthumously." The October issue had originally been planned as "a collection of political manifestoes," but nothing so pointed up the political innocence of its editors as another, exuberantly satirical tribute by Matthew Josephson to Henry Ford, wizard of efficiency and mass production, beneficent symbol of machine-age America; it culminated in Josephson's proposal of Ford as "the people's candidate" for the presidency of the United States.¹³

With Josephson aggressively at the helm, *Broom* managed to attract much—but not always favorable—attention. The magazine was written up in the *New York Tribune* and *Evening Post*, the *Chicago Daily News*, the *Dial*, the *Nation*, and the *New Republic*. Burton Rascoe conducted a lengthy interview with the controversial leader of the "youthful iconoclasts" of *Broom* in his "Bookman's Day Book." From London, John Gould Fletcher wrote to pay his respects to "the new and successfully rejuvenated *Broom*," which he felt was "showing signs of becoming the most interesting periodical in the U. S." Not all, however, were voices of critical acclaim. Edmund Wilson had earlier evinced skepticism about Cowley's and Josephson's dadaist proclivities; recent issues of *Broom* had only strengthened his disapproval: "I can't hand the *Broom* crowd very much," he observed to John Peale Bishop; "Cowley, I think, has some ability but is sort of an ass, and Josephson is an ass with practically no observable ability." Several months later, assuming an attitude of above-the-battle impartiality in the *New Republic*, Wilson incorporated his views on the merit as well as the naivety of Josephson's ideas in "An Imaginary Conversation" between the editor of *Broom* and one of his favorite punchbags, Paul Rosenfeld.¹⁴

The *Dial* took a more subtle and ambivalent attitude toward the writers whom, following Gorham Munson, it dubbed "skyscraper primitives." In contrast to the members of the *Seven Arts* group, whose humanism had bred a mostly negative criticism of American culture, the writers of *Broom* appeared to the editors of the *Dial* to have come up with a program of "dogged optimism" incorporating "the entire futurist credo": "They can find, in advertising, movies, political buncombe, jazz, corrupt business tactics, bootleg, Billy Sunday, and so on, an endless 'wealth' of striking and picturesque material." But such an aesthetic veneration of machine-age America, the editors saw, conveniently sidestepped "the humanistic consideration." Between the "humanistic approach" and a celebratory aestheticism, however, they had trouble forging a reconciliation: "One can enjoy the whirr of a smoothly running motor, or one can see only the wreckage in human life which lies behind that motor—and one is respectively skyscraper primitive or Seven Arts." The *Broom* group had chosen to pursue "the harder task," the editors granted: even if they must be "content to leave art on the plane of chessplaying or baseball," a relatively pure display of "skill without content," still they deserved praise for recognizing that "the machine is the dominant factor in contemporary life, and that America is the most highly mechanized country in the world, so that for better or worse the course of society for the next era is most likely to be settled in American terms." [15]

The *Dial*'s criticism was presciently relevant to the development of Cowley's position. Over the next few years he became increasingly aware of the "missing" dimension of humanism—so central a tenet of his classicist aesthetics—in his and Josephson's celebration of machine-age America. Concomitantly he grew increasingly disturbed by the modernist tendency toward a "pure" or "absolute poetry" and by the futility of a literature that more and more became a self-contained mode of lexical game-playing. [16] A growing concern with the artist's social and human responsibility paved the way for his radical commitments of the 1930s.

Despite Cowley's hopes that even adversarial publicity might work in *Broom*'s favor ("it is busy making enemies, and if it lasts long enough its enemies will put it over," he told Loeb), financially the magazine continued in a sorry state. Rising printing debts, dwindling resources, and a shortage of new subscriptions were perpetual worries. A vigorous circulation campaign momentarily revived the editors' hopes, but by the fall even the indefatigable Josephson was losing heart. In Europe, Loeb, too, seemed ready to throw up his hands: "I have no more opinions about *Broom*'s chances but let my spirits rise and fall in accordance with [the] last letter from New York." In October, Cowley met with Josephson to decide upon the future course of the magazine. In order to limit expenses to five hundred dollars or less per issue, they decided to again reduce *Broom*'s size (to forty-eight pages), abandon halftones, and stop paying contributors, thus allowing Josephson to take a job on Wall Street and edit the magazine in his spare hours. Cowley confessed to Loeb that he felt "sceptical about the success of the undertaking, for a magazine needs one man's time. It might be better to go down in the glory of a last number."[17]

Even more disillusioning than *Broom*'s practical difficulties was the waning enthusiasm of the magazine's circle of friends and contributors. In early September Josephson complained to Loeb that "the 'group' which is roughly associated with *Broom* is in a remarkably sterile mood. The absence of any real cooperation . . . on the part of the younger generation is highly discouraging." Some time later Cowley wrote to Loeb in much the same spirit: "The crowd seems willing to help, but most people are in a condition where they can't write much. To get good material seems to be the hardest problem." A month later he voiced his growing exasperation with the apparent apathy of his literary friends: "the people I meet in New York seem to have lost all capacity for indignation and are content to accept the unimportance of their lot or to solace themselves with piddling drunks."[18]

Cowley was not prepared to stand by passively and watch the magazine founder on the rock of its precarious finances or the indifference of its friends. If *Broom* must die, at least its ending "must not be ignoble," he told Burke. "To die gently on an ebb tide is not my idea of death." Mindful of his Paris days Cowley still hoped to buck the rising tide of apathy and to infuse the literary atmosphere with new excitement. "Cowley believes *Broom* should have a spectacular end," Josephson reported to Loeb. Indeed, Cowley had plans galore. Handbills were to be passed out and soapbox orations to be held in Union Square; a dadaist manifestation was to be staged at a New York theater, complete with "violent and profane attacks" on famous writers, mock trials of prominent critics, and burlesques of cherished enemies like Anderson, Dell, Mencken, and Rosenfeld— "anything," he later wrote, "that would add to the excitement of living or writing" and that would display disdain for the "sanctity of American letters." Such stunts, he hoped, might gain publicity for *Broom* and help to keep the magazine afloat.[19] Most of Cowley's plans, however, were fated to remain in blueprint.

As a first step Cowley decided to call a meeting of all the writers and artists, friend and foe, who had contributed to *Broom* and *Secession*. In part, Cowley wanted to gauge and, if possible, reactivate the commitment of *Broom*'s supporters; more broadly, his aim was to try to find a communal platform on which to proceed. Without defining his objectives precisely, Cowley was yet persuaded that some form of "joint action" was necessary, if anemia was to be remedied and new ideals were to be given a lease on life. Thus he wanted the meeting to be a "catholic," nonpartisan one, which would "clear the air" and compose factional quarrels. Sending out an urgent invitation to Burke, Cowley explained: "If we can get together in one room, we can at least define our positions, if we can make no plans to go ahead. Piddling Jesus. The people who can be content with art-for-art's-sake, three issues of a magazine composed of essays by G[orham] B. M[unson] and stories by W[aldo] F[rank] and an occasional glass of synthetic gin, will continue to be content. For God's sake, let's brew some stronger liquor." [20]

Cowley's hopes for unified cooperation in an atmosphere filled with rankling personal conflicts and sharply diverging artistic positions were naively high. Josephson, not on the friendliest of terms with either Munson or Crane, was understandably skeptical of Cowley's plans. Though he admitted they were "logical and clearsighted," he had little confidence in the outcome of the "grand powwow" staged by Cowley and went along only with reluctance.[21]

The ensuing meeting took place on October 19 in a small Italian restaurant and speakeasy on Prince Street in "Little Italy." Most of the writers Cowley had invited attended, among them Burke, Crane, Josephson, Light, Sanborn, Schneider, and Wescott, as well as several wives and nonwriting friends; altogether some thirty people were present. Williams, Stevens, Toomer, Brown, and Nagle were out of town; the latter two sent professions of loyalty to be read at the meeting. Waldo Frank declined to attend, as did Gorham Munson, who was recuperating from an illness in Woodstock, in upstate New York. With Frank and Toomer absent, Hart Crane was left as Munson's sole supporter, a position he viewed with some misgiving. As Crane told Munson, he came prepared to play "the most contrary rôle." Shortly before, still full of rancor over Wheelwright's butchering of his "For the Marriage of Faustus and Helen" in the recently arrived September issue of *Secession*, Crane had told Cowley that he had only "a very slight interest in the meeting" and was "unconcerned with its issues."[22]

At Cowley's request Munson sent in a statement to be read out at the meeting; it presented, he told Cowley, what he considered "the primary issue." Munson was disturbed that Cowley's invitation failed to advance "good reasons for common action" and in his note sought to redress the absence of a framework of philosophical ideas. He pleaded the necessity of "some conscious life-attitude" and borrowed a phrase from John Middleton Murry ("the passionate apprehension of life") to point up the missing dimension in *Broom's* approach. In the process, however, Munson also launched a personal diatribe against Josephson, denouncing him as a "literary opportunist" and "an intellectual faker," one who was dishonest, cunning, treacherous, and notoriety-seeking, and proclaiming that any self-respecting modern movement must part from such as Josephson.[23]

Munson's statement implicitly reflected his and Crane's growing interest in the mystical and visionary idealism of the Russian logician P.D. Ouspensky and the Russian mystic G.I. Gurdjieff. Ouspensky's conception of the imminent emergence of a new order of consciousness, his view of poetry as the visionary medium for spiritual revelation, and his belief in the need for a new use of metaphor and syntax, were deeply congenial to Crane. For a while, Ouspensky's *Tertium Organum* became a "common bible" for Crane and a small circle of friends—Munson, Frank, and Toomer—who felt tacitly leagued in spiritual brotherhood. Ouspensky was a supporter of the more outlandish Gurdjieff who, after peregrinations through Asia and Turkey, had established the Institute for the Harmonious Development of Man at a chateau at Fontainebleau-Avon in France, where he subjected his pupils to cultish exercises in philosophical and practical mysticism aiming to induce new spiritual states through ancient sacred dances, religious rites, and a return to rural fundamentals. Munson, in particular, became a fervent disciple.[24] Such an artistic and philosophical direction was strongly at odds with Cowley's and Burke's hard-edged intellectualism and the formalist exploration of the aesthetic potential of machine-age America advocated in the pages of *Broom*; Gurdjieff, in particular, was a recurrent target of ridicule. It was this basic divergence in artistic orientation that formed the deeper cause for the ensuing quarrels and raised them above the level of a mere conflict of personalities.

Cowley's reading of Munson's letter proved the dubious highlight of the meeting on Prince Street. In the middle of his reading, struck by Munson's pompous rhetoric, Cowley could not refrain from letting his personal prejudices get the better of him and "began to declaim it like a blue-jawed actor reciting Hamlet's soliloquy." As a result, the meeting dissolved into a cacophony of insults and protestations. Crane, as promised, played a leading part in the pandemonium and rushed to Munson's defense. Several days later Josephson reported to Loeb that the evening had been much like "a Tzara-Breton (Dadaist) affair," except that Americans proved "very emotional and less logical than Dadas." "It turned into a riotous party after a while. Attempts by Cowley and me to control it were pathetic. Attempts by the members to discuss their common problems concertedly failed through the inertia of intoxication. Yet many things were clarified. Principally that if anything is to be done here (Cowley admits), three or four of us must go ahead and then tell the others about it. Artists, like other humans, are sheep, only controversial and ill-controled sheep." [25]

What seriousness of purpose the meeting might have had was lost in partly self-instigated dadaist futility. The projected general discussion never got off the ground. Cowley was deeply disappointed. "The question of personal quarrels seemed to overshadow everything else," he reported to Wheelwright, still in Europe to survey the printing of *Secession*. Cowley's efforts at unified cooperation had miscarried, but at least now battle lines were drawn and writers openly took sides with either *Broom* or *Secession*. At the end of October Cowley described the new alignments to Loeb:

> Hart Crane elected to stand by Munson, which disappointed me, for although Munson would be no asset to Broom if he did cooperate, Crane can write. As a result of the meeting, Burke resigned from the board of Secession, saying that he would not join the staff of Broom, but would contribute impartially to both magazines. Brown and I decided to contribute nothing more to Secession. I wrote Munson and told him that so many real differences of opinion had developed, beyond the personal animosities, that he was justified in continuing Secession; that it was no longer in competition with Broom. I hoped there would be no enmity between the two papers. Munson answered,

why no enmity? I answered nothing. We seem to be enemies now, formally.[26]

Several weeks later the Prince Street meeting had a violent aftermath. The incident belatedly gained anecdotal notoriety, largely as a result of the inflated and contradictory accounts of witnesses and participants; the literary grapevine did the rest. In early November, Josephson, infuriated by Munson's personal attacks, decided that the only honorable way of settling the dispute was to travel to Woodstock, where Munson was staying with the art historian William Murrell Fisher, and challenge him to a bout of fisticuffs. The ensuing battle, refereed by Fisher, took place in an autumn drizzle on a stretch of muddy, marshy pasture and apparently, so Cowley reported at second hand in *Exile's Return*, was but "a dull spectacle, a war fought horizontally more than vertically, a series of slips and wallows that ended when both heroes were too stiff with mud and bruises to battle on." Both Josephson and Munson subsequently boasted pugilistic superiority and claimed a qualified triumph. In New York, Josephson remembered, the "Duel in the Mud" created quite a stir and was set down by literary columnists as possibly "the first time in the history of America that two men of letters came to blows over their opposing critical or aesthetic doctrines."[27]

Eight months after the incident, on July 4, 1924, Cowley visited the scene of the battle, together with Wheelwright and Brown, and, in a mood of dadaist clownery, dedicated a "battlefield monument." He also composed a mocking ode immortalizing the two combatants:

> Know, Muse, that heroes yet exist
> Whose anger brooks no intercession,
> And tooth meets tooth and fist meets fist
> And "Up," cries Munson, "with *Secession*!
> Down *Broom*," he snarls, and warriors pant
> Each to defend his literary slant.[28]

Cowley's immediate response to the fight was less lighthearted. Munson's version of events, in particular, rekindled all of his personal resentment. On November 14, 1923, he voiced his exasperation to William Slater Brown: "People disgust me who try to carry physical matters into the domain of the intellect. Munson keeps repeating . . . that he won a 'moral victory.' If I remember my war, moral victories are the sort which precede strategic retreats. . . . I never saw a man of so little talent who possessed such a capacity for irritation. He never lies. . . . But. The impression he gives is this: I defeated Matty clearly but Fisher, out of politeness, called the affair a draw. By a combination of truths he produces falsehood. Immediately on reading this, the fight changed its values for me. It had seemed a sorry spectacle, completely ridiculous; now suddenly I wanted to punch his pasty face myself." [29]

Following his admittedly "hostile instinct," Cowley sent Munson an acerbic and "unambiguous" note, explaining that he had declined to answer his epistolary statement because it consisted of "unsupported assertions based on your personal prejudices," accusing Munson of making "garbled quotations" from other people's letters, including Cowley's, and expressing a clear preference for Josephson "because he has infinitely more talent as a writer." Reversing the charges, Munson promptly returned Cowley's "testy and confused document," accused its author of conducting "a persistent whispering propaganda" against him, and requested not to be approached on "a plane of bickering." From this point on, Cowley's connections with Munson and his magazine were definitely severed. As he told John Wheelwright, who from Florence was fighting his own battle with Munson over *Secession*: "Console yourself, Dearie. Munson has also broken off Relations with me. The protection of the Methodist Church (or is it Baptist?) is henceforth denied us. Why don't you write your companion in the outer darkness?" By this time Wheelwright had come to feel personally wronged at having allowed himself to be associated with a "movement" wrecked by futile bickerings resembling nothing so much as "a church sociable squabble." He had long decided to stand by Cowley, Burke, and Josephson, and on November 23 summed up his frustrations to Cowley: "I don't understand the lack of cooperation. In union is strength, etc. I should think this precious study of ad. slogans would teach you that. For God's sake! Is no one 'who writes' impersonal enough to put through a little enlightened selfishness? This futility gets my grab." Like Burke, he resigned from *Secession*. Munson, now left in sole control of the magazine, published two more issues, in which he made a concerted effort to shift its course "from experimental aestheticism to a kind of Stieglitz-Frank mysticism," a literary path obviously divergent from Cowley's. [30]

Despite his aesthetic and philosophical affinity with Munson and Frank, Crane continued to seek out the less solemn companionship of Cowley and his friends. He relished the spirit of camaraderie and buffoonery that prevailed among the *Broom* group, finding that their company offered him compensations for the frustrations of a business job and that they had an easygoing tolerance for his "Rabelaisian humors and drunken rages."[31] Though temperamental and artistic differences gave cause for friction, Cowley's friendship with Crane, based as it was on mutual respect and admiration for each other's poetry, remained intact.

At the beginning of November, Cowley and Crane traveled to Woodstock, where Crane, having recently resigned from a copywriting job, was to spend part of the winter at a farmhouse rented by Brown and Nagle. En route they stopped off at the country house of Eugene O'Neill in Ridgefield, Connecticut. Shortly before, Crane had met O'Neill in New York and been invited for the weekend. Peggy, an old Village friend of O'Neill's, earlier that week had traveled ahead to Ridgefield with Agnes Boulton, the playwright's second wife. Though Cowley knew O'Neill—he had seen him several times in Village speakeasies and had consorted in the circle of O'Neill's friends at the Provincetown Playhouse—he never was a close or personal friend. During the weekend, O'Neill broke his habitual taciturnity and talked freely to Cowley about the literary concerns close to his heart, in particular the work of German expressionist playwrights, as well as his new play in progress, *Desire Under the Elms*. Though O'Neill was kind enough, the two found it difficult to establish a sense of rapport. "Eugene O'Neill, Mr. O'Neill the playwright, Gene, . . . speaks a language so different from ours that I seemed to converse with him from different worlds," Cowley remarked to Burke several days after the visit. If, as he recalled in a late memoir, he had sensed in the older writer "a need to explain himself to a new generation of writers," Cowley had made little effort to bridge what he later felt was also a gulf between "fame and obscurity"; instead, he had been defensively reticent. The weekend took a rather bizarre turn when Cowley, priding himself on his country knowledge, explained to O'Neill how to tap one of the barrels of hard cider stored in the cellar, thereby starting O'Neill on a rather dramatic course of alcoholic misadventures, which ended a week later when Agnes Boulton found the playwright in a comatose state in one of the upstairs rooms of the Hell Hole, his favorite hangout in the Village.[32]

The failure of Cowley's efforts to gather all behind a common literary program could not diminish his commitment to *Broom*. He had a strong hand in the makeup of its November 1923 issue, which, retrospectively, he rated as the best of the five American numbers. There were poems by

Stevens, Cummings, and Williams, as well as a poem by Cowley satirizing Munson's philosophical pomposity, "Towards a More Passionate Apprehension of Life." In addition, the issue featured two of Cowley's translations of Aragon and Roger Vitrac, book reviews by Wescott, Josephson, Robert A. Sanborn, and B. H. Haggin, the music critic, as well as two pieces of experimental fiction, one a satirical fantasy about a Wall Street speculator by Slater Brown, the other, "An Awful Storming Fire or, Her and I on a Journey to the Secret of the Sun, by the Author Who Solved the Mysterious Riddle," a story by Charles L. Durboraw about a street-corner pickup, which modulated from sharp vernacular realism into an apocalyptic sexual fantasy. This story was titillating enough to draw the attention of the postmaster general: on December 8, 1923, the editors of *Broom* were informed of censorship regulations and warned that "if there is doubt as to the mailability of any matter that appears in your publication, the copies mailed will be withheld from despatch." Though the editors suffered a momentary pang of disquietude, they took the warning in a spirit of levity and Slater Brown composed a mock editorial satirizing "SEC 480" of the postal laws as "one of the most perfect specimens of indigenous American Folk Lore." [33]

Through November and December, Cowley and Josephson fought, against odds, to keep the magazine afloat. Cowley pumped all his spare time and most of his personal savings into the venture. "I personally should be very sorry to see Broom go under, for I think all of us need an organ in which to print," he told Loeb. Brown, too, had recently renewed his pledge of allegiance in a personal letter to Cowley and from Woodstock offered what help he could. Josephson by this time had become convinced that "a career in business with independent and detached position in literature" was his best bet and had taken a job on Wall Street, "pimping" (in Cowley's words) for a brokerage firm, which left him less time for *Broom* than before. To make matters worse, Maxwell Geffen, the magazine's printer and financial backer, withdrew his subvention after the November issue, thereby taking most of the wind out of *Broom's* already tattered sails. The editors dolefully struggled on. Brown negotiated terms with a new printer in Kingston, New York—manufacturing costs per issue were to be limited to $250, *Broom's* format was to be further reduced (to thirty-two pages), the subscription rate lowered from $5 to $3 a year—while Cowley and Josephson searched for new benefactors, issued appeals to readers, started subscription campaigns. Cowley, always good for a practical plan in time of need, devised a scheme to back up the magazine by a system of patronages, suggested a one-evening literary performance, and proved a tireless canvasser and fund-raiser. *Broom's* December issue, originally planned as "a bang-up issue," was silently omitted. In late November, Cowley grandiloquently voiced his mounting disillusionment as well as his bitter determination to Loeb: "the general situation is so discouraging at the present time—Dial gone over to the fairies, Secession to Munson and Frank, no other magazine on the horizon—that we are forced to continue to save our collective face and the respectability of American letters." Meanwhile, nearing the point of exhaustion, the editors were busily, if unwittingly, preparing *Broom's* last issue.[34]

The contents of the January 1924 number of *Broom* had already been made up and the issue sent to press by the time the editors received the postmaster general's reminder of censorship regulations. *Broom's* twenty-first issue, its slenderest, featured contributions by Cummings, Ramon Guthrie, Williams, and (in Cowley's translation) Soupault. Slater Brown wrote a sensitive review of Cummings's *Tulips and Chimneys* and, with Cowley, composed an open letter to the editors of the *Dial*, challenging its decision to present its 1923 award to Van Wyck Brooks, an established critic with a wide audience, rather than an important new talent like Cummings. Cowley and Brown attacked the *Dial* for its cowardly eclecticism and its lack of a "positive standard" in choosing its awardees. In mock retaliation, they announced the presentation of a *Broom* award to "a young American writer who, in our opinion, has done a significant service for American letters." The award for 1923 (consisting of two dollars) went to Sinclair Lewis.[35]

On the basis of these contents, *Broom* stood in no danger of postal censorship. But in preparing the January issue, Cowley and Josephson had also accepted, if with "a passing moment of anxiety," a philosophical tale by Kenneth Burke, "Prince Llan," containing, in condensed fictional form, many of the author's theories about art and life. Though the editors suspected that Burke's "ethical masque" might in places be "too outspoken to meet the requirements of the postal authorities," they naively trusted that it was also too abstruse to catch the vigilant eye of the postmaster general. In effect, they made it a matter of principle to print the story: if *Broom* could no longer publish the daring, innovative material for which it had been called into existence, it seemed to lose its raison d'être.

On January 14, 1924, the editors received word that the last issue of *Broom* had been judged "unmailable" by the Post Office Department in Washington and that the magazine had been suppressed under section 480 of the postal laws, prohibiting the mailing of obscene material (which included pornography and contraceptives). Though no official motives for the suppression were given, the editors could only assume that it had been caused by Burke's tale, which referred explicitly to women possessing "breasts" that stood out "firm like pegs," as well as "sitters" that "undulated" as they walked. Postal employees dumped 1,500 copies of *Broom*'s January issue in the cellar of Cowley's house on Dominick Street. A few hundred of them could be delivered by taxi to New York bookshops; the remainder was disposed of as waste paper.[36]

The suppression of *Broom* caused much excitement, indignation, and publicity. Expressions of commiseration and support came in from many of *Broom*'s friends, among them Crane, Williams, and Fitts, the editor of *S4N*, who was convinced that, after recuperation, *Broom* would "again stick up its horrid head." O'Neill wrote an indignant letter of protest to the postmaster general in Washington, denouncing the censorship decision as one "unjust at any time." Burton Rascoe criticized the suppression in the *New York Herald Tribune* and praised the editors' "refreshingly unorthodox" policy. The American Civil Liberties Union offered free legal aid.[37]

But Cowley and Josephson, feeling "utterly tired and discouraged," lacked the resiliency to put up an effective fight. With the withdrawal of Geffen's support after the November issue, *Broom*'s debts had grown practically insurmountable. Josephson had vainly hoped to clear most of them by translating Apollinaire's *The Poet Assassinated*, but its proceeds were minimal and his job on Wall Street left him with little or no time for *Broom*. Though contributions from Williams and Stevens had helped to print the $200 January issue, in three weeks Cowley's bank account had dropped to $30 from $120. Faced with bankruptcy and plagued by battle fatigue, Cowley and Josephson had to admit defeat. In mid-March 1924 Cowley reported to Loeb in Europe: "It took us some weeks to realize that everything was ended, but when the letters piled up without our being able to answer them; when we were suppressed with a chance for big publicity, and could not take advantage of the chance, we began to see how hopeless was the affair. It is still a nightmare to me, for it was the first time I found myself absolutely impotent, absolutely unmeasured to the work in front of me."[38]

‹ ‹ ‹   Cowley's sense of defeat upon the demise of *Broom* was aggravated by a recent series of simultaneous incidents that pointed up the failure of his efforts to enact the iconoclastic ethics of Dada in New York. Weeks of canvassing for *Broom*, he remembered, left him mentally and physically fatigued and absolutely strained his nerves. Overly susceptible to hints and innuendoes, Cowley suspected "a general conspiracy of slander" against contemporary art and saw insidious attacks against the young avant-garde writers where none were intended. By all accounts it was a hypersensitive and distrustful Cowley who, in late December 1923, read the much-publicized first issue of the *American Mercury*, edited by H. L. Mencken and George Jean Nathan, and who overreacted to its principal feature, "Aesthete: Model 1924," a satirical attack on the modern aesthetes by Ernest Boyd.[39]

Boyd's article presented a "composite" caricatural portrait of a young aesthete that, though ostensibly imaginary, contained so many recognizable touches of so many of the writers associated with *Broom* or *Secession* that each could justifiably feel personally attacked.[40] Boyd pictured his aesthete as a foppish, slightly effeminate creature, whose dreams of literary grandeur outstripped his achievements and whose writings were flawed by fake erudition and facile scholarship. At Harvard he exhibited aristocratic, racial prejudices, wrote sonnets to Boston debutantes, and indulged in the "fleshy sins" of that "decayed city." When he went off to war, he surrendered his "collegiate patriotism" to become a slacker. After the war he resorted to Paris, met Pound and the French dadaists, and wrote a tribute to Proust before returning to Greenwich Village to edit "one of the little reviews making no compromise with the public (or any other) taste." In its pages he printed prose and verse "remarkable chiefly for typographical and syntactical eccentricities, and a high pressure of unidiomatic, uninspired French." In fiction he seemed obsessed by "a breathless phallic symbolism," while in criticism he evolved "an ingenious style, florid, pedantic, technical," but meaningless and incomprehensible. His articles consisted mostly of "esoteric witticisms and allusive gossip about fourth-rate people."

Boyd's article contained more serious charges, some of which struck at the fundamentals of Cowley's and Josephson's literary program for *Broom*. Boyd accused his aesthete of trying to "monopolize the field of contemporary foreign art," and pictured him as "the literary counterpart of the traditional American tourist in Paris," one "glamored by the gaudy spectacle of that most provincial of all great cities." With venom Boyd mocked the avant-garde interest in the popular arts and its aesthetic veneration of machine-age America, "this new-found delight in publicity experts, election slogans, billboards and machinery," the "cult of the movies." With pertinence he exposed the divided loyalties of the aesthete, which forced him (as it had recently forced Cowley and Josephson) to adopt a split mode of existence: "His allegiance is torn between the sales manager's desk, where, it appears, the Renaissance artist of to-day is to be found, and the esoteric editorial chair where experiments are made with stories which 'discard the old binding of plot and narrative.'" In malicious conclusion, Boyd pictured the aesthete as about to abandon his avant-garde idealism for the commercial standards of a consumer culture: "There is pep in the swing of his fist upon the typewriter as he sits down to a regular and well-paid job, convincing others, as his employer has convinced him, that he really knows what the public wants."[41]

Whatever the ironic exaggeration of Boyd's charges, there was enough venom in them to kindle the wrath of an oversensitive Cowley, who seized upon the incident as an opportunity for provocative dadaist posturing in America, a "significant gesture" in line with his performance and arrest on Bastille Day in Paris the previous summer. "It seemed to me," he recalled in *Exile's Return*, "that a critic of some distinction was taking sides with the philistines against his natural allies, was appealing to dangerous forms of prejudice, was making implications about the personal lives of people, many of whom were my friends. 'He ought to be punched in the jaw,' I said." Rumors of Cowley's threat of physical violence had already reached Boyd, a man of reputedly bookish and timid character, even before the latter received a phone call from Cowley demanding an apology for offensive passages. When Boyd professed not to know who Cowley was and to see no reason for an interview, Cowley (in Boyd's version of events) "expressed his opinion of me in language so filthy that, when his oaths and obscenities were exhausted, I asked him if he had not written a poem for one of the esoteric magazines with the modern aesthetes' weakness for what is dirty. Upon which Mr. Cowley offered to come around and 'beat me up.'" Shortly after, Cowley, who claimed never to have made a threat of fisticuffs but merely to have delivered "three round oaths before hanging up," sent Boyd a note, putting him down for "a sneak, a coward and a liar." At this point Cowley's friends took up his dadaist gesture. They sent Boyd "anonymous telegrams, facetious and abusive," and beleaguered him with phone calls from Josephson's apartment, with Burke, Cowley, Crane, and Josephson taking turns. Accounts vary as to the messages conveyed. Where Boyd claimed to have heard "threats and abuse" conveyed in a "vigorous, hooligan style," Cowley remembered the séance as "a pompous, leg-pulling conversation," in which Boyd showed himself the "master at repartee." [42]

Even here the Battle of the Aesthetes, as it was subsequently dubbed, was not allowed to rest. The literary grapevine eagerly took up the incident; gossip pictured Boyd as endangered by "hard-boiled, furious blackjack-toting aesthetes." Burton Rascoe presented an inflated embroidery of the affair in the *New York Herald Tribune*, in which he hyperbolically attacked both sides:

> Two hours after the edition of the magazine appeared on the stands Greenwich Village was in an uproar. The whole literary left wing, which had hitherto been disorganized by internecine strife, solidified against the perpetrator of the article . . .
>
> East Nineteenth Street swarmed with the younger poets, and when the venerable Boyd set out on his morning constitutional he was greeted with a fusillade of ripe tomatoes, riper eggs, sticks, stones and copies of 'S4N', and barely escaped back into his home with his life. There he was kept a prisoner by expediency for three days while Dadaists pushed his door bell, kept his telephone abuzz, scaled the walls to his apartment and cast old cabbages and odor bombs through the windows, sent him denunciatory telegrams, and rigged up a radio receiving outfit with an amplifier through which they broadcast the information that he was a liar, sneak, thief, coward and no gentleman. . . . Barricaded behind his books, subsisting on depleted rations and grown wan and weary under the assaults and harassments, Boyd called Heaven to witness that he had never heard of or read anything by any one of some dozens of his most revengeful assailants and that they had read into his article hints about their private life which he had no intention of putting there nor on re-reading could discover. . . . [43]

In the end, Cowley's "significant gesture" backfired painfully: the sale of the first issue of the *American Mercury* far surpassed the editors' expectations, and Ernest Boyd, as a result of his well-publicized martyrdom, became "a literary hero and a commercial success." Boyd had stolen the thunder of the American dadaists. Instead of arousing a lethargic literary milieu from its apathetic slumbers, Cowley had carried his dadaist propensity into the realm of the ridiculous: conceiving of himself as "a sort of West Texas sheriff sworn to uphold a code of literary conduct," he had rather well succeeded in making a fool of himself. A decade later, he acknowledged that what in Paris had seemed a "noble disinterestedness," in New York had become "a meddlesome effort to push myself forward, to break the front page." In America, Cowley's *"significant gesture"* became "a silly touchiness," his *"manifestation"* a "flop." When, in the wake of such grotesque failure, *Broom* breathed its last, Cowley's sense of defeat was complete.[44]

The entire fracas surrounding "Aesthete: Model 1924" drained the best of Cowley's energies. When, immediately afterward, a more serious opportunity presented itself to engage in "significant" action—a protest against the censorship regulations under which *Broom* was suppressed—Cowley and Josephson had no spirit left to make an effective stand.

‹ ‹ ‹ Five months after his return to America, Cowley had to acknowledge the failure of his efforts at Dada in Manhattan. "We had tried," he noted in *Exile's Return*, "to write and publish a new sort of literature celebrating the picturesque qualities of American machinery and our business civilization, and we found that American businessmen in the age of machines were not interested in reading poems about them." Josephson, too, retrospectively granted the futility of their endeavors: "We had bravely announced our 'acceptance' of the Machine Age, without much analysis or thinking through the matter. We had the effect of a few people firing off peashooters at the unbreakable plate glass-and-steel façade of our civilization." For the moment Cowley's and Josephson's understanding of contemporary urban-technological America remained superficial and, in essence, "spectatorial." With the demise of *Broom*, they confronted with renewed poignancy what Brooks had termed the failure of American culture. Finally—as much as by the problems of personal conflicts, slanderous attacks, financial bankruptcy, and censorship regulations—the editors felt defeated by the general cultural climate that made such censorship decisions possible: the moral, religious, and political conservatism of the Coolidge years, a cultural atmosphere that fostered, in the words of Arthur Schlesinger, Jr., "a literature of complacency, . . . an economics of success and a metaphysics of optimism."[45]

Though *Broom* died in a whimper of editorial frustration, it had lived long enough to make its mark. If, in its early phase, it had perhaps been less pioneering than other little magazines, eventually it helped introduce to America some of the foremost members of the international avant-garde. Always sensitive to the internationalism of modernity, the magazine (particularly in its New York period) provided a radical forum for many of the experimentalist writers in America, both those of Cowley's generation and those slightly older, like Williams, Stevens, and Moore. Under the editorship of Cowley and Josephson, *Broom* persistently sought ways of meaningfully relating literature to contemporary life and gave an important stimulus to a serious artistic negotiation of an American society governed by business and technology. If it failed to answer all the questions raised by its unorthodox and combative platform, it played a flamboyant and vital part in urging the need for an authentic American culture, one fully responsive to the pressures of contemporary life and not inherently inferior to that of Europe. As such *Broom*, and Cowley with it, had consistently been in the vanguard of the modern movement of the 1920s.[46]

12

The City of Anger
New York,
1924–1925

The demise of *Broom*, so painfully symbolic of Cowley's failure to "remake" the American cultural milieu by substituting "moral for mechanical values," impressed upon him with renewed poignancy the need to organize his life along more efficient lines. In early 1924 he entered in his notebook a confessional, stocktaking "Epistle to Malcolm Cowley by Malcolm Cowley," in which he acknowledged his mistakes and admitted the impossibility of being simultaneously a copywriter in the service of a business culture and "editor, free lance, drunkard, literary polemist." Instead, he saw, he "must confine [himself] to essentials: thinking, reading, conversation, writing, friends, livelihood" and arrange his life "against interruptions." "Too many excitements," he concluded; "at this moment you are tired and discouraged. . . . You have left the stage and you did not even bow."[1]

Increasingly aware of the missing dimension of humanism in his celebration of machine-age America, Cowley now sharply saw how different was the reality of New York from the picturesque image of a dynamic urban-technological spectacle he had naively clung to since his return from Europe. New York, it turned out, was "the least human of all the babylons," its values antihuman, its standards commercial and anti-artistic: "Its life is expressed in terms of geometry and mechanics: the height and cubical content of its buildings . . . the lines of force radiating from subway stations, the density of traffic. Its people have a purely numerical function. . . . Their emotions are coefficients used in calculating the probability of trade. . . . Just what is the coefficient of art?"[2]

Even in the fall of 1923 he had experienced moments of anxiety about the alienating effect of life in the city. "[The] advantage of living in New York is the fact that one is so chronically busy that one does not think, or if one thinks, does not feel," he wrote to Hart Crane in late November 1923. "Sometimes in a sudden rush of emotion you discover yourself to be bored, sad, violently goodhumored." New York, he complained to

Loeb, left one "no time for the simplest actions, the most simple emotions." Instead, it roused extremes of paradoxical and nervous feeling: "It is the city without landmarks," he wrote in *Exile's Return*, "the home of lasting impermanence, of dynamic immobility."[3]

Cowley's letters and notebooks give evidence of the unsettling and contradictory impact of his urban experience in the winter of 1924. At times the city fanned his dadaist propensity for iconoclastic activism: "Violent physical exertion when drunk is the solution of every moral problem," he wrote to Burke. At other moments he sought consolation in a mood of "stoical indifference" derived from his reading of Paul Elmer More's *Hellenistic Philosophies*: "The aim of the complete man is not writing but ataraxy." In his notebook he observed how New York itself induced a form of "mysticism": "one reacts against the crowds, the drinking, the atmosphere of business, and with nerves whittled to a fine point, retires into the secret places of his mind, creates a quiet that is more hysterical than the crowds, the atmosphere of business, the hysterical drinking." At times the frantic pace of New York drove Cowley to seek refuge in the deceptive quietude of a museum, to contemplate the "cruel and gothic mythology" of primitive cultures. At other times a longing "to be classical" inspired him with a "hysterical desire" to read Plato. At still other times he seemed to hear in the rumble of trucks the sound of "doom approaching." In his notebook he jotted down apocalyptic visions of urban destruction: "the buildings tumble, the seas rush in, and the waters lap against the subway walls." Always, there was the pastoral dream of "a quieter land."[4]

For the moment, however, Cowley remained disturbed by the lack of continuity and coherence in his life. "It is astonishing to learn how my opinions change from month to month," he observed in his notebook. "Is there any character constant beneath them?" Writing to Burke, he voiced his discontent with the fragmentary, disjointed nature of his life: "I live by clocks which deceive me. I rise at 8.45 and reach the office at 8.45. I rise at 9.05 and reach the office at 9.20. I rise at 8.00 and reach the office at 9.30. I never keep engagements, but on no principle. I have time for nothing." In his notebook he gave vent to his intellectual waverings and his confusion about the contours of his personality: "It frightens me how [my days] are episodic. Yesterday I was going to write a novel. Day before yesterday I was studying to write an essay on aesthetics. To discover what I was last month, I have to re-read my own letters. . . . My character is the color of my surroundings. Am I Epicurean, Stoic, Platonist, Classic,

Modernist, Rebel, Academic? I could tell you if I kept a diary, or if, by laying my hands on the elements of the past, I could lay one on the other and
call them Malcolm Cowley." Marked by conflicting aims and discontinu-
ous activities, his life seemed "held together only by the calendar," he told
Burke. Speaking as if about a distant friend, he made a mock evaluation of
himself: "Cowley—Is busy denying everything he did before Xmas, with
the belief that everything he did was right. Simply, the standard was higher
than he could maintain alone, when most of his time was taken by an
office. He writes amiable reviews, and for the first time has the sensation of
walking backwards." He ended his litany of lamentation with a half-ironic
cry for salvation: "Messiah—Wanted Badly." [5]

Cowley's sense of dislocation surfaced intermittently during the decade;
in effect, it was not healed until he found himself drawn into the radical movement in the early 1930s. Then his commitment to a unifying
political vision was partly based on such hopes for messianic salvation
as he expressed in early 1924. As he explained much later, in being attracted to political radicalism, many writers (including himself) were "also
unconsciously seeking a religious solution, a faith that would supply certain elements heretofore lacking in their private and professional lives as
middle-class Americans." Marx, he wrote elsewhere, was revered by writers
less as an economist, philosopher, or scientist of revolution than as "a
prophet calling for a day of judgment and a new heaven on earth." [6] In
1924, however, he was content to pour out his disgust with the commercial and utilitarian standards of writing that prevailed in America under
Coolidge in his notebook: "I utterly hate and despise the trade and trades-
men of letters. Your typical writer—I beg pardon, your Creator, for writers
have assumed the attributes of God—is a child spoiled by his audience, a
vanity parading before comic mirrors, a prima donna arguing for another
curtain call. . . . If I associate with him it is only for professional reasons,
as thieves for their own protection are forced to band together." [7]

For all his indignation Cowley was slowly accommodating to Manhattan. If the city often seemed unbearable, he now also felt that it harbored
a "strong and vulgar poetry," an urban "folklore" of sex, jazz, and dazzling
skylines, of Halloween office parties, Harlem dancing parties, and Village speakeasy drinking parties. Believing that "the function of poetry is to
make the world inhabitable," as he told Burke, he could now feel that even
the presence of prostitutes made the city appear more human and "more
livable." To Loeb he observed how the irregular Manhattan landscape,

enveloped in "a haze of ragtime tunes," appeared magically transformed: "The brick house, the empty lot, the skyscraper, juxtaposed, become an organic whole."[8]

Gradually, Cowley rediscovered "that the city was less inhuman than it seemed . . . that New York had another life, too—subterranean, like almost everything that was human in the city." Meeting with writers in restaurants and coffeehouses, or congregating with returning expatriates in speakeasies, Cowley joined the anonymous hordes of writers peopling Manhattan and settled down to "the simple business of earning a livelihood," laying more modest literary plans for the future, yet always dreaming of a farm of his own.[9]

‹ ‹ ‹ In late February 1924 Cowley made a trip to Woodstock, in the Catskill mountains, to spend a long weekend with William Slater Brown, who was living a primitive, solitary life there in a drafty shack converted into a studio. For three days Cowley shared Brown's invigorating country routine: in the mornings they chopped wood, in the afternoons they took long walks, tramping the snow and talking aesthetics, in the evenings they drank hard cider. Once they tried out the dadaist experiment of automatic writing but were disappointed by its results. Despite the cold, Brown was "writing with immense vigor," Cowley reported to Loeb, and for the moment seemed "the one man in whom there is any hope." His three days at Woodstock, Cowley felt, were "the highlight of a rather somber three months."[10]

Against odds, Cowley and Brown spent part of their time endeavoring, as Brown had put it in a letter, "to stew up together some fitting Marche Funèbre, Will, or Lament for *Broom*." They considered the leftover manuscript material but agreed that most of it was "undistinguished." Partly to meet outstanding subscription obligations, they planned a small "suppression issue," to consist of the personal manifestoes of the *Broom* contingent. Invitations were sent out to Burke, Loeb, and others, but, ironically, only Munson sent in a manifesto-like statement, advancing in germinal form the division of the contemporary literary situation into an Elder, Middle, and Youngest Generation, which he expounded more fully in *Destinations: A Canvass of American Literature Since 1900* (1928). Though Cowley remained eager to put the failures of the recent past behind him, for the moment he lacked the energy to concretize his halfhearted idealism: the plans for a suppression issue of *Broom* were silently shelved, to be resuscitated later in a different form.[11]

Returning to 16 Dominick Street, Cowley reluctantly resumed his fragmented life of routine-like busyness. At Sweet's the prepublication rush for the engineering catalogue, a light undertaking compared to the huge architectural catalogue, kept him working nights and soon he wrote to Loeb in a familiar vein of complaint: "The key to ¾ of my actions at present is the fact that I have time for nothing." He regularly consorted with Burke, Crane, Josephson, and Coates, recently returned from Giverny, where he had taken over Cowley's studio, but the tone of his social life was depressing: "The chief topic of conversation is wanting to be somewhere else. . . . Coates, who is free-lancing, seems to be contented and says, 'I am very happy in New York. I never look in people's faces.'"[12]

Cowley's search for an anchorage in the spinning currents of modernism had not ceased with his departure from France. Through the fall and winter following his return he continued to feel his way toward a personal collection of aesthetic "maxims." His thinking remained marked by a propensity for broad, axiomatic definition, which at times served to conceal the logical weaknesses in his argument. One of his "maxims" was geared toward machine-age America, but also implied a reaffirmation of his classical ideal of elegance: aesthetic value, Cowley noted, resided in "efficiency" and "utility," beauty being "the shortest distance between two points: the satisfaction of hitting the ball with the bat." An important concern remained the seemingly irresolvable dualism of form and matter, but he now explored a variation on the theme: art, he advanced, was *both* "disinterested creation" *and* "the expression of a sensibility." In several notebook entries he examined the contradictory implications of such a definition: "Literature is divided between creation and expression. The class of writers I prefer are those who *build* an emotion instead of expressing it. The test of a book is whether it has any life independent of the man who wrote it. And yet a worthless man can write only a worthless book."[13] In a lengthy entry he deepened his definition and reached for a synthesis: "The desire to make; in other words to give life to something organic, which, deriving from one's self can still exist outside one's self, is the basis, perhaps, of all art, for the Expressionist desires to create a personality which shall become a legend and thus live on." Cowley was persuaded that his reformulation of the antinomy of form and matter in terms of the contrast between creation and expression had helped to solve a crucial difficulty; as he wrote to Burke, copying from his notebook, "if only a Neo-Platonist could imagine the wedding of Form and Matter, a more direct mind can see that, on a higher plane, creation is expression and expression creation." Loyal to his belief in the communicative function of art, he now added a third term: "Expression is communication. Robinson Crusoe singing on a desert island is not, in our sense, expressing himself, nor is the unintelligible writer a poet." [14]

In a series of consecutive notebook entries, written partly in the form of an imaginary dialogue between Burke and himself, Cowley acknowledged that his aesthetic antinomies were interrelated with similar dichotomies in other branches of human knowledge: "An interest in aesthetics is like a crevice through which one slips to the domain of philosophy as a whole." Problems in aesthetics had correlating problems, he observed, in metaphysics, ethics, politics, sociology, or logic. In the same spirit, he noted in another entry: "to separate, arbitrarily, 'poetry' or 'art' from the rest of life, and to erect aesthetics into a metaphysic or pseudo-science without relation to other philosophies and sciences, leads to the most sterile and ridiculous of commonplaces." On a higher plane an aesthetic differentiation between expression and creation, he now saw, was but a manifestation of "the opposition of two attitudes fundamental in man—the fatalistic and the volitional," determinism and free will. Thus, he reasoned, "creation requires a conscious act, a choice, an exercise of the will. Whereas expression is generally only a record of experienced (i.e. passive) states." Equating determinism with a critical and philosophical monism, Cowley advanced his personal credo: "any monistic conception of the universe is infinitely less rich, less complex than the real world. By conviction, point of view, *Weltanschauung*, I am pluralistic and believe in free will." [15] Over the next few years such aesthetic notions as Cowley was developing in his notebooks formed the critical foundation for his practice as a literary journalist.

‹ ‹ ‹ For a young ambitious poet-critic, the literary situation in the spring of 1924 seemed hardly encouraging. Recent changes in the New York literary scene had not brightened Cowley's prospects. Not only had Canby announced his resignation from the *Literary Review of the New York Evening Post*, but Burton Rascoe, sympathetic to contemporary literature and the younger generation, had been fired from the *New York Herald Tribune*, to be replaced by Stuart P. Sherman, an older critic whose more conservative leanings aligned him with the New Humanists. Moreover, Brooks's *Freeman* had been forced to suspend publication. And whatever hopes Cowley had invested in Norman Fitts's *S4N*—during the previous fall Fitts had printed three letters by Cowley praising the magazine— were badly dented when guest-editor Gorham Munson devoted an entire double issue of *S4N* to essays on Waldo Frank, making it, as Cowley told Loeb, "the most outrageously silly piece of backscratching I have seen in long years." With *Broom* gone, too, and only the *Dial* open for briefers and an occasional poem or review, Cowley seemed momentarily deprived of literary outlets: "There is nowhere to write," he complained on May 9. For the moment, the only things that held out hope were Canby's plans for a new independent literary weekly (in the summer he would launch the *Saturday Review of Literature*), and Edwin Seaver's announcement that he was starting a new magazine from Woodstock, to be called, simply, 1924.[16]

In such a situation Cowley was determined to remain on good terms with the editors of the *Dial*. Eager to work off arrears in writing briefers— "It is depressing to feel that I have accepted responsibilities which I cannot fulfill," he wrote to managing editor Alyse Gregory—by early April he had cleared up some eight books for brief review and was ready for new assignments. Eventually the *Dial* published seventeen of Cowley's briefers in 1924; the previous year, from France, he had contributed twenty-two, a personal record. Typically, the briefers covered a wide range of literary modes and genres: from books on bootlegging and boxing to volumes of English and American poetry, translations of Greek and Chinese verse, and French and Russian novels.[17]

For all his complaints Cowley was busily plying the literary trade. During the spring he corresponded with John Wheelwright about the publication of a joint book of poems to perpetuate the relative success of their appearance in *Eight More Harvard Poets* a year before. When he reflected, however, that a joint book might preclude the publication of a volume of his own, he proposed instead an anthology of "the younger poets" (he named, beside himself, Crane, Cummings, James Daly, Damon, Ramon Guthrie, Josephson, Schneider, Tate, Wescott, Wheelwright, and Yvor Winters as the poets of promise), to be introduced by an older poet (preferably Williams), and to be published by either Albert and Charles Boni (who were bringing out Burke's *The White Oxen*) or Norman Fitts (who had just published Guthrie's *Trobar Clus*). Cowley, who expected the volume to "outrage critics" and "start a great many controversies," could barely contain his ardor: "I haven't come into a more practical idea these long months," he wrote to Wheelwright; "I hope you agree with me, for here I think, is a venture which will help all of us and be fun for all of us." Though, from a practical perspective, Cowley's plan seemed nothing if not viable, and though Crane and Tate responded enthusiastically to his invitation, the anthology remained in blueprint.[18]

Cowley's efforts on behalf of Harold Loeb were more successful. Through the spring, summer, and fall of 1924 he acted as a mediator between Loeb and his New York publishers, negotiating terms for the American publication of Loeb's novel *Doodab* and offering extensive criticism and suggestions for improvement. In early May he promised Loeb that he would "do any dab" to get the novel published, though he was doubtful as to the extent of his influence with New York publishers. By late June he reported on the progress of his negotiations with Boni & Liveright, with whom he had established contact through Isidor Schneider, then an employee at the newly amalgamated publishing house. In September he personally talked with Horace Liveright about Loeb's novel and discussed changes required by the publisher. By late November 1924 Cowley could send Loeb his "congratulations on the signing of the contract" and compliment the newly launched novelist in glowing terms: "I find your style marvelously improved. . . . You could never have a really bad style because you think clearly, and sloppy thinking is at the base of sloppy writing. . . . A good book, Harold. It surprised even me, and I was expecting it."[19]

Cowley's efforts on behalf of Loeb were exemplary of many such literary services to follow: over the years he was often instrumental in getting young or established writers published, recognized, or awarded. It was not the least, if perhaps the lesser-known, of Cowley's merits to function as a "middleman" of letters and be the personal critic, confidant, advisor, and exhorter of many writers, unrecognized and established, inside and outside the professional publishing circuit.

In the spring of 1924 Cowley undertook the first in a series of translations from the French that, in the course of the decade, brought him an established reputation in the field. In the recent past he had intermittently rendered work by French writers for *Broom* and, once, had translated Paul Morand's "Paris Letter" for the *Dial*, but now for the first time he tackled a complete novel, by Pierre MacOrlan. Cowley had interviewed MacOrlan in Paris for the *Bookman*, obtained six months' translation rights, and already done four episodes of *A Bord 'L'Etoile Matutine'* for Loeb's *Broom*.

In April 1924 he contacted MacOrlan again to renew translation rights for England and America and for one hundred dollars contracted to translate the novel as *On Board the 'Morning Star'* for Albert and Charles Boni. The book appeared in the late fall of 1924, copiously illustrated with wood-cuts by Daragnès, so as to make it, in the eyes of Foster Damon, "an exceedingly handsome book." Cowley's lucid and elegant translation of MacOrlan's eery fantasy tale received favorable notice in the *Dial*, which praised it as a "suave" rendering of a book full of "grotesque, cruel and supernatural adventures."[20]

By the summer of 1924 Cowley was becoming, as Robert N. Linscott told Damon, "perfectly well-known as a competent reviewer." His critical articles and reviews were now appearing regularly in the book sections of the *New York Evening Post* and *New York Herald Tribune*, in Canby's newly launched *Saturday Review of Literature*, and, as always, in the *Dial*. The reviews he wrote between the fall of 1923 and the winter of 1925 exempli-fied Cowley's ongoing concern with contemporary letters, mostly if not exclusively American, and underlined the contradictory premises of his literary taste. In September 1923, writing for the *New York Evening Post*, Cowley rather summarily dismissed *The Nuptial Flight*, a novel by Edgar Lee Masters, as "a problem novel of which the subject is the sex instinct." Typically, the review betrayed a greater fascination with the dynamics of Masters's career than with the specific novel, but it was conspicuous for Cowley's denunciation of platitudinous, "journalistic" prose and for his demand that fictional characters be above all human and alive, and not, as in *The Nuptial Flight*, "laboratory specimens."[21] A similar emphasis on the creation of "living" characters pervaded Cowley's overly eulogis-tic considerations of two novels by Harry Leon Wilson, former editor of *Puck* and, to Cowley, "the most considerable of our humorists." Though he acknowledged that Wilson often failed to give depth to his characters, Cowley found his humor "dry, mellow, and purely American" and did not hesitate to place him in the "great tradition" of Sterne, Fielding, Dickens, and Twain.[22] By contrast, Cowley gave short shrift to Theodore Dreiser, whose influence as a novelist he deemed almost disastrous. As "the model of a whole generation of realists who strive to be as ugly and apathetic as the worst of [their master]," Dreiser had become responsible for "the literature of mediocre defeat" and the mood of "inane despair" marking much of the fiction of his imitators. However, Cowley ended his review with a bal-anced appraisal of Dreiser that today seems valid enough: Dreiser's stylistic infelicities—"No sophomore could write more awkwardly than Dreiser at his worst"—were compensated for by a "power of tragic pity" that gave his language "the rhythm of life" and lent his characters an unexpected "dignity."[23]

Cowley could muster greater sympathy for *The Eleventh Virgin*, a semi-autobiographical novel by Dorothy Day, a close friend of Peggy's and a frequent visitor of the Cowleys. He praised the novel as an accurate and authentic rendering of the mood of artistic life in Greenwich Village on the eve of America's entrance into World War I and added personal impressions already tinged with nostalgia: "The Village of those days had a charm which it lost with the introduction of tea rooms, jazz pagodas and exorbitant rents." In a manner anticipating his analysis of "The Greenwich Village Idea" in *Exile's Return*, he concluded his review by pointing up the declined importance of the "former people" of 1917: by 1924, he observed ironically, the principal topic of Village conversation was no longer radical politics but sex and psychoanalysis.[24]

In more substantial articles Cowley examined two unambiguously modernist writers: Guillaume Apollinaire and Kenneth Burke. The first review, of Josephson's translation of *Le Poète Assassiné* (*The Poet Assassinated*), incorporated some of the "dope" on Apollinaire that Cowley had received from André Salmon two years before in Paris. He took Apollinaire as an "expressionist" artist, whose personality overshadowed his work and whose controversial influence persisted beyond his life: "Five years after his death he is still too contemporary for his work to be estimated justly." Cowley used the example of Apollinaire to denounce the symbolist ideal of literature as "an almost monastic profession" demanding renunciation of the world, and betrayed his sympathy for Apollinaire's involvement with contemporary life and for his capacity for change and self-renewal: "Poverty, chastity and obedience: Apollinaire made no such vows. It pleased him better to be violent and worldly; to be feared by his enemies like a melanite bomb. He multiplied himself, created artistic movements and personalities, exploded with new ideas, and wherever he passed by commotion threatened, followed, grew." Impressed by Apollinaire's astoundingly varied achievements, Cowley noted his influence on painting (cubism), music (Les Six, a group of six modern composers including Georges Auric, Darius Milhaud, and Francis Poulenc), and literature (Dada and "super-realism") and admiringly concluded: "He extends across the whole symphony of modern art like a full stop." Cowley's appraisal of *The Poet As-*

sassinated was curiously at odds with the conservative emphasis his other reviews had laid on traditional elements of realistic fiction. Apollinaire seemed to have written his novel as "a defiance to all the conventions of realism"—he thwarted artistic representationalism, set aside consistency of plot, coherence of characterization, narrative logic and chronology. Cowley ended his review with an insight that owed much to his recent failure to transplant Dada to New York: "In one sense the novel is impossible to translate. It depends on its literary background, and, despite all contrary efforts, Paris is Paris and New York remains New York . . . literature is still a national affair and . . . carrying over experiment from one literature to another leads to a senseless confusion." [25]

In the *Dial* of December 1924 Cowley reviewed *The White Oxen*, a collection of Kenneth Burke's experimental short fiction. Over the years Cowley had closely followed his friend's progress as a fiction writer and in his critical response had oscillated between skepticism and enthusiasm. In preparing to review the book for the *Dial*—he had personally asked Alyse Gregory to assign the book to him—Cowley carefully reread Burke's stories and found his admiration, in particular for "My Dear Mrs. Wurtelbach" and "The Book of Yul," persisting: the two stories, he wrote to Burke, satisfied "both formal and associational logic" and were "the completest justification of a method to which you no longer adhere." [26]

Cowley's consideration of *The White Oxen* was a crucial early review. Not only was it written well enough to catch the appreciative eye of Allen Tate, who recommended it to Donald Davidson as an example of "fine, simple, lucid prose"; more pointedly, it comprised Cowley's examination of what he saw as one of the essential features of the modernist creed. In line with his earlier appraisal of Eliot, Cowley presented Burke as a ceaseless explorer of new paths who never repeated himself but always moved on in search of "new discoveries." The modern writer, Cowley wrote, sought "those territories of the imagination which lie across the border of the last formula." It was Burke who exemplified preeminently this modernist tendency toward "a perpetual grailism," the perennial search for "the next phase." Cowley analyzed the progression of method within Burke's volume as an evolution from realism to "accuratism"—"the aim is no longer to make an image of life; but rather, through the combination of observed facts, to create another reality corresponding to nothing outside the author's mind." Dismissing "Flaubertian realism" as merely a literary commodity, Cowley noted how Burke pushed fiction "beyond the limits of pure realism" into a self-conscious, foregrounded formalism. In *The White Oxen*, he concluded that Burke had realized, with complete success, the aims he had set for himself; the book, he felt, marked the close to a "cycle" in Burke's development and raised the question of where the author's next phase would lead him: "Burke can write adventure stories or psychological novels; abandon fiction for poetry or metaphysics; go Dada or Gaga, but his grailism makes him incapable of going back."[27]

Cowley's sympathetic treatment of Apollinaire and Burke showed his continuing ambivalence about literary modernism. In theory he might endorse an experimentalist divagation into nonrealistic, nonrepresentational art, but in his criticism he continued to judge novels by the standards of conventional realism. At times the contradictory assumptions behind his approach to literature made Cowley feel uncomfortable. Publicly he announced the exhaustion of "Flaubertian realism" and acknowledged instead that "the tradition of St. Apollinaire" seemed "on the point of being accepted," but in the privacy of his correspondence with Burke he confessed to the fundamental conservatism of his taste: "the thing I chiefly admire in literature is the creation of characters. Thus, I have an immense subconscious respect for writers like Duhamel, Proust, Galsworthy: a respect which becomes outspoken in the case of men one can safely admire, like Dickens, Mark Twain, Harry Leon Wilson." Though he feared that he possessed "no special talent for creating characters," he toyed with the idea of writing a novel and, in his criticism, decided to "try more for character studies and interviews than plain reviews."[28]

The ambition to write a novel persisted through the decade; it surfaced intermittently in the 1930s and 1940s, before he came to accept the proper bent and limitations of his talents. As early as 1917 he had spoken to Burke of his "unquenchable" desire to write a novel of "the Galsworthy, George, Maugham type." Four years later he had finished a complete outline for a novel set in Greenwich Village in the Prohibition atmosphere of dissipation and sexual profligacy that he had known before he left for France. A thinly disguised fictionalization of Cowley's early life with Peggy in the "Crooked Streets" of the Village, the novel remained in blueprint; as an accompanying note to the outline explains: it was "too autobiographical to be written."[29] Aborted fictional sketches among his papers and lengthy drafts in his notebooks testify to the persistency of Cowley's hopes for a novel dealing with the lives of young ambitious men and women in the carefree and hedonistic atmosphere of 1920s New York. What fragments he wrote suggest that Cowley conceived of the book as a collective novel about the drifting, empty lives of the "lost people," as he later came to call them, a book thematically concerned with the wastage of artistic genius, the corruption of talent and moral character, and the dynamics of literary failure and success.[30] In the end, what novelistic talents Cowley possessed—a capacity for evoking mood and emotion, a gift for building narrative and bringing to life the complex nuances of a writer's literary personality— were channeled into the writing of literary criticism, where it could be made to serve his sensitivity to the interweavings of character, art, and milieu and help to make him an outstanding memoirist and biographical critic. Likewise, the principal thematic concerns of his projected novel— a collective portrait of the younger literary generation of the 1920s, a study of the "ordeal" by success and failure—were transmitted to his critical and historical writings and remained central to his interests.[31]

‹ ‹ ‹   The summer of 1924 saw the beginning of two cherished literary friendships: Hart Crane became a regular companion, and in June, Allen Tate made his first visit to New York from Nashville, Tennessee. Cowley and Crane had corresponded about poetry before they first met in August 1923, shortly upon Cowley's return from Europe. In March, Crane arrived in New York from Cleveland, Ohio, took a job as copywriter with the J. Walter Thompson agency, and fell in with the group around *Broom*, though at first, with Crane electing to stand by Munson and Frank, his relations with Cowley were rather strained. "I like Crane," Cowley told Burke at the time, "but every time I see him we fight on another subject." Crane expressed similarly ambivalent feelings about Cowley to Munson: "I wouldn't make any compromises with C[owley]. I like many things about him, but he is still in his adolescence when it comes to certain reactions." In early January, learning of the failure of Cowley's "significant gesture" against Ernest Boyd, Crane observed to Munson: "Cowley's gaucheries in admitting his mistakes and *tactics* are really funny."[32]

In early 1924, however, with Munson becoming more deeply involved with the Gurdjieff movement than Crane cared to follow and Crane spending more of his time with the writers of Cowley's less solemn circle, Crane's friendship with Munson markedly cooled, while he grew proportionally closer to Cowley. In April 1924 Cowley helped Crane get a position as a copywriter at Sweet's; for almost a year they worked together, behind adjoining desks, helping to bring out the firm's architectural and engineering catalogues, lunching together two or three times a week. Cowley did not rate Crane's talents for copywriting too highly and was surprised to find unexpected lacunae in the reading of a poet whose single-minded and perfectionist devotion to his art he admired immensely. Crane, in turn, was happy enough about the job at Sweet's, without regarding it as more than a practical necessity. His heart was in his poetry—he was already contemplating a poem to be called *The Bridge*—and he responded enthusiastically when, in May 1924, Cowley invited him to contribute to his projected anthology of the younger poets.[33]

It was through Crane that Cowley first met Allen Tate. The occasion was a party at 30 Jones Street, the Village apartment of Susan Jenkins (who had separated from James Light the year before) and the temporary sanctuary of Crane. Tate, on his first visit to New York from the provincial, genteel South, recalled being slightly daunted by Cowley's parade of snobbish cosmopolitanism: "I appeared neatly dressed in a dark suit, carrying a preposterous walking-stick and wearing a Phi Beta Kappa key. I was completely unsophisticated. You were already a man of the world." Tate had joined forces with a group of southern poets, critics and novelists— among them John Crowe Ransom, Andrew Lytle, Donald Davidson, and Robert Penn Warren—who together had founded a magazine, the *Fugitive*, in which, beside a commitment to modernism in art and letters, they advocated a modern mode of southern regionalism (later in the decade they became known as the Agrarians). From the South, Tate and his fellow Fugitives had closely followed the vicissitudes of *Broom* and *Secession*. In the summer of 1922, at Crane's suggestion, Munson had invited Tate to contribute to *Secession*. Tate had sent in "Elegy for Eugenesis." When Munson rejected his poem, Tate had observed to Donald Davidson: "I fear that I can't compete with those *Secession* birds for all my ultra-modernism." Tate's sympathy for the cerebral aesthetics exemplified by *Secession* had been strongly qualified. In July 1922, while Cowley was touring Europe, Tate had explained the grounds of his ambivalence to Davidson: "The chief point of my disagreement with [the critic-poets of *Secession*] is their effort to get away from the connotative and ideational (idea-emotions) in poetry. . . . These fellows are simply trying to do in poetry what has been done in the last twenty years in painting and music . . . abstraction." At roughly the same time, Cowley had expressed similar reservations about a pure or abstract art to Burke. For all his skepticism, however, Tate had had high hopes for Crane, whom he deemed "the best of the lot," and in

March 1924 had considered asking Crane to contribute to the *Fugitive*, which he was editing. Earlier that same year, unaware of the magazine's recent suppression, Tate had submitted a poem to *Broom* but had been informed by Cowley: "There's no use accepting your manuscript, as God knows when we'd be able to print it. We're closing up shop, and will have to perpetuate *Broom* in other forms. Come to New York when you can, and, also, try writing some prose, having mastered the easier art of verse." Even in his discouragement Cowley could not resist being flippant.[34]

In June 1924, when Tate met the writers of the *Broom-Secession* group in person, he was surprised to find them "much less theory-ridden" than the Fugitives. "Don't think these people are an organized group of aesthetes," he reported to Davidson. "They're the simplest and least given to 'organization' of all people I've seen and far less conscious of being 'poets' than we are as a group." His impressions of Cowley, who had escorted Tate through the Bronx Zoo, were rather mixed: "Cowley refuses to talk literature, looks like a truck-driver, and was educated at Harvard . . . the type of snob that becomes a snob himself by giving one to understand that he deprecates all other snobs: but a very keen and refreshingly unpretentious person withal. . . . It seems, by the way, that Crane, Burke, and Slater Brown are the large boys here. Cowley said this, naturally leaving himself out."[35]

It was a later meeting with Tate that, in retrospect, stood out as the more memorable occasion. It began in the late afternoon of June 24, 1924, with a gathering at 110 Columbia Heights in Brooklyn, where Crane not long before had rented a back room with a resplendent view of the Brooklyn Bridge. Cowley and Tate were duly impressed by the splendor of the view, which gave focus to the literary talk that followed. At one point, in response to derogatory remarks by Crane about the poetry of Edgar Allan Poe, Cowley read out loud "The City in the Sea." The contemporary relevance of Poe's nightmarish evocation of the doomed city of death, with its "time-eaten towers" and "Babylon-like walls," was not lost on a poet who, not long before, had written down his own apocalyptic visions of urban inundation in his notebook and who had once evoked New York as a city of the "living dead." Crane was thrilled to hear the poem read aloud to so much effect. Later, Cowley, Crane, and Tate wandered down to the waterfront and climbed to the edge of a scow at the end of a pier on the Brooklyn side of the bridge. There they continued talking, sat listening to the black water lapping the pier, and watched the myriad early lights flash on in the "proud towers" of Manhattan, while across the river an enormous electric sign proclaimed the virtues of "Waterman's Fountain Pens." The moment made an indelible impression. It left Cowley with an exhilarating sense of united literary effort, as if with Crane, Tate, and others he were bound by an unspoken "oath of comradeship"—"Suddenly we felt," he remembered, "that we were secretly comrades in the same endeavor: to present this new scene in poems that would reveal not only its astonishing face but the lasting realities behind it." [36] The afternoon with Crane and Tate may well have inspired a perfectly finished and classically elegant sonnet like "Those of Lucifer," a poem in ambivalent celebration of Manhattan's powerful but possibly diabolical skyscrapers. Its visionary lyricism perhaps inspired by Poe's "The City in the Sea," the poem stands as one of Cowley's finest achievements. An early version, submitted to Alyse Gregory in February 1925, was published in the July 1925 issue of the *Dial*:

Out of an empty sky the dust of hours
a word was spoken and a folk obeyed
an island uttered incandescent towers
like frozen simultaneous hymns to trade

Here, in their lonely multitude of powers
thrones, virtues, archangelic cavalcade
they rise
        proclaiming Sea and sky are ours
and yours O man the shadow of our shade

Or did a poet crazed with dignity
rear them upon an island to prolong
his furious contempt for sky and sea

To what emaciated hands belong
these index fingers of infinity

O towers of intolerable song [37]

Working at Sweet's for nine hours a day kept Cowley from writing as much as he wanted to write. Once again brought up against a faulty "mechanics" of living, he saw his summer lassitude aggravated by a rising sense of frustration. In August his letters to Burke reached new depths of ironic lamentation. "During the last month I've been as near absolute o as one gets without a more serious consideration of the relative merits of pistols, gas, poison and heavier-than-air flight without wings," he wrote hyperbolically on August 12. A week later he complained that unfinished work, domestic chores, and hot weather had brought him to the point where he would "go walking on the roof and be afraid to approach the parapet for psychological reasons." With mounting seriousness he contemplated quitting his job at Sweet's and resuming an independent free-lancing life away from New York.[38]

To finance such a move Cowley now undertook, if not without misgivings, the sort of hackwriting work that under different conditions he would have denounced as an unacceptable form of compromise. At fifty dollars a month he agreed to write on a regular basis for *Charm*, a rather copious magazine published by L. Bamberger's department store in Newark, New Jersey, for distribution to its mostly female charge-account customers. Subtitled "The Magazine of New Jersey Home Interests," *Charm* was modeled after *Vanity Fair* and catered to the interests of New Jersey housewives. For its first few years the magazine was edited by Bessie Breuer, an old Village friend of Peggy who later ventured into novel writing without attaining much recognition; she was succeeded by Lucie Taussig, an editor who gave Cowley more freedom to write on subjects of his own choosing.[39]

Between 1924 and 1928 Cowley wrote more than thirty-five articles for *Charm*; in August 1925 he became book editor and was commissioned to write a monthly book page. Over the years Cowley wrote on an astounding variety of subjects, ranging from aspects of the literary life in Greenwich Village and Montparnasse to reading habits, personal libraries, detective stories, American humor, American history, travel books, and biographies. At his own suggestion he wrote a series of articles dealing with New Jersey history and geography, local places of interest, and industries or crafts peculiar to the region. Thus he wrote on William Franklin, the last Loyalist governor of New Jersey and the son of Benjamin Franklin; composed a historical guide to the Quaker settlements in western New Jersey; presented surveys of churches remaining from colonial times and ancient trees that had witnessed the American Revolution; wrote a history of one of the region's oldest waterways; surveyed the cluster of beautiful lakes in northern New Jersey; and reported on the plentiful fishing trade in Barnegat Bay, off Long Beach Island. In addition, he wrote regular omnibus reviews of "books of the season," discussed various aspects of the literary trade, and recommended books for summer reading or giving at Christmas.[40]

The articles, lavishly illustrated by photographs, drawings, and cartoons, appeared duly flanked by advertisements for real estate developments, new-fangled household appliances, refrigerators, radios, egg noodles, cutlery, shoes, rugs, trunks, hair tonics, body lotions, dental creams, and mosquito nets for baby carriages.

Cowley's first few articles for *Charm*, written and published in 1924, set the tone and pattern for the many that followed. "Parnassus-on-the-Seine," an article on American expatriate life in Montparnasse, was popular and lightly satirical in tone. It resurrected the figure of Young Mr. Elkins but hardly rose above the kind of articles in the *Saturday Evening Post* that helped to fix the stereotypical image of the expatriate as a nonwriting, café-sitting wastrel. Intended first of all to exploit the entertainment value of its subject, it also tried to suggest a little of the serious impact of Montparnasse on the artist; its "real charm," Cowley told the housewives of New Jersey, lay in the international exchange of culture and in "the battle of ideas" waged there, a battle of modernists against conservatives, of romanticism against classicism and realism.[41] A second article broached a subject guaranteed to capture the interest of *Charm*'s readers: "Do Artists Make Good Husbands?" Clever, witty, and amusing, it challenged the conventional view that marriage interfered with an artist's liberty and pushed him toward conformity and caution. Instead, a flippant narrator distinguished between artists proper and people possessed of merely "the artistic temperament," and argued that "an artist's marriage is usually happy." The article surrendered any opportunity for a serious treatment of its subject, but the interference of the exigencies of an artist's personal life with the pursuit of his professional ideals was an aspect of the literary life that continued to fascinate Cowley.[42] Indeed, his articles for *Charm*, however limited their intrinsic value, allowed him to pursue in popular, lightweight fashion, broader interests that surfaced in more serious and complex forms in his more mature years.[43]

These articles for *Charm* were written for money; they lack the distinction of rising above incidental opinions. Yet they possess certain redeeming features not untypical of the best of Cowley's writings. A natural gift for storytelling stood him in good stead in entertaining his New Jersey readers; many of his articles were cast in the form of miniature stories and portrayed imaginary or real characters. His easy narrative style proved a tool adaptable to virtually any subject. Writing in simple language, with a deliberate avoidance of specialized vocabulary, Cowley aimed to introduce new

literary ideas to his unsophisticated readers. Hoping to instruct and entertain, he retained an almost eighteenth-century respect for his "common
reader"—"O Gentle Reader" was his occasional form of address—and regarded writing for *Charm* as something of a "challenge" ("much as if I had
been an engineer asked to design an outlandish bridge"), an exercise in capturing a segment of the American reading public entirely different from the
sophisticated readers of the *Dial* and the *New Republic*. It was a challenge
that fit in with his admiration for a writer like André Salmon, who wrote
with equal success for a mass audience on Parisian murder trials as for a
specialized public on serious literary matters. Fifty years later he confessed
to having shared "that 18th-century ambition to write for the intelligent
but unspecialized reader, the audience that Diderot had in mind for the
Encyclopédie."[44] Throughout his career Cowley occasionally alternated his
writings for highbrow periodicals and specialized academic quarterlies with
articles for mass-circulation magazines. It was in part because the best of
Cowley's work was easily accessible and without compromise in standards
of complexity and depth that he could become an influential and widely
read literary critic and historian.

In 1924, however, Cowley embarked upon his *Charm* adventure almost
against his better judgment. He knew, as he confessed to Jane Heap of
the *Little Review*, that measured by the literary standards he had evolved
in France, such work reeked unforgivably of compromise; Aragon, he
acknowledged, would consider it "very unethical." When Burke, speaking with the voice of literary conscience, objected that in working for
Sweet's and hacking for *Charm* Cowley seemed to have capitulated to pragmatic and commercial motives, his friend had trouble defending himself.
Cowley admitted that the articles in *Charm* were "wrong," "bad policy,"
and "hardly excused by the prompt checks which answer them," but in-
dignantly denied any concern for his "commercial name." His trouble, he
explained, lay in the combination of a "constitutional need to write" with
a wasteful and "faulty methodology"; the principal excuse for *Charm* was
that it promised to help him leave New York to become a free-lance writer.

Against Burke's objections Cowley advanced that his reading, at least,
was as earnest and disinterested as ever: recently he had read several of
Plato's dialogues, Paul Elmer More's *Hellenistic Philosophies*, Sir Thomas
Mallory's *Morte d'Arthur*, Byron's *Beppo*, Poe's *Narrative of Arthur Gordon
Pym*, Matthew Lewis's *The Monk*, Twain's *Life on the Mississippi*, Frazer's
The Golden Bough, and novels in French by Joseph Delteil and Maurice

Barrès. He also reaffirmed his belief in the natural beauty of plain, simple things—"Kitchen chairs are more beautiful than overstuffed library lockers. A Pennsylvania farmhouse is more beautiful than the Wurlitzer Building"—and denounced Burke's concern with "pure" literature as a serious "defection from the classical standard, in which literature is a part of life like the other parts"—"You have a tendency . . . to divide things printed from things merely existing, and to worship the printed word. Personally I endeavor to place books in the midst of life." [45]

‹ ‹ ‹   At the end of August, Cowley made a trip to Belsano to spend a long weekend with his parents. He fished the Cambria County trout streams, played Chopin waltzes on the family grand piano ("echoes out of a past"), and climbed to the attic of the farm, where he rediscovered all the letters Burke had written him since 1915: rereading them was like reliving his own adolescence. In mid-September, back in New York, he found himself caught up once more in the annual prepublication rush for Sweet's big architectural catalogue, due on the first of October. Working overtime till late at night precluded any social or intellectual activity, and Cowley's spirits sank accordingly: "Writing nothing, seeing minus nobody and thinking very little," he complained to Wheelwright. To Harold Loeb, still in Europe, he voiced his frustration in a long litany of lamentation: "The disgusting feature of New York is its professional writers, who are venial to the last degree. Out of business, into literature, there is nobody to respect. One doesn't demand Apollinaire or the Dadas in every city, but there should be at least, in the older generation, a Paul Valéry. The Brouns, Boyds, and Canbys are international. . . . The atmosphere of this city is exhausting. I feel the need of nine hours of sleep, evenings at home, a mind walled up like the entrance to a deserted subway. I have done, during the year, nothing, and will do, during the year, nothing. To quit the job is my only hope, and that hope, considering the amount of hack work it involves, is not bright. Nowhere else in the world have I been brought so blankly against the mechanics of living." [46]

A month later Cowley's spirits rose considerably. After Sweet's catalogue went to press, he went north to spend a month's vacation in Woodstock. By 1924 Woodstock, an artists' colony of some history, had become a favorite place of refuge from the city for the writers of Cowley's circle. Slater Brown had been living there for some time, first renting a house with Edward Nagle, later cohabiting with Susan Jenkins, whom he married shortly after.

Munson had sought out Woodstock for convalescence, fought his battle with Josephson there, and in the summer of 1924 again resorted to it as the place where "the electrifying impulses" of the 1920s could most advantageously be felt. The poet Edwin Seaver was launching his new magazine 1924 from Woodstock; Crane had spent six weeks there during the previous fall; and the Cowleys, too, had paid several weekend visits to the hilly countryside around the village for invigoration and refreshment.[47]

In October 1924 Cowley enjoyed Woodstock to his heart's content. He relished the biting air and the splendid colors of autumn in the Hudson Valley, gathered walnuts, butternuts, and hickory nuts, sampled the cider made by the local farmers, and sawed logs for the open fireplace. The country revived his rural tastes and renewed his awareness of the divided loyalties in himself. "Part of me is still a farmer, and the part is complete. Part of me is a New Yorker," he wrote to Burke from Woodstock; "The parts have little connection. The rural part is a woodsman, proprietor and miser. The New Yorker is an unhappy spender, tainted with an alcoholism which disappears in the country. . . . This country is very satisfying. Nice brooks, mountains rising to 3200 feet from valleys of about 600; pine growing plentifully and spruce on the higher ridges; a great cider country; no swamps."[48]

With the revival of his energies came a renewed desire for action and a new determination to rekindle the combative, iconoclastic spirit of earlier days. "We are like tinder, we need a spark, but the tinder is wet," he exhorted Burke from Woodstock. What was missing, he said, was "a new romanticism. A certain brave defiance." Acting on the upsurge of his moral fervor, he wrote an open letter to the editors of the *New York Herald Tribune Books*, taking issue with such critics of the old guard as Stuart P. Sherman, H. L. Mencken, and, more mildly, Henry Seidel Canby, while speaking up for the literary "moderns," whom he described as people "without compromise; perpetual extremists who are fundamental in a fashion which is not that of academy or church."[49]

A more serious conflict arose over the issue of Dada in America and was fought out with Waldo Frank. In effect, Cowley's debate with Frank reenacted in real life the imaginary conversation between Josephson and Rosenfeld staged by Edmund Wilson in the pages of the *New Republic* in April of that year.[50] In the September issue of 1924 Frank finally retaliated against the attacks leveled against him by Cowley and Josephson. Dada, Frank argued, had perhaps worked well as a "salutary burst of laughter" in a moribund Europe, but it had no relevance for American civilization: "For America *is* Dada. . . . Dada spans Brooklyn Bridge; it spins round Columbus Circle; it struts with the Ku Klux Klan; it mixes with all brands of bootleg whisky; it prances in our shows; it preaches in our churches; it tremulos at our political conventions. . . . We are a hodgepodge, a boil. We are a maze of infernos and nirvanas. Our brew of Nigger-strut, of wailing Jew, of cantankerous Celt, of nostalgic Anglo-Saxon, is a brew of Dada." What America needed, Frank believed, was the "antithesis" of Dada: seriousness, order, and tradition, a sense of wholeness rather than chaos and fragmentation. The American dadaists were simply too caught up in the anarchy of American life to exert control or direction over its course; they were its slaves, not its leaders. Dada in a Dada world stood "in danger of becoming narcissistic: of growing infatuated with its own twitching image." [51]

In late October, Cowley wrote to Frank from Woodstock; his letter, with Frank's reply, was published in the November issue of 1924. Cowley granted that Frank's attack on "a hypothetical group of American Dadas" was justified insofar as it concerned the impossibility of transplanting features of one national culture to another but pointed out that Frank had failed to consider the liberating and innovative impact of Dada: "Dada was also a discovery: that nonsense may be the strongest form of ridicule: that writing is often best when it is approached in a spirit of play; that associational processes of thought often have more force than the logical; that defiance carried to the extremes of bravado is more to be admired than a passive mysticism. Dada was the sense of exhilaration which was born when our old shackles were tested and found to be rusted away." (Thus, Cowley had added in an early draft, Dada was "living still," and gave evidence that the romantic movement was "not dead.") Concluding in a spirit of perverse mockery, he now publicly proclaimed himself the "butt" of Frank's attack: "the clever but not coruscant, smart or swift young man who clutters our more serious magazines, the American Dada." [52]

Cowley's polemic conclusion was more convincing as a specimen of dadaist posturing than as a logical refutation of Frank's position. The weakness of his response lay in its failure to address the serious issue concerning the deficiency of American culture that lay at the heart of Frank's critique; instead, in a manner more emotive than precise, Cowley quarreled with isolated points and used them as stepping-stones to a defiant proclamation. Moving on a different temperamental and literary wavelength, Cowley was unable to rise far enough above personal bias to accurately read Frank's meaning.

In reply Frank pointed out that Cowley's propensity for broad definition had led him into "juvenile" thought. Unable on his side to keep the exchange on rational grounds, Frank took offense at Cowley's use of the term "passive mysticism" and convicted his opponent of "an ignorance so essential as to disqualify you in your present temper from true intelligent discussion." Cowley's advertisement of himself as the American Dada, Frank abrasively concluded, was hard to accept; his poetry alone gave evidence that Cowley was "fit for better things," provided he could muster "the moral courage to confront the reality of our world, and the spiritual energy to take issue with it; instead of permitting yourself to be flung off by its centrifugal action, in the fond belief that because you fly off to Nothing in a graceful pirouette and with a foreign oath upon your lips you are being any the less booted and beshat by the very elements of life which you profess to despise."[53] Frank's angry words contained enough truth to make them painfully pertinent; not only did he reverse Cowley's charge of a lack of moral courage, he also, in effect, reiterated the complaint made earlier by the editors of the *Dial*, that the "skyscraper primitives" failed to engage the human reality below the picturesque surface of modern life.

William Carlos Williams, who had followed the exchange from Rutherford, New Jersey, acknowledged that Frank showed "more energy in his comeback than I had thought possible," but believed that nothing conclusive had been proved against Cowley: "After scraping away the mud and shit I think the judges will have to give you the decision." Cowley had reason to feel less confident. The altercation with Frank was now carried over into private correspondence, where it dragged on through several rounds of epistolary debate, its focus shifting from Dada to mysticism. Private continuation of the argument, however, did little to resolve the issues and the debate ended in a stalemate. Though by his own admittance, Cowley now realized that his attacks on Frank had been founded on at best a limited grasp of "true mysticism," he still ridiculed the overblown rhetoric of Frank's prose style, voiced his exasperation at his assumption of intellectual superiority and continued to resent the obscurantist privatism of Frank's beliefs: "I have never been told his lodge-rites or those of any other Masons."[54]

Indirectly, Cowley's quarrel with Frank also disrupted his relations with Edwin Seaver's 1924 and dashed his high hopes for the magazine. From the first Cowley's enthusiasm for 1924 was mingled with suspicion as to "the omnipresence of Munson's influence." Seaver, indeed, was clearly sympathetic to Frank and Munson; he had been impressed by Frank's "For a Declaration of War" in *Secession* 7 and had granted Munson ample space to expound his views in the first two issues of 1924. When Seaver invited Cowley to contribute—"it seems to me that you are one of the few writing in this country today who have something to say and know how to say it"— Cowley found it hard not to "smell politics" but was willing to give Seaver the benefit of his doubts. During the summer Cowley had assured Seaver that 1924 would have "everybody's support as long as it didn't take sides in our factional quarrels." [55] Seaver, however, was unable, or unwilling, to steer his magazine clear of factionalism. When, in the midst of his debate with Frank, Cowley asked Seaver to make a minor textual change in his open letter and add a footnote clarifying his use of the offensive term "passive mysticism," Seaver tartly refused, arguing that to comply with Cowley's request would "place Frank in an embarrassing position" and give Cowley an undue advantage. In a diplomatic letter Cowley reminded Seaver of the dangers of factionalism and the necessity of editorial impartiality. To Burke he uttered his disappointment that 1924 ("an excellent magazine, the most interesting we have at present") seemed destined to perpetuate old quarrels instead of terminating them. On the basis of his recent experiences he could only conclude that Seaver's editorial "standard of selection" was "something else than literary," and that in "this little teapot-tempest with Frank," Seaver was taking Frank's side, both personally and editorially. [56]

Disheartened by the unwanted revival of polarizing factional bickerings ("Everywhere I turn, another fight"), Cowley was eager enough to dissociate himself from "the whole dirty series of arguments" but found it as hard as before to remain *au dessus de la mêlée*. When Burke appeared unwilling to favor one group over another, preferring rather, in Cowley's words, to be "not so much a neutral as a partisan of both sides," all Cowley's old resentments against Munson flared up. "It would amuse you to hear that Munson is a gurgeyite, galooshiously gurgling Gurdjieff growling Gurdjieff gargling Gurdjieff," he wrote to Harold Loeb and Kitty Cannell in Europe. Munson's type of mind, he confessed to Burke, was to him "profoundly antipathetic." Cowley's animosity toward Munson went beyond a conflict of literary ideologies or aesthetic assumptions; it was, at least in part, personally motivated and admixed with a strongly moral component. "I think

Munson pious, mean-spirited and sly; a man whose every act is in strict accordance with a moral code which is determined by his every action," he observed to Burke. In general, he felt, Munson's behavior was marked by backstairs dealings and malicious talebearing. More than anybody else, it was Munson whom Cowley held accountable for sowing mutual distrust among his literary friends and undermining even his own self-esteem.[57]

It was not long, however, before discouragement once more gave way to a desire for action and cooperation. His recent experiences with Frank and Seaver had strengthened Cowley's belief that "people only fight on moral grounds" and he had found that he thrived on moral indignation. As he fulminated to Burke, he would rather fight and fail than resign himself to living in an atmosphere poisoned by "small tattlings, small mistrusts": "we have stood silent too long under insults; it is not good for a man; it spoils his temper, makes him mean-spirited, checks the flow of his words. To be beaten and turn the other buttock was never our nature, nor was it our nature to be beaten, run away, and shoot jelly-beans from ambush."

When Josephson, too, seemed ready for some form of irreverent group action, the two met with Crane to lay plans for a combative group manifesto. The recent publication of Ernest Boyd's *Portraits: Real and Imaginary* (which included the infamous "Aesthete: Model 1924" as well as Boyd's personal version of his ensuing battle with the aesthetes and Burton Rascoe's double-edged satirical account from the *Herald Tribune*) had revived public interest in the dadaist fracas and rekindled Cowley's anger. When the editors of the *New York Evening Post* first gave Boyd's book to Josephson for review, then hastily withdrew the commission for fear of causing scandal, Cowley and Josephson felt they had perfect proof of the anemic cowardice of literary New York. On November 22, 1924, Cowley wrote an exhilarated letter to Wheelwright in Boston: "Everything points to our getting out some sort of single-issue magazine venture, a revival of Broom or Secession, anything to startle, amuse and answer back." The issue, Cowley announced to Burke, was to be entitled "Contribution to a Literary History of Our Times" and was to contain letters, reminiscences, and polemics, "anything which bore on our thesis that the Great Literary Politicians of New York were a bunch of worms, afraid of shadows because they cast none, anxious to kiss the feet that trampled on them."[58]

From the first Kenneth Burke had responded with bemused skepticism to Cowley's trumpet calls for activism and polemics. In February, when the turmoil about Boyd's "Aesthete: Model 1924" had barely subsided, he had advanced his belief that, at any time, Plato was preferable to polemics and had issued an "appeal for the catacombs," urging Cowley to withdraw from his strategies of futile pea-shooting at negligible journalists into a serious and disinterested pursuit of art and aesthetics: "Let each man . . . see to his private still and his private printing press, that he may live like a gentleman in the midst of prohibition and journalism." In America today, he had concluded, there was "but one magazine where the study of letters [might] occasionally be pursued in public," and that magazine was the *Dial*. In late November, when Cowley was urging him to leave his aesthetic hermitage and participate in a new attack on Boyd, Burke again responded with cautious reluctance: "one can answer Boyd only by Boyd tactics, and I think it less compromising to let him go unanswered than to answer him in his own damned bickering fashion." Burke, for one, believed that "one reputable article, on any reputable subject, appearing in any reputable paper, [could] do more to repair whatever slight damage Boyd may have done than all the broadsides in the world directed against him." Though he was persuaded that "one cannot sling mud, even victoriously, without getting dirty," in the end Burke consented to be publicly aligned with the offended "aesthetes" and promised an article exemplifying more serious concerns.[59]

By early December 1924 preparations for the issue were progressing speedily. A name had been chosen (*Aesthete 1925*); Cowley and Josephson had enlisted the cooperation and financial support of most of their friends; and a fictitious editor and angel had been invented in the figure of Walter S. Hankel, a retired manufacturer from Dayton, Ohio. Preparations proceeded in a spirit of general agreement; the only dissonant note serving as a reminder of recent factional bickerings was the early withdrawal from the roster of Hart Crane, who had made his participation contingent upon a unanimous pledge that none of the contributors would ridicule Munson or Frank—all promised to agree, except, perversely, Wheelwright.[60]

By mid-January 1925 the redoubtable *Aesthete 1925* was at the press; in early February copies were distributed to the New York bookstores and city editors were telephoned in an effort to "break into the news columns."[61] *Aesthete 1925*, indeed, aimed to be shocking and controversial; every article in its thirty-two pages was "guaranteed to be in strictly bad taste." Its chaotic but kaleidoscopically colorful contents—anonymous, pseudonymous, or signed—seemed out to prove that Dada in America was still alive and kicking. Charles Sheeler's cover design, a pen-and-ink drawing of skyscrapers and city tenements, recalled the Dada-inspired fascination with machine-age urban America propagated in *Broom*; the back cover featured a satirical letter to the censor by Walter S. Hankel, spoofing section 480 of the postal laws, ironically reminding the reader how drastically *Broom*'s literary program had failed in America.

A pencil drawing by Peggy Cowley featuring a bald and mustached Walter Hankel suggested that the fictitious editor of *Aesthete 1925* was partly modeled upon "the corpulent ghost of Munson," but the bulk of the issue's satirical venom was at the expense of Mencken and Boyd. A note by William Carlos Williams denounced Mencken's influence as nefarious and negligible, and voiced his disrespect for those who took Mencken's intellectual and linguistic pretenses seriously. A more scathing indictment of Mencken was cast in the form of a full-page "advertisement" for the "Mencken Promotion Society." Dadaistically mocking the consumerist slogans and typographical conventions of American advertising—"Get Self-Respect Like Taking a Pill / MENCKENIZE!"—it presented Mencken as the panacea for a middle-class sense of cultural and intellectual inferiority. "Can't you understand modern art? / Let Mencken show you the absurdity of the Ku Klux Klan. / Can't you follow modern philosophy? / Let Mencken snigger with you at William Jennings Bryan." The advertisement trenchantly pointed up the conservative allegiance to American values underlying Mencken's debunking: "Mencken has been called a radical. This is a DIRTY LIE. Mencken is a conservative. Mencken expresses the conservatism of revolt."[62]

Ernest Boyd could vie with Mencken for receiving the most incisive ad hominem attacks. In an open letter to Walter Hankel, Allen Tate attacked Boyd for catering to the moral and intellectual prejudices of "the great hordes that swarm the plains from Wisconsin to the Gulf of Mexico," and for making it "deliciously and abhorrently understood by the ministers in Guthrie, Kentucky, that all young American writers are given to the varieties of enjoyment derivable from the ritual of lily-carrying and of an effete satanism." Cowley, too, attacked the excessive publicity accorded Boyd as a result of the misguided response to "Aesthete: Model 1924" and, in a mock advertisement, formally proclaimed that "Mr. Ernest Boyd is not employed by me as personal press agent, his activities in this capacity being undertaken solely on his own initiative." Matthew Josephson launched the most venomous attack on Boyd. In "Dr. Boyd Looks at Literature," the review of *Portraits: Real and Imaginary* first commissioned, then retracted by the "affable worms" directing "one of our outstanding literary supplements," Josephson marshaled his powers of hyperbolic rhetoric in order to annihilate Boyd's book through excessive praise. He loudly proclaimed the deserved success of Boyd's "daring exposé of our young aesthetes" and complimented him "for importing into American letters the spirit of controversy. His blows fell upon the heads of the generation of Younger Writers at a moment when they had become far too snug, far too happy in their eccentricities, and were basking much too luxuriously in the warm sunshine of the public's approval." Boyd proved, Josephson charged, that with "very little concern for ideas or clear thinking" one could still write "an epochal essay like 'Aesthete: Model 1924.'"[63]

Illustrative of the spirit of subversive buffoonery animating *Aesthete 1925* was a piece of humorous nonsense fiction by William Slater Brown, postmodernist *avant le mot*, who, in a manner anticipating the more extravagant experiments of Vladimir Nabokov and John Barth, explored the possibilities of parodistic lexical game playing and fictional self-referentiality in "An Interplanetary Episode." John Brooks Wheelwright staged "Little Moments with Great Critics," which, in a manner adumbrated in France by *Littérature* and in America by *Vanity Fair*, presented the average ratings by the aesthetes of virtually all the established critics and literary journalists of the older generation. Predictably, Boyd, George Jean Nathan, and Mencken were at the lowest point of the scale; more interestingly, crowning the ranks were George Santayana, T. S. Eliot, and Paul Elmer More. The dadaist zaniness of "Little Moments with Great Critics" could not obscure an underlying serious concern with literary criticism. Not only did Cowley and Burke conduct an earnest behind-the-scenes correspondence about the value of such ratings, at Burke's suggestion a pseudonymous footnote analyzed the hierarchy of critical types implicit in the ratings.[64]

Kenneth Burke's principal contribution to *Aesthete 1925* was a direct offshoot of Cowley's altercation with Waldo Frank in 1924. His "Dada, Dead or Alive" proved, again, that underneath the issue's overall zaniness lay a serious, if largely unarticulated, concern with art and criticism. Wittily taking issue with Frank, Burke defined Dada as "perception without obsession" ("Dada is the child who, seeing a lame man hobble down the street, attempts through neither sympathy nor mockery, but sheer curiosity, to hobble"). Burke rejected Frank's ideal of wholeness and integration as a "deliberate ruling out of certain predominant factors in life." What was needed was not, as Frank proposed, the contrary of Dada, but precisely

"Dada aggrandized": an ideal of integration encompassing *all* factors of contemporary life—"supernal beauty AND the brass band"—and that was, in effect, "Dada plus."[65]

Burke's article underlined how much of the satire in *Aesthete 1925* had a double edge, striking both at the group's literary opponents and at themselves. Burke's plea for "Dada aggrandized" was accompanied by his declaration that "Dada, like God, is dead." Another, pseudonymous, contribution by Burke mocked the expatriate experience of France from which so many of the collaborators had recently returned.[66] The advertisement promoting Mencken was in itself a parody of Dada stunting. Wheelwright's critical stageshow of quasi-scientific percentages self-mockingly played into the hands of those (Brooks, Lowell, Untermeyer) who had criticized the younger generation for practicing criticism as if it were a branch of mathematics. Even the pamphlet's title was self-ironic: not only did it update Boyd's "model 1924" to suggest that the prototypical aesthete set his sails to the current literary winds, it also self-mockingly advertised as "aesthetes" a disparate group of writers whose divergent literary values and beliefs belied any such common denominator.

Aesthete 1925, for all its larkiness, did not nearly cause as much of a stir as the first issue of the *American Mercury*. Its six hundred copies created a brief flurry of publicity and warmed the heart of William Carlos Williams: "The invigorating thing is that you have succeeded in making SOMETHING live in the poison gas atmosphere of New York. It is astonishing." If Williams was right, then Cowley had attained his aim of rousing a lethargic literary milieu from its torpor; Williams, for one, had no trouble recognizing Cowley's animating spirit behind the venture and personally sensed the dawn of a new era: "I get a good flavor of COWLEY from this AESTHETE. It's wonderful! It seems to me that there's something here that I have been watching for for a long time. I think that damned slow thunder-on-the-horizon COWSTENCH is beginning to seep-sound through the skyscraper. It looks to me as if this is a beginning." John Brooks Wheelwright, who had the biggest financial stake in the magazine (he had contributed twenty-five dollars toward meeting a total expense of seventy-five dollars; others had donated ten dollars each), found *Aesthete 1925* "most satisfactory and effective," but regretted that his projected ridicule of Waldo Frank had been shelved in favor of Burke's more serious article. Cowley had his own interpretation of the effectiveness of *Aesthete 1925*. It had to do, he explained to Burke, with the superior literary ethics of the aesthetes, who were "more interested in literature than in success." Once successful, he feared, they might be "more obnoxious than the Boyds, Menckens and Shermans." Hence, the "virtue" of Aesthete 1925 was that it was bound to be dismissed as "a mere childishness," and thus would serve to "retard" the success of its creators.[67]

The ultimate significance of Aesthete 1925 was limited; what serious literary concerns it exemplified remained submerged in a pervasive tone of prankish inanity. Though it helped to strike some sparks in the "wet tinder" of literary New York, its explosive light flared too ephemerally to constitute a beacon for the future. The group it brought together was too loose and disparate in its literary assumptions to provide a focus for future action; shared hostility toward Menckenism and a desire to thumb its collective nose at its literary elders could hardly form the intellectual foundation of a movement. The contributors to Aesthete 1925 were united by the exuberant feeling of belonging to a defiant league of youth, by a common plight of poverty, and an intense literary ambition; for the rest, beyond a general concern with literary form—a concern diametrically opposed to the formlessness of Dada—there was more to distinguish than to unite the individual participants. Only a momentary willingness to band together in a spirit of good fun—and fun the launching of Aesthete 1925 certainly was— could have bundled the divergent talents of men like Tate and Williams, Wheelwright and Burke. The spontaneous energies released by Aesthete 1925 were largely expended in a mood of playfulness and glee, a mood still possible in the winter of 1924–25 but soon to give way to a more neurotic atmosphere of hysteria, bewilderment, and self-destruction. Aesthete 1925 could still take innocent pride in its carefree and immature iconoclasm. Even here, however, as Dickran Tashjian has suggested, the magazine was "not so much a culmination of American interest in Dada as it was symptomatic of the failure to engage an American Dada." In this respect Burke's proclamation of the death of Dada, coming three years after the movement had been pronounced dead in France, was timely and appropriate. For, precisely because Aesthete 1925 offered "no climactic argument, only explosion and dispersion," it could take its place in literary history as "the last Dada fling in America."[68]

‹ ‹ ‹ Organizing and publishing Aesthete 1925 was a bracing experience for Cowley. For once it had proved possible to assemble a motley group of young writers behind a common literary program and to show that a spirit of united endeavor could, if only temporarily, put an end to factional quarreling and clear the air for serious literary discourse. In December, invigorated by the prevailing mood of literary community and good-fellowship among his friends, Cowley wrote to Burke: "this winter there is more social life, including more intelligent conversation, than I have encountered since leaving Peabody High School. Nobody has been very brilliant, coruscating, coruscant, smart or even clever, but one encounters a vehemence of belief in literary questions that gives one a sense of—shall I say—well-being." In nostalgic retrospection Cowley recurrently spoke of this period as "the good winter" of 1924–25. After work he regularly met with friends for Prohibition drinks at the Poncino Palace, a Village speakeasy nicknamed "Punchino" Palace. Once or twice a week he joined his literary companions for wine and dinner at the Italian restaurant of John Squarcialupi, first located in a large basement on Waverly Place, later on Perry Street. Susan Jenkins Brown has recalled how, at the end of a "gay, impromptu, Dutch-treat dinner party" "the onerous task of figuring out who owed what always fell to patient Malcolm Cowley." After dinner the company would reconvene in the back room, to talk literature and read aloud their latest poems. Harold Loeb remembered an evening at which Hart Crane declaimed a new section of *The Bridge*, then announced he was "through with poetry for life," and Allen Tate recited a satirical piece of verse entitled "The Earnest Liberal's Lament." These were festive, rowdy occasions at which heated literary debate easily gave way to horseplay and jesting. Climactic was the New Year's Eve party that winter, when Cowley's circle was assigned a special room to celebrate at Squarcialupi's and Crane, in an ecstasy of delight, was brought to the point of singing Gregorian chants. There was, Cowley sensed in retrospect, a touch of innocence about these informal literary gatherings: "We were all about twenty-six, a good age, and looked no older; we were interested only in writing and in keeping alive while we wrote, and we had the feeling of being invulnerable—we didn't see how anything in the world could ever touch us, certainly not the crazy desire to earn and spend more money and be pointed out as prominent people." Burke, always argumentative, strove to "outquibble and outcavil" his companions, while Tate, "studiously polite," displayed an unexpected talent for "comic inventions and pure impishness." Crane often banged away at an old upright piano, sometimes playing *Très Moutarde*, a tune with a nostalgic appeal for Burke, Cowley, and Susan Jenkins Brown, since to its melody had been set the words of a Peabody football song. Later in the evening Crane might sink into moroseness or stalk among the tables, growling snatches of poetry, before storming out to roam the Brooklyn docks—storm warnings of his suicide seven years later. In "The Flower and the Leaf," a moving poem published more than forty years later, Cowley, with a mature understanding of the "tangled reasons" for the ordeal by failure and success of his literary companions, cast a nostalgic and sacramental aura about the gay gatherings of this "omnicolored crew" at Squarcialupi's during that "good winter":

> All of an age, all heretics,
> all rich in promise, but poor in rupees,
> I knew them all at twenty-six,
> when to a sound of scraping shovels,
> emerging from whatever dream,
> by night they left their separate hovels
> as if with an exultant scream,
> stamped off the snow and gathered round
> a table at John Squarcialupi's
> happy as jaybirds, loud as puppies.[69]

Much of the groundwork for *Aesthete 1925* was laid during the dinner meetings at Squarcialupi's, the drinking sessions at Poncino's, or occasional gatherings at the office of the pulp magazine *Telling Tales*, on East Eleventh Street, where Tate had meanwhile succeeded Hannah Josephson as editorial assistant to Susan Jenkins Brown. At Squarcialupi's one chair at the long table was ceremoniously kept vacant for the magazine's mysterious Maecenas, Mr. Hankel. *Aesthete 1925* gave some focus to the loose gatherings, but the issue was finally rounded off in one marathon session, held on Sunday, November 30, 1924, at the Broadway Central Hotel, the group working together "in excellent ensemble" for a day and a night.[70]

The preparatory meetings for *Aesthete 1925* released so much good verse and prose that immediate plans were laid for a creative, nonpolemic, second issue. At Cowley's insistence an announcement to such intent was printed in the opening number; the follow-up issue, it stated, was to contain verse and prose by the original contributors, augmented by Robert Coates, Hart Crane, Charles L. Durboraw, and Isidor Schneider. Harold Loeb, before sailing back to Europe, promised to supervise the printing of the issue. There, however, matters rested. A meeting held at Allen Tate's in early March, at which Brown, Cowley, Crane, and Josephson were present, revealed considerable "bashfulness" on the part of Brown, Crane, and Tate, all of whom dreaded the work involved. Discouraged by the lack of response and reluctant to carry through their plans without the assured support of all involved, Cowley and Josephson decided to assemble material and to print a second issue as a group-manifesto under the aegis of another magazine—Jane Heap had expressed interest in such a possibility for the *Little Review*.[71] Thus *Aesthete 1925* remained a one-issue occasion. The product of an ephemeral resuscitation of esprit de corps among Cowley's literary friends, it foundered on lack of agreement and sustained commitment among its participants: in its wake the "Aesthetes" once again dispersed and went their separate ways.

The disbanding of the Aesthetes coincided with a resurgence of frictions between Cowley and Burke, who from the first had been less wholeheartedly committed to *Aesthete 1925* than Cowley had hoped. More seriously, Burke now seemed to question the purity of Cowley's literary motives and, charging that Cowley was "no longer the man [he was] in high school," felt that henceforth he "must be treated with tact." The latter charge hit hardest. As Burke confessed: "To me, the employment of tact is a subtle method of denigration, which, if it implies no absolute discredit to the persons involved, does certainly imply discredit to their relationship." An honest altercation ensued—"our correspondence could be culled to prove that we were the most faithful of enemies"—during which Cowley reaffirmed the necessity of abstaining from tact in their friendship ("the only friendship to me is to tell me, when you think I'm running off at a tangent, that you think I'm running off at a tangent") and rejected Burke's aim to "live by philosophy or aesthetics" as an attempt to do the impossible: to make "the world safe for aesthetics," he was convinced, it was necessary to make some degree of "compromise" with it.[72]

Cowley's falling-out with Burke, concomitant with his friends' failure to perpetuate *Aesthete 1925* in more serious form, revived his former skepticism about the utility of literary groups. In one of his periodic stocktaking letters to Burke he reviewed the progress of his career since his arrival in New York twenty months before. Then, he observed, he had wanted "to help to start a—something—in New York that would incorporate the better features of Dada," to wit "its ethics, assertions and adventures." These, he now realized, had been far from definite plans ("I should be rather ashamed of them as such"), but had rather served to give "a sort of emotional direction" to his endeavors. Looking back on the quarreling and backbiting that had ensued, but also on the invigorating atmosphere of cooperation in which *Aesthete 1925* had been born, Cowley realized with renewed poignancy the introverted, narcissistic character of any literary coterie or school: "Here at last is a Group," he observed to Burke, "but we never really wanted a group, except for social purposes. What we wanted was a direction. A group stares at its navel and lives in an atmosphere of self-congratulation. Its direction is centripetal." For the moment, he thought, "we had better make every effort to continue some sort of magazine of our own," while trying to restrict the function of "groups" to the social rather than the literary sphere.[73]

Typically, Cowley tended to blame his ambivalence on the impact of the city. The nervous intensity of urban life, he felt, diminished one's "interior resources," fostered an "inability to stay alone," and drove writers to huddle together in a manner that clashed with their strongly individualistic bent. Living in the country, he was convinced, he would no longer be disturbed by the question of "groups." Later, writing *Exile's Return*, Cowley realized that his aversion to the city was symptomatic of a broader disgust with a culture governed by a creed of industrial and commercial consumerism. After the failure to establish Dada in New York his literary life lost the sharp individuality of its outline, and his adventures came to lack an element of "freedom" and "novelty." Significantly, it was at this point that, so he judged in retrospect, his experiences as a writer stopped being representative of his literary generation; it was here, also, that he left the stage as a leading actor in his generational drama, *Exile's Return*, to take up a position in the wings. Looking back to the years after 1924, Cowley saw himself as an anonymous face in a crowd, merely one of the countless young people on the fringes of the arts, who had come flocking to Manhattan from the Midwest, to live and write in the margin of a booming business culture in need of "propagandists"—advertising copywriters, designers, stylists, and editors who discontentedly served the cause of business, technology, and consumerism. All of them, Cowley observed in *Exile's Return*, were "individualists by theory, yet they lived the life of their social order as strictly as Prussian officers." Cowley's description was infused with an undertone of guilt and distaste about his personal situation in the mid 1920s: "all these people were living a series of contradictions. They prided themselves chiefly on their professional competence, their skill with words or lines or colors, their ability to gauge the public taste, and yet their skill was devoted to aims in which none of them believed. Their function as a class was to be the guardians of intellectual things, and yet they were acting as propagandists for a way of life in which their intellect played a minor part. They were selling their talents."[74]

The mood of carefree innocence marking the "good winter" of 1924–25 could not obviate an underlying feeling of subtle alienation from prevailing cultural values in America, which, growing stronger in the second half of the decade, formed the seedbed of Cowley's subsequent political radicalism. As did many of his literary friends, Cowley increasingly felt himself a stranger on native grounds—"The financiers, the salesmen, the prophets of success were our enemies." In the spring of 1925, however, Cowley's sense of cultural estrangement was less a fully articulated intellectual attitude than an "obscure" feeling of dislocation and rejection, complicated by a deep attachment to the American land and, ultimately, American society. Beset, as always, with an "instinctive fear of being successful" ("It didn't seem to me possible to be successful in America and at the same time be a good writer"), Cowley now sought a way out of the dilemma that had been plaguing him since his return to America in 1923. Inexorably tied to New York for his income from writing, yet dreaming of an independent and untainted literary life in the country, he decided on a compromise that would combine the "advantages of two worlds."[75]

In April 1925 the Cowleys moved to Staten Island, where they rented a dilapidated five-room house, with heat, electricity, and bath, for thirty dollars a month. Cheap carfare and easy commuting to New York were compensations for the "high" rent. In late March, Cowley described the place to Burke and indulged in the anticipatory pleasures of semirural living: "Yes, we took a house. It is one mile from the Annadale Station in the south-central portion of the island. From the window of what will be my study there is a middling view of the sea. The lot is about 30 × 200; it has some young bearing plum and cherry trees, a grape arbor, and plenty of garden space. . . . From the exterior, it looks pretty shacky and run down, but it will not be uncomfortable. . . . The country is not altogether raw; there are plenty of broad fields and oak woods, and it is only two miles to the sea." The move to Staten Island was a double experiment: it was an intermediary step toward a definitive removal to the country, projected for the following spring; and it enabled Cowley to check out the feasibility of making his living entirely by writing. Besides the purchase of a secondhand Ford, a primary necessity of country living, Cowley planned to commute to New York for several months longer, retaining his job at Sweet's until he could be sufficiently assured of literary markets for his writings to "safely embark on [his] new free-lancing career."

Given his rural background and his persistent ambivalence about urban life, Cowley's semideparture from New York seemed a predestined move. In the mid 1920s he hoped it would help to assuage his sense of alienation from a business culture whose dominant values clashed with what was, after all, his only real interest—the pursuit of literature. Rerooting himself in the country, while retaining his economic ties to the city, catered to Cowley's "obscure need to be an outsider" in American society in Coolidge's New Era; it would allow him, so he hoped, to retain a degree of independence and integrity impossible in New York.[76]

13

Free Lance

1925–1927

At the end of June 1925 Cowley resigned as a copywriter for Sweet's Catalogue Service to become a full-time free-lance writer. From the summer of 1925 on, his output as a critic, reviewer, and translator steadily increased: over the next four years he wrote more than 125 essays and reviews, translated seven books from the French, and published some twenty-five poems; in addition, his first book of poetry, *Blue Juniata*, appeared in 1929. For much of the second half of the 1920s Cowley's literary career was dominated by a precarious struggle to remain financially afloat. As a free lance with a rising reputation he could count on having access to many avenues of publication.[1] Wide as it was, however, the range of Cowley's literary activities was circumscribed by the need to carry his writings to market. A separate notebook devoted to a meticulous account of his literary earnings testifies to his persistent worries over money. With fees for articles and translations, publishers' advances for books to be written, edited, or translated, and reader's reports for firms like Macaulay and Harcourt, Brace, Cowley's monthly income for these years ranged between a high of $583 in May 1926 and a low of $120 in May 1929, averaging between $250 and $275.

Productive as he was, the lists of projected books and articles he incorporated into his notebooks suggest that his achievements fell far short of his ambitions. Though he was writing enough to be assured of a modest income, he remained discouraged about his inability to do the kind of writing by which he set great store. Intermittently he lapsed into moods of lamentation and bleak self-assessment, as he found himself still incapable of resolving the ambiguities that had been the principal "motifs" of his career so far. Throughout the decade he struggled to maintain the relative purity of a rural literary life against the compromises of an urban culture of consumerism, fighting to uphold a principled integrity against the practical necessity of hackwriting.

In the latter half of the 1920s Cowley's career continued to revolve about the pivotal concerns of the early years of the decade: a search for a personal aesthetics, an attempt to define and approximate the ideal of the man of letters, a process of uneasy accommodation to a radical literary modernism, a persistent concern with the mechanics of literary failure and success, the establishment of a congenial literary climate and a sustaining sense of literary community. But his pursuit of these concerns was now marked by a diminished sense of excitement and discovery. The watershed years in France and their turbulent aftermath in New York were followed by a calmer period of consolidation and gestation, as Cowley mostly lived a quiet rural life, spending only his winters in New York. Though he was busy and resilient enough, the four years between 1925 and 1929 constituted a less dramatic (if still crucially formative) intermezzo in his critical and intellectual development. Though he took his stand in most of the literary and intellectual controversies of the time, it was not until the end of the decade that a new phase of fermentation and progression began.

‹ ‹ ‹   During the summer of 1925 the mood of carefree invulnerability of the preceding winter was perpetuated some seventy miles upstate near Patterson, in Pawling County, New York. Here Squarcialupi's "omni-colored crew" habitually reconvened for weekend parties on Tory Hill, just across the state line from Sherman, Connecticut. Slater Brown and Susan Jenkins, now married, had bought an unremodeled pre-Revolutionary farmhouse there, surrounded by an old apple orchard and some eighty acres of overgrown land. After resigning from Sweet's, Hart Crane had joined the Browns to help with repairs. Here, at Robber Rocks—as the place was named, after a nearby cave that during the Revolution had been a refuge for local Tories—Malcolm and Peggy Cowley regularly got together with Crane, the Browns, the Tates, the Josephsons, and, later in the de-cade, Robert Coates, the painter Peter Blume, and the novelist Nathan Asch, all of whom lived in the neighborhood at one time or another. Cowley fondly recalled "the general atmosphere of youth and poverty and good humor" as the crew played a rowdy game of croquet, a pitcher of hard cider hidden in the grass, or, driven inside by a drizzling rain, sat swap-ping stories or reciting poetry beside the fireplace in the big, low-ceilinged kitchen. Particularly memorable was that year's Fourth of July celebra-tion, in effect a three-day saturnalia, involving, Crane told his mother, "an omnibus-full of people from New York," a case of gin, and jugs of locally brewed hard cider. Cowley vividly remembered Crane's "pagan ecstasy" as he capered on a stone fence, a nail keg perched on his head, a pair of "cerise drawers" on his legs, his face luridly painted, dancing like an African cannibal. "We went swimming at midnight," Crane reported,

"climbed trees, played blindman's buff, rode in wheelbarrows, and gratified every caprice for three days." Later that weekend Crane lapsed into
one of the meditative silences preceding the state of frenzied exultation in
which he composed his poems; he pounded out magical, opaque phrases
on the typewriter, a phonograph blasting in his ears, and finally submitted
to his well-meaning but half-comprehending friends a draft of an obscure
visionary poem, "Passage." Later, Cowley understood that Crane's idiosyncratic behavior—which so heavily taxed his friends' capacity for tolerance,
with its sudden shifts of mood from ecstatic exhilaration to sullen moroseness or glittering violence—was in effect a necessary part of his method of
writing poetry, a Rimbaud-like "derangement" of the senses followed by a
calculated exercise of the critical faculty. Witnessing Crane's quirky and
tempestuous conduct helped Cowley understand the connections between
Crane's complex sensibility, the process by which he wrote his poetry, and
his ultimate suicide: Crane's "method of self-induced frenzy" could be
successful only for short spurts of time and carried within it the seed of
self-destruction.[2]

August 1925 was a month of miscellaneous activities. With Peggy,
Cowley made a trip to the farm in Belsano, but the journey was hardly a
success. Seventy miles from Staten Island the self-starter on the Cowleys'
rickety Model-T Ford refused to work and Cowley broke his arm trying to
crank "Little Eva," as the car was nicknamed; in the end he had to hire a
driver to complete the trip and drove back after two weeks with a bandaged
arm. Cowley's visit to his childhood country was less invigorating than
usual. Peggy did not get along easily with Cowley's mother, and Cowley
himself felt ambivalent about the inbred conservatism of the Pennsylva-
nians: "The people are stingy, inquisitive and very kind-hearted. They all
belong to the Ku Klux," he told Josephson.[3]

That summer the Cowleys also toured the lake district of northwestern
New Jersey, to gather material for an article for *Charm*. The piece, lavishly
illustrated with photographs, appeared in August 1925. That same month
Cowley was made "book-editor" of *Charm* at fifty dollars a month. Over
the next three years, writing a regular book page, he brought a wide variety
of books to the attention of his readers: biographies of American historical
figures (Carl Sandburg's *Abraham Lincoln* receiving special praise); books
catering to the public's thirst for "general knowledge," like Mark Sullivan's *Our Times*, Will Durant's *The Story of Philosophy*, or Charles and
Mary Beard's *The Rise of American Civilization*; and, most interestingly,

a galaxy of contemporary American fiction, including Anderson's *Dark Laughter*, Aiken's *Blue Voyage*, Willa Cather's *The Professor's House*, Carl van Vechten's *Nigger Heaven*, Fitzgerald's *All the Sad Young Men*, Thornton Wilder's *The Cabala*, and Hemingway's *The Sun Also Rises*. Cowley's *Charm* book page bore witness to his conviction that, in recent years, the novel form had grown "incredibly rich and diversified" and had become "capable of expressing almost the whole of modern life."[4]

Cowley's career as a free-lance reviewer received an important stimulus when, during the summer, he wrote his first review for Irita Van Doren, who had succeeded Stuart P. Sherman on the *New York Herald Tribune Books*. In a consideration of George Moore's *Anthology of Pure Poetry* Cowley analyzed a cherished passage from Baudelaire's "Femmes Damnées" to prove that the emotion of aesthetic delight engendered by the poem was "our tribute not so much to the violence of the poet's feeling as to the perfection which his form achieves." Cowley's analysis, interestingly enough, seemed predicated on Kenneth Burke's definition of "form" in terms of "the psychology of the audience," which appeared almost simultaneously in the *Dial* for July 1925.[5]

Irita Van Doren—who, with her husband Carl and his younger brother Mark, formed the "Van Doren dynasty" on the *Nation* (she had served as its literary editor from 1922 to 1924)—was quick to recognize the competence and critical promise of Cowley at the age of twenty-seven. Over the next six years Cowley wrote some fifty articles and reviews for her, including a series of lead essays in 1929, the *New York Herald Tribune* in effect forming the financial backbone of his precarious free-lancing life. Irita Van Doren valued especially Cowley's expertise in French literature and for years she assigned to him the majority of books in the field. Through his translations and critical reviews Cowley now gained a solid reputation as an "authority" on French letters; it persisted through the decades, as he continued to follow with a loving, critical eye the fate of French writing, through the Depression, the war years and beyond, and to produce authoritative translations of Gide, Aragon, and Valéry.[6]

Cowley's translations and reviews not only filled the need for the type of criticism he called for in 1927, one that could "interpret the aims of modern French writers in terms which an American layman [could] understand"; he was also regularly consulted by American publishers—including Harcourt, Brace, as well as Macaulay and, as early as 1929, Viking Press—on the advisability of translating French books into English. He could thus function as a cultural mediator, helping to familiarize an American audience with a wide range of French poets and novelists, and to remedy a backward cultural situation in which modern French poetry remained "a vague sort of Thibet, an unvisited province of the mind."[7]

Between 1925 and 1930 Cowley's reviews, marked by an unobtrusive erudition and a solid grasp, both scholarly and imaginative, of the history and spirit of French letters, spanned the whole range of French writing, from the Middle Ages to the complex and confusing present. He reviewed the works of François Villon, the fifteenth-century poet and scoundrel whose early death at thirty had been evoked in Pound's "Hugh Selwyn Mauberley"; he considered four novelists of the *ancien régime* (Crébillon, Laclos, Diderot, and Restif de la Bretonne); and he discussed *The Charterhouse of Parma*, the first volume in a new edition of the complete works of Stendhal, confessing to a preference for *The Red and The Black*. Several reviews exemplifying a growing interest in romanticism dealt with Gautier, Baudelaire, de Gourmont, and Villiers de L'Isle-Adam. Baudelaire received an ample share of Cowley's critical attention: he reviewed translations of his poetry, prose, and letters, as well as two recent biographies of the French poet. The majority of reviews, however, introduced American readers to contemporary French writers: Jean Cocteau, Henri Barbusse, Roger Martin du Gard, Blaise Cendrars, Julien Green, Paul Morand, Alain-Fournier, Joseph Kessel, François Mauriac, André Chamson, and, receiving special attention, André Gide. Though the limited scope of a review often precluded in-depth examination of his subject, Cowley's considerations of French writing evinced the talent for "disinterested appreciation" that he demanded of the critics of his generation. In several reviews, also, Cowley sidled into his role as the literary historian of his generation, as when he discussed, with a half-ironic, self-mythologizing touch that became typical, the impact of modern French poetry on the members of his age group: "New horizons were opening before our astonished, blue, empty, nordic eyes. We were so many Keatses confronted with half a dozen Homers."[8]

Cowley's concern with French literature and European modernism made some of his contemporaries feel that he did not give the literature of his own country equally serious attention. Carl Sandburg, for one, put him down as one of "the few American writers meant by the left oblique in Emerson's remark, 'There are persons born and reared in this country who culturally have not yet come over from Europe!'" Sandburg should have known better, for when *The Prairie Years* was published, Cowley had written him: "By God you pulled it off. Your *Lincoln* is good; it belongs with *Moby-Dick* and *Leaves of Grass* and *Huckleberry Finn*; it is the best piece of American prose which has been written in the last —— years. Fill in the blank yourself, but use at least two figures." Though Cowley might occasionally speak, not without irony, of France as "the country where good Americans go when they die and where literary Americans go when they wish to become conscious of their own land," his commitment to raising America's estimate of its own literature was indisputable and in no way at odds with his interest in a French culture that he saw as an important "challenge to our own civilization of flivvers, skyscrapers and business organization." Indeed, as the 1920s proceeded, he grew ever more skeptical of the cultural benefits of expatriation and proved as much of a literary nativist as Sandburg or William Carlos Williams. Thus, in late 1926, he observed that since the war, American travelers to Europe had been shedding their ancient sense of cultural inferiority and that American writers increasingly aimed at creating "a rich panorama of everything colorful in American life." Two months later he interpreted the current "craze" for biographies of prominent figures from American history as a mode of cultural stocktaking symptomatic of "America's coming of age."[9]

From the first Cowley's reviews were conspicuous for his serious concern with the standards of translation. Cowley was in the position to offer authoritative criticism, ranging from a translator's idiomatic errors and stylistic infelicities to a more serious failure of sensitivity to the nuances of cultural difference. He generally spoke well of notable translators like Lewis Galantière and C. K. Scott Moncrieff who showed "the rare ability to make a liaison between two cultures," but came down with particular harshness on Arthur Symons's translation of Baudelaire, which he dismissed as "inexact, awkward where it should be graceful, and partial where it claims to be complete." Symons's faulty rendering of Baudelaire supported Cowley's conviction that translation always implied interpretation and that in essence poetry was untranslatable: "At best we can render only such qualities of the original as we possess already . . . the translator's work is a mirror to his own mind, rather than to the author's." Cowley found ample proof for such a thesis among the many translators of François Villon who had subjected the rascal-poet to a "process of sentimentalization" in their Victorian hopes of rendering him into "a fitting poet for the parlor, the matinee and even the dame-school."[10]

Malcolm Cowley and his mother,
Josephine Hutmacher Cowley.

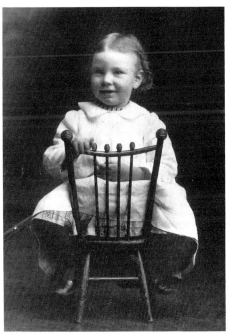

Cowley, circa 1900 (Newberry Library).

Cowley, circa 1902 (Newberry Library).

Cowley, circa 1903
(Newberry Library).

Cowley, age nine: "at the farm in
November when I wore shoes."

"Maple Home," the Cowleys' farmhouse near Belsano, in
western Pennsylvania.

Cowley's fifth-grade class at Shakespeare School, Pittsburgh. Cowley is in the first row, fourth from left.

Cowley, age eleven: "In a fat boy's suit that mother bought me."

Josephine Cowley with her adopted daughter, Ruth, 1911.

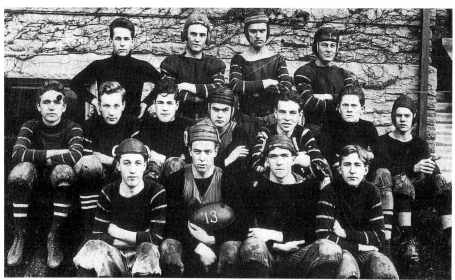

Top: Photographs from the 1914 and 1915 Peabody High School yearbooks. *Clockwise:* Malcolm Cowley, Susan Jenkins, James Light, and Kenneth Burke (Historical Society of Western Pennsylvania). *Bottom:* The 1912 Academy of the New Church in Bryn Athyn football team. Cowley is in the second row, third from right.

Cowley in his American Field Service
uniform, 1917.

Cowley in Paris, 1922 (Sylvia Beach
Collection, Princeton University Libraries).

The foreign class at the University of Montpellier, spring 1922. Cowley is in
the second row, center.

Cowley in 1929. Photograph by
Jim Casey.

Cowley's first wife, Peggy Baird, 1930.

Peggy Cowley and Hart Crane in
Mexico, 1932.

Cowley with Robert Penn Warren in
Kentucky, 1933.

Cowley and Allen Tate at a Confederate
memorial, 1933.

Cowley fishing at Cloverlands, in Tennessee.

Cowley's parents, Josephine and
Dr. William Cowley, 1931.

Cowley in his New York apartment,
circa 1932.

Cowley at his desk at the *New Republic*, 1934.

Of all the French writers he reviewed for the *Herald Tribune* it was André
Gide who came closest to attaining for Cowley a literary ideal and to resolving the incongruities in his attitude to modernism. Gide loomed for
him as "the greatest man of letters in France, perhaps in all Europe." With
Burke and Eliot, Gide shared a "perpetual grailism," that perennial desire
to "launch out on unknown seas," which Cowley had repeatedly posited
as an essential feature of the "modern" sensibility. Insisting on his "liberty
to experiment in different fields," Gide showed an admirable aversion to
"specialization," adopting rather "the whole of literature for his province."
Between 1926 and 1929 Cowley reviewed three of Gide's novels, as they
appeared in English translations: *Les Caves du Vatican* (1914; *The Vatican
Swindle,* 1926), *Les faux-monnayeurs* (1925; *The Counterfeiters,* 1927) and
L'Ecole des femmes (*The School for Wives,* 1929). He delighted in Gide's
attitude of "freedom" toward the conventions of the novel, relished the liberties taken with characters and plot, verisimilitude, and chronology, and
felt his fiction radiated a refreshing "sense of liberation from troublesome
and unnecessary bonds of fact." Cowley's recent readings in the literature
of romanticism had engendered a more open-minded attitude to experimentalist fiction, without making him shed a deeply ingrained predilection
for the novel's traditional virtues. It was Gide who proved that the two
were not mutually exclusive. *The Counterfeiters,* in particular, convinced
Cowley that the deluge of radically experimental novels since 1900 did not
inevitably signify the death of the genre, as he once feared; it was "a vastly
reassuring book," since it proved that the novel could be "born anew without being false to its own nature." Gide's search for a new "pure" novel
had led him back to "the old traditions of European fiction," to Fielding, Dickens, and Dostoyevski. *The Counterfeiters* was "genuinely great,"
Cowley claimed, by virtue of a paradox: it was an indubitably modern
experimental novel, which, "by deliberately avoiding realism," managed to
create "the effect of life." [11]

Gide's appeal to Cowley went beyond formalist aspects and had direct
bearing on his own difficulties with the apparent irreconcilability of aesthetics and morality. Gide, indeed, provided the same "undying answer to
those who believe that no sort of moral judgment has a place in art" as did
Baudelaire. *The Vatican Swindle,* he felt, contained the clearest expression
of a "new system of morality," one that placed Gide at the opposite end
from writers like Sherwood Anderson or D. H. Lawrence. Gide saw man
as foremost "a creature of free will," Cowley insisted, one whose highest

good was "to exercise this will, to control his destiny, to make decisions. Any action which is dictated merely by necessity is contemptible. Any action performed *without motive* should be commended, because it is a defiance of cause, heredity, environment—all the factors which limit the free exercise of the will." Cowley praised Gide's "habit of passing moral judgments on his characters" and sympathized with his disdain for what he called "the 'unmoral' novel . . . the novel of indifference." Gide thus confirmed Cowley's belief, now publicly proclaimed, that "any question which really excites us becomes a question of morality." [12]

For Cowley, Gide's force of moral conviction was a quality sorely absent in contemporary American writing. In two reviews, one for the *Saturday Review of Literature*, the other for the *Dial*, Cowley took Conrad Aiken's *Bring! Bring! And Other Stories* as a case in point. Aiken's characters were "static almost without exception," he criticized; they surrendered "active" thought to a passive emotional life governed by "a desperate futility, a search for pleasant physical sensations, and the fear of death." Cowley's concern, however, extended beyond the idiosyncracies of Aiken's art to the entire realm of contemporary letters. "This dangerous passivity, the neglect of logical thought, the distaste for action (growing into a contempt for action): all these are the symptoms of the malady which afflicts the more intelligent writers of our time. Their books are concerned with people who drift, accept, surrender to their passions. A strain of inherited agnosticism, applied first to God, then to society, has finally centered in the self. They are palsied with doubt; afflicted, characters and authors, with an atrophy of the will." Boldly applying aesthetic criteria to life itself, Cowley displayed an impatience with the subjectivism and moral paralysis of modern writing, which before long propelled him toward a recognition of art's social function and relevance. As early as the fall of 1925 he opposed "a personal mysticism which often seems anti-social" to "the impulse to reform society." [13]

By contrast Cowley praised *Doctor Transit*, a first novel by Isidor Schneider, for its "glorification of the will," a quality "rare in serious fiction," and hoped the characters in Schneider's "epic of the will" would prove symptomatic of a "new attitude," in art and in life. As an attempt to "imagine new characters, new motives and events, a new society" Schneider's novel was a healthy antidote to the underlying mood of much of contemporary writing, which Cowley described elsewhere as "bitter, agnostic or ironic." [14] Cowley now showed a much greater liking than before for "purely imaginative," daringly fantastic writing that wilfully departed from the standards of conventional realism. In a time when the realistic novel had been "formularized," it was refreshing to read a novel like *Doctor Transit*, a book built on an "absurdly" irrational plot, filled with "miraculous" incidents, "unreal" writing, and "imaginary" rather than "observed" characters, but which still retained the formal and stylistic qualities of "an epic poem." Cowley's growing appreciation of contemporary romanticism was a mark of his eclectic open-mindedness to the rich diversity of modern writing and in no sense impaired his neoclassical concern with formal elegance and control. Emblematic of the latter was his review of *The Bridge of San Luis Rey* by Thornton Wilder, a novel he judged "perfect in itself"—"the texture is completely unified: nothing falls short of its mark; nothing exceeds it; and the book as a whole is like some faultless temple erected to a minor deity." [15]

‹ ‹ ‹   By the summer of 1925 the "general exodus" of writers and artists from New York City was well under way. Many of Cowley's literary friends took part in this move of "escape" from a business-oriented urban culture dominated by a hypocritical morality and a pervasive materialism. As early as 1922 Kenneth Burke, once more the pioneer, fled from his Village basement to a dilapidated farmhouse in Andover, New Jersey, some fifty-five miles from the city, where he lived a rustic Spartan life, planting his own garden, dispensing with electricity and running water, hoping to remain untainted in the serious pursuit of art and criticism. In the spring of 1925 Matthew Josephson turned his back on Wall Street and purchased four acres and a country cottage at Katonah, New York, about an hour from New York. In August, Josephson confessed to Cowley that his removal had given him a badly needed stimulus: now that he had renewed his commitment to "following an art rather than a business," Josephson felt his new life-style placed it within his power "to do the things I love to do, more than before." Two months later, as if in proof, he solicited Cowley's criticism of parts of a novel he was writing. Josephson's place was about an hour from Tory Hill, where Slater and Susan Brown provided a place of merry rural refuge for their friends and displayed much converts' zeal in tempting them to settle in the area. In the autumn Allen Tate and Caroline Gordon, married and expecting their first child, rented eight semifurnished rooms from Mrs. Addie Turner, a sixty-year-old widow who lived in a converted barn half a mile from the Browns' cottage. There, living on a monthly income of less than forty dollars, mostly from book reviews, they struggled through the winter, meanwhile providing accommodation to Hart Crane, with whom they managed to live in "comparative harmony" for nearly four months.[16]

A romantic *malgré lui*, Cowley, too, had long shared his friends' Thoreauvian idealism. "Although we didn't read Emerson," he recalled in 1959, "we had the Emersonian dream of establishing ourselves in some untouched Concord not too far from the city, but closer to the wilderness, where we could write in the morning, roam the hills in the afternoon, and sometimes gather in the evening round the fire in a chunk stove." Cowley's naive dream of a life of rustic simplicity and untainted literary pursuit soon proved impossible to maintain without some degree of compromise; his experiences as a free-lance reviewer served to remind him daily of his economic ties to a literary marketplace governed by the same laws and principles as the larger system he despised. As he later granted: "We became part of the system we were trying to evade, and it defeated us from within, not from without; our hearts beat to its tempo." Such realizations, however, could only come by hindsight. In the summer of 1925, with all his friends joining the "exodus" from New York and Cowley remaining mired in his "dinky little white house" on semisuburban Staten Island, he was busily scraping together funds to realize his plan of moving permanently to the country; he had already settled on the area around Patterson, New York, where the Browns, he granted, had found "the right neighborhood."[17]

In September, Cowley returned for a month to Sweet's to help out in the annual prepublication rush. In October, swamped with reviewing obligations, he complained to Allen Tate of being once again submerged in a "great lassitude." During the late fall he took time out to make a tour of Monmouth County, New Jersey, visiting the region's historic churches and talking to the local clergy for a *Charm* article on "Churches Which Remember the Revolution." Unable to do the work he truly valued, Cowley relapsed into a mood of self-ironic lamentation. "When I shuffle my head sounds like a great resounding cavern," he told Burke in early November. When John Brooks Wheelwright announced that he was abandoning the "profession" of literature (though not the writing of poetry) in order to study architecture, Cowley replied despondently: "We all have to face the problem of making literature a vocation or an avocation. I've tried them both, and have been unhappy both ways. Perhaps living and thinking are the only vocations." What was needed, he said, was "some sort of external discipline, without which we mope." [18]

With his friends dispersing into separate rural enclaves, Cowley missed the sense of literary community that had sustained him through the previous winter and summer. At the end of November, eager for the stimulus of disinterested literary conversation, he took Josephson on a visit to Wheelwright in Boston. The occasion proved as exhilarating as Cowley had expected. "I feel like a man who has just had a cataract removed from his eyes," he wrote to Wheelwright upon his return. "In a sober life, devoted to Art, Letters and Money, I [had] forgotten the strange countries which lie over the border of work and sleep." Wheelwright's effervescent companionship impressed upon Cowley the "necessity of a salon—some place where people could meet with a pretense of breeding and a reality of conversation." Such a salon, Cowley hoped, could have "the effect of a whetstone: it sharpens people's minds against each other." The project, viable as it seemed, stranded for lack of a "hostess" who was willing to invite and entertain "the froth of the whipped cream of the Artists and Writers of the nation," but the impulse behind the plan, symptomatic of Cowley's efforts to maintain a precarious sense of united literary effort among the members of his age group, remained, to be resuscitated in the future and expanded to encompass what Cowley came to think of as the "commonwealth of letters." Even in the 1920s he and Tate "speculated about the possibility of putting out a magazine of sorts, to be called 'News of the Republic of Letters.'" Cowley's later efforts on behalf of Yaddo, the League of American Writers, and the National Institute and American Academy of Arts and Letters were a natural exfoliation from his early efforts to sustain a sense of common literary purpose among his coevals. [19]

In the closing days of 1925, however, Cowley had to make do with occasional weekend trips to Robber Rocks and weekly or biweekly lunches with his friends in New York City. His trip to Boston, followed by a visit to S. Foster Damon in Providence, Rhode Island (Damon had lately been appointed a professor of English at Brown University), had been merely an exhilarating intermezzo. Back in New York, Cowley had difficulty resuming his "practical affairs," which he confessed to Wheelwright were in a "terrible" state: "I haven't been so poor since I left college, ill, with Peggy ill, and with just money enough for a train and a taxicab to Greenwich Village." [20]

When, shortly after, Allen and Caroline Tate invited the Cowleys to spend Christmas up at their new domicile on Tory Hill and Tate offered to take Cowley hunting ("You can't walk a quarter of a mile without raising partridge; rabbits almost trip you up every step"), he jumped at the proposal. Tate also reported that Crane had received one thousand dollars from financier and art patron Otto Kahn. On December 12 Crane arrived at Addie Turner's in excellent spirits, and with ambitious plans for work. With the Cowleys driving up from Staten Island to stay in "Mr. Crane's part" at the Turner house, and the Josephsons being accommodated at nearby Robber Rocks, Tory Hill that year witnessed one of its merriest Christmas reunions. At one of the festive get-togethers, Cowley remembered, Crane read out his "Voyages II." It may well have been Crane's reading of this poem (in which "sleep, death, desire / close round one instant in one floating flower") which moved Cowley to compose "The Flower in the Sea," a poem both about and dedicated to Crane, which beautifully captures the peculiar mixture of the sexual and the religious in Crane's visionary poetry. Cowley mailed the poem to Crane upon his return to New York after Christmas. It imagines Crane speaking:

> Jesus I saw, crossing Times Square
> with John the Baptist, and they bade me stop;
> their hands touched mine:
>
> visions from the belly of a bottle.
>
> The sea, white, white,
> the flower in the sea,
> the white fire glowing in the flower,
> and sea and fire and flower one,
> the world is one, falsehood and truth
> one, morning and midnight, flesh and vision
> one.
>
> I fled along the avenues of night
> interminably, and One pursued,
>
> my bruised arms in His arms nursed,
> my breast against His wounded breast,
> my head limp against His shoulder.

Crane was pleased with the tribute and in a letter to Cowley praised it as a poem "flatteringly apocalyptic," with just "the proper nautical slant." "The Flower in the Sea" seemed "to stand on its own feet as a poem," Crane judged; he appreciated "a very great deal the tonality and direction of it in its more intimate aspects." [21]

Before going off to spend Christmas with the Tates, Cowley had put out feelers for a new free-lance job. In mid-December 1925 he wrote to Lowell Brentano, an acquaintance from Harvard and a scion of the family who owned the largest book store in New York and the publishing firm that had brought out *Eight More Harvard Poets*. Cowley proposed to write a series of portrait interviews of "distinguished American authors" for *Brentano's Book Chat*, the firm's bimonthly house organ, founded in 1922, which under the editorship of Bellamy Partridge cherished literary aspirations beyond the mere promotion of new books. [22] Cowley's proposal was well, even enthusiastically, received. In early February 1926, even before his first article had appeared in its pages, he was asked to become contributing editor, together with Gilbert Seldes, the novelist Samuel Ornitz, and others. Barely two months later he was offered the job of writing, under a nom de plume, "The Tower of Babel," a column in which he was expected to review the current stock of foreign books in French, German, Spanish, and Italian. Cowley accepted the assignment—though, as he admitted to Tate, with his "rusty" German and his "nonexistent" Spanish and Italian the job was "something of a joke"—and for some two years filled a considerable part of the contents of *Brentano's Book Chat* with his pseudonymous writings; he even took a course in Italian at Columbia University. For a while his work for Brentano's yielded an assured income of another fifty dollars a month. [23]

Between 1926 and 1928 *Brentano's Book Chat* featured ten of Cowley's portrait-interviews of contemporary American writers: Willa Cather, Sinclair Lewis, Eugene O'Neill, William Beebe, Ring Lardner, H. L. Mencken, Edwin Arlington Robinson, Conrad Aiken, Carl Sandburg, and Ernest Hemingway. In addition, he wrote on a variety of subjects, from the "fine art" of giving books, to the special appeal of the Nick Carter stories, and the disappearance of a once-popular type of verse, the "harbingers" of spring. Cowley tried to improve the literary tone of *Book Chat*, but editorial demands prevented him from rising far above the level of middlebrow comprehension. Editor Partridge consistently enjoined him to write in a light and humorous vein and, wherever possible, to "inject a little of the mysterious stuff called popularity."[24]

Cowley's pen-portraits of American writers, even more so than his *Bookman* series on French authors, were distinctly popular in tone and did not shun the anecdotal; some of them, he admitted to Maxwell Perkins at Scribner's, read "very much like a publisher's brochure." Yet they exemplified, embryonically, many of Cowley's ongoing critical concerns and illustrated a typical approach that persisted beyond such admittedly "apprentice stuff." Their most conspicuous characteristic was Cowley's objective "to describe an author's work from the standpoint of his personality and his personality from the standpoint of his work." As such, the portraits gave evidence of Cowley's intention to "try more for character studies" in his writings and adumbrated his maturer explorations of the complex interweavings of personality and literary art.[25]

In a manner anticipating his later "empathetic" mode of criticism, Cowley built each portrait around personal reminiscences or observations of the author. He recalled first meeting Sinclair Lewis on the terraces of the Dôme in Paris in 1921—when the author of *Babbitt* was satirically impersonating his own Babbitt—and set his reminiscences against the impressions he had gleaned on a visit with Josephson to Lewis's country estate in Katonah, in the summer of 1925. Likewise, he pictured O'Neill as he had first seen him in the back room of the Hell Hole in the Village, after his return from the war in 1917; he recalled "an evening of animated conversation" with Edwin Arlington Robinson in the spring of 1919, when with Foster Damon he had sought him out in Brooklyn; and he remembered his first meeting with Hemingway in the Paris apartment of Ezra Pound, antecedent to reconstructing what, barely two years later, had become "the Hemingway legend." To complement his memories, Cowley sought out most of the writers in person. In January 1926 he talked to Cather in her comfortable Village apartment and met with Lewis in a New York hotel. In July he gained access, through Maxwell Perkins, to Lardner and interviewed the writer in his home in Great Neck, Long Island ("You can tell him that I promise not to ask too many questions, not to treat him as one of the Seven Lively Arts, not to handle his Puppets with dirty fingers and not to drain the family cellar," Cowley had promised Perkins). In January 1927 he talked to Robinson. In the spring of that year he escorted Sandburg during a performance of his "ril Amurricn" poetry and songs before an incongruous audience of rich and elegant Eastern ladies at the New York

Junior League, and during the summer spoke with Aiken while visiting his friends John and Elinor Nef on Cape Cod.[26]

Cowley transformed each of his *Book Chat* portraits into an opportunity for discussing an aspect of literature or the literary life that he saw reflected in the writings and career of his subject. Among contemporary American writers Cather stood out as "the finest example of the classical ideal," one existing, paradoxically enough, amid "the broken debris of the romantic tradition." Cowley's appreciation of Lewis as a writer who had profoundly affected America's understanding of itself paralleled his aversion to "pure literature" as "abstract, tedious and dead." William Beebe, the popular ornithologist and explorer of tropical wild life, was the odd man out in the series. Cowley examined the "aesthetic" implications of Beebe's adventurous, "strenuous" life-style and found him an exemplar of a "classical" ideal of universality sharply at odds with the contemporary tendency toward specialization. Like Edmund Wilson, Cowley dealt with Lardner as a serious writer at a time when his critical reputation suffered from his popular success as a sportswriter with a gift for sardonic humor.

Predictably, Mencken received short shrift. Mencken, Cowley acknowledged, was the Voltaire of his time, the "voice" and "prophet" of an "age of gin, Freud, knickerbockers, sex, the Charleston, boyish bobs and revolt against all forms of puritanism," but as a critic he was "tremendously overrated." Cowley's biggest grievance against Mencken was that he diminished contemporary American literature: "our writers are strong enough to stand on their own feet, to be praised only for their virtues and damned for their faults." Robinson impressed Cowley as a poet uncompromisingly devoted to his art in a commercial culture in which poetry was "not counted among the useful arts." In an age of "intensive specialization," when literature stood in danger of becoming a "great Fordized industry," Aiken likewise was one of the few American writers who did not "confuse art with business" but who remained "strictly a man of letters." Cowley's portraits of Robinson and Aiken were symptomatic of his growing impatience with an American culture that failed to recognize the function and validity of art and could not provide its artists with adequate spiritual or economic sustenance.

Cowley's last *Book Chat* portrait was advertised as "the first real pen-picture of Ernest Hemingway that has ever appeared in print." By the time of its appearance, in the fall of 1928, Hemingway had already become "a legendary figure," and Cowley did his best to boost the legend, painting a colorful and anecdotal picture of Hemingway's charismatic personality and successful career. Cowley's portrait of Hemingway was one of his earliest attempts to define the leading characteristics of his generation; it was a "practical" generation, he wrote, one "energetic in the attainment of its limited ends," "candid in the pursuit of pleasure," and, in its own way, "fundamentally religious." Unlike their elders, the writers of Hemingway's generation were no longer plagued by "the relationship of man to the machine," Cowley claimed with boldness; "they have mastered the machine; they sit unheedingly at the wheel of a high-powered automobile or the joy-stick of an airplane; they have become the primitives of a new age." Theirs, Cowley noted, was "the sort of deliberate innocence which is the goal of sophistication." Their themes were "simple," unlike those of their predecessors, who were "so obsessed with the complexity of their age and so bitterly determined to be original that most of their stories were written, as it were, on the very margins of experience. Hemingway is convinced of his originality; he does not need to prove it by being finical or obscure. Having found a new manner of writing, he dares to attack the ancient themes of love and death." It was Hemingway, Cowley acknowledged, who "expressed his generation better than any other writer." [27]

Here, in all its crude and elementary simplicity, were the nebulous contours of the picture of the lost generation that Cowley presented with more persuasiveness, depth, and complexity in *Exile's Return*. His early analysis displayed a characteristic inclination to define his generation in contrast to its immediate elders and exemplified a naively self-confident indifference, so typical of a generation buoyantly committed to the present, to a native American tradition in writing that extended backward from Eliot through James to Hawthorne.

Cowley's pen-portraits were generally well-received. There were letters of appreciation from Cather, Beebe, and Robinson, who felt they had been treated with tact and generosity; only Aiken complained, grumbling that Cowley had misjudged his novel *Blue Voyage*. Whatever his misgivings, by October 1927 Cowley still saw enough in his portraits to suggest a continuation of the series to Partridge on the understanding that he would be allowed to write on up-and-coming younger writers and be permitted to exchange his strategy of "unmixed praise" for one of frank reaction: "The stunt is not to leave people in a mood of dumb acquiescence, as if they were sitting in church, but to get them in a state of mind in which they approve, disapprove, shout and get generally excited." He projected future profiles of, among others, Dreiser, Booth Tarkington, Anderson, Amy Lowell, the "Younger Dramatists," and the "Expatriates." Conjointly, Cowley was persuaded, the *Book Chat* portraits might encompass "a pretty complete survey of American literature since the war" and could be published as a book.[28] Though, in the end, none of the proposed portraits were written, Cowley was conceiving of himself with growing self-assurance as the chronicler and historian of his literary times.

‹ ‹ ‹   In February 1926 Cowley took time out from his regular free-lancing to complete a translation of Joseph Delteil's controversial "novelized biography" of Joan of Arc. Cowley had made the acquaintance of Delteil's work through Louis Aragon who, at one of the dadaist gatherings in Paris in the spring of 1923, had enthusiastically declaimed a passage from Delteil's first novel, *Sur le fleuve Amour* (*On the River Amour*, 1929), which had impressed Cowley as "all very barbarous, imaginative, and lyrical, and new." Delteil's *Joan of Arc* was a rhapsodic, unabashedly personal re-creation of a cherished historical legend, written from a modernist perspective. Cowley relished Delteil as an author who showed a refreshing disdain for popular success and who spoke his own mind "with malice and gusto" regardless of established opinion. Most of Delteil's novels, Cowley noted in his introduction, exemplified "the revolt of the individual against a standardized society" and as such seemed pertinent to his own day and age. As he listed the qualities for which he liked Delteil—"A vast weariness with the ratiocination, the profound aesthetics of the last generation. A departure from realism, idealism, naturalism; all are equally boring. A revolt in favour of lyrical freedom and the imagination. Finally a taste for adventure, action"—it became clear that Delteil's appeal fit in with Cowley's growing appreciation for a contemporary romantic literature daringly inventive and unorthodox, but above all unmistakably, even shockingly, "modern."[29]

The book received wide and favorable notice. Most reviewers followed Cowley's lead that the book was to be seen less as a biography than as a modern "lyrical novel." Praise for Cowley's translation was unanimous. Matthew Josephson, writing for the *Saturday Review of Literature*, regarded the book as "a test of the modern style" and commented: "The text with its mixture of the latest colloquialisms and the most obsolete terms, its brood of quarrelsome metaphors which are like angry bedfellows, seemed veritably inaccessible. It needed much nimbleness and virtuosity to attack this French and create the illusion of something written in English." In a lengthy review for the *Herald Tribune Books* Harrison Smith considered Delteil "fortunate to have found a translator who could mirror his sustained lyric outbursts so that the English version rises to the level of an interpretation and recreation." Together with the translation of MacOrlan's *On Board the 'Morning Star'*, Smith believed, this rendering of Delteil "should establish a reputation for [Cowley] that is to be envied." [30]

In March of 1926 Cowley was invited by none other than the redoubtable Ernest Boyd to contribute a biography of his own to the "International Men of Letters Series," which Boyd was editorially supervising for Little, Brown and Company. Any misgivings Cowley may have had about writing for Boyd were obviated by Hart Crane, who persuaded him that, far from "implying any concessions," to accept Boyd's proposal was "a fine weapon against further attacks from that gent." Cowley jumped at Boyd's proposal and suggested Baudelaire as "the man I am most anxious to write about," followed by Stendhal and de Gourmont. Baudelaire, Cowley argued, was quite simply "the great poet of his century, and one of the great precursors" of modernism. The background to his life, moreover, was "rich in tragic, and even more in comic effects," and Cowley was confident of his ability to dig up hitherto unused material, in particular on the subject of French satanism. Boyd accepted Baudelaire as an "excellent" choice for the series. Exhilarated by the sudden prospect of another trip to Europe to gather new material, Cowley applied for a Guggenheim Foundation fellowship. He asked Marianne Moore to be his reference—he sent her a copy of his *Racine* as proof of his competence—and indicated how he hoped to fit in Baudelaire with his present literary preoccupations: "Any study of Baudelaire must touch several questions which are fundamental in literature:— one's judgment of romanticism considered in its most extreme manifestations; one's judgment of the relation between morality and aesthetics; and finally the interplay between the artist and his environment, particularly interesting in the case of Baudelaire." [31]

Cowley's critical biography of Baudelaire was never written: the Guggenheim fellowships for the year had already been awarded. Though his enthusiasm for the project lingered on, his fascination for the French poet had to be channeled into reviews of books on Baudelaire by others. These reviews suggest that at least part of Cowley's biographical thesis would have revolved around the "reciprocal" connection between the poet's life and work, an interest consonant with the themes he was developing in other reviews at the time. In 1929 he observed how "in Baudelaire's case we cannot forget . . . the double contrast, first that his life was disordered, chaotic, full of trivialities, whereas his poems are purified, disciplined, *composed*, to the highest degree, and, second, that in life he suffered from atrophy of the will, whereas his poems represent . . . his incessant exercise of the faculty of choice, his determination to achieve perfection at any cost—in a word, the will itself, in one of its noblest manifestations. We can subtract his life from his poems and they remain. We cannot . . . subtract his poems from his life, for in a sense they *are* his life." The artist as constructionist and expressionist, a defense of the conscious intelligence against a psychoanalytic explanation of literary genius as "a form of abnormality," the contrast between the poet's personal morality and his literary ethics—these were presumably the leitmotifs of Cowley's treatment of Baudelaire.[32]

His trip to France having fallen through, Cowley relapsed into discouragement. At the end of March 1926 he addressed one of his periodic letters of plaintive, doleful stocktaking to Allen Tate. Tate, he knew, had long been vexed by problems of poverty, hackwriting, and the lack of opportunity for truly creative work; the year before, Cowley had banded together with friends, including Edmund Wilson, and appealed to the Personal Service Fund in New York for financial aid for "a poet of unusual talent," but one in "exceptionally hard straits." Unburdening himself to Tate, he measured his present life against the high ambitions with which he had returned from France:

> Three years ago, when I came back from France, I had very different plans. I was going to take a job so that all my writing could be disinterested. I also felt (and feel today) that the grave weakness of the literary life in New York was the fact that it was unimportant. For unimportant read "had no moral value." Anything to which we attach importance becomes a moral question. . . . And we were going to change all that. . . . We would be passionate, ridiculous and undignified. We were. And we became profoundly discouraged, not so much by general hostility as by our own tepidity and quarrels.
>
> According to my own standards, everything I'm doing now is rotten. The articles for Charm are rotten. The articles for Book Chat are rotten. . . . I see nothing else to do but compromise. Some people are saved by a sort of divine dumbness which makes them incapable—

not morally, but intellectually—of successful hackwork. I've always lacked that defense.

Lack of talent isn't one of our chief problems. Almost any of our friends has as much talent as André Gide or Joseph Conrad. The problem is living such a life as to develop our talents. Until forty, at any rate—afterwards things are easier. To reach forty with clean hands. I can't see myself doing it.[33]

As often in his moods of despondency, Cowley was inclined to exaggerate the misery of his plight and the degree to which he had allowed his integrity to be corrupted. When he went so far as to criticize the withdrawn, bucolic type of life away from New York led by the Browns and Tates—"I admire it from a distance, but think it a mistake to retire, to narrow your circle of experiences"—Tate took his friend sharply to task for falsely bemoaning a partly self-inflicted fate: "I can't see the advantage of working like hell at a great variety of hack jobs just in order to stay bewildered and in New York. . . . On a hundred dollars a month six persons could live out here, and have enough left to buy stick-candy. But you make more than that; and you complain that you are broke. You deserve to be. And all for the illusion of wide experience. As long as you're living in a fashion that requires two hundred dollars a month, you will manage to make that much; you will manage it by writing essays 'of no value'; and you will reflect on the misery of a mechanical life, which gives you no spare time, and, moreover, corrupts your moral hands with dirty jobs . . . but why abet the criminal? Why make it worse? . . . Facts sir, nothing but facts . . . will puncture an illusion." Tate's criticism was well-taken, not in the last place because it implied an admonition to stop wallowing in self-complaint and begin to exert that capacity for directing one's own life through conscious choice for which Cowley had been calling in his notebooks and reviews. Though Tate agreed that the present literary scene was "intolerable" and devoid of "moral value," he believed that his "temporary choice" of living in the country was preferable to Cowley's ambivalent loyalty to New York.[34]

As Tate well knew, Cowley's reluctance to exchange the possibility of "wide experience" in New York for a rural existence in closer proximity to his friends was hardly a dilemma. In May 1926 Cowley moved to Sherman, Connecticut, where Charlie Jennings, a local farmer, had located a suitable house owned by his old friend Akin Briggs, at a walking distance

of five miles from Addie Turner's. Cowley's move to Sherman was one further step toward a permanent year-round residence in the country. For the
moment he resumed the life-style of his youth, summering in the country from May through October, spending his winters in an apartment in
downtown Manhattan. In early June he described his new rural environs
to Harriet Monroe, who had just accepted a group of Cowley's pastoral
poems for publication in *Poetry*: "This is a magnificent country, full of
deer, trout, granite and poison ivy. I hope I'll be able to stay out of the
woods long enough to complete some work. 'The woods' are not a figure
of speech. They are acres of oak, elm, hemlock, black, white and yellow
birch surrounding the bed of a stream where trout sleep in pools below the
falls. Before writing the last sentence I looked out of the window, sniffed
the breeze and decided the fish would be biting. Then conquering temptation, I returned to the machine." Without a doubt, Cowley had returned
to homelike territory.[35]

‹ ‹ ‹   The spring of 1926 witnessed the birth of another group manifesto
by Cowley and his friends, when Jane Heap made good her promise to
open up the pages of the *Little Review* for a reprise of *Aesthete 1925*. From
the first the *Little Review* had been sympathetic to the spirit of youthful
iconoclasm of Cowley's literary circle. Its founder, Margaret Anderson,
had published Aragon, Picabia, and Soupault as early as 1921, and Heap
had welcomed Dada to America in the spring of 1922, giving it credit for
introducing "ridicule into a too churchly game" and for flinging "its crazy
bridges to a new consciousness." She had also greeted "the new epoch"
buoyantly ushered in by *Secession*. Though she had criticized *Aesthete
1925* as an ineffectual polemical magazine conceived under "the auspices
of poverty" ("wasn't it rather a poverty of spirit to devote an entire magazine to Mr. Ernest Boyd?"), she had retained enough confidence in the
"aesthetes" to solicit the help of Cowley and Josephson for a special issue
she was preparing on the French surrealists. Despite misgivings, Cowley
helped out by translating verse by Tristan Tzara as well as an "innocuous"
article on the paintings of Joan Miró by Michel Leiris.[36]

By April 1926 Heap had decided, as she told Matthew Josephson, that
"it would be fun to publish your group and the French group against each
other," and invited Cowley to write one of his "mad outbursts" for the
issue. Cowley thought Heap's idea for a joint French-American issue "excellent," and he submitted a group of poems about his literary friends as

well as "Race between a Subway Local and a Subway Express," a fictional experiment with motion and structure in the spirit of Marinetti's futurism. As with *Aesthete 1925*, the final push to the group manifesto was given during an all-day session at the old-fashioned Broadway Central Hotel in New York. There, the one-time Aesthetes cooperated in a spirit of good fun and lively camaraderie on the issue's American section before, late in the afternoon, they resorted with their wives to jollier quarters, the Savoy Ballroom in Harlem.[37]

The 1926 spring-summer issue of the *Little Review* featured an assembly of European surrealists and former dadaists—among them René Crevel, Michel Leiris, Tzara, Arp, Delteil, Ribemont-Dessaignes, and Marcel Arland—as well as work by Joan Miró and L. Moholy-Nagy. The American section featured most of the contributors to *Aesthete 1925*, as well as work by Crane ("Voyages"), Hemingway ("Banal Story"), Charles Durboraw ("Colors of Life"), Munson, Nagle, and John Riordan, a young disciple of Williams. Conspicuously absent were Burke and Tate, though the latter had submitted his poem "Idiot" (which Cowley deemed "a tremendous and impressive piece of work") to Josephson for inclusion in the group manifestation. An editorial note by Heap set the tone of irreverent iconoclasm in which the issue was conceived and voiced a typical lament: "We are all too serious about art in America . . . we treat it as we treat the dead . . . with respect and no attempt at communication." As long as the artist was "either treated as a god or as a rather ridiculous and useless member of society," there was, Heap felt, "little hope for art in America."[38]

Not all American contributors were persuaded by Heap's claim of artistic kinship with the European surrealists. Josephson, for one, launched a caustic attack on his "anciens amis," which pointed the direction in which Cowley, too, was steadfastly, if more slowly, moving. In "A Letter to My Friends" he attacked the surrealists and one-time dadaists for their irrational and antisocial attitudes to art and life; he mocked their veneration of Freudian psychoanalysis, urged them to stop retreating into the private recesses of the self, and admonished them to face the realities of modern life: "Revolution, the race-track, the political arena, the stock market." In America, Josephson fulminated, writers could not afford to withdraw into the pursuit of "pure literature," but were forced to "live in storm-cellars or country-retreats. It is bitter to survive; it is bitter to find ears." Still, it was "a thrilling struggle" to be a writer in America: "Stealthily, to have done something well in the line of our own traditions remains a secret delight and a social crime." It seemed only a matter of time before Josephson's impatience with a culture in which art was "a secret delight" but "a social crime" would break out into political radicalism.[39] In 1926 his transitional stance was roughly consonant with Cowley's, though the latter's nascent social consciousness remained as yet publicly unarticulated.

Cowley's contribution was "Anthology," a group of portrait-poems about his literary friends. While each poem captured the nuances of a distinct style and personality, conjointly the poems stand as Cowley's study in verse of the dilemmas and ambiguities plaguing the writers of his age group in the mid 1920s. Thus, "Kenneth Burke," later renamed "The Narrow House," expresses Cowley's fear that a permanent residence in the country might, as he had told Tate, "narrow" the circle of one's experience; the poem points up the discrepancy between Burke's idyllic pastoral existence and his driven pursuit of chimerical hopes and dreams. "Matthew Josephson," later retitled "Buy 300 Steel," captures his friend's inner conflict between the earnest, moneymaking Wall Street speculator and the poet longing for a peaceful rural residence devoted to writing. "Walter S. Hankel" presents a bizarre apocalyptic vision of the destruction of Manhattan (later, retitled "The Death of Crowds," it was dedicated to the painter Peter Blume). The poem on Robert Coates evokes the wistful sadness and near-suicidal melancholy that marked the writer's life in New York; later it was renamed "The Eater of Darkness," after Coates's first novel. A satirical poem on Gorham Munson, an earlier version of which had appeared in *Broom*, mocks the rhetorical and dignified pomposity of his criticism. "The Flower in the Sea," the splendid poem on Hart Crane, forms the highlight of the group. "Malcolm Cowley" captures the sense of life as a pointless, hurried pursuit of "nothing" that had intermittently plagued its subject in New York: "Hurry / at a quarter after seven / nothing, at a quarter after eight / nothing, the aim is nothing, the pursuit / hurried. . . ." Cowley, mercifully, never reprinted the poem.[40]

Cowley's "anthology" had a comical aftermath. In March 1926 he had been invited by Eugene Jolas to contribute a selection of his poems to an anthology of modern American poetry, which Jolas hoped to publish in Paris in a French translation. When, during the summer, Jolas read Cowley's poems in the *Little Review*, he assumed it was an actual anthology and, through his wife Maria Jolas, sent Cowley questionnaires asking for biographical information on each of the seven poets, including the fictitious Walter S. Hankel. For a moment Cowley contemplated the perpetration of another Dada prank and, as he wrote Crane, "thought seriously of letting Jolas remain in ignorance, and of having us all prepare fictitious biographies to send him." In early November an enlightened Jolas admitted he had made quite a "gaffe," but voiced his admiration for Cowley's adept poetic performance: "I think you did an amazing work in the quality of your empathy." When Jolas's *Anthologie de la Nouvelle Poésie Américaine* finally appeared in Paris in 1928, it included "The Urn" and "Blue Juniata."[41]

Jolas was sufficiently impressed by Cowley's poetry to want to secure his contributions for *transition*, the new radically experimental magazine he was starting from France with Elliot Paul. In early January 1927 he and Paul sent separate invitations to Cowley to write for an early issue of *transition*: the new magazine intended, Paul explained, to present "the modern writers of America" side by side with translated work by continental European writers, and it had already secured contributions from Joyce, Stein, Anderson, Hemingway, Coates, Aragon, Jean-Richard Bloch, and Paul Eluard. When, by May 1927, the editors had not heard from Cowley—it is not unlikely he distrusted their search for a literature that was "a lyrical expression of the subconscious"—Jolas more insistently urged Cowley to "send us something to help demoralize all the literary sows both here and in America." This time Cowley complied: the January 1928 issue of *transition* featured "The Hill above the Mine," a poem about the destruction of the Pennsylvania landscape of his childhood, as well as "Race between a Subway Local and a Subway Express," a story combining a realistic rendering of Cowley's experience as a subway traveler with the futuristic demand that literature reflect the accelerating speed of a chaotic modern technological society.[42]

❮ ❮ ❮ In May 1926 Cowley undertook his most ambitious and influential translation, a rendering of *Variété* (1924), a book of essays by Paul Valéry. Cowley had secured the job with some difficulty. In December 1925 he had recommended the book for translation to Harcourt, Brace and Company, but no action was taken by the publishers. In March he more insistently urged publication, with success: at the end of April, Harrison Smith, who had been favorably impressed by Cowley's earlier renderings from the French, informed him that Harcourt, Brace was willing to have him translate *Variété* at a fee of $450. "I am delighted that you have undertaken this for us," Smith wrote; "there is no one in this country who I think can handle French as you can." An advance of one hundred dollars came in handy, on the eve of the Cowleys' removal to Sherman, and the translator started work. Then, out of the blue, the publishers received word that Valéry had personally arranged for *Variété* to be translated by Lewis Galantière, whose rendering of Jean Cocteau's *Le Grand Ecart* Cowley had favorably reviewed the year before. On May 7, 1926, Cowley learned that Harcourt, Brace had notified Galantière that an American translation had already been contracted for. Not having been consulted in the matter, Cowley immediately wrote to Valéry and Galantière, both in Paris, to explain his predicament and straighten out the situation. "How would *you* feel," he asked Galantière in an angry, yet polite, letter, "if you got a publisher to accept a book, studied for your translation, wrote part of your introduction, got an advance and spent it, planned your life on it, and then somebody else stepped in?" In a more studiously diplomatic letter to Valéry, Cowley recalled the circumstances of their first meeting in Paris— "I carried a letter of introduction from Georges Duthuit. I came from the University of Montpellier, where I had met your brother and your nephew. You talked to me about your poetry, and spoke of observing all the rules of verse as one would observe the rules of tennis"—and adduced all possible arguments to convince Valéry that his arrangement with Harcourt, Brace was in the best interest of author, publisher, and translator.[43]

Galantière gallantly withdrew as a translator (even though he had already completed nearly half of *Variété* in a first draft) and promised to assure Valéry of Cowley's equal competence: he wished Cowley "good luck" with the book, which, he granted, was "a wonderful nut to crack." But Valéry was stubborn. He resented the "cavalier fashion" in which he had been treated by Harcourt, Brace—they had informed him of their decision to go ahead with Cowley as a translator and had seemed reluctant to submit the manuscript of the translation to him for review—and threatened to stick to Galantière, even though the latter had relinquished all claims to the work. It needed all of Galantière's tactful diplomacy to get Valéry to agree to a workable compromise, by which Cowley would do the authorized translation and Galantière review the manuscript in Valéry's name.[44]

Cowley spent most of the summer of 1926 "slaving over Valéry," as he put it to Hart Crane. On September 1 he reported the completion of the manuscript to Burke, and shortly after sent his translation to Galantière in Paris. "Get down on your knees and lift your voice to Heaven, saying: O Lord, I thank Thee that I didn't go ahead with that translation," he commented. If the Delteil had seemed difficult, *Variété* was "the toughest piece of work that one could hope to find." Cowley had spent a disproportionate amount of time and energy on the job and, though he granted that *Variété* was "a tremendously fine book" ("the more time I spent with it, the more I admired it"), he was "far from satisfied" with his English rendering, *Variety*. Setting aside his pride—"ordinarily I'd be furious to think that some one else was going over one of my translations"—he urged Galantière to critically review his manuscript ("It takes something of a collaboration to render Valéry in English"), sending along a list of "doubtful" passages and explaining that in places he had "departed pretty far from the original," but always "to obtain greater clarity." A literal translation of the many "shortcuts and elliptical expressions" would make Valéry only more difficult than he already was in the original, he reasoned. He asked Galantière to make but a sparing use of the "unlimited opportunity for change" offered by any translation but emphasized that he was "more anxious that the manuscript should be correct than that it should preserve my own precious individuality of style." He concluded by pointing up the conscientious and disinterested effort made by all involved: "I hope that Valéry has ceased to think that he's being treated cavalierly. We're all trying to do the best possible work with the English version. And nobody's making a profit out of it. . . . We're all acting out of respect for a magnificent volume of essays."[45]

In mid-October 1926 Cowley completed an introductory essay on Paul Valéry that revealed why, as he had told Marianne Moore, he considered the essays in *Variété* so "extremely important." Through Allen Tate he submitted his introduction to Mark Van Doren at the *Nation*. When Van Doren reluctantly rejected the essay (he had already contracted for an article on Valéry by the French critic René Lalou), Cowley sent it on to Edmund Wilson, who promptly accepted it for the *New Republic*—he had recently been made an editor—and offered to publish some of Valéry's essays translated by Cowley, notably "The Intellectual Crisis."[46]

Cowley's "Toward a Universal Man" appeared in the *New Republic* on December 8, 1926. One of his crucial early essays, it brought into focus many of his fundamental critical concerns of the time. Like André Gide, Paul Valéry helped to resolve many of his ambiguities about specific tendencies of literary modernism and, by precept and example, presented a solution to a personal problem that had haunted him for years: the episodic and fragmentary nature of his literary endeavors, and the disturbing lack of focus and direction in his literary life. For all Cowley's current interest in romanticism, Valéry appealed to his deepest classical and intellectual instincts. In addition, he gave intellectual and philosophical sanction to Cowley's own loose bundle of aesthetic beliefs.

In his essay Cowley presented Valéry as the "constructionist" par excellence, a type of artist whose poems "exist independently" of his person and are "not necessarily an expression of himself"; Valéry wrote poems, as he had told Cowley in 1923, as "a laboratory experiment in thought." With a splendid disdain worthy of Rimbaud or Aragon, he had abandoned a prospectively brilliant career as a young symbolist poet of the circle of Mallarmé and Gide, and for twenty years had stopped writing for publication to devote himself to a more essential aim: the search for "a fundamental attitude underlying all the operations of the mind." For Valéry, one of the fathers of "pure poetry," literature had ceased to be "an end in itself" and become "simply a form of mental exercise." The essays in Variété, likewise, were intellectual exercises of an "instrumental mind" of exquisite and mathematical precision. What was remarkable, Cowley felt, was that none of the essays dealt with themes of the author's choosing but that all subjects were assigned; yet in each case Valéry admirably managed to recover "the natural direction of his thought," thus preserving its "essential unity." Here, indeed, lay the possibility of an intellectual methodology that promised to put an end to Cowley's feeling that his life and writings lacked coherence and direction:

> Valéry is not alone in possessing an "instrumental" mind. In our stage of civilization we find numbers of men who can solve any problem set them, but cannot set themselves problems. They lack direction. Independence they also lack, since their careers are determined by outside influences—the books they are asked to write, the formulae they are asked to discover, the portraits they are asked to paint, the trades to which they are apprenticed. If the objects set them are unworthy, their minds deteriorate, and in a period of idleness, will rust as quickly as a piece of complicated machinery left standing in the rain. . . . But Valéry alone has discovered a solution: that is, by making the instrumentality of his mind an end in itself, by seeking continually to develop and protect it, he has recovered his independence.[47]

Writing to Burke, Cowley revealed how strongly pertinent to his own life and career was this notion of "the Instrumental Mind." He himself, he believed, possessed "an instrumental mind . . . of excellent quality." There were moments when his mind seemed capable of independently engendering ideas, but he feared that he often lacked "the gift of spinning these moments into days or months." As he correctly sensed, his mind was not of the type of Burke's, one capable of building a self-conceived framework of synthetic thought. The trouble with such an instrumental mind as his own, Cowley confessed, was that its quality was "determined by the objects given it; a poor object, such as my articles for *Charm*, will blunt the tool." For one who conceived of "the good life" as "one in which all one's powers are exercised to the most dangerous degree," the example of Paul Valéry took off the sharp edges of the much lamented frustrations of a book reviewer's life. After all, Cowley, too, had often written on subjects not of his own volition, and in each specific instance had struggled to transform his assignment into a consideration of his central preoccupations. Valéry, in effect, endowed Cowley's own admittedly diffuse and fragmentary efforts in criticism with a new intellectual and moral respectability. As he reminded himself in his notebook two years later: "Valéry has been more than a literary training to you; he has given you a methodology, which you are trying to apply in your own life; he has been a guide to conduct."[48]

Beyond resolving the personal literary ethics of Malcolm Cowley, Valéry loomed as a quintessential force in modernism, one whose intellectualism was profoundly appealing to Cowley in the 1920s. Everything in Valéry, he noted with approval, was "directed toward a defense of the intellect, of the conscious mind." As such his essays marked a necessary antidote to all those forces in contemporary culture which, conjointly, represented "a pretty general attack on the freedom of the intellect." The conscious human intelligence, Cowley explained,

> has need of defenders in our time. Against Freudianism. . . . Against the Superrealists. Against that school of writers led by Anderson and Lawrence which counsels drift and surrender to our instincts. Against the metaphysics of Behaviorism. Against the sociological theory of art. . . . Against determinisms in general. Against Spengler's idea that, ours being a declining civilization, we have nothing left but to sail ships and make ourselves millionaires. . . .
>
> But among all the enemies of conscious thought, it is specialization which is the most paralyzing. It leads to the belief that a real gulf exists between the different activities of the mind; as, for example, between

the arts and the sciences . . . a specialization, any specialization, becomes a fixed idea, which is a form of hypnosis.

Here lay the cornerstone to the thought of Valéry, and to Cowley's aesthetics in the 1920s; here, also, lay the possibility of "an ideal to be pursued by our own generation." That ideal was represented by Leonardo da Vinci, the "universal man" of the Renaissance, whose methodology, in the words of Valéry, was rooted in a pursuit of "the central attitude from which all the enterprises of learning or science and all the operations of art are equally possible, and a successful cooperation between analysis and action is singularly probable." Yearning for the possibility of intellectual synthesis in an age of fragmentation and specialization, Cowley hoped "a new Leonardo" would arise "to include the whole field of intellectual activity in his scope."[49]

Critical interest in Paul Valéry was at its height in the mid 1920s,[50] and when Cowley's translation of *Variété* appeared in March 1927, it could count on receiving wide and serious attention. "*Variety* is off to more than a fair start," Harrison Smith reported to Cowley; "The critics show every sign of being wildly enthusiastic about it." Carl Van Doren told Smith that *Variety* was "one of the best books published by anybody this year" and went about reading parts of it out loud. Christopher Morley sent "a most enthusiastic and lyrical outburst" to the publishers and spoke highly of Cowley's translation. Harry Hansen devoted an entire column to the book in the *New York World*. "I think that it really will cause the critical stir that we hoped it might," Smith exulted, "and it will certainly go down to our credit and to yours."[51]

The publishers' enthusiasm was borne out by the critical response. Eugene Jolas wrote Cowley from France, complimenting him on a "superb" translation: "You are the only American I know whose translation and interpretation of the modern French writers is congenial." Most American reviewers had similar words of praise for Cowley's "excellent" rendering of Valéry's difficult French into lucid English and took *Variety* as a seminal book in modernist literature. Matthew Josephson and Lewis Galantière, both critics with an expert knowledge of French writing, transformed their reviews into personal essays on the significance of Valéry, thereby acknowledging the invaluable service of Cowley's rendition to contemporary letters. Both pointed up Valéry's continuation in "the classical tradition of Racine" and emphasized the relevance of his efforts at intellectual unification in "the age of the quantum theory and relativity." Clifton Fadiman, too, granted that in *Variety* Valéry addressed "the most important contemporary critical problem: that of analyzing the exact extent and seriousness of the dissolution we see around us." Valéry's "brilliant war" on behalf of the intellect, he agreed with Cowley, was "a tonic antidote for current literary and philosophical romanticism." The young Thornton Wilder, whose novels *The Cabala* and *The Bridge of San Luis Rey* had been received enthusiastically by Cowley, described Valéry's primary objective as a poetic "reintegration of the Symbolist aims into the classic tradition," but, in a manner that anticipated Cowley's strictures against Valéry in *Exile's Return*, took him to task for pushing the French genius for logic and clarity to extremes: "Here the play of ideas has charm and weight and even excitement, but the mind remains an instrument and not a force; everywhere there is light without warmth. The book remains a monument to the pride of intellect." Alyse Gregory of the *Dial* was the only critic who publicly questioned the "punctiliousness" of Cowley's translation in specific instances. Though Cowley was aware that he had opened himself up to such charges by translating freely, he had done so in an effort to attain lucidity where Valéry remained obscure. In response to Gregory's critique Cowley sent an indignant letter to Marianne Moore, protesting the "demonstrable injustice" of several of Gregory's criticisms, granting the legitimacy of others, but toning down his anger by praising her review as "a superb piece of writing, and probably the most intelligent comment which *Variety* has received in this country . . . one is always grateful for good writing in a desert of commonplaces."[52] Cowley's curiously double response to Alyse Gregory's review was symptomatic of his steadily deteriorating relations with the editors of the *Dial*, in particular Marianne Moore. He still made diplomatic efforts to remain on good terms with a magazine he valued highly, but frictions would soon come to a head.

At intermittent periods during his long career Cowley returned to Valéry and resumed his struggle with the latter's "cold, glittering intellect." In 1928 he translated four of Valéry's essays—"My Work and I," "Pure Poetry," "The Future of Literature," and "The Question of Europe"—published in March and April of that year in Irita Van Doren's *Herald Tribune Books*, their first appearance in English. Once again, the essays drew wide attention. Lewis Galantière, unaware that Cowley had translated the essays, wrote an open letter to the editor of *Books* ranking the anonymous translator with Scott Moncrieff as one of the best in the field. Clifton Fadiman expressed his personal admiration for Cowley's "beautiful rendering" of the essays and, on behalf of the publishers Simon and Schuster, invited him to undertake a French novel. Edmund Wilson, about to embark on *Axel's Castle*, remembered Cowley's rendering of the essays and asked to borrow the originals for his chapter on Valéry. Cowley himself devoted a section to Valéry when he came to write *his* study of the symbolist religion of art in *Exile's Return*, in which he strongly qualified his earlier endorsement. Thirty years after *Variety* Cowley was invited to translate Valéry's essays on Leonardo, Poe, and Mallarmé for the standard English edition of the *Collected Works of Paul Valéry* (1972). A slow but perfectionist worker, Cowley struggled with the "fantastically" difficult job during much of the late 1950s and early 1960s; several of his renditions appeared in the *New Republic* and the *Kenyon Review*. In 1969 Cowley wrote a last essay on Valéry for Louis Kronenberger's *Atlantic Brief Lives* (1971), which formed a testimony to the persistent fascination of Valéry's disciplined and luminous intellect for Cowley: "I translated a book of [Valéry's] essays in 1926, then retranslated some of them along with others in 1958, so that I have lived with them for more than forty years. Sometimes on rereading them I find myself still puzzled by a passage in which I know perfectly what every word should mean. Sometimes I am shocked again by an opinion, for this author dislikes everything that is copied from life or that rises from the subconscious. Always I am held by the exact but graceful language, the breadth of vision, and the interplay of well-meditated ideas. Valéry did create a music of ideas, and the best of his essays—which are also the best of our time—are as soundly constructed as a Beethoven sonata." [53]

As late as 1970 Cowley singled out Valéry as "the strongest influence on my prose work." That influence, however, resided less in the substance of Valéry's thought (about which he later repeatedly expressed reservations) than in its methodology, and in the quality of his prose. In part Cowley was deeply attracted to Valéry because he possessed a type of mind radically unlike his own, a mind that, in its perennial search for underlying principles of unity and synthesis, resembled rather his friend Burke's. Valéry's aesthetics, too, correlated to a surprising degree with those of Burke; both, for example, shared a fascination with the *process* of literary creation rather than the finished product; Valéry's notion of "the poet of the hypothesis" seemed to tie in with Burke's "perpetual grailism," while Burke's idea of "perspective by incongruity" seemed foreshadowed in Valéry's observation that "nine times out of ten, every great improvement in a field of activity is obtained by the introduction of alien and unexpected methods and notions." In the course of their friendship Cowley recurrently urged Burke to read Valéry, intuitively sensing their intellectual and methodological kinship, but Burke remained remarkably silent on Valéry throughout his voluminous writings.[54]

‹ ‹ ‹   In 1926 Valéry might loom as "the saint of all hack writers, the exemplar of the dream that they can do works of genius to order," but his example could not preclude Cowley's intermittent periods of discouragement. In the very letter to Burke in which he had advanced the consoling notion of the "Instrumental Mind," Cowley bemoaned his present lack of accomplishment: "To take stock. Twenty-eight, good biceps, bad constitution, nothing accomplished. Or seemingly nothing accomplished. What frightens me is that I have no margin. Having finished one poem or one essay, I have no plans for another; I am a perfect vacuum, like a man after copulation who is very doubtful whether he will ever be able to copulate again." For the moment, not even the company of literary friends could rekindle confidence. "Slowly our friends assume their wooden functions," he wrote Burke in the summer of 1926. The annual Fourth of July party on Tory Hill was "rather less drunken and less successful" than that of the year before. Slater Brown was immersed in writing the novel that became *The Burning Wheel* (1942), Susan Jenkins Brown was in ill health, Hart Crane was on the Isle of Pines composing parts of *The Bridge* (at the end of July he sent Cowley the section "Cutty Sark"), and Caroline Gordon and Allen Tate more than ever gave Cowley the impression of "babes in the wood, unable to cope with the complexities of modern life."[55]

Over the autumn months of 1926 Cowley critically reviewed the bulk of his varied writings to see if he could collect or rework them into one or more publishable books. In November he drew up a list of six projected volumes in his notebook: "1. Traders in Darkness; 2. Charles Baudelaire; 3. A volume of Poems—Blue Juniata; 4. A volume of serious essays; 5. A volume of portraits; 6. A novel."[56] For all his complaints, Cowley was seething with plans and projects. And for all his persistent fear of the compromise of success, he in effect deeply desired the sense of accomplishment that could come with the publication of a book. Publishers seemed willing enough, but a combination of stubborn skepticism and lack of disciplined endeavor prevented Cowley from bringing his plans to fruition.

For the time being his ambitions continued to outrun his achievements, and magazine publication remained the only outlet for his writings.

The poetry reviews Cowley wrote between 1925 and 1927 revealed his continuing struggle to accommodate his classicist predilections with a growing appreciation of the current and historical manifestations of romanticism. Increasingly he understood the latter as an inextricable component of the modern spirit. Increasingly, also, he saw that neither classicism nor romanticism was an ideal to be pursued exclusively, but that either might lead to unacceptable extremes. Simultaneously, he continued to seek ways of engrafting a classicist concern with formal elegance and control upon a modern sensibility essentially romantic;[57] after all, even his personal campaign against contemporary extremes of romanticism had been infused with a romantic moral fervor.

In the late 1920s Cowley's interest in romanticism led him to explore its historical origins through considerations of such precursors of contemporary romanticism as Baudelaire, Poe, Shelley, and Théophile Gautier. Gautier, one of the originators of the *l'art pour l'art* school in French letters, formed the subject of "The Art of Visible Things," a review published in the March 1927 *Dial* that contained the germ of Cowley's analysis of the "religion" of art (as he here called it for the first time) in *Exile's Return*. Cowley argued that Gautier's attitude to art was "still a living force" and that there were "features of modern literature and literary theory" that could not be understood "without reference to his work." Mindful of the circumstances under which *Broom* had been suppressed, he used Gautier as the occasion for a plea against the dissociation of art and morality: every time a book fell victim to censorship, he wrote, "art for art's sake comes forward, in its revised and strictly modern form, to state that no harm was intended, that morality still reigns unchallenged, that the book in question, being a work of art, could have no possible effect on what people think or do. . . . But Plato, when he banished poets from his commonwealth as being dangerous to the established order, was paying them a less ambiguous compliment."[58]

Almost a year later he took a more outspoken stand on the subject, one not entirely consistent with his contention that Gautier's beliefs were a continuing influence, but indicative of his increasing hostility to such a pure aesthetics. "Among the ten million casualties of the war, less bitterly mourned than the others but less quickly forgotten, was the doctrine of art

for art's sake," he observed; today it was "only a ghost speaking in echoes."
In its place Cowley welcomed the refreshing "new voices" of European
writers like Franz Werfel, who were "unconscious of the boundaries between art and morality which once were drawn with such confidence,"
and with obvious relish noted that "the faded garlands of Walter Pater are
gathering dust on the wall." [59] By fits and starts, without as yet a great deal
of consistency or systematic effort, Cowley's thought was evolving toward
the thesis he developed in *Exile's Return*.

In the summer of 1927 Cowley again took up in the *Dial* the question
of classicism and romanticism. At the end of June, Kenneth Burke, back
on the editorial board of the magazine, asked him to do a long review of
an anthology of Chinese and Japanese poetry, a subject that he knew held
Cowley's interest. Soliciting the review, Burke criticized, albeit tongue in
cheek, what he viewed with increasing misgivings as Cowley's critical impressionism, his inclination to judge a book on the basis of his literary taste
and intuitions rather than by a priori formulations of general critical principles and assumptions: the anthology, Burke prodded wittily, "seems like
a fair opportunity for summing up on western Asiaticism, Schopenhauer,
Spengler, Benda, *Masses*, Amy Lowell and *The Quill*. Or has the 'I like'
triumphed?" [60]

"The Golden House" took its title from *Fir-Flower Tablets*, the collection of Chinese verse that only five years before had delighted Cowley as
the epitome of classical elegance. This time he arrived at a different estimate. Explaining the special appeal of Oriental poetry to modern writers as
a reaction against a standardized culture ridden by the tiring complexities
of science, business, and technology, Cowley remained deeply appreciative of the elegant serenity and imagistic concreteness of Chinese poetry,
but was now much more aware of its limited range of subjects and its correspondent "poverty of emotions." Where, he wondered, were the poems
on love and death, "the two great subjects of our lyric verse," where the
sense of epic "struggle"? Chinese poetry expressed "neither the sense of sin
nor the sense of the infinite; neither the romantic revolt against society nor
a romantic exultation in the terrors of nature." Above all, what was lacking
was "that search for the *new* which is the underlying motive of so great a
part of modern poetry." Clearly, what Cowley missed in Chinese verse was
precisely the whole range of themes and emotions that of late had propelled
him toward romanticism. In the *Dial* he concluded on a cautiously non-
committal note: "if Baudelaire is one of our favourite poets (or Rimbaud,

Shelley, Byron, Coleridge, Poe)—then we are likely to encounter Chinese poetry with tempered admiration. On the other hand, if we are attracted by the classical qualities of definiteness, harmony and restraint, we are apt to value it more highly . . . and to exult in the popularity of T'ang poets as evidence that the Augustan qualities are once more returning to favour."[61]

Ever since his adventures among the European avant-garde writers Cowley had been struggling to find a common denominator to the seemingly contradictory manifestations of literary modernism. In 1923 he had posited its "intellectualism" as a unifying principle, but three years later had come to feel the need to modify and subtilize his earlier conclusions. In the spring of 1926, prompted by his recent consideration of an anthology of modern French poetry in the *Herald Tribune Books*, he began a more in-depth examination of the influence of French modernism on contemporary American poetry. After a mortifying publication history involving rejections by the *New Republic* and the *Dial*, the essay appeared, with much delay and some damage to the topicality of its interest, in the *Saturday Review of Literature* for May 7, 1927.[62]

"French Poetry and the New Spirit" was Cowley's most elaborate effort to date to come to a broadly inclusive definition of modernism. It aimed to look beyond individual and often paradoxical manifestations to the essential "spirit" of modernity. The "modern," Cowley argued, was not primarily a question of poetic technique or the search for a new idiom. Nor did modernism primarily define itself in terms of "a new mechanism of thought" in which "logic" was replaced by "associationalism." The one fundamental characteristic unifying all modern French poets, Cowley advanced, was "a state of mind, a certain moral attitude towards letters and the world. . . . The race of poets, who began by slowly purging their aesthetics of every moral element, have ended by developing aesthetics into a new moral code, which they applied first to letters, then to the literary life, and finally to life in general. . . . The moral principle which underlies the modern spirit is a belief in the viciousness of formulae; in the inherent virtue of search and discovery."

Cowley located the essence of modernism in the moral and aesthetic imperative he had first discovered in a cherished line of Baudelaire's poem "Le Voyage"—"Au fond de l'Inconnu pour trouver du *nouveau!*" It was Baudelaire's "desperate descent" into the frightful maelstrom of the "unknown," in order to discover what was *new*, which had first signaled the modernist "morality of search." In art it had led to a conception of poetry as no longer "a vale of refuge" but "a chain of mountains to be climbed, a dangerous archipelago to be explored"; carried over into life, it had led to "acts and theories of violence." Here, Cowley found, lay the common impulse behind such apparently disparate acts of the mind as Rimbaud's abandonment of poetry to smuggle rifles into Abyssinia, Georges Sorel's *Réflexions sur la violence* (1908; *Reflections on Violence*), Paul Valéry's detached pursuit of pure or abstract consciousness, and Tristan Tzara's cheerfully nihilistic *Sept Manifestes Dada* (1924; *Seven Dada Manifestoes*). Simultaneously, it helped to explain such sharply divergent phenomena as the recent revival of neo-Catholicism and the embracing of bolshevism by surrealists and onetime dadaists. Once the principle had been discovered, the applications, both in art and life, seemed endless, and the effect of literature on human conduct unquestionable. Cowley's claim that the modernist French writers had "begun perceptibly to influence our own literature" was not substantiated in his essay, but had been amply borne out by his earlier considerations of American modernists: Baudelaire's imperative, after all, lay equally behind Eliot's consistent urge to move into new territories of form and the imagination, and behind Burke's "perpetual grailism." Later, Cowley discovered the same impulse in Crane's frenzied derangement of the senses and in Aiken's "religion of consciousness."[63]

In November 1926, months before his essay appeared in print, Cowley sent a copy to Allen Tate, who had meanwhile exchanged his domicile at Addie Turner's for a janitor's existence in a basement apartment in Greenwich Village. Tate's response was bracing: "Your essay is excellent, the best statement on the subject I've seen," he wrote to Cowley in Sherman. He took issue, however, with what he misread as "the main idea of the essay— the technical definition of modernism, where you distinguish between the logical procedure of traditional poetry and the associational methods of modernism." Modernism, Tate countered, arose from "the application of the historico-scientific method to the past" and was "simply the temporary, or permanent, chaos" following the exposure of the relativity of tradition. As a result, in modern poetry the focus had shifted to the personal "vision" of the poet and themes had become "casual, arbitrary and invented." Modernism, Tate argued, was marked by an essential "discrepancy between vision and subject" and he proposed "subjectivism" as a better phrase than Cowley's associationalism. What especially disturbed Tate was that, as a result of the failure of early nineteenth-century romanticism to stem "the tide of the scientific spirit," the expected restoration of classical order and balance had failed to come about and that, instead, there had appeared "a still more violent Romanticism in the Symbolists."[64]

In reply, Cowley pointed out that the heart of his essay lay, not in associationalism, but in an attempt to define the "moral attitude towards letters and the world" underlying modernism. His response to Tate revealed how strongly indebted Cowley remained to the literary ethics he had imbibed from Louis Aragon (all he had done, he claimed, was "to state the theory which is implicit in all the criticisms I've heard Louis Aragon making"). It also testified to the influence of Valéry, and showed a growing impatience with the moral conservatism of Eliot. "Remember that I'm talking about French poetry. In poets like Stevens or Eliot the moral attitude is different or lacking. Eliot impresses a French modernist as being pathetic or old-fashioned. Valéry, however, belongs to the modern spirit. . . . Valéry is accepted as a modern largely because of the fashion in which he abandoned literature, then returned to it merely as an exercise. He is accepted because of his moral attitude." Cowley granted that Tate's "vision-subject theory" had the advantages of greater subtlety and exactitude, but the distinction, he felt, hardly applied to the literary history of the last hundred years: not only did it seem impossible to "subtract the subject from most of the romantic poets," but cherished poems like Byron's "Don Juan," Shelley's "Ode to the West Wind," or Baudelaire's "Femmes Damnées," exemplified a perfect integration of subject and vision. Nor was there, as Valéry had taught him, "any radical difference between the scientific spirit at its best and the spirit of poetry. Monks of art and monks of the laboratory—both are discoverers." Tate's definition of classicism as "the state in which poetry most closely meets the spiritual structure of society," however, seemed "excellent."[65]

Cowley's response to Tate showed how much his effort to find a common denominator of modernism correlated with his personal desire to unify the disparate elements in his own life and writings. His exchange of letters with Tate contained the germs of their future divergence (Tate moving toward a reactionary traditionalism, Cowley toward a radical politics) but it also indicates how closely, for the time being, Tate and he were moving along parallel literary tracks, each trying to come to terms in his own way and against the background of his own needs with the crucial literary and intellectual issues of the time: the conflicting claims of science and poetry, classicism and romanticism, aesthetics and morality, the subconscious and the conscious mind. During the 1920s, notwithstanding their temperamental and intellectual differences, Cowley and Tate were engaged in a united literary endeavor; they felt that at heart they shared the same literary values and beliefs, and this feeling proved a cementing force of friendship strong enough to survive the polarizing political storms and enmities of the next decade.

‹ ‹ ‹   By 1926 Cowley was gaining wider recognition as one of the most promising "modern" poets of the young generation. Early that year William Carlos Williams had asked him to send several of his poems—"such especially which seem to you tentative toward new forms"—for inclusion in a *Contact* collection of modern verse he was helping to put together. Cowley had submitted two groups of poems (subsequently published as "Anthology" and "Leonora") as representative of "the sort of work I'm doing now" and had commented: "I'm more interested in new forms of thought than new forms of verse. By new forms of thought I don't mean new ideas, but new ways of connecting ideas or impressions. Or images." [66]

There were other signs of recognition, not all of them welcome. William Stanley Braithwaite, the popular anthologist, invited Cowley to be represented in his *Anthology of Magazine Verse for 1926* and solicited biographical information to be included in *Who's Who in American Poetry, 1912–1926*. Inclusion in the volume was made contingent upon each poet's willingness to put in an advance order, at three dollars, for at least one copy of the anthology. In an acerbic letter to the editors of the *Herald Tribune Books* Cowley expounded his motives for not complying with Braithwaite's request: "There is something about the whole proposition which shows the low estate of contemporary verse." He declined to be included in Braithwaite's *Who's Who*, since it was bound to be "confused with a sucker list." [67]

A more respectable venture was being prepared by Edmund Wilson and Allen Tate. In December 1925 Wilson had written to Tate that there was "quite a good deal of American poetry which ought to be published" and had singled out Cowley, Tate, and Phelps Putnam as eligible poets, followed by Crane, Rolfe Humphries, Laura Riding, John Peale Bishop, and himself. He had urged Tate to help him launch a new series of poets and considered approaching Boni & Liveright. Tate was enthusiastic about the venture, which promised to lead to the publication of "a good deal of fine poetry which, under the Untermeyer dictatorship, had little chance to appear," as he told Donald Davidson. He promptly invited Cowley, who two years earlier had proposed a similar plan to Wheelwright. At the end of February 1926 Wilson reported that he had met with "absolutely no success" with the publishers, who seemed reluctant to bring out a series of which there was "no chance of a large sale." Wilson and Tate, however, were persistent and in May 1927, having found a new prospective publisher, Tate wrote to Cowley: "The poetry series comes nearer and nearer. . . . You are down, so far, for the first splash. Can you let me have the ms.? Red tape requires that it pass on to Wilson and [Mark] Van Doren, but Wilson and I are already for you; so the rest is courtesy." For reasons that remain unexplained, "the rest" was never done and the planned series of poets never launched. The need for it was obviated shortly afterward, when several of the poets initially proposed for the series published their first books of verse: Laura Riding and Hart Crane in 1926, Phelps Putnam in 1927, and Allen Tate in 1928.[68]

Cowley's book lagged behind but was gradually taking shape. In April 1926 he had submitted a group of seven Pennsylvania poems to Harriet Monroe for ensemble publication in *Poetry*. Monroe had printed groups of his poems twice before—once in November 1919, once in February 1923—and to much effect; on the latter occasion Cowley's appearance in *Poetry* had elicited an invitation from London magazine editor Harold Monro to contribute to the *Chapbook*, yielded an "Honorable Mention" from *Poetry* itself, and led to his election to the Poetry Society of America. Publication in *Poetry* ensured a high degree of visibility and Cowley, accordingly, was "tickled to death" when Monroe accepted his new batch and agreed to print them as a group, as he had emphatically requested: "in the case of long-winded, unemphatic, unfigured work like mine . . . several poems together are required to create an atmosphere, to cause a state of mind." The following spring, he added, he hoped to bring out a book, and a group appearance in *Poetry* would be "the very best introduction to that book, the best assistance to its publication." He suggested that the group of poems in *Poetry* carry the title of the prospective book, "Blue Juniata."[69]

"Blue Juniata"—comprising "Bones of a House," "Chestnut Ridge," "Laurel Mountain," "Empty Barn, Dead Farm," "Bill George," "The Urn," and "The Streets of Air"—appeared in *Poetry* in November 1926. Conjointly, they formed the heart of the first section of the 1929 book and set the tone of wistful sadness that was to mark the entire volume.

They stood as a poetic tribute to a macabre, death-haunted landscape of youth, sprinkled with empty, abandoned farms as symbolic reminders of a vanished past:

> Farmhouses curl like horns of plenty, hide
> lean paintless shanks against a barn, or crouch
> empty in the shadow of a mountain. Here
> there is no house at all—
>
> only the bones of a house,
> lilacs growing beside them,
> roses in clumps between them,
> honeysuckle over;
> a door, a crooked chimney,
> mud-chinked, a yawning fireplace,
> the skeleton of a pine;
>
> a railroad thirty yards from the empty door.

The sole inhabitants of this lost country are the last survivors of a life-style receding into history: dying old farmers like Bill George, Simon Eliot, or the nameless father in "Laurel Mountain," accidentally killed by the slipping axe of one of his sons and buried with improvised ceremony in the rain-drenched, almost pantheistic hemlock woods.

> The rain
>
> beat steadily on our shoulders hunched in prayer
> against a tall God like a hemlock tree,
> his arms like crooked branches, his head bare,
> his voice a cold rain dripping in the moss,
> and hemlock needles tangled in his hair.

Severed from a landscape once rich and fertile, the poet now can hear only "rumors of home" and finds his imagination teeming with images of emptiness and drought, as he evokes in poem upon poem an emotional wasteland where no spiritual salvation is forthcoming and man becomes "an empty sacrificial vessel waiting / without patience to be filled with God."[70]

Over the years Cowley continued to use more or less traditional poetic forms, such as blank verse or the sonnet, but in many of his poems (and a few of his prose sketches) he revealed himself as a more unambiguously "modernist" writer than in his criticism and his letters, where he recurrently expressed his skepticism about certain features of modernism. Thus, for all his distrust of the subconscious, early poems like "Nocturnal Landscape" (retitled "The Cast-Iron Panthers") or "Into That Rarer Ether" (retitled "Sunrise over the Heiterwand") exemplified precisely the "associationalism" he had posited as one of the manifestations of the modern spirit. For all his continuing skepticism, in his critical writings and his acts of literary rebellion Cowley also recurrently displayed a defiant exuberance that rather easily accommodated an appreciation of the technical experiments and formal novelties of modernist writing. Yet what often seemed lacking was an understanding of the mood of spiritual despair and cultural disaster underlying modernism. Embracing Dada, Cowley borrowed its rebellious stance and moral fervor but, like Josephson, intuitively sidestepped its nihilistic despair. Admiring T. S. Eliot's technical poetic innovations, he was brashly impatient with the older poet's upholding of the superior, fertile past over a barren present, and "instinctively" rejected the sense of contemporary history as "an immense panorama of futility and anarchy," as Eliot had put it in his review of *Ulysses* for the *Dial*. He translated Valéry's "La Crise de l'Esprit" ("The Intellectual Crisis") but seemed unable to accept Valéry's doom-ridden perception of the mortality of modern civilizations. Nor did he have much patience with the apocalyptic prophecies of Oswald Spengler, which he experienced as false to his sense of the present.[71] In his poetry, however, Cowley often, as in the sequence "Blue Juniata," exemplified a personal and symbolic vision of spiritual bleakness and emotional drought, a poetics of loss and alienation from the nourishing roots of his childhood country, which marked him out as a quintessentially modernist poet, in sensibility as well as in technique.

With sixteen of his poems published, 1926 was a good year; only 1923 had witnessed the appearance of a larger number. During 1927, fewer poems reached print, though at least one of them belongs with Cowley's finest. In September 1927, the *Dial* published "Leander." The poem, written in the early spring of 1926, elicited an enthusiastic response from friends. Both Tate and Brown considered it one of Cowley's best poems to date. Tate felt it displayed "a fine harmoniously functioning structural rhythm throughout," while Brown praised its lack of "self-conscious virtuosity" (a feature that he felt marred some of Cowley's other poems). He detected the influence of Marlowe, but felt Cowley had finally struck his "real idiom." Tate, uncannily, heard echoes of Hart Crane, especially in its concluding line. Wheelwright belatedly thought the poem possessed a music "finer than anything Poe wrote except 'To Helen.'" "Leander" carried an epigraph from Rimbaud ("*Un noyé pensif parfois descend*") and re-created the classical myth of the man who nightly swam the Hellespont to his beloved Hero but drowned one night when Hero's guiding lamp was blown out. Not only did the poem's diction, rhythm, and nautical motif recall Crane's denser and more complex verse but its apostrophe in retrospect seems eerily prophetic of Crane's death at sea in 1932:

> Regal and tired, O corpse that mapped the countries
> of ocean, saw pelagic meadows where
> the sea-cow grazes, traveller who skirts
> the unicellular gardens of the foam—
>
> southward you drift, where archipelagoes
> of stars deflect the current, and waters boil
> with Lava, through indefinite Marquesas,
> spinning in the typhoon, and off Cape Stiff
> in westerly gales your eyes commemorate,
> still tropical, the wax and wane of moons.
> Time is a secret frozen in your smile.[72]

‹ ‹ ‹   The Cowleys spent the winter months of 1927 in New York. In February Cowley was hospitalized for several weeks in Pittsburgh, having to undergo "a not very dangerous operation" to remove a tumor on the bladder. On February 18, from the Wallace Building, he told Marianne Moore of the success of his operation, and of his discharge from the hospital. Four days later, prodded by the environs of his adolescence, he dashed off an indignant letter to Burke signaling what he took to be another crisis in their friendship. Though both men had continued to meet regularly in New York, their correspondence had conspicuously fallen off since Cowley had moved to Staten Island in the spring of 1925 to embark on a free-lancing life. Burke, meanwhile, had seemed to withdraw more and more into a life devoted to aesthetic contemplation and the writing of the essays that became *Counter-Statement* (1931). He had followed with bemused contempt the sort of compromises Cowley was permitting himself to make and had periodically reminded his friend of the higher duties of a disinterested pursuit of letters. He himself had refrained from participating in the 1926 group manifestation in the *Little Review* and allowed his correspondence with Cowley to become perfunctory, despite the fact that the latter, as he now pointed out in anger, had periodically "staked out a portion of [his] Soul" to his friend without receiving much of a reply. Cowley confessed himself "incapable of preserving an indifferent neutrality" in the face of Burke's silence: "By the simple process of not writing and not talking, we have got ourselves into a situation where we have our choice of talking it out or fighting it out." The "vague dissatisfaction" of their present relations was "worse than hostility," he wrote: each of his efforts to reestablish epistolary contact had run up against Burke's "indifference" or, worse, his "sense of duty," so that Cowley now felt "replaced by Friendship or Loyalty in the abstract." This time Burke responded promptly; his silence, he explained, was not to be attributed to indifference but to his present state of intellectual crisis—"I am battling like a fiend, battling for nothing less than my mind itself"—which had made him slink away from "the complications of friendship." With a good deal of implicit criticism, however, he also notified Cowley that for him any future relationships could only be rooted in a serious and uncompromising pursuit of intellectual matters: "I feel certain that there can henceforth be no decent contact between any of us, except on the basis of research and study. The psychology of the free lance has given us a society of dogs." [73]

Burke's letter hit hard. With the exception of letters pertaining to *Dial* reviews, both friends relapsed into epistolary silence. In the late summer of 1927 they went on a long hiking trip together, during which Burke promised to "lay it all out" to Cowley, but their correspondence was not restored to anything resembling its former footing until the summer of 1928, when there was talk of repeating the sort of walk they had undertaken the year before. At the occasion Burke explained how, for him, a friend was "none other than that person whom one treats with all the shabbiness and dilatoriness that he scrupulously rules out of his business relationships," and Cowley, in a spirit of mocking banter, proposed to resume debating the eternal questions of adolescence from their present perspective as adult writers: "Is it not time for us to moot the world once more? Would eternal life be desirable if it existed[?] Who is God? Is space limited? Why literature, and is poetry more to be admired than prose? Is love really wonderful? Now that we have a good five-cent cigar, what does the country really need? If a bandit approached you with drawn revolver and announced that he was either going to shoot off your nuts or blow out your brain, would you kiss him? For answers see next week's *Saturday Evening Post*." [74]

In early May 1927 the Cowleys left New York to spend the summer at the Briggs farm in Sherman. Before their removal they spent most of their savings to rent and furnish a new apartment on Sutton Place, at 501 East Fifty-fifth Street, which they planned to maintain for business trips and pleasure dips into the city. Their new "palatial tenement," Cowley mockingly observed to Tate, rented for eighteen dollars and featured three rooms, gas, a fireplace, and "an unlimited supply of cold water." It was located on the fifth floor in a building without an elevator. Back in Sherman the Cowleys resumed the life of country summer people, trying to regain a sense of rootedness in the land, to counteract "the absolute past-lessness of life in New York." One of Cowley's first acts upon arrival was to obtain a fishing license in the village and search the local brooks for trout, while Peggy delved into the Connecticut loam to restore her winter-ruined flower garden.[75]

Over the summer Cowley made a trip with Foster Damon along the Jersey coast to investigate fishing conditions in Barnegat Bay for an article for *Charm*. They explored tiny fishing villages, talked to local Jersey fishermen, and sailed out with them onto the open sea. The experience inspired the idea of similar articles in the future. In August Cowley wrote a long letter to Lucie Taussig, the editor of *Charm*, outlining a series of articles on New Jersey "special industries," on fighting forest fires, on historic Jersey trees, and (with particular insistence) on slavery. Of the articles proposed, three were actually written. Cowley's letter coincided with the end of his connection with *Charm*. In the fall Taussig was succeeded by a new editor, Elizabeth D. Adams, who discontinued the magazine's book page, thereby depriving Cowley of an assured fifty dollars a month.[76]

Cowley's upsurge of journalistic inspiration came in the wake of two "delightful" weeks spent on Cape Cod, eating lobsters and quahogs, visiting with the Nefs, acquaintances from Paris days, and talking with Conrad Aiken. In September, Cowley spent two weeks in New York—visiting publishing houses, trying to "sell ideas" and to "get drunk on watered whiskey"—and emerged with a contract for a new job for Boni: editing the account of a slave trader's life. He attended the celebration of the 250th anniversary of a Quaker town in western Jersey and made a tour of Quaker settlements for his *Charm* article. His operation in Pittsburgh had put him $250 in debt, the purchase of a new car had added another $100, and late September found Cowley back in Sherman, "writing articles in black letters to blot out the red of my account books," as he told Josephson. Over the summer he had made some extra money from laboriously rewriting, for the publisher Macaulay, "a very bad translation" of Barbusse's novel *Jésus*. Once more, Cowley was brought face to face with the oppressing compromises of a free-lance existence. "There is nothing to do, these days, except to write one's books and become successful: to accept new responsibilities and to write more books in order to keep up with them."[77]

In the fall of 1927 Cowley reviewed, for *Charm*, a new "yearbook" of contemporary American writing, *The American Caravan*, edited by Brooks, Kreymborg, Mumford, and Rosenfeld. The volume, so the editors explained in a foreword, was the result of "a spiritual as well as geographical canvas" of the nation. It hoped to "accommodate a progressively broader expression of American life" and to serve as "an affirmation of the health of the young American literature." The encyclopedic work offered a representative selection of over seventy American writers, established and unknown, and Cowley sympathetically considered the new publishing venture for *Charm*, singling out for special mention the "brilliant younger writers"—Schneider, Wilson, Crane, Williams, O'Neill, Hemingway, Tate, and Dos Passos.[78]

Cowley was represented in the book by "Biography," a collection of poems and prose pieces he had written during slack office hours at Sweet's and submitted first to Williams for inclusion in his *Contact* collection, then, in April 1926, to Ernest Walsh for publication in *This Quarter*. Three of Cowley's poems, later included in *Blue Juniata* as "Leonora" and dedicated to Peggy, re-create the mood and circumstances of their courtship in the Village. They were published in alternation with two fictional sketches, which contrast the experiences of a naive rural boy of fifteen undergoing his sexual awakening at the hands of a miner's wife with those of the "lost" adult writer, absorbing the melancholy, jazzy poetry of life among the skyscrapers and tenements of Manhattan, dreaming of "women who carry dogwood from the country," and cynically struggling to maintain the integrity of his imaginative vision against the commercial encroachments of the city: "When I was twenty-eight, I came to Manhattan, city of journalists, factory where ideas are duplicated under the Taylor System. No admittance, if you have nothing to sell. But critics can be bribed to let you ride in the caboose of letters; and on every street corner there are ambulant poets who sell glimpses of the stars or moon, through a brass telescope, for ten cents, two nickels, the tenth part of a dollar. Allagazam, ladies and gents, step up, ladies and gents, see the rings of Saturn, the

eclipse of Venus, the dry craters of the moon, the death of lyric verse. . . .
We are the realtors of literature. . . . We are the pimps of culture."[79]

That Cowley was not alone among the younger writers to suffer from
occasional delusions of literary persecution was shown by Allen Tate's response to *The American Caravan*. When he saw the book, which featured
two of his own poems, he angrily solicited Cowley's cooperation against
"one of the foulest outrages of our time." Tate's wrath was roused by the
editors' dedication of the volume to "Alfred Stieglitz, Teacher" and by
their foreword, both of which, Tate felt, exuded "the most hellish stink
of Word-Fellow-ism." He proposed to offer "armed resistance" in an open
letter to the editors: "It's a good chance to give the Brooks-Mumford school
a blow." In a more dispassionate reply Cowley granted that the dedication
was an "imposition" to the contributors, making it "seem that Stieglitz was
the teacher of you and me and God knows who besides," but agreed to
sign an open letter only on condition that it "render justice to the disinterested labor performed by the editors." In other words, he recommended,
"shit on them if we can, but let's not lose our pants." Cowley's strategy
of caution—he *had* learned his lesson from the bickerings of the past—
was persuasive and Tate decided to "let word-fellowism hang itself on its
own error of taste." *The American Caravan*, he granted, was a "good book"
despite the editors. If he had mistaken the book for a "high-handed *coup de
main*" on the part of the critical establishment against the younger generation, he still resented that he and his friends had been "misrepresented as
(1) sympathetic with the aims of *that* generation or (2) as its acknowledged
vassals having no aims of our own and contented to let Mumford give us
his fuddled ideas." Such a misapprehension, he persisted, needed to be
combatted "with the life's blood"—"The longer we wait . . . the greater
fools we become. Those fellows are our superiors in economy; we can't get
money; and they command us by publishing us." Tate's temper was not
easily calmed.[80]

In late October 1927 Cowley received the Levinson Prize from *Poetry*.
The award, consisting of one hundred dollars, was named after Salmon O.
Levinson, one of the Chicago magnates who sponsored Monroe's magazine, and was given in recognition of the distinguished quality of Cowley's
contributions to *Poetry*, in particular his latest batch of poems, "Blue
Juniata." Cowley first learned of the award through long-distance phone
calls from several Connecticut newspapers, whose copy-desk men, he
wrote to Monroe, "were evidently eager to write the headline, HOME TOWN

BARD WINS POEM PRIZE." Cowley felt "honored by the choice" but applied his first prize money to a prosaically practical purpose: he took out twenty-five dollars for groceries and used the remaining seventy-five as part of a down payment on "sixty acres of abandoned farmland and a hungry-looking house half a mile from Addie Turner's," just across the state line from Sherman.[81] He had been but a tenant on the Briggs place; now he finally had a farm of his own.

This time, however, neither poetic recognition nor the actual posses-sion of a country home alleviated Cowley's sinking hopes about the lack of progress and achievement in his career. As usual, he poured out his misery in his notebooks. At a particularly somber moment in late 1927 he observed: "Since last February I have written nothing in prose or verse of which I can be proud, and very little of which I should not be ashamed." Despite the methodology exemplarily offered by Paul Valéry, Cowley still despaired of finding a "common denominator" to his life, his "own win-dow on the universe." In his notebook he tried to find "certain experiences in my youth which set a pattern, and to which I shall always return." He searched in his poems for "the images that set my unconscious into fabri-cating lines"—symbols that recurred with a persistent emotional force and that, like "fetishes," had a "mysterious charm": words like "parade" or "pro-cession," images of abandoned houses, receding mountain ranges, slow, cold rains. He noted the curious (and incorrect) fact that, with the excep-tion of a "fairly admirable but fabricated" poem like "Those of Lucifer," "Leander" was the first of his poems "not based on an experience of child-hood" that went beyond the emotion of "primitive nostalgia" in his earlier verse. In an entry entitled "Meditations on My Not Writing," he expressed his poignant awareness that he remained, irremediably, one of the "wan-derers outside the gates," and gave vent to his despair about himself: "With the realization that I should probably never return to Belsano, an epoch closed in my career as a poet. . . . I have questioned God, but not the virtue of writing. . . . I am still, as I was five years ago, helpless and confused in the face of life. I act on instincts, and my choices are not deliberate. In my own eyes I am unadmirable. And, thinking of some of my meaner actions, I am led from the recognition of evil into that of good—of the supreme Good—of perhaps God. And the 'perhaps' was an afterthought."[82]

Battling what he felt were the weaknesses of his own character—stub-born inertia and a self-indulgent lack of disciplined endeavor—Cowley determined once again to aim for greater efficiency and purposiveness in his life, to resist more strongly the hedonistic temptations of his day, and to set apart a segment of "appointed time" for serious work of his own. In a moment of greater self-confidence he reflected upon his various motives for writing in a more positive vein, but one still marked by deprecatory self-irony:

> Reader, if I yield sometimes to the vice of writing, it is out of the desire to create you in my image. I write to impose my point of view. . . . I write to expand my stature at the expense of yours, . . . I write from selfishness and conceit. . . . But there are many other reasons why I write.
>
> To make enemies, for example: no form of flattering one's self is a more violent pleasure. I write sometimes to amuse my friends, but more often in the hope of puzzling them, to make them less eager to abandon me. I write to make myself attractive to the women I like, and so that I need not be introduced three times to strangers. I write also to earn money, but since I earn more money by working in an office, this can not be called a principal motive.
>
> Often I write to collect my memories, and so form in my own mind an idea of the sort of man I have been. I try to gather the elements of my personality out of the past. . . .
>
> I write out of a desire to build, with the same purpose I had when a boy and built mud dams in the ditches after a rain. . . . One has a carpenter's pride in doing a good job, in turning a graceful line. One hopes to make something complete, organic, which will have a history separate from one's own. . . .
>
> The pleasure I take in reading my own work is rarely equal to the discomfort. What irritates me most are the little mannerisms, the simpers, which pleased me so much when I wrote. And besides, it is not always agreeable to recall one's past.
>
> . . . Writing is a vice, and I can take it or leave it alone. But when I leave it alone, my vanity begins to suffer. I think, "You are losing your ability to write." And to prove my own talent to my own satisfaction, I return to the typewriter. Mostly, however, I write because it is a habit, like cigarettes, like marriage, and like fishing down a stream instead of up, because all my life I have fished down a stream.[83]

By the end of 1927 Cowley had still not succeeded in finding a solution to the dilemmas that had plagued him since his return from France. It was only by closing the doors to "certain rooms of my soul," as he confessed to himself, and by cynically pursuing aims in which he did not truly believe, that he managed to remain afloat, intellectually, emotionally, and financially, in the "atmosphere of frustration and purposeless tension" which, by 1927, had begun to mark his life in New York. "I feel in an evangelical mood; I feel like preaching some new gospel to you, but I have absolutely nothing to preach," he moaned to Josephson. Whenever he *could* muster the moral courage to examine his personal situation with unsparing self-criticism, he lapsed into a mood of bleak disillusionment and, as his friends had come to expect, complained of dissipating his energies and wasting his talents on insignificant work. Even Josephson, who had suffered from similar self-questionings, found a temporary solution to the intellectual frustrations of a poet's life in late 1920s America and over the summer escaped to France to do research for his biography of Emile Zola, vicariously realizing Cowley's hopes for a life of Baudelaire. From Paris, Josephson wrote exhilarating letters home, celebrating his miraculous progress on his book and, in savory terms, describing his meetings with his former dadaist friends to Cowley. Immersed in the fascinating life story of Zola, Josephson responded to Cowley's complaints with ironic but severe advice: "I have known for months that you Go Out on Parties with Nice People and Drink Drinks. But where is the old sparkle when I sent you messages on t[oilet] p[aper]? . . . going out night after night and Drinking Drinks is not after all preferable to being buried in a book."[84] It was high time, Josephson implied, for Cowley to stop wasting his talents on a host of trivial things, to consolidate his literary energies, and to finally settle down to the serious business of writing.

14

Toward a Critique of American Culture

1927–1929

In April 1928 Cowley finished "The Edgar Allan Poe Tradition." One of his more important essays of the decade, it brought together many of his literary preoccupations around a timely and controversial subject. So far, Cowley had approached the subject of literary modernism mostly from the perspective of French poetry; it was only natural that he would now examine an American precursor of modernism who could be placed beside Rimbaud and Baudelaire. Poe was very much in the limelight of critical attention in the 1920s, but he remained, as T. S. Eliot was to write, "a stumbling block for the judicial critic." In the years after World War I, research had brought to light a substantial body of new biographical information, but a proper appreciation of Poe's literary merit remained hindered by a moralistic suspicion that he was a man of weak, amoral, morbidly unwholesome character and that such a personality was by definition incapable of producing serious art. The early 1920s, it is true, saw the emergence of critical studies of considerable depth and originality: D. H. Lawrence in his *Studies in Classic American Literature* (1923), Paul Valéry in his essay on Poe's *Eureka* in *Variété*, and William Carlos Williams in his *In the American Grain* (1925) had, each in his own fashion, argued for a recognition of Poe as a serious literary artist. The same period also witnessed the appearance of a spate of new Poe biographies, many of which drew heavily on newly available psychoanalytic insights. One of the more sensitive of these was Joseph Wood Krutch's *Edgar Allan Poe: A Psycho-Analytic Interpretation* (1926), which explained Poe's literary genius as the result of psychological, social, and sexual maladjustments that forced him to seek compensation in an abnormal emotional world of terror, phantasmagoria, and doom.[1]

Poe lay at the heart of Cowley's critical concerns in the 1920s. Cowley had long been aware of Baudelaire's fascination with the American poet and in May 1922 had reminded American readers that the "reclamation" of Poe from the French was "the basis of our contemporary poetry." In his notebook he regarded Poe as an important initiator of "monistic formalism" and singled him out as "the classical American example of the constructionist." On a memorable day in Brooklyn in June 1924 he read aloud "The City in the Sea" to Tate and Crane.[2] The three men subsequently formed a secret "Poe Society" as proof of their sense of aesthetic affinity with a poet whose career seemed appropriately symbolic of the fate of the modern artist amid inimical social and cultural forces; "[Poe] is with us like a dejected cousin," Tate later wrote in a famous essay. In November 1926 Edmund Wilson sought admittance to their informal lodge and participated in what Tate soon referred to as a "fateful evening" of discussion about the recent deluge of Poe biographies.[3]

The Winter 1926 literary supplement of the *New Republic* opened with Wilson's "Poe at Home and Abroad." The essay launched a caustic attack on Joseph Wood Krutch's psychosexual interpretation of Poe and on "the modern school of social-psychological biography," which, so Wilson advanced, did not merely misunderstand and underestimate Poe's works "from the point of view of their literary value" but led to complacent "caricature" of his personality and career. Wilson stood up against the criticism that regarded Poe as "a freak," and he presented him instead as "a thorough romanticist" who, in his striving for "spiritual *effect*" and his attempt to make poetry approach "the indefiniteness of music," had formed a "bridge" between nineteenth-century romanticism and "modern symbolism." Wilson's essay was a brilliant apologia, but it owed much to recent talks with Cowley and Tate on the subject. "I hope I haven't stolen your thunder," Wilson wrote to Cowley in late November 1926, admitting that he "should never have thought of writing" the essay "if it hadn't been for that conversation with you." He signed his letter "Yours for the Poe Society." Tate was furious about Wilson's borrowing of ideas from private conversation, in particular since he could name at least four instances in which Wilson had played similar tricks: only a week before, Tate wrote to Cowley, he himself had proposed an article on the biographers of Poe for the *New Republic*, only to find the idea rejected by Wilson; two days later the magazine miraculously changed its mind. Perhaps, Tate observed, he ought to intimate "to Brother Herbert that I appear in The New Republic oftener than he imagines" (Herbert Croly was the magazine's founder and chief editor). Wilson's shameless exploitation of "the economic value of an idea" was "really humiliating," he told Cowley; the "new brother" should be "expelled" from their Poe Society, or at least "disciplined."[4]

In early January 1927, when Krutch answered Wilson's attack with what even Wilson granted was a moderate "counterblast" in the *Saturday Review of Literature*, the critical debate among New York literati reached the height of controversy and Cowley was not prepared to stand by passively. Krutch, rather indiscriminately, took Wilson's essay as an example of "the newest school of criticism," one that aimed to "elevate aesthetics to the position of a separate science" and that cast out "psychology quite as definitely as it casts out sociology or morality." The most vital question in contemporary criticism, Krutch observed, was whether literature should be discussed *"in its relations or in itself,"* a question particularly ticklish in the case of Poe, whose life and art urgently invited psychological criticism: "whatever quarrel the aesthetician and the psychologist may have, there is no place where it may be more conveniently fought out than over the dead body of Poe." Krutch ended his essay with a plea for the validity of psychological criticism as an attempt "to bridge, in some fashion, the gulf between aesthetics and the various other sciences which deal with the phenomena of human life," though he granted that it had little to say on "the art of rhetoric or effective expression." [5]

Cowley's thoughts on Poe crystallized even before Wilson and Krutch publicly took their stands. In early October 1926 he wrote to Marianne Moore that he was eager to review for the *Dial* a new Poe biography by Hervey Allen, *Israfel: The Life and Times of Edgar Allan Poe,* because it considered Poe "as a writer, instead of treating him as a psycho-analytic case." In November and December he wrote again to Moore to tell her how "tremendously pleased" he was with Allen's book and in January 1927, shortly after the appearance of Krutch's essay, urged speedy publication of his review in the *Dial*: "I think I advanced several ideas which are important as ideas, and ought certainly to be expressed before the present Poe controversy dies down." Moore, however, did not make much haste in printing the review but suggested minor stylistic revisions that, together with Cowley's departure for Pittsburgh to undergo his operation, caused publication to be further delayed. On February 18, 1927, Cowley sent corrected proofs to Moore and again commented: "I hope you won't keep this review in the icebox; there has been considerable discussion of Poe since the recent biographies; what I have said belongs to that discussion; and if publication is too long delayed, my review is in danger of being outmoded, like Secretary Kellogg's war on the Bolshevists." [6]

Impatiently awaiting publication of his review in the *Dial*, Cowley spoke out on the current Poe controversy in *Charm* and in *Brentano's Book Chat*. In February 1927 he drew the attention of his *Charm* readers to the apparent irreconcilability of Poe's dissolute living and his artistic worth; he recommended Allen's *Israfel* as an accurate biography that advanced "no clever little theory—no secondhand Freudianism" but presented Poe's life and career as a story "just as relentless, just as pitiful and proud as one of Shakespeare's tragedies." A month later, in *Brentano's Book Chat*, he recalled how, as early as 1919, his own "taste had been formed by reading Poe and Baudelaire," from whom he learned to demand "a sort of ecstasy"—what Valéry had named "*pure poetry*—something which is separate from plots, characters, ideas—something which, on the rare occasions when I encountered it, sent shivers of delight along my spine."[7]

Cowley's Poe review did not appear until the *Dial*'s August 1927 issue. Tate shared Cowley's irritation and felt that the delay in publication, with Moore's refusal to let Cowley expand his review into a full-fledged essay, was symptomatic of the younger generation's lack of power to resist the conservatism of the literary establishment. "The best piece of Poe criticism ever written by an American appeared recently in the Dial," he observed to Cowley in hyperbolic praise. "It should have appeared six months ago; it should never have been stuck in the back of the magazine. It can be conveniently overlooked for many years. . . . Because we had no magazine to print it in, at the right time, in the right place."[8]

Cowley's *Dial* review suffered from the limitations imposed by Moore's astringency but conveyed the gist of his position. Most biographers of the time, he observed, faced with the discrepancy between the young writer of promise and proud force of character and the unbalanced drunkard plagued by dreams of insane grandeur and paranoiac delusions, tried to give a simplified interpretation of Poe's deterioration: "Heredity, a weak heart, a 'mother fixation,' opium, alcohol, sexual impotence, or general waywardness: each has been advanced . . . as the reason both for his literary achievements and the disintegration of his character." They had disregarded "the value of literature as such" and treated genius as "a mental or physical disease." Though Hervey Allen still wavered between "the psychological attitude of Mr. Krutch" and "the aesthetics of M. Valéry," he deserved credit, Cowley thought, for admiring Poe's poetry "for what it is." Probing into the causes of "our strange misapprehension of Poe's genius," Cowley pointed to the critics' general failure to "grasp the importance of his work as a whole." Following, and possibly anticipating, Wilson, he insisted Poe must be seen as "a product of international romanticism and the precursor of a symbolism which is nearly as universal." Had he been given the opportunity, Cowley was persuaded, Poe's most important work would have been "in the field of aesthetics and pure philosophy" and would have yielded answers to "the great questions which have been troubling our minds since his day." In conclusion he acknowledged a personal indebtedness: "[Poe's] work has helped shape our own attitude toward the art of letters. When we try to find the origin of our problems—such problems as the relation between poetry and science, the nature of pure poetry, the attitude of the poet to his audience, the proper function of psychology in criticism—we follow a path which leads from country to country and from author to author; from M. Valéry we proceed to Mallarmé, and from Mr. Eliot to Laforgue; but always, at the end of a vista, we find the proud, the still mysterious figure of Edgar Allan Poe."[9]

Cowley had more to say on Poe than was possible in the *Dial* review. An opportunity for more elaborate discussion came early in 1928, when he was asked by the editor of the *Outlook* to write the first essay in a series of "revaluations, by contemporary critics, of the great figures of America's literary past." The magazine advertised Cowley as "one of the most brilliant of our younger critics." Cowley's contribution to the series, "The Edgar Allan Poe Tradition," was a restatement and expansion of the position he had taken in his review and exhibited the influence of Burke's theories of form and of Valéry.

For all the research since Poe's death, Cowley observed, the "mystery" of his genius remained "as deep as ever" and the misjudgments, especially by "professors of literature, moral philosophers, and critics in general," as persistent: "Like carrion birds, they have gathered about [Poe's] carcass, choosing each a portion for attack, and leaving nothing but his bleached gigantic bones to be studied and reconstructed like those of some palaeozoic monster." Cowley repudiated the notion that Poe's appeal, like Shelley's, was foremost to the adolescent sensibility and that his poetry and criticism was of no "use" for the mature and serious literary artist. He ascribed the contemporary misapprehension of Poe to current "literary fashions," which demanded a strict realism and looked askance at the rich inventiveness, wide learning, and exotic imagination of Poe.[10]

The core of his essay, however, was a belated attack on critics who, like Krutch, sought to attribute Poe's genius to "an almost unparalleled collection of mental, physical, and environmental troubles and infirmities." When, almost eighteen months before, Krutch publicly announced the existence of a "quarrel" between the aesthetician and the psychologist, Cowley had privately objected to the distinction. In an unpublished manuscript he criticized Krutch for failing to differentiate between those critics interested in "the psychology of the writer" and those interested in "the psychology of the audience," a notion he had derived from Burke or, as seems more likely, that both Burke and Cowley had first discovered in Poe's own writings. Poe, after all, Cowley had written in his manuscript, was "so little concerned with the psychology of the writer, and so deeply interested in the psychology of the audience, that when he set out to explain how he wrote 'The Raven,' his explanation was entirely mistaken and disingenuous—as concerns himself; but it is a masterly presentation of the psychological methods by which an author *affects an audience.*"[11] In his essay for the *Outlook* Cowley explained why a concern with "the psychology of the writer" (as in most recent psychoanalytic studies of Poe) could never lead to "the highest type of criticism." By definition, he wrote (borrowing his differentiation from one of the essays by Valéry he had translated for the *Herald Tribune Books* that spring), such criticism was "confined to the psychological *causes* of literary works, whereas the more important function of criticism is first to study, and then to judge, their psychological *effects.* The causal critics have no real standards of judgment." They had, he implied, nothing to say on the aesthetic properties of a work of art: "its symmetry, its luster, its color, its texture, and all the elements which give effect to its beauty."

Granting the restricted validity of psychological criticism, Cowley yet acknowledged that Poe's physical and psychical infirmities helped explain the narrow range of his emotions, the limited number of his effects, and his failure to "transcribe the real world or to create living characters." In one important respect, Cowley believed, Poe's maladjustments had "encouraged" his genius by providing him with a "motive" for developing his "bitter ambition" for artistic success. Here, as in the case of Baudelaire, Cowley was led to the conclusion that personal morality did not inevitably coincide with literary ethics: "Just as the virtues of the king may be the vices of the man, it is sometimes possible for vices of character to become literary virtues." Such early insights into the discrepancy between an artist's character flaws and his "saintlike dedication" to his art proved axiomatic; half a century later they formed the basis of Cowley's more subtle and profound formulation of the five "commandments" persisting in the depths of any artist's mind, a "pentalogue" that, though it offered no guide to daily conduct, was in itself "a moral code" of art.[12]

Like Wilson's essay, "The Edgar Allan Poe Tradition" was in essence an apologia for a misunderstood and underestimated American artist. But Cowley, more so than Wilson, was also critical of the technical weaknesses in Poe's poetry. Two of Poe's more serious "faults" were his "lack of visualization," which engendered a style "almost purely auditive," and an element of "theatricality." Cowley accepted Poe's conception of a poem as "a machine for producing emotions" (it was another notion he reverted to in his later criticism, as when in A Second Flowering he analyzed Hemingway's "system of practical aesthetics" in terms derived from Poe), but he acknowledged that Poe was "sometimes guilty of constructing his emotive machine with shoddy materials, and sometimes . . . adopted the methods of a charlatan"; as a result, Poe was capable of "magnificent artifices" but also of "mere tricks."[13]

In conclusion, Cowley more precisely related the current misapprehension of Poe to the neglect of a large portion of his writings, in particular the "Marginalia," Eureka, and The Narrative of Arthur Gordon Pym. If we would base our appreciation of Poe on his entire oeuvre, Cowley was convinced, we should find that, despite his "narrow emotional range," Poe possessed "an exceptionally wide range of intellectual interests"— from literature, the arts and history, through landscape gardening and interior decoration, to mathematics, physics, meteorology, psychology, and astronomy. Poe was "not only one of the first American writers to state the opposition between science and poetry, but also the very first to reconcile these hostile departments of the modern mind. He was the enemy of inordinate specialization, that vice of the nineteenth century which threatens to persist into the twentieth." In the late 1920s Edgar Allan Poe loomed for Cowley as "the most important American man of letters," one whose unparalleled influence made him "a part of the traditions of modern literature in half a dozen countries."

Cowley's plea for a consideration of Poe's merit on the basis of his total literary output was an early manifestation of a persistent belief: as he put it in 1961, it is "a mistake to approach each work as if it were an absolutely separate production, a unique artifact, the last and single relic of a buried civilization. . . . It seems to me that any author of magnitude has his eye on something larger than the individual story or poem or novel . . . [and] wants it to serve as a chapter or aspect of the larger work that is his lifetime

production, his *oeuvre.*" It is precisely this "larger work"—considered both
in its intrinsic and its extrinsic aspects—that Cowley increasingly strove to
make into the subject of his most substantial essays, both those on earlier
American writers like Poe, Hawthorne, or Whitman, and those on literary contemporaries like Faulkner, Fitzgerald, Hemingway, Dos Passos,
Cummings, and Aiken.[14]

In 1927–28, taking his cue from the French perspective on Poe and
choosing Baudelaire and Valéry for his critical lodestars, Cowley was able
to anticipate, admittedly in elementary fashion, the important revaluation
of Poe that reached its height in the late 1940s in influential essays of
greater depth and perspicacity by T. S. Eliot and Allen Tate. Like Cowley
twenty years earlier, Eliot, in a famous 1948 Library of Congress lecture,
discovered that "by trying to look at Poe through the eyes of Baudelaire,
Mallarmé, and most of all Valéry, [one became] more thoroughly convinced of his importance, of the importance of his *work* as a whole." Allen
Tate's two major lectures on Poe—"Our Cousin, Mr. Poe" (1949) and
"The Angelic Imagination: Poe as God" (1952)—likewise examined neglected or misapprehended aspects of Poe germinally suggested by Cowley.
The latter essay, in particular, referred to *Eureka*, one of the works Cowley
had singled out as being "unjustly neglected," to fathom and formulate
the quasi-theological cosmology implicit in Poe's writings, and recapitu-
lated the gist of Cowley's attack on Poe's psychoanalytic critics.[15] Even in
1928 Tate felt that Cowley and he were engaged in a collective endeavor
to stem the tide of a nefarious mode of criticism. In May of that year Tate
submitted an early version of his essay on Emily Dickinson to the *Outlook*
and commented to Cowley: "What little previous criticism of her there has
been, has in effect argued that she would have been better off if she had
indulged occasionally in sexual intercourse. In effect, I combat that view.
If I remember the drift of your Poe essay, it does the same thing. Two essays
in that direction may count a little in checking the tide of opinion to the
contrary."[16]

In the late 1920s Cowley's interest in the origins of contemporary romanticism was further exemplified in two articles examining the tradition of the
Gothic novel and the life and works of Percy Bysshe Shelley. Both, Cowley
advanced, stood in need of just appreciation. "The Haunted Castle," published in the fall of 1928 in *New Republic*, displayed what became two
articles of critical faith: first, Cowley's belief that a critic should "select
works of art worth writing about, with special emphasis on works that

are new, not much discussed, or widely misunderstood"; and second, a deliberate effort to read "with a sort of innocence . . . with a lack of pre-conceptions." In substance, his 1928 article contended that the Gothic novel (as written by Horace Walpole, Ann Radcliffe, and Matthew Gregory Lewis) was "perhaps today the most neglected field of English letters." Taking Lewis's *The Monk* (1796) as a case in point, Cowley found that, read "without preconceptions," the book possessed "an astounding power of imaginative evocation" as well as "a violent realism . . . a naturalism of the passions, an accuratism of horror." Arguing that this mixture of the imaginary and the real foreshadowed the literary methods of the Roman-tics, he pointed out how for them *The Monk* had been "a talisman, a magic mirror: it revealed new worlds of mystery, passion, terror, forbidden dreams." The haunted castle had been a "symbol of liberation" for the writers of the Romantic era, but it had persisted into modern literature, where, merging into "the conceptions of abnormal psychology," it had as-sumed a new symbolic function: "we have learned that the mind, too, has its passages and labyrinths . . . no less terrifying than those dungeons of Santa Clara where lizards crawled, where ghosts came stalking, and where a sudden gust of wind blew out the lamp." [17]

Among the English Romantic poets Shelley held undoubtedly the strongest fascination for the young Cowley—perhaps proof of a linger-ing touch of adolescent romanticism in his own sensibility. Not only did echoes of Shelley's rhetorical lyricism steal into his poetry ("Leander," par-ticularly, seemed indebted to poems like "Alastor" and "Ode to the West Wind"), Cowley also intermittently mentioned Shelley in his reviews, and quoted from his *Defence of Poetry*. In the *Dial* for June 1928 he consid-ered a massive life of Shelley by Walter Edwin Peck. Peck's "authoritative" biography, Cowley granted, might be "a labour of disinterested scholar-ship," but it was fatally lacking in "creative sympathy" and marred by the author's attitude of "a hostile judge, who, having weighed the evidence and balanced probabilities, now rises to pronounce his sentence." Peck's critical stance was one that consistently irritated Cowley; throughout his career Cowley emphasized the need of humility and respect on the part of the critic before works of art. Judgment was subordinate to interpretation and definition, he observed in 1961. Peck, however, not only committed the sin of critical pride, he also showed considerable "critical ineptitude" in pronouncing judgment on Shelley's flaws of moral conduct, an aspect disconnected with his achievement as a poet: after all, Cowley advanced, "among modern authors, Shelley was preeminently a man of works, a man who lived in his poems." Shelley's dramatic death by drowning already seemed anticipated in his finest poems, notably "Alastor." In effect, Cowley concluded, Shelley had sacrificed his life to "a symbol"—"very much as if William Jennings Bryan had really been crucified on a cross of gold," he noted in a letter to Marianne Moore.[18]

Cowley's letter was his last communication with Moore as editor of the Dial; his Shelley review marked the end of his connection with the magazine. The long delay between Cowley's first request for the review in August 1927 and its final appearance in June 1928 crowned a dissatisfaction that had been steadily mounting ever since Moore had been appointed editor in the spring of 1925. Though Cowley had warmly greeted her accession to the editorial chair—"It will be extremely interesting to write for the Dial under your editorship"—in the summer of 1926, he told Burke that he could not, in all honesty, congratulate him on returning to the Dial: the magazine, he felt, was "getting Awful." Cowley's personal disappointment in the later Dial was representative of a wider critical response. The magazine's alleged opposition to experimentalism, its staid catholicity of taste, and its reputed partiality toward established European writers had been a thorn in the side of the pugnaciously modernist younger generation ever since the days of Broom and Secession; after 1925, such objections only seemed to gain pertinency and the magazine, consequently, estranged quite a few of its earlier sympathizers. Williams, recipient of the Dial Award for 1926, two years later told Pound that he was "disgusted with the Dial for its halfhearted ways" and felt the magazine was "a dead letter among the publisher crowd." With the general falling off of excitement in the literary climate (there was, in the late 1920s, no annus mirabilis like 1922, which saw the appearance of Ulysses and The Waste Land) the Dial seemed only to become more precious and sedately dignified. When the Dial ceased publication in 1929, Cowley commented that "even during its lifetime it had ceased to be receptive to new ideas; it published Cummings when he first appeared, but six years later it was closed to Hemingway."[19]

The merit of Moore's editorship of the Dial was hardly undisputed even at the time, but Cowley had his own reasons for being unhappy with her treatment of his work. One of Moore's first acts had been to reject, in a tone irritatingly judicial, the group of pastoral Pennsylvania poems that later appeared in Poetry: "Although we enjoy in your poems the exact rendering of atmosphere, and feel the definiteness of your intention in the determining of cadence and of pattern, we feel nevertheless a lack of cumulative force," she had informed him in the fall of 1925. The only one of Cowley's poems to meet with her strict and esoteric standards was "Leander." Not only had Moore rejected Cowley's essay on "French Poetry and the New Spirit," she had also printed Alyse Gregory's niggardly appreciation of his translation of *Variété*, had unforgivably held up the publication of his Poe review, and, of late, had let him slave over a translation of an installment of Proust's *Le temps retrouvé* (1927; *The Past Recaptured*, 1941), which was never published in the *Dial*. Repeatedly Cowley's efforts had not elicited the kind of hospitable response that he had hoped for.[20]

But Cowley was particularly irked by Moore's habit of making or proposing changes in his manuscripts. She approached the art of editing her magazine with the same punctiliousness she bestowed on the composition of her poems and repeatedly suggested alterations, even in Cowley's brief reviews. Mostly, Cowley politely acknowledged that her proposals were improvements, but occasionally he resented the implication of carelessness and curtly referred her to the Oxford English Dictionary for arbitration. Moore's solicitude for good writing collided with Cowley's own standards of craftsmanship and the conscientiousness with which he wrote his critical prose. "In general I feel very nervous when someone starts in to change my work," he observed to Burke in 1927. A year later he was more explicit: "I don't work very well when I'm Marianne-Moore'd." Burke enjoyed the high respect of Moore—she spoke of him affectionately as "our critic" and proposed him for the *Dial* award of 1928 over Wallace Stevens—and he may well have tactfully alerted Moore to his friend's sensitivity about her treatment of his work. By the spring of 1928, at least, she seemed to have become aware that some of her suggestions rubbed Cowley the wrong way and told him that she wanted to be assured of his approval of her alterations in the Shelley review: "We cannot buy contentment with tyranny." Cowley, however, decided to break off relations with the magazine and henceforth submitted his more substantial essays and reviews to Edmund Wilson and to Irita Van Doren; the latter, at least, rarely altered his manuscripts and instantly published what he wrote. When the *Dial* breathed its last in the summer of 1929, Cowley belatedly explained his step to Burke, granting it entailed "a confession of weakness": "I ceased to write for the Dial, but only after long and conscientious efforts to get along with Marianne Moore; fundamentally she didn't like me, and fundamentally I need to be liked if I'm going to do my best work."[21]

Though Cowley's grievances were partly justified, on the whole Moore had been generous and conscientious in her dealings with a touchy contributor. She had agreed to serve as Cowley's reference for his Guggenheim application, over the years had been patient with the arrears and delays resulting from his laborious working habits, and had displayed a continued, if discriminating, hospitality to his writings.[22] For all Cowley's grumblings, the *Dial* had played a significant role in establishing his reputation as a poet and a practitioner of "modern" literary criticism. The *Dial*, moreover, paid well—twenty dollars a page for poetry, two cents a word for prose, and two dollars for brief reviews, rates unmatched by other, comparable magazines of the time. As Cowley, oblivious of his earlier strictures, observed in 1958: "On the whole [the *Dial*] was the best magazine of the arts that we have had in this country. For the young American writer of the time, it was marvelous to have a magazine that would publish his best work, and pay him for it." [23]

‹ ‹ ‹   In early 1928 Cowley began writing regularly for the *New Republic*. Two years before, Edmund Wilson had joined the staff of the magazine, to serve as an associate editor and principal book reviewer for the next five years; in 1928 he was about to take over the literary editorship from Robert Morss Lovett, who later that year was ushered out of office by Herbert Croly. At the time, Wilson already enjoyed considerable prestige and authority as a professional critic and in the eyes of many seemed on his way to becoming "the Sainte-Beuve of a new literature." [24]

Cowley's connection with the liberal weekly that was to play such a decisive role in the shaping of his subsequent career was off to a confused start. Memories of the unfair, indifferent, or inconsistent manner in which the editors had treated several of his earlier articles and proposals still rankled, and when, in late October 1927, Wilson invited Cowley to review on a regular basis for the magazine, Cowley entered a lengthy "bill of complaints." Repeatedly over the last few years, Cowley told Wilson, his suggestions for articles had been coldly received, his writings "published, lost, altered, neglected," until he could no longer be certain of the fate of what he submitted. Still, Cowley granted, "I should be glad to be connected with any periodical which you help to edit, and in spite of all difficulties I should like to write for the New Republic." All he asked was fair treatment and a reasonable assurance that what he wrote would be paid for, whether printed or not. Wilson repaid Cowley in kind. He dismissed the latter's letter as "a great farrago and galimatias of poppycock and balderdash" and regretted to see Cowley develop "literary delusions of persecution similar to those which afflict Ernest Boyd." Patronizingly, he warned Cowley that most editors were "unbusinesslike persons" subject to "all kinds of manias, abstractmindedness, metaphysical prejudice [and] partisan feeling." He guaranteed that any commissioned review would be paid for, and again expressed his eagerness to have Cowley, whom he believed to be "one of the best writers in the country," contribute regularly to the New Republic. In reply an undaunted Cowley pointed out that Wilson would do well to "distinguish between neurosis and superstition." He simply felt that "a jinx sat on [his] shoulders" every time he had tried to write for the magazine. Wilson, however, had managed to pour balm into his correspondent's soul. Cowley not merely confessed himself ready to write for the magazine; he even considered dropping his present reviewing work for Irita Van Doren and the Herald Tribune Books, in deference to Wilson's superior editorial and literary standards.[25]

Cowley's early reviews for the New Republic were assigned a modest place in "the back of the book," but they were precisely the sort of thing Wilson was looking for. "Your capacity for doing these trivial things well is astonishing," he observed in March 1928 apropos of a short one-column review. Wilson's growing confidence in Cowley's ability to produce "first-rate" reviews to order soon led to requests for "leading" reviews and contributions to the magazine's more elaborate literary supplements, which Wilson hoped to make into "all-star affairs." As always, Cowley approached his reviews with an attention to craftsmanship and style that earned him the admiration not only of Wilson but also of Herbert Croly and Bruce Bliven, then managing editor (he became editor in chief upon Croly's death in 1930). The short book review was rapidly developing into Cowley's special "art form." By making high demands on himself, he not only became an eminent practitioner of what Henry Dan Piper has called "the art of literary journalism" but also helped to raise the standards of professional book reviewing in America. Edmund Wilson, for one, was quick to recognize Cowley's special talents in the field; in May 1928 he spoke of the usual "elegance and perspicuity" of Cowley's reviews and praised his ability to give them "that kind of independent existence as an article which is just what is lacking in most reviews."[26] When, two years later, the New Republic was on the lookout for a new literary editor, Cowley was naturally foremost in Wilson's thoughts.

For the *New Republic* Cowley now also began reviewing occasionally the sort of books that had left him indifferent before, those dealing with specific social, political, or more broadly intellectual issues of his day and age. While he retained his sensitivity to problems of form and technique, several reviews displayed a dawning awareness of the darker underside of American society in an age of business and technology. It formed an embryonic indication that, by fits and starts, Cowley's critical horizons were broadening to include the public issues of his time, especially as they affected the fate of American writing.

The first series of reviews Cowley wrote under Wilson appeared in the early half of 1928 and included purely literary considerations of books of poetry by Donald Davidson and Humbert Wolfe, the letters of Baudelaire, fiction by Thornton Wilder, Sinclair Lewis, Wyndham Lewis, and Julien Green, and two books of English grammar.[27] The latter review displayed a typical, if somewhat naive, distrust of professorial "authority" in the field of language and stated that Americans badly needed "a final tribunal in all matters affecting the language" consisting of actual "men of letters and men of words," much like the French Academy. Cowley's principal concern in these reviews remained, quite simply, with the quality of good writing. Thus Wyndham Lewis received short shrift for his "seigniorial contempt" for style, while in his reviews of Wilder and Julien Green Cowley betrayed how much the "classical" virtues of Racine remained his critical touch-stone for contemporary writing. At Wilson's special request he wrote a longer review of two books by William Beebe, *Pheasant Jungles* and *The Arcturus Adventure*, for the spring literary supplement. Wilson judged the article "first-rate" and found Cowley "excellent on Beebe's style." A shift of emphasis, however, was noticeable even in Cowley's exclusively literary reviews. In a consideration of Sinclair Lewis's *The Man Who Knew Coolidge* he observed that Lewis's once vitriolic satire had lost much of its force and effectiveness ("this punitive expedition after the average American is no longer so thrilling as it was five years ago") and urged Lewis to widen the scope of his social satire, to turn to "other weapons" and "other objects" for his "distinguished powers of constructive hate."[28]

"Style and Fashion," a review that Wilson praised as "more or less a masterpiece in its way," gave a more explicit indication of Cowley's growing unhappiness with the social and economic factors affecting current American writing. It demonstrated his ability to transform a review of two relatively unimportant books—one a biography of Horatio Alger, the other an account of buccaneers in the Pacific—into an occasion for pointed generalization about larger cultural issues. In effect the review amounted to an attack on the "styling" of books and the extension of commercial principles into the field of literature through the issuing of "yearly models" for fashionable consumption. The application of consumerist criteria to publishing, Cowley charged, led to an unforgivable dilution of literary standards.[29]

Two reviews that appeared in the *New Republic* in June and July 1928 concerned social and political realities formerly outside Cowley's ken. "The Peasants of New York," a leading review, dealt with two books about the problems of Democratic city politics: graft in Tammany Hall and the "gangs" of New York. It entailed a personal recognition of the existence of an urban "underclass" to American capitalist society and implied a humanitarian sympathy, as yet unpoliticized, for this "urban peasantry." Cowley acknowledged that here was a whole class of American citizens who failed to profit from a booming national economy, who remained "the victims of inherited poverty and the subjects of exploitation," but he refrained from pleading the cause of social and political justice. Instead he focused on the exposure of graft and corruption in the Democratic party machine. And even here he refused to accept a "completely damn-ing" picture of Tammany Hall, but, still allowing for "the possibility of change," pointed to "the immediate and sometimes ephemeral benefits which Tammany offers in exchange for the right of imposing distant and abstract wrongs." It was one thing to look at the problem from the stand-point of an abstract political and moral ideology, Cowley observed; it was more complex and ambiguous to consider the matter from the voter's per-spective of pragmatic politics.[30]

At the suggestion of Herbert Croly Cowley reviewed *The Inquiring Mind* by Zechariah Chafee, Jr., a Harvard Law School professor who special-ized in stock issues of liberalism like social injustice and the suppression of civil liberties. Cowley's review evinced a good deal of skepticism about Chafee's political idealism: "true liberalism," he observed, would always be "a doctrine with few adherents." For all Chafee's idealism—he believed a liberal utopia could be "accomplished without revolution, perhaps without legislation; we need merely convert our administrators and judges to the liberal frame of mind"—Cowley remained cynical about the possibility of working social change through current American politics: "our civilization seems unable to produce ['dynamic' liberals] in sufficient numbers, and we are left blundering toward the polls to make our immemorial choice between men who believe in extremes and men who believe in nothing whatsoever."[31] In 1928 Cowley voted for Gov. Alfred E. Smith.

On the wave of his enthusiasm for Cowley's high-quality reviews, Wilson solicited other articles: "we are in the market for all kinds of special sketches, satires, and whatnot. . . . The more amusing, the better." Cowley promptly obliged and wrote "Portrait of a Publisher," a satirical expansion on the central idea of "Style and Fashion," in which he launched a more scathing attack on the spirit of economic consumerism in publishing. Cowley's imaginary publisher, Mr. Pontevedra, conceived of publishing as "the business of marketing beauty," a luxury trade which appealed to his readers' "desire for the exclusive" and their "hopes for social superiority." He established sumptuous offices in fashionable Fifth Avenue quarters and began manufacturing books with an exclusive, snobbish appeal; in the end he had "transformed the publishing of books into the art of producing bibelots." Pontevedra also "manufactured" authors by insidiously controlling and commercially exploiting their attitudes, styles, indeed, their personalities: "Like a great designer among his mannequins, he gave each of his collaborators a character to be worn in public, like a gown." He would begin a book by choosing an exquisite fabric for its binding, then settle on a matching subject with a guaranteed popular appeal and pick out a manipulable writer. Cowley ended his "Portrait of a Publisher" with the picture of a young struggling poet and essayist, the author of a series of studies in contemporary aesthetics, leaving the world of letters (a "small world full of jealousies and arbitrary failures," where books "grew slowly from within and were never tailored to meet a hasty order"), and buckling under the seductive pressures and promises of success held out by Pontevedra.[32]

Cowley's satirical portrait, projected as part of the series that he still hoped to turn into a book, showed an uncanny insight into the psychology of consumerism and an early knowledge of the economics of bookmaking. His critique of prevailing publishing standards, however, was too trenchant to suit the liberal tastes of the *New Republic* editors. Both Bliven and Croly deemed the article too transparent a portrait of Alfred Knopf and feared it would "bring down a lot of trouble on our heads." To Wilson, who had no power to overrule an editorial decision made by his seniors, fell the task of informing Cowley that his portrait could not be printed. "I feel now that I was very foolish to have encouraged you to write it," he wrote apologetically; "I might have foreseen this." He solicited other articles of the kind, with a promise of higher remuneration, and offered to pass on Cowley's portrait to Seward Collins of the *Bookman*.[33]

Here was another article first ordered then rejected by the *New Republic*, and Cowley may well have felt he had again just cause for grievance. Between the summer of 1928 and the fall of 1929 he wrote only five more reviews for the magazine and submitted the bulk of his articles to Irita Van Doren. In October 1928 a personal plea from Herbert Croly was needed to keep Cowley within the flock of *New Republic* contributors: "Everything that you write makes a particular appeal to me personally, and if we could arrange to have more of your MSS. in the paper it would, I am sure, strengthen the New Republic's service to its readers." In late October 1928 Bliven, writing on behalf of Croly, again assured Cowley that "the hospitality of the New Republic towards your work is just as high as you have been given to believe."[34]

Meanwhile, "Portrait of a Publisher," which Cowley had hoped to sell for forty dollars was given, gratis, to the *New Masses*, where it appeared in January 1929. The *New Masses*, a magazine of revolutionary sympathies, was bound to be less ambiguously critical of American culture, and Cowley's portrait was hailed by editor Michael Gold as a devastating critique of publishing under American capitalism: "Many thanks for the portrait of a publisher, or rather, Mr. Knopf-Liveright-Coward McCann," Gold wrote to Cowley; "It's damn good, and just what I hoped for. If we can get a few more as savage and photographic we will have so good a number it will lose us all our book ads, I hope. Damn it, why is there only one poor little magazine like ours in America to print this kind of thing. The country is really too smug for words. Anyone who talks out gets to feel like a kind of freak after a while." Gold hoped Cowley could suggest other contributors with "a really magnificent hate on the whole works."[35]

Cowley could as yet not share the full extent of Gold's radical ardor, but he appreciated the moral fervor of his letter and evinced a mounting concern with the social and economic aspects of the writer's trade. Being dependent for a large part of his income on translation fees, Cowley's concern with rendering foreign works into English went beyond the matter of language and the problem of cultural perspectives. From the first he not only pleaded for the recognition of translation as a serious art but early set himself up as a champion of the legal and economic rights of professional translators. In March 1928, when he received an invitation to join the Authors' Guild of the Authors' League of America, he seized upon the opportunity to draw attention to the "miserable situation" of translators. Speaking as one belonging to "the proletariat of literature," he argued that translators were underpaid and "underrecognized," and badly in need of an "organization of their own" that could protect professional standards. The Guild, he urged, could perform "very great services" on their behalf by drawing up a standard contract for translations, providing guarantees for the translator's share in English rights, protecting his interest in serial rights, and, in general, impressing upon publishers "the idea that they would gain by skilled work." Cowley's plea was symptomatic of his growing concern with the social and economic position of American writers, artists, and translators toward the end of the decade.[36]

‹ ‹ ‹   The summer 1928 issue of *transition* featured another group manifestation by Cowley and friends. In late 1927, working on his Zola biography in Paris, Josephson met Eugene Jolas and Elliot Paul and so infected the editors of *transition* with his optimistic proclamation that an upsurge of literary activity was about to take place in America that Jolas asked him to become contributing editor and to keep *transition* abreast of current developments in the United States. Jolas, very much taken with Joyce, Rimbaud, and surrealism, appears to have hoped that the allegiance of Josephson and Cowley, whose *Broom* and *Secession* had early published an impressive array of dadaists and surrealists, might signal a broader American shift to the sort of neoromantic subjectivism he was propagating in *transition*. His magazine, moreover, had been launched with high hopes for American literature—there were in America "unmistakable signs of artistic awakening," Jolas had proclaimed in the opening issue [37]—and *transition* 13, accordingly, was an "American Number," featuring, among others, Berenice Abbott, Archibald MacLeish, Gertrude Stein, Cowley (his poem "Seven O'Clock"), William Carlos Williams, Man Ray, Kay Boyle, Laura Riding, John Herrmann, Murray Godwin, Paul Bowles, and Katherine Anne Porter. In addition there was a twenty-page group manifestation entitled "New York: 1928."

The project had been initiated by Josephson, who even before his return to America issued a call for joint action in letters to his friends, aiming to demonstrate the infeasibility of expatriation and the need to confront the reality of America at home. Back in New York, Josephson and Cowley organized another all-day writing session comparable to the ones that had given birth to *Aesthete 1925* and the *Little Review* manifestation two years before. In January 1928 Cowley and Josephson, with Brown, Burke, Coates, and three pseudonymous ghosts resuscitated from the past—"Will Bray," "Walter S. Hankel," and "H. L. Mannikin"—reconvened in suites 1711–12 of the Hotel Chelsea, where between jokes and bantering arguments they hammered out the collective statement that Jolas vainly hoped would express a trend of current literary opinion in America sympathetic to *transition*.[38]

"New York: 1928" was a miscellany of satirical pieces of verse and prose that owed much in spirit to *Aesthete 1925* but also showed that, for all its witty and ironic contentiousness, a change in attitude was taking place among the participants. As Josephson told Jolas, the time had been "extremely inopportune" for a group manifestation, since many members "really did not feel the same grievances" they had expressed in *Aesthete 1925*. Among the few features harking back to the lambasting mode of the earlier manifestoes was Cowley's poem "Tar Babies"; it satirized those "talented" poets whose poetic barings of the beauty of their souls were in reality but ill-disguised attempts at sexual conquest, who obsequiously kissed "the hands of the great," and who slickly complained about the manners of critics "in a style that creeps across / your cheeks like a barber's fingers." A series of satirical annotations to the poem contained an exposure, written some four years before, of the literary trappings and "white shirtfront of modernism" and attacked the logrolling practices of such literary journalists as Floyd Dell and Harry Hansen, whose "critical morals," Cowley suggested, existed "no more than do sexual morals among the Papuan aborigines."[39]

Mock advertisements from the "Prince Llan Agency" continued earlier attacks on Mencken and "the Waldo Frank school" of Freudian fiction, but in general the target of satire had shifted and the critique, more serious, had a double aim: savage and comicoserious attacks on notorious expatriates like Pound and McAlmon were counterbalanced by scathing satires on the insipidity of American culture in an age of mass production and consumerism. Much of the project, as Cowley suggested in *Exile's Return*, was an ironically enacted ritual of exorcism of all those forces in contemporary mass culture—standardization, materialism, "the Voice of the Machine, the Tyranny of the Mob"—that the group experienced as antagonistic to the possibility of art and the literary life. Robert Coates contributed a wistful, surrealistic satire about a salesman teetering on the brink of mental collapse, who desperately tries to sell the secret of salvation and success to anonymous faces behind anonymous tenement doors, but is finally overcome by the disorienting, estranging nature of life under capitalist consumerism. Josephson exposed the fallacy of "the positivistic notion of perpetual advance or evolution toward perfection," which he saw underlying the self-confident proclamations by the Ford Motor Company that America stood at the dawn of a new industrial and commercial era. Only five years earlier in *Broom* he had celebrated Ford as the technological wizard of the new America. As "Will Bray" he now attacked the psychology and economy of consumerism, and, posing as the prophetlike founder of a new lodge of "Knights of Press-Agentry," ironically criticized the artist's subservience to machine-age America. "The poets and prophets of industry hold mightier seats of power than the Petrarchs, the Miltons, the Bossuets of an older day." Now was the time, he advanced, for the "strategic power" of this "intellectual class" to be fully exploited: artists must "unite and prepare themselves to taking over control of society in the future," so that new ideals might be propagated and new wants be "conceived in the interest of man, rather than in the interests of purposeless machines."[40]

Revolutionary embers were smoldering underneath the tone of mocking banter. Cowley, in mock-apocalyptic fashion, envisioned the imminent revolution as already having taken place and commemorated the epochal event in a poetic "Tablet," which opened the group manifesto:

TABLET

THERE WAS NO DICTATOR—THE REVOLUTION CHOSE RATHER TO FUNCTION THROUGH EXISTING AGENCIES—LEGISLATIVE RIGHTS WERE USURPED BY ACTORS' EQUITY—THE ADVERTISING MEN'S BRANCH OF THE AMERICAN LEGION BECAME A COMMITTEE OF PUBLIC SAFETY AND PROCEEDED TO EXECUTIONS—THE MAYOR WAS THROWN UNDER THE WHEELS OF THE SUBWAY—THE POLICE FORCE WAS JAILED—THE COMMISSIONER OF THE PORT WAS DROWNED—POETS IN DROVES WERE HANGED TO THE LAMPPOSTS UNDER THE SMALL BRIGHT LEMON-COLORED STARS—THE STREETS WERE LUMINOUS DURING THE EXECUTION WITH RED ORANGE YELLOW BLUE GREEN INDIGO AND DAYLIGHT BULBS FURNISHED BY COURTESY OF THE NEW YORK EDISON COMPANY— BROADWAY WAS CLOSED TO TRAFFIC—AT THE CORNER OF ALL EVEN

NUMBERED STREETS WERE NIGGER ORCHESTRAS—OFTEN WE DANCED
NAKED AT THE BURNING OF A CHURCH—UNDER RED SKIES—IN THE
GUTTERS FLOWING WITH URINE—BLOOD—AND WINE[41]

A substantial part of "New York: 1928" was given over to a bitter renunciation of expatriation by a band of writers who, excepting Burke, had
themselves once lived and worked in Europe but who now, with the zeal of
newly converted nativists, turned upon those who had remained abroad.
The manifesto, indeed, was shot through with the notions of "exile" and
"return." A group of occasional poems written by Slater Brown, including
his famous couplet on McAlmon, set the tone of the attack. An example
entitled "FRY TWO!" reads: "The vulgarity of these United States / Is something every Exile hates. / In Paris, though, they turn the table / And act
as vulgar as they are able."[42] It was Josephson, however, who put his personal stamp on the whole manifesto by its final feature, an "Open Letter
to Mr. Ezra Pound, and the Other 'Exiles.'" He attacked the American
expatriates as a band of "forlorn wanderers" and "fugitives," who vainly
had sought salvation in the "hollow land" of Europe, turned their backs
upon America as "an intolerable land of boobery and buncombe," and
proceeded to surrender to "an ingratiating and inexpensive epicureanism."
For a while, he granted, he and his friends had gone "adventuring along
the same trails," but in the end they had grown "tired" of their "aesthetic
wanderlust" and come to "demand constants." Now they were "once more"
concerned with "the conditions of existence" and were eager to exchange
"the passive principle of flight and exile" for "an *active principle* for the artist." Josephson's attack struck at the heart of the aesthetic program of "The
Revolution of the Word" behind *transition* when it dismissed Pound's elitist, privatist art as "a genteel, bourgeois sport" and denounced "the whole
game of 'making words play with each other'" as a form of "Futurism pro-
longed." It was the obligation of the artist to confront American reality
at home and try to stem the disjointing impact of materialism with the
leavening power of the mind: "We may become centurions of Soap for a
time, pro-consuls of hydro-electricity . . . [but in the end] the dispersed
and scattered beauty of automobiles and spotless kitchens and geometrical office buildings will have been organized and given direction through
our understanding of the ensemble. A spiritual equilibrium will have been
reached, in which we shall have been active factors."[43]

Josephson's thoughts on the artist's position in the urban-industrial

America of the late 1920s and his perception of the inutility of expatriation had been sharpened by his recent revisit to France and his studies of Zola. He had been quick to formulate his thoughts and by January 1928, the time of the group session at the Hotel Chelsea, had arrived at an intellectual stance that was more radical and more articulate than Cowley's but pointed the direction into which he too was slowly moving. As several of his articles indicated, in the early half of 1928 Cowley, like Josephson, was beginning to feel increasingly out of sorts with the political, economic, and cultural situation in America. They rejected "escape" into expatriate life as a viable alternative, were becoming convinced of the writer's duty to actively strive to affect society through his ideas, but as yet refrained from translating their dissatisfactions into political action. It was symptomatic of Cowley's wavering position at the time that his critique of the consumerist "styling" of books in the *New Republic* of April 1928 appeared simultaneously with his translations of Paul Valéry's essays "Pure Poetry" and "The Future of Literature: Will It Be a Sport?"

Later that year Cowley returned to the subject of literary exile in a front-page review of the diary of Dostoyevski's wife, Anna Grigorevna, for the *New York Herald Tribune*. Much expanded the article became the section "Historical Parallel" in *Exile's Return*. In 1928 it fit in with an awakening interest in Russia and the possibility (or impossibility) of culture in the Soviet experiment; more particularly, it explored the parallelism and divergence between the wave of Russian expatriation after the middle of the nineteenth century and that of American writers in the 1910s and 1920s. The problem in the Russia of the 1860s was admittedly "far more acute," but there were pertinent correspondences. Russian writers were inclined to adopt gallicized or anglicized idioms, becoming in effect "workmen struggling with half-foreign tools," much in the manner of contemporary American writers who hesitated "whether to use the English expressions they learned in school or the words they hear on the streets." Cowley was now feeling his way toward the theory of deracination he was to develop fully in *Exile's Return*:

> the members of what might be called the literary middle class led a troubled life: their economic position was uncertain, and almost all the intellectual styles they followed came to them from abroad. If they stayed at home, they had the feeling of being provincials. If they emigrated, many of their troubles were ended: they lived nearer the source

of literary fashions; they lived in an atmosphere that seemed more favorable to art; they lived more cheaply; and finally they acquired a certain distinction at home, a *cachet* derived from the very fact of their expatriation. On the other hand, they lost the close contact with their own people . . . they were uprooted from the soil.

Cowley distinguished between two "generations" of Russian expatriates, symbolized by Dostoyevski and Turgenev, whose meeting in Baden-Baden in the late 1860s he compared to an imaginary encounter between Hemingway and Eliot: the older writer had "definitely cast his fortunes with Europe" and "spoke rather coldly of the homeland," while the effect of expatriation on the younger writer had been "to emphasize his hatred of Europe, his mystical faith in Russia, and every national element in his character." Exile had turned Dostoyevski into a "patriot" *ex patria*, one whose "love for Russia" was "wholly conscious" and who had, in a manner, "invented the Russian soul." The implications remained unstated, but correlated with Josephson's more radical urgings to Pound in *transition*: it was the duty of the American writer to return from exile, in spirit if not in body, and to help invent or create the American "soul." Only then could the "burden of inferiority," as Cowley put it in *Exile's Return*, be lifted and the conviction gain ground that "American themes, like other themes, had exactly the dignity that talent could lend them."[44]

‹ ‹ ‹ Shortly before participating in the group session at the Hotel Chelsea, Cowley finished a long essay on the slave trade, a historical subject combining his taste for romantic, picturesque adventure with a dawning awareness of the cruelty and human expense attending an unjust economic system. While studying up on the subject for his earlier commission to write on the trade for the *Saturday Evening Post*, Cowley had come across a dusty volume in the New York public library: the memoirs of a forgotten slave trader, Théophile Conneau, as told to a Baltimore journalist in 1854. He managed to rouse the interest of the Boni brothers in reissuing the book in modern dress and in the summer of 1928 *Adventures of an African Slaver, Being the True Account of the Life of Captain Theodore Canot, Trader in Gold, Ivory & Slaves on the Coast of Guinea: His Own Story as told in the Year 1854 to Brantz Mayer & Now Edited with an Introduction by Malcolm Cowley* was published. Beautifully illustrated by Miguel

Covarrubias, the book stands as a labor of love and a feat of disinterested historical scholarship on the part of the editor. Cowley poured months of research into an introduction and epilogue and carefully reedited Mayer's "turgid" and "bombastic" sentences, which, he observed in his introduction, "curl their length like serpents over the page. Always he found a moral to adorn their tails." Cowley's concern for style remained a first priority—his own historical introduction was uncommonly well-written—but he also pointed up the romantic ghoulishness implicit in the illegal slave trade. He even added to the glamor of his subject by omitting many of Mayer's moralizings, by playing up Canot as "a more interesting Trader Horn," and by emphasizing his reputation as "Captain Gunpowder," a phrase that occurred only once in the manuscript. But he also drew attention to the extremes of injustice fostered by an exploitative economic system that he compared to "a hothouse in which cruelty flourished, like some cancerous plant of the tropics."[45]

Cowley early displayed a shrewd feeling for what books would do well in the literary market, an intuition that served him well in his later capacity as publisher's editor and literary advisor. *Adventures of an African Slaver* was hailed enthusiastically by reviewers. The *Dial* gave the book only brief mention, but granted that "the modern editor" had done "an excellent job" and wondered why, since this book was "a success," "shoddy like Trader Horn" should also succeed. Harrison Smith wrote a lengthy front-page review of the book for the *Herald Tribune* in which he expressed his admiration for Cowley's resurrection of "Mr. Gunpowder," and in a personal letter admitted he was "sore as the devil" that he had not risen to the bait when Cowley had proposed the book to Harcourt, Brace: "After this when you say a book is good, you will find us hot on the trail." He seriously urged Cowley to take up again his own book on the slave trade. A history of Atlantic slave runners would fit in with the then current interest in primitivism and black culture. Contemporary writers for some years had been seeking out black jazz clubs from Harlem to Paris hoping to recapture a whiff of the black man's supposedly vital and untainted wisdom. A book by Cowley on the slave trade, Smith believed, might "transfer the interest in the negro from Harlem to Africa and the West Indies" by going back to the negro's "native home." There was "dynamite" in such a book, Smith was convinced, but Cowley, though he got a five-hundred-dollar advance, did not return to the subject until more than thirty years later.[46]

For the moment Harcourt, Brace had to make do with Cowley's translation of *Catherine-Paris*, a third novel by a French-Rumanian author, Princess Marthe Bibesco.[47]

In the wake of the *transition* manifesto both Cowley and Josephson decided to investigate the social changes overrunning America in the late 1920s. Josephson embarked on a tour of American cities in the Midwest to write a series on living and working conditions in urban slums and industries. Cowley, characteristically, turned back to his native region to see how it and its inhabitants were holding up under the advance of mass production and technology. In August 1928 he spent two weeks in Belsano and reported on his observations in "My Countryside, Then and Now," an elegiac prose tribute to his childhood country published in *Harper's Monthly Magazine*. After thirteen years Cowley found his home region socially and physically changed in fashions that seemed "typical of a whole cycle in American rural life." At the instigation of his *Harper's* editor he played up the representative nature of the changes in an essay ambitiously subtitled "A Study in American Evolution." He described the article to Burke, somewhat self-deprecatingly, as "a collection of nostalgic rhetoric with a few noble periods, partly inspired by [Maurice] Barrès's *Les Déracinés* [1897; "The Uprooted"]." The notion of deracination infused Cowley's "salute in prose" to Belsano, which combined a rich feeling of lyrical wistfulness for a lost past with an awareness of the havoc wrought by industrial capitalism. It opened with an evocation of Cowley's native soil as he had left it in 1915: its resources of timber exhausted, its deer driven away, its trout streams polluted, its young men faced with the options of becoming imprisoned in a stunting, puritan life or of growing into "landless men, trees without roots—the homeless peasants of the machine." For farmers and miners, he recalled, life had then been a tragic battle against poverty and starvation, in which social feeling was "almost lacking" and the spirit of a rugged individualism still strong; what had counterbalanced such "unsocial harshness" was "a fund of local patriotism" attached to tribal "totems" like trout, white pines, and deer.

Returning in 1928 Cowley noticed many signs of physical improvements—increased population, occupied rather than abandoned farms, well-kept roads, a new brick school—but also found changes in social attitude: a strict and stunting Protestantism had lost influence to a new liberalism in manners and morals, while the "old" individualism had given way to a "new collectivism" and a responsible awareness of belonging to a local community. One of the disturbing effects of the new spirit had been a widespread conservatism and unconcealed membership of the Ku Klux Klan, but by 1928 the Klan seemed "practically dead" and "the group instinct and the spirit of regionalism were being directed toward less questionable ends," such as a better enforcement of forest and game laws and, in general, a greater degree of communal supervision. As a result, forest fires had diminished, the white pines were slowly returning, deer and trout had become again profuse. The country itself no longer lived in the past, but, though its economic problems remained unsolved, had "found salvation of a sort": the young men no longer migrated to the city but stayed "at home." Cowley's article was informed with a cautious optimism for rural America. "Our nation is much less standardized than its critics like to believe; they generally overlook the importance of our regionalistic forces, not all of which are losing their power." Rural communities that managed to tap the resources of local pride and patriotism could very often solve apparently unconquerable economic problems, Cowley believed. His confident hopes for regional America, however, were counterbalanced by a nostalgic realization of what had been lost: "My country had once possessed a tragic power, a sort of cold majesty that was melting in this more genial age." He ended his "salute" with an appropriately elegiac evocation of his childhood past and by proclaiming a faith in the future that would prove unwarranted soon enough. Though the history of his country, like that of the United States at large, had been "a slow exhausting of resources," Cowley had "no fear for what would come"—"the hills had shown a power of recuperation: the trees were creeping back into the desolate choppings where fire had raged; the fields were resting for other tasks under a blanket of white-top and goldenrod. The people, too, were preparing for the future; they felt a common aim; they would find other resources inevitably. Out of the village, borne by the low winds that precede a storm, came the ring of hammers from the carpenters at work on the new school."[48]

This, clearly, was not the voice of an incipient revolutionary persuaded of the need to change or overthrow a viciously corruptive capitalist system. Rather, it was the voice of one who firmly believed in the indestructible resiliency of the regionalist spirit, in conservationism, in the recuperative powers of nature, in the durability of the old pioneer spirit directed toward a new civic collectivism on a small, local scale. Cowley, as he avowed in 1984, always was "a Little American" at heart, "a patriotic native of some American neighborhood," whether Blacklick Township in Cambria County, Pennsylvania, or Sherman, Connecticut. "I like and love America," he affirmed in old age, "but not in any abstract fashion. . . . I like the people, or most of them, I like the landscapes when they aren't defaced, and I feel at home in almost any of the small communities in which Americans flock together. . . . I detest superhighways, shopping malls, Standard Metropolitan Areas, chemical pollution, and international struggles for power. . . . Perhaps the America I love best is the country of my boyhood, with open fields to run barefoot in and never a chainlink fence in days of travel over dirt roads." Regionalism, a harkening back in spirit to an older, more innocent, rural America, remained the moral touchstone, in matters both literary and political. Even at the height of his radicalism in the 1930s Cowley continued to judge the social and political well-being of the nation by its capacity to provide a decent life for its small or marginal farmers, just as he measured the feasibility of plans for social change by its effects on the literary profession and the lives of American writers.[49]

Shortly after returning from his trip to Belsano in 1928 Cowley sent his "congratulations in excelsis" to Allen Tate, whose first book of poems he had just received, and commented: "I think that you are fundamentally, like me, a regionalist poet. Your years in New York—and my years also—are only an extended episode. Eventually," he added prophetically, "I think we shall both retire, you to Tennessee, I to Cambria County, and continue a friendship in letters and visits." Tate replied at once: "I have always believed you were a regionalist poet because you are a good poet. The good in all poetry has a provincial origin, no matter how much it may be disguised. The contemporary menace to poetry lies in the complex causes that force us into an exile from which we can't return." The trouble with an expatriate poet like Eliot, Tate observed, as if in confirmation of Cowley's beliefs, was that he had "dried up his native roots" and expected to "renew them with the urine of St. Thomas."[50] If for the moment Cowley and Tate seemed to be moving along parallel regionalist lines, the underlying differences in their conceptions of regionalism came to the surface soon enough, as Tate began moving toward agrarianism, a mode of regionalism Cowley was not prepared to follow or endorse.

Tate had for some time been struggling to define his personal relationship to the traditions of the Old South—it was in 1928 that he finished his "Ode to the Confederate Dead"—and later that year he carried his personal dilemmas with him to Paris. On April 15 of the following year, writing from France, he confessed to Cowley that he could no longer suppress his "views, or emotions" on the significance of "the late War between the States." In early June, Cowley spoke out against the conservative implications of Tate's evolving agrarianism, differentiating it from his own, more purely local, conception of regionalism, and revealing in the process that his rising social consciousness was aimed at correcting the nefarious industrialist present rather than at recapturing a way of life rooted in the traditions of the past:

> your regionalism, since it extends to eleven states and a whole civilization, is almost a form of nationalism. . . . I myself should approve of it more completely if it were confined to a county or a township. The culture of the old South, like the culture of Athens, was confined to a very small ruling class. It was surprisingly high . . . and at the same time somewhat sterile; only in Poe, an outcast from the ruling class, did it find a satisfactory expression. Since Kant's Critique of Practical Reason, most of us have been obsessed with an idea of social justice—not to employ human beings as instruments—and I doubt that a purely aristocratic society will ever again be possible. . . . As an article of unreasoned faith, faith in the present is pragmatically effective.[51]

In reply Tate insisted that his position was really "much closer" to Cowley's than his friend imagined and that the question of regionalism was "not sectional." The Civil War, he argued, had brought "the defeat of independent agrarian communities everywhere," and the Old South might well be made into "a convenient symbol of the good life for everybody." In 1930, after Tate had joined eleven other southerners in taking a public stand against industrialism, Cowley, by then an editor on the *New Republic*, promised to review the Southern Agrarian symposium *I'll Take My Stand* (1930) in person, rather than assign it to a Northern reviewer whose "city background would make him unable to treat it justly." He commented: "My own answer to the Southern agrarian dilemma is localized machines, operated by electricity, which can change the small plantation once more into an economic unit and fight the factory system with some chance for success." Over the next few years Cowley and Tate continued to debate their different conceptions of regionalism as a viable alternative to the crisis in industrial capitalism. Though they were led into opposite political directions, on a deeper level their literary friendship remained intact, despite recurring frictions; clinging to "the notion that literature was more important than region or politics," both could remain committed to the establishment of a "republic of letters," a dream that originated in their shared experiences in the 1920s.[52]

‹ ‹ ‹ Social life on Tory Hill was hectic during the summer of 1928. The novelist Nathan Asch, then a resident in "the Tates' part" of Addie Turner's house, recalled how "we, the writers rejected by New York booming with the market of the twenties, consoled ourselves with the gaiety we could engender ourselves." Slater and Susan Brown threw their annual Fourth of July party, with lots of dancing, revelry, and liquor from the local bootleggers, and on July 21 a whirling birthday party was thrown for Hart Crane, just returned from a catastrophic six months' stay in California from which he never fully recovered; that summer his friends began to recognize the physiological symptoms of the early stages of alcoholism. Not all was frenzied revelry, however. Cowley remembered "the long, intensely quiet mornings, the games of croquet at the Browns'. . . . the weekday afternoons spent fishing by myself or walking in the woods with Hart, and the talks about poets and poetry." Crane was trying hard to persuade Cowley to collect his poems into a book and both men saw each other almost daily that summer to lay the groundwork for *Blue Juniata*. On top of his regular reviewing Cowley had undertaken to translate Maurice Barrès's novel *La Colline Inspirée* (1913; *The Sacred Hill*), a job that Matthew Josephson, temporarily a book editor at Macaulay's, had helped him secure.[53]

On August 24 Cowley turned thirty. He had contemplated writing a poem on the occasion and told Burke he had already "thought up some melancholy lines to contrast with a jovial metre." In his notebook he entered a less lighthearted letter to himself, reviewing his literary progress over the last two years and sounding a warning against personal pride:

> *Epistle to Malcolm Cowley.* Two years ago the words "Success" and "Failure" were an obsession with you. They are no longer. You are no longer afraid of being a never-was; you are terrified of becoming a has-been. . . . This last year has been my thirtieth, and you have risen, not vastly, but enough to give you infinite hopes. You need those infinite hopes, which you endeavor to translate into possibilities, and some of which you may render into facts. Perfectly American, you are most pleased by receiving large checks. You fancy yourself as a business-man. On this side you are in more than a little danger. . . . There is a

danger, tremendous danger that you will lose the clearness of vision, the judgment of motives on which you depend, in your pride. . . . This pride enables you to form projects, forces you to carry some of them out, and will preserve—perhaps even create—a sort of integrity you prize now more than ever. But if your pride continues to increase as it has during the last year, it will give you all sorts of false values, it will prevent you from judging your effect on others, it will open you to acquaintanceship with stupid people . . . it will make you into an ass. Careful, Malcolm.[54]

Suffering from a feeling that his writings and actions were too dependent on the contingencies of circumstance and inspiration, Cowley now began to make a concerted effort to direct his career toward self-chosen aims. In late 1927 he made the private decision that, with Crane's active help, led to the publication of *Blue Juniata* two years later: "From now on," he wrote in his notebook, "I'm going to endeavor to put my poems before the public. I've hidden them so long that I've almost lost faith in them." He also decided that henceforth he would consciously set himself a subject, then aim to write a poem on it. In later years he realized that such extreme constructionism rarely led to good poetry and that "real poems did not come from a deliberately chosen subject; they had to be waited for; they could not be willed into being."[55] In the late 1920s, however, Cowley approached his poems much in the spirit of Poe and Valéry, as first of all a conscious problem in poetic composition, in the creation of an effect. As a first step in his new poetic program he set out to write a poem on Nicola Sacco and Bartolomeo Vanzetti, admittedly a subject on which he had "thought little and written nothing." He methodically outlined the poem in his notebook in November 1927, beginning, as often, with a passage of poetic prose that he later recast into metrical patterns and stanzaic forms. The poem underwent further polishing and revision before it appeared as "For St. Bartholomew's Day" in the *Nation* of August 22, 1928, to commemorate the execution in Boston of the two Italian anarchists a year before. The poem registered the belated impact of a public tragedy on Cowley's sensibility but, for all its moral and political indignation, left the impression that an artificially worked-up emotion underlay its stirring rhetoric of revolt and disenfranchisement:

> Then die!
> Outside the prison gawk

the crowds that you will see no more.
A door slams shut behind you. Walk
with turnkeys down a corridor
smelling of lysol, through the gates
to where a drunken sheriff waits.

.   .   .   .   .   .

A doctor sneezes. A chaplain maps
the routes of heaven. You mount the chair.
A jailer buckles tight the straps
like those which aviators wear.
The surgeon makes a signal.
                                    Die!
lost symbols of our liberty.

Beyond the chair, beyond the bars
of day and night, your path lies free;
yours is an avenue of stars:
march on, O dago Christs, while we
march on to spread your name abroad
like ashes in the winds of God.[56]

The execution of Sacco and Vanzetti, two men widely believed to be innocent of the crime with which they had been charged, following upon seven years of imprisonment and legal investigations shot through with racial and political prejudice, was the one cause of the late 1920s that brought writers and intellectuals of disparate political plumage together for a common purpose. Mike Gold, Dorothy Parker, John Dos Passos, Katherine Anne Porter, Edna St. Vincent Millay, John Howard Lawson, Lola Ridge, and many others issued protests and appeals, picketed the Boston State House, and engaged in other forms of political action. Matthew Josephson followed the impending execution from Paris and, with other Americans abroad, found himself treated with hostility by impassioned Frenchmen who took a radical stand in what had become an international cause célèbre. To Burke he confessed his sympathy for the protesters and dissenters who had exchanged their artistic isolation for political activism in a manner resembling Zola's stand in the Dreyfus affair.[57]

Like Burke, Cowley had not participated in any of the protest demonstrations but had followed the mounting hysteria in newspapers and periodicals from the position of a quiet observer living and writing in rural isolation; perhaps, as he later remarked, he "never really expected the executions to occur." Though he had talked to several of the writers who had joined in the "strange nocturnal march" on August 22, 1927, there is little in his letters and notebooks of the late 1920s to support the view that Cowley's political radicalism dated from the time of the execution of Sacco and Vanzetti, as was the case for so many future fellow travelers. His poem on the "dago Christs" may have been "the gesture of a shaken writer determined to take a stand on a tragedy he had not publicly protested," as Elinor Bulkin has suggested; still, its radical sentiments seem too much in the nature of a rhetorical pose. It was not until eight years after the tragic events of 1927 that Cowley wrote extensively on the case for the *New Republic* and explained the conversion to radical politics of the "intelligentsia" as, in part, "a sequel to the Sacco-Vanzetti case, a return to united political action" after the defeat of radical protest in 1927. Even *Exile's Return*, the book he published in 1934 at the height of his radical faith, made not the slightest mention of the affair. When, a year later, he argued that "the effects of the Sacco-Vanzetti case [had] continued to operate in a subterranean style," to surface with the Depression, he seemed to be speaking less from personal experience than as the contemporary historian of an entire class of intellectuals, one in whose leftist perspective the case had come to loom with large significance. Still, his general observation may have held a kernel of personal truth. In August 1929, two years after the executions, he confessed to John Brooks Wheelwright: "To tell the truth, I went a little sour on Boston in 1927, and I should remain sour on Boston even if it suddenly appeared that the two Dago Christs were really bandits." Whatever the precise degree of the radicalizing impact of the Sacco and Vanzetti affair on Cowley's thought, undoubtedly the event reinforced his feeling of disaffection with the moral obtuseness and thwarted perceptions of justice displayed by the guardians of the country. To the extent that his future revolutionary stance was rooted in such a feeling of cultural disaffiliation, Cowley's later political commitments were, indeed, the "echoes of a crime." In 1928, however, he could feel at most, with his friend Josephson, that the affair illustrated "the perfect impotence of Individualists in the face of mass-realities," without being propelled into revolutionary activism.[58]

Some of the delayed impact of the deaths of Sacco and Vanzetti became visible in Cowley's long review of Josephson's biography of Zola, appearing in mid-October in the *New York Herald Tribune Books*. *Zola and His*

Time, Cowley wrote, was "vigorous, absorbing, hastily written, superbly documented, and rich, amazingly rich." His sense of style infallibly led him to the heart of Josephson's commitment to Zola and his long discussion of the Dreyfus affair, three chapters written with "the fire that is aroused only by contemporary problems." Cowley devoted nearly half of his review to Zola's role in focusing public attention on the Dreyfus case and played up the parallelisms with the Sacco and Vanzetti affair.[59] "In one case it was the question of an individual against the army; in the other it was a question of two individuals against the judicial system of a state. Into one the Jewish problem entered largely; the problem of unassimilated aliens entered into the other. Both cases attracted political zealots for their own ends and disinterested thinkers for the love of justice. Honest men were divided about them both," he observed, with barely a spark of radical sentiment. He quoted Josephson's lament that there were "no more Zolas today," and acknowledged that Zola's public stand in his famous letter, *J'Accuse,* was "a superb step." In conclusion, he cited Anatole France's honorific description of Zola's behavior as "*a moment of the conscience of mankind.*" Indirectly, in his own cautious and quieter fashion, Cowley was ranging himself on the side of the writer who recognized his responsibility to society. The career of Zola, he wrote in his review, "reveals new judgments of the literary life. It opens horizons."[60]

A week later, reviewing a selection of the works of Remy de Gourmont by Richard Aldington, Cowley revealed how much he had internalized the example of Zola as a new touchstone of the literary life. At one time he and Burke had cherished de Gourmont as a hero of literary art. Now he spoke out with force and self-confidence against the symbolist ideal of a monastic literary life: "We have learned of recent years to consider a man's literary works as part of a larger unity in which his life is also included. In Gourmont's case, his whole career has come to be judged unfavorably; it is found to be too specialized, too lacking in liberality and courage; it represents what we now regard as a false ideal of the literary life. . . . Gourmont spent his workdays in a library and his leisure moments in second-hand book shops. Except for a few bookish love affairs, he lived entirely in the past and in the printed word. At the end of his thirtieth year . . . he yielded completely to his fear of life, and, like a hermit crab, retired into a shell which was not his own. Books were his wall against the world." While his contemporaries were "endeavoring to affect the literary and political life of the time," de Gourmont was writing novels that now seemed "as moldy and airless as the study in which his life was passed." His books, Cowley noted, displayed "merely the unhealthy eroticism of a hermit, of St. Anthony creating his own temptations."

Cowley's insistence that the writer leave his artistic hermitage and become involved in the larger world about him has to be set against his persistent wariness of surrendering a precious individuality and independence to a dogma, creed, school, or .party. For all his criticism, he also upheld de Gourmont as "an enemy . . . of all forces that attack personal liberty," a last defender of individualism against oppressive political systems, be they democratic or socialistic. De Gourmont's skepticism—"Truth tyrannizes; doubt liberates," he had written—was clearly congenial to Cowley; it was a mark of the ambiguity of his position that he ended his review by acknowledging that de Gourmont was "most convincing to our own age" at those moments when he spoke as "a messiah of the skeptics."[61]

Between the lines of Cowley's contrasting evaluations of Zola and de Gourmont a sensitized reader could catch glimpses of another crisis of self-confidence. There was much fearful self-recognition for Cowley in Aldington's observation that, "instead of concentrating his genius, [de Gourmont] dissipated it through a mass of writings all of high quality, but few or none of the highest." Had Cowley, too, possibly "diluted his thought" and "stored it in too many diverse receptacles"? Writing his biography of Zola, Josephson, by contrast, wisely saved his best critical energies for the big job, without dispersing them over a host of little articles and projects, as he himself had been doing. Contemplating his position Cowley once again was besieged with self-doubt: "Should we decide, deliberately, to be Great Men?" he asked Burke, not without irony, on October 16. "The ambition is not impossible. One rationalizes, one learns a methodology, one pursues a course; in a country of drunkards and cretins, the result is not too much in doubt, but is it worth the sacrifices it entails?" A day later, he revealed, with less equivocation than he had in his reviews, precisely where he stood. The example of Zola, amalgamated with that of Valéry, shone radiantly. He wrote to Burke:

It would be nice to be permanently adolescent. Still, I should not like to return to the sense of futility that brooded over our own adolescence. We had determined to be writers, and writers, in America, play no part in public affairs. They are specialists, in other words cripples. I should like to have the courage to proclaim that nothing human is

alien to my interests. Perhaps it is true that if, like Leonardo, we discover a methodology, we can apply ourselves to everything. If some
American writer would take a stand in favor of the widest interests
possible—a stand like that of Zola in the Dreyfus case—he would
improve the status and resolve the doubts of us all. But to reach this
point he would have to have a long training in pride, in the noblest
conception of himself. The pride of a good writer is to be disinterested, to observe everything, to be able to predict economic and social
movements, and yet to draw no profit from his powers of prediction.[62]

The writer's proper place was squarely in the midst of contemporary life;
he should aim to affect the social and economic realities of his time, in
particular as they pertained to the position of the artist in an age of mass culture, but should do so without surrendering his independence, integrity,
and disinterestedness. Only if he stopped being dependent on his writing
for his livelihood, Cowley implied, could such an ideal be attained.

Meanwhile, money was much on Cowley's mind. Two weeks of editorial
work for Harold Loeb in November yielded $250, $150 of which went to
pay off a long-standing debt to Isidor Schneider. Through Loeb, in whose
financial expertise he had enough confidence to swallow his scruples,
Cowley tried for once to seize his share of the "easy money" available
under a boom economy and with Burke invested part of his meager capital
in stocks; within a week their shares had dropped below the profit line.[63]
The free-lance market offered better chances of a profitable return on his
efforts, if hardly satisfaction. He continued to slave over his translation of
Barrès's *La Colline Inspirée* and in October learned that *Harper's* had accepted his essay on Cambria County, at $250. He submitted a proposal for
articles to the *New Yorker* but balked at the magazine's suggestion that he
write one or two of the articles without guarantee of publication. Through
Burke's mediation he received a commission from Donald Freeman, managing editor of *Vanity Fair*, to translate a series of articles by French writers,
including Paul Morand and Valéry. The assignment, which yielded about
$15 a day, soon proved a hackwriter's nightmare. Morand and Valéry ex-
cepted, the articles were trash, and Cowley's translations were subjected to
gratuitous editorial cuts and "improvements" into the bargain. "Me and the
job don't get along extra well," he told Burke in early December. "They'd
have to give me lots and lots of praise and feed my greedy vanity to make
me relish that diet of thin pap. What shit they publish!" He was "coquet-

ting" with translation offers from three different publishers and considered turning over his *Vanity Fair* commission to Slater Brown. But for all his grumblings at the abomination of the undertaking, Cowley did not break off the deal and continued to do occasional translations for *Vanity Fair* until late spring 1929, when Freeman departed for Europe.[64]

With the help of Zola and Valéry, Cowley had arrived at a clearer conception of the ideal literary life, yet he remained unable to work out a practical solution to the frustrations of a free-lancing career. At the end of 1928 he again descended to the depths of self-complaint. He stayed in the country until deep into the winter season, slaving over "The Prophetic Hill," as his translation of *La Colline Inspirée* was provisionally titled, frittering away much of his energy on the chore of keeping the farm comfortably heated in the sub-zero cold. "Sunday night in southern Labrador," he wrote to Burke; "the wind howls around the chimneys; the snow, having softened a little in the sun, even at ten degrees below freezing, is now forming a hard crust; the kitchen stove is swallowing wood like a pack of wolves, and the house is snug. I've spent a purely physical day, not thinking, not reading, but chopping a little wood, eating, playing cards, and stepping outside from time to time to sniff the air like an overdose of cocaine." A study on abnormalities of human behavior had made him realize with renewed poignancy how much of his life was wasted on trivial actions. "Character is a sum of past actions and a potentiality for actions in the future," he observed to Burke, in line with some of his earlier notebook speculations. "I am coming round to behaviorism, not as a philosophy—I detest [J. B.] Watson and his allies—but as a handle by which to move the world." For one who, four years earlier, had written in his notebook, "The good man is the man who makes his own conditions, who makes himself free," Cowley had pathetically failed to live up to his personal standards of morality and he now realized as much: "none of my difficulties will be solved until I learn to plan my day, to be master of my leisure instead of its slave." Once again Cowley stood face to face with his inability to direct his life along the lines of a self-imposed discipline, to withstand the compromises endemic to a free-lance life. He was certain, however, that his troubles were not uniquely his own but were symptomatic of the position of the artist in late 1920s America: "I'm becoming more and more convinced that the principal problem for an American writer is one of living. . . . The authors of intelligence who fail because of aesthetic shortcomings are rare in comparison with those who surrender either to the need for making more money or, in other instances, to the narrower vistas imposed by the effort to spend less."[65]

Six weeks later, reestablished in a cramped apartment at Thirty-three Avenue B in New York, he wrote to Edmund Wilson to express his disgust at the cutthroat competitiveness of literary New York and to voice his hope that Wilson, who was going through a nervous breakdown that winter (the "price," Cowley told Tate, for his "Babylonian and Alexandrian nights" of immoderate living), would recover soon and return to New York "with a new store of malice to join in that battle of malice which is literature." Wilson was fighting his private battle to survive as a writer in America, but to Cowley he seemed one of the very few able to transcend the hampering conditions of the literary life. "Think," he wrote encouragingly to Wilson in mid-February 1929, "you have a special distinction: you're the only writer I know who has been successfully leading a double life—that is, who has been earning a living out of literature and at the same time writing good books. I ought to know the difficulty of this double task, since it seems to me that I've rather failed in both sides of it."[66] In early 1929 it was Edmund Wilson's disciplined professionalism that pointed the way toward a conduct of the literary life.

15

The End of a Literary Apprenticeship

1929–1930

In early April 1929, when the first signs of spring appeared in the streets of New York, the Cowleys fled back to the country around Patterson. It had been a turbulent and disorienting winter in the city. Cowley's marriage had for some time been falling apart. There had been affairs on both sides, and Cowley found it painful to contemplate the contrast between his own relationship, childless and unstable, and those of his friends, most of whom were by now the fathers of steadily expanding families. "Ah, this bloody everlasting talk of gestation and parturition, abortions and diapers. I don't know what to say when I hear it. I sneak off and get tight," he told Tate on the verge of his escape to the country. Having plunged into the social and sexual distractions of winter life in New York, he now turned away in disgust. "Too many parties; too much seduction, sodomy, cunnilinctus and abortion; too much money spent; no sleep," he told Wilson in late March. Increasingly, also, the underside to American prosperity became an oppressing and inescapable reality of life in New York, and Cowley, returning alone from his nightly escapades, felt stirrings of conscience at observing the first signals of an impending economic depression. On April 2, 1929, he wrote to Tate: "What a flurried winter! I've been a rounder; I've seen my old friends seldom and strange faces often; I've come home at seven in the morning to watch the bread lines stretching for three blocks along this Main Street of Jewry. That was on Good Friday; the men standing in line were impassive and averaged from forty-five to fifty years, the cast-offs of our industrial civilization, which hires no men over thirty-five; I had a rather drunken phantasmagoria of being Christ and of descending myself into something or other." Still, he assured Tate, against all odds he had been "working immoderately, working badly," struggling to complete translations, hurrying off "articles for which the figurative presses were waiting," and "thinking hardly at all."[1]

Over the winter Cowley had made significant progress on assembling his book of poems, but yet, with a persistence that at times seemed comical, he continued to bemoan his failure to control the conditions of his life. In early April, Josephson, in the midst of an affair with Katherine Anne Porter, observed to Wheelwright: "I see Cowley now and then. He has magnificent plans: but something always keeps him one gasp behind them. . . . [He] claims passing months without having 'a single idea,' [but] sometimes indulges in remarkable confessions." Shortly after, Cowley admitted to Foster Damon that he was not sure whether he had made the right move in becoming a free lance and depending on "the world of letters and pseudo-letters for a livelihood. I have no time for work that isn't immediately remunerative (in other words, I can't finish a book without going too heavily in debt). I keep loping along, three jumps in front of destitution, like a horse pursued by a pack of wolves, and I must even do my reading as I run. On the other hand, I'm my own boss; I can tell publishers to go to hell, and generally do; I've earned a sort of independence—at what a price in fullness of life." [2]

One redemptive feature of this difficult winter was that Cowley began a new important friendship. On one of his lonely nocturnal ramblings through the city, Cowley had drifted to Lee Chumley's speakeasy in the Village and fallen in with a group of young strangers who were living it up in the hedonistic fashion of the decade. They were the members of a generation younger than Cowley's own, who felt, if possible, more "lost" and who were rebellious in a more uninhibited fashion. It was not the first time that Cowley, so proudly a member of a generation that made a cult of youth, had found himself confronted with youngsters who looked down on him and his coevals as "relics of an age that was passing." At one of the Fourth of July parties on Tory Hill he had met "a delightful flapper," the daughter of George Cram Cook, and had grimly observed to Burke: "She speaks of Her Generation, which makes one feel very old. And it really is a generation, with marked characteristics, chief of which is a total lack of sexual scruples." [3] Among the group at Lee Chumley's one young man stood out, "almost like a young prince, distinguished by his air of affability and his easy self-assurance." Peter Blume, twenty-two, with Roman features and an "aureole of red-gold curly hair," was already determined to become a painter. In 1911, aged five, he had emigrated, Cowley soon learned, from Russia. Since 1925 Blume had been living the penurious bohemian life of a professional artist in the Village and had been associated with the painters of the Daniel Gallery (Sheeler, Demuth, and Kuniyoshi among them), which, with the Stieglitz Gallery, actively sponsored a radically modernist American art. Blume was struggling along on a moderate allowance from the Daniel Gallery, and Cowley was impressed by his absolute imperviousness to money. In early 1929 he described Blume to Burke as "a good painter, a ladies' man, and a deep thinker—as most modern painters insist on being."[4]

Blume had known about Cowley for some time. His literary friends regarded Cowley as "the most promising of poets who were coming along at that time" and Blume had been reading his poetry in the little magazines. He had been impressed by Cowley's translation of *Variété*, in particular by his ability to transform Valéry's abstruse and reflective prose into lucid, natural English without simplifying its complexity. Shortly after their first encounter both men met again, at Romany Marie's and other speakeasies, and began taking long walks together in New York.[5] Cowley and Blume struck up an intimate friendship that was to last the rest of their lives. There was more than a commitment to modernist art and a life-style of financial struggling to draw both men together in the late 1920s. Both had had an affair with the same woman; Blume's had just broken off at the time of his meeting with Cowley, and he was temporarily "roosting" in other people's studios while searching for a place where he could work, without interruptions, on a bigger scale. Through Cowley he learned of four unheated rooms for rent at Addie Turner's for eight to ten dollars a month, which Blume accepted on the spot. Cowley drove him to the country in an old ramshackle Model-T Ford, an expedition on which Blume received his first driving instructions. Over the summer of 1929, living across the hall from Crane's one-time quarters, Blume worked almost uninterruptedly on his first major painting, *Parade*, which he finished in January 1930.

In a special way Blume's picture displayed his aesthetic affinity with Cowley. As Blume explained in a 1981 interview, he too tried to "approach art as a distinctively American art form, that is, with what we learned from European modernism." At the time, Blume was aiming to make his own "new synthesis" of cubist and futurist techniques with a distinctly American realism, one that would surrender "the idea of absolute purity of form" and initiate "the revolution of content." *Parade* depicted a looming urban-industrial landscape of conveyors, big air ventilators, and tenement walls painted over with advertisements, set against a lowering sky darkened over by polluting plumes of smoke. In the foreground marched a human figure bearing aloft an iron suit of armor, the symbol of a threatening dehumanization in an age of mass industry and technology. The figure, wearing a brown beret with a slightly French look, was Malcolm Cowley.[6] *Parade* was the first occasion when Blume had actually realized a "conceptual synthesis," a deliberately chosen "composition," before setting out to paint it, and Cowley, sensing Blume's kinship with Valéry, in his notebook classified him as a "constructionist" artist, together with Dante, da Vinci, Racine, and Flaubert.[7]

Living in the country Cowley found himself more intensely worried about money than before. In early May 1929 he made a big loan to make his final payment of $732 on the farm; he received the deed to the property, but was left "completely, beautifully and prodigiously broke." Once again he was faced with the unpleasant task of having to write himself "out of the hole" at the rate of two cents a word. Cowley's attitude to money was careful and conservative. For all his periodic dissipations, he retained from his middle-class upbringing a hatred of being financially (or morally) "beholden" to anyone and had "a horror of running into debt." Once or twice, he took some of the "quick and easy money" that, as Fitzgerald was to say, was "in such profusion around you" in the Jazz Age, either by speculating on the stock market or by accepting the advances of publishers who looked with kindness on the experiments of his generation. More commonly he retained an attitude of prudence, partly from a fear of becoming too deeply involved in a commercial culture inimical to art. In April 1929, flirting with the idea of accepting another five-hundred-dollar advance on his projected book on the slave trade, he cautioned himself to be "much warier" about such solutions and, in early May, broached the possibility of financial assistance to Burke, whose bank account had recently been fattened by a two-thousand-dollar *Dial* award. His appeal, however, was met with "moral lectures" in which he was urged to bring the conduct and conditions of his life in tune with his precarious finances. In reply to Burke's upbraiding, Cowley acknowledged that his present money worries were the "penalty" for a self-chosen mode of life and determined anew to battle his way out of his bankruptcy. He even toyed with the idea of abandoning his free-lance independence: "Just now," he told Burke on May 8, "I should be willing to take a job if it represented a real financial advance—in other words $100 a week, or, if the position were very easy or had other honors attached to it (like one on the New Republic), $75 a week, but these are my minima." A week later, once more in the dumps, he wrote to Burke: "I have a very bad conscience over being almost thirty-one, and having done really nothing whatsoever, and being broke, and losing part of my interest in general ideas, and this and that and you know the old litany." He hoped that "another bad month" would put him back on his feet financially. After five weeks of strenuous work he completed a translation of *Le Perroquet Vert* (1924; *The Green Parrot*) by Princess Marthe Bibesco for Harcourt, Brace, finished his rendering of Barrès's *La Colline Inspirée* as *The Sacred Hill* for Macaulay, and made substantial progress on a translation of Raymond Radiguet's *Le Bal du Comte d'Orgel* (*The Count's Ball*) for Norton. But shortly, after three days in New York, he again complained of being "broke, completely and definitely broke, starvation broke, with only the rainbow of prosperity in front of me." This time he was so tired of balancing on the check-bouncing edge of bankruptcy that he contemplated taking concrete steps toward leaving the free-lance life: he had been tentatively offered a part-time job as assistant to Carl Van Doren at the Literary Guild, where he would be expected to read manuscripts and interview publishers, at seventy-five dollars a week. Should the job fall through, publisher Harrison Smith had offered to put him on a drawing account in the fall; the second possibility, Cowley granted, was "nearly ideal."[8]

Meanwhile, "the unfaithful slave of the typewriter," he continued to ply the writer's trade. For some time he had been seeing less and less of his friends but found himself clinging more persistently to the past he had shared with them. Their parties, once the light of his life, increasingly seemed to depress him. The annual Fourth of July celebration was "terrible," he told Burke; "too much drunken philandering, too much strong punch." The mood of the times was changing as the decade was spiralling toward a frenzied climax. At the parties Cowley attended, there was harder drinking, more desperately uninhibited lovemaking, more bitter quarreling; the carefree innocence of the "good winter" of five years before was giving way to laughter that was "keyed too high," to horseplay that was strained and hysterical. "It seems to me that this year might well be known as the era of ill feeling," Cowley told Burke at the end of September 1929. "Everybody is quarreling, has quarreled, or is about to quarrel with everybody else." His own immediate future was yet uncertain: the job with the Literary Guild was "still hanging fire," and it was equally undecided if Harrison Smith would actually "subsidize" him. Shortly after, in early October, Cowley was asked by Bruce Bliven to join the staff of the *New Republic*.[9]

‹ ‹ ‹   Cowley's doleful self-evaluations must not be taken at their face value. Though his discouragement was real enough, he had been uncommonly productive and resilient for most of the winter and spring. For one thing, 1929 saw the appearance of three French novels translated by Cowley, one of which affected him profoundly. In May *The Green Parrot*, by Princess Marthe Bibesco, appeared; it was hailed by reviewers as a "just and sensitive" rendering of a "romantic variation" on the incest theme, played out against the background of the exiled Russian nobility in France. Raymond Radiguet's *The Count's Ball*, which appeared in December, was one of two novels by a young author who had died at twenty. Reviewers' comments indicated how much the novel fell in with Cowley's personal literary enthusiasms: the book was greeted as an "interesting specimen of the 'new classicism' in postwar French literature," one "intensely modern in its viewpoint," yet executed on "a highly moral, and at the same time highly sophisticated plane." George Stevens, Cowley's editor at W. W. Norton, was euphoric about his translator's "perfectly gorgeous job." Shortly after, Cowley contracted with Norton for a book of essays that over the next five years would grow into *Exile's Return*.[10]

Cowley's standards of craftsmanship had not suffered from the fact that he had undertaken the translations largely for money. *The Green Parrot* brought in $400; Radiguet's novel $350. His third translation, Barrès's *The Sacred Hill*, yielded more—for six months, between May and October 1928, he registered a $125 advance in his notebook—but it was also a much more arduous task over which he slaved intermittently from the spring of 1928 through the spring of 1929. "It has proved to be incredibly difficult," he told Wilson in the midst of his struggles, "and I'll probably fall dead of poverty over the last page of the manuscript."[11] Cowley was far from happy with his rendering of *The Sacred Hill*. Perhaps Barrès's mannered and rhetorical style clashed too strongly with his own inclination toward elegance and lucidity. In his introduction, completed on June 11, 1929, Cowley described Barrès's style as "supple, grave, musical and complex" but pointed out that it lacked the bright limpidity of the typically " 'French' style." For once, the reviewers' response fell short of the expected unanimity of praise, though even the sternest critic granted that if the book did "not sound quite right in English" the "fault" was less the translator's than Barrès's own.[12]

The Sacred Hill held a particular fascination for Cowley, not so much because it was "a magnificent study of religious aberration" and "a very unusual combination of the imaginative and the real," as because it strongly appealed to his personal regionalist instincts. Not long before, Cowley had relished *Les Déracinés* and found Barrès a congenial author fully aware, like himself, of the dangers of deracination. In his introduction he now praised *The Sacred Hill* as "a study of local patriotism" and betrayed his feeling of affinity with its author: the novel, he observed, "deals with the countryside that was both the birthplace of Barrès and the symbol of his love for the undying past. It deals with people who were so fiercely attached to their own soil that they endowed the landscape with a life of its own; and the author, who shared their emotions, has made [it] perhaps the most important character in his novel." He ended his introduction with a long personal memory of the wondrous ascendancy gained over a western Pennsylvania community close to Belsano by a Protestant clergyman, whose religious rise and subsequent downfall had remarkably resembled that of Barrès's protagonists.[13]

More important than Cowley's translation projects was that he finally took the decisive steps toward the publication of his first book of poetry, *Blue Juniata*, though it needed "a pure act of friendship" on the part of Hart Crane for him to do so. Since the previous summer Crane had unselfishly devoted himself to the project of prodding Cowley into bringing his poems together in a book. On July 16, 1928, he announced to Isidor and Helen Schneider that he intended to do his utmost to find a publisher for Cowley's poems before a year had passed. "He'll never do much about it himself," Crane wrote, "and his collection is really needed on the shelves these days." By the summer of 1928 some ninety-five of Cowley's poems had appeared in magazines and, even after subtracting the thirty-odd discardable juvenilia, a solid sixty poems remained as the core of a book. As Cowley later acknowledged, however, he supposedly felt "no urgent desire" for a book, preferring for the time being to remain "unclassified and free to move in any direction." His actual ambition to attain book publication appears to have been greater than his recollection suggests, for as early as 1926 he had contemplated a *Blue Juniata* in his notebook. Still, he needed Crane as a catalyst. In July 1928, at Crane's repeated insistence, Cowley gathered a group of his poems and with Crane made a selection and thought about structure and sequence. Crane felt the poems would gain by appearing in an emotional sequence that was inevitably "right" and conceived of the book as very much an organic whole. Although Crane had publicly chided as "a genial pedestrianism" Cowley's efforts to keep his lines as close as possible to the rhythms of prose, he respected the integrity of Cowley's verse and was reticent in the matter of alterations, thus proving he was, as John Unterecker called him, "a perceptive and careful editor." [14]

In early August, Cowley went off to Belsano and Crane set himself up in his friend's New York apartment, hoping to find a publisher for the book. At the end of October he urged Cowley to bring the manuscript along on his next trip to the city: "I have a suspicion," he wrote, "that something will come of it now." A month later he dashed off a chaotic letter showing the aftereffects of a drunken night on the town but reported the safe arrival of the poems: "I'll be careful with the mss. And your book'll be out within 7 months. . . . About time!" On December 1, 1928, he had once again carefully gone over the arrangement of the poems, omitted one of them, changed the order of three others, and painstakingly retyped the entire manuscript. He was tickled to death with the success of his efforts: "Certainly I have been on more intimate terms with the poems than ever, and my enthusiasm has been heightened thereby rather than in any way diminished. . . . Really the book as we now have it has astonishing structural sequence. Most of the more doubtfully important poems come in the central section. There is the fine indigenous soil sense to begin with in the Juniata, and the eloquent and more abstract matter mounting to a kind of climax toward the end." On the verge of his departure for Europe, Crane returned the original manuscript, sent one copy to a " 'secret' arbiter" at a New York publishing house, and took another copy along with him to try and place it with an English publisher. The reason for Crane's secrecy about the New York publisher soon became apparent: his "arbiter" was Gorham Munson, then an editorial advisor for Doubleday, Doran. In an in-house memorandum to John Farrar, Munson explained Crane's role in the selection of poems and advised favorably: "I strongly recommend Cowley's work. He is 'modern' in his technique, but lucid, and very able. He is certain to have a *succès d'estime* and will adorn your list in much the same way that Phelps Putnam did." Disinterestedly, Munson put aside the quarrels of the past but emphasized to Farrar that "owing to some past personal differences with Cowley" he was "not to appear in the transactions." In early January 1929 Doubleday, Doran offered Cowley a contract. Within the year, Crane had made good his promise of getting his friend's poems accepted by a publisher. [15]

Now, however, his selfless efforts stranded on Cowley's own admittedly "stiff-necked character": Cowley rejected the offer of Doubleday, Doran, from a proud unwillingness to be obliged to anyone but himself for the structure and publication of his book. Three weeks before, Harrison Smith had left Harcourt, Brace and established a publishing house of his own in partnership with the English firm of Jonathan Cape. Smith was "stealing authors right and left," Cowley told Foster Damon, and when Cowley submitted his manuscript, he found it promptly accepted. Smith had earlier given proof of his belief in Cowley's promise and, only the summer before, had observed: "I have always been confident that all you needed in your career was the completion of a book." Cowley was flattered by the ironic coincidence of finding his book simultaneously accepted by two publishers. Smith offered "much better terms" and "a good sized advance" ($125 against royalties of 10 percent on a first printing of a thousand copies) and promised to really try and sell the book. But Cowley also opted for Cape & Smith for other than material reasons; as he explained to Harriet Monroe, Smith seemed genuinely interested in preserving the art of poetry in an age of consumerism and commercialism: "He no longer intends to treat poetry as a weak sister in the family of books; he intends to publish it in such form and with such advertising that it wins back its popularity and economic self-sufficiency." [16]

Meanwhile Hart Crane had moved on to France, still carrying Cowley's manuscript, and plunged into Parisian bohemian life with his new friends Harry and Caresse Crosby, whom he met through Eugene Jolas. The Crosbys took him up into the circle of American expatriates centering around *transition* and Harry Crosby's Black Sun Press.[17] In Paris, Crane entered upon some of his most notorious drunken brawls and soon, he told Cowley, was gaining a reputation as "the best 'roarer'" in the city. But he had not forgotten his friend's poems: on January 23, 1929, after their second meeting, Harry Crosby noted in his diary that Crane had shown him "a Mss of poems Blue Juniata by Malcolm Cowley." Crane and Crosby discussed the volume on subsequent occasions and Crane was at the point of persuading Crosby to publish the book through the Black Sun Press, when he learned from Cowley that *Blue Juniata* was being brought out in America. Crane hailed "the good news" ecstatically, urging Cowley to at least thank Munson for his interest; Munson deserved "some real credit," Crane felt, since the knowledge that Doubleday, Doran were about to publish the book had probably intensified the interest of Hal Smith and prompted him to offer better terms.[18]

Having picked his own publisher, Cowley took the book home to his

New York apartment and spent much of the winter "once more revising the interminably revised manuscript." Discontented with the shape Crane had given it, he completely recast its structure, placing the poems in a sequence that was "autobiographical" rather than "emotional," and dividing the book into five sections, three of them introduced by prose notes infused with an inescapable note of ironic, elegiac nostalgia. The new arrangement was chronological by subject matter, not by date of composition; the opening section, Cowley's lyrical-poetic re-creation of the country of his childhood, consisted of poems written and revised at various moments between 1919 and 1929, while the last section, a coda entitled "Old Melodies: Love and Death," abandoned chronology altogether; it was held together by more universal or existential themes—love, death, the "tyranny" of time, the emptiness of alienation, the longing for salvation. The new structure enabled Cowley to expand the book from Crane's original selection of thirty-seven to fifty-four poems and to include some poems that, in isolation, did not come up to his rigorous standards. In early April 1929 he explained to Tate in Paris: "in reprinting only poems that reached a certain technical standard, I was giving a false and incomplete picture of the author." The present structure, he hoped, "could give some idea of the development of a poet and produce a book with a unity that a shorter volume would not possess. I think I succeeded to some extent, and I think that the book as a whole is better than any single poem in it. At any rate, it's not a scrapbook, a collection of unrelated poems by the same author." [19]

Blue Juniata was in type by the middle of June. With some trepidation Cowley sent galleys to Crane in Paris. Crane responded with characteristic generosity and without a hint of resentment at Cowley's abandonment of the original structure. On the contrary, he was rather proud that his initial efforts were bearing fruit. In the midst of his roaring revelries—shortly after his letter he was arrested and imprisoned for failing to pay his drinking bill at the Sélect and for knocking down several waiters and a gendarme—he wrote to Cowley on July 3:

> Since reading the proofs I'm certain that the book is even better than before. And the notes!—When you first mentioned them to me I admit having trembled slightly at the idea. But since seeing them I haven't a doubt. The maturity of your viewpoint is evident in every word. Humour and sincerity blend into some of the cleverest and

most adroit writing I know of, leaving the book a much more solidified unit than it was before. . . . Wherever I have noted changes they seem to be for the better. . . . I like the added bulk of the book. Really, Malcolm—if you will excuse me for the egotism—I'm just a little proud at the outcome of my agitations last summer. "Blue Juniata" will have a considerable sale for a long period to come, for the bulk of it has a classical quality—both as regards material and treatment— that won't suffer rejection by anyone who cares or who will later care for American letters.

When *Blue Juniata* appeared on August 8, 1929, Crane was the first to receive an inscribed copy: "If it's bad," Cowley wrote, "the sin be on your head." Crane cherished the book as a prize possession; he carried it with him on his fateful return voyage from Mexico on the *Orizaba* in 1932.[20]

Critically as well as commercially, *Blue Juniata* was quite a success. When Smith's firm went bankrupt in the early Depression, precluding a second printing, all but twenty copies of the original thousand had sold. But it was the critical response that was truly heartening. *Blue Juniata* received wide and responsible critical notice, not all of it unambiguously laudatory, by some of the best critics of the time, and the book clinched Cowley's reputation as one of the significant poets of his generation. Allen Tate gave the book its most thoughtful and eulogistic review. Tate had long admired Cowley's poems and in an article on contemporary American poetry for the *Bookman* had called him "one of the most finished writers in America," "one of those rare American poets genuinely gifted with rural and regional feeling." Tate's own predilections were also strongly reflected in the review he wrote for the *New Republic*. In March, before Cowley had finished transforming Crane's manuscript, Tate had sent Wilson a careful consideration of the book, which Wilson thought gave "an excellent account" of Cowley. Wilson himself considered *Blue Juniata* "certainly a very sound and distinguished piece of work." Tate revised his review to incorporate Cowley's additions and on August 29 Cowley told Wilson: "I read with pink ears the review you published of Blue Juniata; really, Allen overstated the case."

Tate's review was of the sort first-book poets dream of, but it was not uncritically euphoric. Tate presented Cowley as he would have liked to see himself: "a highly trained man of letters," who offered "a fine example of the discipline of craftsmanship" and "successfully cultivated more than one type of literature." But Tate pushed beyond flattery to a remarkably astute estimate of the strengths and limitations of Cowley's writings, both in poetry and criticism: "No American at present writes a more lucid prose than Cowley, and yet it is now clear that prose, certainly critical prose, is not his true medium. His mind is basically concrete and unspeculative; he brings to facts and observations an even emotional tone that is the mark of a genuine style; but in criticism Cowley's instinct for exact definition is not strong; and the necessity for a certain amount of abstraction only violates the even tone of his style. It is in poetry, at least for the present, that Mr. Cowley may be seen at his best." Tate pointed up the beneficial effect on Cowley's poetry of the "long discipline of prose" and singled out "Leander" for its fine display of "the loose orderliness of highly conscious prose— without any falling off in the poetry." Apart from its "high" intrinsic value as poetry, Tate saw *Blue Juniata* as a "unique" document of Cowley's, and his own, generation, "the record kept by a member of this generation who broke with his past, witnessed the moral collapse of Europe, and returned to make the best of the confused intellectual life of post-war New York." Tate astutely diagnosed what Lewis Simpson later described as the poetics of exile (and nostalgic return) at the heart of Cowley's imaginative conception of his, and his generation's, experience. Out of his Pennsylvania childhood, Tate judged, Cowley had "written his best poems." He defined Cowley as essentially "a romantic poet" with an "almost unerring sense of form," whose work as a whole held "no great moments," nor any "disconcerting lapses." Cowley, he concluded, was "one of our most distinguished talents," who, in "The Urn," had created a lyrical poem "unsurpassed in our time."[21]

Kenneth Burke, for much of what Cowley felt was a "pious" and "tactful" review, steered clear of judgment and evaluation but concentrated on the emotional and intellectual autobiographical background to the book. Burke praised specific poems, including "Leander," "Sunrise Over the Heiterwand," "Two Swans," and "Day Coach," and observed how Cowley had supplied to the contemporary world "a Baudelairean corrective of nostalgia." He, too, noted the perennial "hankering after something native" in his friend's verse and deemed it unfortunate that Cowley was best known as a critic and translator; his poetry was "by far his most important contribution" and some ten of the poems in *Blue Juniata* were "permanent acquisitions to our literature." Burke, like Tate, had written a "far too complimentary" review, Cowley told Wheelwright.[22] But more of the same was to come.

In a flowery and impressionistic review for *Poetry*, Harriet Monroe praised Cowley's disciplined craftsmanship—"he beats his poems out of iron, or sometimes bronze, and hammers them into a sturdily beautiful shape, a shape that bears his own impress"—and eulogized his capacity for making his characters "glow with an inner fire, quiver with intensity of life." Cowley had felt "the beauty and lyric agony" of urban as well as rural landscapes; his poems, she rhapsodized in conclusion, "throb to the depths with passion inexplicable, inevitable. Still more when the poet gives us himself, his own intense ecstasy and agony over the rich and violent clashes and harmonies which make up the outrageous magnificent symphony of life . . . he shakes us with a sense of the utterly fantastic grotesqueness of this dance of death on a little ball swinging in space which we dignify and celebrate as human life. . . . We find a thinker in this book, and a man who lives profoundly to the depths of his being. We find also a singer who feels the value of harshness and discords to emphasize his harmonies. . . . These are man-size poems." Somewhat embarrassed, Cowley confessed to feeling "bashful and schoolboyish" upon reading such excessive praise but could not help feeling gratified in his vanity. Monroe's enthusiasm for the book led to its being chosen as the selection for *Poetry*'s book club, the "Poetry Clan," and Cowley was invited to be a judge in a *Poetry* contest, together with Witter Bynner, Padraic Colum, and Sara Teasdale.[22]

Other critics were less indiscriminately enthusiastic. Louis Untermeyer, who had been alerted to the book by Crane, wrote in the *Saturday Review of Literature* of an "auspicious debut." He praised the book's unity and roundness of structure but delicately objected that Cowley penetrated "fewer surfaces than he leaves undisturbed." Though he heard the "accents" of Cummings, Aiken, Eliot, and Laforgue, he judged that in his best poems ("Two Swans," "Blue Juniata," "Mine No. 6," "Day Coach," and "Winter: Two Sonnets") Cowley "grappled with his influences" and seemed "finally to be in possession of himself."[24] John Chamberlain agreed that Cowley had been "so completely honest with himself" that it was now possible to put him "into perspective" as the representative poet of "a generation still imbued with an indefinite sadness and in love with the mood of nostalgia, but more alive and less likely to retreat into the cloister than Mr. Eliot." Cowley, he felt, combined an awareness of tradition with a headlong involvement in contemporary life. He, too, heard echoes, of Masters, of Eliot, of Crane, and felt Cowley was at his best in poems like "There Is a Moment," "Winter: Two Sonnets," and "Leander."[25] Edwin Seaver was struck by Cowley's "genuine and refreshing lyrical gift" as well as his "precision and limpidity of language," but also noted "the eclecticism that for better or worse distinguishes contemporary art as a whole" and hoped a second book of poetry would show a "more definite direction." Horace Gregory, by contrast, believed that Cowley had transformed his various influences into "a distinguished style"—"Not even Hart Crane," he judged, "can surpass Mr. Cowley's verbal excellence." By making "the relationship of humanity to industrial and machine-made life" into the material for "authentic" verse, he felt that Cowley had shown "the potential vitality of contemporary poetry."[26]

A recurrent motif in many reviews concerned Cowley's faculty for absorbing and reflecting the various literary influences to which he had exposed himself over the past ten years. Many critics noted the influence of Sandburg and Masters in the early poems, heard echoes of Eliot and Laforgue, and sensed Cowley's kinship with the dadaists, as well as with Crane, Cummings, and Glenway Wescott. Not all were equally convinced that Cowley had shed his chameleon colors and found his own voice. Several found it difficult to establish the exact point at which the representative quality gave way to unique poetic authenticity. A characteristic, if extreme, complaint was voiced by Ralph Cheney in Contemporary Verse, who described the book as "a record of the spiritual pilgrimage of the sad young men," which led nowhere. He found its poems "exceedingly smart" but "devoid of emotion" and berated Cowley for setting his sails to the shifting winds of literary fashion. In Commonweal, R. Ellsworth Larsson described Blue Juniata as "a sort of handbook of contemporary literary history" and noted that the direction of Cowley's writing was "toward a complete assimilation of the French tradition," something that Larsson thought was "true of the majority of our modern experimentalists." Both complaints were registered in magazines not particularly conspicuous for their hospitality to avant-garde art.[27]

The critical dilemma was voiced with greater urgency in a sensitive and balanced review by the young Morton Dauwen Zabel for the Nation. Cowley was "a new and definitely interesting poet," Zabel felt, one with a "sharp awareness of the characteristic quality of his experience." He strongly stressed the "symptomatic" nature of *Blue Juniata*, variously describing it as "a diagram of the sensations and disillusioning conflicts" of the younger generation, a "self-confessed logbook of literary youth in America," and "a guidebook to an exciting interval of intellectual and aesthetic adventure." Still he judged that Cowley had "kept his own voice among the discordant chorus of voices in which the lyric ambitions of so many youthful poets have been drowned." Zabel was the only critic to single out "Towers of Song" (one of the "imagistic" poems that Cowley himself felt were "false" to the rest of his work) as the "climax" of *Blue Juniata*. Cowley's stature as a poet was "already revealed," but Zabel hoped that the poet would learn to write "somewhat more independently of his generation's peculiar ordeal."[28]

More acerbic criticism came from Yvor Winters and Conrad Aiken. In early August, Cowley sent a copy of *Blue Juniata* to Winters in California. Winters promptly volunteered a review, which he submitted to the *Nation*, but, finding the book already spoken for, turned to R. P. Blackmur, then managing editor of the *Hound & Horn*. Blackmur, six years younger than Cowley, as early as 1924 had expressed a "tremendous" enthusiasm for Cowley's work to Foster Damon.[29] Blackmur's early admiration persisted throughout the decade, and when, on a visit to Damon in Providence in June 1929, he was shown the proofs of *Blue Juniata*, he immediately informed Cowley of his determination to have the book reviewed in the *Hound & Horn*, either by Damon or himself.[30]

In August 1929 Blackmur was busy writing his own review of *Blue Juniata* when he received Winters's unsolicited contribution, which he promptly accepted. In his review Winters, who knew he already had "a slight reputation for a bad disposition," spoke out with boldness. His astringent criticism of *Blue Juniata* clearly reflected his own critical preoccupations. It was not to the book's credit, Winters charged, that "its less successful poems might serve as an outline history of the fashions that [had] risen and fallen" during the past ten years. Cowley had only rarely "mastered" his various influences—in particular those of Laforgue and Eliot—but rather adopted them "from the outside with little or no awareness of their organic causes." In disagreement with most reviewers, Winters did not rate Cowley's Pennsylvania poems his best work: "the group as a whole is more moving than any of its parts, the reason being a kind of stylistic dilution of an emotion that is nevertheless quite genuine of its kind, so that the poetry never permits of very close scrutiny of any given point."

Winters condemned what Tate had praised. He objected to the proselike diffuseness of Cowley's "unorganised catalogues and progressions" (as in "Blue Juniata") and demanded more "firm and closely organized" poems like "William Wilson," "There Is a Moment," and, especially, "The Lady from Harlem," which he quoted in its entirety as a perfect realization of "an organic, not a sought and theoretically correct emotion." It was where Cowley was "endeavoring to study and master himself," Winters observed, that he proved to be "one of the eight or ten most distinguished poets of his generation [who] might become . . . something more." Winters's sharp critique was not wholly unjust; there was in many of Cowley's poems a tendency toward the disorderly looseness of prose as well as an emotional artificiality. What Winters failed to grasp was that the former was part of a deliberate poetic strategy ("my chief interest has always been rhythm rather than image," Cowley had written to Burke) and the latter partly caused by the revisionist zeal of a "constructionist" poet.[31]

"My chief quarrel with you would be that you have tried to find your salvation in so many places other than your own conscience: now in Laforgue, later in Dada, later still in a nostalgic collapse into your native countryside," Winters wrote to Cowley upon finishing his review. Conrad Aiken registered similar objections but did so more violently and without bringing his embarrassing charges before the public. In May, Aiken had promised to review *Blue Juniata* for the *Bookman* but two months later was forced to confess that Cowley's book had failed to live up to his central requirements of good poetry. On July 26, 1929, Aiken poured out his disappointment in a long, anguished letter:

> Damnation! Here for years I've been urging you to get [*Blue Juniata*] out, to get it off your chest, and harboring a clear enough notion that I liked these things . . . and now that they're out, and I re-read them, I disastrously find that they no longer very much move me. . . . But to be seriously truthful: these things seem to me excessively able: they often show a technical brilliance, you can sling almost any manner you want to; and there is a toughish something through all sorts of manners which I can hear as your voice, see as your profile, distinguish as your manner of dressing, your stubborn way of thinking. And yet, there is also the fact that reading them through is disconcertingly like seeing a cross-section of the poetry of the last ten years: as if you had changed your style in accordance with the fashions—no doubt

unconsciously, but detectable all the same. . . . [You have been] so preoccupied with poetry as *technique* . . . that somehow you've forgotten to get down to the real business of the poet: viz., consciously or unconsciously to give the low-down on himself, and through himself humanity. It's as if you come to it from outside. . . . But you? what you think or feel which is secretly you? shamefully you? intoxicatingly you? drunkenly or soberly or lyrically you? This doesn't come out. . . . The stuff is so good, and yet so (somehow) superficial! As if you'd adopted one palette after another and demonstrated your skill, but nevertheless avoided the final business of self-betrayal. . . . I always think of you as the most individual and honest of your generation: all you've got to do is tap *that*. . . .[32]

However much Aiken's critique might reflect his personal aesthetics of ruthless self-revelation,[33] in 1929 there was enough harsh truth in his charges for Cowley to feel pained by the disapprobation of a poet who had been in so many ways his mentor and preceptor. Only two months earlier Cowley had informed Burke of his decision to compose his poems by "deliberate determination" rather than by "inspiration." Shortly after reaching his thirty-first birthday he unwittingly revealed the pertinency of Aiken's observations in his notebook; he had decided, he wrote, to abandon "the idea of writing poems as they come to me" and, henceforth, to apply "all my technical knowledge to the task, deliberately, as if I were a carpenter making a book-case." He had continued: "At 31, what I write will be less personal, more objective. . . . I shall make no attempt whatsoever to be original. From Eliot I shall freely borrow the indirect statement, from Hart a certain handling of images, from Cummings the vocabulary of contemporary life. If I write about myself, I may even borrow Phelps Putnam's fantastic treatment and pedestrian metres. I may possibly use Eliot's treatment of a subject on two or three planes, present and past, fact and dream, incident and emotional reaction. I shall carefully avoid the vocabulary of these poets, and shall hope that by absolutely sacrificing originality, I shall gain it and be admitted into the Heaven of the Beatitudes."[34]

Cowley's half-cynical reflections proved self-defeating; perhaps they were the symptoms of a fear that he was entering a period of infertility as a poet. It was not until six years after the publication of *Blue Juniata* that another new poem by Cowley reached print. It was not until 1941 that a second booklet of poems appeared, significantly entitled (with a wink at T. S. Eliot) *The Dry Season*, including a mere seventeen poems, two of which had appeared in the *Little Review* and *transition* in 1926 and 1928, respectively. Its title poem suggests that "the flow of inspiration" had indeed temporarily run dry:

> The springs were dry,
> the stream bed stony there, its pools half-stagnant,
> with snakes beside them dozing and the trout
> gasping and dying at the water's brim
> . . . .
> It is August, the dry season of your life.
> Take out your heart and wring it between your hands;
> no pain will dart, no blood will drip from it.
> No blood is there.[35]

Like Whitman and Baudelaire, Cowley was essentially a one-book poet, who strove for the duration of his career to perfect and adapt the original fifty-four poems in *Blue Juniata*. In September 1929 he observed to Tate: "My next book of poems, when written, will probably be an expansion of the New York section of Blue Juniata; then I shall perhaps try to expand the country poems; then finally to revise and reissue the whole book." For the next thirty-nine years Cowley followed, sometimes with long interruptions, the "program" outlined to Tate. In 1968 appeared *Blue Juniata: Collected Poems*, which expanded the autobiographical structure of the original book to encompass eighty-six poems, including seventeen new ones besides *The Dry Season*; in 1985 the addition of six new poems completed *Blue Juniata: A Life*, and the book received the subtitle truly befitting "the integrated record of a life."[36]

In 1929 *Blue Juniata* represented Cowley's *testament de sa jeunesse*, his poetic equivalent of George Moore's *Memoirs of My Dead Life*. "Every novel, every poem, every essay, merits just so much of its author's life, and no more," Cowley observed to Wilson in February 1929. "There's a time when everything ought to be published (that is, buried, for publishing a book is exactly equivalent to burying a part of one's past)." *Blue Juniata*, in effect, marked the beginning of a process of retrospective evaluation of his early life which culminated five years later in *Exile's Return*. In the prose notes to his book of poetry Cowley expressed reservations about certain "questionable" qualities in the poems of this "dead adolescent." He may have been wisely anticipating his critics or he may have been voicing a sincere feeling of apologetic self-deprecation when he observed: "I have ceased to value many of these poems; their emotions and their technique are too impermanent. They still impress me, however, as having a certain documentary importance, and as marking a chapter in the history of our wandering, landless, uprooted generation." Cowley's wistfully ironic prose notes were infused with an incipient awareness of the deficiency of his "spectatorial" attitude to art and life. He now acknowledged that his expatriate years in France among "the *Valutaschweine*" had been lived through without much understanding of the realities underlying the frenzied excitement of life among the European avant-garde: "I saw the picturesque rather than the enduring." Before long such a mode of half-nostalgic, half-repudiatory stocktaking would lead to the realization that his "real exile" had been from "society itself." [37]

‹ ‹ ‹ Cowley spent the three weeks before the appearance of *Blue Juniata* in Belsano. There, where the ancestral house was "cool" and the hemlock woods "dark as a cathedral," he hoped to find momentary relief from the summer heat and the mounting strains in his marriage. His trip was in part a "flight from idleness" and he expected that out among "the goldenrods, woodchucks and Methodists" he would be able to finish some articles for the *New Republic* and the *Herald Tribune Books*. He had hopes of enticing Burke to join him on his return expedition to the haunts of childhood and through June and July urged his friend not to miss this occasion for "the fruitful cultivation of an atmosphere that threatens to be forgotten." When Burke seemed to be hedging, Cowley grew more emphatic: "It's an opportunity for a flight backwards into adolescence, into a life with only the future shadow of women (walks along dusty roads, Chopin at twilight on an out-of-tune piano, books, possibilities, Mother in the kitchen)." [38]

Cowley returned from his trip with a renewed determination to consolidate his attainments. But when he surveyed the host of articles and reviews he had written over the years, he was appalled by the ephemerality of many of his writings. "Here I've been writing reviews," he lamented to Burke, "and sometimes very good reviews, for the last ten years, and they're wasted, old, purely topical, occupied with specific books instead of general ideas. I'm not entirely lacking in general ideas, but for proof I can only point to my notebooks, not to my published work." Burke had repeatedly warned Cowley against precisely this sense of futility, urging him to delve for general principles of criticism rather than spend his energies on the more pragmatic (and more quickly remunerative) task of reviewing specific works, and Cowley was now forced to acknowledge that Burke's admonitions had been painfully pertinent. "Reviewing is a form of suicide," he observed to John Brooks Wheelwright.[39]

It was Irita Van Doren who opened a way out of such bleak assessments by commissioning Cowley to write a number of leading essay-reviews for her *Herald Tribune Books* and inviting him to be the magazine's "visiting critic" for the fall. Cowley jumped at the chance to write a series of articles "in the same direction," which he hoped would give unity and focus to a projected book of essays. "It could be either about French or American literature," he speculated in a letter to Burke: "personally I should like to make it American and to deal with the problems that are confronting ourselves." To begin with he contemplated an essay on "The Literary Life," which revealed how much he was moving toward the pursuit, for his own generation, of a line of broader cultural criticism first laid out and then abandoned by Van Wyck Brooks. His essay would be one in which he "described the opportunities afforded by a career of letters, distinguished between men of letters and writers pure and simple, pointed out that very few American writers have achieved a literary career, demanded a higher code of literary ethics, etc."[40]

The extensive outlines and drafts he made in his notebooks indicate that Cowley was now developing many of the ideas he later embedded in a critical-historical framework in *Exile's Return*. Indeed, the later sections of his 1920s notebooks read like first drafts of the book. Conjointly the six major articles he wrote for Irita Van Doren in the second half of 1929, together with a full-length article for the *New Republic*, "The Literary Business," demonstrate that even before the impact of the imminent Depression could make itself felt on his thinking Cowley had come to think of literary culture as indissolubly embedded in a social and economic context. Taken together the essays amounted to his personal stocktaking of American letters in the recent past and an exploration of its prospects for the future as these appeared to him on the threshold of the 1930s. Cowley's impulse to sum up the literary achievements of a passing decade was shared by others of his generation; Tate, Burke, and Munson produced a similar series of essays for the *Bookman*, evaluating the decade's attainment in American poetry, fiction, and criticism, respectively.[41]

Cowley's essays bifurcated quite naturally: three of them comprised his evaluation of the present attainments and future prospects of his literary generation while the others were concerned with the interdependence of the fate of contemporary writing and the state of American civilization. The first two articles appeared in late June 1929 and illustrated Cowley's conviction, voiced three years earlier in *Charm*, that "history is never more fascinating than when it describes the adventures of our own generation."[42]

"Our Own Generation" marked the beginning of *Exile's Return*; its opening sections contain the substance of the "Prologue" and the chapter "Big-Town High School" of the book. By 1929 Cowley's contention that "in a very restricted sense of the word we composed what was probably the first real 'generation' in American letters" no longer sounded as preposterous as it had eight years before in "This Youngest Generation"; nor did his claim that "already it seems that this wartime generation will be rather important in the history of American letters" sound like unwarranted optimism or prejudiced overestimation: Dos Passos, Hemingway, Wescott, and Wilder, Cowley could now claim, had "already established their positions," and Burke and Crane had, likewise, made "permanent contributions to American literature."

In the second half of his essay Cowley probed the reasons why the feeling of disillusionment weighing on his generation at age seventeen had now disappeared. If at thirty the generation was no longer "lost," this was partly the result of the "new forces" in the intellectual world after the war (Einstein, Freud, Proust, Joyce), partly of a new conduct of life adopted by a whole age-group. Cowley did not hesitate to project his personal life's motto—Copey's "solvitur ambulando"—onto an entire generation: "We ourselves have found that most of our philosophical difficulties can be solved, not by philosophy itself, but by living on, by changing one's angle of approach, and often simply by changing one's place." The war itself, he claimed, had had emotional and intellectual consequences that had been "generally disregarded"—"It destroyed our sense of dull security and taught us to live from day to day. It gave us a thirst for action and adventure. It presented us with violent contrasts, with very simple tragedies, and so led us back to the old themes of love and death." The cumulative effect of all those changes had been to destroy "the definite ideas, the purely Anglo-Saxon tradition, the feeling of limited opportunities" of their adolescence and to replace them by "almost nothing—nothing except a vague sense of tremendous possibilities" and a childlike "feeling of wonder" toward life in general.

At thirty, Cowley pictured his generation as standing at "a sort of cross-roads from which any number of paths will lead us toward a variety of destinations." He was reluctant to recommend any path at the exclusion of the others. Cummings and Hemingway were moving toward an "almost pure thoughtlessness" in their efforts to "convey the exact color of the passing moment"; Burke and Tate, by contrast, seemed to be proceeding toward "the pure intellectualism" of Valéry; Wilder and Wescott steered an intermediary course by pursuing "a certain moral tone, a note of personal dignity"; Eliot's classicism had "exercised a very deep influence on half the members of our generation"; and Dos Passos and Mike Gold were guiding themselves "recklessly by the red signboard that points towards Moscow." Less feasible directions were pointed by Joyce's and Stein's experiments with "the abstract value of words" and by surrealist explorations of the subconscious. Cowley's concluding paragraphs bespoke a cautious eclecticism and an open-minded pluralism, but also indicated a need to first digest and evaluate the impact of the modernist upheaval before plunging ahead into new territories of art and life:

> There is a feeling among us that the time for pure experiments has ended and that much of value has been discovered, but not reduced to order, and that our task is rather to consolidate the gains of the last decade and exactly to map the territory which has already been partially explored.
>
> The industrial world spins on toward the future; the world of science questions the fundamental axioms on which it rests; the thunder of new wars, new changes, is heard in a restless sky. We hasten to select a path, any path. . . . For, we have come to believe—most of us have come to believe—that the choice of a literary direction is no longer of fundamental importance to ourselves. . . . It is not a fixed goal, after all; it gleams forth now here, now there; like the holy Grail it appears to some and hides itself from others. And like the knights who pursued the Grail . . . we are undertaking a search which depends not so much on our direction as on our conduct of life itself.[43]

Two years later such an open-ended "grailism" seemed inviable under the impact of his radical political commitments. In 1929 Cowley preferred to keep his options open and shrank from a definitive choice in public.

In the privacy of his notebook, however, he was less unequivocal and summed up his personal beliefs in a "credo" that not only indicated his vacillating awareness that some sort of choice was inevitable but also, for all its lack of political coloration, pointed the direction in which he would eventually move:

Beliefs.
1. The highest ideal for a writer of my generation is to influence the generations that come after him.
2. This influence should have an earthy basis in a regionalism that is neither sectionalism nor chauvinism.
3. It can be exerted through essays, history, fiction, drama, poetry— all the paths are open and I must choose my own.
4. It should involve an interest in social and economic forces.
5. However, it should remain disinterested. Often it may happen that the intellectual may foresee—war in Europe—growth of New York into Nassau or Westchester—further rise or decline of the automobile industry. He can turn this knowledge into essays or even into greater imaginative effort—into novels, plays, poems, but he cannot build munition plants, buy lands in Nassau county, go long or short of automobile stocks, without committing treason to the intellect.
6. Success in one's career as an intellectual should come neither before 30, when one is still unripe, nor after 40, when one is apt to be embittered.
7. It now remains for me to choose my path and go ahead.
8. To be a man means exercising one's power of choice to the fullest.[44]

For all the determination in his articles of faith, for the moment Cowley remained surer of what he rejected than what he was prepared to advocate. His stance was very much that of the writer out of sorts with the prevailing tendencies of contemporary culture but shrinking from commitment to a possibly doctrinaire program of social change.

In his second essay of this period for the *Herald Tribune*, "The New Primitives," Cowley opposed the ethics and aesthetics of his coevals to the cultural pessimism and nihilism exemplified by Aldous Huxley, T. S. Eliot, Oswald Spengler, and Joseph Wood Krutch, whose examination of *The Modern Temper* (1929) was then arousing sharp debate. In his notebook Cowley had already taken his stand on an affirmative humanism that carried the dormant seeds of radicalism:

Our prophets of despair have developed certain functions of the imagination at the expense of others. They can conceive of an inhuman universe; they cannot conceive of a vast human society in relation to which the life of the individual is petty but not without possibility of lasting effect; they lack the concept of history. Greatness is relative. We are little or great in relation to something. We have perhaps lost the concept of God, but we have replaced it by that of society—the existence, the power, the reality of which cannot be questioned. . . . And so, essentially, we are a humble generation; having accepted the theoretical losses of our immediate predecessors, we are consolidating the real and sufficient possessions they have left us, and we are building our own limited happiness among the debris of their illusions, a cottage in the ruins of a palace.[45]

Writing for publication, Cowley took issue with Krutch's belief that modern man had lost the sense of tragedy and human dignity once possessed by the Elizabethans and challenged his conviction that (in Cowley's paraphrase) "aesthetic principles cannot be applied to questions of conduct." Krutch's logic, Cowley pointed out, was refuted by his style: Krutch's language was not that of "an absolute cynic, empty of hopes and aspirations" but betrayed "a high moral purpose" that underlay his ideological indictment. Krutch's pessimistic conclusions, Cowley argued, were belied by a group of younger writers ("the new primitives," he dubbed them) in whose works one definitely found the "note of tragedy" as well as "a feeling that is both modern and strangely Elizabethan."[46] These writers dismissed the cultural pessimism of Krutch and Spengler in a simple but effective fashion: "They proclaim the dignity of life in their own way, by living." As a result their works radiated "the sort of headlong enthusiasm that one associates with the beginnings of things, with the first step towards a new culture." Their work often "avoided the expression of ideas" but was confined to sensuous impressions, simple emotions, and acute perceptions. Aiming to define their commonly held ideas, Cowley observed how the "new primitives" represented "a definite break with literary tradition," by writing as if no one had ever written before them and replacing "the language of Tennyson and Keats" with "the American language as spoken in poolrooms, speakeasies, beauty shops and Pullman smokers." They shunned the Freudian subject of "the human soul, with its dreams, its warped desires, its uncertain flow of consciousness," and turned away from this "misty mid-region of the soul" to "the definite, brightly colored fields of reality." [47]

In the last analysis, however, Cowley dissociated himself from the "new primitive" indifference to the "complicated traditions" of the past and, indirectly revealing his indebtedness to T. S. Eliot, felt his way toward an intermediary position of criticism and endorsement: "more cautious contemporaries," he noted, "are neither contemptuous of the present, like Dr. Spengler and Mr. Krutch," nor are they "willing to dismiss the past. We regard the traditions of literature as a complex and precious system of relationships which we cannot abandon and can alter only laboriously, slowly, with the utmost caution. The task, however, is one that seems worthy of our most patient efforts. And so we proceed on our own difficult path, while we observe the bold progress of [the new primitives] with curiosity and a sort of admiring dismay." [48]

The difficult task Cowley so cautiously set himself was to constitute a lifelong endeavor: his most substantial essays, in particular those written in mid-career, aimed to recover a "usable past" for American literature and to demonstrate the place of the major writers of his generation in an American literary tradition harboring Poe and Emerson, Hawthorne and Whitman. In his conclusion to "The New Primitives" Cowley adopted a critical perspective not unlike Fitzgerald's "double vision." Writing about "his" generation, Cowley typically strove to combine "the maximum of critical detachment" with "the maximum of immersion in the drama" of his literary times; he fused the roles of spectator and participant into a perspective so uniquely his own that it could be representative. [49]

In early October 1929 Cowley discussed at length a new work by the "new primitive" par excellence: Ernest Hemingway's A *Farewell to Arms*. In line with his earlier *Book Chat* portrait Cowley examined the reasons, both literary and extraliterary, for Hemingway's "legendary" fame, and found he "expressed, better than any other writer, the limited viewpoint of his contemporaries." He analyzed the way in which Hemingway's "subtractive" style and "strict behaviorism" led to a general effect of "deliberate unsophistication"—and did so in plain, lucid prose that highlighted the degree to which he shared his generation's distrust of emotional falsification, its effort to "redeem" the American language by discarding "the big words." [50] He also pointed out that Hemingway's style was changing to accommodate more complicated emotional registers as well as a subtler and more sophisticated range of intellectual interests. Already, it did not seem unwarranted to mention Hemingway "in the same breath" with Stendhal.

Cowley's perceptive review of A *Farewell to Arms* also encompassed a critical revaluation of his own and his generation's war experience and its effect on postwar literature and life that later formed the heart of the "Ambulance Service" section in *Exile's Return*. The ambulance service, Cowley now advanced, had in reality been "a sort of college extension course for the present generation of writers." In its way, the service had been "almost ideal," but its most important effect, he now stated for the first time, had been to instill in an entire generation "a *spectatorial* attitude" toward the war. Cowley took A *Farewell to Arms* as exemplary of such a stance—Frederic Henry being "a spectator who was beginning to lose interest"—but his essay also entailed a half-guilty recognition that, insofar as the "curious air of detachment" had continued to mark his and his generation's attitude toward postwar life and society, it had pushed an entire generation of writers into a self-defeating and possibly futile direction.[51]

The four remaining essays testified to Cowley's growing awareness that the fate of writing was inextricably linked up with the social, moral, and economic forces at work in American society. Implicitly they amounted to a personal acknowledgment that insofar as his attitudes had been based on the principle *"art is separate from life; the artist is independent of the world and superior to the lifelings,"* he had steered by a faulty compass. On the threshold of the 1930s Cowley now explored issues that became major preoccupations over the next few years. In a notebook entry on "Propaganda and Art" he observed: "The old idea that literature pure existed merely for entertainment, advanced no thesis, and produced no effect on readers, has been pretty thoroughly exploded." There was little doubt, he reflected apropos of Burke's theories of form, that "art might be judged by the *effect it produces on the reader*" but that certain "types" of effect were "better than others—better, that is, in relation to society as a whole, which is the final creator and criterion of value." With increasing urgency he was feeling his way toward a coherent vision of art and society that could provide a meaningful antidote to his feeling that his early years had possibly been wasted. Several poems in the last section of *Blue Juniata* had pictured the poet as a solitary man waiting vainly for some form of salvation, perhaps religious; in his notebook he confessed himself still searching for "a word, one word to unlock the corridors of dream." One of his last entries for 1929 was entitled, grandiloquently but symptomatically, "Toward a Philoso-phy of American Life"; in it, he considered the thwarting effects of mass consumerism, cultural standardization, and machinery on the quality of human life, was disturbed by the seemingly general breakdown of moral character, and noted that "an increasing number of people seem unable to adjust themselves to modern civilization; they 'break' after thirty; the 'young men on the make' whom we admired in college become simple drunks, or develop strange manias, . . . their wives sometimes change into real monsters of debauchery & self-indulgence." Increasingly he became convinced that "escape"—whether into a pure and purposeless art, into the past, into exotic lands, primitive cultures, private social islands, rural regions, or frenzied sexual abandonment—always boiled down to "a form of treachery" and that one "must, instead of finding backwaters in the river of history, flow with the current and try to direct it."[52]

In public, however, Cowley remained sanely balanced and refrained from taking the stand toward which his private speculations were tentatively pointing. A full-length article for the *New Republic* in early July 1929 indi-cated that Cowley was already conceiving of the man of letters as a mediator between the world of commercial publishing and the literary community at large, a conception that led him to assume an influential position as lit-erary consultant to Viking Press twenty years later. "The Literary Business" examined in more serious fashion the tendencies in American publishing that Cowley had satirized before in his "Portrait of a Publisher," while it probed into the economic conditions producing the new phenomenon of the book clubs. To conceive of publishing as one of the "luxury trades," to apply to it the standards of commercial salesmanship, and to adopt "the sensational methods of the circus and the stage," Cowley observed, had led to a dangerous increase in the promotion of a dull and mediocre (because economically dependable) literature. If the new tendencies had perhaps the "redeeming" effect that publishing was "no longer a corpse floating in the backwaters of American business," they also were marked by an unforgivable "lack of efficiency." Because the "business" of literature was "largely a game of chance," Cowley advanced, books were priced at a level barely justified by their production costs. Here lay the raison d'être for the phenomenon of the book clubs, which to Cowley signified merely one more step in "the gradual 'socialization' of the country, in the process of reducing every citizen to a unit of sales resistance." From here it seemed but a step to a more radical critique of the wasteful and deleterious methods of capitalist consumerism and a plea for efficiency and centralization that Cowley was to advocate, along with others on the *New Republic*, before another two years had passed. In 1929 he hoped the book clubs might lead publishers to "revise their methods" by pruning the "dead wood" from their lists, confining themselves to "books that are really worth publishing" and even reducing their prices.[53]

Three long articles published in the *New York Herald Tribune Books* in November 1929 reflected Cowley's preoccupation with the position of the individual in an industrial society in which the pressures were all toward a dehumanizing standardization. In "Machine-Made America" Cowley aimed to construct "a philosophy of American life" by synthesizing the bleak cultural analyses of James Truslow Adams's *Our Business Civilization*, Ralph Borsodi's *This Ugly Civilization,* and Edward O'Brien's *Dance of the Machines,* three writers who considered the quality of human life under industrial capitalism from the point of view of the intellectual and professional classes, the "quality-minded" people at large, and the creative artists, respectively. Cowley was "impressed" by their unanimous agreement that under the present system, educated and uneducated Americans alike were not only the "slaves" of machinery but were being pressured to sacrifice "all the finer arts of life to the maintenance of a high material standard." But he was not as yet prepared to accept such a "dark picture" of life and argued that there were still "compensations for individuals" in a standardized consumerist society. He now probed more deeply into the question of "style and obsolescence," which he saw as the sine qua non of the modern industrial system: it was only through perpetually creating "new styles" for consumption that the system could maintain itself at all. Believing that "style" represented "the whole element of originality or creativeness in modern life," Cowley affirmed a near-Emersonian faith in the possibilities of individualism against the strong pressures for social and cultural uniformity: "If we are able to trace any style to its source, we usually find that it was created by an individual, by some one so sure of himself that he was able to direct public opinion, instead of being directed by it." It was still possible, Cowley concluded, for "certain gifted individuals to disengage themselves from social uniformity" and attain "the sort of independence that is necessary for the creation of styles." In this way the mass of consumers might be led by a cultural elite, "an aristocracy of style makers, highly rewarded, left in comparative independence, and existing side by side with our present aristocracy of business."[54]

In a companion essay, "The Escape from America," Cowley examined the various modes of "escape" resorted to by American writers in an effort to "achieve independence from mass production and uniformity," but found that whether they fled to tradition and the church (Eliot), the Italian Riviera (Pound), Spain (Hemingway), the South Seas (thus following Gauguin), or a life of "sophisticated savagery" in the shadows of big city skyscrapers, each escape route was "open to individuals, but not to society as a whole." Communism, he believed, was declining and losing the support of the intellectual classes, most of whose members were going for "personal means of salvation." The American writer might agree with the Communists in condemning the social and human injustice of the Sacco and Vanzetti case, the miserable living conditions of the southern textile workers, or the recent bloody strikes at Gastonia, North Carolina, but one could do so without becoming convinced that "such defects of the capitalist system could not be remedied without destroying the system as a whole." Cowley, moreover, was "appalled" by the prospect of America following the Russian example of collectivist management: "What became of personal freedom in a Communist state?" Deadlocked between equally inviable alternatives, Cowley turned to Adams, Borsodi, and O'Brien, each of whom offered a different panacea to current social and spiritual ills. Predictably, he was drawn most strongly to Borsodi's proposal of a return to a self-sufficient, small-scale system of rural household economics. In the final analysis, however, he concluded that even Borsodi's program offered "no solution for society as a whole" but at best "a personal evasion."

In reality, Cowley advanced, there was no need to "escape" from American life. Conditions, after all, were not "so bad that we cannot face them without losing our separate individualities"; there were still sufficient opportunities for a meaningful exercise of the creative spirit within the limits imposed by the social system. Moreover, more was lost than won by cutting one's ties with one's native culture:

> The frantic consumption of factory-made products is not imposed on us by law and neither are we compelled to hold standardized opinions. Without permanently leaving our own communities—unless those communities are worse than any which I myself inhabited—one can achieve a certain measure of individual freedom, of artistic living and even of artistic success.

> Moreover, there is much to be gained by remaining with our own

people and by not departing too widely from their mode of life. The present generation in American letters offers a certain negative proof of this assertion. It is by no means a lost generation, but it is certainly uprooted; and it seems to me that its members have paid a heavy penalty for deserting their own background. They are forced to write about indefinite subjects for an indefinite audience. They are tempted to become either disciples without conviction or prophets without a people. . . . It is entirely possible that the quality of their writing might be improved if they accepted the responsibilities of settled men. . . .

The present system, Cowley concluded, still offered "an extraordinary opportunity for those capable of leadership, and such an opportunity is a sort of duty from which they can escape to other countries or economic systems only at a certain cost to themselves." [55]

On Black Thursday, October 24, 1929, the collapse of the stock market triggered an economic depression that would profoundly affect the nature, if not the substance, of Cowley's literary thought. The articles published in the *Herald Tribune Books* in November 1929 were written before the impact of the economic upheaval could have made itself felt; as Cowley was to write later, the 1930s did not really begin until "several months or more than a year" after the crash, and 1930 itself served in essence as "an epilogue to the Boom." In November 1929 Cowley's essays carried the dormant seeds of a future radicalism in his insistence that the writer could reap artistic profit by maintaining his links with the larger human community around him. Before long such convictions were to be politicized and transformed into the confident (but soon subverted) expectation that American writers would choose the workers' side in helping to change American capitalist society; in 1929, however, Cowley's beliefs pointed less toward Marx's revolutionary vision than toward Hawthorne's nonpolitical awareness of the tension between artistic isolation and a humanizing commitment to maintaining one's place in the "magnetic chain of humanity." By late 1929 Cowley had effectively embarked upon a lifelong endeavor to "redeem" (in Lewis P. Simpson's words) the American writer from his condition of "exile" on native grounds. In "The Escape from America" he had struck a vein that, on a level incorruptible by politics, he continued to mine in his subsequent career as a mediator between the small American "republic" of letters and the larger community of society. By 1929 he had become convinced that the American writer had no business being a refugee, exile, or spectator of contemporary reality and must become involved in the culture of his native land to the benefit of his art and of himself. Implicitly he had already come to recognize that writers, as he formulated it in 1949, had "a double duty," both to "the public" and to "the values of their own profession."[56]

As a coda to his series of essays, in "The Business of Being a Poet" Cowley examined the opportunities offered by American society for the flowering of a mature poetry. For his point of departure he took Alfred Kreymborg's compendious "outline" of American poetry since 1620, *Our Singing Strength* (1929). By being indiscriminately sympathetic to some 450 American poets—including the author of *Blue Juniata*—Kreymborg, Cowley found, had created the "false and unfortunate" impression that American poetry as a whole was "extraordinarily rich." If the present, in particular, seemed "rich in promise," Cowley feared that "most of all promise [was] doomed never to be fulfilled." His most serious objection against Kreymborg's "census" was that he had failed to consider poetry as the outgrowth of a particular situation: he spoke of poets "as if they were divorced from their homes, their daily occupations, their financial worries, their ambitions—from all the sad business of being a poet." At present the social and economic pressures on the young ambitious poet were absolutely stunting; if exceptionally prolific, he might hope at best to earn "approximately as much as the striking mill-hands in North Carolina." More commonly, he was forced to waste his energies on "uncongenial occupations." If poetry remained "the last branch of literature . . . substantially free from commercialization," there also yawned a fatal abyss between artist and audience: the poet's "amateur standing" prevented him from being taken seriously by "a public which sets a cash value on everything." Such a misconception of the value of poetry was due not only to "hostile" social and economic forces but also to critics like H. L. Mencken who insisted that poetry should be abandoned at the age of "intellectual maturity." Too much of American poetry, Cowley acknowledged, was "the result of obvious emotional maladjustments": most American poets "wrote to escape from oppressive realities, but this poetry of escape . . . is usually very bad poetry. The qualities we admire in literature are, after all, the qualities we admire in life. Weakness, infantilism and inability to face reality are virtues of neither. . . . What American literature needs is not more poets . . . but mature poets who are willing to devote their whole time to the most difficult of the arts. The present situation makes them very rare." Cowley could think of only one poet over thirty-five who against all odds had "clung monastically to the writing of verse as his one profession"—Edwin Arlington Robinson. If Robinson, however, was the "nearest approach" to the ideal of the major poet, he had paid the heavy price of a life of poverty and a "corresponding poverty of sensations" in his poetry. "One cannot fail to wonder," Cowley concluded, "whether it might not have been less bleak and rigid if conditions . . . had allowed him to lead a less restricted life."[57]

By the end of 1929 Cowley was convinced that the fate and future of American writing were indissolubly linked with the fate and future of American society. From his awareness that current conditions hampered, even blighted, the fruition of a mature art of poetry, it was but a small step to his belief in the necessity for social change. The final entry in his 1920s notebook showed Cowley wavering on the brink of political commitment. It ended on a questioning note from which flowed all the major political, social, and artistic dilemmas he was to confront in the following decade:

> *The Career Open to Talent.* There is a problem whose social impor-
> tance has often been overlooked: it is that of finding the career open
> to talent—*la carrière ouverte aux talents.* Early in the history of the
> American Republic, this career was sought chiefly in politics. . . . For
> the two generations that followed the Civil War, business replaced
> politics as the surest road to prestige; more recently literature has been
> taking the place of both. For the young man who feels that he is more
> than usually gifted, there is no assurance of political rewards. . . .
> Politics is a game for disreputable bosses or wealthy amateurs. As for
> business, it impresses the young man as being controlled by luck and
> pull and office politics; mere talent is no guarantee of success; it is even
> mistrusted. Ambitious people turn to other careers: motion pictures,
> amateur athletics, aviation, engineering. The more articulate turn to
> literature, a field in which talent is almost certain to be recognized.
>
> All this involves a change in the status of letters as a profession. The
> day of art-for-art's-saking writers has ended. Isn't it time for writers to
> assert themselves and to assume the social responsibility they cannot
> well avoid?[58]

By an ironic twist Cowley's thought by the end of 1929 had swung around to the bleak cultural assessments of the early Van Wyck Brooks, whose indictments of "the failure of American culture" he had deemed far too pessimistic at the beginning of the decade. The pressures of his personal experiences, together with his observations of his friends' struggles to attain a satisfactory conduct of the literary life, now led him to acknowledge, at least by implication, the restricted validity of Brooks's plaint against American culture and his demand for a new leadership in letters. Brooks, however, had long since abdicated his earlier role and turned his energies toward recovering a "usable past" for American literature. At the end of the 1920s Cowley had gained the confidence and maturity to step forth in defense of the writing profession in America and to assume that responsible function for the literature of his own times; it was a function that he never abdicated. Cowley's own explorations of the "usable past" came later, in particular in the 1940s, after he had joined Brooks in a concerted political endeavor to create a viable sense of literary community through the League of American Writers. In a nonpolitical fashion Cowley's efforts to safeguard American writers against the "oppressive realities" of American society and to establish a congenial cultural atmosphere in which writers could "devote their whole time to the most difficult of the arts" were perpetuated in the various offices he fulfilled in his later career.

At the breaking point of the hedonistic 1920s and the sober-minded 1930s, the revival of interest in the New Humanism of Irving Babbitt and Paul Elmer More forced Cowley to formulate his personal philosophy of art and life more explicitly and elaborately than he had done so far. Babbitt (1865–1933), a professor of French and Romance languages at Harvard since 1894, was an outstanding scholar of conservative leanings and a trenchant critic of romanticism, in particular Rousseau. He was the author of *The Masters of Modern French Criticism* (1912), *Rousseau and Romanticism* (1919), and *Democracy and Leadership* (1924). More (1864–1937), a student of Sanskrit and the classics, had been a journalist in New York and editor of the *Nation* from 1909 to 1914 before returning to scholarship at Princeton. Beside the *Shelburne Essays*, which appeared in fourteen volumes between 1904 and 1936, he had published two studies on Plato, *Hellenistic Philosophies* (1923)—the book Cowley had read for consolation in the "city of anger" in 1924—and, most recently, *The Demon of the Absolute* (1928). Against the materialist excesses and moral lassitude of contemporary American culture, Babbitt and More sounded a moral *réveil*. Emphasizing the human over the natural and divine, they took a strongly ethical view of existence, seeking for a unifying and controlling framework of human values (intellectual rather than theological) against what they saw as the chaos and decay of the moral and intellectual life of the present. They found their inspiration in a "classical" past of propriety, reason, and decorum, raised the disciplined Puritan moral sensibility to new heights of respectability, and vituperated against the spontaneous, subjectivist eruptions of present-day modernism and romanticism; instead, they put a high premium on the exercise of moral will and self-control (More spoke of the "inner check," Babbitt preferred *frein vital* or "vital control"). The social implications of the New Humanism were clearly reactionary and traditionalist; as More observed, the "true consummation of a democracy" lay in a "natural aristocracy" of taste, education, manners, and decorum. In literature the New Humanists pleaded for a "classical" rather than romantic mode of writing, one that would enunciate the moral discipline of the author and aim to enhance the moral sensibility of the reader. They displayed a severe hostility to "modern" literature—whether realist, naturalist, or romanticist—and had great difficulty finding any contemporary writer who lived up to their ethical standards. Paul Elmer More typically denounced Dos Passos's *Manhattan Transfer* as "an explosion in a cesspool" and contemptuously spoke of Gertrude Stein as "that adventuress into the lunar madness of literary cubism."[59] It was this pronounced antipathy to contemporary writing that set off the antihumanist reaction on the part of those deeply committed to modern literature.

In early 1930 the New Humanists had taken their stand in a symposium, *Humanism and America: Essays on the Outlook of Modern Civilization*, edited by Norman Foerster, critic and professor of American literature at the University of North Carolina, and a formidable proponent of what in his preface he conceded was assuming the contours of a "movement." A collective act of obeisance to Babbitt and More, its principal contributors, the symposium included essays by More's brother Louis Trenchard More, T. S. Eliot, Frank Jewett Mather, Jr., Harry Hayden Clark, Gorham B. Munson, and seven lesser-known intellectuals, most of them professors of literature or the fine arts. In a pious introduction Foerster defended the New Humanism against the fourfold charge that it was "academic, un-American, reactionary, and Puritanic," and, in vintage New Humanist fashion, reaffirmed his belief that "the quality of all life is higher or lower according as our power of vital restraint is exercised." In early March 1930 Cowley, Tate, and Wilson circulated an open letter addressed to the New Humanists among their friends and literary allies; they ironically presented themselves as critics who, desiring "to study the Humanist principles in practice, would be glad to know of a contemporary work of art either pro-

duced by an American Humanist or encouraged and approved by one."
On March 26, 1930, the letter appeared in the *New Republic*, signed by
thirty-three writers who almost made up a roster of the younger literary
generation. In reply Frank Jewett Mather, Jr., an art critic and Princeton
professor, pointed out that because New Humanism was "not an esthetic
but an attitude in morals, a humanistic masterpiece is likely to emerge only
from a society in which humanistic morals are dominant"; he nevertheless proposed More's *Shelburne Essays* and E. A. Robinson's "Cavender's
House" (1929) as distinguished humanist masterpieces. Both Wilson and
Cowley remained unconvinced. The one contemporary work of creative
imaginative writing deemed worthy of unambiguous praise in the New
Humanist symposium, Cowley noted, was a "dull," "correct," and "didactic" novel by the "estimable" Dorothy Canfield Fisher, *The Brimming Cup*
(1921).[60] Clearly, Cowley felt he had reason to fear that, should the New
Humanism come to rule the waves, literary creativity would be ground to
death between its decorous millstones.

In late January 1930 the literary critic and contemporary historian
C. Hartley Grattan invited Cowley to contribute an essay to an antihuman-
ist symposium on the topic "The Humanists and the Contemporary and
Experimental in Literature." *The Critique of Humanism: A Symposium* ap-
peared in the late summer of 1930. It featured contributions by Grattan,
Wilson, Cowley, Henry Hazlitt (recently appointed literary editor of the
Nation), Rascoe, Tate, Burke, the art critic Henry-Russell Hitchcock, Jr.,
Blackmur, Chamberlain, Bernard Bandler II (editor of the *Hound & Horn*,
who had also contributed to the Humanist symposium), Winters, and
Lewis Mumford. In soliciting Cowley's contribution, Grattan had indi-
cated that he expected an article that would "in some way indicate the
inadequacy of Humanism as a literary philosophy." Each article in the
symposium, Grattan stipulated in a later communication, was to contain "an expression of the author's personal philosophy of criticism."[61]
Cowley took up Grattan's challenge. In taking his stand against the New
Humanism, he arrived at his fullest articulation to date of a personal credo.
Although it underwent subtle modification and deepening over the years,
it remained the cornerstone of his literary and ethical beliefs.

In preparation of his essay Cowley thoroughly studied the subject: in
addition to Norman Foerster's New Humanist symposium, he plunged
into William Graham Sumner's *Folkways* (1907), read Babbitt's *Democracy and Leadership* (1924), several of More's works, and such articles as

Seward Collins's "Farewell to the Twenties" in the *Bookman*, which of late had virtually become a house organ of the New Humanists. Cowley purposed, as he put it in his notebook, to attack the disciples of Babbitt and More "on what I conceive to be humanistic [not Humanist] grounds—namely, that their practice, if not their theory in itself, is hostile to the development of creative writers." "Show us," he orated, "a great American poem or novel based on the philosophy of Babbitt, as Dante was based on the philosophy of Thomas Aquinas, or even as Melville was based on Transcendentalism, and perhaps we shall suspend our disbelief."[62]

In his essay Cowley granted that the more general attitude of "humanism" on which he took his stand was difficult to define: "Partly it is an emphasis on the qualities it considers to be essentially human. Partly it is a defense of human dignity, of human possibilities; partly it is an opposition to all the forces that threaten them, whether these forces be religious, social, governmental, economic, or those of an anti-human philosophy." By contrast, the "doctrinal" New Humanism of Babbitt and More wished to "apply fixed standards to literature" and appealed to the more "conservative" among the younger generation (Munson had devoted two long chapters to Babbitt and More in *Destinations* [1928] and contributed to the New Humanist symposium). The New Humanists, Cowley charged, had "unconsciously confused their specific cult with the general attitude" and thus falsely claimed "all the humanist past for their modern doctrine."

Cowley's critique of the New Humanism was twofold: the doctrine was incomplete as a "system of ethics" (even though it claimed to pursue what Foerster called "the ideal of completeness of life"), and it wholly disregarded the social and economic realities of the present. Both objections were interrelated: it was only by considering "man in relation to society" that a "complete system of ethics" could have been developed, Cowley argued. The failure of the New Humanism was that it had "confined" itself to the morality and psychology of the individual in an age that was "increasingly corporate." Cowley rightly pointed out that the New Humanist emphasis on inner moral regeneration as a cure-all was "perhaps the most unreal" solution for such "realities of the present system" as unemployment, low wages, and unbearable working conditions, but in his eagerness to expose the irrelevancy of the New Humanist prescription, he was inclined to replace his opponents' stock of reactionary presuppositions with the prejudices of his own dawning radicalism.[63] "Economically, socially, [the New Humanist] doctrine is based on nothing and answers no questions,"

Cowley charged. "Out of what society does Humanism spring, and toward what society does it lead? Has it any validity for the mill-hands of New Bedford and Gastonia, for the beet-toppers of Colorado, for the men who tighten a single screw in the automobiles that march along Mr. Ford's assembly belt? Should it be confined to the families who draw dividends from these cotton mills, beet fields, factories, and to the professors who teach in universities endowed by them? Can one be Humanist between chukkers of a polo match, or can the steel workers be Humanists, too—once every three weeks, on their Sunday off?" Humanism, Cowley believed, produced "the lamest utopia ever imagined"; it offered no alternative to the wasteful functioning of capitalism, to the increasing centralization of capital, to the "purely automatic" and "dehumanizing tasks" demanded of factory workers, to the unemployment of two million. Instead, Babbitt seemed to "contemplate the salvation of society through a private-school system culminating in a Humanist university."

Reading the New Humanists, Cowley experienced a curious sense of déjà vu, as if he were "carried back into the atmosphere of the classroom," of the social elite on Harvard's Gold Coast. The New Humanism, he felt, grew from the snobbish moral atmosphere of Eastern university life, in which professors inculcated in their students the timeless values and standards that were, in essence, leisure-class ideals. The New Humanist ideals, Cowley was to write in *Exile's Return*, seemed merely "the student virtues [of Harvard] rephrased in loftier language."[64] Cowley's critique of the New Humanism thus implied a repudiatory analysis of the cultural universalism in which he had been steeped at Harvard and which, shortly after, he posited as a crucial phase in the deracination of an entire generation of writers.

In 1930 a sharp cleavage existed between the world of academic scholarship and the literary profession, and Cowley, with a distrust that persisted even after both worlds had come together in the 1940s through the efforts of such New Critics as John Crowe Ransom and Robert Penn Warren, typically took his stand in defense of the contemporary writer against "angry professors" whose moral, social, and intellectual prejudices distorted their literary judgments. By taking their "Puritanism" to "heights of chaste absurdity," the New Humanists arrived at a reductive approach to literature, Cowley charged; they were incapable of dealing with literature as literature: Babbitt delivered "lectures on the sex-life that could not be surpassed by the professor of Mental Hygiene in a fresh-water college," and More's puritanism led him to elevate Trollope over Poe and to advance the detective story as "the only form of literature today wherein you may be sure that the author will not play tricks with the Ten Commandments."

It was to the credit of the New Humanists, Cowley acknowledged, that they had directed attention toward the past, "toward questions of permanence, toward a judgment based on centuries." In his notebook, however, he avowed that by emphasizing the past at the expense of the present the New Humanists had violated, or at least restricted, a vital function of the critic: "It is pretty obvious that the critic has no single function. He is a prospector, a judge, an interpreter of the creative arts, and he generally insists on being a creative artist himself. He discusses the relations between the art of the present and that of the past; he revalues the past in terms of the present, but he cannot, without the cost to himself of a certain disloyalty, neglect the present entirely, nor always read an old book each time a new book is published."[65]

By reaffirming "the connection between ethics and esthetics," the New Humanists had perhaps helped to "rescue" art from the "moral vacuum" of a pure aestheticism, but they had overreached themselves by making art "the servant of morality." It was, Cowley observed in his notebook, an essential "*humanizing* function" of literature and art to create value; it was, he felt, "extremely doubtful whether anything in the world of nature or of men has any value that men do not put into it. They transform questions of expediency into moral questions—the only sort of questions which have real power over the human mind."[66] In his essay he now publicly enunciated a set of literary beliefs that remained axiomatic through the political turmoil of the 1930s and beyond.

All good art—at least all good literary art—has a thesis. Its thesis is that life is larger than life—that life as portrayed by the creative imagination is more intense, more varied, more purposeful or purposeless, more tragic or comic, more crowded with moral decisions, than is the life we have been leading day by day. Sometimes we are discouraged by the contrast; sometimes we merely escape into the world of art. Sometimes, however, we try to reinterpret our lives in the light of the artist's vision. The new values we derive from his work, when projected into our own experience, make it seem more poetic, dramatic or novelistic, more significant, more sharply distinguished from the world of nature—in a word, more human.

But art has another humanizing function perhaps no less important: it is the humanization of nature itself. The world about us was
alien in the beginning; vast portions of it are alien to us today. Before man can feel at ease in any milieu, whether that of forest, plain
or city, he must transform the natural shapes about him by infusing them with myth. Perhaps I am choosing a too pretentious word;
perhaps I should merely say that certain streets in New York are rendered habitable for me by snatches of old ragtime, that I never saw
a telephone until I saw it in one of Charles Sheeler's drawings, that
my memory of Hawthorne transforms and humanizes a New England
village like this. I might say that this creation of myth, by whatever
name we call it, has continued since the earliest times; that it is, indeed, a necessity of the human mind. It is a sort of digestive process,
one that transforms the inanimate world about us into food without
which the imagination would starve.

The masterpieces of the past could not fulfill these functions for the
present. With Emersonian confidence Cowley proclaimed: "Our own
myths, our values, must be renewed from generation to generation. They
will so be renewed as long as artists live: they will be renewed in spite of
the critics who cling to exiled legends and values long since dead." He
concluded by affirming his conviction that it was "one of the real tasks
for American critics today   to assess our contemporary literature on
the basis of this double humanizing function."[67] It was a task that Cowley
faithfully strove to fulfill for the duration of his career.

‹ ‹ ‹   By 1930 Cowley had come to the end of his literary apprenticeship. He had laid the foundations for the "little bundle of beliefs" he carried
with him through his subsequent career and had established a reputation
as an important practitioner of "modern" criticism. He had gained a distinguished name as a critic and translator of French literature and had come
to be recognized as a dependable historian and chronicler of his literary
times, the self-appointed guardian of the literary talents of his generation.
He had also made his own modest but far from negligible contribution to
the literature of his "lost generation" in a well-received debut as a poet.
Moving at the nerve center of American literary life between 1915 and
1930, both at home and abroad, he had confronted the varied and per-
plexing manifestations of international modernism. In a personal search

marked by contradictions and ambiguities, he had evolved his own kind of critical perspective—humanist, pluralist, and eclectic—from which to judge its attainments and define its effects on contemporary American writing. His personal experiences as a struggling writer in American society, together with his observations of the possibilities of the literary life in France, had led him to a broadly inclusive conception of the man of letters as one who would, ideally, adopt "the whole of literature as his province" and who, by religiously devoting himself to the art and profession of letters, might be a useful mediator between the writer's obligations to his art and the oppressive realities of society. On the threshold of the 1930s such an ideal was as yet more promise than fulfillment. It came under pressure in the following decade, as Cowley for a while thought to have found a viable path to a sustaining sense of literary community through the instruments of revolutionary politics. Divested of its political coloration, however, this ideal came into its own after World War II and reached a second flowering.

Also by 1930 Cowley had embarked on what was to be a distinguished, if not unblemished, career as the last independent literary editor of the *New Republic*. Three weeks before the crash he had been appointed by Bruce Bliven to the modest position of part-time copy editor and proofreader, replacing T. S. Matthews. Already known for his "passion for getting words right," he soon proved a worthy junior editor. When Edmund Wilson took a leave of absence in the summer of 1930 to finish *Axel's Castle*, Cowley was deputed to replace him. The year after, when Wilson left his post to embark on his travels as a roving reporter through a depression-ridden United States, Cowley was the natural candidate to succeed him as presider over "the back of the book." The literary editorship of the *New Republic* also presented a personal solution to the problem of a faulty "mechanics" of living that had plagued Cowley throughout his early life: it provided him with the "external discipline" that, as he had complained to Wheelwright, he so badly needed. As Cowley told Burke in August 1930, working on the *New Republic* was less a job than "a manner of life," and it opened the way toward living the literary life that, with all its drawbacks and limitations, was at least more satisfying than the tribulations of a free-lance existence. As literary editor of an influential liberal "journal of opinion," Cowley found himself in a strategic position to observe and comment on the intellectual, literary, and political crosscurrents of a turbulent era in American history. From his editorial desk at the *New Republic* he could realize a Zolaesque ideal of the man of letters as one who was concerned with "every department of human activity, including science, sociology and revolution" but who also retained a sufficient degree of independence and disinterestedness to take his stand on social and political issues "without committing treason to the intellect." [68] If that ideal was not entirely made good by its actual practice, the internal logic of Cowley's formative years nevertheless pointed toward his assumption of precisely such duties as those of the literary editor and leading critic of the *New Republic*.

Between 1919 and 1929 Cowley had made a complete *volte-face* in his literary beliefs: from an early embrace of a symbolist aesthetics he had moved to a repudiation of its antisocial and antihuman implications and a rejection of the "religion of art" as a false ideal of the literary life. From disaffiliation he had moved toward accommodation, from spectatorial aloofness toward involvement. His literary apprenticeship came to a close with his realization that he must stop being a literary wanderer outside the gates. With the awareness that the American writer had no business being a stranger on native grounds, the literary exile could believe he had come home.

Epilogue

Malcolm Cowley, Man of Letters

It was Malcolm Cowley's luck to come to maturity as a writer during a period of high excitement for American literature and to undergo his literary apprenticeship at a time when "youth in itself was a moral asset."[1] From the first he was an alert and sensitive witness to the complex interplay of cultural and historical forces from which emerged, between 1915 and 1930, a distinctly modern American literature. He registered the impact of European modernism on the writers of his own exuberantly young generation and, by writing its collective literary history as he watched it unfold, helped to establish the premises of critical interpretation of its defiantly new literature. Even before the end of the war he immersed himself in the aesthetics of symbolism in the belief that there, as Edmund Wilson was to confirm in *Axel's Castle*, lay the sources and principles of what he valued in contemporary literature. From the French symbolist poets he recovered, as did Eliot and Pound before him, a near-religious sense of literary vocation together with a high ideal of formalist craftsmanship. Soon, however, he came to the recognition that, as R. P. Blackmur observed in 1934, serious literary art does not ever "escape into thin air without first influencing the moral and spiritual life of its readers."[2] It was a recognition that he shared with Eliot but one that Cowley was determined to understand first of all in terms of the united literary effort of his own generation. Buoyantly committed to the present, he shared its rebellious search for authenticity and originality, its radical revolt against the genteel past, its self-mythologized determination to find new forms and a new voice to celebrate life in its own time. In the process Cowley never lost sight of his formalist ideals; rather, they were engrafted upon a broader endeavor to recover what Lewis P. Simpson has called the "humanistic amplitude" of modern literature, and embedded in a Brooksian concern with the establishment of an organic American culture.[3] Cowley continued to follow critically the internal and external evolutions of American literary modernism throughout his career. As his perspective deepened and matured, his appreciations underwent subtle modification, but the gist of his early critical reservations remained intact.

Cowley was lucky in belonging to a literary generation that produced a body of creative work complex and challenging enough to require a sustained effort at interpretation and elucidation for an American audience largely untrained to appreciate its often idiosyncratic and innovative achievements.[4] In response to the unfolding "second flowering" of American literature, Cowley could thus help to develop the set of critical instruments and the historical perspective necessary for a proper evaluation of its distinctive place in the larger context of international modernism. In the process he could help in his own fashion to make American criticism come of age.

The writers of his generation were fortunate in having Cowley as a conscientious literary chronicler and historian as well as a devoted apologist and loving curator. From the first Cowley was extraordinarily generation-conscious. In "This Youngest Generation" (1921) he was the first to delineate, boldly if tentatively, the moral and aesthetic contours of an emerging literary group. By 1929 his early claim of the prospective importance of his age group had been validated and he could begin, in "Our Own Generation," to estimate its ambitions, its achievements, and its intellectual history. It was a self-imposed literary obligation that he strove to fulfill for more than half a century.

In the 1920s Edmund Wilson, too, alertly scanned the literary horizon for the important writers of the younger generation and by 1929 had written perceptive reviews of F. Scott Fitzgerald, Ernest Hemingway, Hart Crane, E. E. Cummings, and John Dos Passos that helped to mold the public's estimate of these writers in ways the younger Cowley could only hope to emulate.[5] Even as a young man Wilson radiated an air of authority and maturity. As an editor on established journals like *Vanity Fair* and the *New Republic* he found a congenial and influential position from which to speak out on contemporary writing at a time when Cowley was still struggling to resolve the ambiguities of a free-lance existence. Possessed of a "tireless intellectual energy" that Cowley, three years younger, could only envy, Wilson in the 1920s came close to being the intellectual and literary conscience, not merely of his friend Fitzgerald but of an entire generation.[6] But even in his early years Wilson seemed to speak from a different perspective than Cowley. Where Cowley, moving in the circles of the national and international avant-garde, combined an outsider's detachment with an insider's familiarity with the ethics and aesthetics of his contemporaries, Wilson seemed to write from an almost patrician perspective located above his literary subjects. Wilson, only a year older than Fitzgerald, sounded at times much like a member of an earlier generation, one closer in intellectual sympathies to the writers of the Progressive Era than to those of the wild and hedonistic 1920s. Cowley's tone unmistakably aligned him with a disaffiliated and rebellious league of youth. Also, as Henry Dan Piper has noted, whereas Wilson always remained "the metropolitan cosmopolite," Cowley retained a "grass-roots attachment to the land and rural America." If Cowley lacked Wilson's massive erudition, he displayed a greater sensitivity to the technical nuances of poetry. Unlike Wilson, who, in Cowley's words, "never bothered to understand how people act in groups" and whose writings always seemed marked by a touch of aristocratic aloofness, Cowley's work, both in poetry and prose, was from the start infused with a strong sense of literary community and displayed a genial democratic temperament.[7]

Cowley's important evaluations of the specific works of his generation came later, in particular once he had taken over Wilson's editorial desk at the *New Republic* and had found an authoritative platform from which to speak.[8] But if Wilson, in certain respects, had been earlier, Cowley clung to his role more faithfully; and whatever the extent of his indebtedness to Wilson's example, he always remained his own man. In the end, with Wilson moving on into the broader fields of history and economics and evincing a talent for "monumental" scholarship as well as a formidable ambition to preside over "all literature as his imperium," Cowley's critical focus remained consistently on the literary and social record of native American experience. If Wilson was "the Sainte-Beuve of a new literature," Cowley was the Boswell of his generation. A barometric chronicler of his literary times, Cowley first predicted the arrival of a new generation on the literary scene, then aimed to define its achievements at an early stage. Treading later in the footsteps of the early Brooks, he sought to establish its connection with the traditions of the past, and following Eliot, he continued to review its attainments in the light of the shifting present and to judge the present in the light of his changing perceptions of the past. Still later, speaking up as "the Ishmael of his generation," he persistently, with affection as well as critical detachment, defended its achievements against the "jackals" and "parricides" of various critical and political persuasions.[9] At the end of a long career spanning seven active decades he could bask in the glow of the then classic stature of the many writers he had championed.

‹ ‹ ‹   *Exile's Return: A Narrative of Ideas* (1934) was the first book of its kind to give an authoritative design of interpretation to the social, historical, and literary forces at work on the lost generation. To all intents and purposes, Cowley had already begun to write the book in the late 1920s: in the fall of 1929 he opened negotiations with the publisher W. W. Norton for a volume of "Fifteen Essays." *Exile's Return* started concretely as another group manifestation by Cowley and company. In the spring of 1931 Elizabeth Ames, the director of Yaddo, the artists' colony at Saratoga Springs, invited Cowley to organize a writers' conference there. Cowley conferred with Josephson and the plan arose to gather their friends and hammer out "a collective book of memoirs." In early May 1931 Cowley, Josephson, Burke, Coates, and Wheelwright reconvened in upstate New York; they were joined by Evan Shipman, a poet and aficionado of horse racing who had been a friend and drinking companion of Ernest Hemingway in Paris. "At Yaddo we had a high old time," Cowley recalled thirty years later. "Evan Shipman found a horse room and a bootlegger. We talked, we explored the countryside, and I wrote. Some of the others pretended to write, but they didn't get anything done. I was launched on my book. Soon afterwards I signed a contract with W. W. Norton and he picked a title: 'The Lost Generation.'"[10]

Between 1931 and 1934, moving forward by fits and starts, *Exile's Return* slowly took shape. At Yaddo, Cowley wrote first drafts of the sections that became "Case Record," "Significant Gesture," "The French Line Pier, 1923," "Women Have One Breast," and "Manhattan Melody": together, they formed the account of his dadaist shenanigans and their immediate aftermath in New York. Revised and expanded over the summer, they appeared as a series of five articles in the *New Republic* in the fall of 1931.[11] Subsequently, Cowley turned back to his years in high school and college and traced his and his coevals' adventures through the war and in Greenwich Village; in the fall of 1932 the *New Republic* printed the sections "Mansions in the Air" and "Ambulance Service," and in January 1933 an early version of "War in Bohemia" appeared in *Scribner's Magazine*. In May 1933, discouraged by the slow progress of his book, Cowley took a leave of absence from the *New Republic* and spent ten weeks at Cloverlands in Tennessee, near Caroline Gordon and Allen Tate, where, between fishing expeditions on the Cumberland River and visits to the Tates and other Agrarians, he filled out the story and composed his repudiatory analysis of Dada as the culmination of the symbolist religion of art; revised and completed during the fall, "Readings from the Lives of the Saints," "A Discourse over the Grave of Dada," and "The Death of a Religion" were published in the *New Republic* in January 1934. During February, Cowley wrote "Connecticut Valley" and "No Escape," neither of which was published as a magazine article, and in March 1934, after borrowing the diaries of Harry Crosby from his wife Caresse, he spent two lonely weeks at an old inn in Riverton, Connecticut, to write "Echoes of a Suicide," the symbolic account of the end of an era. On May 1, 1934, Cowley finished the epilogue that he would remember as "the high summit of my revolutionary enthusiasm."[12]

The interruptions that marked the writing of *Exile's Return* were only partly caused by the pressures of a busy and responsible job on the *New Republic*. Dramatic changes in Cowley's personal and political life recurrently stalled the writing and laid the foundations for a change of directions. In early 1931 he made the painful decision to separate from his wife. Peggy left for Mexico, where she was joined by Hart Crane; over the winter of 1931–32 they became lovers. Given a new lease on life, Crane again found the strength and inspiration to write poetry, and Peggy's letters to Cowley from Mexico glowed with radiant happiness. Cowley found it difficult to believe, though, that Crane's new life was "anything more than a respite from his private hell." His premonitions proved to be tragically right: in late April 1932, sailing home from Mexico on the *Orizaba*, Crane leaped off the stern of the ship. Death and divorce: the "echoes of an era that had ended."[13]

But the sense of an ending was counterbalanced by the determination to make a new and responsible beginning. In June 1932 Cowley married Muriel Maurer, a beautiful New York fashion editor he had met a year before. Their marriage was to last. During the same time, Cowley's political radicalization peaked in a series of public acts of commitment. In 1931 he protested the torture and killing of twenty-four young Chinese Communist writers in a campaign to suppress the Chinese revolution and joined the National Committee for the Defense of Political Prisoners. In 1932 he was a member of a delegation of writers, including Waldo Frank, Edmund Wilson, and Mary Heaton Vorse, that went on a mission to Pineville, Kentucky, to distribute food to the striking miners. Having witnessed the human misery and the hopelessness of their lives, Cowley made a "public confession of faith" by marching in that year's May Day Parade. In July 1932 he reported on the flight of the Bonus Army, driven out of Washington by federal troops, as it passed through his native Pennsylvania region. That same summer he joined the League of Professional Groups for Foster and Ford and participated in the political campaign for the Communist party presidential candidates by helping to write the campaign pamphlet *Culture and the Crisis*. Later that year he reported on the National Hunger March on Washington for the *New Republic*, together with Robert Cantwell.[14]

In private correspondence, meanwhile, he struck a more ambiguous note, explaining to Burke that he was "not plunging blindly ahead" into communism but "trying to evolve a theory, a hypothesis, that will fit what I see happening." In 1932 a combination of literary reservations and a stubborn need to retain his freedom to criticize—not political caution—kept Cowley from taking the ultimate radical step: he never joined the Communist party. As Daniel Aaron has pointed out, Cowley rarely wrote with the zeal of a convert. Nevertheless, his radicalization was part of a process of personal change that was religious and emotional before it was intellectual. In *The Dream of the Golden Mountains* (1980), Cowley wrote:

> I would never be more than a fellow traveler, and yet I was an ardent one at the time, full of humility, the desire to serve, and immense hopes for the future. Because any disaster seemed possible in that strange year [1932], so did any triumph. Suddenly the range of possibilities had widened and deepened, as had the picture of our relation to history. It was as if we had been walking for years in a mist, on what seemed to be level ground, but with nothing visible beyond a few yards, so that we became preoccupied with the design of things close at hand—friendships, careers, love affairs—and then as if the mist had blown away to reveal that the level ground was only a terrace, that chasms lay on all sides of us, and that beyond them were mountains rising in the golden sunlight. We could not reach the mountains alone, but perhaps we could merge ourselves in the working class and thereby help to build a bridge for ourselves and for humanity.[15]

During the 1920s Cowley had repeatedly sought a unifying principle of order and discipline in his life. In his moments of despair and disorientation he had turned to his notebooks to give voice to his longing for "salvation" and to search for a key "to unlock the corridors of dream." To Burke he had sounded a half-ironic cry for a "messiah." As Hamilton Basso rightly intuited, Cowley's involvement with the radical movement of the 1930s was in part "a religious manifestation: a longing for 'order,'" inspired by a feeling that in the 1920s his life—personal, political, and literary—had been set in self-defeating directions.[16]

To the extent that *Exile's Return* argued the case against the literary past, it amounted to a confession of personal failure and a testimony to a new-found belief. The entries Cowley made in his notebook during his stay at Cloverlands testify to the strong doubts about the value of his earlier beliefs and the validity of his present undertaking that plagued him throughout the writing of the book.[17] The early 1930s, in the words of one historian, were "a time of penance for past sins and declarations of future rectitude." Read in the context of its time, *Exile's Return* was a symptomatic book: a bidding of "farewell to a whole period" in Cowley's life, it breathed a sober air of re-pentance for a misspent past. *Exile's Return* was part of a broader tendency to discredit the moral, political, and artistic courses sailed in the 1920s; it built up to the acknowledgment that "all that is dead now," but it did so with a subtlety of insight and a degree of literary eloquence that raised it far above the level of a crude and intolerant attack. The center of Cowley's critique of the past was his analysis of the symbolist ethics and aesthetics at the heart of modern literature. Though he granted that the religion of art had left "a great heritage," on the wave of his radical enthusiasm he was considerably less certain than before of its lasting contribution. His analysis of the lives of its "saints"—Eliot, Joyce, Pound, Proust, and Valéry—and his discussion of its extreme manifestation in Dada left his readers little room to doubt that Cowley had become thoroughly convinced that in its dissociation of art from life, in its pursuit of a pure and purposeless poetry, in its hermetic and narcissistic subjectivism, the religion of art had proved "essentially anti-human" and "anti-social." As an ideology and an ethics, symbolism was the equivalent in literary art of a bankrupt individualism in the economic and political sphere.[18]

The shedding of "yesterday's burdens" prepared the way for new convic-tions and *Exile's Return* pointed a clear political moral. Active participation in a movement for the revolutionary change of a system that seemed to be "convulsively dying" was only a natural corollary of Cowley's recognition of the futility and aimlessness of his earlier literary ideals. *Exile's Return* greeted the end of the 1920s with visible "relief." It now appeared that the collapse of the stock market promised to put an end to the madness, hyste-ria, and despair of a decade that had culminated in the seemingly symbolic suicides of Harry Crosby and Hart Crane and that the ensuing depression had accelerated the realization that the "real exile" of American writers was "from society itself, from any society with purposes they could share, toward which they could honestly contribute and from which they could draw new strength." Cowley's argument in the book radiated his belief, voiced with didactic eloquence in the epilogue, that involvement in the class struggle could put an end to the enfeebling isolation of the American writer and that "the desperate feeling of solitude and uniqueness" could be redeemed by "a sense of comradeship and participation in a historical process vastly bigger than the individual."[19] It was here, in the search for a nourishing sense of community, that the artist could hope to find surcease from the oppressive sense of alienation endemic to his spectatorial stance.

Cowley's repudiation of symbolism antedated his conversion to radical politics, and even before the stock-market crash of 1929 he had, in opposition to the privatist ethics and aesthetics of symbolism, evolved a broadly humanistic insistence on the inseparability of art and life, on the interdependence of artist and audience, art and milieu. His earlier humanism was now given a new dimension of historical understanding and the pragmatic coloration of a radical political vision, but it remained the premise of his convictions, both literary and political. Cowley's argument against the literary past in *Exile's Return* was only a natural outgrowth of the values and beliefs he had developed during his own odyssey through the postwar years; for all its denunciation of "a literary period that was mistaken in its general aims,"[20] the book also stood as the crystallization of the "little bundle of beliefs" Cowley carried with him as his most essential literary baggage throughout his long career. It was one of the subtle incongruities of the original 1934 edition (one only partly remedied in the 1951 revised and expanded edition) that the curiously trivializing tone in which Cowley described the adolescent irresponsibilities of an earlier time was partly belied by the note of wistful and compassionate regret with which it evoked the intellectual and emotional mood of a literary era now passé. Its tone of ambiguity bespoke the survival of at least a partial allegiance to literary values discredited with such apparent determination.

‹ ‹ ‹   Appearing in the midst of a "violent reaction against the 1920s," *Exile's Return* met with a devastating reception. Many of the younger reviewers hailed it with qualified praise. Older reviewers, writing in established magazines of wider circulation, had "a grand time demolishing the book," so that to Cowley "the weight of hostile opinion seemed overwhelming." Not only did his political opinions come under heavy fire but the brunt of the excoriations was leveled against the book's claim that the achievements and vicissitudes of the 1920s exiles was a story worth retelling at all. Cowley felt much like "a criminal chained and taunted in the marketplace," as all his personal doubts about the validity of the undertaking seemed confirmed by the fusillade of clobbering reviews.[21]

When *Exile's Return* was revised and republished in 1951 it was as lyrically acclaimed as it had once been abusively condemned. The critical somersault was only partly due to the nature and extent of the changes, which mostly served to divest the book of its politics and to place the story in a maturer, if also a more mellow and nostalgic, perspective.[22] This time, however, the literary zeitgeist worked much in its favor: by 1951 Cowley's claim of literary stature for the lost generation had been more than validated (partly as a result of Cowley's own critical efforts on its behalf)[23] and, coming out on the wave of a critical rehabilitation of the 1920s, the book's true meaning and significance were more clearly visible. By 1951 Cowley's perspective, too, had subtly changed. In the wake of the series of revaluations he had edited (and partly written) in 1937 as *After the Genteel Tradition*, he could now acknowledge, more precisely and disinterestedly than before, the influential role played by the writers of an older generation (Mencken, Dreiser, Lewis, Anderson). He could more dispassionately evaluate the nature of the impact of symbolist aesthetics (and, by extension, the whole tradition of European modernism) on the literature of his generation. And he could more clearly recognize its connectedness with an American literary tradition that extended back to Poe, Hawthorne, Melville, James, and Stephen Crane.[24]

Cowley's strategy in *Exile's Return* was highly selective. Writing on the tangent plane of the personal and the communal and adopting the dual perspective of a detached spectator and empathetic participant, he aimed to use his own experience only insofar as it could be made symbolic or representative. Because he had lived through virtually all the formative phases of his generation's literary experience, Cowley, in almost Emersonian fashion, could feel justified in making the self exemplary. The documentary record of his early life reveals that his account is only in a limited sense to be trusted as accurate autobiography. Predictably, and notwithstanding Cowley's acknowledgment that "each life has its own pattern, within the pattern of the age, and every individual is an exception," not all of his contemporaries felt equally comfortable with being fitted into his generational paradigm.[25] In giving imaginative form and structure to real events and experiences Cowley had inevitably done some degree of violence to individual deviations from the overall thematic pattern. Insofar as the writing of history is always an act of imaginative reconstruction, however, it had been Cowley's luck that history and personal experience coincided and helped to give, as he put it to Burke in 1931, "a good novelistic structure" to his critical narrative. The pattern of generational experience outlined in *Exile's Return* is indeed fictional as much as historical; perhaps it is precisely for this reason that it could so influentially shape the public conception of the lost generation and could become, among the countless histories and memoirs of the time, "the one epic-making one."[26]

Drawing on the ancient mythical pattern of exile and reintegration, odyssey and homecoming, *Exile's Return* exemplified a sui generis form of literary history. Infused with a genuine gift for poetic lyricism, it survives as a work of the literary imagination, one that derives much of its effectiveness from the orchestration of interpretative metaphors, the building of dramatic narrative line, and the intensity of Cowley's personal connection with its subject matter. His "narrative of ideas" is informed with an essentially novelistic understanding that abstractions and ideas do not live unless they find concrete embodiment in character, action, and situation. It is this fundamental grasp of the nature of imaginative re-creation that forms the basis of what Kenneth Burke has called Cowley's "personalistic" mode of writing literary history and criticism. It is partly for such literary reasons that *Exile's Return* deserves to be seen, not merely as an "irreplaceable" literary record of what Van Wyck Brooks has called "the most dramatic period in American literary history," but also as an integral part of the artistic legacy of the lost generation.[27]

Part of the ongoing appeal of *Exile's Return* comes from its recovery of a timeless fable from the historical experience of a specific generation. The rite of passage it outlines is one reenacted in one form or another by every new generation as it grows to maturity and finds itself subjected to the alienating realities of modern existence. Because, at its deepest level, Cowley's poetic history of exile exemplifies what Lewis P. Simpson has described as "that curious modern feeling that the self has of being dissociated from an integral self," *Exile's Return* has gained with time something of the timeless appeal of a legend.[28]

Since 1934, and even more so since 1951, our understanding of the nature and necessity of literary exile has changed profoundly. Set against the experiences of Vladimir Nabokov, Thomas Mann, Alexander Solzhenitsyn, Salman Rushdie, and countless other writers and intellectuals for whom exile has been a painful, unwanted, and often politically enforced mode of cultural severance and linguistic dislocation, the expatriate experience of Cowley and his coevals emerges as a particularly happy and luxurious form of literary banishment; it was engaged in with a good deal of bounce, in the full, if partly ironic awareness that their severance from the homeland was voluntary, temporary, and, often, revocable at a moment's notice. As Warner Berthoff has pertinently suggested, for the members of Cowley's generation, "exile" was in part merely "crisis language . . . for the familiar custom of the European *Lehrjahre*." [29] Today we may well feel with Leon Edel that the question of literary nativism or expatriation has "ceased to be a controversial issue" for the American writer. But our changed historical perception of the problem does little to diminish the status of *Exile's Return* as "a classic document of literary history." Even its most fervent detractors, like Geoffrey Wolff and Kenneth Lynn, have had to acknowledge its influence and authority as "the book which did more than any other to popularize [the legend] even as it was among the first to validate the great importance of the literature which made the legend possible." More than half a century after the book's first appearance, the appraisal of Robert E. Spiller, made in the mid 1970s, remains valid: "Anyone who does not absorb and understand *Exile's Return* is not prepared to comment on any American literary event between 1915 and 1975." [30]

‹ ‹ ‹　The complex and painful story of Cowley's literary and political odyssey through the 1930s falls outside the scope of the present narrative. It will not do, however, to trivialize or excuse the political errors into which Cowley allowed himself to fall, in particular in the second half of the decade, once his earlier political idealism had begun to seep away and he had come to feel a sense of disillusionment and moral fatigue. The literary historian or biographer of those years faces the difficult task of disentangling Cowley's often conflicting modes and motives of behavior. He will have to weigh the justice of the serious upbraidings Cowley received from trusted literary friends like Allen Tate, Edmund Wilson, and Hamilton Basso, who recurrently challenged Cowley's pursuit of what Alfred Kazin has euphemistically called "a sophisticated literary Stalinism." [31] He will also have to find a dispassionate answer to the fierce attacks leveled against Cowley by a long line of often overzealous political enemies, from Trotskyist sympathizers like Felix Morrow, Eugene Lyons, and James T. Farrell in the late 1930s to such neoconservatives as Kenneth Lynn and Joseph Epstein in the early 1980s. Their bitter critiques will have to be considered in the light of their own literary and political presuppositions and be set against more balanced appraisals of Cowley's radical years by Daniel Aaron, Alfred Kazin, Robert Alter, George Core, and Lewis P. Simpson. Cowley's own memoirs and historical accounts of the tangled reasons for his conversion to and subsequent disaffection from his radical hopes will have to be measured against the historical documentary record of his published writings and his unpublished journals and correspondence. Such an effort may reveal why a man of good will, who tried to maintain "a shop-keeper's honesty" about his beliefs, was unwillingly led into false positions because he failed to voice in public the doubts and reservations he confided to his notebooks. It may help to establish the reasons why, in their cumulative effect, Cowley's self-confessed "sins of silence, self-protectiveness, inadequacy, and something close to moral cowardice" left him with a sense of guilt about the second half of the 1930s.[32] Perhaps it may also help to estimate the extent to which Cowley allowed his literary values to be distorted by his political convictions.

What needs to be emphasized is that Cowley, like Wilson, remained at heart "a man of the twenties." Even at the height of his radicalism he never truly abdicated from the ethical and aesthetic standards and the ideal of the man of letters that he had evolved by 1929. If we examine the many reviews Cowley wrote in the 1930s under the aegis of a radical literary criticism—as he told Burke, he was "driven toward" Marxian criticism because it considered "art as organically related with its social background, and functionally affecting it"—we find that underneath the glowing fervor of his often naive political sentiments Cowley's basic literary beliefs remained surprisingly intact. Alfred Kazin has not been the only one to feel that in the 1930s Cowley seemed "to unite, through his love of good writing and his faith in revolution, the brilliant Twenties and the militant Thirties."[33] Tendentious as some of his literary judgments may have been, he mostly did not confuse "correct" political opinions with literary gifts. Undue emphasis on Cowley's political mistakes, real enough though they were, obscures the fundamental soundness of his literary intuitions and fails to register the many and repeated reservations he expressed about the crudity of revolutionary writing, the dogmatism of leftist literary thought, and the limitations of Marxian criticism.[34] If Cowley's lack of political prescience made him cling to a Stalinist line long after more perceptive fellow travelers had seen through its fallacies, in the literary realm he mostly retained his independence of judgment and remained loyal to a critical pluralism and eclecticism. Even in 1934 he maintained that "there is no single theory of the function of art that has not finally confined and narrowed and impoverished art, whether the theory be that of Plato, Aristotle, Kant, Schopenhauer, Mallarmé, Plekhanov or the Russian Association of Proletarian Writers."[35] To denounce Trotsky for his "archidiabolical pride" and elevate the personal qualities of Stalin was ultimately, as Wilson saw, less "real" to Cowley than to explore the enriching impact on William Butler Yeats's poetry of his "baptism of the gutter," or the humanizing effect on Baudelaire's art of his revolutionist *engagement*. Typically, Cowley wrote on Karl Marx, not primarily as a strategist of revolution, but as "a man of letters, . . . the spiritual contemporary of Baudelaire and Flaubert."[36] For all his belief in the bankruptcy of the religion of art, Cowley continued to seek ways of accommodating the dubious technical attainments of symbolism with the benefits to be reaped from involvement in the revolutionary movement. The latter, he said in a speech at the American Writers' Congress on May 1, 1935, could offer the writer not merely an indispensable sense of a responsive audience and a whole new range of subject matter in the sorrows and sufferings of the working class, most importantly it could give the artist "a new perspective on himself" by providing a "sense of human life, not as a medley of accidents, but as a connected and continuing process. . . . It gives the values, the unified interpretation, without which one can write neither good history nor good tragedy."[37] Literature, not politics, remained the touchstone.

Throughout the 1930s Cowley remained consistently concerned with the creation of a sustaining cultural climate for the American writer. Persuaded that the revolutionary movement could put an end to an impoverishing artistic isolationism, he gave it his seemingly unambiguous allegiance as long as he remained convinced that it offered the best practical instrument to foster the "double humanizing function of art." His efforts as vice-president of the League of American Writers were but a natural continuation and expansion of his earlier, nonpolitical efforts to maintain a viable sense of literary community among his friends; they take on a wider resonance of meaning when placed in the context of Cowley's ongoing endeavors on behalf of the "commonwealth of letters," both at Yaddo and at the National Institute and American Academy of Arts and Letters.

In 1936 the Cowleys, by this time the parents of a two-year-old son, Robert, moved to a remodeled barn in Sherman, which over the years Cowley transformed into a beautiful farmhouse, planting his own pine forest and maintaining his professional links with New York. During the second half of the 1930s Cowley's hopes for a united endeavor on the left—he actively endorsed the cultural policies of the Popular Front— were thwarted by vicious factional bickerings, notably between Trotskyites and Stalinists. Nor was he always able to preserve the above-the-battle impartiality befitting his position as a *New Republic* editor. He allowed his name to be used in public support of radical organizations affiliated with the Communist party (many of them relief committees for victims of the war in Spain), chaired meetings with party speakers, once or twice wrote for the *Daily Worker,* took a stand against the American Committee for the Defense of Leon Trotsky, controversially defended the official version of the Moscow Trials, and quarreled with the editors of *Partisan Review.* Though often his position was more subtle (and, as his notebooks testify, more ambivalent) than it was made out to be by overzealous opponents, in a climate of political polarization Cowley was easily identified with the party line in politics.

Still, literature came first. *After the Genteel Tradition* (1937), edited and partly written by Cowley, was a compilation of essays on American literature between 1910 and 1930 that began as a series of "Revaluations" in the *New Republic*; beside introductory and concluding essays by Cowley, it featured appraisals of John Dos Passos (again by Cowley), of Van Wyck Brooks (by Bernard Smith), of Carl Sandburg (by Newton Arvin), of Willa Cather and Eugene O'Neill (by Lionel Trilling), of H. L. Mencken (by Louis Kronenberger), of Sinclair Lewis and Upton Sinclair (by Robert Cantwell), of Hemingway (by John Peale Bishop), of Sherwood Anderson (by Robert Morss Lovett), of Theodore Dreiser (by John Chamberlain), of "the James Branch Cabell period" (by Peter Munro Jack), of Robinson Jeffers and Edna St. Vincent Millay (by Hildegarde Flanner), and of Thomas Wolfe (by Hamilton Basso). An expanded version, published in 1964, added a long essay by Cowley on Edwin Arlington Robinson. The original series, though not conceived as such, fit in with the Popular Front emphasis on the "defense of culture" and with the nascent mood of literary nationalism in the late 1930s. Its counterpart in intellectual and cultural history, *Books That Changed Our Minds,* edited by Cowley and Bernard Smith, likewise ran in the *New Republic* in late 1938 and 1939. Beside a lengthy foreword and afterword by Cowley, it included essays by Lewis Mumford (on Oswald Spengler's *Decline of the West*), C. E. Ayres (on John Dewey's *Studies in Logical Theory*), Charles A. Beard (on Frederick Jackson Turner's *The Frontier in American History*), Bernard Smith (on Vernon Louis Parrington's *Main Currents in American Thought*), David Daiches (on I. A. Richards's *Principles of Literary Criticism*), Louis Kronenberger (on *The Education of Henry Adams*), Rexford G. Tugwell (on Thorstein Veblen's *Theory of Business Enterprise*), Paul Radin (on Franz Boas's *The Mind of Primitive Man*), Max Lerner (on Beard's *Economic Interpretation of the Constitution* and Lenin's *The State and Revolution*), John Chamberlain (on William Graham Sumner's *Folkways*), and George Soule (on Freud's *Interpretation of Dreams*).

In the summer of 1937 Cowley traveled to Europe, where he renewed his friendship with Louis Aragon, now a leading figure in the literary and Communist world in France, and personally witnessed the havoc caused by the war in Spain. Later he dated the beginning of his disenchantment with communism from attending the Second International Writers' Congress in Madrid that summer. His reservations were fanned by "the big sellout" in Munich in 1938 and by the Nazi-Soviet Pact of August 1939. A long letter to Edmund Wilson, written in early February 1940 and reprinted in —*And I Worked at the Writer's Trade*, evinced his troubled state as a mixture of frustrated hopes, a harassing uncertainty about the future, an angry disillusionment with communism, and a persistent loyalty to the idealism and self-sacrifice of the best of the radicals. In May 1940, later than most, he resigned from the League of American Writers and publicly broke with radical politics. Perhaps more than anything else it was the fall of France in June that destroyed the last vestiges of his faith in the radical movement. His defection from radicalism, and his early interventionist sentiments, exposed Cowley to fierce attacks in the leftist press—he was caricatured as a renegade in the *New Masses* and lambasted in the *Daily Worker*—while, privately, he was engaged in a painful process of self-examination, marked by a "double drive" of guilt and self-justification.[38]

At heart, Cowley's commitment to the revolutionary ethos of Marxism had been part of a larger attempt to recover, in the words of Lewis P. Simpson, "the humanistic amplitude of literature" and to incarnate "the moral polity of letters." As long as this seemed feasible Cowley was content to work within the League of American Writers and endorse the moral prestige of communism. When he finally withdrew his support of revolutionary politics, he did so less for political reasons than because he had come to feel that the movement no longer seemed beneficial to writers but had succumbed to an "academic and inhibited" doctrinalism, a "mental inertia" that precluded "the capacity for fresh observation or independent thinking," which he believed indispensable for a living and human art.[39] In 1941, when he came to settle his intellectual accounts in a sober investigation of communism as a "religion," he rejected it essentially because it had come to violate his deepest humanist beliefs: not only had it failed to develop a sense of human limitations, it had also proved incapable of offering a safeguard against pride, a restraint against egotism and lust for power. Most seriously, by using "living men and women" as political instruments, by recognizing "no absolute value except society," and by clinging to a "bare and simplified picture of the individual," it had become impervious to human dignity and proved itself "inferior to even the decayed and diluted Christianity of the western world."[40] Cowley's "religion of humanity" had lain at the heart of his attraction to revolutionary communism; it likewise formed the core of his rejection of it.

‹ ‹ ‹ In late 1940 an internal reorganization at the *New Republic* relieved Cowley of editorial responsibility, but he continued to write a weekly book page through the war years, in which he reviewed books on the international situation, considered the effects of the war on American writing, remained sensitive to new directions in poetry, and defended the writers of his generation against attacks by Archibald MacLeish and Bernard DeVoto. As early as 1940 he projected a book on "the writers' crusade" of the 1930s, but the subject was fraught with too many painful and conflicting feelings for early summation and responsible digestion; the first part of his memoirs of the 1930s, *The Dream of the Golden Mountains*, did not appear until 1980. Further pain was caused by his experiences in Washington in 1942, when attacks in *Time* magazine and on the floor of Congress (by the Dies Committee on Un-American Activities) made Cowley decide to resign as chief information analyst for Archibald MacLeish's governmental agency, the Office of Facts and Figures, where he had hoped to make a constructive contribution to the war effort. After what he remembered as "the worst two years" of his life, Cowley remained sensitive to the social and historical ramifications of American writing but avoided political controversy, though not always successfully, and aimed to survive the expected counterpurge with grace and self-respect from his position as a "Little American" in Sherman. With a "sense of release and opportunity" he now returned to his "proper" field of interest: the history of American letters, of the present and the past. As his letters to Burke and others indicate, Cowley's political concerns in the McCarthy years did not so much disappear as become subterraneous. He sharply felt the paralyzing effect of "the need to keep silent" in public, but in private correspondence showed himself intensely worried about the atrophy of liberty, the emasculation of the liberals, and the lack of effective resistance. His political aberrations cast a long shadow over his subsequent career. He had to fight the forces of reaction that tried to prevent his appointment as Walker-Ames lecturer at the University of Washington in Seattle in 1949, was called up twice to testify at the Alger Hiss trials, and was denied a teaching assignment at the University of Minnesota in 1950. As late as 1980, the publication of *The Dream of the Golden Mountains* engendered attacks by neoconservative descendants of onetime anti-Stalinists.[41]

From a literary perspective, the period between 1944 and 1954, when he published *The Literary Situation*, were "high years" for Cowley.[42] Released from his weekly obligations to the *New Republic* and supported by a generous five-year grant from the Mellon Foundation, he now joined in the large-scale critical-historical endeavor of those years to recover a "usable past" for American literature. Helping to define the contours of a national literary tradition, he wrote sensitive and influential revaluations of Hawthorne, Whitman, James, and the naturalists, as well as of Hemingway, Faulkner, and Fitzgerald. From the 1920s Cowley retained an awareness of the inevitable and paradoxical tension in American writing between isolation and community, romanticism and classicism, expression and construction. If in the 1930s he had overemphasized the writer's obligation to portray the meaning and dignity of the "outer" world, he now sought to redress the balance and, in the mid 1940s, arrived at a subtler perception of the problem. In Hawthorne, especially, Cowley discovered a congenial writer obsessively aware of the paradoxical "relation between the inner and the outer world." But Hawthorne, as if in disproof of Cowley's earlier admonitions, had created his greatest art in a state of hermitlike isolation: while being a "mere spectator, condemned to live in the world without any share in its joys or sorrows," he had written a rich store of moral fables dramatizing the evil of solipsistic pride and urging involvement with the democratic community of mankind. He had, repeatedly and guiltily, confessed his inability to portray, imaginatively and realistically, the "outer" world of contemporary reality and produced instead a "literature of loneliness . . . in which persons, however real in themselves, tend[ed] to dissolve into symbols and myths." In this, Cowley saw,

Hawthorne had been the precursor of "a continuous literary tradition" in American writing, one "deep," "lyrical," "psychological," and symbolic, rather than broadly democratic, optimistic, epical, and realistic.[43]

From the 1930s Cowley retained his conviction, now deepened and depoliticized, that an artist gained in compassion and human understanding by being wrenched out of an often necessary spell of loneliness and alienation, by learning to reconnect himself to humanity at large through some profoundly moving experience. But such a recovery of a new sense of human involvement, he now saw, did not always work unambiguously to the advantage of his art. Hawthorne had been drawn out of his desperate isolation by the discovery of human love, but his greatest work was the product of his dark and brooding Salem years. At the polar opposite of the tradition established by Hawthorne stood Walt Whitman, reputedly the optimistic and epical bard of American democracy, the singer of the self containing the vast "multitudes" of the outer world. Whitman, indeed, by the end of his life had "moved from his private world into a stable relation with society." But his greatest poems, paradoxically, had emerged from the experience of a personal *saison en enfer*, from a period "when he stood apart from society with the sense, at times, of belonging to a confraternity of the damned." Underneath the public "mask" of the healthy, virile celebrant of democracy lay the "real but almost unknown" poet, one "wounded and alone," "a democrat . . . from below, feeling his brotherhood with the crippled and diseased."[44]

In the 1940s, besides translating André Gide's *Interviews Imaginaires* (1942; *Imaginary Interviews*, 1944) and the war poems of Louis Aragon (*Aragon, Poet of the French Resistance*, 1945), Cowley helped to initiate and give prestige to the Viking Portable Library series, by editing interpretative collections of Hemingway (1944), Faulkner (1946), and Hawthorne (1948). *The Portable Faulkner*, issued at a time when most of Faulkner's works were effectively out of print, helped to bring a great writer's reputation in line with his achievement. Cowley told the story of his role in Faulkner's reclamation and published the pertinent correspondence in *The Faulkner-Cowley File* (1966). In 1949, when the Mellon subvention expired, Cowley went to work as publisher's advisor for Viking Press, a mutually profitable association that lasted far into Cowley's old age. That same year he wrote, for *Life*, the first extended biographical essay on Hemingway, having personally sought out "Papa" in Key West and in Havana. In the early 1950s, riding the wave of the "boom" of interest in the 1920s,

Cowley republished *Exile's Return*, edited *The Stories of F. Scott Fitzgerald* for Scribner's, and prepared what he felt was the "final version" of Fitzgerald's novel *Tender Is the Night*, an edition long in print but now generally rejected in favor of the original 1934 edition.

Throughout the postwar decades Cowley hoped to avert what he saw as a fatal "divorce of contemporary literature from contemporary life" and continued to admonish American writers to make an effort toward "intellectual and emotional understanding of what was happening in the world." For better or worse, however, he now also recognized that it was Hawthorne who was the archetypical American artist, who stood "at the beginning of a double line that runs through James to Eliot . . . and through Stephen Crane to Faulkner and Hemingway." Hemingway, Cowley had already perceived in 1944, for all his deliberate effort to write "truly" of the "real" world, had been wrongly placed in the naturalist tradition; in essence he belonged with "the haunted and nocturnal writers, the men who dealt in images that were symbols of an inner world." Faulkner, like Hawthorne, was "a solitary worker by choice," Cowley observed in his introduction to *The Portable Faulkner* (1946); his works, he reaffirmed twenty years later in *The Faulkner-Cowley File*, were produced in accordance with an essentially "Symbolist system of values." [45]

In mid-career Cowley wrote sensitive critical and historical studies of American literary naturalism (Theodore Dreiser, Frank Norris) and explored its continuance in contemporary writing (Nelson Algren, Ralph Ellison, Saul Bellow). His reappraisals of Hemingway, Faulkner, Hawthorne, and Whitman, however, had persuaded him of at least the restricted validity of the symbolist aesthetics he had once so fiercely repudiated. The best writers of his own generation seemed to have followed the line of Hawthorne, admixed with a hopeful Emersonian democratic individualism, rather than the deterministic line of Dreiser and Norris; they had combined symbolist standards of craftsmanship and perfection with a buoyant determination to be the "true" and "honest" historians of their own time and to speak in their own, often vernacular, language. By reading the past in the light of the present and by reconnecting the literature of his own times to that of the past Cowley had helped to "clear away important misconceptions"—a favorite phrase—and aimed to redeem his generation's "detachment from the native traditions." [46]

The insights Cowley developed in his "middle years" were a natural outgrowth and modification of his earliest beliefs; they remained the basis of his later interpretation and evaluation of the attainments of "his" lost generation. A *Second Flowering* (1973), the culmination of a lifetime of thought about the literature of his age-group, was infused with Cowley's double perception of the writers of his generation as both individualistically oriented and tribally inclined; they were isolated and autonomous artists unswervingly committed to the production of high art (an image rooted in the romantic or symbolist tradition) but also, in essence, "historians . . . of a living community in a process of continual and irreversible change" (an image rooted in Cowley's classicist perception of culture as the outgrowth of a larger-than-personal situation).[47]

A *Second Flowering* also testified to the persistence of its author's concern with the morality of artistic production and the correlation between art and character. In the final analysis, Cowley pictured the writers of his generation as "heroes" of the literary vocation, an "elite" by virtue of their intensely moral dedication to the production of enduring works of art as well as by "such inner qualities as energy, independence, vision, rigor, an original way of combining words (a style, a 'voice'), and utter commitment to a dream." Determined at all cost to carefully husband their talents and preserve the integrity of their aesthetic purpose, all of them, Cowley felt, tried to maintain a very high standard of professional ethics, even if the price to be paid in terms of human companionship, personal disaster, or mental equilibrium often seemed exorbitantly high.[48]

Insofar as A *Second Flowering* posited these writers as loyal adherents to a moral code of art originating in the tradition of symbolism, it signaled Cowley's modified return to the religion of art and completed the curve of his literary development from the 1920s to the 1970s. —And I Worked at *the Writer's Trade* (1978) was even more explicit on this point. Ending with Cowley's attempt to formulate a "pentalogue" of art, the moral "commandments" persisting in "the depths of an artist's mind," the book amounted to a belated renewal of faith in the ethical premises of the religion of art and rehabilitated the image of the artist as a "saint" or "martyr." Once denounced as an anachronistic ideal of the literary life, Marcel Proust was now assigned a place of honor in the "Book of Martyrs," together with other "priests of consciousness" like Flaubert, James, Mallarmé, Mann, and Aiken. In his late years Cowley thus came to reaffirm a set of moral and aesthetic imperatives for the literary artist, imperatives first discovered in the 1920s. In the late 1970s, as if in testimony to the remarkable consistency of his conception of the writing profession as "a priestly vocation with its own strict ethical code," he explored, in effect, the implications of an aesthetic maxim he had first jotted down in his notebook in the early 1920s: "No complete son-of-a-bitch ever wrote a good sentence."[49]

In the practice of his criticism Cowley remained loyal to the values and beliefs he developed in his early years. When, in "Criticism: A Many-Windowed House" (1961), he explicitly formulated the theoretical and methodological assumptions underlying a lifetime of writing about literature, his critical credo formed a testimony to the pluralism, humanism, and eclecticism that had formed a persistent trait of his critical approach. Cowley's writings continued to reflect his early conviction that any single point of view is inevitably narrow, incomplete, and ultimately false, whether it is founded on historical, biographical, psychoanalytical, expressionist, moral, or political principles. He likewise rejected an exclusively textual approach because to view the work of art as "pure" and completely autonomous would involve "a disturbing amount of make-believe." The critic would have to disregard not only the particular time and place of composition but also the interrelations with other works by the same author and the peculiar tendencies prevailing in a certain group of writers; to Cowley this would simply be the creation of another critical fallacy: "Literature is not a pure art like music, or a relatively pure art like painting and sculpture. Its medium is not abstract like tones and colors, not inorganic like metal and stone. Instead it uses language, which is a social creation, changing over the years with the society that created it. The study of an author's language carries us straight into history, institutions, moral questions, personal stratagems, and all the other aesthetic impurities or fallacies that many new critics are trying to expunge." Written at a time when the New Criticism had gained dominion over the field of literary criticism, Cowley's essay struck a note of mild rebelliousness that seems outdated today, but it anticipated the subsequent interest in recovering the possibilities of historicism for literary criticism.

In Cowley's view criticism was best approached as one of the literary arts, if a minor one; consequently it should be well written, in an articulate and literary fashion of its own. The attitude for the critic to take was one of humility in the face of the works he was criticizing. Although criticism could never be entirely impersonal and never reach a scientific degree of objectivity, it should nevertheless be based on verifiable information in order to be persuasive. Aware of the possible unreliability of an author's statement of intentions, Cowley found his "probative evidence" primarily in an author's personal testimonies—letters, notebooks, outlines, public statements. If the critic rejected these sources as insubstantial or immaterial, he ran the risk of falling into an "unintentional fallacy": he might impose on a work meanings that are not there, or substitute his own fantasy or creation for the author's.

For all his skepticism about the restrictions imposed upon the critic's liberty and usefulness by any exclusive approach, in principle Cowley started and ended with the text and was willing to accept the adage of the textual critic that "the principal value of a work lies in the complexity and unity of its internal relations." Simultaneously, however, he moved beyond the possibly confining implications of such a notion: "It is a mistake to approach each work as if it were an absolutely separate production, a unique artifact, the last and single relic of a buried civilization. Why not approach it as the author does? It seems to me that any author of magnitude has his eye on something larger than the individual story or poem or novel. He wants each of these to be as good as possible, and self-subsistent, but he also wants it to serve as a chapter or aspect of the larger work that is his lifetime production, his *oeuvre*."

For Cowley this larger work was an essential part of the critic's subject matter. By studying the interconnections between separate works of art and analyzing the progression of recurrent themes through the entire oeuvre, the critic was able to chart the development of a career, to distinguish between phases within that career, and, consequently, to avoid the mistake of viewing an author as "a single and permanent aggregate of qualities." An important part of Cowley's critical effort was directed toward establishing what he called a writer's central "fable": the central truth (embodied in a recurrent situation, theme, or symbol) around which everything in the oeuvre falls into place and for the expression of which the whole life's experience of the writer becomes available. In order to diagnose the "fable" the critic needed to consider "internal questions" of style, structure, and imagery, but also had to take into account "external relations": the nature of the audience, the regional and social background of the author, the implied moral of the fable. He might even be obliged to study the society in which the author wrote and lived, if this would help to elucidate or establish his meaning.[50] Cowley's approach thus often led him into the extraliterary fields of history, biography, psychology, or sociology. The approach went back to one of Cowley's earliest and most fundamental convictions: the complex relationship existing between literature and life. Although at different moments in his career he interpreted that relationship in different ways and with different degrees of loyalty to each specific solution—from a relatively pure aestheticism to a view of art as a potential instrument of political revolution—he remained antagonistic to any critical method that extricated or dissociated the element of human life from art.

"Criticism: A Many-Windowed House" was written partly in response to what Cowley viewed as the excesses of the New Criticism in the 1940s and 1950s, a period when the "career open to talent" was preeminently the critical consolidation of the modernist attainment, rather than vigorous experimentation in the creative arts, as had been the case in Cowley's formative years. In these years, inevitably, Cowley's approach fell into critical disfavor and at times came under heavy fire. The case against his "historical" and contextual criticism was made most fiercely in 1954 by a onetime critical disciple, John W. Aldridge, who, in his search for modes of critical "heresy," thought he had found a perfect specimen in Cowley's *The Literary Situation* (1954).[51] With the New Critical mode of highbrow criticism at the peak of its prestige, Cowley's reputation suffered and he was sometimes condescendingly dismissed as a "middlebrow" or "sociological" critic. At the same time he enjoyed a high respect in academe on the basis of his reclamation of Faulkner and his pioneering studies of Hemingway and Fitzgerald, while founding fathers of the New Criticism like Allen Tate, Kenneth Burke, Robert Penn Warren, Cleanth Brooks, and R. P. Blackmur, unlike more zealous and dogmatic disciples, continued to recognize the soundness and solidity of his literary criticism.

Aiming to remain impervious to the shifting tides of critical and literary fashions, Cowley mostly steered clear of what he called "critical endogamy" and resisted any monolithic or reductive approach, whether he found it in the distortions of literary nationalism in Bernard DeVoto's *The Literary Fallacy* (1944), in the psychoanalytical excesses of Leslie Fiedler's *Love and Death in the American Novel* (1960), or in the "meta-Freudian" reading of Faulkner in John T. Irwin's *Doubling and Incest—Repetition and Revenge* (1975).[52] Distrustful of the tendency to make criticism into a separate and autonomous genre, Cowley always insisted on its dependency on the primary arts. Alive to the diversity of American writing and skeptical of the exclusivism of literary canon-making, he deemed it an essential task of the critic to discover new or underestimated writers (though he did not often write on women or writers from cultural minorities) and to explore neglected aspects of the literary life and profession. Thus, he wrote on

Horatio Alger, Lafcadio Hearn, S. Foster Damon, Robert Coates, Erskine Caldwell, James Thurber, Nelson Algren, and was not afraid of voicing "dissenting opinions" on canonized authors like Robert Frost and Ezra Pound.[53] He also continued to look with an open mind at modes of writing, both historical and creative, outside the range of attention of the New Criticism—as witness his critical homage to Van Wyck Brooks, his exploration of "the middle-American prose style," and his reclamation and authoritative interpretation of Whitman's *Leaves of Grass: The First (1855) Edition* (1959).[54]

‹ ‹ ‹   By the mid 1970s Cowley could look back on a long career in which, like Poe, he had "worked hard to establish professional standards of authorship." As a man of letters of a by then vanishing species, he had consistently worked in a vein of literary endeavor extending back to Poe. As Allen Tate acknowledged in 1968, Poe had been "the first committed and perhaps still the greatest American literary journalist on the high French model: a critical tradition represented today by Edmund Wilson and Malcolm Cowley." Over the years Cowley remained faithful to the ideal of the man of letters he first evolved in the 1920s, an ideal rooted in the "classical" tradition of the Renaissance and the Enlightenment. Following the French encyclopedists, he aimed to create, for his own times, *une société de gens des lettres* and to act as a sensitive mediator between "high" literary art and the "common reader." As Lewis P. Simpson has pertinently suggested, Cowley's endeavor to assuage the American writer's seemingly ineluctable condition of alienation infused his approach to the literary profession with "a poetics of literary community," together with a pragmatic understanding of the interrelatedness of all aspects of the literary trade. From his earliest experiences in the Village, Cowley was concerned with the living and working conditions of American writers, and with their opportunities to pursue a fruitful career. In this context he wrote with equal expertise on the "business" of literature, the sociology of the writing profession, the economics of book production, and the changing state of the publishing world; to alert a larger audience to the importance of an editor like Maxwell Perkins came rather naturally to him. "A Natural History of the American Writer," a near book-length study of the literary profession in America included in *The Literary Situation*, perhaps best illustrated Cowley's pragmatic perception of the professional literary artist as also a member of the living human community and as such subject to regular domestic, marital, social, economic, and psychological pressures. If his approach seemed partly to emerge from the conformist zeitgeist of the 1950s and at times lapsed into the sociological, it remained a characteristic feature of Cowley's broadly eclectic vision of the American writer.[55]

In a literary career spanning over seven active decades, Cowley combined an impressive multiplicity of functions: he was poet, critic, literary historian, editor, literary consultant to publishers, and, in general, "middleman" of letters. His awareness of the literary profession as "interdependent at all its levels" prompted him to speak up in its defense whenever he saw it threatened. On behalf of the "little American republic of letters" he took his own firm stand against the "Philistines" in the controversy over the Bollingen Award to Ezra Pound in 1949.[56] At the same time, he recurrently expressed his skepticism about the inroads made into the writing trade by commercialism and collectivization and voiced his fear that writers might lose their status as "independent craftsmen" to become officials in a bureaucratic structure, possessing technical virtuosity but paralyzed by timidity, conventionality, and lack of personal courage. During the McCarthy years he was disturbed by the pervasive mood of anti-intellectualism, by the decline of the reading habit, and by the potentially dangerous effects of an alliance between creative writing and academic careerism.[57] At the same time, he worked within academe as a teacher, writer in residence, and lecturer at writers' conferences.[58] Always, however, he felt slightly out of place among academic scholars; even as a participant in *The Literary History of the United States* (1948), he felt odd man out among professors of literature. He was most at ease among writers, artists, publishers, and editors. It was as characteristic of Cowley to devote his Hopwood lecture at the University of Michigan in 1957 to "The Beginning Writer in the University" as it was to edit the first in a series of literary conversations on the practical and technical problems of the "craft" of writing in *Writers at Work: The Paris Review Interviews* (1958).

Few have had Cowley's talent for friendship and the geniality of temperament to associate on terms of equality (and often intimacy) with a wide and varied circle of literary friends and acquaintances, from Faulkner, Hemingway, Crane, and Tate, to younger writers like John Cheever, Tillie Olsen, and Ken Kesey, or visual and sculptural artists like Peter Blume, Arshile Gorky, and Alexander Calder. Though some of his literary friends must have strained his capacity for tolerance and compassion, Cowley, in his dealings with writers, often showed (in the words of George Core) "an uncommonly even disposition, a remarkable ability to forgive, and a wise but not uncritical acceptance of human fallibility." As critic, teacher, and roving scout of new talent for Viking Press, Cowley continued to exhort, advise, and practically assist young writers, urging them to meet the challenges of contemporary reality, to find new forms, and to speak in their own voices.[59] His early discovery of John Cheever, his efforts on behalf of Jack Kerouac's *On the Road,* and his encouragements of Ken Kesey, Larry McMurtry, and Peter S. Beagle (students in Cowley's class in creative writing at Stanford in 1961) are merely the better-known examples of a long list of services rendered to numerous writers.[60]

By the mid 1950s, however, the newer forms of fiction he himself had called for were not much to Cowley's liking. Though his conception of the novel remained open and flexible enough, he insisted too strongly on a mimetic, realistic, humanist art to accommodate the bulk of postmodernist experimentation. Rather than to a John Barth, Donald Barthelme, or Thomas Pynchon, Cowley found himself attracted to a classical realist like Thornton Wilder or conservative writers who intuitively grasped the shaping force of social reality in individual life (one thinks of his essays on John P. Marquand, John O'Hara, James Gould Cozzens, Willa Cather, and John Cheever, but also of his encouragement of Mary Lee Settle and Tillie Olsen). He wrote a flamboyant defense of the ancient art of storytelling and found himself sharply at odds with the newer developments in criticism: approaches like structuralism, poststructuralism and deconstructionism were regarded as modes of critical heresy by Cowley, "a humanist by instinct" who by 1978 had come to feel "increasingly alone and beleaguered."[61]

Toward the end of the 1950s Cowley's role as the barometric chronicler of his literary age, one possessed of an almost "seismographic" sense of shifting cultural forces, began to lose much of its dramatic momentum, as he felt himself slowly growing out of touch with the literary temper of the times. "A deaf man gardening in the country and writing about books," he was a bemused but detached observer of "the unbelievable 1960s." In literary criticism his career became increasingly dominated by retrospection and the ongoing critical revaluation of the high years of American literary modernism, the living heart of Cowley's career. His account of the "love generation" of the 1960s in —*And I Worked at the Writer's Trade* evinced the troubled perplexity of a man of letters confronted with a generation desirous of social change but impervious to the order of literary ethics and aesthetics in which Cowley breathed most naturally: the instruments of cultural change no longer seemed primarily literary. It also showed that Cowley's best critical and historical writing depended on a degree of personal and imaginative connection with its subject matter.[62]

The 1960s were for Cowley a time of critical consolidation and of revaluations of his radical past. The latter were now given a new impetus by the emergence of the New Left and a concomitant revival of interest in the "old" left. Cowley participated in symposia on the 1930s, wrote "remembrances" of his "red romance," as well as much of what later became *The Dream of the Golden Mountains,* and with the help of Henry Dan Piper collected his *New Republic* articles of the 1930s in book form.[63] He also gathered the best of his other past writings into what he tried to make into unified books. He revisited and revalued his efforts on behalf of Faulkner, assembled and revised his collected poems, and, once more with the help of Piper, compiled A *Many-Windowed House* (1970), a volume containing some of his best essays on classical and modern American writers. Two later compilations, subsequent to —*And I Worked at the Writer's Trade: Chapters of Literary History, 1918–1978* (1978), were edited by Donald W. Faulkner, *The Flower and the Leaf: A Contemporary Record of American Writing Since 1941* (1985) and *The Portable Malcolm Cowley* (1990). A selection of his correspondence with Kenneth Burke was published in 1988.

By the mid 1960s Cowley had become an official member of the literary establishment. He had been elected to the National Institute of Arts and Letters in 1949, served as its president from 1956 to 1959 and again from 1962 to 1965, and in 1964 had been "elevated" to the American Academy of Arts and Letters, serving as its chancellor from 1967 to 1976. Though, with advancing age, he found himself increasingly besieged by ailments and infirmities, he almost naturally became a wise and genial chronicler of the experience of old age in the beautifully written *The View from Eighty* (1980). As far as age permitted he remained an active force in the "commonwealth of letters." He continued to conceive of American writers as a community of individual craftsmen, each fiercely devoted to his or her special talent and vision yet all engaged in a united literary endeavor. For Cowley, as for Edmund Wilson, the advancement of literature was "in great part a collaborative venture." Like Allen Tate's, his "true home" was in the timeless and placeless Republic of Letters, a realm which he defined, in typical pluralistic fashion, as a "loose federation composed of many dukedoms and principalities."[64] As its "roving diplomat" he moved with ease, tact, and generosity between the realm of serious criticism, literary history, and academic scholarship, and the pragmatic world of publishing, editing, writers' conferences, and artists' colonies, mediating, as few have been capable of, between a disinterested pursuit of letters and the literary marketplace.[65] Outliving most of his coevals, as well as many a younger literary friend, he became in old age, naturally if sadly, the retrospective celebrant and elegiac obituarist of the community of letters.

In his last decade Cowley's stature and influence were confirmed by honorary academic degrees and literary awards, among them the Hubbell Medal of the Modern Language Association for service to the study of American literature and *Who's Who in America*'s 1983–84 Achievement Award for Arts and Communication. The honors culminated on May 20, 1981, when he received the Gold Medal for Belles Lettres and Criticism of the American Academy and Institute of Arts and Letters. Appropriately the award was presented to him by Kenneth Burke. "That's the way we ought to structure our lives," Cowley wrote to Burke in 1981, "with the best coming last, in a graded series."[66] With typical modesty Cowley spoke of himself as a "poet and critic," never as a "man of letters." Nevertheless, at the end of his life, after a "second flowering" in his own career that saw the publication of nine books after his sixty-eighth year, Cowley could look back on a literary life in which, in his own fashion, he had fulfilled the ideal of the man of letters he had first developed as a young man. It seems a graceful irony of literary history that in the 1980s Cowley's status came to approximate that of William Dean Howells, who once symbolized all that his generation was in revolt against: that of Dean of American Letters.

Notes

Unless indicated otherwise, all references are to letters and unpublished manuscript material in the Malcolm Cowley Papers in the Newberry Library in Chicago, Illinois. Magazines, newspapers, and periodicals are referred to by their full titles throughout the notes; the titles of secondary works appear in shortened form after first mention. All correspondents are indicated by full names, with the exception of Malcolm Cowley (MC) and Kenneth Burke (KB). All quotations have been taken from the original manuscripts, even when these have been published. Cowley's notebooks of the 1920s are in the Newberry Library; the new series of notebooks started in 1933 are in possession of Robert Cowley and are referred to as "n.s." For a virtually complete bibliographical listing of Cowley's published writings, see Diane U. Eisenberg, *Malcolm Cowley: A Checklist of His Writings, 1916–1973* (Carbondale and Edwardsville, Ill., 1975) and the preliminary updated version of the checklist by Ruth M. Alvarez and Diane U. Eisenberg in the "Special Malcolm Cowley Issue" of *The Visionary Company: A Magazine of the Twenties* vol. 2, no. 2/vol. 3, no. 1 (Summer 1987): 205–30.

The following abbreviations have been used to denote works by Malcolm Cowley.

BJ	*Blue Juniata* (1929)
BJCP	*Blue Juniata: Collected Poems* (1968)
CMC	*Conversations with Malcolm Cowley.* Edited by Thomas Daniel Young (1986)
DGM	*The Dream of the Golden Mountains: Remembering the 1930s* (1980)
ER	*Exile's Return: A Literary Odyssey of the 1920s* (1951)
ER (1934)	*Exile's Return: A Narrative of Ideas* (1934)
FCF	*The Faulkner-Cowley File: Letters and Memories, 1944–1962* (1966)
FL	*The Flower and the Leaf: A Contemporary Record of American Writing Since 1941.* Edited and with an introduction by Donald W. Faulkner (1985)
LS	*The Literary Situation* (1954)
MWH	*A Many-Windowed House: Collected Essays on American Writers and American Writing.* Edited and with an introduction by Henry Dan Piper (1970)

SC   *The Selected Correspondence of Kenneth Burke and Malcolm Cowley, 1915–1981.* Edited by Paul Jay (1988)

SF   *A Second Flowering: Works and Days of the Lost Generation* (1973)

TBOU   *Think Back On Us: A Contemporary Chronicle of the 1930s.* Edited by Henry Dan Piper (1967)

VE   *The View from Eighty* (1980)

WT   *—And I Worked at the Writer's Trade: Chapters of Literary History, 1918–1978* (1978)

LOCATION OF MANUSCRIPT COLLECTIONS
REFERRED TO IN THE NOTES:

American Review and *Bookman* Papers: Collection of American Literature, Beinecke Rare Book and Manuscript Library, Yale University, New Haven, Connecticut

Benét Papers: William Rose Benét Papers, Collection of American Literature, Beinecke Rare Book and Manuscript Library, Yale University, New Haven, Connecticut

Brooks Papers: Van Wyck Brooks Collection, Department of Special Collections, Charles Patterson Van Pelt Library, University of Pennsylvania, Philadelphia, Pennsylvania

Burke Papers: Kenneth Burke Collection, Fred Lewis Pattee Library, Pennsylvania State University, University Park, Pennsylvania

Contempo Papers: Harry Ransom Humanities Research Center, University of Texas at Austin, Texas

Damon Papers: S. Foster Damon Papers, Brown University Library, Providence, Rhode Island

Dial Papers: Collection of American Literature, Beinecke Rare Book and Manuscript Library, Yale University, New Haven, Connecticut

Dos Passos Papers: John Dos Passos Papers, Poetry Collection, Lockwood Memorial Library, State University of New York, Buffalo, New York

Galantière Papers: Lewis Galantière Papers, Rare Book and Manuscript Library, Columbia University, New York, New York

Hicks Papers: Granville Hicks Papers, George Arents Research Library for Special Collections at Syracuse University, Syracuse, New York

Josephson Papers: Matthew Josephson Papers, Collection of American Literature, Beinecke Rare Book and Manuscript Library, Yale University, New Haven, Connecticut

Kenyon Review Papers: Olin Library and Gordon Keith Chalmers Memorial Library, Kenyon College, Gambier, Ohio

Little Review Papers: Archives, Golda Meir Library, University of Wisconsin-Milwaukee, Wisconsin

Loeb Papers: Harold Loeb Papers, Princeton University Library, Princeton, New Jersey

Lowell Papers: Amy Lowell Papers, Houghton Library, Harvard University, Cambridge, Massachusetts

Poetry Papers: *Poetry Magazine* Papers, 1912–35, Joseph Regenstein Library, University of Chicago, Chicago, Illinois

Rascoe Papers: Burton Rascoe Collection, Department of Special Collections, Charles Patterson Van Pelt Library, University of Pennsylvania, Philadelphia, Pennsylvania

Sandburg Papers: Carl Sandburg Collection, Library of the University of Illinois at Urbana-Champaign, Illinois

Schneider Papers: Isidor Schneider Papers, Rare Book and Manuscript Library, Columbia University, New York, New York

Scribner's Archives: Charles Scribner's Archives, Princeton University Library, Princeton, New Jersey

Stallman Papers: Robert W. Stallman Collection (# 6778), Clifton Waller Barrett Library, Manuscripts Division, Special Collections Department, University of Virginia Library, Charlottesville, Virginia

Tate Papers: Allen Tate Papers, Princeton University Library, Princeton, New Jersey

Warren Papers: Robert Penn Warren Papers, Collection of American Literature, Beinecke Rare Book and Manuscript Library, Yale University, New Haven, Connecticut

Wheelwright Papers: John Brooks Wheelwright Papers, Brown University Library, Providence, Rhode Island

Williams Papers: William Carlos Williams Papers, Collection of American Literature, Beinecke Rare Book and Manuscript Library, Yale University, New Haven, Connecticut

Wilson Papers: Edmund Wilson Papers, Collection of American Literature, Beinecke Rare Book and Manuscript Library, Yale University, New Haven, Connecticut

I thank the libraries mentioned above for granting me permission to quote from the Cowley material in their various collections, as specifically indicated in the notes.

PROLOGUE: AN URN OF NATIVE SOIL

1. VE, 12–13; *SF*, p. 30.

2. Cowley's later essays on Aiken, Cummings, Damon, and Wilder are his explorations of the continuity of the spirit of New England transcendentalism in modern times. See *SF*, 90–113, 114–29, and *WT*, 35–50, 231–48. As literary advisor at Viking Press Cowley worked with enthusiasm on Gay Wilson Allen's biography of Emerson (dedicated to Cowley) and collaborated with Carl Bode on a revised edition of *The Portable Emerson* (New York, 1981); the quotation from Emerson appears on page 11

of *The Portable Emerson*. For a consideration of Cowley as the "spiritual heir" of Emerson, see Adam Gussow, " 'Whatever Roots We Had in the Soil': Malcolm Cowley and the American Scholar," *Horns of Plenty: Malcolm Cowley and his Generation* 1 (Spring 1988): 5–15, 19–24.

3. "Mother and Son," 9. The essay was written in May 1982 and published in *American Heritage* 35, no. 2 (February–March 1983): 28–35. Quotations in the text are from the original typescript.

4. MC to Robert Penn Warren, July 9, 1967; MC to Henry Rago, September 28, 1967. The poem was published in *Poetry* 112 (June 1968): 149–50.

5. *BJCP*, 3. The charred landscape of Cowley's poem bears an interesting resemblance to the "burned-over country" in which Nick Adams finds himself in the opening scenes of Ernest Hemingway's "Big Two-Hearted River." I shall return to the special importance of Hemingway to Cowley below.

6. MC to Conrad Aiken, January 14, 1961; *ER*, p. 14; " 'Boy in Sunlight' was written in the fall of 1967, but it is based on a vivid memory that goes back sixty years. It was a rite of initiation: the countryside marked me as its own, as if a surveyor had scarred a witness tree." Talk to the people of Sherman, August 30, 1968, unpublished. The poem, though not written until 1967, was projected much earlier, possibly as a result of Cowley's readings of Walt Whitman. In a notebook entry for November 27, 1955, Cowley observed: "I keep thinking about the poems. In a sense it is the return of age to scenes of youth—I remember those scenes more vividly than I see today the Connecticut countryside. But also it is the craftsman's desire to get things right—to take those intimations of poetry and give them a permanent expression. . . . I must do the poem (my 'There Was a Child Went Forth') about the position of the boy by the landscape" (Notebook 7, n.s., August 9, 1954–February 14, 1957). In 1955 Cowley's attention had been focused on Whitman by the appearance of Gay Wilson Allen's biography *The Solitary Singer*, which he had reviewed for the *New York Times Book Review* on February 6. Several months later he had edited a "little anthology" of Whitman's poems for the *New Republic* of July 25, on the occasion of the centennial of the publication of *Leaves of Grass*. His critical commentary was later expanded into the introduction to the reissue of the first (1855) edition of *Leaves of Grass* (Viking Press, 1959), edited by Cowley.

7. *BJCP*, p. 28; *ER*, p. 13; Allen Tate to MC, n.d. [September 1968]; *BJCP*, p. 5.

8. The nearest equivalent to a full account is a moving tribute to his mother, "Mother and Son," written in May 1982; the most expansive evocation in prose of the country of his youth can be found in "My Countryside, Then and Now," *Harper's Monthly Magazine* 158 (January 1929): 239–45.

9. MC to Margaret Binney Smith, June 17, 1966; MC to Donald C. McKenna, March 31, 1967; MC to George Swetnam, October 22, 1968; "Mother and Son," p. 5. Cowley was named David after his father's brother; he dropped the name after high school, presumably because his uncle was "something of a no-count" and "hardly a model to emulate." Robert Cowley to author, November 7, 1990.

10. "My Countryside, Then and Now," *Harper's Monthly Magazine* 158 (January 1929): 239.

11. *ER*, p. 15; "The Pyre," *BJCP*, p. 27.

12. "Mother and Son," pp. 7–9; Robert Cowley, "Malcolm Cowley: Countryman," *Country Journal* (October 1983), pp. 63–64, reprinted in *CMC*, pp. 182–92; "Continental Highway," *New Republic* 66 (February 25, 1931): 34.

13. "My Countryside, Then and Now," p. 243; "The Living Water," *BJCP*, p. 131. An earlier version of the poem was published as "The Source" in *Poetry* 72 (April 1948): 18–19.

14. Talk to the people of Sherman, August 30, 1968, unpublished; *SF*, p. 208.

15. *SF*, pp. 149, 248, 255; *FCF*, pp. 151–52.

16. "My Countryside, Then and Now," p. 240; Introduction to *The Portable Hemingway* (New York, 1944), pp. xix, xxi–xxii. Compare *ER*, p. 289.

17. MC to KB, May 16, 1929; MC to Margaret Binney Smith, June 17, 1966; "My Countryside, Then and Now," pp. 244–45; Notebook 7, n.s. (August 9, 1954–February 14, 1957), entry for September 2, 1955; for the aspects of Hemingway discussed here, see Scott Donaldson, *By Force of Will: The Life and Art of Ernest Hemingway* (New York, 1977), pp. 72–77, 230–40; and Carlos Baker, *Hemingway: The Writer as Artist* (Princeton, N.J., 1972), pp. 82–86; MC to Allen Tate, April 21, 1966, Tate Papers.

18. "Continental Highway," p. 35; "My Countryside, Then and Now," pp. 240, 245; "Malcolm Cowley: Countryman," p. 64.

19. "The Waste Land," *New Republic* 88 (September 2, 1938): 187; *BJ*, p. 2.

20. "My Countryside, Then and Now," p. 240; "Dan George," *BJCP*, pp. 7–8.

21. *BJCP*, pp. 15–18.

22. "My Countryside, Then and Now," p. 239; "The Waste Land," p. 187; *ER*, p. 28.

23. MC to Mrs. David Thompson, November 17, 1967; MC to Robert W. Stallman, July 22, 1960, Stallman Papers; talk to the people of Sherman, August 30, 1968; *BJCP*, p. 9.

24. "The Hill above the Mine," *BJCP*, pp. 10–11. A similar promise is held out to the farmers of "Poverty Hollow" (*BJCP*, p. 12), who, against odds and fate, have continued to fight an exhaustive but losing battle against the dwindling resources of nature. The closing stanza of "The Hill above the Mine" compares illuminatingly with the epigraph from Ecclesiastes to Hemingway's *The Sun Also Rises* ("but the earth abideth forever").

25. "My Countryside, Then and Now," p. 239.

26. "The Blown Door," *BJCP*, p. 25.

27. Lewis P. Simpson, "Malcolm Cowley and the American Writer," *Sewanee Review* 84 (April–June 1976): 225.

28. *BJCP*, pp. 21–24.

29. *BJCP*, pp. 27–29; "Continental Highway," p. 34; MC to KB, July 27, 1970; MC to Margaret Binney Smith, August 6, 1970.

30. MC to Margaret Binney Smith, July 21, 1968; *BJCP*, p. 26. Published in *Poetry* as "Poem for Two Voices."

31. Allen Tate to MC, November 27, 1973; MC to Walter Snow, August 27, 1971; *BJCP*, p. 142.

32. Lewis P. Simpson, "Malcolm Cowley and the American Writer," p. 225.

33. *ER*, pp. 32–33.

34. *DGM*, p. xi.

35. *DGM*, p. 227.

36. *MWH*, p. 24.

37. *SF*, p. 149; Bishop's epithet is quoted in *DGM*, p. xi; Alfred Kazin, *Starting Out in the Thirties* (Boston and Toronto, 1965), p. 19; *DGM*, p. xi.

38. Notebook 6, n.s. (August 25, 1950–July 16, 1954), entry for August 28, 1950; "Continental Highway," p. 35; *FCF*, p. 152. See also Hans Bak, "Malcolm Cowley: The Critic and His Generation," *Dutch Quarterly Review of Anglo-American Letters* vol. 9, no. 4 (1979): 261–83.

1. PITTSBURGH AND PEABODY HIGH, 1898–1915

1. "Mother and Son," typescript, p. 5.

2. Ibid., pp. 3–4.

3. MC to Stanley Young, April 11, 1944.

4. MC to George Swetnam, October 22, 1968. The six original Carnegie partners had agreed that if anyone should leave the business prematurely he was to be repaid his initial investment. For his share in the Carnegie Iron Works William Cowley's estate received close to $4,000, which his mother, Cowley's great-grandmother, spent on a trip back home to County Down in Northern Ireland. See also MC to Donald C. McKenna, March 31, 1967.

5. For Swedenborg's following at the time, see Austin Warren, *The Elder Henry James* (1934; rpt., 1970), pp. 65–69.

6. MC to Stanley Young, April 11, 1944; "Mother and Son," p. 2.

7. MC to Donald C. McKenna, March 31, 1967; Warren, *Elder Henry James*, p. 158; "Mother and Son," pp. 4–5.

8. "Prayer on All Saints' Day," *Sewanee Review* 86 (Fall 1978): 563. The poem was reprinted in *Blue Juniata: A Life. Collected and New Poems* (New York, 1985), pp. 151–53.

9. MC to author, March 23, 1980.

10. Cited in Warren, *Elder Henry James*, p. 240.

11. Ibid., pp. 82, 91–96, 244.

12. Leon Edel, *The Life of Henry James*, Vol. 1: 1843–89 (New York, 1977), pp. 31–34; Cowley first advanced his notions about God and Society in his Notebook 1 (1922–1924), pp. 50–51; he reverted to his ideas, adapting them to explain communism as a religion, in a letter to Granville Hicks, July 11, 1941, Hicks Papers.

13. *TBOU*, p. 387.

14. "Mother and Son," pp. 10–11; MC to Harry [Duncan], October 5, 1943; MC to KB, September 1, 1924.

15. MC to Harry [Duncan], October 5, 1943; *SF*, p. 234.

16. MC to author, March 23, 1980; *DGM*, pp. 51–52.

17. Edel, *Life of Henry James*, p. 95; Notebook 1 (1922–24), p. 53; MC to author, March 23, 1980; *WT*, p. 99.

18. "Mother and Son," pp. 5, 6, 10–11; *The Standard Edition of the Complete Psychological Works of Sigmund Freud* (London, 1953), p. 26; MC to author, June 4, 1982.

19. "Mother and Son," pp. 8–12.

20. *DGM*, p. xi; "Mother and Son," pp. 7, 9–10, 16; "Chopin," *Peabody* 3 (March 1915): 5. The poem is quoted in the special Cowley issue of *The Visionary Company* (Summer 1987): 69.

21. "Mother and Son," p. 9; MC to Alfred Kazin, May 18, 1962; *LS*, p. 146.

22. "Mother and Son," pp. 7, 9–10; MC to author, June 4, 1982.

23. MC to Alfred Kazin, May 18, 1962.

24. "Aspects of the American Scene," *Charm* 8 (November 1927): 30.

25. MC to Evelyn B. Byrne, March 21, 1969.

26. *LS*, pp. 144, 147.

27. MC to Carsten Ahrens, August 12, 1961; MC to Mary Whoully, July 14, 1966; *LS*, p. 145.

28. *ER*, p. 15; MC to Hannah Josephson, May 16, 1936, Josephson Papers.

29. MC to Stanley Young, April 11, 1944; MC to Betty Cox, September 8, 1960; "School News," *Peabody* 3 (January 1915): 24.

30. "To Lotta on Her Double Chin," *Peabody* 3 (January 1915): 14; "True to Art," *Peabody* 3 (February 1915): 18; "The Best Story of the Year," *Peabody* 3 (June 1915): 95–98. For Cowley's other contributions to the *Peabody*, see the updated bibliography in the special Cowley issue of *Visionary Company* (Summer 1987): 226, 229.

31. Susan Jenkins Brown, *Robber Rocks: Letters and Memories of Hart Crane, 1923–1932* (Middletown, Conn., 1969), pp. 26–27; MC to KB, July 29, 1966; MC to Jake Davis, July 28, 1966.

32. MC to Allen Tate, May 18, 1973.

33. *SF*, pp. 244–45; MC to KB, June 2, 1932 (SC, p. 201).

34. MC to KB, [1916] (SC, p. 19).

35. KB to MC, October 2, 1959.

36. Donald G. Parker and Warren Herendeen, "KB & MC: An Interview with Kenneth Burke," *Visionary Company* (Summer 1987): 88–89, 96. The memory of their walks and talks together, the melody of their adolescent voices, would still reverberate in both men's minds sixty-five years later, even though by then their hearing had become considerably impaired. In a 1981 poem, "An Epistolation," dedicated to Cowley, Burke claimed that he could still perfectly understand his ancient friend's voice, even when, as at a recent meeting of the National Institute and American Academy of Arts and Letters, he was surrounded by a host of others talking loudly and he had neglected to bring his hearing aid: "hence missing an awful lot of the verbatims / put forth by the various thinkeroos / as the official meeting doodled on / I natheless understood sans effort every word / that you as Ipse Dixit judgmentally pronounced / during our severely

498 | NOTES TO CHAPTER 1

solemn deliberations." Malcolm Cowley, "Notes to a Poem by Kenneth Burke, 'An Epistolation,'" *Visionary Company* 1 (Summer 1981): 5–7.

37. Stanley Edgar Hyman, *The Armed Vision* (1948; rev. ed., 1955), p. 384; *SF*, p. 245; Allen Tate, "A Regional Poet," *New Republic* 60 (August 28, 1929): 51–52.

38. For a discussion of their friendship and correspondence, see the present author's "'Contest in Vilification': The Literary Friendship of Kenneth Burke and Malcolm Cowley," *Southern Review* 26 (Winter 1990): 226–35.

39. Van Wyck Brooks, *The Confident Years, 1885–1915* (New York, 1955); "Letter to England," *New Republic* 82 (February 13, 1935): 22 (*TBOU*, p. 255); *SF*, p. 26; compare Henry F. May, *The End of American Innocence* (New York, 1959), pp. 9, 22, 29, 112.

40. *ER*, p. 18; "Prayer on All Saints' Day," *Sewanee Review* 86 (Fall 1978): 564 (reprinted in *Blue Juniata: A Life*, p. 152).

41. *ER*, p. 19; "My Countryside, Then and Now," *Harper's Monthly Magazine* 158 (January 1929): 239–40.

42. Alfred Kazin, *On Native Grounds* (1942; New York, 1970), p. 92; May, *End of American Innocence*, pp. 121, 141.

43. "Letter to England," p. 22 (*TBOU*, p. 255–56); "The Smart Set Legend," *New Republic* 81 (January 16, 1935): 281 (*TBOU*, p. 249).

44. "Wowsers on the Run," *Brentano's Book Chat* 6 (January–February 1927): 30–33. *Book Chat* 6 (January–February 1927): 30–33.

45. *ER*, pp. 19–20, 27–28; MC to Cynthia A. Rusick, December 13, 1970.

46. "Two Gentlemen on Literati Road: Cowley Interview (August 30, 1975)," *Lost Generation Journal* 3 (Fall 1975): 6. Reprinted in *CMC*, pp. 129–37.

47. *SF*, p. 235.

48. *ER*, pp. 21–22; Notebook 1 (1922–1924), pp. 24–25.

49. *ER*, pp. 17, 21.

50. MC to KB, June 24, 1915; July 20, 1915; July 27, 1915; August 2, 1915.

51. MC to KB, July 20, 1915.

52. MC to KB, August 18, 1915; August 25, 1915.

53. MC to KB, September 3, 1915; September 7, 1915.

54. MC to KB, May 2, 1949; "Mother and Son," pp. 10–11; MC to Stanley Young, April 11, 1944.

2. THE EMERGENCE OF A HARVARD POET, 1915–1917

1. For Harvard University under President Eliot, see Samuel Eliot Morison, *Three Centuries of Harvard, 1636–1936* (1936; Cambridge, Mass., 1965), pp. 323–99, and Herbert Howarth, *Notes on Some Figures Behind T. S. Eliot* (Boston, 1964), pp. 64–113. Also see Richard S. Kennedy, *Dreams in the Mirror: A Biography of E. E. Cummings* (New York, 1980), pp. 52–100; Townsend Ludington, *John Dos Passos: A Twentieth-Century Odyssey* (New York, 1980), pp. 50–85; May, *End of American Innocence*, p. 56.

2. For Harvard University under President Lowell, see Morison, *Three Centuries of Harvard*, pp. 439–50.

3. "Toward a Universal Man," *New Republic* 49 (December 8, 1926): 69–71.

4. See Ronald Steel, *Walter Lippmann and the American Century* (Boston, Toronto, 1980), pp. 17–22; May, *End of American Innocence*, pp. 142–47. James had died in 1910; Santayana had retired in 1912 to spend the remaining forty years of his life in Europe; Royce was still alive during Cowley's freshman year, but died in September 1916.

5. May, pp. 58–61; Ludington, *Dos Passos*, p. 53.

6. Howarth, *Notes on Some Figures Behind T. S. Eliot*, pp. 89–94. Eliot's observation is quoted in Richard Ruland, *The Rediscovery of American Literature* (Cambridge, Mass., 1967), p. x.

7. "Hemingway's Wound—And Its Consequences for American Literature," *Georgia Review* 38 (Summer 1984): 235; see also *FL*, pp. 253–54.

8. *LS*, p. 158. For a fuller listing of Cowley's Harvard predecessors, see Kennedy, *Dreams in the Mirror*, p. 67; Edward Weeks to MC, January 29, 1957.

9. *LS*, pp. 164–65; notes for a speech to the Signet Society, February 8, 1974.

10. Compare Kennedy, *Dreams in the Mirror*, p. 66.

11. Morison, *Three Centuries of Harvard*, pp. 445–46; notes for speech to Signet Society, February 8, 1974, p. 2; MC to Fredson Bowers, August 12, 1967.

12. MC to KB, October 3, 1915; [October 21, 1915].

13. Notes for speech to Signet Society, pp. 1–2.

14. MC to KB, October 3, 1915; October [November?] 22, 1915 (*SC*, pp. 10–11).

15. MC to KB, postcard, October 26, 1915; November 9, 1915; November 14, 1915.

16. KB to MC, November 6, 1915 (*SC*, pp. 7–9).

17. MC to KB, [November 1915]; "Backstairs," *New York Herald Tribune Books*, October 7, 1928, p. 4.

18. MC to KB, November 9, 1915; November 14, 1915; [early December, 1915]; postcard December 4, 1915; January 18 [1916].

19. Matthew Josephson, *Life Among the Surrealists* (New York, 1962), p. 36; MC to KB, [November 1915].

20. KB to MC, November 6, 1915 (*SC*, p. 9).

21. MC to KB, [early December, 1915].

22. MC to author, May 12, 1984; KB to MC, December 10, 1915 (*SC*, pp. 14–15); MC to KB, December 15, 1915 (*SC*, p. 15).

23. MC to KB, January 5, 1915 [1916] (*SC*, p. 16); MC to Phillip McKenna, June 17, 1966.

24. MC to KB, January 5, 1915 [1916] (*SC*, pp. 15–16); January 18, [1916]; January 26, 1916.

25. MC to KB, January 26, 1916.

26. MC to KB, [January 1916]. Part of the letter appears in *SC*, pp. 18–19.

27. MC to KB, November 9, 1915; February 13, 1916; March 9, 1916 (partly published in *SC*, pp. 21–22). See also Morison, p. 420.

28. MC to KB, February 13, 1916; March 9, 1916.

29. *ER*, p. 35; *TBOU*, p. 203.

30. Ludington, *Dos Passos*, pp. 56–57; Charles Norman, *E. E. Cummings: A Biography* (New York, 1969), p. 45.

31. MC to KB, March 26, 1916; Norman, *Cummings*, p. 45; *WT*, pp. 37–38. For Cowley's contributions to the *Advocate*, see Eisenberg, *Malcolm Cowley*; for Cowley's evaluation of the Harvard Aesthetes from his 1930s perspective, see *TBOU*, pp. 211–13, and *ER* (1934), pp. 37–39.

32. MC to KB, March 26, 1916.

33. MC to KB, March 9, 1916 (*SC*, p. 22); April 5, 1916.

34. *Harvard Advocate* 101 (March 31, 1916): 42; Ernest Hemingway, *Death in the Afternoon* (New York, 1932), p. 2.

35. Morison, *Three Centuries of Harvard*, p. 430; Donald Hall, "Introduction," *The Harvard Advocate Anthology* (New York, 1950), p. 14 and passim; Jonathan D. Culler, "Introduction," *Harvard Advocate Centennial Anthology* (Cambridge, Mass., 1966), pp. xx–xxvi; *SF*, p. 91. The rivalry between both magazines persisted through the years. As late as 1951 Cummings, who had served on the staff of the *Monthly*, protested in a letter to Cowley that "our unhero [Cummings himself] wrote for a literary mag called The Harvard Monthly, not for a social sheet called The ditto Advocate." E. E. Cummings to MC, April 30, 1951.

36. Culler, "Introduction," *Harvard Advocate Centennial Anthology*, pp. xxvii, xx.

37. MC to KB, January 26, 1916; [May 1916] (*SC*, p. 28); "Execution," *Harvard Advocate* 101 (June 5, 1916): 114; "On Rereading Wordsworth," ibid., 109.

38. MC to KB, May 3, 1916 (*SC*, pp. 24–25).

39. For anti-Semitism at Harvard, see Stephen Steinberg, "How Jewish Quotas Began," *Commentary* 52 (1971): 67–76. Steinberg observes that "a climate of intolerance prevailed in many Eastern colleges long before discriminatory quotas were contemplated by college officials. From the turn of the century anti-Semitism was a common feature of campus social life" (p. 71). On November 2, 1971, Cowley wrote to his former classmate Jake Davis: "Yes, that Commentary article tells it as it was. I had forgotten what a prejudiced man A. Lawrence Lowell was, though I hadn't forgotten social anti-semitism at Harvard." Lowell, presumably motivated by a desire to preserve Harvard's historical identity as a repository of New England protestant values and upper-class standards, and presenting his proposal as a way of restricting the growth of anti-Semitism, in 1922 initiated moves to curb the enrollment of Jews at Harvard.

40. MC to Mrs. Andys K. Allport, May 21, 1976; MC to Joel Townsley Rogers, September 13, 1961.

41. MC to KB, September 27 [1915]; November 9, 1915; July 21, 1916.

42. MC to KB, April 5, 1916.

43. MC to KB, May 3, 1916 (*SC*, p. 25).

44. MC to KB, [May or June, 1916] (*SC*, pp. 28–29).

45. MC to KB, [June 1916].

46. MC to KB, July 4, 1916; MC to author, May 12, 1984; MC to KB, March 9, 1916; August 12, 1916; [August 1916].

47. MC to KB, July 21, 1916.

48. MC to KB, August 12, 1916.

49. MC to KB, July 21, 1916; August 31, 1916; September 8, 1916.

50. MC to KB, October 11, 1916; October 12, 1916; November 28, 1916.

51. MC to KB, November 1, 1916 (partly published in *SC*, p. 32).

52. KB to MC, November 7, 1916 (*SC*, p. 32).

53. MC to KB, November 11, 1916 (partly in *SC*, p. 33). Cowley's personal experience ties in with Samuel Eliot Morison's observations on the prerequisites for social success at Harvard. See *Three Centuries of Harvard*, p. 422.

54. Notes for speech to Signet Society, February 9, 1974, p. 3.

55. The basic society was a social organization called The Institute of 1770. Each year from 15 to 18 percent of the sophomores were admitted in elections organized in tens. Election to the Institute was the first social sifting among the sophomores and up until 1904 its list of members, printed in the local papers, served as an index of social rating. In their junior and senior years, members of the Institute could be elected to the Hasty Pudding Club. The first seven or eight "tens" automatically belonged to the D.K.E., the "Dickey." From there a socially ambitious climber would move on to a "waiting club," as a preliminary step toward election to one of the prestigious "final clubs," such as the elitist Porcellian Club. See Morison, pp. 422–27.

56. MC to KB, November 11, 1916.

57. MC to KB, October 24, 1916; November 11, 1916; December 14, 1916.

58. Compare Culler, "Introduction," p. xxi; *TBOU*, p. 273.

59. Alan M. Wald, *The Revolutionary Imagination: The Poetry and Politics of John Wheelwright and Sherry Mangan* (Chapel Hill and London, 1983), pp. 22–25; Norman, *E. E. Cummings*, pp. 48–58.

60. *Harvard Advocate* 102 (October 10, 1916): 4.

61. MC to KB, November 11, 1916; *Harvard Advocate* 102 (November 8, 1916): 42. "To a Girl I Dislike" was reprinted in *Harvard Advocate Anthology* (1950), pp. 151–52.

62. MC to KB, November 28, 1916; *Harvard Advocate* 102 (December 20, 1916): 82.

63. MC to KB, December 14, 1916; Lowell's compliment is quoted in S. Foster Damon, *Amy Lowell: A Chronicle* (1935; Hamden, Conn., 1966), pp. 398–99; *TBOU*, p. 280.

64. *Harvard Advocate* 102 (November 22, 1916): 62–63; see also the review of William McFee's *Casuals of the Sea*, in *Harvard Advocate* 102 (January 17, 1917): 124.

65. MC to KB, November 28, 1916; December 9, 1916; December 14, 1916.

66. MC to KB, January 10, 1917.

67. MC to KB, [January 1917]; January 22, 1917; January 31, 1917; Matthew Josephson, *Life Among the Surrealists* (New York, 1962), pp. 36, 41.

68. MC to KB, [January 1917]; *Slate* 1 (January 1917): 14 and (April 1917): 87; Frederick J. Hoffman, Charles Allen, Carolyn F. Ulrich, *The Little Magazine: A History and a Bibliography* (Princeton, N.J., 1947), p. 253; Max Lincoln Schuster to MC, June 17, 1953.

69. "James Thurber and the Avant Garde," unpublished lecture delivered at Ohio

State University, March 21, 1970, at the dedication of the James Thurber Collection, p. 1.

70. *Sansculotte* 1 (January 1917): 1.

71. "James Thurber and the Avant Garde," p. 1; Burton Bernstein, *Thurber: A Biography* (New York, 1975), p. 52; MC to Mr. Bergman, March 31, 1967; MC to Lewis C. Branscomb, February 19, 1970.

72. MC to KB, January 22, 1917; February 26, 1917; *Sansculotte* 1 (April 1917): 2.

73. *Sansculotte* 1 (January 1917): 5.

74. Ibid. (February 1917): 7.

75. *Harvard Advocate* 102 (February 7, 1917): 152.

76. MC to KB, January 22, 1917; *Harvard Advocate* 103 (February 28, 1917): 3. Reprinted in *Harvard Advocate Anthology* (1950), pp. 152–53.

77. MC to KB, March 21, 1917; *Harvard Advocate* 103 (February 28, 1917): 5.

78. *Harvard Advocate* 102 (January 10, 1917): 105–6.

79. See J. Donald Adams, *Copey of Harvard* (Boston, 1960), pp. 150–51; WT, p. 55; Morison, p. 402.

80. MC to KB, March 15, 1917; "The Beginning Writer in the University," *Michigan Alumnus Quarterly Review* 64 (1957): 67; MC to J. Donald Adams, July 25, 1957. See also Adams, *Copey of Harvard*, p. 180.

81. MC to KB, March 31, 1917; [April 1917] (SC, p. 35).

82. MC to KB, [March 1917]; a holograph copy of "Copey's Room" is among the Cowley Papers.

83. MC to J. Donald Adams, July 25, 1957; "The Beginning Writer in the University," p. 70; MC to author, March 23, 1980.

84. See ER (1934), pp. 31–37; ER, pp. 28–34.

85. ER (1934), p. 34; ER, p. 32.

86. KB to MC, November 6, 1915 (SC, p. 9); "On Rereading Wordsworth," *Harvard Advocate* 101 (June 5, 1916): 109.

3. THE SPECTACLE OF WAR—FRANCE, 1917

1. Morison, *Three Centuries of Harvard*, pp. 438, 451, 456–59.

2. SF, pp. 9, 92; the *Advocate* editorial is quoted in *Harvard Advocate Centennial Anthology* (1966), p. xx.

3. Kennedy, *Dreams in the Mirror*, pp. 136–37; SF, p. 80; Ludington, *Dos Passos*, pp. 124–64.

4. For Burke's attitude to the war, see his letters to MC between May 27 and September 18, 1917, in SC, pp. 35–38, 40–43, 46–49, 51–53. Also see Josephson, *Life Among the Surrealists*, pp. 38–39, 53–54; review of *Egotism in German Philosophy*, by George Santayana, *Harvard Advocate* 103 (May 14, 1917): 73–74; MC to KB, May 3, 1916; March 31, 1917.

5. Harvard itself had produced a mythical example of wartime heroism and romance

in the poet Alan Seeger, whose "I Have a Rendezvous with Death" was already a famous war poem. Seeger was mortally wounded on July 4, 1916, and became one of the earliest American martyrs of the war. His collected poems appeared in the fall and his *Letters and Diary* were published in May 1917. Seeger's poetry was widely known and admired at Harvard and encouraged those of literary sensitivity and ambition in particular to seek some form of military service. See *SF*, pp. 6–7. For the response of the younger literary generation to the war, see Frederick J. Hoffman, *The Twenties: American Writing in the Postwar Decade* (1962; New York, 1965), pp. 71–77; *ER*, p. 37; Stanley Cooperman, *World War I and the American Novel* (Baltimore, 1967), pp. 44–56. David C. Duke, *Distant Obligations. Modern American Writers and Foreign Causes* (New York and Oxford, 1983) has an illuminating chapter on Cowley's experience of the war in comparison with Edith Wharton's and Alan Seeger's.

6. *Harvard Advocate* 103 (May 14, 1917): 7.

7. As David C. Duke has pertinently suggested, "[t]he educational dissatisfaction that so many of [Cowley's] younger generation of writers felt helps explain why they so eagerly rushed from the halls of academe to what they believed was a truer kind of classroom." *Distant Obligations*, p. 83.

8. MC to J. Donald Adams, July 25, 1957; MC to KB, March 31, 1917; [April 1917] (*SC*, p. 35). Schenck, a protégé of Barrett Wendell and a literary acquaintance of T. S. Eliot, had done similar services to others.

9. Josephson, *Life Among the Surrealists*, p. 40; David E. Shi, *Matthew Josephson, Bourgeois Bohemian* (New Haven and London, 1981).

10. Burke's observation is quoted in Shi, p. 25. Josephson's first meeting with Burke and their subsequent friendship is described in his *Life Among the Surrealists*, pp. 30–32, 53–55. See also Shi, *Matthew Josephson*, pp. 25–26, 29–30.

11. MC to KB, April 24, 1917; May 11, 1917; "Camion Service Notes," May 18 [1917]; MC to Charles Norman, November 10, 1962, Humanities Research Center, University of Texas at Austin; Brown's and Cummings's subsequent adventures laid the foundation for Cummings's *The Enormous Room* (1922). See also Kennedy, *Dreams in the Mirror*, pp. 138–58. For a description of the American Field Service headquarters, see Geoffrey Wolff, *Black Sun: The Brief Transit and Violent Eclipse of Harry Crosby* (New York, 1976), p. 41.

12. Charles A. Fenton, "Ambulance Drivers in France and Italy: 1914–1918," *American Quarterly* 2 (1951): 327, 331, 336–38; *ER*, pp. 37–38; for the precise number of the participants, see *History of the American Field Service in France* (Boston, 1920), vol. 3, appendix C, pp. 440–41. Harvard men numbered 325; Yale, 198; Princeton, 181; Dartmouth, 118.

13. MC to KB, May 11, 1917.

14. As A. Piatt Andrew, evaluating the service of the volunteers in March 1919, observed: "Their work was often hard and fraught with difficulties. It sometimes seemed to its participants inglorious and uninspiring, though never to those who observed them toiling through crowded traffic and endless clouds of dust. But like prisoners in unexplored regions they . . . built better than they knew, . . . and helped substantially in

blazing the way towards victory." A. Piatt Andrew, "The Origin of the American T. M. Sections," *American Field Service Bulletin* (Mallet Reserve Number), no. 84 (March 8, 1919), n.p.; see Fenton, p. 339; MC to KB, June 20, 1917.

15. MC to parents, May 20, 1917; "The Transport Sections of the American Field Service in France," brochure, May 1917, n.p.

16. The war diary, a handwritten sheaf of loose sheets of paper, is among Cowley's papers at the Newberry Library. Entitled "Camion Service Notes," it is a rather slender and chaotic affair, but is important because it contains rough drafts of many episodes that later found their way into the American Field Service Bulletin; it forms the source of the section "Ambulance Service" in *Exile's Return*.

17. "Camion Service Notes," May 18 [1917]; Fenton, pp. 329–30.

18. "Four Books About Ourselves," *Charm* 5 (June 1926): 33; "Camion Service Notes," May 19 [1917].

19. "Camion Service Notes," May 20 [1917].

20. MC to KB, June 1, 1917; June 7, 1917 (SC, p. 39); June 26, 1917 (SC, p. 43); see "Camion Service Notes," May 31 [1917]; MC to parents, May 20, 1917; May 22, 1917.

21. "In 'Le Pays Reconquis,' " *American Field Service Bulletin*. Reprinted in the section "Camion Sidelights" in *History of the American Field Service in France*, vol. 3, pp. 88–90; "U. S. Volunteer Tells of French Battle Front Visit—No Union Hours," *Pittsburgh Gazette Times*, January 6, 1918, p. 3. Quotations in the text are from the latter, more elaborate, account.

22. *History of the American Field Service in France*, vol. 3, p. 259; quoted in Fenton, p. 340.

23. *ER*, pp. 38–39.

24. "Camion Service Notes," June 12 [1917]; "U. S. Volunteer Tells of French Battle Front Visit," p. 3; MC to parents, June 11, 1917; MC to KB, June 7, 1917 (SC, p. 39); see also Cowley's 1933 memories of mutinies among French soldiers in "The Dead of the Next War," *New Republic* 76 (October 4, 1933): 216 (*TBOU*, p. 46).

25. William E. Leuchtenburg, *The Perils of Prosperity* (New York, 1958), pp. 35–36; MC to "Popsie," July 9, 1917; *ER*, p. 40.

26. "Camion Service Notes," June 12 [1917], different entry; MC to parents, June 11, 1917; MC to "Popsie," July 9, 1917; "Camion Service Notes," June 15 [1917].

27. "On the Road with T.M.U. 526" appeared in the *American Field Service Bulletin* and was reprinted in the *History*, vol. 3, pp. 72–77. For an early draft, see "Camion Service Notes," June 20 [1917]. Quotations in the text are from the *History*.

28. MC to KB, June 7, 1917 (SC, p. 39).

29. "On the Road with T. M. U. 526," *History*, pp. 75–76.

30. *BJ*, pp. 63–64.

31. MC to "Popsie," July 9, 1917; MC to KB, June 26, 1917 (SC, p. 44); MC to KB, July 4, 1917 (SC, pp. 45–46).

32. MC to KB, July 4, 1917 (SC, p. 45); July 24, 1917; July 31, 1917 (SC, p. 50).

33. "Books for Your Christmas List," *Charm* 4 (December 1925):84; MC to KB, June 7, 1917 (SC, p. 39); June 20, 1917; June 26, 1917 (SC, p. 43); July 12, 1917; July 31, 1917 (SC, pp. 50–51).

34. MC to KB, July 12, 1917.

35. MC to KB, July 24, 1917; "Fourth of July in the Old T. M.," *American Field Service Bulletin*, no. 51 (June 29, 1918), n.p. Reprinted as "Fourth of July, 1917" in *History*, pp. 91–96. Quotations in the text are from the *History*. "Camion Service Notes," July 6 [1917].

36. *History*, pp. 97–99; *ER*, p. 40.

37. MC to KB, July 24, 1917; "Camion Service Notes," June 25 [1917].

38. MC to "Popsie," July 28, 1917; [July 1917]; MC to KB, July 24, 1917; August 25, 1917.

39. MC to KB, June 26, 1917 (*SC*, pp. 43–44); August 20, 1917.

40. MC to KB, September 11, 1917; September 18, 1917.

41. MC to KB, September 2, 1917; September 23, 1917.

42. MC to KB, September 18, 1917; September 23, 1917. See especially Bourne's "The War and the Intellectuals," *Seven Arts* 2 (June 1917): 133–46, and his "Twilight of Idols," *Seven Arts* 2 (October 1917): 688–702. Bourne's articles are reprinted in *The War and the Intellectuals: Collected Essays, 1915–1919*. Edited with an introduction by Carl Resch (New York, 1964). For Burke's comments on the war, see KB to MC, September 18, 1917 (*SC*, p. 52).

43. Fenton, p. 339; MC to KB, September 11, 1917.

44. *American Field Service Bulletin*, No. 13 (September 29, 1917). Reprinted in *Harvard Advocate* 104 (February 1918), 280.

45. Paul Fussell, *The Great War and Modern Memory* (New York and London, 1975), p. 8; *Harvard Advocate* 104 (February 1918), 280.

46. MC to KB, September 11, 1917.

47. MC to KB, September 23, 1917; October 19, 1917; November 2, 1917; December 14, 1917.

48. MC to KB, October 3, 1917; October 9, 1917 (*SC*, p. 54); October 13, 1917; October 19, 1917.

49. MC to KB, October 13, 1917. As noted above, Cowley's correspondence does not reveal any such anti-Semitic expressions beyond this point in time.

50. MC to KB, October 29, 1917 (partly in *SC*, p. 55); MC to mother, October 9, 1917; "Both Sides of a Push," in "Camion Service Notes," n.d.; "The History of a Push," *Harvard Advocate* 104 (January 1918): 241–42.

51. MC to KB, October 29, 1917; November 2, 1917; November 3, 1917.

52. *ER*, pp. 38, 41.

53. *ER*, pp. 41–43, 46.

54. See Cooperman, *World War I and the American Novel*, p. 227, and Fussell, *The Great War and Modern Memory*, pp. 191–230. In *Exile's Return* Cowley mostly used Dos Passos's *1919* and Hemingway's *A Farewell to Arms* to buttress his claim of a "spectatorial attitude." For his use of the writings of other coevals to support his interpretation of the war, see his "Après la guerre finie," *Horizon* 10 (Winter 1968): 112–19, and his "American Writers and the First World War," *Proceedings of the American Academy of Arts and Letters and the National Institute of Arts and Letters*, second series, no. 18 (1968), 25–46. Instructive, also, is a comparison between Cowley's account in *Exile's*

Return and the reminiscences of John Dos Passos in *The Best Times* (New York, 1966), especially pp. 56–57, 64, 68, 71.

55. Not only was the book written, as Cowley told Warren I. Susman (March 8, 1965), "in the midst of a violent [literary] reaction against the 1920s," historians, too, by 1934 were inclined to believe that the United States had been "tricked into the war by the twin forces of profiteering and Allied propaganda." Early that year the Nye Committee had turned up startling evidence that economic interests had largely determined American intervention in 1917. William E. Leuchtenburg, *F. D. R. and the New Deal: 1932–1940* (New York, 1963), pp. 198, 217–18.

56. *New Republic* 76 (September 20, 1933): 161 (*TBOU*, p. 41).

57. Fenton, p. 334. Out of some 2,100 American Field Service volunteers in France, 127 were killed, a death rate of more than six percent, 230 received the *croix de guerre* and five the *médaille militaire*. Cooperman, p. 227. (Compare *Exile's Return*, p. 41: "seldom were there more than two or three serious casualties in a section during the year"). For comparable accounts of camion drivers, see the section "Camion Sidelights" in *History*, 3, pp. 66–114.

58. Though, from the perspective of half a century, Cowley was "tempted to postulate a death wish in an entire culture," he saw no reason to revise his earlier diagnosis of the spectatorial attitude—"You went to the war and it was like going to a theater that advertised the greatest spectacle in history." American volunteers, even in the face of death, had remained "the spectators of somebody else's war" and death itself had largely been "a spectacle . . . with aesthetic properties." *SF*, pp. 5, 9–11.

59. Cowley used the phrase "organized Byronism" in a letter to David C. Duke, May 2, 1968. As Duke subsequently noted, it was "a most paradoxical turn of events that activism abroad ultimately led to social detachment rather than commitment" (*Distant Obligations*, p. 99).

4. HARVARD AND NEW YORK, 1918

1. "Eugene O'Neill, Writer of Synthetic Drama," *Brentano's Book Chat* 5 (September–October 1926): 19; *MWH*, p. 191; Josephson, *Life Among the Surrealists*, pp. 33–34.

2. MC to KB, December 7, 1917; December 14, 1917.

3. The pocket diary is among the Cowley Papers at the Newberry Library. The outline for "A Son at Harvard" appears on pp. 3–6.

4. MC to KB, December 14, 1917; January 13, 1918 (*SC*, p. 59); Eisenberg, *Malcolm Cowley*, p. 99; "U. S. Volunteer Tells of French Battle Front Visit—No Union Hours," *Pittsburgh Gazette Times*, January 6, 1918, sec. 5, p. 3, reprinted in the special Cowley issue of *Visionary Company* (Summer 1987): 75–80; MC to Richard C. Johnson, April 13, 1972; *Harvard Advocate* 104 (January 1918): 240–42.

5. MC to KB, December 14, 1917; "Ostel 1917" was republished as part of "Two French Towns" in *Youth* 1 (October 1918): 5; pocket diary, p. 2; MC to KB, January 13, 1918 (*SC*, p. 59).

6. Josephson, *Life Among the Surrealists*, p. 41; KB to MC, January 6, 1918 (SC, p. 56); MC to KB, January 13, 1918 (SC, pp. 58–59).

7. Louis Sheaffer, *O'Neill: Son and Playwright* (London, 1968), pp. 396–97; Arthur Gelb and Barbara Gelb, *O'Neill* (New York, 1962), pp. 343–44; Josephson, *Life Among the Surrealists*, pp. 40–41, 271; Susan Jenkins Brown, *Robber Rocks*, pp. 10, 12–13, 26. In the early 1920s, after her divorce from Light, Susan Jenkins became an editor at *Telling Tales*, a pulp magazine publishing risqué fiction and "true confessions," a position at other times held by Hannah Geffen, Matthew Josephson's wife, and for a while by Allen Tate.

8. MC to KB, February 17, 1918.

9. MC to KB, February 17, 1918; February 25, 1918 (SC, p. 62); notes for a speech to Signet Society, February 9, 1974, pp. 3–4.

10. MC to KB, February 25, 1918 (SC, p. 61); "The Way Out," typescript of unpublished review of *The Charnel Rose* (1918) by Conrad Aiken, n.p.

11. "Conrad Aiken: A Man of Letters," *Brentano's Book Chat* 6 (September–October 1927): 32; "The Way Out," n.p. Aiken's work, Cowley later wrote, was unified by a central principle of "candor," which the poet had evolved into a complete "system of aesthetics and literary ethics." In Aiken's insistence that the writer be "a surgeon performing an exploratory operation on himself, at whatever cost to his self-esteem," he had managed to avoid the hermeticism of the "merely private" and given his self-revelation a "public" value. In this, Cowley saw, Aiken was as much Emersonian as symbolist or Freudian: "By finding words for his inmost truth, the writer—especially the poet—has made it part of the world, part of human consciousness. He has become a soldier, so to speak, in the agelong war that mankind has been waging against the subliminal and merely instinctive." In such a way Aiken had fulfilled the supreme task of any writer: that of "broadening, deepening, and subtilizing the human consciousness." *WT*, pp. 233–35.

12. "Biography with Letters," *Wake* 11 (Summer 1952): 26; *WT*, p. 232; Joseph Killorin, ed., *Selected Letters of Conrad Aiken* (New Haven and London, 1978), pp. 13, 25, 38–39.

13. "Biography with Letters," p. 26; MC to KB, March 2, 1918; March 17, 1918 (SC, pp. 62–63).

14. *WT*, pp. 233, 237.

15. *WT*, pp. 35–37, 38, 48.

16. MC to KB, March 9, 1918; *WT*, p. 36; *TBOU*, p. 279; MC to KB, April 27, 1918; May 25, 1918 (SC, pp. 65–66).

17. *WT*, p. 39; Wald, *Revolutionary Imagination*, pp. 36–37, 174; Matthew Josephson, "Improper Bostonian: John Wheelwright and his Poetry," *Southern Review* 7 (April 1971): 509–40.

18. MC to KB, March 2, 1918; March 9, 1918.

19. MC to KB, March 17, 1918 (SC, p. 63).

20. MC to KB, n.d.

21. MC to KB, March 9, 1918; March 25, 1918.

22. MC to KB, March 9, 1918; "Louisburg Square," *Harvard Advocate* 104 (March 1918): 308; "Sentimental," ibid., 324.

23. Ezra Pound, "A Study of Modern French Poets," *Little Review* 5 (February 1918): 3–61; WT, pp. 71–72; MC to KB, March 25, 1918.

24. "A Theme with Variations," *Harvard Advocate* 104 (April 1918): 337–38.

25. MC to KB, April 27, 1918; MC to Mrs. Leo Gurko, August 29, 1960; see also the pocket diary.

26. Interview with author, January 30, 1982; MC to KB, October 22, 1967; notes for a speech to Signet Society, February 9, 1974; MC to KB, February 25, 1918 (SC, pp. 61–62); May 11, 1918.

27. MC to KB, March 2, 1918; April 27, 1918.

28. Lowell's letter is quoted in Damon, *Amy Lowell*, pp. 449–50; WT, p. 39.

29. MC to Charles Fenton, October 17, 1957; MC to KB, May 11, 1918; May 25, 1918.

30. MC to KB, n.d.; "Dear Norma," unpublished poem; William Jay Smith, *The Spectra Hoax* (Wesleyan University Press, 1961) gives an amusing account of both the Spectra and Earl Roppel hoax. See also Damon, *Amy Lowell*, pp. 453–57; MC to Witter Bynner, September 14, 1958; WT, pp. 39–43, gives Cowley's account of the Roppel affair. For the account given here I have depended on these sources, as well as on new material in the Cowley Papers and the Amy Lowell Papers in the Houghton Library at Harvard.

31. WT, pp. 40–41; Earl Roppel to Amy Lowell, June 28, 1918, Lowell Papers; quotations from Roppel's poems are from manuscripts in the Amy Lowell Papers; the letter to Bynner is quoted in a manuscript version of Smith, *The Spectra Hoax*, which is among the Cowley Papers.

32. WT, pp. 41–42; Amy Lowell to Earl Roppel, August 20, 1918, Lowell Papers.

33. "The Real Earl Roppel—The Brief and Meteoric Career of the Genius of the Catatonk," *Literary Review of the New York Evening Post*, July 24, 1920, p. 4.

34. Witter Bynner to Earl Roppel, November 11, 1918; Eric Schuler (secretary and treasurer of the Authors' League of America) to Witter Bynner, October 25, 1918; Nano Loring (librarian, Coburn Free Library, Owego, Tioga County, N.Y.) to Witter Bynner, November 26, 1918.

35. "Sunset" is quoted in full in WT, p. 42; Witter Bynner to Earl Roppel, n.d.; Louis J. Stellman to Witter Bynner, April 7, 1919; a clipping of "Bynner Seeks Lost Mystery Poet in N.Y." is among the Cowley Papers. The complete success of Cowley's and Damon's parodic intent was confirmed by Zoe Burns, who, not long after, wondered in the *San Francisco Bulletin* what happened to "the lad who had such a freshly interesting outlook on life from the narrow confines of a little New York hamlet and to whom the great dreams came thronging while he plowed the fields. . . . And I'm wondering if the war took that fresh fine almost-girlish sweetness out of him and made him bitter as it has so many of our youths. . . . Was the heart of him smitten by the thunder of war? And the melody of his spirit silenced by its horrors? Was perchance his very life blown out like a candle in the blast?" Burns is quoted in WT, p. 43.

36. Here may well have lain a source of the confusion and Roppel's lack of response:

Clemenceau Cottage was at 86, not 186 Greenwich Avenue; Witter Bynner to War Department, Washington D.C., January 28, 1920; Witter Bynner to Major General Commandant, U.S. Marine Corps, September 10, 1920; Witter Bynner to Chief, Bureau of Navigation, Navy Department, September 10, 1920; Witter Bynner to Landlord or Householder, 186 Greenwich Avenue, N.Y., September 10, 1920.

37. Witter Bynner to Earl Roppel, July 25, 1921; Witter Bynner to MC, January 7, 1922; MC to Amy Lowell, August 30, 1921, Lowell Papers; Witter Bynner to MC, [1923]; MC to Witter Bynner, May 20, 1923, Lowell Papers.

38. The documentary record of Cowley's career from August 1918 to the summer of 1921, a period he spent alternately in Cambridge and New York, is sparse and incomplete. A pocket diary, intermittently kept from the time of his return from the war through January 8, 1922, holds but a very fragmentary record of the period. As Cowley saw more of Burke in person in New York, there was less need to keep up a continuous correspondence and more opportunity to talk. For long periods, between August 3, 1918, and June 10, 1919, and again between August 25, 1920, and May 5, 1921, there are gaps in a correspondence which virtually constitutes an intellectual autobiography. Our account of those years, then, will have to rely on scanter documentation.

39. WT, p. 41; Morison, Three Centuries of Harvard, p. 459.

40. Pocket diary, entry for December 4, 1918. The entry retrospectively covers Cowley's activities from September 16.

41. Amy Lowell to MC, July 26, 1918, Lowell Papers; TBOU, p. 280; Amy Lowell to MC, October 24, 1918, Lowell Papers; MC to Harriet Monroe, November 1, 1918, Poetry Papers; MC to Amy Lowell, November 1, 1918, Lowell Papers.

42. Hoffman et al., Little Magazine, p. 255; "Two French Towns, 1: Ostel, 2: Nouvron-Vingré," Youth: Poetry of Today 1 (October 1918): 5; "Bayonet Drill: Two Sonnets," Harvard Advocate 104 (November 1918): 18.

43. ER, pp. 46–47.

5. A HUMBLE CITIZEN OF GRUB STREET—
GREENWICH VILLAGE, 1919

1. Compare Frederick J. Hoffman, The Twenties: American Writing in the Postwar Decade (1962; New York, 1965), pp. 33–43.

2. ER, pp. 66–67; see also James Gilbert, Writers and Partisans: A History of Literary Radicalism in America (New York, 1968), pp. 39–41, 47; pocket diary, first part, p. 27.

3. ER, p. 67; Allen Churchill, The Improper Bohemians: A Recreation of Greenwich Village in Its Heyday (New York, 1959), p. 166; ER, p. 48.

4. ER, pp. 55, 73.

5. ER, pp. 48–50.

6. LS, pp. 162–63; ER, p. 50.

7. WT, p. 51; MC to author, March 2, 1984; for Orrick Johns, see also Churchill, The Improper Bohemians, pp. 23, 69–70, 260. The town clerk at Babylon reports that

a "Marjory Francis" Baird was born in Babylon on November 18, 1887, the daughter of Frank S. Baird, jeweler, and Cecilia M. Brown. If this is Peggy Baird, as seems most probable, then Cowley's first wife was his senior by eleven years and not, as Cowley reported to the present writer in 1984, by eight years. Hunce Voelcker to author, January 29, 1989. I am indebted to Mr. Voelcker for consulting the town clerk at Babylon.

8. Josephson, *Life Among the Surrealists*, pp. 41, 44; Peggy Baird Cowley to John Brooks Wheelwright, September 1921, Wheelwright Papers.

9. MC to author, March 2, 1984; Sheaffer, *O'Neill: Son and Playwright*, pp. 327, 340; the Herb Roth cartoon is reprinted in Albert Parry, *Garrets and Pretenders: A History of Bohemianism in America* (New York, 1933; rev. ed. 1960), p. 271.

10. Harold Loeb, *The Way It Was* (New York, 1959), p. 134; Josephson, *Life Among the Surrealists*, p. 47; Josephson's description of Cowley is quoted in Shi, *Matthew Josephson*, p. 35.

11. MC to author, May 12, 1984; William Carlos Williams, *The Autobiography of William Carlos Williams* (New York, 1951), pp. 135–42. Williams recalled that Cowley was an occasional visitor at Grantwood and even "lived there for a while" with Peggy, but his memory was imprecise. The one visit Cowley paid to Grantwood was in the late spring of 1919, though he was invited to several evenings of the *Others* group in the spring of 1920.

12. *WT*, pp. 51–52; *ER*, p. 51.

13. *WT*, p. 52; Robert Morss Lovett, *All Our Years* (New York, 1948), p. 153.

14. Review of *The Poets of the Future*, edited by Henry T. Schnittkind, *Dial* (April 19, 1919), p. 432. Cowley had first submitted the review to the *Nation*. In February its literary editor had returned the manuscript, explaining there was no opening for poetry reviewers on the *Nation* for the time being. W. R. Brown to MC, February 17, 1919.

15. "Current News," *Dial* (May 17, 1919), p. 526; review of *The Rising of the Tide*, by Ida M. Tarbell, *Dial* (August 9, 1919), p. 122. The Jacquerie was an insurrection of French peasants against the nobility at the time of the Hundred Years' War, in 1358.

16. "Notes on New Books," *Dial* (October 4, 1919); review of *The Writing and Reading of Verse*, by C. E. Andrews and *How to Read Poetry*, by Ethel M. Colson, *Dial* (May 31, 1919), p. 572; "The Tools of Poetry," *Literary Review of The New York Evening Post* 1 (January 29, 1921), 8. Among Cowley's papers at the Newberry Library is a "Scrapbook, 1917–1924," containing clippings of several, but by no means all, of Cowley's unsigned reviews for the *Dial* and the *New Republic*. Since in many cases their running heads are missing, not all clippings can be fully identified.

17. Pocket diary, second part, entry for May 14, 1919; *ER*, pp. 51–52; *WT*, pp. 53–54.

18. Unpublished typescript of speech to Signet Society, dated February 11, 1974, p. 3; "Scrapbook, 1917–1924" contains items from the *New York Central Magazine* and the *Official Metropolitan Guide*; MC to KB, June 10, 1919.

19. KB to MC, June 21, 1919 (*SC*, p. 67); MC to KB, July 8, 1919; pocket diary, second part, various entries, pp. 23–35.

20. Cowley's impressions of Moise appear in *LS*, pp. 162–63, n. 1; his review of Day's novel, entitled "The Village Smell," appeared in *Literary Review of the New York Evening Post* 4 (June 21, 1924), 844; Harold Loeb, *The Way It Was* (New York, 1959), p. 42.

21. "Parting—Gare du Nord" appeared in *Youth: Poetry of Today* 1 (June 1919), 92–93; "Sunday Afternoon (After Jules Laforgue)" appeared in *Little Review* 6 (July-August 1919), 61–62.

22. MC to KB, July 8, 1919; pocket diary, second part, p. 24.

23. For a consideration of the early years of the *New Republic* and an appreciation of Francis Hackett's career, see George Austin Test, "The Vital Connection: A Study of *The New Republic* Magazine as a Literary Journal, 1914–1922," Ph.D. dissertation, University of Pennsylvania, 1960. David Seideman, '*The New Republic*': A *Voice of Modern Liberalism* (New York, 1986) gives a history of the first twenty-five years of the magazine.

24. *WT*, p. 53. By an ironic twist of literary history, their relations would be reversed more than a decade later. In the early 1930s Mary Updike worked for some time as assistant to Malcolm Cowley, then the literary editor of the *New Republic*, until her resignation in 1934. In 1937 Cowley, who as early as 1919 had been impressed by Hackett's gifts as a "stylist," invited him to write for the *New Republic* in an effort to "re-establish continuities." MC to Hylan Packard, July 6, 1967.

25. "Through Yellow Glasses," *New Republic* 19 (July 23, 1919), 401–2.

26. Josephson, *Life Among the Surrealists*, p. 51.

27. Josephson, *Life Among the Surrealists*, pp. 47–49, 67–68.

28. Josephson, *Life Among the Surrealists*, pp. 49–50.

29. MC to author, March 23, 1980, and March 2, 1984.

30. Lovett, *All Our Years*, p. 153; "Wowsers on the Run," *Brentano's Book Chat* 6 (January-February 1927), 30–31; *SF*, p. 14.

31. "A Life in the 1920's," unpublished manuscript, p. 1; *ER*, pp. 101–2.

32. Cowley had already been exposed to French symbolism during his first two years at Harvard, where, in the years before the war, the example of T. S. Eliot had done most to enflame young Harvard poets with enthusiasm for French symbolist verse. Eliot, after all, was writing the sort of modern poetry they all hoped to write. In December of 1908 Eliot had picked up, in the library of the Harvard Union, Arthur Symons's *The Symbolist Movement in Literature* (1899), which had put him on the track of the poets he would strive to emulate. Laforgue, in particular, became for Eliot "the first to teach me how to speak, to teach me the poetic possibilities of my own idiom of speech." Soon after, Eliot was publishing poems in the *Harvard Advocate*— "Nocturne" (1909), "Humouresque (After J. Laforgue)" and "Spleen" (both 1910)— that clearly reflected the new influence. In 1915, the year Cowley entered Harvard, Eliot had published perhaps his most distinctly Laforguean poem, "The Love Song of J. Alfred Prufrock," in *Poetry*; sixty years later its "tangent" ending still impressed Cowley as "one of the great moments in twentieth-century English poetry." *WT*, pp. 70–71; for T. S. Eliot, see John J. Soldo, "T. S. Eliot and Jules Laforgue," *American*

Literature 55 (May 1983), 137–50. Quotations from Eliot are from this article. For the Laforguean poems by Eliot mentioned here, see T. S. Eliot, *Poems Written in Early Youth* (London, 1967), pp. 29–32, 40–41; *WT*, p. 80.

33. *WT*, pp. 35, 72, 81.

34. Pocket diary, second part, p. 38; *WT*, pp. 73–75.

35. *WT*, pp. 74, 81; MC to Warren French, November 12, 1960.

36. When, from a perspective of more than forty years, Cowley came to discuss some of these poems, he modestly took them as representative historical evidence rather than as poems worthy to be judged on intrinsic literary merit. Yet, in the verdict of Warren French, he had been capable of producing "two of the best English renderings of Laforgue." French, *Jules Laforgue and the Ironic Inheritance* (New York, 1953), p. 196.

37. "Sunday Afternoon (After Jules Laforgue)," *Little Review* 6 (July-August 1919), 61–62; MC to Jackson R. Bryer, February 5, 1964.

38. "Romance in a Major Key," *Modern S4N Review* 1 (August 1926), 11–12; *BJCP*, pp. 37–39. Written about 1919, the poem was not published until 1926, when an early version appeared in *Modern S4N Review* as "Romance in a Major Key." Revised as "Nocturne," it was published again in the *Hound & Horn* in 1929. Collected in *Blue Juniata* (1929), the poem struck Yvor Winters, always one to call a spade a spade, as "almost a paraphrase of Laforgue's *Complainte des Pianos* which has the dazzling rapidity of a first-rate xylophone performance: *Nocturne* is slow and limps." Yvor Winters, "The Poetry of Malcolm Cowley," *Hound & Horn* 3 (October-December 1929), 111.

39. "Four Horological Poems," *Little Review* 7 (July–August 1920), 18–21; *WT*, p. 77; MC to author, November 2, 1984; *BJ*, p. 95.

40. *WT*, pp. 78–79; *BJCP*, p. 34.

41. *BJ*, pp. 33–34.

42. "One O'Clock at O'Connor's," *Pagan* 4 (January 1920), 52 (here quoted as revised and retitled "Kelly's Barroom" in *BJ*, p. 35).

43. *WT*, p. 72; "Translucent Fingers" was revised and retitled "Angelica" in *BJ*, pp. 59–60.

44. This is one of many valuable insights in James M. Kempf, *The Early Career of Malcolm Cowley: A Humanist Among the Moderns* (Baton Rouge and London, 1985), pp. 39–40.

45. *ER*, pp. 54–57, 60–61; *ER* (1934), pp. 63–67, 69–71.

46. *ER*, pp. 67, 69; *ER* (1934), pp. 77, 80.

47. *ER*, pp. 69–72; *ER* (1934), pp. 80–83.

48. *SF*, pp. 14–15. As Cowley's differentiation between the older and newer Villagers suggests, rather than to his own generation, the term "lost" or "disillusioned" was more applicable to an older group of writers, artists, and intellectuals. It was they who, in journals like the *Masses*, the *Seven Arts*, and the *New Republic*, had been most vocal in their rebellion against a stunting materialism, puritanism, and provincialism, who had idealistically exposed the failure of American culture, and cherished hopes of a cultural renaissance. Cowley's generation thus constituted what Christopher Lasch has called "the second of the lost generations." Coming in the wake of the prewar social

revolutionaries and cultural idealists, Cowley and his friends inherited the forms and stances of rebellion from their predecessors but soon found themselves left with only the shells and not the substance. Christopher Lasch, *The New Radicalism in America, 1889–1963: The Intellectual as a Social Type* (New York, 1965), pp. 71, 255.

49. Malcolm Cowley (with Howard E. Hugo), *The Lesson of the Masters: An Anthology of the Novel from Cervantes to Hemingway* (New York, 1971), p. 235.

50. As Elinor Bulkin has pertinently observed, Cowley's search for an ideal life of art can best be seen in a religious context. "Malcolm Cowley: A Study of His Literary, Social and Political Thought to 1940," Ph.D. dissertation, New York University, 1973, p. 17; *FL*, p. 234; compare Josephson, *Life Among the Surrealists*, pp. 60–62, 65.

6. HARVARD REVISITED, 1919–1920

1. *BJ*, p. 35; the second quotation is from the original version of "One O'Clock at O'Connor's" which appeared in *Pagan*, p. 52.

2. MC to KB, August 24, 1919 (SC, p. 68); pocket diary, second part, pp. 36–37.

3. "Mother and Son," pp. 11–12.

4. MC to KB, August 24, 1919 (SC, p. 68).

5. MC to KB, August 30, 1919 (SC, pp. 68–69).

6. Notes for speech to Signet Society, February 8 and 9, 1974, p. 3; speech, February 11, 1974, pp. 3–4.

7. MC to KB, October 23, 1919.

8. Josephson, *Life Among the Surrealists*, p. 36; see Shi, *Matthew Josephson*.

9. MC to KB, October 23, 1919.

10. MC to Alfred Kazin, May 18, 1962; *WT*, p. 35.

11. Though Signet was somewhat outside the complex social-club system—less a social club than a society of members with shared literary interests—most of its members were "clubbies." The majority were chosen from the staffs of the *Crimson*, *Lampoon*, or *Advocate*; the editors of the *Monthly* were bypassed on the grounds of social and political deviation. On the whole its membership was staid, aristocratic, and conservative, recruited largely from prep-school graduates—with an occasional exception like Cowley, elected because of his literary standing as a former president of the *Harvard Advocate*. Speech to Signet Society, February 11, 1974, p. 5.

12. Notes for speech to Signet Society, February 8 and 9, 1974, pp. 1–6; Speech, pp. 4–6; MC to Jake Davis, June 1, 1967.

13. Members of Cowley's class who achieved distinction in their respective fields included George Brownell and Lloyd Garrison (law), Royal Little and Fred Warburg (finance), Robert Gross and Robert Hoffman (engineering), and Cass Canfield (publishing). Though Brownell, Garrison, Warburg, and Canfield became, like Cowley, members of the Century Club, Cowley did not readily take to them as friends, with the possible exception of Cass Canfield. MC to Mrs. Andys K. Allport, May 21, 1976; MC to Robert Cunningham, February 2, 1964.

14. MC to George L. Batchelder, Jr., April 11, 1964; MC to Mrs. Andys K. Allport, May 21, 1976; MC to KB, February 6, 1974.

15. MC to Harriet Monroe, August 25, 1919; September 26, 1919; October 14, 1919, all *Poetry* Papers. The poems were "Moonrise," "Barn Dance," and "Danny" and appeared in *Poetry* 15 (November 1919): 76–79.

16. MC to Harriet Monroe, September 26, 1919; November 22, 1919, both *Poetry* Papers. The "Fantastic Etude" presumably was an early version of "Nocturne."

17. "Nantasket," *Harvard Advocate* 106 (November 1919): 51.

18. "Colloquy with Himself," *Pagan* 4 (February 1920): 17. The poem was printed in the Boston *Globe* in early March. Mercifully, Cowley never reprinted the poem.

19. *WT*, p. 54.

20. Review of *A Servant of Reality*, by Phyllis Bottome, *New Republic* 21 (December 17, 1919): 86; review of *Storm in a Teacup*, by Eden Phillpots, and *The Builders*, by Ellen Glasgow, *New Republic* 21 (February 18, 1920): 364, 366; review of *The Little Daughter of Jerusalem*, by Myriam Harry, *New Republic* 22 (March 31, 1920): 168; review of *Short Stories from the Balkans*, translated by Edna Worthley Underwood, *New Republic* 22 (April 7, 1920): 192. In Cowley's scrapbook at the Newberry Library are undated clippings of two unsigned reviews for the *New Republic*, one of *The Four Roads* by Sheila Kaye-Smith, the other of *Tumblefold* by Joseph Whittaker.

21. "Apples of Understanding," unpublished.

22. "Necromancy," *Harvard Advocate* 106 (January 29, 1920): 181; "Agassiz and Agony," ibid. (March 1, 1920): 219; "Eighteenth-Century Sonnet," ibid. (April 1, 1920): 254.

23. MC to KB, October 23, 1919; November 16, 1919 (SC, p. 70).

24. MC to KB, February 9, 1920 (SC, pp. 71–72).

25. Speech to Signet Society, p. 6; MC to KB, January 26, 1920.

26. Speech to Signet Society, p. 6; notes for speech to Signet Society, p. 6.

27. *WT*, p. 55; MC to William Wasserstrom, November 29, 1958. The *Dial*, Scofield Thayer wrote to John Brooks Wheelwright in June 1920, was to be "a literary magazine without precedent in America"; not only was it going to be "exclusively devoted to the arts," but it also aimed to present the finest examples of the old *and* the new in art and letters side by side—"it proposes to combine in one magazine everything that is best in both the accepted and the unconventional forms of expression, without prejudice to either." Scofield Thayer to John Brooks Wheelwright, June 17, 1920, Wheelwright Papers.

28. MC to KB, January 26, 1920. The manuscript of the entire ode is among Cowley's papers at the Newberry Library. Burke remained associated with the *Dial* throughout its existence and served in a variety of critical and editorial capacities. In 1921 he was taken on the editorial staff and two years later replaced Scofield Thayer and Gilbert Seldes during their absence abroad. From 1927 to 1929 Burke succeeded Paul Rosenfeld as the *Dial*'s music critic. Burke's discussions with his fellow editors helped him to work out his literary theories; his indebtedness to the *Dial* appears in part from the dedication of *The Philosophy of Literary Form* (1941) to J. S. Watson, the editor who was most congenial to the younger writers on the *Dial*. The majority of Burke's

early stories, poems, and essays first appeared in the *Dial*, and many of them found their way into his first three books, which in effect were outgrowths of his *Dial* years: *The White Oxen and Other Stories* (1924), *Counter-Statement* (1931), and *Towards a Better Life* (1932). In 1928 Burke received the Dial Award, joining the company of Sherwood Anderson, T. S. Eliot, Van Wyck Brooks, Marianne Moore, E. E. Cummings, William Carlos Williams, and Ezra Pound. See Armin Paul Frank, *Kenneth Burke* (New York, 1969), pp. 22–23, and William H. Rueckert, *Kenneth Burke and the Drama of Human Relations* (1963; 2d, rev. ed., 1982), pp. 296–98.

29. WT, p. 55; MC to KB, June 16, 1923. Cowley repeated his comments on the level of reviewing in the *Dial* in print in "Midsummer Medley," *New Republic* 80 (August 15, 1934): 25.

30. Scofield Thayer to MC, May 25, 1923; G. A. M. Janssens, *The American Literary Review: A Critical History, 1920–1950* (The Hague, 1968), p. 33; Peggy Baird Cowley to Wheelwright, September 1921, Wheelwright Papers; MC to KB, August 25, 1929.

31. In 1932 Cowley first advanced his opinion that the attitudes of the Harvard Aesthetes were "often embodied in *The Dial*, which for some years was almost a postgraduate edition of *The Monthly*." In 1934 he claimed again that "the aesthetic tradition of the Harvard Monthly was later revived by the Dial" under Thayer and Watson. In 1973 Cowley still wrote about the refurbished *Dial* as "the unexpected sequel" to the *Monthly* and repeated that, "in some ways and in some contributors," the *Dial* "carried on the tradition of *The Monthly*, this time with a national audience." "The Poet and the World," *New Republic* 70 (April 27, 1932): 303 (*TBOU*, p. 213); "Midsummer Medley," p. 25; SF, p. 95. Alyse Gregory's description of Scofield Thayer is quoted in William Wasserstrom, *The Time of the 'Dial'* (Syracuse, N.Y., 1963), p. 64. For a balanced and detailed consideration of the influence of the *Monthly* on the *Dial* see Nicholas Joost, *Years of Transition: The Dial, 1912–1920*, pp. 149–53. G. A. M. Janssens has argued that "the significance of the *Monthly* [for the *Dial*] is primarily to be sought in the fact that it brought a number of later *Dial* regulars together and that it gave them an early opportunity of getting their work published . . . but *The Harvard Monthly* can hardly be said to have served as its model." *American Literary Review*, pp. 24–25.

32. WT, p. 55. The publication history of the article reveals a typical strategy on the part of an impecunious but pragmatic apprentice writer. Cowley reviewed Sheila Kaye-Smith's *The Four Roads* in three different ways for three different magazines: first, as an unsigned four-hundred-word piece for the *New Republic*; second, as a "briefer" for the fortnightly *Dial* ("Review later," the note promised); third, as one of two novels by Sheila Kaye-Smith reviewed for the monthly *Dial*. Though he managed to make all three reviews into independent articles with a minimum of overlap, he was remunerated thrice for writing about a single novel. Likewise, Reginald Wright Kaufman's *Victorious* was reviewed in both the *New Republic* and, in an omnibus review of war fiction, for the fortnightly *Dial*; Ellen Glasgow's *The Builders* in both the *New Republic* and as a "briefer" in the fortnightly *Dial*; John Gould Fletcher's *Breakers and Granite* in both the *Literary Review of the New York Evening Post* and (conjointly with a book

by Conrad Aiken) in the monthly *Dial*; Amy Lowell's *Fir-Flower Tablets* in both the monthly *Dial* and Arthur Moss's *Gargoyle*; Conrad Aiken's *Bring! Bring! and Other Stories* in both H. S. Canby's *Saturday Review of Literature* and in the *Dial*. For each publication the review was newly composed and freshly written, so as to form, in effect, an entirely different article. Such practice anticipated Cowley's later habit of "beefing" his longer essays and distributing them over several periodicals. See *FCF*, pp. 20–21.

33. "The Woman of Ihornden," *Dial* 68 (February 1920): 259, 261.

34. "Colas Breugnon," ibid. (April 1920): 513. For MC's observations on the "Art Novel" see *TBOU*, pp. 213–15.

35. MC to KB, February 9, 1920 (SC, p. 72); "A Life in the 1920's," unpublished manuscript; MC to author, November 2, 1984; *WT*, pp. 55–56.

7. GREENWICH VILLAGE, 1920–1921

1. MC to author, November 2, 1984; *WT*, pp. 56, 62; "Winter Tenement," *BJCP*, p. 46. Bessie Breuer later became an amateur novelist and was Cowley's editor at the New Jersey magazine *Charm*.

2. "Mother and Son," p. 11; "The Pyre," *BJCP*, pp. 27–29.

3. MC to author, November 2, 1984. In the course of time Cowley's early experiences helped to give a new dimension of human understanding and compassion to his criticism. More than twenty-five years later he found that a private season in hell also underlay the art of Hawthorne and Whitman and helped to explain the flowering of their genius. Both writers had been wrenched out of loneliness, reconnected themselves to humanity at large, and won a new, darker sense of human community. These later perceptions were given urgency by the literary climate of the 1940s, but the terms in which Cowley then described their "descent into the underworld" suggests that he was writing in the remembrance of the painful experiences of his early years. In all cases, Cowley noted, the writers' descent led to "a double sense, of their isolation first and then of their brotherhood or identity with all the outcast and diseased and rejected of the earth. Later they emerge into sunlight, but for a long time they walk the streets as if in disguise and continue to feel that they belong with the secret people of the caves." There had been a time when Cowley, too, had suffered such a "double sense" of isolation and community, and had walked the streets of Greenwich Village with a feeling of belonging to "a confraternity of the damned." See Cowley's essays on Hawthorne and Whitman in *MWH*, pp. 3–75; the passage referred to above appears on pp. 67–68.

4. "Free Clinic," *BJCP*, pp. 41–42.

5. "William Wilson," *BJCP*, p. 130; "Interment," *BJ*, p. 45; "Winter Tenement," *BJCP*, p. 46.

6. "So Perish Time," *BJCP*, pp. 44–45.

7. "Deathbed," *BJ*, p. 44; "Mortality," *BJCP*, p. 43.

8. "A Solemn Music," *BJ*, pp. 97–98.

9. See, for another example, "John Fenstermaker," *BJCP*, p. 136.

10. "Colonizing Manhattan's Lower West Side," *New York Evening Post*, April 10, 1920, Magazine, p. 5.

11. "The Famous 'Shropshire Lad' and His Brother," *New York Evening Post*, May 8, 1920, Book Review, pp. 1, 11.

12. MC to KB, June 4, 1920; June 9, 1920 (*SC*, p. 72).

13. *WT*, p. 57; MC to author, November 2, 1984; MC to KB, June 4, 1920; June 9, 1920 (*SC*, p. 73); June 19, 1920.

14. MC to KB, June 4, 1920; Norman, *E. E. Cummings*, pp. 110–13; Churchill, *Improper Bohemians*, pp. 255–56, 323, 329, 336–37.

15. MC to KB, June 9, 1920 (*SC*, p. 73); August 25, 1920 (*SC*, pp. 76–77). As an immediate offshoot of his proposal, Cowley set to work on "Day Coach," a poem exemplifying his experiments with structure and motion. A later attempt to realize similar intentions in prose was "Race between a Subway Local and a Subway Express," a prose sketch that appeared in *transition* in January 1928.

16. MC to KB, June 9, 1920; June 19, 1920. Burke was pleased "immensely" by Cowley's proposition: "The Rousseau-ism of the idea is magnificent, especially Rousseau-ism so near to Times Square." KB to MC, June 12, 1920 (*SC*, p. 74).

17. For precise bibliographical citation of *Evening Post* reviews mentioned here, see Ruth M. Alvarez and Diane U. Eisenberg, "Malcolm Cowley: A Checklist of His Writings Updated," *Visionary Company* (Summer 1987): 207–8; MC to author, November 2, 1984; *MWH*, p. 191; "Doing your Play-Going at Home," *Charm* 5 (March 1926): 32; MC to KB, February 9, 1920. A typescript of the play "Barn Dance" is among the Cowley Papers. "Barn Dance" explores the dilemma of a bright local boy whose opportunities for rising above the deadening dullness and narrow morality of small-town life in the Midwest are threatened by his sense of human obligation to a girl he has gotten "into trouble." With gruesome irony the play exposes the reality of sexual passion and man's latent capacity for brutal violence underneath the complacent surface of local pride and moral self-righteousness found in the provinces.

18. MC to author, November 2, 1984; MC to KB, June 19, 1920; July 20, 1920.

19. MC to KB, July 20, 1920.

20. *BJ*, p. 45; MC to KB, August 25, 1920 (*SC*, p. 76).

21. "Dr. Canby and His Team," *Saturday Review* 47 (August 29, 1964): 54–55, 177; *WT*, p. 57.

22. "Mme. Duclaux on France," *Literary Review of the New York Evening Post* 1 (October 2, 1920): 3; "Gaucho Drama," ibid. (November 13, 1920): 3; "The Era of Disillusion," ibid. (November 20, 1920): 4; "The World's Timber," ibid. (November 27, 1920): 4; "Women of Japan," ibid. (December 24, 1920): 9; "Entertaining Plays," ibid. (December 31, 1920): 5; "Motley Verse," ibid. (December 31, 1920): 9; "A War-Time Squad," ibid. (March 26, 1921): 6.

23. *WT*, p. 56.

24. For a discussion of the shifting reputation of the Georgian poets, see Robert H. Ross, *The Georgian Revolt, 1910–1922. Rise and Fall of a Poetic Ideal* (Carbondale and Edwardsville, Ill., 1965), pp. 115–38, 165–200, 237–38, 241.

25. "Against Nightingales," *Dial* 68 (May 1920): 621–22.

26. By 1920, lashing out at the Georgians had ceased to be shocking or revolutionary; T. S. Eliot, John Middleton Murry, and Edith Sitwell had preceded Cowley in exposing Georgian deficiencies. By the time of Cowley's *Dial* attack, with modern poetry moving toward obscurity, privacy, and intellectuality, Georgianism was, in effect, "a dead poetic movement" and considered by many of the newer writers as "positively anti-modern." Ross, *Georgian Revolt*, pp. 190, 193, 238.

27. Ezra Pound, "A Retrospect," in *Literary Essays of Ezra Pound*, edited and with an introduction by T. S. Eliot (London, 1954), p. 12.

28. See, for example, "Colas Breugnon," *Dial* 68 (April 1920): 514. Winking at the classicism and humanism of the eighteenth century, Cowley upbraided modern literature "since Verlaine" for exemplifying "a morbid fear of the platitude," yet granted that "about the important matters of life: about birth, time, love, death, there is little to be said that does not verge on the banal—even this. Authors . . . must confine themselves to smaller themes when they wish to be satisfyingly original."

29. "As to 'Poetic Arrivals,'" *Literary Review of the New York Evening Post* 1 (July 31, 1920): 6; "Georgians and Post-Georgians," *New Republic* 24 (September 15, 1920): 77–78.

30. "Against Nightingales," pp. 621–25.

31. "Random Reflections," *Literary Review of the New York Evening Post* 1 (May 21, 1921): 6. In March 1921 Cowley collaborated with Ronald Levinson, a Village acquaintance of Peggy's, on "a most amusing burlesque" of H. G. Wells's *History of the World*, in rhyming couplets; Canby liked it well enough to publish it in the *Evening Post*. "Wells' Springs of History," *Literary Review of the New York Evening Post* 1 (March 19, 1921): 7.

32. "The Chinless Age," *Dial* 70 (January 1921): 73–76.

33. *The Fourteenth Chronicle: Letters and Diaries of John Dos Passos*, edited and with a biographical narrative by Townsend Ludington (Boston, 1973), p. 302.

34. "The Tools of Poetry," *Literary Review of the New York Evening Post* 1 (January 29, 1921): 8.

35. An avid reader of literary magazines such as *Poetry*, the *Little Review*, and the *Dial*, Cowley was sure to have come across the writings of Pound and Eliot, both of whom had found in Europe a more congenial artistic homeland. Though he would not go so far as either Pound or Eliot in their abhorrence of free verse—vers libre, Eliot had written in an early essay, had "not even the excuse of a polemic; it is a battle-cry of freedom, and there is no freedom in art"—Cowley evinced a strong ambivalence toward it. With Pound he might have insisted that America's literary excellence was to be attained through disciplined craftsmanship and a scrupulous attention to poetic technique. Pound, likewise, emphasized the need for a close study of poetic tradition, though he went to lengths of pedantry and erudite obscurity Cowley could and would not follow. Tradition, Pound had proclaimed in *Poetry* in 1913, is "a beauty which we preserve and not a set of fetters to bind us." The poet should aim to discover an organic form, a rhythm and cadence which "corresponds exactly to the emotion or shade of emotion to be expressed." The serious artist, Pound felt, abjured abstraction, moral up-

lift, rhetorical excess and "emotional slither"; he aimed at precision and control, clarity and simplicity, intensity and concentration, so as to attain a "maximum efficiency of expression." T. S. Eliot, "Reflections on *Vers Libre*," in *Selected Prose of T. S. Eliot*, edited with an introduction by Frank Kermode (London, 1975), p. 32; *Literary Essays of Ezra Pound*, pp. 9, 12, 43, 48–49, 56, 91.

36. Eliot's essay had appeared two years earlier in the *Egoist*. I have found no indication that Cowley had read or even knew of Eliot's essay.

37. "These Things Are Banal . . .," *Dial* 70 (June 1921): 703–4; Babette Deutsch, "Orchestral Poetry," ibid. (March 1921): 343–46. Cowley's review of Aiken and Fletcher had an unexpected aftermath. On June 23, 1921, Fletcher wrote to the editors of the *Dial* disclaiming that he and Aiken had incurred any mutual poetic debts and maintaining that passages quoted by Cowley to illustrate Fletcher's indebtedness were written long before he had either read or met Aiken. A second letter to the *Dial* reached Scofield Thayer in Paris and demanded rectification. The editors "cheerfully" obliged, advertising the Cowley-Fletcher controversy in their September issue and quoting from a letter written by "the penitent Mr. Cowley" from Paris to Fletcher in London. Cowley explained that his inferences of Fletcher's debt to Aiken (and vice versa) were based on—possibly imperfect—memories of conversations he had conducted with Aiken in Boston, admitting he might have strained a point in searching for poetic evidence but assuring Fletcher he had acted "in good faith." Both Fletcher and Cowley, concluded the editors, were "masters of implication." What the editors did not reveal was that Cowley had proposed to prove his honorable intentions by fighting a duel with Fletcher. On August 4, 1921, Cowley received a letter from Fletcher accepting his explanation of the circumstances leading to the *Dial* review, once again denying "deliberate borrowings" and proving that Cowley was "mistaken" in his thesis. As for the proposed duel, Fletcher feared his brash opponent must be content with a "long-range bombardment" by letter. Fletcher's critique of Cowley's argument in the specific instance did little to subvert the general validity of its points, which, the editors of the *Dial* agreed, seemed "well-taken." "Comment," *Dial* 71 (September 1921): 377–78; Scofield Thayer to MC, July 30, 1921, *Dial* Papers; John Gould Fletcher to MC, August 4, 1921.

38. "Adam & Eve & Pinch Me," *Dial* 71 (July 1921): 94–95.

39. "Page Dr. Blum!" *Dial* 71 (September 1921): 365–67; see Kenneth Burke, *Attitudes Toward History* (1937; 3rd ed., Berkeley and Los Angeles, 1984), pp. 308–14; Edmund Wilson, *Axel's Castle* (New York, 1931), p. 13. Cowley had recently been warned against the proliferation of musical terms in his criticism by John Brooks Wheelwright, who detected the influence of Aiken in this. See Wheelwright to MC, [1921].

40. "Programme Music," *Dial* 71 (August 1921): 222–26. Cowley's generous appreciation of *Legends* coincided with Amy Lowell's agreement to act as his literary agent for the time of his French stay. In October 1921 she informed Cowley that she thought his review "an honest and clear analysis of the book" and that he had maintained a precarious balance of judgment, falling into neither of "the pitfalls of over-praise or over-blame." She used part of Cowley's review to advertise her book, together with statements by D. H. Lawrence, John Livingston Lowes, and John Farrar, editor of the *Bookman*. Lowell to MC, October 28, 1921. She also used Cowley's review in de-

fending her book against criticism from Padraic Colum. See Damon, *Amy Lowell*, p. 561.

41. The two poems published in Canby's *Literary Review* were "About Seven O'Clock" and "Wells' Springs of History"; they appeared on January 22 and March 19, 1921, respectively. MC to KB, June 19, 1920; the following items, all unpublished, are among the Malcolm Cowley Papers: untitled play, dated May 25, 1922; outline for a novel, 1921; "The Juneberries Have Withered," unpublished prose sketch.

42. MC to KB, May 5, 1921 (SC, pp. 84–85). Cowley's letter contains early drafts of the poems "For a New Hymnal" and "Poem for Two Voices," both published in 1923 in revised form, and with new titles.

43. *ER*, p. 80; Charles A. Fenton, "Ambulance Drivers in France and Italy: 1914–1918," *American Quarterly* 3 (1951): 334.

44. Peggy Baird Cowley to S. Foster Damon, March 17, 1921, Damon Papers.

45. Amy Lowell to MC, May 10, 1921; June 28, 1921, Lowell Papers. MC to KB, May 5, 1921 (SC, p. 85).

46. MC to S. Foster Damon, May 25, 1921; June 25, 1921, Damon Papers.

47. Peggy Baird Cowley to S. Foster Damon, March 17, 1921, Damon Papers; MC to KB, May 5, 1921 (SC, p. 85).

48. MC to KB, June 17, 1921 (SC, p. 87).

49. MC to KB, June 17, 1921 (SC, pp. 87–88).

50. Harold Stearns, *America and the Young Intellectual* (New York, 1921), pp. 21, 160, 167–68.

51. Harold Stearns, ed., *Civilization in the United States: An Inquiry by Thirty Americans* (New York, 1922), pp. vii, 135, 144, 146–48.

52. Stearns, *Civilization in the United States*, pp. 179–81; Cowley was sufficiently moved by the depth of feeling and conviction in Brooks's statement of the problem to quote an elaborate passage in *Exile's Return*. *ER*, pp. 75–76.

53. *ER*, pp. 74–75, 78–79. In *Life Among the Surrealists* Matthew Josephson, too, took pains to dissociate his motives for expatriation from those advanced by Stearns and his intellectual consorts. Stearns, he objected, could hardly have functioned as "a latter day Mahomet leading a pilgrimage of Yankees to the Left Bank of the Seine" because most of the younger expatriates had never heard of Stearns or his symposium at the actual hour of their departure. Josephson, *Life Among the Surrealists*, pp. 9–10.

54. *SF*, p. 53.

55. For Josephson, see Shi, *Matthew Josephson*, p. 47; George Wickes, *Americans in Paris* (Garden City, N.Y., 1969), p. 3; *Literary Essays of Ezra Pound*, p. 222.

56. In September 1920 Pound had already discussed the "young and very ferocious" group of French dadaists whom Cowley would shortly meet in Paris—Aragon, Breton, Soupault, Tzara—and had wondered "how to introduce them to a society where one is considered decadent for reproducing pictures by Cézanne." The group was carrying on, so Pound reported, "the satiric heritage of Laforgue, and of symboliste sonorities" and was already "taking its place in the sun by right of intelligence, more than by right of work yet accomplished." Ezra Pound, "The Island of Paris: A Letter," *Dial* 69 (October 1920): 408–9; see also Pound's Paris Letter in *Dial* 69 (December 1920): 635.

57. Josephson, *Life Among the Surrealists*, p. 65.

58. *ER*, pp. 79, 102–3.

59. As Frederick Hoffman has observed, for the modern writer of the 1920s "the concern with form was basically a concern over the need to provide an aesthetic order for moral revisions." *The Twenties*, pp. 434–35.

60. Shi, *Matthew Josephson*, pp. 49–51; compare Warren I. Susman, "Pilgrimage to Paris: The Background of American Expatriation" (unpublished doctoral dissertation, University of Wisconsin, 1957), pp. 304–19.

8. PILGRIMAGE TO HOLY LAND—FRANCE, 1921–1922

1. Ezra Pound, "Remy de Gourmont," in *Pavannes and Divisions* (New York, 1918), p. 116; Gertrude Stein, *Paris France* (1940; rpt. New York, 1970), pp. 2, 11; "Exile's Return," *New Republic* 68 (September 23, 1931): 150.

2. James M. Kempf, *The Early Career of Malcolm Cowley: A Humanist Among the Moderns* (Baton Rouge, 1985), p. 53; *ER*, pp. 102–3. For Cowley's intellectual development in France, see also Elinor Bulkin, "Malcolm Cowley: A Study of His Literary, Social and Political Thought to 1940," Ph.D dissertation, New York University, 1973. Bulkin's pioneering study, based on original research, is useful but limited in its focus on Cowley's ideas.

3. MC to KB, [July 14, 1921]; [late August 1921]; MC to John Brooks Wheelwright, October 9, 1921, Wheelwright Papers; MC to KB, November 28, 1921 (SC, p. 107); September 27, 1922.

4. MC to KB, [July 14, 1921].

5. *SF*, p. 54.

6. *SF*, p. 57; MC to S. Foster Damon, September 5, 1921, Damon Papers; MC to KB, August 10, 1921 (*SC*, p. 96); August 17, 1921. For Harold Stearns, compare Dos Passos, *The Best Times*, pp. 162–3.

7. MC to KB, August 17, 1921; Hemingway, in particular, made a point of shunning the noisy idlers at the Dôme, Rotonde, and Sélect, and preferred the quieter Closerie des Lilas to do his writing. He satirized the stereotypical café-dwelling expatriates in *The Sun Also Rises* and, retrospectively mixing bitterness and nostalgia in *A Moveable Feast*, spurned the make-believe artists stacking saucers on Montparnassian terraces as suckers for publicity who, instead of working, sought out their cafés as "daily substitutes for immortality." Ernest Hemingway, *A Moveable Feast* (New York, 1964), p. 81. Cowley, too, would soon come under fire from Hemingway.

8. MC to KB, August 10, 1921 (*SC*, p. 96); MC to S. Foster Damon, September 5, 1921, Damon Papers.

9. Manuscript, dated August 10, 1921; MC to KB, September 17, 1921; MC to John Brooks Wheelwright, October 9, 1921, Wheelwright Papers; "The Journey to Paris," *Gargoyle* 1 (October 1921): 8–12. For Cowley's critique of Burke's early stories, see MC to KB, July 12 and July 13, 1921, both in *SC*, pp. 92–93.

10. MC to KB, August 17, 1921; MC to John Brooks Wheelwright, October 9, 1921,

Wheelwright Papers; undated manuscript draft for *Exile's Return*.

11. MC to KB, September 28, 1921; "Three Americans in Paris," *Literary Review of the New York Evening Post* 2 (January 14, 1922): 351. The poem on Harold Stearns ridiculed the discrepancy between his high-minded, theatrically expounded motives for expatriation and the bibulous reality of his Montparnassian existence. The poem on Ezra Pound, mixing respect with a firm dose of irony, recalled Cowley's meeting with Pound at the Hôtel Jacob on July 23; it was republished, in a much revised version, in *BJCP*, p. 59. His third satire was entitled "Sinclair Lewis Imitates a Member of the Gopher City Rotary Club." It mocked the comical disparity between the sophisticated cosmopolitanism of Paris and the Babbitt-like midwestern chauvinism paraded by Sinclair Lewis on the terraces of Montparnasse. Several years later Cowley recalled how Lewis, then engaged in writing *Babbitt*, had distinctly relished "acting the part of his principal character: the naivety, philistinism, nasal sing-song and all the rest of it." "Garçong! Garçong!," *Brentano's Book Chat* 5 (May–June 1926): 25.

12. *ER*, pp. 97–99.

13. "This Youngest Generation," *Literary Review of the New York Evening Post* 2 (October 15, 1921): 81–82. Among the later famous members of the Lost Generation whom Cowley could not name was Ernest Hemingway, who arrived in Paris in late December 1921 as a promising journalist for the *Toronto Star*; he came armed with letters of introduction from Sherwood Anderson, but was as yet unpublished. William Faulkner, too, had yet to appear in print. F. Scott Fitzgerald, whose first novel *This Side of Paradise* (1920) had been followed the year after by a book of short stories, *Flappers and Philosophers*, was already on his way to fame, but apparently "too popular" for Cowley's then "rarefied taste" (*SF*, p. viii). Hart Crane had been publishing poetry in a variety of little magazines since 1917. Though it seems unlikely that, by 1921, Cowley would not have known of Crane's verse—if only because Crane had been a friend of Josephson's since 1919—he appears not to have taken much notice of Crane as a promising modern poet until the latter's appearance in *Broom* and *Secession* in 1922. Conspicuously absent in Cowley's tentative list of names was Matthew Josephson; in October 1921 he was preparing to come to France and was as yet more promise than fulfillment. It was only after he met the dadaists in late 1921 and became involved with *Broom* and *Secession* that Josephson began to flourish publicly as a writer.

14. "This Youngest Generation," p. 82; MC to KB, December 23, 1921.

15. See *ER*, pp. 101–2; Kazin, *On Native Grounds*, p. 314; MC to KB, January 2, 1922; "The Urn," *BJCP*, p. 142.

16. MC to S. Foster Damon, October 21, 1921, Damon Papers; MC to KB, fragment of undated letter [October 1921?].

17. MC to John Brooks Wheelwright, October 9, 1921, Wheelwright Papers; Peggy Baird Cowley to John Brooks Wheelwright, [1921–1922], Wheelwright Papers; MC to KB, fragment of undated letter [October 1921?]; MC to S. Foster Damon, November 18, 1921, Damon Papers; MC to KB, October 27, 1921.

18. MC to KB, September 17, 1921; MC to Amy Lowell, September 7, 1921, Lowell Papers; James Sibley Watson to MC, October 14, 1921; Lowell to MC, October 28, 1921. The nine poems Lowell sent to the *Dial* were "Mountain Valley," "History,"

"Local Town," "Three Hills," "Poem for Two Voices," "Prophetic," "Deathbed," "Nocturnal Landscape," and "Interment." See also S. Foster Damon to MC, September 19, 1921, and October 15, 1921.

19. MC to S. Foster Damon, November 18, 1921, Damon Papers; MC to Amy Lowell, December 9, 1921, Lowell Papers.

20. Amy Lowell to MC, November 21, 1921; "Mountain Valley," *Dial* 71 (December 1921): 670; MC to KB, December 9, 1921; December 23, 1921.

21. Loeb was a Princeton graduate and wrestling champion, the son of a wealthy Wall Street broker, and a rebellious offshoot of the famous Guggenheim family. After a period of personal questing Loeb committed himself to the life of literature and ideas, bought a partnership in the Sunwise Turn bookshop in New York, and became convinced that a new literary magazine was needed to bring "the good life" a little nearer. Loeb, *The Way It Was*, pp. 3–58.

22. MC to KB, June 17, 1921; Alfred Kreymborg, *Troubadour* (New York, 1957), pp. 287–88; Alfred Kreymborg to MC, September 23, 1921; MC to Alfred Kreymborg, September 27, 1921, Loeb Papers; Alfred Kreymborg to MC, September 30 [1921]; MC to KB, September 28, 1921; [October 1921] (SC, pp. 104–5).

23. MC to S. Foster Damon, October 21, 1921, Damon Papers; "Manifesto 1," *Broom* 1 (November 1921). To underline its international focus *Broom's* first issue featured contributors of thirteen different nationalities. It contained reproductions of works by mostly European avant-garde artists—Pablo Picasso, André Derain, Juan Gris, Albert Gleizes, Jacques Lipchitz—but also featured two Americans: Joseph Stella and Man Ray. The majority of writers represented were Americans and included Conrad Aiken, Amy Lowell, James Oppenheim, Louis Untermeyer, Haniel Long, and Lola Ridge.

24. MC to S. Foster Damon, October 21, Damon Papers; "Broomides," *Broom* 1 (November 1921): 94. The essay that came closest to a statement of editorial policy was an article by Emmy Veronica Sanders, which viewed the American "invasion" of Europe with strong misgivings and deplored the tendency on the part of "the extreme left wing of literary America" to confuse Europe with France. It disparaged the influence of technology and "the American Machine" on avant-garde aesthetics and pleaded for a catholic, cosmopolitan approach to American culture. Cowley appears to have read the Sanders article as a disparagement of his self-chosen mode of expatriation and his strong commitment to French literature. Emmy Veronica Sanders, "America Invades Europe," *Broom* 1 (November 1921): 89–93; Alfred Kreymborg to MC, November 9 [1921]. In an earlier letter to Cowley, Kreymborg had endorsed the central argument in Sanders's essay: "The lady doesn't disparage French literature. She simply warns us against our proverbial knee-bending to Paris (and, may I add, to London). In her zeal, she probably carried her point too far. But it's a healthy one—one I've always accorded in. France isn't Europe—nor Europe, the universe." Alfred Kreymborg to MC, October 25 [1921]. Sanders's article reflected the influence of Kreymborg's internationalist approach in the pages of *Broom*. By contrast, Loeb's orientation was rather one of cultural nationalism. Tensions between Loeb and Kreymborg made *Broom's* editorial direction indeterminate from the start; conflicting attitudes

on the issue of cultural nationalism and internationalism coexisted uneasily through its first four issues. For *Broom's* Italian period, see Marjorie Rose Smelstor, "*Broom* and American Cultural Nationalism in the 1920's," Ph.D. dissertation, University of Wisconsin, Madison, 1975, pp. 34–74.

25. MC to KB, [October 1921] (*SC*, p. 105); a perfected version of "The Willow Branch" appears in *BJ*, p. 13; in a revised form it appears as "The Silvery Fishes" in *BJCP* on pp. 133–34; MC to KB, October 27, 1921; "Rabelais Returns to His Own Home Town," *New York Tribune*, November 21, 1921, p. 3; MC to KB, November 28, 1921.

26. MC to S. Foster Damon, November 18, 1921, Damon Papers; MC to John Brooks Wheelwright, November 3, 1921, Wheelwright Papers; MC to KB, January 2, 1922.

27. MC to KB, November 28, 1921 (*SC*, p. 107); December 23, 1921; January 23, 1922 (*SC*, p. 110). Arthur Moss's *Gargoyle* did not pay for contributions. Cowley, indeed, needed any complement to his fellowship he could find. In early November his financial prospects were so low that he appealed to Wheelwright for a thousand-franc loan: "We are now living on rocky bottom and the bottom is soon going to fall." MC to Wheelwright, November 3, 1921, Wheelwright Papers.

28. MC to KB, January 2, 1922; January 12, 1922.

29. Matthew Josephson to MC, December 5, 1921; for Josephson, see Shi, *Matthew Josephson*, pp. 53–54, 56–57.

30. MC to KB, January 12, 1922; MC to Robert Penn Warren, August 31, 1967, Warren Papers.

31. MC to KB, January 23, 1922 (*SC*, p. 110); MC to KB, February 27, 1922.

32. MC to KB, [October 1921] (*SC*, p. 105); January 28, 1922. Known to his contemporaries as the "legislator of Parnassus," Boileau succeeded in transforming the then current mode of satirical verse from a moral and philosophical genre into an instrument of literary criticism. In the four cantos of *L'Art Poétique* (1674), in particular, he formulated the aesthetic laws and ideals of classicism. Taking nature and reason for his lodestars, he presented his readers with concrete advice on writing and offered precise rules and definitions, thereby helping to make aesthetics into an exact and exacting discipline. *Boileau: Selected Criticism*, translated with an introduction by Ernest Dilworth (Indianapolis and New York, 1965), pp. vii–xii.

33. *Boileau: Selected Criticism*, pp. 11–17.

34. MC to KB, December 1, 1921 (*SC*, p. 108); January 12, 1922.

35. Notebook 1, entry 1, p. 1. For a discussion of Cowley's early notebooks and a presentation of selected passages from them, see Bak, "The Fabulous Ostrich of Art: Malcolm Cowley's Notebooks of the Twenties," *Visionary Company* (Summer 1987): 131–60.

36. MC to KB, January 12, 1922; February 27, 1922 (*SC*, p. 115).

37. Notebook 1, entries 6 and 7, pp. 4–5.

38. MC to KB, January 23, 1922 (*SC*, p. 110); Notebook 1, entry 10, pp. 7–8; MC to KB, January 28, 1922. Burke's response to MC's observations on the religiosity and obscurity of modern art is an instructive qualification (*SC*, p. 111).

39. Cowley's response did not merely anticipate Edmund Wilson's, it dovetailed with Burke's. If symbolism, as Edmund Wilson was to write, encompassed "an attempt by carefully studied means—a complicated association of ideas represented by a medley of metaphors—to communicate unique personal feelings," such an attempt was also leading to the creation of an obscurantist poetry that was "so much a private concern of the poet's that it turned out to be incommunicable to the reader." Burke had pointed out not long before in the *Dial* that symbolism might lead to a form of "intellectual anarchism"—"If each man was his own world . . . it was inevitable that each man should have his own idiom . . . the reduction to absurdity of individualism in art is to spend one's life in talking to oneself." Wilson, *Axel's Castle: A Study in the Imaginative Literature of 1870–1930* (1931; rpt. New York, 1953), pp. 20–22; Kenneth Burke, "Approaches to Remy de Gourmont," *Dial* 70 (February 1921): 125.

40. MC to KB, January 28, 1922; Notebook 1, entries 28 and 29, p. 22.

41. MC to KB, [late August 1921]; Notebook 1, entry 54, p. 36.

42. Notebook 1, entries 13, 21 and 26, pp. 11, 16–17, 20.

43. MC to KB, January 12, 1922; January 28, 1922.

44. MC to KB, February 8, 1922; February 27, 1922 (SC, pp. 114–15); March 12, 1922; March 13, 1922.

45. MC to Amy Lowell, January 24, 1922, Lowell Papers; MC to KB, January 23, 1922; Peggy Cowley to S. Foster Damon, November 16, 1922, Damon Papers.

46. " 'They Have Lived in the Golden House,' " *Gargoyle* vol. 2, nos. 1, 2 (January–February 1922): 24–27; "Bonded Translation," *Dial* 72 (May 1922): 517–21.

47. "Form," Cowley wrote to Burke, was too inclusive a term to be meaningful in critical analysis; it was "dangerously vague" and had better be dissected into its component parts. Cowley distinguished between such elements as "architectural" or "geometrical" form, "motion," "rhythm," and "expression" or "style." To Burke he explained: "Now if you proclaim that the *geometrical form* of a work of art is its most important feature, or if you proclaim that it should be judged by its motion, you are proclaiming something. But if you say that form is more important than matter you are adding only an individual affirmation to a dispute that has lasted since Plato." MC to KB, March 13, 1922; Notebook 1, entries 14 and 16, pp. 11–14. The entries are quoted in full in "The Fabulous Ostrich of Art: Malcolm Cowley's Notebooks of the Twenties," *Visionary Company* (Summer 1987): 142. As James Kempf has pointed out, the ongoing critical dialogue with Cowley may well have helped Burke to develop the theoretic conception of form he later advanced in *Counter-Statement* (1931). In his "Lexicon Rhetoricae" Burke decomposes form into the following elements: "progressive form (subdivided into syllogistic and qualitative progression), repetitive form, conventional form, and minor or incidental forms." As an example of qualitative progression Burke uses Cowley's sonnet "Mine No. 6." See *Counter-Statement*, pp. 124–38; Kempf, *Early Career of Malcolm Cowley*, p. 71.

48. Notebook 1, entry 12, pp. 9–11; see also entry 15, p. 12 ("The Fabulous Ostrich of Art," p. 142).

49. MC to KB, March 30, 1922 (SC, pp. 117–18).

50. MC to John Brooks Wheelwright, April 2, 1922; Notebook 1, entries 4, 5 and

20, pp. 3–4, 15–16. Wheelwright shared Cowley's nascent defensiveness about American culture and subscribed to his repudiation of Stearns's symposiasts, whom he found "too sociologic and Freudian. . . . This school makes a living by insisting evil. They are neurotic, and if the truth be told, rather bourgeois themselves. That is what the 're-volt' in America consists in: the bourgeois denying their environment. They succeed in making acid the soil they must grow in." It was time, Wheelwright implied, to exchange destructive pessimism for constructive criticism. Wheelwright to MC, [1922].

51. MC to Wheelwright, April 2, 1922; "The French and Our New Poetry," *Literary Review of the New York Evening Post* 2 (May 6, 1922): 641.

52. MC to KB, March 30, 1922 (*SC*, p. 117); "A Brief History of Bohemia," *Freeman* 5 (July 19, 1922): 439.

53. "In Vindication of Mr. Horner," *Freeman* 5 (June 7, 1922): 308–9. Cowley's reappraisal of French classicism and his current anti-romanticism might seem to fit in with the critical temper of the times. As Susan Turner has observed, with traditionalism being conceived of in new ways (*vide* Eliot), it was becoming "modern" to explore the literary past; the degree of modernity, however, was dependent upon what segment of the past was held up for scrutiny. Susan J. Turner, *A History of 'The Freeman': Literary Landmark of the Early Twenties* (New York and London, 1963), p. 93.

54. MC to Van Wyck Brooks, November 27, 1920, Brooks Papers.

55. MC to KB, April 12, 1922; Turner, *A History of 'The Freeman'*, p. 95; John Brooks Wheelwright to MC, May 3, 1922; Van Wyck Brooks, *Days of the Phoenix* (New York, 1957), p. 61.

56. For Brooks, see Raymond Nelson, *Van Wyck Brooks: A Writer's Life* (New York, 1981); Paul Rosenfeld, "Van Wyck Brooks," in *Port of New York* (1924; rpt. Urbana and London, 1966), pp. 57, 59, 61; "Benefit Show," *New Republic* 79 (August 8, 1934): 350.

57. See, for example, Cowley's introduction to Brooks's *Autobiography* (New York, 1965), reprinted as "Van Wyck Brooks's 'Usable Past,'" in *MWH*, pp. 213–28.

58. As F. W. Dupee stated in 1939: "When [Brooks] appeals to the work it is in order to confirm some theory about the man. Literature gets dissolved into biography in such a way that the work itself with its four walls and established furniture as given by its author is often quite lost to view." F. W. Dupee, "The Americanism of Van Wyck Brooks," *Partisan Review* 6 (Summer 1939). Reprinted in Morton Dauwen Zabel, ed., *Literary Opinion in America* (New York, 1937; rev. ed., 1951), p. 563.

59. Claire Sprague, "Introduction," *Van Wyck Brooks: The Early Years* (New York, Evanston and London, 1968), p. xxiv; Turner, *History of 'The Freeman'*, p. 69.

60. For Eliot, see John D. Margolis, *T. S. Eliot's Intellectual Development, 1922–1939* (Chicago and London, 1972) and Peter Ackroyd, *T. S. Eliot* (London, 1984). The quotation of Eliot is taken from Ackroyd, p. 75. Whereas Cowley arrived at classicism by way of Boileau and Racine and moved on to a qualified endorsement of communism, Eliot came to classicism through the teachings of his Harvard mentor Irving Babbitt and the philosophy of T. E. Hulme and found a logical path extending from classicism to royalism and Catholicism.

61. MC to KB, April 12, 1922. In 1923 Eliot launched a controversy over romanticism and classicism in the pages of the *Criterion*, which lasted for nearly five years without being resolved. In "The Function of Criticism" (1923) he defined the difference between classicism and romanticism as one between "the complete and the fragmentary, the adult and the immature, the orderly and the chaotic." In 1926 he described the tendency of the *New Criterion* as one toward classicism—"a higher and clearer conception of Reason, and a more severe and serene control of the emotions by Reason." As early as 1922 Cowley was differentiating between both concepts in similar terms. See John D. Margolis, *T. S. Eliot's Intellectual Development*, pp. 52–68; T. S. Eliot, *Selected Essays* (London, 1932), p. 26; T. S. Eliot, "The Idea of a Literary Review," *New Criterion* 4 (January 1926): 5.

62. MC to KB, April 12, 1922; Notebook 1, entries 18, 19 and 27, pp. 14–15, 20–21.

63. In Notebook 1, entry 27, pp. 20–21, Cowley observed that "anything is pertinent to a criticism which aids in conveying to the reader the precise nature of the book in question." Thus it might be desirable to deviate into "psychological criticism," even though such was "only a frill of reviewing." More importantly, it was necessary to consider "what the book means to civilization," a question involving an excursion into "moral criticism." A critical impressionism was deemed permissible, if only as an additional "aid" to definition.

64. "Keats and Hearst," *Dial* 73 (July 1922): 108–11; MC to KB, April 12, 1922; June 2, 1922.

65. Gorham B. Munson to MC, December 6, 1921. When Munson had not heard from Cowley by the end of January 1922, he wrote again, reiterating his proposal and request for advice and soliciting contributions that Cowley valued highly but that were unacceptable for a magazine like the *Dial*. The new magazine, he added, would "ignore rather than combat existing censorship" and was ready to engage in "literary bellicosities." Munson to MC, January 23, 1922.

66. Gorham B. Munson, "The Fledgling Years, 1916–1924," *Sewanee Review* 40 (January 1932): 24–28, 31.

67. Munson, "The Fledgling Years," *Sewanee Review* 40: 28–29; Matthew Josephson to MC, December 5, 1921; Josephson, *Life Among the Surrealists*, p. 154.

68. Gorham Munson to MC, January 23, 1922. The history of the founding, career and demise of *Secession*, its rivalry with *Broom*, and the ensuing feud among editors and contributors, is obfuscated by rankling personal sentiment and contradictory reminiscences. For a reliable and above-the-battle account, see Alvin H. Rosenfeld, "John Wheelwright, Gorham Munson, and the 'Wars of *Secession*,'" *Michigan Quarterly Review* 14 (Winter 1975): 13–40.

69. MC to KB, January 28, 1922.

70. Gorham Munson to MC, February 19, 1922; March 8, 1922; MC to KB, March 13, 1922; Munson, "The Fledgling Years," *Sewanee Review* 40: 32. A copy of the circular is among the Cowley Papers.

71. Matthew Josephson, "Apollinaire: Or Let Us be Troubadours," *Secession* 1 (Spring 1922): 9–13.

72. Gorham B. Munson, "Exposé No. 1," *Secession* 1 (Spring 1922): 22–24; "A Bow to the Adventurous," ibid., 15–19; "Day Coach," ibid., 1–3; Munson, "The Fledgling Years," *Sewanee Review* 40: 32.

73. MC to KB, [late 1922].

74. MC to KB, April 12, 1922; Peggy and Malcolm Cowley to John Brooks Wheelwright, [1922], Wheelwright Papers. "Munson (who seems to have read us very well) has found a couple of sentences which reconcile our aims with Tristan Tzara, but the peace seems a little patched," Cowley wrote to Burke. To Wheelwright he voiced similar objections, emphasizing that Burke and he were "at the opposite poles of literature" from Tzara.

75. Matthew Josephson to MC, April 25, 1922; May 2, 1922; MC to Josephson, May 10, 1922, Loeb Papers; Josephson to MC, May 25, 1922; June 18, 1922; MC to KB, April 28, 1922; May 8, 1922. Cowley's "Poem" appeared in *Secession* 3 (August 1922): 13.

76. MC to John Brooks Wheelwright, April 2, 1922.

77. KB to MC, [1921]. Manuscript versions of several drafts of the play are among the Cowley Papers. The idea of the play may well have derived from Laforgue, whose highly original interpretation of Shakespeare's play, *Hamlet, ou les Suites de la Piété Filiale* ("Hamlet, or the Consequences of Filial Piety") was part of his *Moralités Légendaires* (1887). Cowley had earlier observed to Burke that he had discovered the germ of Laforgue in Shakespeare. MC to KB, January 26, 1920.

78. KB to MC, [1921]; October 21, 1921; MC to KB, May 8, 1922; June 2, 1922.

79. Notebook 1, entries 32 and 33, pp. 23–24; Notebook 5, unpaginated.

80. "Young Man with Spectacles," *Broom* 3 (October 1922): 199–203, reprinted in the special Cowley issue, *Visionary Company* (Summer 1987): 81–86; MC to KB, May 20, 1922; Harold Loeb to MC, May 9, 1922; June 28, 1922; September 12, 1922, Loeb Papers.

81. Loeb, *The Way It Was*, pp. 98–100.

82. Harold Loeb, "Foreign Exchange," *Broom* 2 (May 1922): 176–79. Loeb's essay was partly a rebuttal to a fierce attack on the French dadaists and their aesthetic veneration of American technology by Edmund Wilson. In the February 1922 issue of *Vanity Fair* Wilson lambasted the younger French writers for dismissing the tradition of "perfection and form, of grace and measure and tranquillity." Wilson took a conservative stand, explaining the attraction of the "monstrous" and "vulgar" forms of American popular culture for the French as an antidote of force and vitality to their war-induced exhaustion, a notion soon challenged by Josephson in *Secession*. Wilson sounded a warning against the dehumanizing effects of an urban-industrial technology and pointed to the uncongeniality of an American machine-aesthetics to "*le clair genie français.*" By its very nature, Wilson claimed, the American sensibility was so dadaistic as to make French dadaism appear "a violent, rather sophomoric movement." Edmund Wilson, "The Aesthetic Upheaval in France," *Vanity Fair* (February 1922), pp. 49, 100. Wilson's warnings fell on deaf ears. In the eyes of Josephson, Cowley, and Loeb his deprecation of contemporary American culture aligned him with the older critics of *Civilization in the United States*.

83. MC to KB, May 20, 1922; Harold Loeb to MC, May 2, 1922; May 19, 1922, Loeb Papers.

84. Matthew Josephson, "Made in America," *Broom* 2 (June 1922): 266–70.

85. Under Josephson's editorial influence *Broom* was thus brought in tune with the aggressive modernism of *Secession*. In the same issue that featured Josephson's "Made in America" Loeb had greeted the first issue of *Secession* as a congenial contemporary magazine and had wished it "every success" ("Comment," *Broom* 2 [June 1922]: 271); Josephson, *Life Among the Surrealists*, pp. 187–88.

86. Stewart Mitchell to MC, May 16, 1922.

87. I. L. Kandell, Executive Secretary of American Field Service Fellowships, to MC, May 8, 1922; MC to KB, February 8, 1922; February 27, 1922; May 8, 1922; May 20, 1922 (SC, pp. 120–21).

88. MC to KB, May 20, 1922 (SC, pp. 120–21); June 2, 1922.

9. A SUMMER OF EUROPEAN TRAVEL, 1922

1. MC to John Brooks Wheelwright, June 29, 1922, Wheelwright Papers; MC to Harold Loeb, July 14, 1922, Loeb Papers; MC to KB, July 2, 1922 (SC, p. 122).

2. Ivan Opffer to MC, April 10, [1922]; September 20, 1947; *WT*, pp. 58–59.

3. "Henri Barbusse," *Bookman* 56 (October 1922): 180–82; "André Salmon and His Generation," ibid. (February 1923): 714–17; "Duhamel, M.D.," ibid. 57 (April 1923): 160–62; "Charles Vildrac," ibid. (May 1923): 291–94; "Paul Fort," ibid. 58 (November 1923): 253–54; "James Joyce," ibid. 59 (July 1924): 518–21; "Pierre MacOrlan," ibid. 60 (January 1925): 585–89; MC to John Farrar, July 27, 1922, *American Review* and *Bookman* Papers.

4. "Henri Barbusse," *Bookman* 56 (October 1922): 180–82. For Barbusse as a radical writer, see Daniel Aaron, *Writers on the Left* (New York, 1961), pp. 68–72.

5. Henri Barbusse to MC, July 13, 1922; September 2, 1922; September 12, 1922. Cowley continued to follow Barbusse throughout the decade. In 1926 he wrote a laudatory review of his novel *Chains*, in which he embedded his impressions of their first meeting. Barbusse replied with a letter complimenting Cowley on a "brilliant and amicable" treatment of the book. The year after, Cowley supervised the American translation of Barbusse's novel *Jesus* (1927). In 1935, just a few months before the writer's death in Moscow, Cowley noted with approval in the *New Republic* that Barbusse was part of the "brilliant" French delegation at the Writers' International Congress for the Defense of Culture, held in Paris in June of that year. See "The Road of Excess," *New York Herald Tribune Books*, February 7, 1926, p. 17; Henri Barbusse to MC, March 24, 1926; and "The Writers' International," *New Republic* 83 (July 31, 1935): 339 (*TBOU*, pp. 98–101).

6. Cuthbert Wright, "The Country of Cockayne," *Dial* 72 (May 1922): 493–97; MC to André Salmon, n.d. Cowley presented *Broom* to Salmon as "une revue dans le genre du Dial, mais plus intelligente, plus 'avancée,' et beaucoup plus pauvre. . . . Broom n'est restraint dans son choix que par les difficultés de traduction et par le *puritanisme*

du publique Américain" ("a review in the mode of the *Dial*, but more intelligent, more 'advanced,' and a good deal poorer. . . . *Broom* is only restricted in its choice by the difficulties of translation and the *puritanism* of the American public"); MC to KB, July 2, 1922 (*SC*, p. 123).

7. "André Salmon and His Generation," *Bookman* 56 (February 1923): 714–17.

8. "Duhamel, M.D.," ibid. 56 (April 1923), 160–62; "Charles Vildrac," ibid. (May 1923): 291–94; Charles Vildrac to MC, February 28, 1923; MC to Amy Lowell, January 24, 1922, Lowell Papers.

9. MC to John Farrar, October 28, 1922, *American Review* and *Bookman* Papers; S. Foster Damon to MC, July 15, 1922; MC to Damon, September 9, 1922, Damon Papers; Damon to MC, September 21, 1922. Seven years later Damon's appreciation of *Ulysses* had risen considerably. In 1929 he wrote a eulogistic analysis of the book for the *Hound & Horn*. See S. Foster Damon, "The Odyssey in Dublin," *Hound & Horn* 3 (1929): 7–44.

10. MC to John Farrar, November 12, 1922; John Farrar to MC, December 13, 1922. Both *American Review* and *Bookman* Papers; "James Joyce," *Bookman* 59 (July 1924): 518–21.

11. See *ER*, pp. 115–19. See also Peggy Cowley to S. Foster Damon, September 16, 1922, Damon Papers.

12. MC to S. Foster Damon, August 17, 1922, Damon Papers; for Williams and McAlmon, see Sanford J. Smoller, *Adrift Among Geniuses. Robert McAlmon: Writer and Publisher of the Twenties* (University Park and London, 1975), p. 126.

13. MC to KB, July 22, 1922; MC to S. Foster Damon, August 17, 1922, Damon Papers; Josephson, *Life Among the Surrealists*, p. 174; MC to KB, August 20, 1922; *ER*, p. 133.

14. *BJ*, p. 49; *ER*, pp. 81–82; MC to S. Foster Damon, August 17, 1922, Damon Papers; MC to KB, August 20, 1922.

15. MC to KB, August 27, 1922; *BJ*, pp. 49–50.

16. MC to Harold Loeb, September 9, 1922, Loeb Papers; *BJ*, pp. 51–52; MC to John Farrar, October 28, 1922, *American Review* and *Bookman* Papers.

17. Gorham B. Munson to MC, April 6, 1922; May 26, 1922.

18. MC to KB, July 12, 1921; Munson, "The Fledgling Years," *Sewanee Review* 40: 33; John Brooks Wheelwright to MC, August 31, 1922, Wheelwright Papers.

19. Gorham B. Munson, "Interstice Between Scylla and Charybdis," *Secession* 2 (July 1922): 30–32. Munson's broadside appears on page 33 of the issue.

20. MC to John Brooks Wheelwright, September 12, 1922, Wheelwright Papers; MC to KB, August 27, 1922.

21. Matthew Josephson, "Mr. Blunderbuss," *Secession* 3 (August 1922): 28–31. See also Paul Rosenfeld, "Guillaume Apollinaire," *Vanity Fair* 18 (June 1922): 59, 106, 108. Tristan Tzara's "Some Memoirs of Dadaism" had appeared in a recent issue of *Vanity Fair*; it was reprinted by Edmund Wilson as an appendix to his *Axel's Castle* (1931), pp. 304–12.

22. Josephson was not the only one to miss the joke in Cowley's poem. From Boston, Wheelwright reported that he and Damon had been forced to defend the poem against

attacks by Amy Lowell and Robert Hillyer. Munson, who felt the poem should have stayed in Cowley's "laboratory notebook," received letters from Waldo Frank, Louis Untermeyer, Hart Crane, Jean Toomer, and Leo Stein lamenting its inferior quality to Cowley's earlier *Secession* poems. Cowley perversely refused to publicize its burlesque intent and preferred to accept "full responsibility for writing damned nonsense if I feel like writing damned nonsense." His defense could not undo the backfiring of his satire. John Brooks Wheelwright to MC, December 30, 1922; Gorham B. Munson to MC, February 20, 1923; MC to Wheelwright, January 30, 1923, Wheelwright Papers.

23. MC to KB, September 25, 1922 (*SC*, p. 126).

24. MC to KB, August 27, 1922; "Matthew Josephson," *Book Find Notes* (January 1947), p. 6.

25. MC to KB, September 10, 1922. On January 23, 1922, before he knew Loeb, Cowley had observed to Burke that he "should regret Kreymborg's demise" as a *Broom* editor (*SC*, p. 110). Hemingway presented a rather scathing portrait of Loeb in the figure of Robert Cohn in *The Sun Also Rises*. Kitty Cannell appears in the novel as Frances Clyne. Like their fictional counterparts, Loeb and Cannell were having an affair at the time Cowley met them in Austria.

26. Loeb, *The Way It Was*, pp. 130–31; MC to Harold Loeb, September 9, 1922, Loeb Papers; MC to KB, September 10, 1922. Loeb paid twelve francs a page for translation, four dollars for prose, six dollars for poetry.

27. Loeb, *The Way It Was*, p. 122; Matthew Josephson, "After and Beyond Dada," *Broom* 2 (July 1922): 346–50, and "Exordium to Ducasse," *Broom* 3 (August 1922): 3; MC to KB, September 27, 1922.

28. Loeb, "The Mysticism of Money," *Broom* 3 (September 1922): 115–30. For a brief history of the Nick Carter stories, see Cowley's "Nick Carter," *Brentano's Book Chat* 6 (July–August 1927): 34–37.

29. MC to KB, September 10, 1922; MC to Harold Loeb, September 27, 1922, Loeb Papers.

30. MC to Harold Loeb, September 27, 1922, Loeb Papers; "Young Mr. Elkins," *Broom* 4 (December 1922): 52–56. "Young Mr. Elkins" was headed by an epigraph from Rosenfeld and presented snatches from Rosenfeld's recent *Dial* essay on Sherwood Anderson as the opinions of Mr. Elkins. The latter had appeared in *Dial* 72 (January 1922): 29–42; it was included in his *Port of New York* (1924). On November 1, 1922, Cowley told Loeb that he had bought an Underwood portable from Harold Stearns for 550 francs. The irony would not have been lost on Stearns.

31. *ER*, p. 133; Josephson, *Life Among the Surrealists*, pp. 192–93. See also Harold Loeb, *The Way It Was*, p. 134.

32. See also [Karl] Westheim, "George Grosz," *Broom* 4 (February 1923): 163–69; "Hymn of Hate," *New Republic* 89 (December 23, 1936): 249; "Louis Aragon," *New Republic* 88 (October 7, 1936): 258 (*TBOU*, p. 301).

33. "Louis Aragon," p. 258 (*TBOU*, pp. 301–2); Aragon's impressions of Berlin are quoted in Josephson, *Life Among the Surrealists*, p. 197; *ER*, p. 133.

10. LIFE AMONG THE DADAISTS—FRANCE, 1922–1923

1. MC to Harold Loeb, [November 1922]; November 10, 1922, Loeb Papers; MC to KB, November 10, 1922; "Mortuary" appeared in *Broom* 4 (February 1923): 170; it was collected as "Death" in *BJ* and as "Mortality" in *BJCP*.

2. MC to KB, November 27, 1922 (*SC*, p. 129); MC to KB, undated postcard; "The Butlers of Giverny," unpublished manuscript; *ER*, pp. 32, 134.

3. MC to KB, November 27, 1922 (*SC*, p. 129).

4. Gilbert Seldes to MC, May 31, 1922.

5. "Euphues," *Dial* 73 (October 1922): 447; MC to Scofield Thayer, August 3, 1922, *Dial* Papers; "Two American Poets," *Dial* 73 (November 1922): 563–67. As Nicholas Joost has observed, by pointing up the relativity of nationality in art, Cowley's review exemplified the ideal of a transnational, cosmopolitan culture advanced by Randolph Bourne and Scofield Thayer. Cowley's allegiance to such an ideal, however, was rather short-lived. Nicholas Joost, *Scofield Thayer and 'The Dial': An Illustrated History* (Carbondale and Edwardsville, Ill., 1964), p. 201.

6. MC to KB, January 6, 1923 (*SC*, p. 130); MC to John Brooks Wheelwright, January 30, 1923, Wheelwright Papers. Cowley's letter was a response to an earlier letter from Wheelwright in which he had denounced Cowley's essay as "smart aleck writing" and "extrinsic" criticism and had affirmed his belief in "tradition" over the dangerous "spook" of nationalism. Wheelwright to MC, December 30, 1922.

7. "Pierre MacOrlan," *Bookman* 40 (January 1925): 588–89. Cowley's portrait of MacOrlan, written during December 1922, was the last in his *Bookman* series. "I have been very glad to do this work for you," Cowley told Farrar upon completing his task; "it introduced me to some very fine writers and set me out on a new path." MC to John Farrar, December 29, 1922, *American Review* and *Bookman* Papers. Cowley's conviction of the promise and vitality of American literature had been recently strengthened by a meeting with Ford Madox Ford at the Dôme. Ford, a "pathetic and sympathetic" man, had spoken of his admiration for Ezra Pound and advanced his belief that "everything living in English literature comes, like Pound, from America." MC to KB, December 17, 1922.

8. See, in particular, Enrico Prampolini, "The Aesthetic of the Machine and Mechanical Introspection in Art," *Broom* 3 (October 1922): 235–37; Robert Alden Sanborn, "A Champion in the Wilderness," ibid., 174–79; and Paul Strand, "Photography and the New God," ibid. (November 1922): 252–58.

9. Josephson, "The Great American Billposter," *Broom* 3 (November 1922): 304–12.

10. Pascin was a French painter of Bulgarian birth who left France for the United States at the outbreak of the war. He became an American citizen, traveled extensively through the United States, painting and drawing what he saw, and returned to Paris in 1920, where he consorted with many of the American expatriates. Leading the life of a lonely Bohemian artist, Pascin never foreswore representationalism in painting and was known for his delicate craftsmanship. His sensitive but bitterly ironic studies of women, often prostitutes, betray a tender capacity for humanitarian sympathy. He committed

suicide in 1930. For American reminiscences of Pascin, see Robert McAlmon, *Being Geniuses Together, 1920–1930*, revised and with supplementary chapters by Kay Boyle (Garden City, N.Y., 1968), pp. 123, 300–301, 342; see also Hemingway, A *Moveable Feast*, pp. 101–4.

11. MC to Harold Loeb, July 27, 1922; Loeb to MC, July 31, 1922, Loeb Papers.

12. "Pascin's America," *Broom* 4 (January 1923): 136–37.

13. See, for example, Cowley's "Humanizing Society," in *The Critique of Humanism: A Symposium*, edited by C. Hartley Grattan (New York, 1930), pp. 63–84.

14. *ER*, p. 135; MC to KB, February 8, 1923 (*SC*, p. 136). See also Shi, "Malcolm Cowley and Literary New York," *Virginia Quarterly Review* 58 (1982): 575–93.

15. *Littérature* was the defiant house-organ of the French dadaists, edited by Aragon, Breton, and Soupault, until Breton took over as sole editor in 1922. MC to KB, December 17, 1922; MC to Harold Loeb, December 19, 1922, Loeb Papers; "Locus Solus," *Broom* 4 (March 1923): 281–83. For Josephson's account of the manifestation, see *Life Among the Surrealists*, pp. 132–34.

16. The dadaist interest in America is exemplified in Philippe Soupault's "The 'U.S.A.' Cinema," *Broom* 5 (September 1923): 65–69; *ER*, p. 106; MC to KB, January 28, 1923 (*SC*, pp. 134–35). Cowley was inclined to simplify Burke's not unsubtle analysis of the quality of American culture. See KB to MC, January 18, 1923 (*SC*, pp. 131–32), and February 8, 1923 (*SC*, pp. 138–39).

17. MC to John Brooks Wheelwright, January 14, 1923, Wheelwright Papers. Cowley's phrase "a critical patriot" is quoted from a personal letter to the author in Marjorie Rose Smelstor, "*Broom* and American Cultural Nationalism in the 1920's," Ph.D. dissertation, University of Wisconsin, 1975, p. 118. Cowley discussed his objectives in writing about the Leyendecker man in several letters to Burke. MC to KB, January 6, 1923; January 28, 1923; May 4, 1923; "Portrait by Leyendecker," *Broom* 4 (March 1923): 240–47. For Joseph Leyendecker, see Stephen Fox, *The Mirror Makers: A History of American Advertising and Its Creators* (New York, 1984), p. 44. "Voices from Home: 1923" appears in *BJCP*, p. 68.

18. MC to KB, January 10, 1923; "They Carry Him Off in a One-Horse Hack . . . ," *Secession* 5 (July 1923): 19 (collected as "Memphis Johnny" in *BJ* and *BJCP*); "Love and Death I," *Secession* 5 (July 1923): 18. The latter poem appears as "There Is a Moment" in *BJCP*, p. 127. It is here quoted without its second stanza.

19. Tristan Tzara to MC, February 5, 1923; MC to KB, February 8, 1923. For the internal dissensions among the dadaists, see Josephson, *Life Among the Surrealists*.

20. *ER*, pp. 151, 154; Notebook 1, entry 31, p. 23; MC to KB, February 8, 1923 (*SC*, pp. 136–37).

21. MC to KB, February 8, 1923 (*SC*, pp. 136–37); "A Life in the 1920's," unpublished manuscript, p. 2; *ER*, p. 149.

22. Notebook 1, n.s., June 10, 1933.

23. *ER*, p. 158; MC to KB, January 28, 1923 (*SC*, p. 136); February 8, 1923 (*SC*, p. 137); March 18, 1923. For Burke's hostility to Dada, see KB to MC, January 18, 1923 (*SC*, pp. 132–33).

24. MC to KB, January 6, 1923 (*SC*, pp. 129–30); Notebook 5, n.p. Cowley later used this passage as part of his contribution to a group manifestation in *transition* 13 (Summer 1928): 96–97; see also Notebook 1, entry 42, pp. 28–29.

25. MC to KB, January 6, 1923; January 11, 1923; January 28, 1923; February 8, 1923; April 6, 1923.

26. Loeb, *The Way It Was* (New York, 1959), pp. 145–47; MC to KB, January 6, 1923; Harold Loeb to MC, March 14, 1923, Loeb Papers; Gorham Munson to MC, February 20, 1923.

27. MC to KB, January 10, 1923; Gorham Munson to MC, May 5, 1923; Josephson, *Life Among the Surrealists*, pp. 234–38; *ER*, pp. 180–81. See also Alvin H. Rosenfeld, "John Wheelwright, Gorham Munson, and the 'Wars of *Secession*,'" *Michigan Quarterly Review* 14 (Winter 1975): 26; Munson, "The Fledgling Years, 1916–1924," *Sewanee Review* 40 (January 1932): 39–40; Shi, *Matthew Josephson*, pp. 70–71. Since Wheelwright did not leave for Europe until February 1923, he could not have been present at this editorial conference, as Shi suggests. See MC to John Brooks Wheelwright, January 30, 1923, Wheelwright Papers.

28. MC to KB, January 11, 1923. In a vengeful memoir published eight years later in the *New Republic*, Cowley evoked Munson as a man "singularly empty of literary talent" who nevertheless desired to be "the apostle of a new American literature" (to be produced by Cowley, Josephson, and Burke). He presented Munson as a chameleonlike writer under the successive influence of Josephson, Burke, and Frank, and recalled that in 1923 both he and Josephson felt that for all his intellectual and literary deficiencies Munson possessed a gift for diplomacy and literary politics that might make him a useful *chef d'école* for their literary group. Munson could be manipulated from the wings as "a sort of white shirtfront" of *Secession*, while his managers pursued their independent ways behind the scenes. "Exile's Return: Coffee and Pistols for Two," *New Republic* 68 (October 21, 1931): 259–60.

29. Gorham B. Munson, "The Mechanics for a Literary 'Secession,'" *S4N* 4, no. 22 (November 1922), n.p. *S4N* ran from November 1919 to July 1925. When its first issue was ready to be sent to the printer, no title had yet been decided on, and "Space for Name" was tentatively put on the cover. Its abbreviation remained as the title of the magazine.

30. Louis Untermeyer, "The New Patricians," *New Republic* 33 (December 6, 1922): 41–42.

31. Editorial, "Secession," *Freeman* 6 (January 10, 1923): 414. Through 1923 Brooks recurrently attacked the aestheticism of contemporary letters in his "Reviewer's Notebook." See Turner, *History of 'The Freeman'*, pp. 94–97. See also John Brooks Wheelwright's apologia for *Secession* in "Concerning Secession," *Freeman* 6 (February 7, 1923): 522. Wheelwright took issue with both Untermeyer and Brooks. Untermeyer's supposition of the predominantly critical output of the *Secession* group, he claimed, was "at variance with the facts"; it was only "the niggardliness of editors" that prompted its members to expend their best energies on criticism and reviewing. Wheelwright pointed out that Brooks's understanding of the aesthetic concerns of his generation was limited at best and challenged his indictment that the young writers were "arid

of faith." With impish wit he explained how Damon's work was founded on mysticism, his own on neo-Platonic High Anglicanism, Burke's on "neo-Scholasticism or reworked Spinoza," and Cowley's on a form of classicism.

32. MC to KB, January 11, 1923; March 18, 1923; MC to Norman Fitts, [1923].

33. MC to John Brooks Wheelwright, January 14, 1923, Wheelwright Papers.

34. MC to KB, February 8, 1923; Gorham Munson to MC, February 20, 1923.

35. MC to KB, March 8, 1923; March 18, 1923; MC to Harold Loeb, March 6, 1923, Loeb Papers; Loeb to MC, March 14, 1923, Loeb Papers.

36. Loeb, *The Way It Was*, pp. 142–57; Harold Loeb to MC, November 30, 1922; December 19, 1922; February 9, 1923, Loeb Papers; MC to KB, March 11, 1923.

37. MC to Harold Loeb, February 9, 1923, Loeb Papers; MC to KB, March 11, 1923. Hugo von Hofmannsthal (1874–1929), Austrian poet, dramatist, and essayist, reached international fame through his collaboration with the German composer Richard Strauss, for several of whose operas he wrote the libretti. The "Viennese letters" most likely refer to the correspondence between Hofmannsthal and Strauss. Hofmannsthal's career has been seen as symptomatic of the crisis that terminated the romantic-symbolist movement of the end of the nineteenth century.

38. Gorham Munson, "A Comedy of Exiles," *Literary Review* 12 (1968): 66.

39. S. Foster Damon to MC, September 2, 1922; John Brooks Wheelwright to MC, May 3, 1922; MC to S. Foster Damon, March 23, 1922, Damon Papers. Cowley's selection included "Château de Soupir: 1917," "Two Swans," "Translucent Fingers," "Fifteen Minutes," "Mountain Farm," "For a Georgian Anthology," "Runaway," "Coal Town," "About Seven O'Clock," "Mountain Valley," and "Day Coach," poems which between 1918 and 1923 had appeared in the *Harvard Advocate*, the *Dial*, *Poetry*, the *Little Review*, *Broom*, *Gargoyle*, *Secession*, and the *Literary Review of the New York Evening Post*. Rejected were "To a Dilettante Killed at Vimy," "Eighteenth-Century Sonnet," "On Visiting the Revere," "Sentimental," "Nantasket," "For a Methodist Hymnal," "Deathbed," "Nocturne," "Sudden Encounter," and "Poem for Two Voices." John Brooks Wheelwright to MC, May 3, 1922. Among the poets considered but (partly on Cowley's advice) rejected, were Joseph Auslander, Donald B. Clarke, Malcolm Vaughn, and Charles McVeagh. MC to Wheelwright, November 3, 1921, Wheelwright Papers. Under the pseudonym of "Dorian Abbott" Wheelwright wrote an introduction to the book in which he critically surveyed the history of Harvard anthologies since 1876. He characterized its precursor, *Eight Harvard Poets*, as a book "in the full flood of modernist and Georgian fashion," which had done much to advance its contributors' present literary standing. The new volume lacked its predecessor's homogeneity, he granted, yet it hoped to capture "an essence of the intellectual temper of undergraduate life." Dorian Abbott, Preface to *Eight More Harvard Poets* (New York, 1923), pp. xii, xiv.

40. James Light to MC, n.d.; Stewart Mitchell to MC, January 14, 1923; John Dos Passos to John Brooks Wheelwright, n.d., Wheelwright Papers; Conrad Aiken to Wheelwright, March 7, 1923, Wheelwright Papers; Conrad Aiken to MC, March 27, 1923, *Selected Letters of Conrad Aiken*, p. 75; Wheelwright to MC, February 8, 1923.

41. Milton Raison, "Poets and Pheasants," *New York Tribune* (January 28, 1923),

p. 22; Mark Van Doren, "Genevieve Taggard and Other Poets," *Nation* 114 (February 28, 1923): 246; "Poetry," *Times Literary Supplement*, April 12, 1923, p. 250; William Rose Benét, "Some Recent Poetry," *Literary Review of the New York Evening Post* 3 (March 10, 1923): 516; "Briefer Mention," *Dial* 74 (March 1923): 314; Newton Arvin, "Shorter Notices," *Freeman* 7 (May 2, 1923): 190; Gorham B. Munson, "Harvard Poets," *New Republic* 36 (October 3, 1923): 160. See also "Recent Books in Brief Review," *Bookman* 57 (April 1923): 221, and "Shopgirls, Farms and Ghosts," *New York Times Book Review* (January 28, 1923), p. 2.

42. For Crane's awareness of Cowley's poetry as it appeared in magazines, see *The Letters of Hart Crane, 1916–1932*, edited by Brom Weber (Berkeley and Los Angeles, 1965), pp. 42, 75, 84, 97, 113. Crane's review is collected in *The Complete Poems and Selected Letters and Prose of Hart Crane*, edited with an introduction and notes by Brom Weber (Garden City, N.Y., 1966), pp. 214–15. Crane's review first appeared in *S4N* 4 (March–April 1923): n.p.

43. MC to Hart Crane, May 20, 1923, in Susan Jenkins Brown, *Robber Rocks*, p. 10.

44. The poems—"Poem for Two Voices," "Nocturnal Landscape," "Interment," "Sudden Encounter," "Prophetic," and "Three Hills"—appeared in *Poetry* 21 (February 1923): 233–39. Amy Lowell to MC, July 25, 1922, and MC to Amy Lowell, August 25, 1922, Lowell Papers.

45. "Prophetic," *Poetry* 21 (February 1923): 237. Revised and collected as "Ten Good Farms" in *BJ* and *BJCP*.

46. With the sale of two poems to the *Bookman* and the *Double Dealer*, Amy Lowell's services as Cowley's informal literary agent came to an end; she had sold ten out of the original batch of twenty-five poems Cowley had sent her. In January 1923 Cowley expressed his formal thanks to Lowell for having done "big things" for him (MC to Amy Lowell, January 11, 1923, Lowell Papers). By this time, too, Lowell had begun to lose interest in the poetic efforts of her one-time protégés. Though she granted that, among the "Eight More Harvard Poets," Cowley and Wheelwright had "some good things," she could not see "enough in their work to warrant them much of a future." She distrusted the cerebral experimentalism of the *Secession* group and disapproved of their propensity for critical theory. Among the younger poets, she preferred the group of "Lyrists" led by Elinor Wylie and Edna Millay. For Lowell's critique of the Secessionists, see her "Two Generations in American Poetry," *New Republic* 36, pt. 2 (December 5, 1923): 3; S. Foster Damon, *Amy Lowell: A Chronicle*, pp. 637, 642; Norman Fitts to MC, September 14, 1922; MC to KB, n.d.

47. MC to KB, n.d.; Edmund Wilson to MC, March 27, 1923, in Edmund Wilson, *Letters on Literature and Politics, 1912–1972*, edited by Elena Wilson (New York, 1977), p. 104.

48. MC to Burton Rascoe, March 23, 1923, and May 11, 1923, Rascoe Papers; MC to KB, May 16, 1923, and June 9, 1923.

49. MC to KB, March 1, 1923, and March 11, 1923; MC to Scofield Thayer, May 18, 1923, *Dial* Papers; Scofield Thayer to MC, May 25, 1923.

50. MC to KB, February 4, 1923; March 17, 1923 (SC, p. 140); April 28, 1923 (SC,

p. 141); June 16, 1923; for a listing of Cowley's briefers, see Nicholas Joost and Alvin Sullivan, *The Dial: Two Author Indexes* (Carbondale and Edwardsville, Ill., 1971), pp. 14–15; the poem quoted in the text appeared in *Dial* 74 (May 1923): 494; MC to KB, March 8, 1923.

51. The other essay was Francis Birrell's "Marcel Proust: The Prophet of Despair," *Dial* 74 (May 1923): 463–74.

52. MC to S. Foster Damon, April 26, 1922, Damon Papers; MC to KB, April 28, 1923.

53. MC to KB, November 27, 1922 (SC, pp. 128–29).

54. Cowley's early analysis of Proust's style and vision was astute enough. The "secret" of Marcel Proust, he argued, lay in a "decomposition of life into an infinity of situations." Each situation was minutely analyzed and in turn decomposed into its "constituent elements." For Proust, however, all situations appeared to exist simultaneously; though his real subject was "the stream of personal consciousness," his situations had "a causal, but no temporal connexion." For Proust, Cowley implied, time was truly lost. "A Monument to Proust," *Dial* 74 (March 1923): 237–39.

55. "A Monument to Proust," pp. 234–40. Compare *ER*, p. 125.

56. MC to KB, March 17, 1923 (SC, pp. 139–40).

57. *ER*, p. 120; "The Hemingway Legend," *Brentano's Book Chat* 7 (September–October 1928): 25–29; MC to Harold Loeb, October 18, 1969; Nicholas Joost, *Ernest Hemingway and the Little Magazines: The Paris Years* (Barre, Mass., 1968), pp. 135–36.

58. The reference reads "And there in the café as he passed was Malcolm Cowley with a pile of saucers in front of him and a stupid look on his potato face talking about the Dada movement with a Roumanian who said his name was Tristan Tzara, who always wore a monocle and had a headache." See Philip Young, "For Malcolm Cowley: Critic, Poet, 1898– ," *Southern Review*, n.s., 9 (Autumn 1973): 778–79. As Young reminds us, Alfred Kazin remembered Cowley's as "the face which so startlingly duplicated Hemingway's handsomeness" (*Starting Out in the Thirties*, p. 15).

59. MC to John Dos Passos, December 7, 1934, Dos Passos Papers; Joost, *Hemingway and the Little Magazines*, pp. 129–54.

60. Notebook 1, entry 45, pp. 30–31; Cowley incorporated his notebook description of the prevailing intellectualism of modern writing in a review of Elinor Wylie's *Black Armour* written in early spring 1923 for the *Dial*. In his review he presented Eliot as a mastertype of the modern artist: "intellectual," "perfectly conscious," and "never quite the same." "The Owl and the Nightingale," *Dial* 74 (June 1923): 624–26; MC to KB, March 11, 1923, and April 5, 1923.

61. *ER*, pp. 110–15.

62. "Phantasus," *Dial* 75 (August 1923): 196–99. Compare *TBOU*, pp. 89–90.

63. MC to KB, March 18, 1923; see Notebook 1, entry 47, pp. 32–33.

64. MC to KB, March 18, 1923, and May 4, 1923.

65. Noel Riley Fitch, *Sylvia Beach and the Lost Generation: A History of Literary Paris in the Twenties and Thirties* (1983; New York and Harmondsworth, 1985), p. 172; Man Ray, *Self Portrait* (1963; rpt. New York, 1979), p. 190; MC to KB, March 1, 1923; March 11, 1923; March 17, 1923; April 5, 1923; May 16, 1923; May 20, 1923;

MC to Harold Loeb, May 27, 1923, Loeb Papers; Elinor Nef to MC, March 21, 1934; "Toward a Universal Man," *New Republic* 49 (December 8, 1926): 69–70.

66. For some years Van Doesburg had been experimenting with geometrical abstractions in the style of Piet Mondriaan, and by 1923 he was making concerted efforts to launch a Dada movement in the Netherlands. He had made the acquaintance of dadaists of various European nationalities, including Tzara, Ribemont-Dessaignes, and Kurt Schwitters, and had staged Dada manifestations in The Hague, Haarlem, and Amsterdam. MC to Hannah Hedrick, December 4, 1970; Hannah Hedrick to MC, February 2, 1971; *WT*, pp. 59–60; "Madrigals," *Mécano*, nos. 4, 5 (1923), n.p.; Kurt Schwitters, "Theo Van Doesburg and Dada," *De Stijl* Dernier Numéro [no. 90] (January 1932): 24–30, reprinted in Robert Motherwell, ed., *The Dada Painters and Poets: An Anthology* (New York, 1951), pp. 275–76; MC to KB, March 1, 1923, and March 17, 1923 (*SC*, p. 139); MC to Harold Loeb, March 18, 1923, and May 27, 1923, Loeb Papers.

67. John Brooks Wheelwright to MC, December 30, 1922; Gorham B. Munson to Wheelwright, December 14, 1922; February 5, 1923; October 18, 1923, Wheelwright Papers.

68. MC to KB, April 5, 1923; MC to John Brooks Wheelwright, May 9, 1923, Wheelwright Papers; "Comment," *Secession* 5 (July 1923): 20–23.

69. MC to KB, April 5, 1923; MC to John Brooks Wheelwright, May 9, 1923, Wheelwright Papers; *ER*, p. 160.

70. John Brooks Wheelwright to Gorham B. Munson, October 22, 1923; Munson to Wheelwright, October 19, 1923, and November 17, 1923; MC to Wheelwright, n.d., Wheelwright Papers; Wheelwright to Peggy Cowley, n.d.

71. Munson, "A Comedy of Exiles," p. 60; MC to John Brooks Wheelwright, May 9, 1923.

72. For a detailed discussion of the Munson-Crane-Wheelwright "imbroglio" see Alvin Rosenfeld, "John Wheelwright, Gorham Munson, and the 'Wars of Secession,'" *Michigan Quarterly Review* 14 (Winter 1975): 30–36. Munson's resentment flared up and throughout the fall he conducted a pained and angry correspondence with Wheelwright, trying to regain control of his magazine and forcing Wheelwright to suspend printing. His rancor was slow to subside and in later reminiscences was aimed rather indiscriminately at Josephson, Wheelwright, and Cowley. He spoke of acts of "sabotage" and of "the virtual hijacking of *Secession* by Wheelwright and Cowley" and denounced Cowley and Josephson as "machiavellians" with an "unscrupulous attitude" toward *Secession*. To Alfred Stieglitz he observed that both had become "active and venomous enemies." See Gorham Munson, "The Fledgling Years," pp. 40–43, and "A Comedy of Exiles," pp. 60–62.

73. MC to Harold Loeb, March 6, 1923, Loeb Papers; Loeb to MC, March 14, 1923, and March 24, 1923; MC to Loeb, April 11, 1923, Loeb Papers; Loeb, *The Way It Was*, pp. 162–63; Josephson, *Life Among the Surrealists*, pp. 246–48; MC to KB, April 28, 1923, and May 20, 1923; MC to Harold Loeb, May 27, 1923, Loeb Papers.

74. MC to KB, May 4, 1923; June 4, 1923.

75. "Exile's Return," *New Republic* 68 (September 23, 1931): 152–53; *ER*, p. 161.

76. Notebook 1, entry 52, pp. 34–35. Cowley's observation proved prescient: not long after, many one-time dadaists and surrealists converted to political radicalism.

77. Ibid., entry 57, pp. 37–38.

78. Ibid., entry 56, p. 37; MC to KB, June 29, 1923 (SC, p. 143). An ironic and indignant, but unsent, letter to the postmaster general on literary censorship appears in Notebook 1, part 2, entry 44, pp. 90–91. The letter is quoted in full in Bak, "The Fabulous Ostrich of Art: Malcolm Cowley's Notebooks of the Twenties," *Visionary Company* (Summer 1987): 147.

79. MC to M. A. Abernethy, July 29, 1932, *Contempo* Papers; *ER*, pp. 158–59; Loeb, *The Way It Was*, pp. 167–70; Dos Passos, *Best Times*, pp. 150–51; Norman, *E. E. Cummings*, pp. 138–40. Aragon's memory of the event, as related to Samuel Putnam, is given in the latter's *Paris Was Our Mistress: Memoirs of a Lost and Found Generation* (1947; rpt. Carbondale and Edwardsville, Ill., 1970) and deviates in details.

80. This composite account of events is based on the following sources, which are neither entirely consonant in matters of detail nor entirely devoid of subjective coloration; they are, however, the best and only documents of a wild night at the disposal of the historian: *ER*, pp. 164–70; Loeb, *The Way It Was*, pp. 176–79; McAlmon, *Being Geniuses Together*, pp. 113–15; André Salmon to MC, two undated letters [1923]; for Munson's retrospectively dim view of the "significance" of Cowley's gesture, see "A Comedy of Exiles," pp. 69–70.

81. *ER*, pp. 169–70.

82. "Prize American Literary 'Eggs' Boil Over in Paris Latin Quarter," *New York Tribune*, July 19, 1923; Munson, "The Fledgling Years," *Sewanee Review* 40:46–47.

83. Harold Stearns, *The Confessions of a Harvard Man: 'The Street I Know' Revisited*, edited and introduced by Hugh Ford, with a preface by Kay Boyle (Sutton West & Santa Barbara, 1984), pp. 298–300.

84. For McAlmon, see Smoller, *Adrift Among Geniuses*, pp. 26, 46; Josephson, *Life Among the Surrealists*, pp. 74, 77; McAlmon, *Being Geniuses Together, 1920–1930*, revised and with supplementary chapters by Kay Boyle (New York, 1968), p. 42. McAlmon claimed he had played a leading role as a witness in achieving Cowley's release and, commenting on Cowley's subsequent return to the United States to assume an editorial post on the *New Republic*, scathingly described him as one "duly ponderous, the young intellectual fairly slow on the uptake." When *Being Geniuses Together* was to be reissued in a new and revised version more than thirty years later, Cowley commented that McAlmon, for all his ability to make shrewd and scathing judgments, was essentially "lacking in imagination and blind to anything beyond the end of his own nose" (MC to Ken McCormick, December 9, 1967). In a prejudiced review, he portrayed McAlmon as a man whose capacity for generosity to young and needy writers tended to be overshadowed by his lack of humility and his inability to "bear his sorrows like a Christian." The book belatedly struck Cowley as "McAlmon's revenge on almost all the writers he had known." "Those Paris Years," *New York Times Book Review*, June 9, 1968, p. 1 (*FL*, pp. 244–45).

85. Compare Elinor Bulkin, "Malcolm Cowley: A Study of His Literary, Social, and Political Thought to 1940," Ph.D. dissertation, New York University, 1973, pp. 19–20.

Bulkin was the first to note the discrepancy between *Exile's Return* and the historical record on this point. Humphrey Carpenter's more recent *Geniuses Together: American Writers in Paris in the 1920s* (Boston, 1988) rather faithfully follows Cowley's account in *Exile's Return* and, hence, is typical in the way it overplays Cowley's involvement with Dada at the expense of his classicist predilections. See especially pp. 111–34. Carpenter's finely written book is useful and illuminating for the way it embeds Cowley's French venture in the general expatriate experience of Americans in Paris in the 1920s.

86. MC to KB, June 16, 1923; June 29, 1923; July 5, 1923; Notebook 2 (1922).

87. *Racine* (Paris, 1923); MC to KB, June 16, 1923; Cowley's essay on Racine was reprinted in *The World of Tragedy*, edited by John Kimmey and Ashley Brown (New York, 1981), and again, with an afterword by Ashley Brown, in *Horns of Plenty* vol. 1, no. 3 (Fall 1988): 26–39.

88. MC to author, August 31, 1985. The letter to Gertrude Stein is quoted in full in "The Fabulous Ostrich of Art," *Visionary Company* (Summer 1987): 139–40.

89. WT, p. 61; MC to Harold Loeb, August 31, 1923; September 14, 1923; October 12, 1923; November 22, 1923; November 29, 1923, all five Loeb Papers; Loeb to MC, September 30, 1923; November 5, 1923; November 19, 1923; MC to Van Wyck Brooks, September 14, 1923, Brooks Papers. After distributing the pamphlet to friends and acquaintances who he felt might share an interest in Racine, Cowley was left with a hundred-odd copies of the pamphlet, which for years he saved in the closets of his various habitations, until he finally discarded them. The dozen or so surviving copies became collectors' items. In 1960, a "slightly foxed" copy brought thirty-five dollars, about the price he had paid for the entire batch in 1923; in 1970 it was offered at the price of seventy-five dollars.

90. Charles Townsend Copeland to MC, n.d.; Glenway Wescott to MC, October 10 [1923]; Scofield Thayer to MC, January 3, 1924; S. Foster Damon to MC, January 9, 1924; Willam Slater Brown to MC, n.d.; Gorham B. Munson to MC, January 24, 1924. Though the enmity between both men had come to a head in the fall, Munson's critique was ostensibly devoid of rancor and seemed largely inspired by his exploration of a literary path opposite from Cowley's, one that would soon lead him to the mysticism of Ouspensky and Gurdjieff.

91. See, for example, "The Caged Osprey," *New Republic* 55 (July 4, 1928): 179; "Angry Author's Complaint," *New Republic* 80 (January 22, 1934), 51–52; "The Good Earthling," *New Republic* 81 (January 23, 1935): 309–10; "Voodoo Dance," *New Republic* 82 (April 10, 1935): 254–55; "Second Thoughts on 'Joseph,'" *New Republic* 94 (March 23, 1938), 198–99. See also *LS*, p. 141; "Five Acts of *The Scarlet Letter*," in *Twelve Original Essays on Great American Novels*, edited by Charles Shapiro (Detroit, 1958), p. 36.

92. MC to Harold Loeb, February 9, 1923, Loeb Papers; MC to KB, n.d.

93. MC to Harold Loeb, February 26, 1923, Loeb Papers; Cowley translated "The Extra" by Louis Aragon (*Broom* 5 [November 1923]: 211–16), "Poison" by Roger Vitrac (*Broom* 5 [November 1923]: 226–28), and "My Dear Jean" by Philippe Soupault (*Broom* 6 [January 1924]: 6–9); MC to KB, n.d.; March 1, 1923.

94. MC to KB, March 8, 1923; May 4, 1923; May 16, 1923; May 20, 1923; June 4,

1923; June 9, 1923; MC to KB, July 5, 1923 (SC, p. 144); MC to John Brooks Wheelwright, July 10, 1923, Wheelwright Papers.

95. MC to KB, June 4, 1923; June 9, 1923; MC to John Brooks Wheelwright, May 18, 1923, Wheelwright Papers; MC to KB, January 28, 1923 (SC, p. 135); February 4, 1923.

96. Notebook 4, entry 71, p. 39; pt. 2, entry 78, p. 62.

97. MC to KB, June 4, 1923; Notebook 4, pt. 2, entry 76, pp. 58–59. Compare ER, p. 161.

98. Notebook 4, pt. 2, entry 75, p. 57; ER, p. 160.

99. MWH, p. 252; WT, p. x.

100. ER, pp. 196, 83, 170; Shi, Matthew Josephson, pp. 76–77; BJCP, pp. 66–67.

101. Compare R. P. Blackmur, "The American Literary Expatriate," in David F. Bowers, ed., Foreign Influences in American Life (Princeton, N.J., 1944), p. 140.

11. DADA IN NEW YORK, 1923–1924

1. ER, pp. 170, 174–75; "Exile's Return," New Republic 68 (September 23, 1931): 151.

2. ER, pp. 171–72.

3. BJ, p. 73.

4. MC to Harold Loeb, August 31, 1923, and October 12, 1923, Loeb Papers; ER, p. 175.

5. ER, p. 176; MC to Harold Loeb, August 31, 1923, Loeb Papers; SF, p. 197; MC to John Brooks Wheelwright, [August 1923], Wheelwright Papers; MC to Loeb, October 12, 1923, Loeb Papers.

6. SF, p. 197; Notebook 1, entry 60, pp. 41–42.

7. ER, pp. 174–78; Notebook 1, entry 59, pp. 39–40.

8. MC to Witter Bynner, May 20, 1923, Lowell Papers; Notebook 4, pt. 2, entry 77, pp. 59–60.

9. Among them were the painter Edward Nagle, stepson of sculptor Gaston Lachaise and a college friend of Cummings and Dos Passos, who served as advisor and contributor on art; Glenway Wescott, the young novelist from Wisconsin, recently returned from France; Jean Toomer, the young black novelist and poet, parts of whose Cane appeared in Broom; the poet Isidor Schneider, then an employee at Boni & Liveright; and Charles Sheeler, one of America's leading avant-garde painters. William Carlos Williams pledged his continuing allegiance and contributed several poems as well as sections from his In the American Grain. Hart Crane continued to move in the circle of writers associated with Broom, but his relations with Josephson were strained and he did not contribute to any of the magazine's American issues. Cowley had enlisted the support of Ramon Guthrie, a poet, one-time ambulance driver, and aviator, whom he had met during his voyage home. Josephson, Life Among the Surrealists, pp. 243–54; ER, p. 172. For Guthrie, see VE, pp. 58–60.

10. Matthew Josephson to Harold Loeb, September 3, 1923, quoted in Loeb, *The Way It Was* (New York, 1959), p. 186; Loeb, "Comment: Broom: 1921–1923," *Broom* 5 (August 1923): 55–58. Though nominally he remained chief editor, Loeb's position in Europe made it practically impossible for him to play an active part in the process of editorial decision making in New York. Loeb's actual editorial involvement with *Broom* fell off sharply during the fall, as he was more and more absorbed in writing his novel *Doodab*. Though he remained strongly committed to the magazine, a series of misunderstandings about the serialization of parts of *Doodab* in *Broom* created tensions between the three editors and hurt Loeb's feelings to the point where he threatened to resign. In effect, as Loeb rightly if painfully suspected, his editorial title was rapidly becoming "merely honorary." Loeb to MC, November 19, 1923; Loeb, *The Way It Was*, p. 187.

11. "Snapshot of a Young Lady," *Broom* 5 (August 1923): 3–10; MC to KB, May 4, 1923.

12. "Memphis Johnny," *Broom* 5 (September 1923): 97–98; Josephson, "Brain at the Wheel," *Broom* 5 (September 1923): 120; MC to Harold Loeb, August 31, 1923, Loeb Papers.

13. *ER*, pp. 178–79; Josephson, "Henry Ford," *Broom* 5 (October 1923): 137–42.

14. Loeb, *The Way It Was*, p. 187; Josephson, *Life Among the Surrealists*, p. 256; Burton Rascoe, "A Bookman's Day Book," *New York Herald Tribune*, September 30, 1923, p. 15; John Gould Fletcher to *Broom*, October 23, 1923; Edmund Wilson to John Peale Bishop, January 15, 1924, in *Letters on Literature and Politics, 1912–1972*, p. 119; Edmund Wilson, "An Imaginary Conversation: Mr. Paul Rosenfeld and Mr. Matthew Josephson," *New Republic* 38 (April 9, 1924): 179–82. Wilson's article was reprinted in his *The Shores of Light: A Literary Chronicle of the Twenties and Thirties* (New York, 1952), pp. 125–40.

15. "Comment," *Dial* 75 (September 1923): 311–12.

16. See, for example, Cowley's translations of two of Paul Valéry's essays, "Pure Poetry" and "The Future of Literature: Will It Be a Sport?," which appeared in the *New York Herald Tribune* in March and April 1928.

17. MC to Harold Loeb, August 31, 1923; September 14, 1923; Loeb to MC, September 30, 1923; MC to Loeb, October 12, 1923, Loeb Papers.

18. Matthew Josephson to Harold Loeb, September 3, 1923, quoted in Shi, *Matthew Josephson*, p. 85; MC to Loeb, September 14, 1923, and October 12, 1923, Loeb Papers.

19. MC to KB, October 11, 1923; Matthew Josephson to Harold Loeb, October 20, 1923, quoted in Loeb, *The Way It Was*, p. 194; *ER*, pp. 179–80; Josephson, *Life Among the Surrealists*, pp. 260–61.

20. MC to Harold Loeb, October 12, 1923, Loeb Papers; MC to KB, October 11, 1923.

21. Matthew Josephson to Harold Loeb, October 20, 1923, quoted in Loeb, *The Way It Was*, pp. 194–95.

22. *ER*, p. 180; Loeb, *The Way It Was*, pp. 195–96; Crane's grumblings to Mun-

son and Cowley are cited in John Unterecker, *Voyager: A Life of Hart Crane* (1969; London, 1970), p. 314.

23. Gorham B. Munson to MC, October 15, 1923; Munson, "The Fledgling Years," *Sewanee Review* 40: 49–50; Loeb, *The Way It Was*, p. 196.

24. Gurdjieff's preachings were championed in America by A. R. Orage, the British man of letters, and given publicity by Gorham Munson. For a while, Gurdjieff had quite a following among American bohemians and avant-gardists—Margaret Anderson and Jane Heap of the *Little Review* were not the only ones to found a "Gurdjieff Circle." In the spring of 1924 Gurdjieff held a series of lectures and demonstrations in New York. The performance of his troupe of dancers elicited as much scornful ridicule as worshipful admiration. As Munson later observed, in the spring and summer of 1924 "the question of Gurdjieff—a new Pythagoras or charlatan?—was the most controversial topic at intelligentsia gatherings." Unlike the enthusiastic Munson, Crane was appalled by Gurdjieff's New York performances and turned away in disgust from the mystic's insistence upon disciplined commitment to the creed. From early 1924 on, as Crane's friendship with Munson, and his spiritual bond with Frank and Toomer, began to dissolve, he became progressively closer to the circle around *Broom*—Cowley, Burke, Josephson, and Brown. For Crane, see Philip Horton, *Hart Crane: The Life of an American Poet* (1937; rpt. New York, 1976), pp. 154–56. For Munson and A. R. Orage, see Munson's *The Awakening Twenties: A Memoir-History of a Literary Period* (Baton Rouge and London, 1985), pp. 253–83. For disparagings of Gurdjieff, see Boyle and McAlmon, *Being Geniuses Together*, pp. 95–96, and Putnam, *Paris Was Our Mistress*, pp. 82–83.

25. *ER*, pp. 181–82; Matthew Josephson to Harold Loeb, October 23, 1923, quoted in Loeb, *The Way It Was*, pp. 195–97.

26. MC to John Brooks Wheelwright, October 25, 1923; MC to Harold Loeb, October 30, 1923, Loeb Papers. In *Exile's Return* Cowley noted how the whole experience made him realize "the pathos and absurdity of the fierce individualism preserved by American writers in the midst of the most unified civilization now existing. . . . In the struggle we had lately undertaken we were beaten almost before we began. We should have realized that there was no chance of imposing our ideas on others when we couldn't agree among ourselves, or even preserve the decorum customary in an Italian speakeasy." *ER*, pp. 182–83.

27. *ER*, p. 184; Josephson, *Life Among the Surrealists*, p. 267. For the varying and conflicting accounts of the muddy scrap at Fisher's Field, see Josephson's *Life Among the Surrealists*, pp. 265–67; Munson's "The Fledgling Years," *Sewanee Review* 40:50–52; Loeb's *The Way It Was*, pp. 200–201; and *ER*, pp. 183–85.

28. The entire ode appears in *ER*, pp. 184–85.

29. MC to William Slater Brown, November 14, 1923.

30. MC to Gorham B. Munson, November 14, 1923; Munson to MC, [November 1923]; MC to John Brooks Wheelwright, November 18, 1923, Wheelwright Papers; Wheelwright to MC, November 17 and November 23, 1923; Munson, "A Comedy of Exiles," p. 62.

31. Horton, *Hart Crane*, pp. 156–57.

32. MC to KB, November 8, 1923 (SC, p. 147); for Cowley's retrospective account of the weekend, see *MWH*, pp. 191–200.

33. MC to Harold Loeb, October 30, 1923, Loeb Papers; *ER*, p. 186; E. M. Morgan to "Publishers of 'Broom,'" December 8, 1923; Josephson, *Life Among the Surrealists*, p. 270; William Slater Brown to "Matty Malcolm Josephson Cowley," [December 1923].

34. MC to Harold Loeb, November 22, 1923, Loeb Papers; William Slater Brown to MC, [November 1923]; Matthew Josephson to Harold Loeb, October 23, 1923, quoted in Loeb, *The Way It Was*, p. 197; *ER*, p. 189; Brown to Josephson, n.d.; MC to Loeb, November 29, 1923, Loeb Papers.

35. Prior to the issue's publication Cowley had written to Brooks, assuring him that the forthcoming open letter was in no way to be construed as an oblique attack on Brooks himself, whom Cowley referred to as "a critic of integrity" deserving of "a more definite award." Brooks took the open letter, as well as Cowley's explanation, in a spirit of good sportsmanship. MC to Van Wyck Brooks, December 18, 1923, Brooks Papers; Brooks to MC, December 28, 1923; "Comment," *Broom* 6 (January 1924): 30–31.

36. Josephson, *Life Among the Surrealists*, pp. 272–73; *ER*, pp. 189–90, 195.

37. Hart Crane to "Broom," n.d.; William Carlos Williams to MC, n.d.; Norman Fitts to MC, n.d.; Eugene O'Neill to Postmaster General Harry S. New, n.d. (In a private, undated letter to Cowley, O'Neill added: "I'm rather a weak asset on this brand of protest because I'm so 'suspect' myself, that they'll think it's my own axe I'm grinding." O'Neill's play *The Hairy Ape* had recently been censored in New York, Boston, Philadelphia, and Detroit, and all his works "blacklisted" by the Catholic Church); Burton Rascoe, "A Bookman's Day Book," *New York Herald Tribune*, January 27, 1924, p. 26.

38. *ER*, p. 196; MC to Harold Loeb, March 14, 1924, Loeb Papers.

39. *ER*, p. 190.

40. Cowley thought he recognized, besides himself, Gilbert Seldes, Edmund Wilson, Burke, Josephson, Dos Passos, Cummings, Munson, and John Farrar. Josephson, in addition, spotted features of Loeb, Waldo Frank, and Hart Crane. Munson, rather perversely, maintained that Boyd's portrait was "entirely imaginary and related to no writer and no review that I could identify." Yet he denounced Boyd's article in *Secession* 7 as "a piece of mud-slinging bristling with gratuitous inferences of log-rolling, ignorance, perversity, etc" and calculated to make the existing literary situation only "murkier"—he hoped that the "few writers" whom it annoyed would prove "intelligent enough to disregard derisive gestures of this calibre." *ER*, pp. 190–91; Josephson, *Life Among the Surrealists*, p. 268; Munson, "A Comedy of Exiles," *Literary Review* 12 (1968): 73, reprinted in Munson's *The Awakening Twenties*, pp. 157–88; Munson, "The American Murkury," *Secession* 7 (Winter 1924): 32.

41. Ernest Boyd, "Aesthete: Model 1924," *American Mercury* 1 (January 1924): 51–56, reprinted in Boyd's *Portraits: Real and Imaginary* (1924; rpt. New York, 1970), pp. 11–25.

42. Cowley's account appears in *ER*, pp. 190–95; Ernest Boyd's version of events is

given in his *Portraits: Real and Imaginary*, pp. 153–55; see also Josephson, *Life Among the Surrealists*, pp. 268–69.

43. *ER*, p. 195; Burton Rascoe, "A Bookman's Day Book," *New York Herald Tribune*, January 6, 1924, p. 23, reprinted in Boyd's *Portraits*, pp. 155–61.

44. *ER*, pp. 194–95. Cowley's account of the Battle of the Aesthetes in *Exile's Return* is informed with a trivializing and laconic tone, which occasionally rings false. From his radical perspective Cowley was inclined to tone down the angry exuberance of his dadaist posturing in the winter of 1924. While he rightfully exposed some of Boyd's "purely tactical misstatements," he tended to overplay the implications of homosexuality in Boyd's caricature and seemed to conveniently sidestep the more serious of Boyd's charges, notably those concerning the aesthete's split position as both an avant-garde artist and a servant of a business culture. Moreover, his contention that Boyd's attack must be explained on economic grounds—an insight too obviously born of his radicalized consciousness—rests on at best a half-truth: if Boyd had reason to fear competition in the field of contemporary foreign art, Cowley, too, had his reasons for professional jealousy. As he later confessed to Burton Rascoe: "In 1921, when I began writing for *Broom*, I discovered what was to me a new literary genre, the composite portrait." He had written several such portraits for *Broom* and entertained hopes of publishing them, with his portrait-interviews for the *Bookman*, as a series of "Portraits: Real and Imaginary." When, in late 1923, he saw the first issue of the *American Mercury*, containing the "composite portrait" by Ernest Boyd, Cowley was "moderately incensed" to find that his literary device had been "borrowed" and used against him and his friends. Indeed, Boyd was doing to Cowley and his friends much more effectively what Cowley had hoped to do to Stearns and Rosenfeld in "Young Mr. Elkins." In late 1924 Boyd published *Portraits: Real and Imaginary*, thereby preempting the field. MC to Burton Rascoe, October 30, 1931, Rascoe Papers.

45. *ER*, p. 196; Josephson, *Life Among the Surrealists*, p. 261; Arthur M. Schlesinger, Jr., *The Crisis of the Old Order: 1919–1933* (Boston, 1957), p. 71.

46. See also Hoffman et al., *The Little Magazine*, pp. 101–7, and Marjorie Rose Smelstor, "'Broom' and American Cultural Nationalism in the 1920s," Ph.D. dissertation, University of Wisconsin, 1975.

12. THE CITY OF ANGER—NEW YORK, 1924–1925

1. *ER*, p. 202; Notebook 4, entry 54, p. 12; a slightly revised version of the "Epistle" appears in *ER*, p. 201.

2. *ER*, pp. 201–2.

3. MC to Hart Crane, November 28, 1923, published in Susan Jenkins Brown, *Robber Rocks*, p. 19; MC to Harold Loeb, November 22, 1923, Loeb Papers; *ER*, p. 201.

4. MC to KB, November 8, 1923 (*SC*, p. 147); Notebook 4, entry 54, p. 12; Notebook 1, entry 63, p. 43; MC to KB, November 18, 1923; Notebook 4, entry 56, pp. 18–19; MC to KB, February 1, 1924 (*SC*, pp. 155–56).

5. Notebook 1, entry 59, pp. 38–39; MC to KB, February 1, 1924 (SC, p. 155 [compare ER, p. 202]); Notebook 4, entry 56, pp. 18–20; MC to KB, February 19, 1924 (SC, pp. 158–59).

6. DGM, p. 37; WT, pp. 99–100.

7. Notebook 4, entry 75, p. 45 (compare ER, p. 203).

8. MC to KB, November 8, 1923 (SC, p. 147); November 18, 1923; February 19, 1924 (SC, p. 159); MC to Harold Loeb, November 22, 1923, Loeb Papers.

9. ER, pp. 204–5.

10. A notebook entry apropos of Cowley's trip to Woodstock indicates that one of the topics of discussion with Brown had been the pertinence of T. S. Eliot's "Tradition and the Individual Talent" to the practice of criticism: "Literature exists for us (as Eliot pointed out) as a series of relations, and each new work modifies not only the present and the future, but the series of relationships which make up the past. When Ulysses appeared, it was time to write a criticism of Sterne or Fielding or Flaubert. In the case of Ulysses we could tell what it was but not how good it was, for our standard of good and evil is really nothing more than our judgment of the effect of a book on the history of literature." Whether it was Brown who brought Eliot's essay to Cowley's attention remains uncertain; the notebook entry from 1924 is the earliest evidence available that Cowley had read "Tradition and the Individual Talent." For Cowley's visit to Brown, see ER, pp. 197–99; MC to Harold Loeb, March 14, 1924, Loeb Papers.

11. William Slater Brown to MC, [January–February 1924]; ER, p. 198; MC to Harold Loeb, March 14, 1924, Loeb Papers; Munson's statement is among the Cowley Papers. Gorham B. Munson to MC, March 9, 1924. For Munson's generational division see especially chapter 1, "The Pattern of Our Milieu," Destinations: A Canvass of American Literature Since 1900 (New York, 1928), pp. 1–10. Burke outlined a never-sent statement for Broom in a letter to Cowley; see SC, pp. 160–61.

12. ER, p. 200; MC to Harold Loeb, March 14, 1924, Loeb Papers.

13. Notebook 1, entries 61 and 62, p. 42, and separate unpaginated entry. The correlation between art and character, literary and personal ethics, continued to preoccupy Cowley. He embedded his final thoughts on the subject in the last chapter of —And I Worked at the Writer's Trade (1978), which he ended with a statement adapted from his notebook: "No complete son-of-a-bitch ever wrote a good sentence." WT, pp. 256–66. See also "Artists, Conscience and Censors," Saturday Review 45 (July 7, 1962): 8–10, 47; and "Ethics in the Arts," in Ethical Problems for the Sixties, by Malcolm Cowley, Robert Lewis Shayon, John Smith, and Charles Frankel (New Britain, Conn., 1962), pp. 1–15.

14. Notebook 1, entry 64, pp. 44–47 (see "The Fabulous Ostrich," p. 144, for a longer quotation); MC to KB, February 1, 1924 (SC, p. 156). For Burke's critique, see KB to MC, February 5, 1924 (SC, pp. 157–58). Cowley continued to explore the interconnections between the various sets of antinomies throughout the decade. In a later entry he replaced the term "creationist" by "constructionist," following Paul Valéry's use of the term "construction." In an interesting "addenda" he admitted that his critical practice was not always consistent with his theoretical observations: "The classical

American example of the constructionist is Poe, and Whitman of the expressionist. Examples of expressionism are plentiful today; the constructionists, except Eliot, are second-rate: Cather, Hergesheimer, Cabell. . . . by temperament, I incline to constructionism, but sometimes write expressionistically and do not always prefer Valéry to Joseph Delteil. And rarely Cather to Anderson. Perhaps I only detest expressionism when it is followed blindly, and not when it is embraced as the result of reflection and a choice." For Valéry's use of the term "construction," see his *Variety* (New York, 1927), pp. 260–63; Notebook 4, entry 80, pp. 70–71.

15. Notebook 1, entry 65, p. 48; Notebook 4, entries 78, 79, pp. 61–70.

16. MC to John Brooks Wheelwright, May 10, 1924, Wheelwright Papers; Cowley's letters in praise of *S4N* appeared in volume 4, nos. 26–29 (May–August 1923), [87], [100], [109]. The double issue of *S4N* on Frank was that of September 1923–January 1924. Munson had recently published a book on the subject, *Waldo Frank: A Study* (1923); MC to Harold Loeb, May 9, 1924, and June 24, 1924, Loeb Papers; MC to KB, June 24, 1924.

17. MC to Alyse Gregory, January 3, 1924; January 19, 1924; February 17, 1924; and April 5, 1924, all *Dial* Papers. For a full listing of Cowley's briefers, see *The Dial. Two Author Indexes*. Compiled by N. Joost and A. Sullivan (1971).

18. MC to John Brooks Wheelwright, May 10, 1924, and May 11, 1924, Wheelwright Papers; Wheelwright to MC, April 29 [1924], May 3 [1924]; Norman Fitts to Wheelwright, [1924], Wheelwright Papers; Norman Fitts to MC, n.d.; Hart Crane to his mother, May 11, 1924, in *The Letters of Hart Crane, 1916–1932*, edited by Brom Weber (Berkeley and Los Angeles, 1965), p. 184; Allen Tate to Donald Davidson, June 15, 1924, in *The Literary Correspondence of Donald Davidson and Allen Tate*, edited by John Tyree Fain and Thomas Daniel Young (Athens, Ga., 1974), p. 20.

19. MC to Harold Loeb, May 9, 1924; June 24, 1924; September 15, 1924; September 17, 1924; November 23, 1924, all Loeb Papers. Reviewing *Doodab* for the *New York Herald Tribune*, Cowley adopted a more critical tone, but still spoke of a promising first novel and praised Loeb's "exact fancy" and his ability to create "living characters." In acknowledgment of services rendered Loeb dedicated his second novel, *The Professors Like Vodka*, to Cowley, who again had critically reviewed the manuscript. "Exact Fancy," *New York Herald Tribune Books*, November 22, 1925, p. 8; for Cowley's supervising of Loeb's second novel, see Loeb's afterword to *The Professors Like Vodka* (1927; rpt. Carbondale and Edwardsville, Ill., 1974), pp. 253–66.

20. "Paris Letter," *Dial* 75 (November 1923): 473–79; Pierre MacOrlan to MC, February 4 [1923]; Albert and Charles Boni to MC, April 19, 1924; Pierre MacOrlan to MC, April 28, 1924; MC to Harold Loeb, May 9, 1924, Loeb Papers; S. Foster Damon to MC, December 4, 1924; "Briefer Mention," *Dial* 78 (March 1925): 246. The appearance of Cowley's rendering of *On Board the 'Morning Star'* in late 1924 was given added publicity by the neatly timed publication by John Farrar of Cowley's *Bookman* portrait of MacOrlan in January 1925.

21. S. Foster Damon to MC, June 24, 1924; "Family Adventures," *Literary Review of the New York Evening Post* 4 (September 22, 1923): 61.

22. "The Best of Medicine," *Literary Review of the New York Evening Post* 4 (October 27, 1923): 184; "A Lamb Among Wolves," *Saturday Review of Literature* 1 (November 15, 1924): 279–80.

23. "Black and White," *Literary Review of the New York Evening Post* 4 (February 16, 1924): 520. Cowley's review was of *The Color of a Great City*, a collection of early newspaper sketches, but branched out into a consideration of the general influence of Dreiser.

24. "The Village Smell," *Literary Review of the New York Evening Post* 4 (June 21, 1924): 844.

25. "St. Apollinaire," *Literary Review of the New York Evening Post* 4 (June 21, 1924): 835; for Apollinaire's role as "the impressario of the avant-garde," see Roger Shattuck's excellent *The Banquet Years: The Origins of the Avant-Garde in France, 1885 to World War I* (1958; rev. ed. 1968), pp. 253–322.

26. MC to Alyse Gregory, September 15, 1924, *Dial* Papers; MC to KB, October 22, 1924.

27. Fain and Young, eds., *The Literary Correspondence of Donald Davidson and Allen Tate*, p. 132; "Gulliver," *Dial* 77 (December 1924): 520–22.

28. MC to KB, August 19, 1924.

29. MC to KB, July 12, 1917; a four-page outline of the novel is among the Cowley Papers. The projected novel centered on the turbulent fluctuations in the relationship between an ambitious but naive young writer—"He was a gentle young man, transversed by storms of moral indignation. He had written poems, but his character was a form of protective coloring. . . . His most American characteristic [was] that of blundering ahead without stopping to analyse his motives"—and an experienced, hard-drinking and not too faithful divorcee, who "had a knack for picking out men for their outstanding qualities, . . . had learned a little about writing, a little about drawing, a little about decoration," and who introduced the young apprentice writer to New York editors.

30. By the summer of 1925 Peggy could report to Damon that Cowley had made a definite start on a novel, found a publisher, settled on a title, and finished two chapters and part of a preface; several newspapers, she said, had announced the forthcoming book, but the novel remained unfinished. Peggy Cowley to S. Foster Damon, [summer 1925], Damon Papers. Five years later, Cowley's desire for a novel still unquenched, he drew up a new prospectus: "The novel I want to write should belong to the Fielding-Dickens-Dostoevski type—a large canvas, many people moving in different directions, the whole bound together by some big and moderately simple theme." The "fairly simple ideas" around which the novel was to revolve had obvious pertinence to Cowley's personal life in the 1920s: "(1) Character, more than ability, is the key to success in the arts. Every year there are graduated from our universities, art schools, conservatories, Greenwich Villages and Montparnasses, hundreds of young men and women with the ability to be great. They fail because life is too hard for them, or because they are too weak for life. (2) We pay for our vices. However, I have my own definition of vice. I think there are two great crimes for an ambitious young man: one is selfishness, or rather self-centredness, and the other is surrender, taking the easier of

two possible courses instead of the more difficult." "A Novel," three-page manuscript, dated September 17 [1929?], reprinted in *Horns of Plenty* 1 (Summer 1988): 6–7. In May 1934, in the immediate wake of finishing *Exile's Return*, Cowley returned to the idea of writing a novel about "the break-up of a group [of young writers in New York], as some of its members are snatched into fame and others decline into alcoholism, so that their relative positions are completely changed at the end of the story." Three years later he again projected a novel about the "roots" of literary failure and success and recurrently considered the tragic life story of Hart Crane as a potential subject. He continued to waver, however, between "a simple love story" and a "group novel." It was not until 1952 that he admitted to himself, in the confessional of his notebook, that he had "more or less decided not to be a novelist," but that perhaps his memoirs and poems might have "the same value" as the by now chimerical novel. Notebook 1, n.s., entry for May 12, 1934; Notebook 1, n.s., entries for January 2, 1937, and November 10, 1937; Notebook 6, n.s., entry for February 21, 1952.

31. *ER*, p. 244. The question of "the mechanics of literary reputations" was an important leitmotif of the "chapters" of literary history published in —*And I Worked at the Writer's Trade* (1978). The closest he eventually came to writing his collective novel about literary life in the 1920s was in *Exile's Return*, a sui generis book that not only possessed the stylistic virtues of a well-made novel but also, while concerned with real events and characters, was built on "a good novelistic structure," as Cowley explained to Burke in 1931. Not without justification he could in 1967 point to *Exile's Return* as "a non-fictional novel . . . done rather deliberately in that form." MC to KB, August 6, 1931; Page Stegner and Robert Canzoneri, "An Interview with Malcolm Cowley," *Per/ Se* 2 (Winter 1967–1968): 34–39, rpt. in *CMC*, pp. 92–104.

32. MC to KB, October 11, 1923; Weber, ed., *Letters of Hart Crane*, pp. 155, 166.

33. For Crane's shifting allegiance to Munson, see John Unterecker, *Voyager*, pp. 358–60; *SF*, p. 192; Hart Crane to Waldo Frank, April 21, 1924, and Crane to his mother, May 11, 1924, in Weber, ed., *Letters of Hart Crane*, pp. 182, 184.

34. Allen Tate to MC, June 8, 1958 (see also *SF*, pp. 192, 194); Fain and Young, eds., *Literary Correspondence of Donald Davidson and Allen Tate*, pp. 8, 16, 17, 18, 20, 27, 100; MC to Allen Tate, [1924], Tate Papers.

35. Fain and Young, eds., *The Literary Correspondence of Donald Davidson and Allen Tate*, pp. 119–20.

36. For Crane's appreciation of his view of Brooklyn Bridge see Weber, ed., *Letters of Hart Crane*, p. 183; *SF*, p. 194.

37. Originally entitled "Skyscrapers" and included as "Towers of Song" in *Blue Juniata* (1929), the poem was subsequently dedicated to Allen Tate. MC to Alyse Gregory, February 12, 1925, and March 7 [1925], *Dial* Papers.

38. Apart from a handful of book reviews he was less than usually productive in 1924. That year, for the first time since 1916, none of his poems reached print; 1923, by contrast, had seen the appearance of twenty poems in as many as ten different magazines, in addition to the publication of *Eight More Harvard Poets*. MC to KB, August 12, 1924; August 19 [1924].

39. *WT*, p. 62.

40. For a virtually complete listing of Cowley's articles for *Charm*, see Eisenberg's *Malcolm Cowley*, pp. 30–37, 101–6.

41. "Parnassus-on-the-Seine," *Charm* 1 (July 1924): 19, 80, 83.

42. "Do Artists Make Good Husbands?" *Charm* 2 (August 1924): 28–29, 83, 91. In more serious form the interest surfaced again in "A Natural History of the American Writer" in *The Literary Situation* (1954), a near book-length study of the living and working conditions in the writing profession in America; there, in a manner anticipated by his *Charm* article, Cowley presented himself as a literary anthropologist reporting on the personal and professional customs and folkways of American writers as a special tribe. *LS*, pp. 132–228.

43. Thus several articles evinced a bibliophilic delight in books as made objects and displayed a wide-ranging interest in aspects of the literary trade, from seasonal fluctuations in the publishing world to prices, editions, lettertypes, and the quality of printing paper. Others exemplified an early interest in arboriculture, the preservation of the American landscape, the public management and conservation of natural resources. In later life Cowley planted his own little forest of pine trees on his acreage in Sherman, Connecticut, and, for twenty years, served the local community as chairman of the zoning board, helping to preserve the regional landscape against commercial encroachments (see, for example, Cowley's 1973 stand against a new lakeside development in the vicinity of Sherman in the *New York Times*, November 4, 1973, sec. 8, pp. 1, 12, 16); he also regularly reviewed the state of farming in New England for such regional magazines as *Country Journal*.

44. *WT*, p. 62; MC to James M. Kempf, November 23, 1974.

45. MC to Jane Heap, October 24, 1925, *Little Review* Papers; MC to KB, August 23, 1924; August 29 [1924].

46. MC to KB, September 1, 1924; MC to John Brooks Wheelwright, September 17, 1924, Wheelwright Papers; MC to Harold Loeb, September 15, 1924, Loeb Papers. The letter is reprinted in Loeb's *The Way It Was*, pp. 222–23.

47. Munson, *The Awakening Twenties*, p. 291; Susan Jenkins Brown, *Robber Rocks*, p. 38.

48. MC to KB, October 22, 1924; October 30 [1924].

49. MC to KB, October 22, 1924; a clipping of Cowley's open letter "To the Editors of Books," dated October 20, 1924, is among the Cowley Papers.

50. See Dickran Tashjian, *Skyscraper Primitives: Dada and the American Avant-Garde, 1910–1925* (Middletown, Conn., 1975), pp. 135–37.

51. Waldo Frank, "Seriousness and Dada," 1924, no. 3 (September 1924): 70–73. Frank's position on American Dada was in line with Wilson's earlier attack on Dada in *Vanity Fair*.

52. "Communications on Seriousness and Dada," 1924, no. 4 (November 1924): 140–41; MC to Waldo Frank, [late October 1924].

53. Waldo Frank to MC, November 3, 1924. The altercation with Cowley in 1924 was reprinted in Frank's *In the American Jungle* (New York, 1937), pp. 128–35.

54. William Carlos Williams to MC, December 24, 1924; Waldo Frank to MC, November 9, 1924, and November 21 [1924]; MC to KB, November 22 [1924].

55. MC to Harold Loeb, September 15, 1924, Loeb Papers; Gorham Munson, *The Awakening Twenties*, p. 292; Edwin Seaver to MC, [1924]; MC to KB, June 24, 1924 (SC, p. 161); MC to KB, October 22, 1924; MC to Edwin Seaver, November 15, 1924.

56. Edwin Seaver to MC, [November 1924]. Cowley wanted to have inserted as a footnote: "Bertrand Russell says, 'Traditional mysticism has been contemplative, convinced of the unreality of time, and essentially a lazy man's philosophy.' It has always seemed to me that the mysticism of Mr. Frank's novels was of this traditional type." The footnote was included in the reprinted version of the exchange in Frank's *In the American Jungle*, p. 132. As Cowley's subsequent correspondence with Frank made clear, addition of the footnote to Cowley's open letter in 1924 would have done little to lessen Frank's fury. When Seaver refused to print the note, Cowley offered to sign and date it (November 8), to make clear that it had "no connection with [Seaver's] editorial policy, unless that policy is simply to praise Frank." MC to Edwin Seaver, November 15, 1924; MC to KB, November 16, 1924 (SC, p. 164).

57. MC to KB, November 16, 1924 (SC, p. 165); November 22 [1924]; MC to Harold Loeb, September 15, 1924, Loeb Papers; MC to KB, October 30 [1924].

58. MC to KB, October 22, 1924; November 22 [1924]; Shi, *Matthew Josephson*, p. 99; MC to John Brooks Wheelwright, November 22, 1924, Wheelwright Papers; MC to KB, November 16, 1924; November 22 [1924] (SC, pp. 164–65). Cowley's moral anger was admixed with a longing to resuscitate the exciting European days of *Broom*. To Loeb he sentimentally confessed: "Harold, you don't know how we regret Broom; if only some copper magnate would die and leave you Fifty Thousand Dollars, wouldn't you like to contribute a tithe of it to renewing the good fight? In the same case, I should like nothing better: to write and edit, moving from capital to capital with the valuta, cursing the Dawes plan and browbeating the miserable printers who think that typographical errors in foreign English are of no account. The two years of Broom were not two years to the wind; it still makes more stir than the continuing Dial." MC to Harold Loeb, November 23, 1924, Loeb Papers.

59. KB to MC, February 21, 1924 (SC, pp. 160–61); November 25, 1924, Burke Papers.

60. MC to Harold Loeb, December 8 [1924], Loeb Papers; MC to KB, [December 1924]. The "Agenda" of a group session held in late November lists Crane's "Fantasia in the National Arts Club" as one of the features in the issue. MC to KB, November 29 [1924], Burke Papers. Misunderstanding about the extent of Crane's alliance with the makers of *Aesthete 1925* further strained his friendship with Munson. When Crane was thought to have contributed to the issue a poem ridiculing Munson's recent interest in mysticism and mocking his pompous critical rhetoric—a poem actually written by Slater Brown—disagreement between both men rose to a peak, and Crane, much to his discomfort, found himself caught in the crossfire between two opposed literary groups. See Hart Crane to Gorham B. Munson, December 5, 1924, and December 8, 1924, in Weber, ed., *The Letters of Hart Crane*, pp. 195–97. See also Brom Weber to MC, September 2, 1948, and Brown, *Robber Rocks*, pp. 42–43.

61. MC to KB, January 15, 1924 [1925] (SC, p. 169); MC to KB, February "something," 1925 (SC, pp. 172–73).

62. Josephson, *Life Among the Surrealists*, p. 291; William Carlos Williams, "[Letter to Walter S. Hankel]," *Aesthete 1925* 1 (February 1925): 9–10. The "advertisement" for Mencken appeared on the inside back cover.

63. Allen Tate, "[Letter to Walter S. Hankel]," *Aesthete 1925*, pp. 10–11; "To Whom It May Concern," *Aesthete 1925*, p. 28; Matthew Josephson, "Dr. Boyd Looks at Literature," *Aesthete 1925*, pp. 29–31. Cowley also contributed a series of "meditations" on art and criticism supposedly written by Walter S. Hankel, including diatribes against "popular critics" and a plea for the immature and amateurish in criticism as more healthy and vital than a deadly "professional spirit." In a letter Tate objected that Hankel's observations failed to do justice to their author: he hoped it was not too late "to remove the stigma of mere aestheticism from Mr. Hankel's reputation" and to have him parade before the public in his true nature as "one of those rare spirits whose harmony of parts is most aptly described by the term Humanist." Allen Tate to MC, February 11, [1925].

64. William Slater Brown, "An Interplanetary Episode," *Aesthete 1925*, pp. 12–20; John Brooks Wheelwright, "Little Moments with Great Critics," *Aesthete 1925*, pp. 1–8; MC to KB, [December 1924]; KB to MC, December 19, 1924, Wheelwright Papers. Highest scored "academic critics, devoted to standards of morality and scholarship"; they were followed by the psychological and sociological critics (led by Van Wyck Brooks—"For the finding of sociological evidence, 98%. For the use of it as literary criticism, 0"); next came the editors and publicists, "inclined to the conservatism of compromise"; and, at the bottom, the impressionists and columnists: Heywood Broun, John Farrar, Burton Rascoe. Burke's hierarchy conspicuously omitted a formalist or aesthetic mode of criticism, implying that only the younger generation as represented in *Aesthete 1925* were writing criticism proper. The footnote by Walter S. Hankel appeared on page two of the issue. As Dickran Tashjian has pointed out, such analyzing as Burke's "looked forward to the academic orientation of the New Criticism and its opposition to impressionistic surveys of literature." *Skyscraper Primitives*, p. 141.

65. Kenneth Burke, "Dada, Dead or Alive," *Aesthete 1925*, pp. 23–26.

66. [Kenneth Burke], "French Letter," *Aesthete 1925*, p. 28.

67. William Carlos Williams to MC, [February 1925]; John Brooks Wheelwright to MC, February 16, 1925; MC to KB, February "something," 1925 (SC, p. 172).

68. Tashjian, *Skyscraper Primitives*, p. 142.

69. MC to KB, [December 1924]; ER, pp. 222–23; Brown, *Robber Rocks*, pp. 26–27; Harold Loeb, "Mid-Atlantic Letter," *This Quarter* 1 (1928): pp. 211–12; Weber, ed., *The Letters of Hart Crane*, p. 198; SF, pp. 195–96; "The Flower and the Leaf," BJCP, pp. 139–41.

70. Josephson, *Life Among the Surrealists*, pp. 289–91; MC to KB, November 29 [1924], Burke Papers.

71. MC to KB, December 6 [1924]; February "something," 1925; March 22 [1925].

72. KB to MC, January 14, 1925 (SC, p. 168); MC to KB, January 15, 1924 [1925] (SC, p. 169); February "something," 1925 (SC, pp. 172–73).

73. MC to KB, March 7 [1925] (partly in SC, pp. 173–74).

74. MC to KB, March 7 [1925]; WT, p. 91; ER, pp. 207–9.

75. "A Life in the 1920s," unpublished manuscript, pp. 2–3; *ER*, p. 210.
76. MC to KB, March 7 [1925]; March 22 [1925].

13. FREE LANCE, 1925–1927

1. Between 1925 and 1929 Cowley's poems appeared in, among others, *Poetry*, the *Little Review*, *transition*, the *Dial*, the *Nation*, and the *Hound & Horn*. For *Charm* he continued to write on an assortment of topics and books, while for *Brentano's Book Chat* he did a series of profiles of contemporary American writers. For the *New York Herald Tribune Books* he regularly reviewed French literature, while he continued to write, if less frequently, for the *Literary Review of the New York Evening Post* and Canby's *Saturday Review of Literature*. The *Dial* remained open for brief reviews and longer review-essays on modern European and American literature. In early 1928 Cowley began writing regularly for the *New Republic* under Edmund Wilson. His translations, meanwhile, appeared in the *Dial*, the *New York Herald Tribune Books*, and *Vanity Fair*.

2. Brown, *Robber Rocks*, pp. 27–30; Weber, ed., *The Letters of Hart Crane*, p. 212; *ER*, pp. 227–35; *SF*, pp. 198–200, 207–11.

3. MC to Matthew Josephson, August 12, 1925, Josephson Papers; Peggy Cowley to S. Foster Damon, [August 1925], Damon Papers.

4. "Beavers, Builders and Lakes," *Charm* 4 (August 1925): 14–17, 83, 90; "A Miscellany of Winter Books," ibid. (January 1926): 50; "A Few Novels Worth Keeping," ibid. (November 1925): 34, 64; "The Reviewer Cleans House," ibid. 7 (February 1927): 81. The latter review was Cowley's first consideration of Hemingway in print and contained his earliest analysis of Hemingway's style, a style that seemed "ridiculously simple," yet managed to convey "a complicated feeling of pity, sadness and passion." Cowley's discussion typically relied on empathy and personal experience to explain Hemingway's "hardboiled sentimentality."

5. "Mr. Moore's Golden Treasury," *New York Herald Tribune Books*, August 2, 1925, p. 5; Kenneth Burke, "Psychology and Form," *Dial* 79 (July 1925): 35, 42–43. Burke used the same quotation from Baudelaire to demonstrate the psychological workings of "form." Cowley's analysis, however, remained his own.

6. William Rose Benét to MC, April 16, 1947, Benét Papers. In 1944 Cowley translated Gide's *Imaginary Interviews*; a year later appeared *Aragon: Poet of the French Resistance*, edited by Hannah Josephson and Cowley, who translated a substantial number of Aragon's poems; Cowley also translated most of the essays in *Leonardo, Poe, Mallarmé*, the eighth volume in the collected works of Valéry published under the auspices of the Bollingen Foundation in 1972.

7. "Poets March in the Van," *New York Herald Tribune Books*, October 16, 1927, p. 4; "French Poetry and the New Spirit," *Saturday Review of Literature* 3 (May 7, 1927): 810; Marshall Best to MC, October 10, 1929.

8. "Grosse Margot's Lover," *New York Herald Tribune Books*, July 15, 1928, p. 3; "That Excellent Blackguard," ibid., September 9, 1928, p. 3; "Haloes for the Damned," ibid., May 9, 1926, p. 10; "Stendhal Complete," ibid., May 23, 1926, p. 12; "The Art

of Visible Things," *Dial* 82 (March 1927): 247–49; "A Messiah of the Skeptics," *New York Herald Tribune Books*, October 21, 1928, p. 7; "Untranslatable Genius," ibid., January 31, 1926, p. 19; "From 'Flowers of Evil' to the Super Realists," *Literary Review of the New York Evening Post* 7 (January 29, 1927): 1, 14; "The Apron-Strings of Vice," *New Republic* 53 (February 8, 1928): 328; "The Voyager of Dreams," *New York Herald Tribune Books*, February 10, 1929, p. 3; "The Victim of a Mask," ibid., April 13, 1930, p. 8; "Cocteau's First Novel," *Saturday Review of Literature* 2 (November 28, 1925): 335; "Lightning in a Mist," *New York Herald Tribune Books*, April 10, 1927, p. 2; "The Road of Excess," ibid., February 7, 1926, p. 17; "A Few Translations and Reprints," *Charm* 7 (March 1927): 39, 84, 87; "A Fourth Brontë," *New York Herald Tribune Books*, October 23, 1927, pp. 5–6; "The Caged Osprey," *New Republic* 55 (July 4, 1928): 179; "The Geographer of Love," *New York Herald Tribune Books*, December 4, 1927, pp. 6–7; "As If Written by Starlight," ibid., December 2, 1928, p. 4; "A Talented Subaltern," ibid., August 26, 1929, p. 4; "The Curse of Beauty," ibid., June 16, 1929, p. 4; "The Men of the Road," ibid., July 7, 1929, p. 4; "A Man of Letters," ibid., January 17, 1926, pp. 4–5; "The Coin of Greatness," ibid., September 25, 1927, pp. 1–2; "Albumblatt," ibid., October 20, 1929, pp. 5–6; "The Problems of André Gide," ibid., July 22, 1934, p. 4; "French Verse in English," ibid., April 25, 1926, p. 12.

9. Carl Sandburg to MC, May 18, 1926; MC to Sandburg, [1926], Sandburg Papers; "What is a Show Boat, Anyway?" *Charm* 6 (November 1926): 31; "Four Biographies and a Novel," ibid. (January 1927): 49.

10. "Marcel Proust's Unfinished Symphony," *New Republic* 81 (December 12, 1934): 139–40; "Cocteau's First Novel," *Saturday Review of Literature* 2 (November 28, 1925): 335; "Stendhal Complete," *New York Herald Tribune Books*, May 23, 1926, p. 12; "From 'Flowers of Evil' to the Super Realists," *Literary Review of the New York Evening Post* 7 (January 29, 1927): 1, 14; "French Poetry and the New Spirit," *Saturday Review of Literature* 3 (May 7, 1927): 810; "Grosse Margot's Lover," *New York Herald Tribune Books*, July 15, 1928, p. 3.

11. "A Man of Letters," *New York Herald Tribune Books*, January 17, 1926, pp. 4–5; "The Coin of Greatness," ibid., September 25, 1927, pp. 1–2; "Albumblatt," ibid., October 20, 1929, pp. 5–6. "During our own century," Cowley opened his 1927 review of *The Counterfeiters*, "the history of the novel has been distinguished by experiments of every conceivable sort. We have been given Freudian novels, Expressionist or Dada novels, stream-of-consciousness novels, lyric novels, super and infra-realistic novels. We have grown familiar with very strange techniques, some . . . borrowed from the cinema, others from machinery, and still others from the world of dreams. It seems that every writer has a new remedy, a patented pulmotor of his own, with which he guarantees to resuscitate the art of fiction. And the novelists themselves are at fault if we come to suspect, sometimes, that an art which requires so many doctors must be nearly on its deathbed."

12. "From 'Flowers of Evil' to the Super Realists," p. 1; "A Man of Letters," pp. 4–5. Eventually, Cowley followed Gide on the path toward communism. Just as, in the late 1920s, he admired Gide for his ability to harmonize the conflicting forces of tradition and experiment, morality and art, so in 1934, at the height of his political radicalism,

he could praise Gide for his ability to "take an interest in collective matters, to work for judicial reforms, for better treatment of African natives, then finally to proclaim his sympathy with Communism—and to do all this without damage to his literary work" and without surrendering his "fierce individualism." "The Problems of André Gide," *New York Herald Tribune Books*, July 22, 1934, p. 4.

13. "The Dark City," *Saturday Review of Literature* 1 (June 27, 1925): 851; "The Orange Moth," *Dial* 79 (December 1925): 507–9; "Some Interesting Biographies," *Charm* 4 (September 1925): 86. Cowley related the moral attitude of Aiken's characters to the form of the short story, which he defined in terms to which he would remain surprisingly faithful. "Ideally considered," he wrote in the *Dial* for December 1925, "the short story is a plot which contains four elements. There is a situation (or event); an emotion which the event calls forth; an idea crystallized from the emotion; finally an action." Compare Cowley's early formulation with his definition of the story as given in "A Defense of Storytelling," *WT*, p. 204: "A *person* (or group of persons) is involved in a *situation* and performs an *act* (or series of acts, or merely undergoes an experience) as a result of which *something is changed.*"

14. "Frankenstein; or, the Poetical Faculty," *New York Herald Tribune Books*, November 1, 1925, p. 10; "Two Anthologies," ibid., February 21, 1926, p. 6.

15. "Frankenstein; or, the Poetical Faculty," p. 10; "The Bridge of San Luis Rey," *New Republic* 53 (December 28, 1927): 173–74.

16. MC to S. Foster Damon, November 1, 1925, Damon Papers; *ER*, pp. 216–17; Josephson, *Life Among the Surrealists* (New York, 1962), pp. 300–303; Matthew Josephson to MC, August 2, 1925, and September 30, 1925; "Two Winters with Hart Crane," *Sewanee Review* 67 (Autumn 1959): 547–56; *SF*, pp. 200–204.

17. "Two Winters with Hart Crane," p. 550; *ER*, pp. 226–27; MC to S. Foster Damon, April 6, 1925, and November 1, 1925, Damon Papers.

18. Allen Tate to MC, October 20, 1925; "Churches Which Remember the Revolution," *Charm* 4 (December 1925): 12–17, 78; MC to KB, November 9, 1925; John Brooks Wheelwright to MC, November 7 [1925]; MC to Wheelwright, November 17, 1925, Wheelwright Papers.

19. MC to John Brooks Wheelwright, November 28, 1925, Wheelwright Papers; MC to James M. Kempf, April 20, 1975. Yaddo is the name of a mansion and estate in Saratoga Springs, New York, originally owned by the Trask family; it was endowed as a literary and artistic retreat in 1926 and still serves as a place of work and refuge for writers and artists. From the early 1930s on Cowley was a regular guest at Yaddo (part of *Exile's Return* was written there); later he served on its admissions committee and as a director. The League of American Writers, a loose organization of writers with radical sympathies, was founded at the American Writers' Congress in New York in 1935; its aim was to coordinate and further contributions American writers could make to a revolutionary solution of the crisis in capitalism. Cowley served on its executive committee; he resigned in 1940. The National Institute of Arts and Letters is an honorary society of writers, artists, and intellectuals. Cowley was elected in 1949 and served as its president from 1956 to 1959 and from 1962 to 1965. In 1964 he was elevated to its upper chamber, the American Academy of Arts and Letters, serving as its chan-

cellor from 1967 to 1976. The two bodies were later amalgamated into the American Academy and Institute of Arts and Letters.

20. MC to S. Foster Damon, November 18, 1925, and November 28, 1925, Damon Papers; MC to John Brooks Wheelwright, November 28, 1925, Wheelwright Papers.

21. Allen Tate to MC, [1925]; *SF*, pp. 201–2; *BJ*, p. 82; Hart Crane to MC, January 3, 1926, in *Robber Rocks*, p. 47.

22. Lowell Brentano to MC, December 28, 1925. In origin the *Book Chat* recalled the *Chap-Book* (1894–98), a magazine that also began as a house organ of Stone and Kimball, Chicago book publishers of Harvard extraction, but grew into a self-consciously avant-garde little magazine of the "purple" 1890s. Unlike its more illustrious predecessor, however, *Brentano's Book Chat* was never important or influential enough to earn a place in the literary annals of its time. For the *Chap-Book* see Larzer Ziff, *The American 1890s: Life and Times of a Lost Generation* (New York, 1966), pp. 134–38; MC to author, March 2, 1980.

23. Bellamy Partridge to MC, February 9, 1926, and April 2, 1926; MC to Joel Townsend Rogers, September 13, 1961; MC to Allen Tate, March 27, 1926, Tate Papers. By 1927 Cowley had grown tired of a hackwriting job that yielded pay but little honor, and turned over "The Tower of Babel" to the destitute Allen Tate. By May 1928 Tate, too, had reached the limits of his tolerance for such work and in turn passed on the column to another set of destitute friends, Susan and Slater Brown. Tate to MC, May 16, 1928, and May 23, 1928.

24. "Lost! A Lady. Found! An Artist," *Brentano's Book Chat* 5 (March–April 1926): 19–23; "Garçong! Garçong!" ibid. (May–June 1926): 24–29; "Eugene O'Neill, Writer of Synthetic Drama," ibid. (July–August 1926): 17–21; "The Real Jungle King," ibid. (September–October 1926): 17–21; "How to Interview Ring Lardner," ibid. (November–December 1926): 25–30; "Wowsers on the Run," ibid. 6 (January–February 1927): 30–33; "Edwin Arlington Robinson: The Person and the Poet," ibid. (March–April 1927): 24–28; "Decadent Spring," ibid. (May–June 1927): 37–41; "Nick Carter," ibid. (July–August 1927): 34–37; "Conrad Aiken: A Man of Letters," ibid. (September–October 1927): 29–32; "Smash Your Guitar!" ibid. (November–December 1927): 33–36; "On Giving Books," ibid. 7 (January–February 1928): 38–40; "The Hemingway Legend," ibid. (September–October 1928): 25–29; Bellamy Partridge to MC, January 27, 1925 [1926?].

25. MC to Charles Scribner's Sons, March 8, 1926, Scribner's Archives; MC to author, March 2, 1980; MC to KB, August 19 [1924].

26. *SF*, p. 248; Josephson, *Life Among the Surrealists*, pp. 303–4; MC to Charles Scribner's Sons, March 8, 1926. See also Maxwell Perkins to MC, May 11, 1926; MC to Perkins, May 14, 1926; Perkins to MC, May 17, 1926; May 19, 1926; MC to Perkins, May 22, 1926, all Scribner's Archives. Further details have been taken from Cowley's articles on the respective authors.

27. "The Hemingway Legend," pp. 25–29.

28. Willa Cather to MC, January 17 [1926]; William Beebe to MC, August 2, 1926; E. A. Robinson to MC, January 3, 1927, and March 7, 1927; Conrad Aiken to MC,

August 26, 1927, and September 12, 1927; MC to Bellamy Partridge, October 6, 1927. The book here tentatively outlined eventually became *After the Genteel Tradition*.

29. Introduction to Joseph Delteil, *Joan of Arc* (New York, 1926), pp. xiii–xix.

30. Josephson, "A Modern's Joan of Arc," *Saturday Review of Literature* 2 (June 19, 1926): 869; Harrison Smith, "A Poet's Joan," *New York Herald Tribune Books*, May 16, 1926, p. 7. Reviews also appeared in the *Dial*, the *New Republic*, the *Literary Review of the New York Evening Post*, the *New York Times Book Review*, *New York World*, *Boston Transcript*, and the *St. Louis Post Dispatch*. To Marianne Moore, Cowley had observed that the Delteil book, because it was "composed in the French vernacular . . . in a syntax as far from English as the Semitic or Turanian tongues," was "the most difficult problem in translation" he had yet encountered. MC to Moore, February 16, 1926, *Dial* Papers.

31. Ernest Boyd to MC, March 11, 1926; Hart Crane to MC, March 28, 1926, in *Robber Rocks*, p. 52; MC to Boyd, March 13, 1926; Boyd to MC, March 20, 1926. The subject of French satanism had been thoroughly researched by one of Cowley's professors at Montpellier, who had intended to present Baudelaire "in the new role of a reformer," but whose findings had remained unpublished at his death. MC to Marianne Moore, April 3, 1926, and Moore to MC, April 7, 1926, *Dial* Papers.

32. "The Voyager of Dreams," *New York Herald Tribune Books*, February 10, 1929, p. 3; see also "The Apron-Strings of Vice," *New Republic* 53 (February 8, 1928): 328, and "The Victim of a Mask," *New York Herald Tribune Books*, April 13, 1930, p. 8.

33. MC to Anna B. Davis [Personal Service Fund], [1925]; Edmund Wilson to MC, August 21, 1925; MC to Allen Tate, March 27, 1926, Tate Papers.

34. MC to Allen Tate, March 27, 1926, Tate Papers; Tate to MC, March 30, 1926.

35. MC to Harriet Monroe, June 3, 1926, *Poetry* Papers. For Cowley's description of the life of "summer people," see *ER*, 211–12.

36. Jane Heap, "Lost: A Renaissance," *Little Review* 12 (May 1929): 5–6; Jane Heap, "Dada," ibid. 8 (Spring 1922): 46; Jane Heap, "Exposé," ibid. (Spring 1922): 46–47; Jane Heap, "Comments: Aesthetes 1925," ibid. 11 (Spring 1925): 19; Jane Heap to MC, [late 1925], *Little Review* Papers; Matthew Josephson to MC, [early 1926?]; MC to Heap, October 24, 1925; November 1, 1925; December 27, 1925, *Little Review* Papers.

37. Jane Heap to Matthew Josephson, April 8, 1926, quoted in *Life Among the Surrealists*, p. 291; Matthew Josephson to MC, [early 1926?]; MC to Heap, April 26, 1926, *Little Review* Papers; MC to KB, April 16, 1926; MC to Jackson R. Bryer, February 5, 1964; *ER*, p. 225.

38. For John Riordan, see Paul Mariani, *William Carlos Williams: A New World Naked* (New York, 1981), pp. 248–51; MC to Allen Tate, March 27, 1926, Tate Papers; Tate to MC, April 28, 1926; "Notes on Contributors," *Little Review* 12 (Spring-Summer 1926): 1–2.

39. Josephson, "A Letter to My Friends," *Little Review* 6 (Spring–Summer 1926): 17–19. Josephson's admonitions to his former friends were rather prescient: as he noted in a footnote to his open letter, recent events had endowed his words with "an air

of prophecy"—by mid-1926 many of the surrealists had shifted their objectives from aesthetic subjectivism to political revolution, the majority turning "Bolshevist," a few others, Fascist.

40. "Anthology," *Little Review* 12 (Spring–Summer 1926): 33–36.

41. Eugene Jolas to MC, March 27, 1926; Maria Jolas to MC, September 9, 1926; MC to Hart Crane, October 8, 1926, in *Robber Rocks*, pp. 65–67; Eugene Jolas to MC, November 7, 1926; January 8, 1927.

42. Eugene Jolas to MC, January 8, 1927; Elliot Paul to MC, January 8, 1927; Dougald McMillan, *'transition': The History of a Literary Era, 1927–1938* (Amsterdam and London, 1975), p. 37; Eugene Jolas to MC, May 12, 1927; "The Hill above the Mine," *transition* 10 (January 1928): 90–91; "Race Between a Subway Local and a Subway Express," ibid. (January 1928): 51–54. Futurism was an early twentieth-century avant-gardist movement founded and named by the Italian poet and editor F. T. Marinetti (1876–1944) that called for a radical discarding of past traditions and the creation of new forms of expression exalting modern technology, speed, violence, and war. A forerunner of Dada and surrealism, it celebrated motion ("dynamic sensation"), glorified the machine, and preferred subjects like speeding automobiles, trains, racing cyclists, dancers, animals in motion. Marinetti exulted in the outbreak of World War I ("the only true hygiene of the world") and, later, saw in Fascism a natural extension of futurism. Unaware of the political implications of the futurist creed, Cowley had earlier shown himself sympathetic to its artistic aims when he advanced his plans for a new "school" in art in a 1920 letter to Burke: "Up to this time, practically all the motion expressed in art has been the motion of the object; the motion of the observer and its curious effects remain practically unwritten and unpainted. Also double motions and triple motions, as, for example, a subway express passing a local while the posts seem to stride backwards at a terrific rate. Or the unrolling of a landscape like a reel of film. Or the queer going sour of a sound as your train moves away from it. . . . We should have one or two poets, one or two prosateurs, a sculptor, a painter. And then hold an exhibit. The prose and poetry would be cast by the sculptor; for example a poem expressive of spiral motion would be engraved on a sort of circular staircase. . . . The sculpture would concern itself with moving trains, and perhaps we would even have a few pieces of real machinery. . . . Notice how well this new school would fit in with futurism and unanimism." MC to KB, June 9, 1920 (partly in *SC*, p. 73).

43. Harrison Smith to MC, April 29, 1926; MC to Lewis Galantière, May 7, 1926, Galantière Papers; MC to Paul Valéry, May 7, 1926.

44. Lewis Galantière to MC, May 17, 1926, and June 16, 1926. It is not unlikely that Valéry's acerbity was partly caused by his reading of the American translation, by J. H. Lewis, of "Note and Digression," part of his "Introduction to the Method of Leonardo da Vinci," the first installment of which appeared in the June 1926 *Dial* with the announcement that "the present translation is published by permission of Harcourt, Brace and Company who will shortly bring out a translation of the volume, *Variété*, in which this essay is included." Galantière, who had seen the *Dial* issue in Paris, denounced Lewis's rendering as one teeming with "inaccuracies" and thought it gave "evidence of bad translator-judgment" (at one point, indeed, Cowley discovered that

Lewis had spoken of Hercules's *"modi operandi"* where Valéry referred to his twelve "labors"). If this was the sort of treatment to be expected from an American translator, no wonder, then, that Valéry bristled. J. H. Lewis's translations appeared in *Dial* 80 (June 1926): 447–57, and *Dial* 81 (July 1926): 47–58.

45. MC to Hart Crane, October 8, 1926, in *Robber Rocks*, p. 65; MC to KB, September 1, 1926; MC to Lewis Galantière, September 12, 1926, Galantière Papers. Eventually Valéry informed Cowley through Julien P. Monod, his "minister of the quill," that he felt happy about the arrangements made for the translation of his book. Julien P. Monod to MC, November 1, 1927. Compare James R. Lawler, "Introduction" to *Paul Valéry: An Anthology*. Bollingen Series 15-A (Princeton, N.J., 1977), p. viii.

46. MC to Marianne Moore, April 16, 1926, *Dial* Papers; Allen Tate to MC, n.d.; Mark Van Doren to MC, October 20, 1926; Edmund Wilson to MC, November 17, 1926. See also Wilson to MC, November 27, 1926, in *Letters on Literature and Politics*, p. 139.

47. "Toward a Universal Man," *New Republic* 49 (December 8, 1926): 69–71. Reprinted as introduction to *Variety*, pp. v–xv.

48. MC to KB, July 26, 1926 (SC, pp. 176–77); Notebook 4, entry 85, pp. 76–77.

49. "Toward a Universal Man," pp. 70–71; Paul Valéry, *Variety*, pp. 181–82. In the 1920s, reading Valéry in the light of his own preoccupations, Cowley was perhaps overly inclined to project personal dilemmas onto his subject; as a result, his interpretation was slightly distorted. Mostly he seemed to overemphasize Valéry's intellectualism. If he justly presented Valéry as a "constructionist" in his essays, he did not fully acknowledge the extent to which Valéry's poetry exemplified a tension between intellectualism and a sensuous rootedness in this world. As T. S. Eliot (and the young Thornton Wilder) perceived more correctly, in his poetry Valéry aimed to reintegrate the ideals of symbolism into the classical tradition. Later, Cowley saw that for Valéry "inspiration" was fundamental; the crucial factor lay in "the conscious reworking of inspiration into an intellectual construction" (MC to KB, March 10, 1969 [SC, p. 366]). In his later writings Cowley was sharply skeptical about Valéry's striving for the "pure" and "detached" consciousness, which could only lead, Cowley believed, to the extrication of the human element from art. Likewise Cowley was increasingly critical of the extreme formalism that made Valéry a precursor of postmodern critical theorists like Gérard Genette. Predictably Cowley could muster little sympathy for a mode of criticism that abolished the author, saw the text as completely autonomous, and reduced literature to a self-referential mode of linguistic sport. For a later appreciation of Valéry and his influence, see Charles G. Whiting, *Paul Valéry* (London, 1978), especially pp. 46–65, 78–84, 110–18.

50. Symptomatic was the generous attention given Valéry in the pages of the *Dial* during 1925 and 1926. In March 1925 Paul Morand had announced the recent publication in France of a new edition of *Variété*; in his "Paris Letter" he had singled out "La Crise de l'Esprit" as "without doubt the most important essay which has appeared in Europe since the war." The June 1925 issue of the *Dial* contained Lewis Galantière's translation of "A Letter from Madame Emilie Teste" as well as a combined review-essay

by Edmund Wilson of a book on Valéry by Albert Thibaudet and the English edition of Valéry's *Le Serpent* containing T. S. Eliot's "A Brief Introduction to the Method of Paul Valéry." In December of that year Wilson discussed the symbolic significance of Paul Valéry's recent succession of Anatole France to the French Academy in the *New Republic*, a treatise later incorporated into *Axel's Castle*. In January 1926 the *Dial* published J. H. Lewis's translation of Valéry's "Pierre Louÿs," while in June and July it printed Lewis's faulty rendering of "Note and Digression." In late 1926 Edmund Wilson solicited several essays from the forthcoming *Variety* for advance publication in the *New Republic*. Paul Morand, "Paris Letter," *Dial* 78 (March 1925): 222–23; "A Letter from Madame Emilie Teste," ibid. (June 1925): 465–74; Edmund Wilson, "Paul Valéry," ibid. (June 1925): 492–97; Edmund Wilson, "Paul Valéry in the Academy," *New Republic* 45 (December 23, 1925): 134–35; J. H. Lewis's translations appeared in *Dial* 80 (January 1926): 43–46; ibid. (June 1926): 447–57; ibid. 81 (July 1926): 47–58; Edmund Wilson to MC, November 17, 1926; November 27, 1926, in *Letters on Literature and Politics*, p. 139.

51. Harrison Smith to MC, March 4, 1927.

52. Eugene Jolas to MC, May 12, 1927; Matthew Josephson, "Intellectual Comedy," *Saturday Review of Literature* 3 (April 16, 1927): 725–26; Lewis Galantière, "'Consciousness and X,'" *New York Herald Tribune Books*, March 20, 1927, pp. 5–6; C. P. Fadiman, "Essays by Paris's New Deity of Letters," *Literary Review of the New York Evening Post* 7 (March 12, 1927): 3, 11; Thornton Wilder, "Pride of Intellect," *Yale Review* 17 (October 1927): 178–80. See also [anon.], "Paul Valéry's Essays in an English Translation," *New York Times Book Review*, March 20, 1927, p. 5, and S. H., "Paul Valéry and Variety," *Boston Transcript*, April 27, 1927, p. 4. Other reviews appeared in *Outlook*, 146 (May 4, 1927): 28; *Living Age*, 332 (May 15, 1927): 747; *Independent* 118 (April 9, 1927): 400; *American Review of Reviews* 76 (July 1927): 107; Alyse Gregory, "A New Academician," *Dial* 83 (November 1927): 429–33; MC to Harrison Smith, December 2, 1926; MC to Marianne Moore, November 14, 1927, *Dial* Papers.

53. Lewis Galantière to Editor of "Books," April 1, 1928; Clifton Fadiman to MC, May 9, 1928; Edmund Wilson to MC, September 17, 1928, in *Letters on Literature and Politics*, p. 151; for Cowley's later strictures against Valéry, see *ER*, pp. 126–32; MC to John Crowe Ransom, June 22, 1956, *Kenyon Review* Papers; MC to George Lanning, October 1, 1964; October 13, 1964; October 31, 1964; Cowley's translations of Valéry appeared in *Kenyon Review* 19 (Summer 1957): 425–47 ("The Existence of Symbolism"), *Kenyon Review* 27 (Winter 1965): 94–112 ("I Sometimes Said to Stéphane Mallarmé . . ."), and *New Republic* 137 (March 3, 1958): 17–19 ("Leonardo da Vinci"); the extensive correspondence about the Bollingen translation between Jackson Matthews and MC is among the Cowley Papers; "Paul Valéry," *Atlantic Brief Lives*, edited by Louis Kronenberger (Boston, 1971), pp. 819–22. For Cowley's continuing fascination with Valéry, see also "What Are the Qualities That Make an Author Modern?" *New York Herald Tribune Book Review*, July 27, 1952, pp. 1, 10, and "Gide as Friend and Colleague," *Washington Post Book Week*, May 1, 1966, p. 2. Cowley's *Variety* (1927) retained a solid reputation through the decades. In 1949 James Laughlin

requested permission to include parts of it in a volume of Valéry's *Selected Writings* to be published by New Directions. In 1956 Harcourt, Brace and Company seriously considered reissuing the book in combination with *Variety 2*, translated by William Aspenwall Bradley, and asked Cowley to expand his original introduction to encompass both volumes; the gist of his essay, Cowley felt at the time, still had contemporary relevance after thirty years. As late as 1968 Kraus Reprints considered doing an offset of *Variety*. Both plans for reissuing the book were obviated by the Bollingen series in progress. James Laughlin to MC, November 25, 1949; MC to Margaret Marshall, June 21, 1956; MC to Jackson Matthews, June 25, 1956; MC to KB, November 9, 1968; October 4, 1964.

54. MC to Melvin B. Yoken, April 17, 1970; "Toward a Universal Man," p. 70; MC to KB, June 23, 1929; April 5, 1966. For all his aversion to abstraction, in the course of time Cowley, too, found himself moving closer to Valéry's fascination with the "process" of art: thus, in 1949, he observed in his journal: "Year by year the *problem of writing* an essay, book, poem, becomes more interesting to me, and the answer to the problem—that is to say the finished essay, book, poem—seems less important in itself." Notebook 5, n.s., entry for January 22 [1949].

55. MC to KB, April 5, 1966; MC to KB, July 26, 1926 (SC, p. 176); Hart Crane to MC and Peggy Cowley, July 29, 1926, in *Robber Rocks*, pp. 64–65.

56. The list needs annotation. In May 1926 Cowley had secured a commission from the *Saturday Evening Post* to write a series of five articles on the African slave trade; over the summer he had begun assembling materials for a book, "Traders in Darkness," and had actually reached an agreement with Harcourt, Brace and Company. The articles for the *Post* were never written, but his book on the slave trade thirty-six years later became *Black Cargoes: A History of the Atlantic Slave Trade* (1962), written in collaboration with Daniel P. Mannix. The biography of Baudelaire was never written, but Cowley had already decided on the title of his first book of poems, *Blue Juniata*, which slowly took shape over the next three years. The volume of "serious essays" was to include his articles on Racine, Proust, Gide, Valéry, as well as essays still to be written, including one variously entitled "We Romantics" or "In Defense of Romanticism." Though the book here projected suffered from a fatal lack of focus, in embryonic form it anticipated *Exile's Return*. The book of portraits was to contain the profiles, real and imaginary, he had written for *Broom*, the *Bookman*, and *Brentano's Book Chat*, in addition to a follow-up series—including studies of Anderson, Frank, Ernest Boyd, and, interestingly, the novelist Dawn Powell—about which he was negotiating with Edmund Wilson for publication in the *New Republic*. His projected novel, for the time being, was accorded relatively low priority. Notebook 4, pp. 98–104; Harrison Smith to MC, May 7, 1926; Edmund Wilson to MC, November 1, 1926; November 17, 1926.

57. See, for example, his review of the *Collected Poems of H. D.*, "Icy Fire," *New York Herald Tribune Books*, October 11, 1925, p. 5. The poetry of H. D., Cowley noted, seemed to reach out toward a paradoxical but possibly ideal synthesis, its "icy fire" combining the "cold" sobriety and "flawless" restraint of classicism with the subjective emotional intensity of romanticism.

58. "The Art of Visible Things," *Dial* 82 (March 1927): 247–49.

59. "Death of a Nobody," *New York Herald Tribune Books*, December 18, 1927, p. 5.

60. KB to MC, June 29, 1927, *Dial* Papers.

61. "The Golden House," *Dial* 83 (October 1927): 339–42.

62. In April 1926 Cowley submitted an early version, a consideration of Joseph T. Shipley's *Modern French Poetry: An Anthology*, to Robert Morss Lovett at the *New Republic*. Lovett rejected the article because Cowley, in unknowing conflict with the magazine's policy, had already done a different review of the book for Irita Van Doren, but he promised to "consider" an independent essay by Cowley on the subject. Cowley reworked the review into a full-length essay and resubmitted it to the *New Republic* in the fall, but this time met with Edmund Wilson's hesitation: "I like it, but . . . it's hard to get in a long literary essay which is not hung on some recent book, or, like the Valéry, on some particular brilliant writer." Lovett finally rejected the piece on the grounds that it was "a hard subject to handle for our particular constituency." Angry at the treatment his essay had received at the hands of Lovett and Wilson, Cowley submitted the piece to Marianne Moore of the *Dial*, but again it was rejected. Finally Canby accepted the essay. See Robert Morss Lovett to MC, April 28, 1926, May 10, 1926, and December 9, 1926; Edmund Wilson to MC, November 27, 1926, in *Letters on Literature and Politics*, p. 139; MC to Marianne Moore, October 4, 1926, and December 17, 1926, *Dial* Papers; Moore to MC, December 27, 1926, *Dial* Papers.

63. "French Poetry and the New Spirit," *Saturday Review of Literature* 3 (May 7, 1927): 810; *WT*, pp. 233–35. Cowley continued to use Baudelaire as a "touchstone" of modernism. See his "What Are the Qualities That Make an Author 'Modern'?" *New York Herald Tribune Book Review*, July 27, 1952, p. 1.

64. Allen Tate to MC, November 19, 1926. Tate had also touched upon the distinction between subject and vision in his foreword to Hart Crane's *White Buildings* (1926).

65. MC to Allen Tate, November 24, 1926, Tate Papers. Cowley appears to have slightly misread Tate's point about the "discrepancy" between vision and subject.

66. William Carlos Williams to MC, December 31 [1925]; February 3 [1926]; February 12 [1926]; MC to William Carlos Williams, January 3, 1925 [1926], Williams Papers. Williams's "Contact Collection" was presumably a venture of Contact Editions, the publishing firm of Robert McAlmon, named after *Contact*, the little magazine edited by Williams and McAlmon between 1920 and 1923. The collection was never published.

67. A copy of the circular and questionnaire are among the Cowley Papers; MC to Editors of "Books," n.d.

68. Edmund Wilson to Allen Tate, December 11, 1925, in *Letters on Literature and Politics*, p. 128; Allen Tate to MC, December 23 [1925]; Allen Tate to Donald Davidson, January 3, 1926, in *The Literary Correspondence of Donald Davidson and Allen Tate*, p. 156; Edmund Wilson to Tate, February 24, 1926, in *Letters on Literature and Politics*, p. 129; Tate to MC, May 24, 1927. Riding's *The Close Chaplet* appeared in 1926, as did Crane's *White Buildings*. Putnam's *Trinc* appeared in 1927, Tate's *Mr. Pope and Other Poems* in 1928.

69. MC to Harriet Monroe, April 27, 1926; May 22, 1926; June 3, 1926; October 3, 1926, all *Poetry* Papers. "Bones of a House" was an early title of "Blue Juniata," "Empty Barn, Dead Farm" of "Overbeck's Barn," "Bill George" of "Dan George," and "The Streets of Air" of "John Fenstermaker."

70. "Blue Juniata," *Poetry* 29 (November 1926): 61–71. When Ronald Levinson, who five years before had collaborated with Cowley on a satirical poem on H. G. Wells, saw the assembly in *Poetry*, he wrote: "I read with reverence your 'ghostly' epic of Pennsylvania. There is a nostalgic ache in whatever you write of that state. She gave you birth with groaning and travailing; you are, so to say, returning the compliment." Levinson to MC, November 2, 1926.

71. For the mood of despair underlying modernism, see Malcolm Bradbury and James McFarlane, eds., *Modernism* (1976), p. 26; T. S. Eliot, "*Ulysses*, Order, and Myth," *Dial* 75 (November 1923): 480–83. From Kenneth Burke's translation of *The Decline of the West*, installments of which had appeared in the *Dial* between November 1924 and January 1925, Cowley retained the overall impression that "the morphology of history is a conception with many virtues—of which truth may be one—but that Spengler, as soon as he gets down to specific examples, is the same sort of ass as Max Nordau. Spengler is a journalist when he speaks of contemporary events." MC to KB, [late 1924].

72. Allen Tate to MC, April 28, 1926; William Slater Brown to MC, [1926]; John Brooks Wheelwright to MC, [late 1929]. René Taupin detected the influence of Rimbaud's "Le Bateau Ivre" in the poem (as well as that of Laforgue, Tailhade, and Soupault in other poems) and quoted extensively from "Leander" in his *L'Influence du Symbolisme Français sur la Poésie Américaine de 1910 à 1920* (Paris, 1929), pp. 290–91. "Bon poète et critique de goût," Taupin observed, "[Cowley] possède les meilleurs qualités françaises et en particulier l'élégance d'esprit" ("A good poet and critic of taste, Cowley possesses the better French qualities, in particular the elegance of spirit"). "Leander" appeared in *Dial* 83 (September 1927): 199–200.

73. MC to Marianne Moore, [January 1927], and February 18, 1927, *Dial* Papers; MC to KB, February 22, 1927 (SC, pp. 178–79); KB to MC, February 24, 1927.

74. KB to MC, July 21, 1928 (SC, p. 180), and August 1, 1928, Burke Papers; MC to KB, July 24, 1928 (SC, p. 181).

75. MC to Allen Tate, May 7, 1927, Tate Papers; "Two Winters with Hart Crane," p. 550.

76. "Fisherman's Luck on Barnegat Bay," *Charm* 8 (September 1927): 13–15; MC to Lucie Taussig, August 21, 1927; Taussig to MC, October 6, 1927. The three articles actually written were "The Oldest Quaker Colony," *Charm* 8 (December 1927): 11–13, 83–84; "Our Last Royal Governor," ibid. 9 (February 1928): 18–20, 77–78; and "Last Veterans of the Revolution," ibid. (May 1928): 24–25, 76, 78.

77. MC to KB, July 31, 1927, *Dial* Papers; MC to Matthew Josephson, September 26, 1927, Josephson Papers; Barbusse's *Jesus*, translated by Solon Librescot and supervised by Cowley, appeared in late 1927.

78. *The American Caravan*, edited by Van Wyck Brooks, Paul Rosenfeld, Alfred

Kreymborg, and Lewis Mumford (New York, 1927), pp. ix–x; "Aspects of the American Scene," *Charm* 8 (November 1927): 30, 80.

79. MC to KB, April 26, 1926; "Biography," *The American Caravan*, pp. 52–58.

80. Allen Tate to MC, card postmarked August 30, 1927; MC to Allen Tate, August 30, 1927; Allen Tate to MC, September 2, 1927.

81. Notebook 3, financial record for October 1927, n.p.; Harriet Monroe, *A Poet's Life* (1938; rpt. New York, 1969), p. 334; MC to Harriet Monroe, June 28, 1928, *Poetry* Papers; Brown, *Robber Rocks*, p. 102; *WT*, p. 64; *ER*, p. 207.

82. Notebook 4, entry 77, pp. 46–50.

83. Notebook 5, entry 1, pp. 3–5. The entry, entitled "I Write Because . . ." is quoted in full in "The Fabulous Ostrich of Art," pp. 153–54.

84. Notebook 6, entry 77, p. 48; *ER*, p. 243; MC to Matthew Josephson, September 26, 1927, Josephson Papers; Josephson to MC, June 24, 1927; November 15, 1927; [late 1927].

14. TOWARD A CRITIQUE OF AMERICAN CULTURE, 1927–1929

1. T. S. Eliot, "From Poe to Valéry," in *To Criticize the Critic* (London, 1965), p. 27; Eric W. Carlson, ed., *The Recognition of Edgar Allan Poe: Selected Criticism Since 1829* (Ann Arbor, Michigan, 1966), p. ix.

2. "The French and Our New Poetry," *Literary Review of the New York Evening Post* 2 (May 6, 1922): 641; Notebook 1, entry 16, p. 13; Notebook 4, entry 80, p. 70; *SF*, p. 194. Later, in *The Bridge*, Crane incorporated a passage on Poe that questioned whether the contemporary artist, in the midst of a hostile consumerist environment, would be able to preserve his integrity in the face of death and disintegration. See "The Tunnel" section of *The Bridge* in *Collected Poems* (New York, 1933), pp. 51–52.

3. Allen Tate to MC, [1926]; Tate, "Our Cousin, Mr. Poe," *Collected Essays* (Denver, 1959), p. 458.

4. Edmund Wilson, "Poe at Home and Abroad," *New Republic* 49 (December 8, 1926): 77–80; Edmund Wilson to MC, November 27, 1926, in *Letters on Literature and Politics*, p. 129; Allen Tate to MC, [November 1926]; November 19, 1926. Herbert Croly, author of *The Promise of American Life* (1909), had founded the *New Republic* in 1914 as an organ of the younger progressive intellectuals.

5. Edmund Wilson to MC, January 6, 1927; Joseph Wood Krutch, "An End and a Beginning," *Saturday Review of Literature* 3 (January 8, 1927): 493–94.

6. MC to Marianne Moore, October 4, 1926; November 13, 1926; December 17, 1926; January 13, 1927; February 18, 1927, all *Dial* Papers. Frank P. Kellogg, secretary of state under Coolidge, for a while was favorably disposed to U.S. military intervention in Mexico, where President Calles, a devotee of the anti-capitalist ideals of the Mexican Revolution, had recently enacted legislation threatening American oil interests. The threat of war with Mexico, real enough in late 1926, was averted when on January 25, 1927, the U.S. Senate unanimously resolved that American differences with Mexico be settled by arbitration. By this time Kellogg, too, supported a peaceful

solution. In 1928 he negotiated the Kellogg-Briand Pact outlawing war as "an instrument of national policy." See John D. Hicks, *Republican Ascendancy, 1921–1933* (New York, 1960), pp. 151, 154–57.

7. "The Reviewer Cleans House," *Charm* 7 (February 1927): 33; "Edwin Arlington Robinson: The Person and the Poet," *Brentano's Book Chat* 6 (March–April 1927): 25.

8. Allen Tate to MC, September 2, 1927.

9. "Israfel," *Dial* 83 (August 1927): 168–71.

10. "The Edgar Allan Poe Tradition," *Outlook* 149 (July 25, 1928): 497.

11. Untitled and unpublished manuscript, n.d. Cowley had found the same idea in Valéry, who, in his masterly "Introduction to the Method of Leonardo Da Vinci" had written: "What critics call a *realization*, or a successful rendering, is really a problem of efficiency . . . in which the only factors are the nature of [an author's] materials and the mentality of the public. Edgar Allan Poe . . . has clearly established his appeal to the reader on the basis of psychology and probable effects." The quotation from Valéry is from *Variety*, p. 281.

12. "The Edgar Allan Poe Tradition," pp. 498–99, 511; *WT*, pp. 256–66.

13. *SF*, p. 63; "The Edgar Allan Poe Tradition," pp. 499, 511.

14. *MWH*, p. 251. The essay on Poe was seriously considered by Henry Dan Piper for inclusion in *A Many-Windowed House*, but was finally omitted for reasons of space. Henry Dan Piper to MC, March 4, 1969.

15. T. S. Eliot, "From Poe to Valéry," in *To Criticize the Critic*, pp. 27–42; Allen Tate's two essays on Poe were included in his *Collected Essays*, pp. 432–54, 455–71. Cowley himself continued to consider Poe as an important precursor of modern literature, if difficult to fit into the main current of American literature. Between 1941 and 1944, and again in 1952, he named his *New Republic* column of miscellaneous critical commentary after Poe's "Marginalia," and in the mid-1940s he wrote major essays on Hemingway and Faulkner in which he acknowledged their kinship with the "haunted and nocturnal" spirit of Poe (see Cowley's introductions to *The Portable Hemingway* and *The Portable Faulkner*). In late 1945 he again wrote on Poe for the *New Republic*, emphasizing that most appreciation of Poe in America was "of the wrong sort" and pointing up Poe's importance in the history of European and world literature: "He stands at the exact beginning of the doctrine of art for art's sake (or life for art's sake); he stands at the exact point of transition between the Gothic romance, set in a haunted German castle, and that modern type of story in which the terror, as Poe said, 'is not of Germany, but of the soul'; and he also stands at the exact point where Romantic poetry is transformed into Symbolist poetry." See "Aidgarpo," *New Republic* 113 (November 5, 1945): 610 (*FL*, p. 199). In 1949, the centennial year of Poe's death, Cowley spoke on Poe at the Grolier Club in New York, expanding and deepening his earlier analysis of Poe's influence on avant-garde writing, from French symbolism to Crane and Hemingway; it was one of several lectures delivered in the late 1940s exemplifying Cowley's continuing fascination with "the passage back and forth of literary ideas between France and the United States." Though he continued to regard Poe as primarily a "constructionist," by 1949 his early distrust of the role of the subconscious in literary creation had diminished and he could more readily acknowledge Poe's influence

on surrealism: his "real originality," Cowley then saw, lay in his combination of "the maximum of logic and intellection with a maximum use of subconscious material." See "Poe's Influence on Europe" and "Notes on a Literary Balance of Trade," unpublished lectures, 1949. Twenty years later, in 1969, he remarked to Burke that, *pace* Valéry's "anti-inspirationism," he had come to believe that the important factor about the use of dreams or the subconscious in writing was "the conscious reworking of inspiration into an intellectual construction." MC to KB, March 10, 1969 (SC, p. 366). Still later, when, as literary editor at Viking Press, he was working with enthusiasm on Gay Wilson Allen's life of Ralph Waldo Emerson, Cowley belatedly recognized that Poe's constructionist approach to poetry (and, with it, the entire line in American poetry extending from Poe to Eliot and Wallace Stevens) was counterbalanced by an "expressionist" tradition which originated with Emerson and ran through Whitman to Crane, the Beats, the Black Mountain poets, and the San Francisco poets. In opposition to Poe's "mechanistic" view of art as expressed in "The Philosophy of Composition" (1846) he then placed Emerson's "The Poet" (1844) as a magisterial if extreme statement of "the inspirational view of poetry," the belief that "poetry comes from the unconscious and that conscious form is secondary." MC to Gay Wilson Allen, February 7, 1978, and March 18, 1978, personal files of G. W. Allen. Emerson looms conspicuously in several of Cowley's later essays, notably those on Aiken, Cummings, Damon, and Wilder, as if in counterpoint to the haunting presence of Poe in his early writings.

16. Allen Tate to MC, May 23, 1928. The full version of Tate's 1928 *Outlook* essay on Emily Dickinson is included in his *Collected Essays* (Denver, 1959), pp. 197–213.

17. *MWH*, pp. 250–51; "The Haunted Castle," *New Republic* 56 (October 31, 1928): 300–301. If Cowley's tone here seems to imply an acknowledgment of the subconscious as a force in modern writing, in other articles he continued to lash out at critics who approached poetry "with Freud and a flourish," and who proceeded "from assumption to hypothesis, without ever finding a plausible basis in fact." As he remarked acerbically in a review of a new translation of Villon, he himself was "not endowed with the sort of second-sight which my contemporaries seem to acquire from reading one or two volumes of psycho-analysis." The popular tendency to "prove by numerology, psycho-analysis, hypnotism, and rather questionable scholarship that genius and inversion are only two sides of a coin" was a thesis to which he would not cease to object, he wrote to Irita Van Doren in the summer of 1928. "Gross Margot's Lover," *New York Herald Tribune Books*, July 15, 1928, p. 3; MC to Irita Van Doren, [late July 1928?].

18. For an example of Cowley's use of Shelley as a touchstone, see "Frankenstein; or, the Poetical Faculty," *New York Herald Tribune Books*, November 1, 1925, p. 10; for Cowley's 1961 observation on the proper critical stance, see *MWH*, pp. 248, 250; "Alastor," *Dial* 84 (June 1928): 475–78. Cowley attacked Munson's criticism, likewise, for being "judicial, hierarchic and discipular." He warned Munson against the danger "of being pedantic, of lacking both humility and humor and of becoming intolerant toward other systems of judgment than his own." See "A Theologian of Letters," *New York Herald Tribune Books*, September 1, 1929, p. 5; MC to Marianne Moore, April 11, 1928, *Dial* Papers.

19. MC to Marianne Moore, May 13, 1925, *Dial* Papers; MC to KB, July 26, 1926 (SC, p. 175); William Carlos Williams to Ezra Pound, August 11, 1928, in John C. Thirlwall, ed., *The Selected Letters of William Carlos Williams* (New York, 1957), p. 103. For the declining reputation of the *Dial*, see G. A. M. Janssens, *American Literary Review*, pp. 79–89. As Janssens has noted, "with the new editorial policy [after 1925] controversy was so completely banned from its pages that, apart from the *Dial* Awards, the magazine seemed to move in a vacuum, a world completely its own." "Hard-Boiled and Romantic," *New Republic* 60 (November 6, 1929): 326.

20. For Marianne Moore's editorship of the *Dial*, see Janssens, pp. 84–87, and Wasserstrom, *The Time of 'The Dial'*, pp. 115–22; Marianne Moore to MC, October 9, 1925; MC to Moore, October 12, 1927; October 27, 1927; March 23, 1928, all three *Dial* Papers; MC to KB, August 21, 1927.

21. Marianne Moore to MC, October 21, 1925; MC to Moore, April 3, 1926, *Dial* Papers; MC to KB, August 16, 1927; December 8, 1928; for Burke's position on the *Dial*, see Wasserstrom, *The Time of 'The Dial'*, pp. 125–29; Moore to MC, April 19, 1928; MC to KB, August 25, 1929.

22. "You know, do you not," she had written at one point, "that we are delighted to consider any work which you would offer? The submitted work of no one of our contributors is invariably published by us and it is with the utmost loyalty and respect that we suggest that work be offered rather than bespoken." Marianne Moore to MC, October 9, 1926, *Dial* Papers. Cowley's relations with Moore remained somewhat problematical. As an editor of the *New Republic* he was eager to have her represented in the book department but found her not politically astute enough to review on a regular basis. In 1936 he described her to Burke as "the very last of the Puritans," whose very conventionality had become "unconventional." MC to KB, Memorial Day [1936?]. Still Cowley remained on good terms with Moore professionally. In the early 1950s he closely cooperated with her on her translation of the fables of LaFontaine for Viking Press, painstakingly supervising and revising her work, so as to clarify the meaning of her idiosyncratic style and bring the renderings closer in spirit to the original French. In her foreword to *The Fables of LaFontaine* (New York, 1954), Moore acknowledged her indebtedness to Cowley for his services as "linguistic Seeing-Eye dog" of Viking Press. The extensive correspondence between Cowley and Moore pertaining to the LaFontaine translation and running from April 1952 to August 1954 is in the archives of the American Academy and Institute of Arts and Letters in New York.

23. Janssens, *American Literary Review*, p. 34; MC to William Wasserstrom, November 29, 1958. In the minds of many Malcolm Cowley remained associated with the *Dial*. In 1931, two years after its demise, rumors circulated in New York that James Sibley Watson was "backing" Cowley, Burke, and Josephson "on another Dial," so Lincoln Kirstein, editor of the *Hound & Horn*, intimated to Roger Sessions (Janssens, *American Literary Review*, p. 89). In 1946 Allan Dowling, a wealthy banker and amateur avant-garde poet, planned to apply a considerable part of his money to reviving the old *Dial* and turned to Cowley as his "first choice" for general editor. Cowley gave the proposal, which included a yearly salary of $10,000, serious thought, gauged the willingness to cooperate of friends like Burke, Tate, and Robert Penn Warren, but in the

end decided against accepting the editorship. In 1947 Dowling transferred his money to *Partisan Review*. It seems an ironic twist of literary history that Cowley's decision indirectly enabled the editors of *Partisan Review* to expand the influence of a magazine that had been bitterly hostile to Cowley's brand of radicalism in the late 1930s and was hardly friendly to him in later years. See Allan Dowling to MC, August 22, 1946; September 3, 1946; September 22, 1946; October 16, 1946; October 31, 1946; November 14, 1946. Also MC to Allen Tate, November 3, 1946, Tate Papers, and MC to Mary Mellon, October 5, 1946. Dowling's sponsorship of *Partisan Review* is announced in "Angel with a Red Beard," *Time* 49 (June 30, 1947): 64. Cowley's 1937 controversy with *Partisan Review* is reprinted in Jack Salzman and Barry Wallenstein, eds., *Years of Protest: A Collection of American Writings of the 1930s* (New York, 1967), pp. 297–307.

24. DGM, pp. 8–9; David Seideman, *'The New Republic': A Voice of Modern Liberalism* (New York, 1986), p. 95; "A Reminiscence: Edmund Wilson on *The New Republic*," *New Republic* 168 (July 1, 1972): 25.

25. Edmund Wilson to MC, October 17, 1927; MC to Wilson, October 20, 1927; Wilson Papers; Wilson to MC, October 26, 1927; MC to Wilson, November 2, 1927; January 7, 1928, both Wilson Papers.

26. Edmund Wilson to MC, March 26, 1928; April 13, 1928; April 27, 1928, all three in *Letters on Literature and Politics*, pp. 143–44; TBOU, p. 385; Henry Dan Piper, Introduction, TBOU, p. xiii; Wilson to MC, May 23, 1928.

27. "The Tall Men," *New Republic* 53 (February 15, 1928): 355; "Humbert Wolfe," ibid. (February 1, 1928): 304; "The Apron-Strings of Vice," ibid. (February 8, 1928): 328; "The Bridge of San Luis Rey," ibid. (December 28, 1927): 173–74; "Babbilogues," ibid. 54 (April 25, 1928): 302; "The Wild Body," ibid. (April 11, 1928): 253; "The Caged Osprey," ibid. 55 (July 4, 1928): 179; "The Chaos of English Grammar," ibid. (July 18, 1928): 232; "Junketing for Science," ibid. 54 (May 16, 1928): 393–94.

28. Edmund Wilson to MC, April 27, 1928, in *Letters on Literature and Politics*, p. 144; "Babbilogues," *New Republic* 54 (April 25, 1928): 302.

29. Edmund Wilson to MC, March 26, 1928, in *Letters on Literature and Politics*, p. 143; "Style and Fashion," *New Republic* 54 (April 18, 1928): 278.

30. "The Peasants of New York," *New Republic* 55 (June 6, 1928): 74–75.

31. Edmund Wilson to MC, May 23, 1928; "Dynamic Liberalism," *New Republic* 55 (July 11, 1928): 104.

32. Edmund Wilson to MC, March 26, 1928, in *Letters on Literature and Politics*, p. 144; "Portrait of a Publisher," *New Masses* 4 (January 1929): 5–6.

33. Bruce Bliven to Edmund Wilson, June 29, 1928; Edmund Wilson to MC, July 9, 1928.

34. Herbert Croly to MC, October 18, 1928; Bruce Bliven to MC, October 31, 1928. Croly's personal communication with Cowley was one of his last: shortly after, he suffered a stroke that forced him to abdicate from editorial responsibility; he withdrew to California, where he died in May 1930. See David Seideman, *'The New Republic': A Voice of Modern Liberalism*, p. 89.

35. Michael Gold to MC, [fall 1928].

36. MC to Authors' Guild, March 20, 1928; Ivan von Auw [Authors' Guild] to MC, March 28, 1928. Cowley's endeavor to attain professional recognition for translators was not an incidental one. Sixteen years later he conducted an acrimonious correspondence with, ironically, Alfred Knopf about his rendering of André Gide's *Imaginary Interviews* (1944)—a difficult job on which Cowley had spent more work than was justified by Knopf's meager remuneration of five hundred dollars—in which he sharply criticized the prestigious publisher's underestimation of the art of literary translation, and, in effect, was forced to reiterate the substance of his 1928 plea to the Authors' Guild: a sad reflection on the lack of improvement in the social and professional position of translators since the late 1920s. Twenty years later, in 1964, he responded with enthusiasm to a proposal of Lewis Galantière for the formation of "a group of literary translators" and promised to bring to bear his influence as president of the National Institute of Arts and Letters. MC to Alfred Knopf, August 12, 1944; Knopf to MC, August 16, 1944; August 21, 1944; MC to Lewis Galantière, November 16, 1964, Galantière Papers.

37. Jolas's proclamation is quoted in McMillan, *transition: The History of a Literary Era, 1927–1938*, p. 27.

38. Shi, *Matthew Josephson*, p. 115; "New York: 1928," *transition* 13 (Summer 1928): 83–104; Eugene Jolas, "Glossary," ibid. (Summer 1928): 271. The group manifestation, Josephson reported to Jolas, had been "executed against great odds." Proceeding in the manner of a court deposition, he declared that "although America suggests mass life primarily, individuals seem to be exasperated to greater egotism, and, unlike our Parisian friends, work with difficulty in a common cause; that all of the men contributing had taken a day off from their jobs; that some wanted to drink and make merry in hedonistic style rather than write; that some wouldn't come at all; that one man kept telephoning all day, etc. A great many *Meisterstuecke* were ferociously torn up after a day of intense excitement."

39. "Glossary," p. 271; "Tar Babies," in "New York: 1928," pp. 96–97.

40. ER, p. 217; Robert Coates, "Letter-Carrier," in "New York: 1928," pp. 90–93; Josephson's attack on Ford appears on p. 95; Will Bray, "Knights of Press-Agentry," pp. 88–89.

41. "Tablet" appears in "New York: 1928" on p. 85; it was reprinted as "Commemorative Bronze: 1928" in *BJCP*, p. 84.

42. "Seven Occasional Poems," in "New York: 1928," pp. 86–87.

43. Josephson, "Open Letter to Mr. Ezra Pound and the Other 'Exiles,'" pp. 98–102. *transition*'s program appeared in issue 16/17 (June 1929). It is quoted in *ER*, pp. 276–77. Eugene Jolas was disappointed in the group manifesto, which in his eyes fell barely short of a call for revolutionary social action. In an accompanying "glossary" he grudgingly admitted that the "critical categories" worked out in "New York: 1928" were to be accepted as "an important document of the new American spirit, although one may disagree with them." At heart, indeed, Jolas did not believe that "the poet's task [was] to use whatever force there is in him for the dissemination of subversive ideas," as he wrote in another place; "I regard it as a waste of time for the poet to let himself be deviated from his most important business—that of creating." In the following

issue of *transition* he probed further into the question of expatriation and conducted an "inquiry" among American expatriates into their reasons for living in Europe. Jolas, "Glossary," *transition* 13 (Summer 1928): 271; Jolas's response is quoted in McMillan, *transition: The History of a Literary Era*, pp. 43–44; "Why Do Americans Live in Europe?" *transition* 14 (Fall 1928): 97–119.

44. "Patriot and Expatriate," *New York Herald Tribune Books*, December 30, 1928, pp. 1, 4. Dostoyevski had preferred to speak, not of the Russian "soul," but of the Russian "God," a concept he defined as "the synthetic personality of the whole people, taken from its beginning to its end." Cowley himself had earlier found substantiation for a similar belief in the anthropological writings of Emile Durkheim, from whom he had derived the notion that "God is identical with society" and that "our only immortality is to become part of the race mind." Before long he would explain in similar terms the appeal of communism as a religion, but in 1928 he was content to note that it was only through "an act of religious faith performed while abroad" that Dostoyevski was able to solve the literary problem of expatriation and provincialism. Notebook 1, entry 68, pp. 50–51; for Cowley's explanation of the appeal of communism as a religion, see "Faith and the Future," in *Whose Revolution?*, edited by Irving Dewitt Talmadge (New York, 1941), 135–65. A shortened version is reprinted in *FL*, pp. 12–24. As Cowley confessed to Granville Hicks, his interpretation was partly indebted to Durkheim. MC to Hicks, July 11, 1941, Hicks Papers; *ER*, pp. 93, 95–96.

45. MC to Albert Boni, [1928]; Introduction to *Adventures of an African Slaver* (New York, 1928), pp. xvii, xxi. Trader Horn was the nickname of Alfred Aloysius Horn, a late-nineteenth-century British Ivory Coast trader whose reminiscences, edited by South African novelist Ethelreda Lewis, were published in 1927, with a foreword by John Galsworthy, as *The Ivory Coast in the Earlies*. The book went through eleven printings between July 1927 and February 1929. It was reissued in October 1930 as *Trader Horn*.

46. "Briefer Mention," *Dial* 75 (October 1928), 358; Harrison Smith, "Mr. Gunpowder," *New York Herald Tribune Books*, July 29, 1928, pp. 1–2; Harrison Smith to MC, July 27, 1928; for the contemporary interest in primitivism, see Frederick Hoffman, *The Twenties*, pp. 306–8; other reviews of *Adventures of an African Slaver* appeared in *Outlook* 149 (July 25, 1928): 513, and *Time* 12 (September 10, 1928): 46. The book did so well that Cowley felt justified in asking Albert Boni for an additional two hundred dollars. MC to Albert Boni, [1928]. In 1962 appeared *Black Cargoes*, written in collaboration with Daniel P. Mannix. Partly as a result of Cowley's resurrection of "Mr. Gunpowder" Mannix was able to point out that Canot's personal narrative had "been reprinted many times in many languages, besides providing material for scores of novels in which Canot is the villain or the hero." *Black Cargoes*, p. 235.

47. The novel, which appeared in late May 1928, painted a portrait of life in the international milieux of the East-European aristocracy on the eve of the war, as seen through the ironic, witty eyes of an intellectual girl raised in Paris, but, as most reviewers noted, it was less a novel of character than a hymn to the City of Light. Cowley's

rendering of the book, which received wide critical attention, was welcomed as, "for American readers, a perfect translation." Lewis Galantière spoke representative words of praise in the *Herald Tribune Books*: "I hope *Catherine-Paris* will be read widely, for it is the product of a fine analytical intelligence, an exquisite sensibility and a superior gift for the writing of delicately cadenced prose. As concerns this last, we owe our appreciation of it to Mr. Cowley, of course, from whom we have learned to look for irreproachable translations." Frances Lamont Robbins, "Aristocratic Authoress," *Outlook* 149 (June 20, 1928): 314; Lewis Galantière, "The True Little French Girl," *New York Herald Tribune Books*, May 20, 1928, p. 3.

48. Josephson, *Life Among the Surrealists*, p. 362; T. Wells [*Harper's*] to MC, September 14, 1928; MC to KB, postcard, August 18, 1928; MC to George Swetnam, October 22, 1968; "My Countryside, Then and Now: A Study in American Evolution," *Harper's Monthly Magazine* 158 (January 1929): 239–45.

49. "Hemingway's Wound—And Its Consequences for American Literature," *Georgia Review* 38 (Summer 1984): 233–34; for the persistence of Cowley's regionalism in the radical 1930s, see "Continental Highway," *New Republic* 66 (February 25, 1931): 34–37 (*TBOU*, pp. 14–15, reprints part of the article), "Homesteads, Inc.," *New Republic* 77 (November 15, 1933): 22–23 (*TBOU*, pp. 51–55), and "How Far Back to the Land," *New Republic* 75 (August 9, 1933), 336–39. As Lewis P. Simpson has pertinently suggested, Cowley's 1930s radicalism was in part an attempt to recover a Jeffersonian pastoral vision of America. Simpson, "Cowley's Odyssey: Literature and Faith in the Thirties," *Sewanee Review* 89 (Fall 1981): 527–28.

50. MC to Allen Tate, August 28, 1928, Tate Papers; Tate to MC, August 29, 1928.

51. Allen Tate to MC, April 25, 1929; MC to Tate, June 3, 1929, Tate Papers. Cowley thought the ideas expressed to Tate important enough to enter them into his notebook under the title "Letter to a Poet from Tennessee." Notebook 4, entry 90, pp. 84–85.

52. Allen Tate to MC, June 14, 1929; MC to Tate, December 15, 1930, Tate Papers. Contrary to his promise, Cowley did not write the review, so that, much to Tate's chagrin, *I'll Take My Stand* did not receive the critical attention it deserved in the *New Republic*. MC to Tate, August 28, 1931, Tate Papers; *DGM*, p. 199; for Cowley's views on Tate in 1936, see his review of Tate's *Reactionary Essays on Poetry and Ideas*, "A Game of Chess," *New Republic* 86 (April 29, 1936): 348–49. In the early 1930s Cowley paid several longer visits to the Tates in Tennessee, wrote part of *Exile's Return* at Cloverlands, and became friendly with many of the Southern Agrarians, including Andrew Lytle and Robert Penn Warren. As Warren emphasized in 1982, Cowley was one of the few radicalized New York liberals who actually came down south to seek out the Agrarians in their own den. In 1973, contemplating the decline of farming in his part of Connecticut, Cowley acknowledged, in a half-serious, half-mocking spirit, his kinship with Tate: "I'm an agrarian, a defeated agrarian. Except for the accident of being born in Pennsylvania, I too would be an anti-Slavery Southern Nationalist." *DGM*, pp. 192–206; interview with Robert Penn Warren, January 28, 1982; MC to Tate, August 29, 1973.

53. Josephson, *Life Among the Surrealists*, pp. 351–52. Josephson was doing other friends similar services and would be instrumental in publishing first novels by Robert Coates and Hamilton Basso, as well as *Flowering Judas*, by Katherine Anne Porter, the latter published through his mediation by Harcourt, Brace. Crane remained a source of solicitous concern for his friends, who commonly took his transgressions with a generous dose of humorous tolerance but were growing increasingly worried. Once, after a bibulous evening at the Browns', Cowley and Peggy woke up to find Crane lying face-down between them, embracing both. It was one of the less violent and more tender manifestations of the erratic behavior of a poet already irredeemably lost. *WT*, pp. 64–65.

54. MC to KB, July 24, 1928; Notebook 4, pt. 2, entry 85, pp. 76–78.

55. "Meditations on My Not Writing," Notebook 4, entry 77, p. 47; compare *SF*, p. 201.

56. Notebook 4, entry 79, pp. 51–56; *BJ*, pp. 104–5.

57. For the impact of the Sacco and Vanzetti affair on American writers, see Frederick Hoffman, *The Twenties*, pp. 400–408; Daniel Aaron, *Writers on the Left*, pp. 185–90; *ER*, pp. 218–21. A full account of the Sacco and Vanzetti case, as well as of the literary record of the affair, is given in Louis Joughin and Edmund M. Morgan, *The Legacy of Sacco and Vanzetti* (1948; rpt. Chicago, 1964), which includes a discussion of Cowley's views on the case as exemplified in *Exile's Return* and his poem "For St. Bartholomew's Day"; Josephson, *Life Among the Surrealists*, pp. 346–48; Shi, *Matthew Josephson*, p. 112. For Burke's response, see his letter to MC, August 23, 1927 (*SC*, p. 179).

58. Elinor Bulkin, "Malcolm Cowley: A Study of His Literary, Social, and Political Thought to 1940," Ph.D. dissertation, New York University, 1973, p. 60; Daniel Aaron, *Writers on the Left*, p. 189; "Echoes of a Crime," *New Republic* 84 (August 28, 1935): 79; MC to John Brooks Wheelwright, August 28, 1929, Wheelwright Papers; Matthew Josephson, "American Letter," *transition* 14 (Fall 1928): 57.

59. The Dreyfus affair, Cowley noted in his review, "came to a first climax on December 22, 1894, when Captain Alfred Dreyfus, of the French artillery, was convicted of having sold military secrets to the Germans, stripped of his rank, and condemned to solitary imprisonment for life in French Guyana. . . . His brother, in 1897, found proof that the list of military secrets, the famous *bordereau* on which Dreyfus had been convicted, was not in his handwriting. A senator got wind of the same information. Even the new chief of the Secret Service was convinced of Dreyfus's innocence, but this officer was almost immediately dispatched on a dangerous mission to Africa as punishment. Matters had reached such a point that it seemed necessary to keep Dreyfus on Devil's Island in order to preserve the prestige of the French General Staff." At this point, Cowley noted, Zola "took a superb step. In order to transfer the affair from a courtmartial to those civil courts where every piece of evidence could be openly discussed, he wrote and published his famous letter 'I Accuse'. In it, after reviewing the case, he charged the General Staff with deliberately convicting an innocent man— thus throwing himself open to prosecution for libel. He was tried in a civil court; the most famous novelist in Europe was sentenced to a year's imprisonment; his life was

threatened; his income nearly vanished; he had to flee the country; but it was the open discussion of evidence in Zola's trial that eventually brought Alfred Dreyfus back to Europe absolved of guilt. This was the masterpiece of the thin Zola."

60. "Excessive and Colossal," *New York Herald Tribune Books*, October 14, 1928, p. 3.

61. "A Messiah of the Skeptics," *New York Herald Tribune Books*, October 21, 1928, p. 7.

62. "A Messiah of the Skeptics," p. 7; "'Excessive and Colossal,'" p. 3; MC to KB, October 16, 1928; October 17, 1928 (SC, pp. 182–83).

63. Isidor Schneider to MC, [1928]; MC to Schneider, two undated letters [early 1929?], Schneider Papers; Cowley's financial arrangement with Loeb is registered in Notebook 3, account for November 1928; MC to KB, December 9, 1928.

64. In December 1928, reviewing his income through writing (including reviews, articles, translations, publisher's reports, and advances) over the past year, Cowley calculated that he had earned an average of $267.50 a month. Notebook 3; KB to MC, October 15, 1928, Burke Papers; MC to KB, October 17, 1928 (SC, p. 182); December 9, 1928; December 30, 1928 (SC, p. 183); April 10, 1929.

65. MC to KB, December 9, 1928. J. B. Watson was the author of the influential *Behaviorism* (1925). Notebook 1, entry 68, p. 51; MC to KB, December 30, 1928.

66. MC to Allen Tate, April 2, 1929, Tate Papers; MC to Edmund Wilson, February 13, 1929, Wilson Papers.

15. THE END OF A LITERARY APPRENTICESHIP, 1929–1930

1. MC to Allen Tate, April 2, 1929, Tate Papers; MC to Edmund Wilson, March 30, 1929, Wilson Papers.

2. Matthew Josephson to John Brooks Wheelwright, April 4, 1929, Wheelwright Papers; MC to S. Foster Damon, April 18, 1929, Damon Papers.

3. *ER*, p. 224; MC to KB, July 26, 1926 (SC, p. 176).

4. Details of Cowley's first meeting with Blume are taken from his "Peter Blume: Painting the Phoenix," *Virginia Quarterly Review* 61 (Summer 1985): 529–36. Blume's memory of his first meeting with Cowley differs at various points; he remembered, for instance, that Cowley was not alone on the occasion but came to Lee Chumley's accompanied by Nathan Asch and William Slater Brown. Interview with Peter Blume, January 31, 1982. See also "Malcolm & Muriel, Peter & Ebie: An Interview with the Cowleys and the Blumes," *Visionary Company* (Summer 1987), 30–31; MC to KB, [April 10, 1929?].

5. Interview with Peter Blume, January 31, 1982.

6. "He never sat for a portrait," Blume remembered, "but I had Malcolm definitely in mind, . . . not symbolically but actually." Cowley also was the model for the dummy in Blume's *Light of the World* (1932). After finishing *Parade*, Blume moved to Sherman, first to a one-time wooden chapel, which he converted to a studio, then to a little house on Church Road. In 1931 he married Grace Douglas Craton, a southern

girl nicknamed "Ebie," Cowley serving as best man. A year later Blume returned the service, being best man at the occasion of Cowley's second marriage, to Muriel Maurer, whom he had met through the Blumes. Later in the decade the Cowleys, at the Blumes' suggestion, bought an old barn across the street on Church Road, which they remodeled into the house they would live in for the rest of their lives. —*And I Worked at the Writer's Trade* (1978) is dedicated to Peter and Ebie Blume, "Neighbors and friends since always." For Cowley's reminiscenses and evaluation of Blume, see his "Peter Blume: Painting the Phoenix," *Virginia Quarterly Review* 66 (Summer 1985): 529–36. Quotations in the text are from this article and from "An Interview with Peter Blume" by Donald G. Parker and Warren Herendeen in *Visionary Company* 1 (Summer 1981): 56–76. See also the 1985 interview with the Cowleys and Blumes in the summer 1987 Cowley issue of *Visionary Company*, pp. 29–53.

7. Notebook 5, entry 93, p. 13. Blume would go on to become a modern painter of international renown. His second big painting, *South of Scranton*, won first prize at the 1934 Carnegie International Exhibition of Painting and Sculpture in Pittsburgh; it is on permanent display in the American wing of the Metropolitan Museum of Modern Art in New York. Many of his paintings, which include *The Eternal City* (1937), *The Rock* (1948), *Tasso's Oak* (1960), and *From the Metamorphoses* (1979), are owned by major American museums and private collections. Donald G. Parker and Warren Herendeen, "An Interview with Peter Blume," p. 56.

8. MC to KB, May 5, 1929; MC to KB, December 30, 1928; Fitzgerald is quoted in *SF*, p. 25; *SF*, p. 35; MC to KB, [April 10, 1929?]; May 5, 1929; May 8, 1929; May 15, 1929; June 23, 1929 (*SC*, p. 186); June 28, 1929.

9. MC to KB, August 25, 1929; May 23, 1929; July 9, 1929; *ER*, p. 243; MC to KB, September 30, 1929 (*SC*, p. 189); *DGM*, p. 12.

10. *The Green Parrot* received laudatory reviews in the *New York Times Book Review*, the *New Republic*, the *Outlook*, the *Saturday Review of Literature*, and the *New York Herald Tribune Books*. *The Count's Ball* was reviewed in *Bookman* and in the *Outlook*. George Stevens to MC, September 25, 1929; Cowley's correspondence with W. W. Norton about *Exile's Return* (1934) is in the Norton Archives at the Butler Library, Columbia University, New York.

11. Notebook 3, accounts for May 1928 through October 1928; MC to Edmund Wilson, January 7, 1928 [1929?], Wilson Papers; Cowley had contracted for the translation of *La Colline Inspirée* (*The Sacred Hill*) through Josephson, then at Macaulay's, as early as October 1927. MC to Matthew Josephson, September 26, 1927, Josephson Papers; Josephson to MC, November 25, 1927; [late 1927?].

12. "The New Books," *Saturday Review of Literature* 6 (January 4, 1930): 624. More representative was the praise Cowley's rendering received in the *Nation*: "Mr. Cowley not only translates idiomatically and accurately but he achieves the most difficult goal of all—the reproduction of the rhythm of the original, the quiet power of Barrès's clear but ladened prose." Florence Codman, "Prose in the Grand Manner," *Nation* 130 (January 8, 1930): 50. In his introduction Cowley gave his readers a glimpse of the trials and rewards of the translator's job: "During the long process of translating a novel, one lives in a state of dangerous intimacy with the author. One learns his thoughts

and half-thoughts, including a few that were never set down on paper; one adopts his mannerisms for the moment, and appreciates his virtues; but especially one comes to detest his literary vices. Sometimes an author may be pretentious, illogical or hasty without revealing these faults to the public, but he can scarcely conceal them from a man who is forced to analyze his work sentence by sentence before recasting it into another language. Few authors pass through this ordeal without suffering to a degree in the eyes of their translators. Maurice Barrès is one of the few, and the more one labours over his prose, the more one learns to respect his solid attainments" (p. vii).

13. "Introduction," *The Sacred Hill* (*La Colline Inspirée*) (New York, 1929), pp. vii–x. Cowley had repeatedly urged Burke to read *La Colline Inspirée*. On July 24, 1928 (SC, p. 181), he had described it as "an admirable novel, parts of which you [Burke] would have liked to write," and a year later, on June 23, 1929, had observed that from Barrès one could learn "how a man who is not a novelist can write a novel that is like a big chunk of lyric granite." Burke let himself be tempted to read the novel, but was disappointed for his own idiosyncratic reasons: "The book was a major disappointment to me," he wrote Cowley on October 3, 1929 (Burke Papers); "His comic relief is shameless, his concepts of rhetorical effectiveness are frequently hackneyed." In his review, too, Burke exemplified his particular concerns with Barrès's "rhetoric." See "The Eloquence of Barrès," *New York Herald Tribune Books*, November 10, 1929, p. 4. Other reviews worth considering, besides those in the *Nation* and the *Saturday Review of Literature*, are: [Anonymous], "Religious Fanaticism," *New York Times Book Review* (October 20, 1929), p. 7; A. C., "The Sacred Hill," *Boston Transcript*, November 9, 1929, p. 5. In addition to *Les Déracinés* and *La Colline Inspirée*, Cowley had earlier relished Barrès's *Du Sang, de la Volupté et de la Mort* (1893; "Of Blood, Lust, and Death") and *Un Jardin sur l'Oronte* (1922; "A Garden on the Oronte"), MC to KB, August 23, 1924.

14. MC to S. Foster Damon, April 18, 1929, Damon Papers; Crane's letter to the Schneiders is quoted in John Unterecker, *Voyager: A Life of Hart Crane* (New York, 1969), p. 561; WT, pp. 65–66; Unterecker, *Voyager*, p. 561.

15. Hart Crane to MC, October 24, 1928; November 20, 1928; December 1, 1928, in *Robber Rocks*, pp. 99–101; Gorham B. Munson to John Farrar, Memorandum, December 27, 1928.

16. WT, p. 67; MC to S. Foster Damon, April 18, 1929, Damon Papers; Harrison Smith to MC, July 27, 1928; MC to Harriet Monroe, January 29, 1929, *Poetry* Papers. In the same letter Cowley told Monroe how grateful he was to her and to *Poetry* for having helped to boost his confidence in his own poetry: "Nowhere else could I have seen enough of my poems printed together to think that they justified a book, and to feel what sort of book they would justify."

17. Harry Crosby (1898–1929), the son of a wealthy Boston banker and a cousin of J. P. Morgan, was a Harvard graduate and a volunteer ambulance driver during World War I who caused a scandal among the Back Bay high bourgeoisie by marrying a divorcée and throwing over the banking career eked out for him to become an expatriate poet in Paris in the 1920s. There he cultivated a life of feverish hedonism and established the Black Sun Press, which, beside his own poetry, published parts of Joyce's

"Work in Progress" (the later *Finnegans Wake*), poems by D. H. Lawrence, and, eventually, Hart Crane's *The Bridge*. Through the 1920s he kept a famous diary, *Shadows of the Sun* (published in installments by Black Sun Press between 1928 and 1930), containing the record of his pursuit of "sun-worship," a privatist cult of mystical and sexual ecstasy that culminated in a suicide pact with another woman upon his return to New York in December 1929. When Crane met Crosby in Paris in early 1929 the latter was already flirting with the thought of a supreme "Sun-Death" in his diary. Cowley met the Crosbys on December 7, 1929, a few days before Harry's suicide, at a party in New York thrown for them by Hart Crane. In *Exile's Return* Cowley took Crosby's life as exemplary of the extremes of isolation, frenzy, and madness to which the religion of art could drive an obsessive adherent, and—by default, for he had really wanted to write about the death of Hart Crane—made Crosby's suicide symbolic of the end of an era.

18. For Cowley's account of Crosby, see *ER*, pp. 246–88. For Crosby, see also Geoffrey Wolff, *Black Sun: The Brief Transit and Violent Eclipse of Harry Crosby* (New York, 1976). Harry Crosby, *Shadows of the Sun*, edited by Edward Germain (Santa Barbara, Calif., 1977), p. 234; Unterecker, *Voyager*, p. 580; Hart Crane to MC, February 4, 1929, in *Robber Rocks*, pp. 112–13.

19. MC to Harriet Monroe, January 29, 1929, *Poetry* Papers; *WT*, pp. 67–68; MC to Allen Tate, April 2, 1929, Tate Papers. Tate agreed to the wisdom of Cowley's changes: "Up to now we have all, to an extent, been duped by an excessive zeal for perfect writing. . . . Every book, prose or verse, should represent a mind at its fullest within the limits of the subject; and if our craft is too weak for this, the weakness should be exposed." Tate to MC, April 15, 1929. Cowley's emphasis on the book's unity was in line with the comments he had expressed in earlier reviews. In the *Dial* of May 1920 he had pleaded for a chronological arrangement of the poems of Siegfried Sassoon so as to reveal "the steady development of a mind" ("Against Nightingales," *Dial* 67 [May 1920]: 623). Five years later, advising S. Foster Damon about the structure of his book of poems, he had urged Damon to select his poems "from the point of view of one dominant mood, probably the mystical frenzy of your apocalyptic poems. Everything else could be arranged from its bearing on that one theme." (MC to S. Foster Damon, November 28, 1925, Damon Papers.) In early 1928, writing for the *New Republic*, he had praised Humbert Wolfe's feeling for structure and unity in terms which anticipated his own efforts with *Blue Juniata*: Wolfe, he observed, "has that rare degree of facility which enables him to draw the plans for a volume, to erect the framework, and then to write the poems which will serve as shingles, sash, and clapboarding. Thus his books . . . are really books of verse, and not mere anthologies of poems by the same author" ("Humbert Wolfe," *New Republic* 53 [February 1, 1928]: 304).

20. Unterecker, *Voyager*, pp. 596–97; Hart Crane to MC, July 3, 1929, in *Robber Rocks*, p. 114; *WT*, p. 68.

21. MC to Mr. Schlanger [Octagon Books], June 1, 1967; Allen Tate, "American Poetry Since 1920," *Bookman* 68 (January 1929): 507; Edmund Wilson to Allen Tate, March 21, 1929, in *Letters on Literature and Politics*, p. 162; Allen Tate, "A Regional Poet," *New Republic* 60 (August 28, 1929): 51–52. Both Tate's *Bookman* article and his *New Republic* review are reprinted in *The Poetry Reviews of Allen Tate, 1924–1944*,

edited with an introduction by Ashley Brown and Frances Neel Cheney (Baton Rouge and London, 1983), pp. 78–88, and 89–91. Cowley was pleased with Tate's review but acknowledged that he could only agree with Tate's "flattering judgment" in his "most sanguine moods." Earlier, he had admitted to the justness of Tate's strictures: "I have not a wide range of emotional or intellectual interests; I have a wide range of factual interests and a considerable intensity of emotion that I don't often manage to express." With typical self-deprecation he had added: "I think you exaggerate the quality of my craftsmanship. Certainly, in revising my poems, I found much that grieved me." From Paris Tate had replied: "I don't believe I exaggerate the quality of your craftsmanship. It is perfectly consistent of you to underestimate it." It was a "ticklish" business, he granted, to review books by friends, but "when the books are good, I think we are obligated to review them." MC to Allen Tate, September 9, 1929; April 2, 1929, Tate Papers; Tate to MC, April 15, 1929; September 20, 1929. Josephson, too, considered reviewing his friend's book a "dangerous and delightful prospect." He intended to review *Blue Juniata* for *transition*, but no such review appeared in its pages. Matthew Josephson to MC, July 31, 1929.

22. MC to KB, August 25, 1929; Kenneth Burke, "An Urn of Native Soil," *New York Herald Tribune Books*, August 18, 1929, p. 2; MC to John Brooks Wheelwright, August 28, 1929, Wheelwright Papers.

23. Harriet Monroe, "Man-Size Poems," *Poetry* 35 (October 1929): 45–49; Harriet Monroe to MC, September 4, 1929; MC to Monroe, September 9, 1929; October 17, 1929, *Poetry* Papers.

24. Louis Untermeyer to MC, July 14, 1929; July 22, 1929; Untermeyer, "Auspicious Debut," *Saturday Review of Literature* 6 (September 28, 1929): 178. Untermeyer promptly asked Cowley for permission to include several of his poems in a revised edition of his *Modern American Poetry—A Critical Anthology* (New York, 1930); it would contain "The Farm Died," "Mine No. 6," "Blue Juniata," and "Winter: Two Sonnets." Louis Untermeyer to MC, August 10, 1929.

25. John Chamberlain, "Modernism in Malcolm Cowley's Poems," *New York Times Book Review*, September 18, 1929, pp. 2, 10.

26. Edwin Seaver, "Cowley's Experiments Suggest Poe, Also Irving Berlin," *New York Evening Post*, August 17, 1929, p. 7; Horace Gregory, "Vital Contemporary Poetry," *New York Sun*, August 17, 1929; a clipping of the latter is among the Cowley Papers.

27. Ralph Cheney, "Labels and Libels," *Contemporary Verse* 25 (September 1929): 15; R. Ellsworth Larsson, "Mementoes," *Commonweal* (December 4, 1929): 150–51.

28. Morton Dauwen Zabel, "The Poems of Malcolm Cowley," *Nation* 129 (August 21, 1929): 200; MC to KB, May 8, 1929.

29. S. Foster Damon to MC, December 4, 1924. Damon voiced his enthusiasm about *Blue Juniata* to Cowley personally. He felt that, collectively, the poems seemed "stronger and more authentic than ever," but wondered what "the N.Y. logrollers" would do with it. He called for "another Amy Lowell" (she had died four years before, in 1925) who would "say what is good and what is bad, and punctuate inflations on both sides, and be a center for theorizing and attack! Since her death, American criti-

cism has collapsed; nobody seems to have any principles except 'I like' and 'They say.' " Damon to MC, July 6, 1929. In *Blue Juniata* Cowley, too, acknowledged his gratitude to Lowell for her "assistance and very practical advice" during the last six years of her life. *BJ*, p. 111.

30. In the summer issue of the *Hound & Horn* Blackmur printed three of Cowley's poems—"Kelly's Barroom," "Nocturne," and "The Rubber Plant"—which would shortly appear in *Blue Juniata*. In the same letter Blackmur made it clear that, with the recent demise of the *Dial*, he hoped to have "a first lien on all the material written for God by Kenneth Burke and yourself." Cowley responded guardedly; he distrusted the magazine's subtitle—"A Harvard Miscellany"—fearing it might be too exclusively hospitable to Harvard writers, but consented to appear in its pages and suggested that Blackmur broaden its boundaries by soliciting contributions from Josephson, Tate, Wilson, Putnam, Crane, and Cummings, most of them not Harvard-grown. By the fall of 1929 the *Hound & Horn* had itself become embarrassed by its subtitle, and dropped it. Shortly after, the *Hound & Horn* merged with the *Symposium* and Blackmur's position as managing editor was terminated. In November 1929 he informed Cowley that the proposed merger had not changed "the tentative arrangements" between the *Hound & Horn* and Cowley and Burke, but Cowley did not contribute any further poems (or articles) to the *Hound & Horn*, even though the projected unification of the two magazines fell through. By then he was too busy writing for the *New Republic* and was no longer dependent on other magazines for publication. R. P. Blackmur to MC, June 26, 1929, and November 12, 1929. For an account of the projected merger between the *Hound & Horn* and the *Symposium*, see Leonard Greenbaum, *The Hound & Horn: The History of a Literary Quarterly* (The Hague, 1966), pp. 44–46, and Janssens, *American Literary Review*, pp. 109, 148–50. Blackmur, who regarded himself as "being in the literary generation which is so to speak immaturely your own," remained sympathetic to Cowley. In his double review of Cowley's *Exile's Return* (1934) and T. S. Eliot's *After Strange Gods* (1934), he aligned himself, subtly and not uncritically, with Cowley rather than Eliot. See his chapter "The Dangers of Authorship" in *The Double Agent: Essays in Craft and Elucidation* (1935; Gloucester, Mass., 1962), pp. 172–83. Cowley lost much of his sympathy for the *Hound & Horn* when he adopted a near-Marxian viewpoint in the 1930s. See "Midsummer Medley," *New Republic* 80 (August 15, 1934): 24–25.

31. Greenbaum, *The Hound & Horn*, p. 162; Yvor Winters to MC, September 11, 1929; Yvor Winters, "The Poetry of Malcolm Cowley," *Hound & Horn* 3 (October–December 1929): 111–13; MC to KB, May 8, 1929. Other reviews of *Blue Juniata* appeared in *Outlook* 152 (August 21, 1929): 671; *Symposium* 1 (January 1930), 135–38; *Virginia Quarterly Review* (1930): 151–60. The latter two were omnibus reviews of recent poetry.

32. Yvor Winters to MC, August 13, 1929; Conrad Aiken to MC, May 23 [1929]; July 25, 1929. In 1952, recalling Aiken's harsh comments on *Blue Juniata*, Cowley observed: "I am conceited or humble enough to think that Conrad was wrong in this instance. The poems were me, or as much of me as I was then capable of putting on paper. For all my talk about technique I wrote—always emotionally, often awkwardly—

those poems only that forced me to write them, and that was a bad habit I should have learned to overcome." "Biography with Letters," *Wake* 11 (Summer 1952): 29.

33. In a 1927 letter Aiken had explained his aesthetic credo to Cowley in terms that seemed to reach for a synthesis between "expressionist" and "constructionist" art: "I can't feel any aesthetic or moral error in the casting of an autobiographical theme into the third person; in fact I believe it is possible to be more *detachedly* honest in this form (if you insist on honesty as a prime criterion) than in straight confession. At all events, I am much interested in *this* form—the autobiographical turned novel, given shape and distance. And it seemed to me a useful thing to do, at this point in my life: I mean, to give myself *away*, for the benefit of any stray psychologist of literature who might be interested in diagnosing the case of the author of Forslin, et al. And incidentally, to twist the thing into a design of its own, to make it stand on its own legs as an organism." Conrad Aiken to MC, August 26, 1927.

34. MC to KB, May 23, 1929; Notebook 4, pt. 2, entry 86, pp. 79–80.

35. "The Dry Season," *BJCP*, p. 90; The fifth section, "The Dry Season," of *Blue Juniata: Collected Poems* (1968) is prefaced by a prose note that reads in part: "By 1930 or thereabouts we were men on the threshold of middle age, each with a household to support. We had ceased to be a generation of friends inscribing poems to one another, and of sometimes bitter rivals united by their distrust of older persons; instead we were busy with our separate jobs. . . . It was exciting to have a share in the business of the world, perhaps in shaping its future, but some of us came to feel that we were not dealing with persons any longer; there was no time for that. More and more we dealt with categories and convenient abstractions. . . . From those years I remember looking for simple emotions that would, at any cost, reassure me that I lived. There was not much time for writing poems, less even than for truly personal relations, but I tried to say in all simplicity that black is black, that love is good, and that home is something you can never go back to. What I feared most and sometimes detected was a dryness of the heart." *BJCP*, p. 88.

36. MC to Allen Tate, September 9, 1929, Tate Papers; MC to Walter Snow, August 27, 1971.

37. MC to Edmund Wilson, February 13, 1929, Wilson Papers; *BJ*, pp. 33–34, 49–50; *ER*, p. 214.

38. MC to KB, May 16, 1929; June 11, 1929; June 23, 1929; July 9, 1929; July 11, 1929; MC to Edmund Wilson, July 17, 1929, Wilson Papers.

39. MC to KB, August 25, 1929; MC to John Brooks Wheelwright, August 28, 1929, Wheelwright Papers. In his notebook he registered his doubts about the value of a career in which he had written enough articles to fill three or four volumes, without having the substance of a book. Notebook 5, entry 94, pp. 13–15, reprinted in "The Fabulous Ostrich of Art," pp. 155–56.

40. MC to KB, June 23, 1929 (SC, p. 186).

41. Tate, "American Poetry Since 1920," *Bookman* 68 (January 1929): 503–8; Burke, "A Decade of American Fiction," *Bookman* 69 (August 1929): 561–67; Munson, "The Young Critics of the Nineteen-Twenties," *Bookman* 70 (December 1929): 369–73. The widespread feeling that an era in literary history was ending did not only induce a mood

of literary stocktaking but also led several of the dominant literary magazines of the 1920s to suspend publication, most notably the *Dial* and the *Little Review*. See, in this light, Jane Heap, "Lost, A Renaissance," *Little Review* 12 (May 1929): 5–6.

42. When Henry Dan Piper collected Cowley's articles and reviews of the 1930s in *Think Back On Us . . .* (1967), he naturally divided the book into two parts, "The Literary Record" and "The Social Record"; "Four Books About Ourselves," *Charm* 5 (June 1926): 33.

43. See *ER*, pp. 4–7, 18–23; "Our Own Generation," *New York Herald Tribune Books*, June 23, 1929, pp. 1, 6.

44. Notebook 4, pt. 2, entry 88, pp. 82–83.

45. Notebook 7, entry 85a, pp. 12–14.

46. Cowley named the following works as marked by the "new primitive" element in contemporary writing: Cummings's *The Enormous Room*, *Him*, and *VI Poems*; *Orient Express* by Dos Passos; *The Sun Also Rises* and *in our time* by Hemingway; *The Office* by Nathan Asch; *Nothing Is Sacred* by Josephine Herbst; and *Engagement* by John Herrmann.

47. Before long Cowley urged American writers at large to abandon the portrayal of man's inner world in favor of the outer world. "If one reads very many of the 'Freudian' novels which have been published during the last ten years," Cowley observed in his 1929 essay, "one is forced to conclude that the subconscious is gray and formless; that one man's subconscious too often resembles another's." His observations anticipate his later distrust of such devices of "the Art Novel" as the "interior monologue." In his speech before the 1935 American Writers' Congress he observed that "the inner world which [the device of the interior monologue] was supposed to illuminate was really not very interesting, not very fresh. The inner world of one middle-class novelist was very much like the inner world of another middle-class novelist. And the liberating effect of the revolutionary movement has been to carry the interest of novelists outside of themselves, into the violent contrasts and struggles of the outer world." *TBOU*, p. 90.

48. "The New Primitives," *New York Herald Tribune Books*, June 30, 1929, pp. 1, 6.

49. *SF*, pp. 31–32.

50. *SF*, p. 16. The distrust, Cowley wrote in *A Second Flowering* (p. 17), "also helped to shape the prose style of a generation which, as a rule, preferred the colloquial tone even in critical essays." Cowley named the example of Edmund Wilson, but the observation seems equally pertinent, if not more so, to his own critical practice. Interestingly enough, Kenneth Burke's stylistic propensity was diametrically opposite to Cowley's (or Hemingway's): from the very first he seemed bent on developing a language and a critical idiom so uniquely and subjectively his own that certain of his critics have come to feel that Burke was, in effect, increasingly enveloping himself in a solipsistic linguistic universe (See Grant Webster, *The Republic of Letters: A History of Postwar American Literary Opinion* [Baltimore and London, 1979], pp. 174–75). On October 3, 1929, having read Cowley's essay-review of *A Farewell to Arms* and recognizing its pertinency to his friend's own stylistics, Burke commented in a letter: "I do not have so strongly as you the test of naturalness in writing—for it leads too inexorably to Hemingway, whom I hate as though sent upon the earth to hate him. . . .

There is no particular virtue attached to naturalness, except where it is a hit, where the naturalness is exceptional in its enlightenment." KB to MC, October 3, 1929 (SC, p. 190).

51. "Not Yet Demobilized," *New York Herald Tribune Books*, October 6, 1929, pp. 1, 6. Robert O. Stephens, ed., *Ernest Hemingway: The Critical Reception* (New York, 1977) reprints extracts dealing specifically with *A Farewell to Arms*, but omits the crucial middle section which became "Ambulance Service" (*ER*, pp. 36–47).

52. *ER*, p. 144; Notebook 5, pp. 21–22; ibid., "Judgment by Effect," p. 20; "Winter: Two Sonnets" and "The Streets of Air," *BJ*, pp. 102–3, 108; Notebook 7, entry 82, p. 3; Notebook 6, entry 4, p. 9; ibid., entry 9, p. 14.

53. "The Literary Business," *New Republic* 59 (July 3, 1929), 172–74. As early as August 15, 1930, Cowley observed to Tate: "I take the New Republic view of anti-industrialism, and believe that we can no more defeat present tendencies than we can make water run uphill—we can merely deflect them." MC to Allen Tate, August 15, 1930, Tate Papers.

54. "Machine-Made America," *New York Herald Tribune Books*, November 3, 1929, pp. 1, 6.

55. "The Escape from America," *New York Herald Tribune Books*, November 10, 1929, pp. 1, 6.

56. *WT*, pp. 92, 97; Lewis P. Simpson, "Malcolm Cowley and the American Writer," *Sewanee Review* 84 (April–June 1976): 225; "The Battle over Ezra Pound," *New Republic* 121 (October 3, 1949): p. 20 (*FL*, p. 106).

57. "The Business of Being A Poet," *New York Herald Tribune Books*, November 17, 1929, pp. 1, 6. In *Our Singing Strength*, Kreymborg singled out Cowley as the most "significant" among the poets brought forth by Harvard, and commented that it was "nothing less than exasperating" that Cowley wrote "only on rare occasions." *Our Singing Strength: An Outline of American Poetry, 1620–1930* (New York, 1929), p. 583.

58. Notebook 6, pp. 30–32.

59. For a discussion of the New Humanism, see Hoffman, *The Twenties*, pp. 165–72, and, in particular, J. David Hoeveler, Jr., *The New Humanism. A Critique of Modern America, 1900–1940* (Charlottesville, Va., 1977), pp. 81–106.

60. Norman Foerster, "Preface," *Humanism and America: Essays on the Outlook of Modern Civilization* (New York, 1930), pp. xi, xiii; "Wanted: A Humanist Master-piece," *New Republic* 26 (March 26, 1930): 153; "Correspondence," ibid. (April 16, 1930): 247–48; "Humanizing Society," in C. Hartley Grattan, ed., *The Critique of Humanism: A Symposium* (New York, 1930), pp. 79–81.

61. C. Hartley Grattan to MC, January 27 [1930]; [early February 1930?]. Grattan had written a critical biography of Ambrose Bierce, a book on Australian literature, and a political and economic study entitled *Why We Fought* (1929). Cowley's contribution was entitled "Humanizing Society." It appeared in a shorter version in the *New Republic* of April 9, 1930, as "Angry Professors." The version reprinted in *TBOU*, pp. 3–13, omits the crucial sixth section of the symposium essay, which it replaces by section 5, which did not appear in the *New Republic* version.

62. The *Bookman* was soon transformed into the *American Review*, which would

come under fire as a reactionary, fascist, and racist periodical; Notebook 6, "Humanism," pp. 18–19.

63. See also Hoeveler, *New Humanism*, p. 131.

64. *ER*, p. 34.

65. Notebook 6, "Humanism," p. 26.

66. Notebook 6, "Humanism," p. 24.

67. "Angry Professors," *New Republic* 62 (April 9, 1930): 207–11; "Humanizing Society," in *The Critique of Humanism*, pp. 63–84. For an earlier notebook version of the extended quoted passage, drafted in late 1929 or early 1930, see "The Fabulous Ostrich of Art," pp. 158–59.

68. *DGM*, p. 12; MC to John Brooks Wheelwright, November 17, 1925, Wheelwright Papers; MC to KB, August 8, 1930; *ER*, p. 160; Notebook 4, pt. 2, entry 88, p. 83.

EPILOGUE: MALCOLM COWLEY, MAN OF LETTERS

1. *FCF*, p. 172.

2. R. P. Blackmur, "The Dangers of Authorship," in *The Double Agent: Essays in Craft and Elucidation*, p. 172. Blackmur's essay originally appeared in *Hound & Horn* 7 (July–September 1934): 719–26.

3. Lewis P. Simpson, "The Decorum of the Writer," *Sewanee Review* 86 (Fall 1978): 569.

4. Compare John W. Aldridge, "Malcolm Cowley at Eighty," *Michigan Quarterly Review* 18 (Summer 1980): 486.

5. For Wilson's reviews, see *The Shores of Light: A Literary Chronicle of the Twenties and Thirties* (New York, 1952).

6. "A Reminiscence: Edmund Wilson on *The New Republic*," *New Republic* 167 (July 1, 1972): 25–28. Parts of the article were incorporated in the final chapter of *SF*, pp. 236, 241–42.

7. Henry Dan Piper to MC, March 4, 1969; *DGM*, p. 12. For Cowley and Wilson, also see Leonard Kriegel, "Art and the Book Reviewer," *Nation* 204 (June 5, 1967): 732.

8. Of the major works of the lost generation published in the 1920s, Cowley reviewed at length only *The White Oxen* and *A Farewell to Arms*, though he wrote extensively about the writers of his age group in other ways. His first serious consideration of Crane came in 1930 ("A Preface to Hart Crane," *New Republic* 62 [April 23, 1930]: 276–77); of Cummings and Dos Passos in 1932 ("The Last of Lyric Poets," ibid. 69 [January 27, 1932]: 299–300, and "The Poet and the World," ibid. 70 [April 27, 1932]: 303–5); of Fitzgerald in 1934 ("Breakdown," ibid. 79 [June 6, 1934]: 105–6); of Wolfe and Faulkner in 1935 ("The Forty Days of Thomas Wolfe," ibid. 82 [March 20, 1935]: 163–64, and "Voodoo Dance," ibid. [April 10, 1935]: 254–55).

9. "A Reminiscence: Edmund Wilson on *The New Republic*," p. 25; *SF*, p. 242. The phrase "Ishmael of his generation" is Robert E. Spiller's in *Milestones in American*

Literary History (Westport, Conn., 1977), p. 41. Just as in 1928 Cowley defended Poe against the critical "jackals," so fifty years later he spoke up on behalf of Hemingway in "Mr. Papa and the Parricides," *WT*, pp. 21–34.

10. Cowley's correspondence with W. W. Norton is at the Butler Library, Columbia University, New York. MC to Warren I. Susman, March 8, 1965; CMC p. 171. Evan Biddle Shipman (1904–1957) was the author of a book of poems, *Mazeppa*, and a novel about horse racing, *Free for All*. He had first met Hemingway in Paris in October 1925, when Shipman was serving as European correspondent for the *American Horse Breeder*. Hemingway dedicated *Men Without Women* (1927) to Shipman. For Hemingway's reminiscences of Shipman, see *A Moveable Feast* (New York, 1964), pp. 131–40. It was probably Josephson, also an acquaintance of Shipman's, who brought the poet and horse-trotting columnist to Yaddo in 1931. For Josephson's reminiscences, see his "Evan Shipman: Poet and Horseplayer," *Southern Review* n.s., 9 (Fall 1973): 828–56.

11. For fuller bibliographical information concerning these and subsequent previous publications of parts of *Exile's Return*, see Eisenberg, *Malcolm Cowley*, pp. 109–14. The third article in the series, Cowley's account of the Munson-Josephson fisticuffs in Woodstock, N.Y., in the fall of 1923, caused a brief but intense flare-up of all the old animosities between Cowley and Munson. Cowley's "Exile's Return III: Coffee and Pistols for Two," *New Republic* 68 (October 21, 1931): 259–62, contained a spiteful caricature of Munson's literary character and his role in the founding of *Secession* in which Cowley let himself be carried away by the self-satirical, trivializing mood of his retrospective evaluations. It was much toned down in *Exile's Return* (1934), possibly as a result of a polemical debate Cowley and Munson conducted over *Secession's* past in the pages of *Sewanee Review* and *Contempo* during the winter of 1931–1932. Munson attacked Cowley's "extravagant fiction" in "Questions for Cowley," *Contempo* 1 (December 15, 1931): 1, 4. Cowley defended his account of the "ludicrous and dead" quarrels of the past in "Munsoniana," *Contempo* 1 (January 1, 1932): 1, 4. Munson, in turn, answered Cowley's attempt to "hoodwink" his readers in a later issue of *Contempo*, and in "The Fledgling Years, 1916–1924," *Sewanee Review* 40 (January 1932): 24–54, presented his own version of events, in which he retaliated with an even more extravagantly spiteful portrait of Cowley that did not have the excuse of deliberate caricature. In a later version of the article, "A Comedy of Exiles," *Literary Review* 12 (1968): 41–75 (reprinted in *The Awakening Twenties* [1985], pp. 157–88), Munson, too, toned down his original attack. In the summer of 1932 Samuel Putnam challenged Cowley's contention that he and his friends had brought Dada to America and presented the anecdote of the urinating incident in Cowley's studio at Giverny (as told to him by Louis Aragon) as "the Secessionists' culminating achievement." Samuel Putnam, "If Dada Comes to America," *Contempo* 2 (July 15, 1932): 1, 3, 5. Cowley answered with a letter to the editor in which he presented *his* memory of the notorious evening ("not to be printed"), and concluded: "As for the question WHO BROUGHT DADA TO NEW YORK? the answer is WHO THE HELL CARES?" MC to M. A. Abernethy, July 29, 1932, *Contempo* Papers.

12. The final stages of the writing of *Exile's Return* can be reconstructed from the new series of more elaborate notebooks Cowley started during his stay at Cloverlands.

Notebook 1, n.s., entries May 17, 1933 through May 12, 1934. See also *DGM*, pp. 192–206, 219–24.

13. *DGM*, pp. 51–55, 63–67, 77–82.

14. "Twenty-Four Youngsters," *New Republic* 77 (July 8, 1931): 205–6; "Kentucky Coal Town," ibid. 70 (March 2, 1932): 67–70; "The Flight of the Bonus Army," ibid. 72 (August 17, 1932): 13–15; "Red Day in Washington," ibid. 73 (December 21, 1932): 153–55. The Bonus Expeditionary Force, popularly called "Bonus Army," consisted of World War I veterans who early in the depression had become impoverished, hungry, and jobless. In June 1932 thousands of them, from every state, marched on Washington to demand full payment of the "adjusted compensation certificates" to which they were entitled under a law passed in 1924. Numbering over ten thousand, including wives and children, they took over unoccupied buildings near the Capitol or built shacks on Anacostia Flats. At the end of July, President Hoover, contending that the Bonus marchers had been infiltrated by Communist revolutionaries and criminals, called out the federal militia—cavalry, infantry, and tanks—to clear out the remaining veterans from the District of Columbia, thereby antagonizing many to whom the marchers seemed to be speaking on behalf of all the unemployed. The story of Cowley's radicalization is told at length in *DGM*. Cowley's pledge of allegiance to the Communist party presidential candidates was reported in "Writers in Support of Communists," *Daily Worker*, September 14, 1932, p. 1, and, more elaborately, in "2,000 Professionals, Writers, Artists, Pledge Support to Communists in Elections," *Daily Worker*, October 14, 1932, p. 1. The latter quoted from a speech Cowley made at an election dinner held under the auspices of the Independent Committee for Foster and Ford on October 13: "It wasn't the depression that got me. It was the boom. I saw all my friends writing the tripe demanded by the present order, stultified and corrupted and unable to make real use of their talents. After that, I had to discover the reason for this state of affairs, which comes from the nature of a ruling class which lives by exploiting everyone else. Then I went through the South, and saw how cleverly the rulers try to divide white and black workers by giving the whites a trifle more than the black sharecroppers. That taught me the necessity of unity of white and black workers and professional workers under the leadership of the Communist Party."

15. MC to KB, June 2, 1932 (*SC*, p. 201); Daniel Aaron, *Writers on the Left* (1961; Avon Books, 1965), p. 348; *DGM*, pp. 117–18.

16. Hamilton Basso to MC, July 17, 1939. On February 16, 1931, Cowley had written to Burke that "a whole scheme of life" had "collapsed" and that he was convinced he would have to "find a new one and find it for myself. . . . I don't think my troubles are peculiar to myself. A lot of people I know have been moving in what now seems to be the wrong direction; they too will have to change or go bust" (*SC*, pp. 191–92).

17. "Never so much as during the writing of this book have I been troubled by doubts concerning myself," he noted on June 2, 1933. "All my fine, simple prescriptions to younger writers . . . all these obvious truths are forgotten and I wonder whether I really have or have ever had anything to say. . . . I don't know whether it is worthwhile setting down this history of people most of whom will be forgotten along with the decade in which they flourished—floruerunt circa 1920–1930." Two weeks later he had become

convinced that "the book should end with a personal confession of belief." Notebook 1, n.s., June 16, 1933.

18. Richard H. Pells, *Radical Visions and American Dreams: Culture and Social Thought in the Depression Years* (New York, 1973), p. 153. Pells's study contains an illuminating discussion of the place of *Exile's Return* in the context of its times; see pp. 154, 156–59. Notebook 1, n.s., entry for May 12, 1934; *ER* (1934), pp. 12, 123–40, 146–67, 286.

19. *Yesterday's Burdens* is the title of the novel by Robert Coates published in 1933 and reissued in 1975 by Southern Illinois University Press. *ER* (1934), pp. 287–88, 294, 223, 302. The epilogue to the original edition is reprinted in *TBOU*, pp. 56–62.

20. *ER* (1934), p. 240.

21. MC to Warren I. Susman, March 8, 1965; *DGM*, pp. 227–32.

22. Representative reviews were the following: Arthur Mizener, "Home Was the Stranger," *New York Times Book Review*, June 10, 1951, p. 9; Lloyd Morris, "Most Vivacious Account of Literary Life in the Twenties," *New York Herald Tribune Book Review*, July 8, 1951, pp. 1, 10; Maxwell Geismar, "Cowley and the Lost Generation," *New York Evening Post*, June 9, 1951, p. 3; F. W. Dupee, "Still a Good Book," *American Scholar* 20 (Autumn 1951): 480, 482. Robert E. Spiller's review for *American Quarterly* 3 (Fall 1951): 273–75, is reprinted in *Milestones in American Literary History*, pp. 39–41. See also Mizener's "The Long Debauch," *New Statesman* 62 (September 29, 1961): 433–34, which considers the belated appearance of the revised edition in England. The principal additions and deletions were the following: the section "Political Interlude" and the epilogue were dropped from the original edition; a new foreword and epilogue were added; the section on Harry Crosby was revised at the request of Caresse Crosby; and new sections were added on Hart Crane and the Sacco and Vanzetti case. In addition there were revisions of style and perspective throughout. Thus the section "Historical Parallel" was rewritten and expanded to incorporate the changed perspective on Russia in 1951.

23. Cowley had not only continued to review with critical loyalty the works of the lost generation published between 1934 and 1951, he had also spoken up in its defense (see, for example, "In Defense of the 1920's," *New Republic* 110 [April 24, 1944]: 564–65, reprinted in *FL*, pp. 179–84) and helped to bring its critical reputation up to par with its achievement by editing *The Portable Hemingway* (1944) and *The Portable Faulkner* (1946), compiling *The Stories of F. Scott Fitzgerald* (1951), and editing what he thought was the "final version" of *Tender Is the Night* (1951). He had also assembled much original biographical information on Hemingway, part of which went into "A Portrait of Mister Papa," *Life* 26 (January 10, 1949): 86–90, 93–94, 96–98, 100–101.

24. *ER* (1951), pp. 296–300.

25. *ER* (1951), p. 291. Peter Blume remembered that Robert Coates, whose *Yesterday's Burdens* Cowley had taken as a representative account in his section "Connecticut Valley," registered objections (interview with Peter Blume, January 31, 1982). Katherine Anne Porter as late as 1965 protested at being classified as an "exile" (Katherine Anne Porter to MC, March 3, 1965) and Kenneth Burke ironically complained in 1985 that in the original *Exile's Return* Cowley was "obviously phasing me

out" ("KB to MC: An Interview with Kenneth Burke," *Visionary Company* [Summer 1987]: p. 89). Cowley's symbolic use of Harry Crosby's life story—a vicarious use, since he had really meant to write about Hart Crane—has particularly come under fire. The case against Cowley's generational paradigm of exile and homecoming and his use of Crosby's life was stated forcefully, but hardly conclusively, by Geoffrey Wolff in his *Black Sun: The Brief Transit and Violent Eclipse of Harry Crosby* (New York, 1976), 114–17, 306–8. Wolff's initial inspiration for writing the life of Crosby had been Cowley's account in *Exile's Return*, which he credits with gracefully keeping alive the memory of Crosby. For Cowley's refutation of Wolff, see his foreword to Karen Lane Rood, ed., *American Writers in Paris, 1920–1939* (*Dictionary of Literary Biography*, vol. 4; Detroit, 1980), pp. xi–xiii. Leon Edel, too, has wondered whether Cowley's choice of Crosby was "genuinely relevant," but finds that Wolff's supposedly corrective biography provides "only a larger picture of what Cowley in essence discerned" (introduction to *Exile's Return*, Limited Editions Club, 1981, p. xviii). Edward Germain, who edited Crosby's diaries for the Black Sparrow Press, saw no reason to challenge Cowley's interpretation of Crosby (introduction to *Shadows of the Sun: The Diaries of Harry Crosby* [Santa Barbara, Calif., 1977], pp. 7–17).

26. MC to KB, August 6, 1931. The qualification of *Exile's Return* as "epic-making" was made by Burke in an interview with the editors of *Visionary Company* for the special Cowley issue (Summer 1987), p. 93.

27. Burke made his comment in a speech on the occasion of the presentation to Cowley of the Gold Medal for Belles Lettres and Criticism, May 20, 1981. The speech is reprinted in the Cowley issue of *Visionary Company*, pp. 9–10. Brooks's comment appeared as a blurb on the jacket of *Exile's Return* (1951).

28. Lewis P. Simpson, "Malcolm Cowley and the American Writer," *Sewanee Review* 84: 237.

29. Warner Berthoff, "Modern Literature and the Condition of Exile," in *Fiction and Events: Essays in Criticism and Literary History* (New York, 1971), p. 78. Berthoff's essay contains a valuable discussion of Cowley's "saga" of exile and return in the context of the international experience of literary expatriation.

30. Leon Edel, Introduction, *Exile's Return* (Limited Editions Club, 1981), p. xi; Robert E. Spiller, *Milestones in American Literary History*, p. 39. Wolff's critique is given in his biography of Harry Crosby (see note 25 above). Lynn's excoriation of *Exile's Return* appears in *The Air-Line to Seattle: Studies in Literary and Historical Writing About America* (Chicago and London, 1983), pp. 94–96. His embittered and biased denunciation departs from the premise that "no other interpretation of American literature has more engaged the national mind, or more thoroughly stultified it, than the legend of the lost generation that Cowley wove from the warp of the Communist line and the woof of his own romanticism"; the last quotation but one is from John Aldridge, "Malcolm Cowley at Eighty," p. 481. Spiller's comment appears in *Milestones*, p. 39.

31. Kazin, *Starting Out in the Thirties*, p. 16. For Wilson's sharp upbraidings, see *Letters on Literature and Politics*, pp. 286–88, 309–10. Tate's and Basso's letters to Cowley have not been published; Daniel Aaron quotes from several of them in his chapter on Cowley in *Writers on the Left*, pp. 347–55.

32. Felix Morrow, "Malcolm Cowley: Portrait of a Stalinist Intellectual," *New Militant* 2 (April 18, 1936): 2–3. Eugene Lyons excoriated Cowley in "Malcolm Cowley: 1938," *Modern Monthly* 5 (June 1938): 6–8. James T. Farrell criticized *Exile's Return* in *A Note on Literary Criticism* (New York 1936), pp. 157–74, and attacked Cowley's review of Dos Passos's *Adventures of a Young Man* (*New Republic* 99 [June 14, 1939]: 163) in "Dos Passos and His Critics," *American Mercury* 17 (August 1939): 489–94, besides being generally hostile to Cowley in the late 1930s. Joseph Epstein, ("The Literary Life Today," *New Criterion* 1 [September 1983]: 13) thought that "nearly every one of the printed literary opinions of Malcolm Cowley . . . needs to be fumigated for possible political motive." Kenneth Lynn's excoriations can be found in *The Air-Line to Seattle*, pp. 108–31, 163–71. For Cowley's answer, see "Hemingway's Wound—And Its Consequences for American Literature," *Georgia Review* 38 (Summer 1984), 223–39. The debate was continued in "Reader's Forum," ibid. (Fall 1984): 668–72, with responses from Lynn, Philip Young, and Cowley. For Kazin on Cowley, see *Starting Out in the Thirties*, pp. 15–20. Aaron's views are given in *Writers on the Left*, pp. 347–55. Robert Alter, "The Travels of Malcolm Cowley," *Commentary* 70 (August 1980): 33–40; George Core, "Malcolm Cowley and the Literary Imperium," *Visionary Company* (Summer 1987): 16–28; Lewis P. Simpson, "Cowley's Odyssey: Literature and Faith in the Thirties," *Sewanee Review* 89 (Fall 1981): 520–39; *WT*, p. 139.

33. *SF*, p. 241; MC to KB, October 20, 1931 (*SC*, p. 197); Kazin, *Starting Out in the Thirties*, p. 15.

34. See, for example, "To a Revolutionary Critic," *New Republic* 76 (November 8, 1933), 368–69; "Art Tomorrow," ibid. 79 (May 23, 1934): 34–36 (part of the original epilogue to *ER* [1934]); "Literature and Politics," ibid. 81 (January 2, 1935): 224; "A Note on Marxian Criticism," ibid. (January 30, 1935): 337; "What the Revolutionary Movement Can Do for a Writer," *New Masses* 15 (May 7, 1935), 20–22; "Marx and Plekhanov," *New Republic* 89 (December 30, 1936), 277–78. Reprinted in *TBOU*, pp. 47–51, 56–62, 78–80, 81–83, 87–94, 130–35.

35. "Art Tomorrow," p. 35.

36. "The Art of Insurrection," *New Republic* 74 (April 12, 1933): 248 (*TBOU*, p. 28); "Fellow Traveler," *New Republic* 82 (May 1, 1935): 346; Edmund Wilson to MC, October 20, 1938, in *Letters on Literature and Politics*, p. 310; "Poet in Politics," *New Republic* 96 (September 21, 1938): 191–92 (*TBOU*, pp. 324–28); "Baudelaire as Revolutionist," *New Republic* 86 (April 15, 1936): 287–88 (*TBOU*, pp. 283–87); "Footnotes to a Life of Marx," *New Republic* 86 (February 26, 1936): 79 (*TBOU*, p. 105).

37. "Socialists and Symbolists," *New Republic* 96 (September 28, 1938): 218–19 (*TBOU*, pp. 328–32); "What the Revolutionary Movement Can Do for a Writer," *New Masses* 15 (May 7, 1935): 20–22 (*TBOU*, pp. 87–94).

38. MC to KB, October 7, 1938 (*SC*, p. 223); *WT*, pp. 154–57; MC to KB, December 17, 1940 (*SC*, p. 234).

39. Lewis Simpson, "The Decorum of the Writer," pp. 569–70; "The Michael Golden Legend," *Decision* 2 (July 1941): 44–45 (*TBOU*, pp. 194–95).

40. "Faith and the Future," in *Whose Revolution?*, edited by Irving Dewitt Talmadge (New York, 1941), pp. 135–65. A shorter version is reprinted as "Communism and

Christianism" in *FL*, pp. 12–24.

41. A selection of Cowley's reviews from the war years appears in *FL*. MC to KB, October 14, 1940 (*SC*, p. 230). Cowley's experiences in Washington, D.C., in 1942 are described in *WT*, p. 158; by Donald Faulkner in his introduction to *FL*, pp. xiv–xvi; and by George Core in "Malcolm Cowley and the Literary Imperium," pp. 24–25. MC to KB, September 4, 1952 (*SC*, p. 307). For Cowley's experiences in Seattle, see *FL*, pp. 107–11. The trials of Alger Hiss, who had been a State Department official with an apparently impeccable record before he became president of the Carnegie Endowment of International Peace, originated in August 1948 when Whittaker Chambers, a repented ex-Communist who later became editor of *Time* magazine, accused Hiss before the House Committee on Un-American Activities of having been a Communist party member and a spy. Hiss denied the accusations, was indicted for perjury, and in two trials in the spring and fall of 1949 was found guilty and sentenced to five years in prison. Cowley was summoned to testify at both trials on the basis of a record he had kept in his notebook of a lunch meeting with Whittaker Chambers in December 1940, at which Chambers had named names, displayed an expert knowledge of the tactics of Communist infiltration, and advanced his intention to use his knowledge against ex-radicals. Cowley's testimony served less to establish the guilt or innocence of Hiss than to point up the deceitful tactics of Chambers, who had also been responsible for the attacks on Cowley in *Time* magazine in 1942. Cowley's testimony once again raised the specter of his own radical affiliations. For an account of the Hiss trials and (not entirely consonant versions of) Cowley's role in them, see Alistair Cooke, *A Generation on Trial: U.S.A. v. Alger Hiss* (New York, 1950), John Chabot Smith, *Alger Hiss: The True Story* (New York, 1976), and Allen Weinstein, *Perjury: The Hiss-Chambers Case* (New York, 1978).

42. A valuable first consideration of Cowley's "middle years" is James M. Kempf's "Cowley's 'Middle Career': In Defense of the 1920's at the American Mid-Century," *Visionary Company* (Summer 1987): 121–30.

43. Cowley's essay on Hawthorne, the introduction to *The Portable Hawthorne* (1948), appeared first as two articles: "Hawthorne in Solitude," *New Republic* 119 (August 2, 1948): 19–23, and "Hawthorne in the Looking-Glass," *Sewanee Review* 56 (Autumn 1948): 545–63. Reprinted integrally in *MWH*, pp. 3–34.

44. Cowley's reconsideration of Whitman, the introduction to *The Complete Poetry and Prose of Walt Whitman* (1948), appeared first as four articles: "Walt Whitman: The Miracle," *New Republic* 114 (March 18, 1946): 185–88; "Walt Whitman: The Secret," ibid. (April 8, 1946): 481–84; "Walt Whitman: The Philosopher," ibid. 117 (September 29, 1947): 29–31; "Whitman: The Poet," ibid. (October 20, 1947): 27–30. Reprinted integrally in *MWH*, pp. 35–75.

45. "The Dispossessed," *New Republic* 116 (June 22, 1942): 865–66 (*FL*, pp. 36–40); "American Literature in Wartime," *New Republic* 109 (December 6, 1943): 800–803 (*FL*, pp. 3–11); *MWH*, p. 34; "Introduction," *The Portable Hemingway* (1944), p. vii; "Introduction," *The Portable Faulkner* (1946), p. x; *FCF*, pp. 153–57. Cowley's role in reclaiming Faulkner has recently come under fire from Frederick Crews in his "The

Strange Fate of William Faulkner," *New York Review of Books*, March 7, 1991, pp. 47–52.

46. Cowley's articles on naturalism appeared mostly in 1947: "Naturalism's Terrible McTeague," *New Republic* 116 (May 5, 1947): 31–33; "Sister Carrie's Brother," ibid. (May 26, 1947): 23–25; "The Slow Triumph of Sister Carrie," ibid. (June 23, 1947): 24–27; " 'Not Men': A Natural History of American Naturalism," *Kenyon Review* 9 (Summer 1947): 414–35. Collected in *MWH*, pp. 116–52, 153–65. For the persistence of naturalism into American fiction at mid-century, see "Naturalism: No Teacup Tragedies," in *LS*, pp. 74–95. *MWH*, p. 74. The last phrase quoted is Alfred Kazin's in *On Native Grounds*, p. 314.

47. *SF*, p. 124.

48. *SF*, p. 249.

49. *WT*, pp. 256–66.

50. "Criticism: A Many-Windowed House," *Saturday Review of Literature* 44 (August 12, 1961): 10–11, 46–47. Reprinted in *MWH*, pp. 244–52.

51. John W. Aldridge, *In Search of Heresy: American Literature in an Age of Conformity* (1954; Port Washington, New York, 1967), pp. 166–76. Aldridge's earlier book *After the Lost Generation: A Critical Study of the Writers of Two Wars* (New York, 1951) is much indebted, especially in its opening chapters, to *Exile's Return*. For Aldridge's finely balanced later appreciation of Cowley, see his "Malcolm Cowley at Eighty," *Michigan Quarterly Review* 18 (Summer 1980): 481–90.

52. "In Defense of the 1920's," *New Republic* 110 (April 24, 1944): 564–65 (*FL*, pp. 179–84); "Exploring a World of Nightmares," *New York Times Book Review*, March 27, 1960, pp. 1, 40 (*FL*, pp. 236–40). For Cowley on Fiedler, see *MWH*, p. 249; "Faulkner: The Etiology of His Art," *WT*, pp. 214–30.

53. For Alger and Hearn, see *MWH*, pp. 76–88, 100–115; for Damon, Coates and Caldwell, see *WT*, pp. 35–50, 82–94, 113–32; for Thurber and Algren, see *FL*, pp. 200–209, 349–53; for Pound and Frost, see *MWH*, pp. 178–90, 201–12.

54. For Brooks, see *MWH*, pp. 213–28; for the "middle-American prose style," see *FL*, pp. 185–93; the introductory essay to *Leaves of Grass* is reprinted in *FL*, pp. 140–68. It must be said that Cowley's open-mindedness was in turn circumscribed by his own literary values and presuppositions and his empathetic method of criticism. For all his skepticism of the exclusivism of literary canon-making, Cowley himself helped establish a canon of the lost generation that implicitly reflected many of his personal preconceptions about literary ethics and aesthetics. A *Second Flowering* authoritatively focused on a galaxy of eight "representative" writers born between 1894 and 1900—Fitzgerald, Hemingway, Dos Passos, Cummings, Wilder, Faulkner, Wolfe, and Crane—and hence could not accommodate, as Cowley acknowledged, "other representative figures" born either before or after those boundary years. Among them were not only Henry Miller, Archibald MacLeish, John Steinbeck, James Gould Cozzens, James T. Farrell, Nathanael West, and Robert Penn Warren (to name only the better known), but also a large contingent of women writers, some of whom were born *within* the timespan of Cowley's generational paradigm: Katherine Anne Porter, Elizabeth

Madox Roberts, Djuna Barnes, Edna St. Vincent Millay, Caroline Gordon, Louise Bogan, Josephine Herbst, Dawn Powell, and Kay Boyle. Women writers might constitute a numerical minority—of the 385 writers born between 1891 and 1905 whom Cowley listed in the appendix to his book, 74 (nearly twenty percent) were women—but Cowley justified his exclusion largely on historical grounds: "the admired writers of the generation were men in the great majority. The time of famous women storytellers and poets was, in this country, either a little earlier or twenty years later. I feel a lasting gratitude for the work of Caroline Gordon, Louise Bogan, Dawn Powell, and one or two other women of the generation, but they have been less widely read than male contemporaries of no greater talent." Nor were there "representatives" of ethnic, racial, or cultural minorities. Sexually, racially, and socially Cowley's eight representative writers formed a fairly homogeneous group: "the men of the Lost Generation were white, middle-class, mostly Protestant by upbringing, and mostly English and Scottish by descent." *SF*, p. 240.

55. "Aidgarpo," *New Republic* 113 (November 5, 1945), 608; Allen Tate, *Memoirs and Opinions, 1926–1974* (Chicago, 1975), p. 119. Lewis Simpson, "The Decorum of the Writer," pp. 567–68; Cowley's two-part portrait of Maxwell Perkins appeared first in the *New Yorker* 20 (April 1, 1944): 28, 32, 35–36, and (April 8, 1944): 30–34, 36, 39–40. It was reprinted in *FL*, pp. 55–66, and reissued, with a "Prefatory Note," as a little book, *Unshaken Friend: A Profile of Maxwell Perkins*, in 1985 by the publisher Robert Rinehart; "A Natural History of the American Writer" appears in *LS* on pp. 132–228. For Cowley's expertise in the field of publishing, see the chapters "Cheap Books for the Millions" and "Hardbacks or Paperbacks?" in *LS*, pp. 96–114, 115–31. It was again typical that for *The Literary History of the United States*, edited by Robert E. Spiller, Willard Thorp, Thomas H. Johnson, and Henry Seidel Canby (New York, 1948), Cowley wrote the chapters "Creating an Audience" (with Canby; pp. 1119–34), "How Writers Lived" (pp. 1263–72), and "American Books Abroad" (pp. 1374–91).

56. The Bollingen Prize in Poetry was established in 1948 by the Bollingen Foundation, financed by Paul Mellon, to be given annually to the best book of poetry by an American citizen. The first award (1949), recommended by the Fellows in American Letters of the Library of Congress, was given to the *Pisan Cantos* of Ezra Pound, then confined to St. Elizabeths mental hospital in Washington, D.C., and under indictment for treason on account of his Fascist radio broadcasts during World War II. Awarding the prize to a poem which could be shown to contain Fascist and anti-Semitic sentiments triggered a controversy that peaked when Robert Hillyer in two articles for the *Saturday Review* denounced the prize as part of a fascist conspiracy to seize power in the literary world and establish "a new authoritarianism." Cowley took a sharp stand against Hillyer in the *New Republic*, affirming the artistic and political integrity of the jurors (among them Conrad Aiken, W. H. Auden, Louise Bogan, T. S. Eliot, Robert Lowell, Archibald MacLeish, Katherine Anne Porter, Karl Shapiro, Allen Tate, and William Carlos Williams), and challenging the award to Pound on literary rather than political grounds. His article was reprinted in *The Case Against the "Saturday Review"* (1949), a pamphlet published under the auspices of *Poetry* magazine, and containing a statement by the Fellows of the Library of Congress waylaying the charges as well

as supportive articles, editorials, and letters by, among others, MacLeish, Mark Van Doren, William Meredith, William Van O'Connor, Cleanth Brooks, and Yvor Winters. "The Battle over Ezra Pound," *New Republic* 121 (October 3, 1949): 17–20 (*FL*, pp. 99–106).

57. "Some Dangers to American Writing," *New Republic* 131 (November 22, 1954): 114–17 (*FL*, pp. 112–18).

58. Cowley taught at the University of Washington in Seattle in 1950; Stanford University in 1956, 1959, 1960–61, and 1965; University of Michigan in 1957; University of California at Berkeley in 1962; Cornell University in 1964; University of Minnesota in 1971; and University of Warwick, England, in 1973.

59. George Core, "Malcolm Cowley, 1898–," in *American Writers: A Collection of Literary Biographies*, edited by A. Walton Litz. Supplement 2, part 1 (New York, 1981), p. 153. "Invitation to Innovators," *Saturday Review of Literature* 37 (August 21, 1954): 7–8, 38–41, incorporated into the concluding chapter to *LS*, "The Next Fifty Years in American Literature," pp. 229–46.

60. For Cheever, see *FL*, pp. 360–74. Cowley's efforts on behalf of Kerouac are recreated in lively detail in Adam Gussow's "Bohemia Revisited: Malcolm Cowley, Jack Kerouac, and *On the Road*," *Georgia Review* 38 (Summer 1984): pp. 291–311. For an account of Cowley and Kesey at Stanford, see *FL*, pp. 324–27. Cowley's services to writers have included critics and literary historians or biographers like Philip Young, Larzer Ziff, Michael Millgate, Gay Wilson Allen, A. Scott Berg, and countless others.

61. For Wilder, Marquand, O'Hara, Cozzens, Cather, and Cheever, see *FL*, pp. 309–13, 291–94, 319–23, 285–90, 299–303, 360–74. For Cowley's lack of appreciation for postmodernist "anti-fiction," see *WT*, pp. 194–213; *WT*, p. x.

62. The word "seismographic" is used by John Aldridge in his "Malcolm Cowley at Eighty," pp. 482–83. Aldridge speaks of Cowley's ability "to sense and report the psychic weather, the dominant moods and styles, the subtle forces that shape the collective state of mind of the historical moment very often while the moment is still in the process of being formed and he himself is being formed by it." *WT*, p. 249; MC to KB, June 21, 1977 (*SC*, p. 407).

63. For Cowley's revaluation of the radical past, see, besides *DGM*, *WT*, pp. 95–112, 133–58. Between 1980 and a few years before his death in 1989 Cowley worked on a sequel to *DGM*, dealing with the second half of the 1930s. See "No Homage to Catalonia: A Memory of the Spanish Civil War," *Southern Review* 18 (January 1982): 131–40; "Echoes from Moscow: 1937–1938," ibid. 20 (January 1984): 1–11; "Lament for the Abraham Lincoln Battalion," *Sewanee Review* 92 (Summer 1984): 331–47; and "A Time of Resignations," *Yale Review* 74 (Autumn 1984): 1–14.

64. *FL*, pp. 328, 338, 341.

65. For a sensitive appreciation of Cowley's activities in the various "dukedoms and principalities" of the Republic of Letters, see George Core, "Malcolm Cowley and the Literary Imperium," *Visionary Company* (Summer 1987), pp. 16–28. Core, like Simpson and Aldridge, felt that Cowley may have been the last of a vanishing type and pointed to the serious loss for the literary commonwealth: "The man or woman of letters is not only a writer of many parts (poet or fictionist, essayist, correspondent)

but is often a secretary and diplomat who serves the literary polity by acting as a mediator between writers and publishers (frequently as an unpaid agent), by working as an editor (again often unofficial and unpaid), by addressing the world at large on behalf of Literature (either in person or on paper), and by performing in many other salutary ways to promote writers and their work. Were this office abolished or were its holders to vanish, the Republic of Letters would be gravely threatened, and professional writers would be little more than a mob with many individuals and numerous cliques but no center, and the literary imperium, which I take to embrace all the chaotic possibilities of the realm of letters at its widest and most primitive, would be disorderly to the point of verging on pandemonium" (p. 20). See also Aldridge, "Malcolm Cowley at Eighty," pp. 487–90; Simpson, "The Decorum of the Writer," p. 570, and "Cowley's Odyssey: Literature and Faith in the Thirties," pp. 534–39.

66. MC to KB, April 17, 1981 (SC, p. 425).

Index

James, Henry, Sr., 20, 21
James, William, 39, 235, 499 (n. 4)
Jammes, Francis, 112
Jeffers, Robinson, 475
Jenkins, Susan. *See* Brown, Susan
  Jenkins
Jennings, Charlie, 354
Johns, Orrick, 105, 125, 126, 127, 158
Johns, Peggy. *See* Baird, Marguerite
  Frances (Peggy)
Johnson, Martyn, 116, 127
Jolas, Eugene, 357, 358, 363, 401, 402,
  429, 569 (nn. 38, 43)
Jolas, Maria, 357
Jones, Robert Edmond, 40
Joost, Nicholas, 532 (n. 5)
Josephson, Hannah. *See* Geffen,
  Hannah
Josephson, Matthew, 97, 105, 145, 176,
  177, 180, 193, 210, 211, 219, 257,
  258, 266, 271, 285, 287, 289, 295,
  296, 303, 305, 308, 331, 336, 345,
  346, 348, 355, 356, 383, 412, 414,
  417, 465, 507 (n. 7), 522 (n. 13), 534
  (n. 28), 541 (n. 9), 543 (n. 24), 544
  (n. 40), 567 (n. 23), 571 (n. 53), 574
  (n. 11), 577 (n. 21), 578 (n. 30), 583
  (n. 10); on MC, 77, 102, 127, 208,
  223, 351, 383, 422; MC's friendship
  with, 77–78, 132, 169, 242; and
  Kenneth Burke, 78, 94, 164; marriage
  of, 132; and symbolism, 142; and
  expatriation, 176, 191, 401, 404–5,
  520 (n. 53); and Dada, 191, 205, 206,
  208, 220, 223–24, 229, 236, 239,
  242, 375, 522 (n. 13); and feud with
  Gorham Munson, 205, 242–44, 246,
  285, 288, 319, 538 (n. 72); and
  Secession, 205–6, 208, 223–24, 243–
  44, 259, 260, 528 (n. 82), 530 (n. 22);
  conflict with MC, 207–8; and *Broom*,
  212, 226–27, 228–29, 234, 235, 243,
  261, 279–80, 281, 282, 283–84, 287,
  291–93, 294, 297–98, 529 (n. 85);

MC on, 225, 245, 246; and Waldo
  Frank, 243, 246; and Louis Aragon,
  262; Harold Loeb on, 281; and
  Aesthete 1925, 323, 324, 325–26;
  MC's letters to, 337, 378, 383; refuge
  in country, 343; and radicalism, 357,
  403, 404–5, 406, 415; and surrealism,
  356, 557–58 (n. 39); and Valéry, 363;
  and Zola, 383, 414, 415–16; and
  transition, 401–2, 404, 569 (n. 38); as
  critic of American culture, 403, 408
Journal, 90
Joyce, James, 33, 136, 179, 201, 215,
  220, 245, 358, 401, 441, 442, 468,
  575–76 (n. 17); MC's views on, 218–
  19; *Ulysses*, 218–19, 375, 393, 530
  (n.9), 546 (n. 10)

Kahn, Gustav, 90
Kahn, Otto, 346
Kansas City Star, 130
Kant, Immanuel, 106, 151, 411, 474
Kaufman, Herbert, 152
Kaufman, Reginald Wright, 132, 515
  (n. 32)
Kaye-Smith, Sheila, 155, 514 (n. 20),
  515 (n. 32)
Kazin, Alfred, 16, 25, 33, 184, 472,
  473, 537 (n. 58)
Keats, John, 34, 118, 339, 444
Kellogg, Frank Billings, 386, 564–65
  (n. 6)
Kempf, James M., xi, 525 (n. 47)
Kennerley, Mitchell, 124
Kenyon Review, 365
Kerouac, Jack, 487
Kesey, Ken, 486, 487
Kessel, Joseph, 339
Kipling, Rudyard, 34, 70
Kirk, G. B., 77
Kirstein, Lincoln, 567 (n. 23)
Kittredge, George Lyman, 41, 52
Kling, Joseph, 113, 204

Mitchell, Stewart, 61, 155, 189–90, 196, 212, 213, 248; MC's impressions of, 190

Modernism: in MC's poetry, 10, 45, 113, 136, 149, 207, 248, 374–75; MC's early exposure to, 33, 35, 44–45, 100, 109; MC's ambivalence about, 36, 37, 56, 104, 107, 149, 155–56, 167, 170–71, 193–95, 202, 205, 212, 218–19, 230, 241–42, 253–57, 268, 269, 283, 308–10, 341–42, 342–43, 360–63, 375, 417, 442, 462, 518 (n. 28); appeal of, 106, 110, 136, 162–63, 216, 351; and music, 106, 113, 170, 171, 195; religiosity of, 194; Rosicrucianism of, 194–95, 196, 201; intellectualism in, 217, 253, 255, 362, 369, 537 (n. 60), 559 (n. 49); MC as critic of, 220, 459–60, 462, 463, 470, 487; definition of, 255, 309, 369–71; MC's approach to, 384; New Humanism and, 454. *See also under* Aiken, Conrad; Baudelaire, Charles; Burke, Kenneth; Eliot, T. S.; Gide, André; Tate, Allen

Modern S4N Review, 512 (n. 38)

Moholy-Nagy, László, 356

Moise, Lionel, 125, 130

Molière, 190, 192, 194, 208, 267

Moncrieff, C. K. Scott, 340, 364

Mondriaan, Piet, 538 (n. 66)

Monet, Claude, 105, 231, 232

Monod, Julien P., 559 (n. 45)

Monro, Harold, 251, 373

Monroe, Harriet, 13, 110, 119, 121, 122, 148, 149, 189, 250, 373, 380, 575 (n. 16); MC's letters to, 121, 355, 380–81, 429; on MC's poetry, 433

Montpellier, 184–85, 188, 189–91, 196, 213, 231

Moody, William Vaughn, 52

Moore, George, 338; *Memoirs of My Dead Life*, 49, 438

Moore, Marianne, 211, 235, 298, 352, 515 (n. 28); as editor of *Dial*, 155, 255, 364, 386, 387, 393–95, 562 (n. 62), 567 (n. 22); MC's relations with, 155, 364, 567 (n. 22); MC's letters to, 360, 376, 386, 393, 557 (n. 30)

Morand, Paul, 306, 339, 418, 559 (n. 50)

More, Louis Trenchard, 454

More, Paul Elmer, 326, 453–54, 455, 456, 457; *Hellenistic Philosophies*, 300, 317, 453

Moréas, Jean, 112

Moreau, Gustave, 96

Morison, Samuel Eliot, 39, 40, 501 (n. 53)

Morley, Christopher, 165, 363

Morrow, Felix, 472

Moscow Trials, 475

Moss, Arthur B., 180, 181, 197, 516 (n. 32), 524 (n. 27)

Mowry, Margaret, 19

Mumford, Lewis, 175, 379, 380, 455, 475

Munson, Gorham B., 204, 283, 302, 311, 319, 322, 324, 325, 356, 440, 531 (n. 22), 544 (n. 40); as editor of *Secession*, 204–7, 208, 222–23, 224, 243–44, 244, 258–61, 289, 292, 312, 527 (n. 65), 538 (n. 72); and Waldo Frank, 204, 243, 246, 305; and Matthew Josephson, 205, 242–43, 246, 286, 288–89, 538 (n. 72); on MC's poetry, 207, 223, 246, 249, 428, 540 (n. 90); MC's relations with, 244, 245–47, 260–61, 285, 286–89, 291, 322–23, 357, 528 (n. 74), 534 (n. 28), 538 (n. 72), 566 (n. 18), 583 (n. 11); on MC and Dada, 266; on MC and classicism, 270; and Gurdjieff, 286, 311, 322, 540 (n. 90), 543 (n. 24); and *Blue Juniata*, 428, 429; and New Humanism, 454, 456.